Copyright © 2012 Kurt Brandle. All rights reserved.
Brandle Publishing LLC, Ann Arbor, Michigan.

ISBN: 978-0-9847271-1-7 (paperback)

Meaning and Aesthetics in Architecture

Kurt Brandle

Preface

We are all involved with architecture. We live in it and usually enjoy it. To get the best out of it through successful design is another matter. For this we must try to understand it as fully as we can which implies careful evaluation. Particular understanding becomes meaning with our choices based on aesthetics, the latter taken more broadly than the reference to being beautiful. To enlighten the process of understanding architecture – in terms of meaning and aesthetics – is the subject of this book. Its discussions range from philosophical foundations to architectural realizations. Many examples are discussed with an abundance of illustrations. The concept of design narratives is developed as the dialog between content and form of architectural objects.

Book Format

The book was written with emphasis on electronic format and distribution. This paperback version is a duplicate with differences in format only.

It still shows in blue color the poles of hyperlinking between the text and the end notes as well as the bibliographic references. Additional links are shown for sources on the web. As the latter change frequently, the references may not always connect but still should be helpful for search purposes.

Open numbers in the text or in parenthesis just before the period sign at the end of sentences refer to figures without mentioning 'figure'. Example: 2.10 or (2.10) refer to the 10th figure in the 2nd chapter.

The elevated numbers at the end of quotes and other text point to their references located toward the end of the book, beginning on page 323. There, the items are ordered by chapters and show, for return to the text, their location by page numbers in the footer.

Quotes which follow each other closely in the text and are also close together in the original text are referenced together by the reference number at the end of their sequence.

Images not by the author and under copyright are identified at the end of the image captions by (© permission). Other source information about images is identified by (source). The image numbers of both kinds connect with the information at the end of the book, beginning on page 371.

Acknowledgements

An account of this magnitude would not have been possible without the inspiration and help from the many philosophers, architects, colleagues and students who I met through their thoughts in books, buildings, and personal encounters.

Todd Schliemann and Susan Strauss gracefully provided the narrative case study about the Biomedical Science Research Building, University of Michigan (Ennead Architects, formerly Polshek Partnership). Jaime Magiera helped me greatly to avoid pitfalls in electronic formatting.

To my wife Judith belongs special gratitude for challenging me often – over half a century – to focus on how complex architecture is and thoughts about it are. Many times she helped me to put such thoughts into words of the present language, which is not the one I learned first.

Any mistakes, inaccuracies and omissions in this text are obviously mine. When you find any, please let me know about them at kbrandle@umich.edu .

Contents

Preface
    Book Format
    Acknowledgements

1 Introduction   1

2 From Things toward Meaning   11
   2.1 Things and things in themselves   12
   2.2 Objects and concepts   18
   2.3 Understanding and judgment   21
   2.4 Observable and relational properties   25
   2.5 Function and complexity   36

3 Our World of Signs   47
   3.1 Signs and communication   48
   3.2 Iconic, symbolic and indexical signs   51
   3.3 Semantics, pragmatics and syntactics   58
   3.4 Interpretation and metaphor   72
   3.5 Unity of content and form   86

4 The Aesthetics of Experience   95
   4.1 Emotions and feelings   95
   4.2 Aspects of beauty   108
   4.3 Aesthetics and the aesthetic   119
   4.4 Objects and 'their' aesthetic   130

5 Type, Style and Ornament   139
   5.1 Concepts and resemblances   139
   5.2 Type and objectivity   146
   5.3 Style and subjectivity   157
   5.4 Configuration and ornamentation   164

6	Cause and Effect in Design	191
	6.1 Cause, effect, change and event	192
	6.2 World and mind in causation	195
	World-to-world causation	197
	World-to-mind causation	199
	Mind-to-world causation	202
	Mind-to-mind causation	205
	6.3 Powers of preference	205
	6.4 Purpose, context and realization	218
	Programming for purpose	222
	Realization in context	227
7	Language, Meaning and Design Narratives	237
	7.1 Language and thought	237
	7.2 Language *of* and language *about* architecture	248
	7.3 'Measurements' of meaning	259
	7.4 Design narratives	262
	From form to content and from content to form	262
	A Stair in the Roth Residence, Weil am Rhein	266
	The Philharmonic Hall, Berlin	270
	The Biomedical Sciences Research Center, University of Michigan, Ann Arbor	273
8	Meaning as Zeitgeist	279
	8.1 Virtuality and reality	280
	8.2 Complexity and inclusion	291
	8.3 Sustainability and outlook	302
Notes and Bibliographical References		323
Illustration Credits and Information		371
Index		375

1 Introduction

Meaning is one of the most important forces in our lives. It arises from understanding and is what we emphasize when we communicate. We all have an idea of what it is, but to explain it is another matter. So it is hardly surprising that meaning is one of the most addressed yet unresolved and controversial issues in philosophy. But often even long texts on meaning do not ponder its very nature, evidently assuming that this is unnecessary. Sometimes it is thought to be the sense of utterance in a language. At other times it is thought to be the sense of a nonlinguistic sign. But these explanations do not bring us much further, especially when we get to the specifics of a particular endeavor. In architecture, few attempts have been made to explain in detail what it is and how it comes about.

Years ago, walking to the University of Stuttgart, where I taught as a guest in the design studio of Peter Faller, I was wondering why, with basically the same program requirements, so many rather different solutions emerged. Where does expression in architecture come from? I did, what sometimes helps, think about the opposite: impression. Are expression and impression really opposites? Is there a link of the two which may be of interest? In a preliminary way, we may say that they are opposites but not in the sense of equivalents. In the flow of events, there is no expression to be had without an impression. We cannot express anything but on the basis of a previous impression or impressions. Now, where does impression come from? From expression. This sounds rather circular. It is not so, however, because there is progress and change between them. In architectural design, as with anything we do, we are involved with chains of cause and effect over time. To become informed, we break the chains of events for contemplation at crucial points. In a present project, the given conditions of the world are the background for impressive and expressive potential. Our minds cause impressions from existing expressions to develop new expressions. At the center of the process is understanding translated into design. What we select then as a particular understanding from often many possible ones is meaning – to be given in the form of design.

The discussion of meaning in architecture has been concerned mainly with the analysis of it as artifacts. It is the view of architecture as history. While this is important here as well, it is not my aim to add to such work to any large extent. I address meaning primarily as process rather than as product.

The present text may be considered a sequence of discussions toward grasping what meaning is in architectural design. Much of it is in contrast to meaning in language. My preliminary view in a nutshell: Meaning is understanding perceived or conceived. How and what I experience is obviously quite similar to how and what we all experience, which indicates that our ways of thinking are similar, a wondrous capacity given to us for communication. But similar does not mean being same. I believe that there is no understanding ever the same as another, as subtle as the differences may be. This is how individuality finds itself within universality and where the semantics of variety have part of their fertile ground.

To look at the subtle elegance of a wildflower with its tenderness outlined on a rock by the sun cannot but evoke a positive experience in each of us, though individually variant (see 1.1). It is similar with the plain but powerful massing of a well built barn where not only nature but human minds and hands have been at work (1.2). The flower grows out of its seed because soil, water, air and light nourish it. We may name it, describe its color and shape, may even know its genetic makeup. This is what it means to us in addition to its gracious beauty, which is pleasure – a meaning as well. The materials for the barn are taken from nature, put together by purpose to fulfill need and desire. Different from the flower, we grasp its practicality and how it turned into form, here represented by roofs, walls, the embracing structural cable around the silo, etc. Again, the farm's beauty is our pleasure.

1.1 In the Albion Basin, Utah

1.2 Near Ellsworth, Michigan

To enlighten meaning as understanding in architectural design is at the center of my interest. Therefore, the emphasis on comprehending it as such takes us in quite different directions than earlier work by Charles Jencks and George Baird, ed., *Meaning in Architecture*; Christian Norberg-Schulz, *Meaning in Western Architecture*; Amos Rapoport, *The Meaning of the Built Environment* and Linda Groat, ed., *Giving Places Meaning*; among others. My efforts are theoretical in their search for a working model of understanding and they are practical in their concentration on architectural design with emphasis on the understanding of understanding. I accept and document help from philosophical and other inquiries wherever I can find it.

We usually grasp meaning best when we understand how we and others relate to present environments, outside or inside. Walking through the contrasts of Louis Kahn's Salk Institute, from sun shine into shadows and back again, or looking around the undulated forms of Frank Gehry's Weatherhead School, from below and from above, brings this point home vividly (1.3 and 1.4) and (1.5 and 1.6).

Salk Institute for Biological Studies
La Jolla, CA

1.3 Courtyard toward west and ocean

1.4 West end of courtyard

Weatherhead School of Management
Case Western University, Cleveland, OH

1.5 From below

1.6 From above

In architecture and all other physical environments, meaning develops in two ways: as outcome of perception or as premise of conception – perception being instrumental for impression and conception being instrumental for expression. We *mean* in these two ways, observing architecture and designing it. Therefore, my approach will begin, in Chapter 2, with a hypothesis of meaning as presently considered understanding either *from* impression or *for* expression. Much of the rest of my enterprise is to underpin this contention.

It is our consciousness which allows us to gain understanding in general and meaning in particular. Thereby, it lets us negotiate between ourselves and other people as well as things. I will elaborate on how we do understand physical and nonphysical things, that is, by means of mental representations. Involved are our sensation and perception of them, leading to their appearance in our mind and to conceptualization by means of our judgment. In fact, what we call conceptualization is usually reconceptualization. I do not believe that we are born with concepts, but with instincts. From infancy on we develop with every experience concepts and accumulate them in memory. What we encounter are properties of objects. What we understand, however, are attributes which we associate with these objects by means of our memory. Still, by convention, we call them properties. My explanations will be carried out with the help of some who have made thinking about the relationship of mind and matter the work of their lives, though I may or may not agree with their views: Descartes, Locke, Hume, especially Kant, then Peirce and James, Wittgenstein, Heidegger, Rescher, Searle, Edelman and Damasio, to name a few. Where I feel that quoting them is most appropriate, I see no reason not to do so.

We think about what we sense which leads to understanding. For reasons of practicality, I differentiate what we can directly sense from objects and what we infer from these sensations indirectly: observable and relational properties. Relational properties are secondary, not in importance, but in the sequence of conceptualization. They are what observable properties represent beyond their own being. When encountering an unpainted concrete column, we see its shape and color as observable properties. Its load-bearing ability we infer as relational property. That it contains steel reinforcement we also infer as relational property. But we may have seen the reinforcement as an observable property before the concrete was poured and now remember it. We may consider the observable properties as more objective than the relational ones as they are what we directly encounter and experience physically in one way or another.

The world is full of complexity, including architecture. Therefore, to end Chapter 2, I address complexity and function as I believe that sorting out functions of what exists and of what we develop is the precondition of well-founded understanding. Functions are relationships which we infer from the behavior of the physical properties of things. For design we may view them as meanings how building systems and components relate to each other. As reality is complex, even in quite limited frames of reference, these relationships are generally also complex. Constraints and conflicts arise which demand resolution in the arrangement of the physical components – one of the central and most difficult tasks in the design process. Every building has functions, internal and external. Only a rather few can find emphasis in expression. Which are given preference is crucial decision making and has an important impact on the overall identity of the building and on many details, such as in spatial organization and facade arrangement. Properties of things and their relationships become through intentions and motivations what I call design factors – the factors which bring architecture about.

To view objects and their properties as signs, especially for communication, has long been found to be extremely helpful. But since the turn of philosophy toward examining language thoroughly as a system of signs early in the last century an important but still insufficiently explained opposition developed of words as signs and objects as signs. This problem leads us, in Chapter 3, to explore semiotics as a field of inquiry and to touch in a preliminary way on meaning *with* words versus meaning *without* words. The characterization of signs as iconic, symbolic and indexical proves very helpful, especially in the comparison of linguistic and nonlinguistic application. Language as such is symbolic, although it is obviously used in constructing text which may describe and refer to the content of all three kinds of signs. Architecture and its design is iconic, often also symbolic or indexical, sometimes all three. Resemblance plays a role. Icons refer to their referents by means of some similarity. Symbols and indexes do not. Another triad, called semantics, pragmatics and syntactics, enlightens how the sign nature of icons, symbols and indexes applies in the practice of communication.

Our mental representations of objects require interpretation which is often helped by thinking in metaphors. We use them to explain what we observe and what we want to communicate. Three concepts are involved: a basic, a declarative and an ensuing one, the latter arising from the association of the other two. The basic concept connects to the declarative concept by means of some similarity in such a way that we infer the ensuing concept. In this roundabout way, metaphors add to our understanding and knowledge of concepts which cannot be or which are not desired to be explicitly given. Metaphors to succeed require that the recipient knows, at least in general, what the meanings of the three components are which the speaker or writer had in mind. So far about language.

In architectural design metaphors arise and are used somewhat differently. Language presupposes thinking, here toward metaphors. Design presupposes thinking as well, but here instead of metaphors embedded in words we consider and think about metaphors embedded in physical objects. Other than with language, the basic and the declarative concepts collapse into the unity of the architectural expression. The metaphor 'the roof is a hat' collapses into whatever expression we give to the cover of the building with the metaphoric connotation being, for example, 'protection from rain and snow'. Observers, here again, must have the capacity to understand what the constituent concepts of the metaphor mean and must, at least to some extent, be able to infer the meaning of the ensuing concept. We may view this concept as a reference, a relational property of the others, the connected ones. Metaphors are very helpful by fostering inspiration and imagination which results in creativity, perhaps otherwise not experienced.

Out of these discussions emerges the view that understanding can only be grasped as mental representation of the object. On the other hand, we can perceive what we want to understand, the content, only by means of its form which is the realization of the object and thus its existence accessible to our senses and thoughts. Content and form are in unity. They are inseparably linked. Our only way to get at their origins is a 'despite-of-their-unity' effort to sort out the impressions which the underlying properties and the relationships among them evoke in us. In *impression from observation* we infer from form toward content. In *expression for design* we infer from content toward form. This view is instrumental for everything else which follows.

Perhaps most difficult to grasp and widely controversial is the role which emotion and feeling play in understanding. There is rather general agreement that all understanding originally comes from experience which begins with sensation. It is also increasingly clear, not only for philosophers and psychologists, but many other researchers of the interdependence of body and mind, like biologists and neurologists, and obviously artists, that feeling influences experience before we come to understanding in any depth. Before we are in a state of reasoning we are in a state of emotion and perhaps feeling because of sensation. In turn, however, when concepts have developed and inspire us they influence our emotions and feelings accordingly. This dual view is the basis for developing Chapter 4. The two foundations for emotion and feeling originate, like conceptualization, from our exposure to the presence of worldly reality and from representation in our memory. As conceptualization needs to be viewed as more or less enhanced by the powers of emotion, there is no understanding which is not in association with feeling. Even dreaming comes to us via emotion, a kind of inner resensation from memory. There is also never, for the fully conscious and conceptually rich mind, feeling which is not influenced by reason.

Out of this line of thinking it is only natural that we are prompted to address what we call aesthetic aspects. Simply from common sense, few of us would doubt that emotion and feeling play a crucial role in it. The concept of 'aesthetic', in ancient Greece associated with perception in general, has crucially changed during the eighteenth century by direct association with beauty. What is aesthetic and what constitutes it is controversial to this day. In this discussion I will clearly differentiate between aesthetics as the field of studies toward enlightening us about what is commonly called the beauty of objects and the aesthetic as the state of mind of pleasure or displeasure. I will back up my belief that there are no aesthetic properties in objects but only properties which we call aesthetic because of our judgment on pleasure or displeasure about them. Everything we perceive lets arise in us an aesthetic whether we are particularly aware of this resulting component of our cognitive processes or not.

As judgment is subjective there can be no generally valid rules on the aesthetic of properties but only collective, sometimes long lasting agreements about it, as was the case with the Golden Section. In the design of objects we have to a certain extent freedom of choice to emphasize or even especially embed properties which we judge to be pleasant and which others then for themselves judge to be pleasant (or perhaps not so). The aesthetic is not equal to beauty. The former is our state of mind with regard to pleasure or displeasure of anything experienced. The latter is our linguistic characterization which we give to objects which evoke pleasantness in us. The aesthetic is in architectural design, as in all other projecting enterprises, part of our state of meaning in our mind. It is inevitably a component of all of our understanding. We come to understanding as emotional, aesthetically experiencing beings.

Type, style and ornament are the focus of Chapter 5. In many respects it is a continuation of the discussion about aesthetics. Types arise from resemblances of objects which provides the basis for conceptualization and classification. They are also fundamental for how we put things together, how we order our world, in our case architectural design. There is repetitiveness of parts but also much variety among them and in the ways we can put them together for larger assemblies. Types have histories of utility. They are objects of cultural, social and formal preference. In architectural design, more than in other artistic endeavors, we think in terms of prototypes and how we can adapt them to particular purposes and environments. In the ways we combine types, which have partial meaning, overall meaning emerges.

Styles are derived from typologies to create repetitively particular themes. They combine types in variation though with recognizable patterns, that is, stylistic resemblances, based on personal choice or, in the wider framework of cultures, based on tradition which is the manifestation of collective choices over time. Styles are the physical answer, the particular formation, individuals or societies give in response to their needs and desires in given environments. Strong styles of individuals eventually determine the societies of which they are part.

With the advent of the industrial revolution and its emerging technologies, especially with the opportunities which mass production offered, the question of style led to answers never possible before. Long before Louis Sullivan arrived at his dictum on form and function, "purposiveness" and its consideration in design had been demanded. It figured prominently in the discussions about styles of neogothic and neoclassical genres throughout the 19th century and is helpful for explaining what has become known as the Modern Movement. I believe that this movement is not finished at all because of the ever more daring possibilities of realization which, however, will be increasingly subject to limitation forced by ecological sustainability.

Freedoms and constraints in style are reflected in ornament, that is, configuration beyond fundamental purposiveness. From this point of view, I see in ornamentation a much more basic function of how forms of architecture come about. In one sense, I consider ornament to be variation as amplification of form beyond pure necessity to facilitate favorable design solutions. In the other, I consider it to be embellishment as decoration, solely added to enhance sensual appeal and sometimes narrative enrichment beyond that which the building itself provides.

Causation, the subject of Chapter 6, is a fundamental condition of understanding and prediction. We consider everything we encounter to be an effect of a cause. When we look for an explanation of meaning, it being effect, we search for properties in objects, they being cause. These properties are effects of even earlier causes. Everything is part of chains of causes and effects. So, overall we have causes that produce effects and, in turn, these effects become causes for further effects. Causation is relational. We cannot observe cause and effect directly, only observe changes in chains of events. We observe cause and effect through the occurrence of difference from what was before.

Strictly viewed, there is only world-to-world causation as we can draw understanding from physical manifestations only. But mentality is involved. Therefore, a fourfold conceptualization of causation is very practical: world-to-world, world-to-mind, mind-to-world and mind-to-mind. When we view aspects of the world as physical and aspects of the mind as nonphysical, it is purely a thought construct and must not be considered to indicate a dualism of body and mind in any Cartesian sense.

World-to-world causation indicates the cause-effect relationship among physical objects or properties. World-to-mind causation indicates the relationship from physical causes to mental effects, producing impressions. Mind-to-world causation indicates the relationship from mental causes to physical effects, producing expressions. Unless one believes in telepathy, pure mind-to-mind causation is not conceivable, which means that it requires intermediate physical cause and effect occurrences. World and mind in these four aspectual arrangements point in a general way to the beginning and end points of partial chains of events.

Architectural design is a teleological process. We start with present impressions of what is given, then simulate future expressions on which, in turn, we make judgments on impressions from them. If we are satisfied, we stop. If not we look back for additional properties which provide, in combination with those already influencing us, further impressions for expressions. These many properties and their highly diverse combinations represent in effect the factors which cause architectural design to move forward. The process is like a spiral movement of a changing target with eventual resolution.

When we ask for causes we ask for observable and relational properties which have influence as design factors. That implies questions about their origins. I believe we can associate them best with the three categories of purpose, context and realization. All three consist of object properties and their functional relationships, and let design factors arise. Purposive design factors arise from programmatic needs or desires of the project, such as social and psychological criteria, organizational and operational guidelines, stylistic and other aesthetic preferences, but also financial targets. Contextual design factors arise from the setting in which the project finds itself, such as historical, cultural and economic conditions, freedoms and limitations of site, adjacent building and neighborhood characteristics, climatic conditions and solar access, even availability of construction labor and local materials. Design factors of realization arise from choices for building the project, such as construction systems and material selection, mechanical and electrical services, project complexity, but also building codes and other regulations.

Design factors from all three categories are constitutive in each architectural project. They are highly interdependent. Because of their nearly infinite variety they usually demand but also allow great flexibility in finding design solutions. All design factors contribute aspects of meaning and with them aesthetic evocation. Combined in whatever way, they should be considered the content in the content-form unity of particular projects. In its entirety, we may hold that the design and building process is the realization of purpose in the given context.

Description of architecture through language is one way of representation. Depiction of architecture through design is another by very different means. Both have architectural reality as reference for understanding. The purpose of Chapter 7 is to suggest a practical framework for how we may acquire meaning from and for specific designs. It builds on what I discussed in the previous elaborations on the sign natures of language and reality.

The linguistic turns of philosophy during the past century brought an enormous increase of our understanding about the structure and utilization of language, and its great impact on nearly everything we undertake. But language does not constitute reality nor does it determine thinking as some of the strongest 'linguistic turners' advocate. It is only referential. It is, however, the most common medium to order our thinking, communicate what we think and understand in highly effective abstraction. In this capacity it compliments visual representation, our main way of communication through physical things, including architecture. Both, language and architecture, allow by their particular capacities and efficiencies to improve on incapacities and inefficiencies the other has. As result, overall thinking is enhanced.

For grasping these differences, I elaborate first on the concepts of language thinking and design thinking. The referential nature of language provides its greatest value in architectural design through the description of purposive and contextual conditions, and that of conceptual developments, derived from these factors in combination with those from memory – all in the process from impressions to expressions, from analysis to synthesis. Language is an excellent 'prompter'. The revelation and clarification process takes place with the progress of design iteration from forms of what exists (with content) to new forms of what may become (with additional content).

While content and form are intimately unified, we may view content as the semantic component and form as the syntactic component. This view provides my foundation for design narratives: descriptions that observe form for content analysis and content for form synthesis. We look for what we want to understand – all described depending on the object or project – as existing properties or wanted properties. The general outline of design narratives is

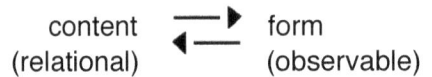

content ⇌ form
(relational)   (observable) .

Design narratives represent the unique process of design thinking as meaning in dialectical action. In every instance of a project the design narrative always pertains to one design factor or a combination of them in a wide or narrow frame of reference. The narratives follow our process of inspiration and decision making in design. They help to document why and how we, as designers, change existing states of affairs to produce new results. They are useful as memorized understanding for future projects. Their descriptions are usually less elaborate on the content side than the form side, as what now exists is easier accessible than what we remember from where it came. This difference decreases with doing such documentation often and systematically, especially when we make it routinely during design development, while content leading to form is still fresh in our mind.

Analysis aspects tend to be especially prominent when design narratives of existing buildings are done by laypersons rather than designers. Form description by clients and the general public, which is strongly influenced by related practical aspects of operation, gives designers much understanding of the thoughts of laypersons about architectural design issues. Professional design narratives foster through their structure design thinking in an organized way. They leave a trace of what happened during the synthesis of a particular project and help us to make design factors and their effects explicit and understood.

What architecture means to us and what we mean through it depends on the time of our involvement. Therefore, my account ends in Chapter 8 with thoughts about meaning in architectural design as part of the broader realm of Zeitgeist – our present understanding of being and culture. Post-structuralist tendencies have given rise to a great diversity in views about content and form in architectural design. With all the individuality in positions we can observe two main camps. On the one side are those who attempt to carve out a strongly independent role of architectural form in relation to a priori constraints of purpose and context, taking advantage of ever bolder virtual design approaches and high-technology realizations. On the other side are those who stay with more conventional approaches of giving purpose and context a role which is as explicit as possible when influencing the design process and its result. For whatever attitude one may assume on this issue, there should be no doubt about the fact that all architecture eventually has to play functional roles for which we must care in design. Some of these roles usually change over the life cycle of buildings. The more design can facilitate such change the better.

Architecture operates in an ever more integrated global environment of design, manufacturing and construction. On one side, we have highly consumption oriented, largely democratic societies, driven by free market and profit thinking, with tensions between common need and individual desire. On the other, we have a rising challenge by the dynamics of developing nations with large population increases and associated demands. Signs of stress because of enormous wealth in contrast to enormous poverty are evident.

A powerful shift of the architectural design and engineering processes from largely parallel to more integrated is ongoing, made possible through the many advances in computerized representation and exchange of information which also influence profoundly manufacturing and construction. That these procedures allow to design and build ever more daring objects presents not only great opportunities but great dangers. 'Everything-goes' excesses can be observed worldwide with little disguise of 'form follows ego'. When deconstruction is not, as Heidegger saw it, a careful method of analysis to build upon because of better understanding, but is deemed a result, then it breeds confusion rather than avoids it. I claim here that reasoned philosophical discourse and reasoned architectural design have more in common than justification of the indeterminacy of an undefined "other". Together they can go far to understand what exists in order to better understand what may become. Simulacrum cannot serve as a comprehensive design paradigm.

On a very different but not separated level a long overdue trend of responsibility is taking hold toward sustainability in all life-cycle phases of architecture from inception to demolition. Except for the enduring input of solar energy, our earth has only finite material resources. A major part of them is consumed by the built environment for construction, operation and disposal. If mankind is to survive, sustainability close to an absolute condition must be achieved in the not too distant future, which means that close to zero sum resource maintenance must be our central concern.

The only way to succeed is to make ecological efficiency and sustainability also in design the central principle.

To conclude this discussion, recent examples are given which indicate various paths architecture can take to reinforce the now inevitable shift towards a culture of sustainability. We have entered a new modernity or, if you will in Habermasian terms, another chapter in the never ending project of modernity. The very fundamentals of human being do not change and, therefore, the fundamental role of architecture does not change, that is, to help provide the best of possible environmental conditions for life to flourish. What sustainability means to us in this sense of critical understanding and which consequences we draw for architectural design will determine how history will look at what we contributed to our time. Today and then, meaning in architectural design needs to be responsive understanding of content in its form.

At the end of this introduction it should be helpful to say a word about the examples used in the following chapters. Overall, meanings are highly heterogeneous. Individually, they are particular understanding. My descriptions and illustrations reflect this duality, having arisen from personal and, therefore, specific encounters. The examples are my choices to reinforce the more general text and are meant to indicate directions, in no way completeness, an impossibility for the breadth of the topics. Other examples will well be found by your own inspiration. What ties all together in their variety is being part of representing the wholeness of things and life.

2 From Things toward Meaning

Meaning is a term with many meanings. It is typically used without further explanation but with the assumption that its particular content becomes eventually clear from the present context. This is acceptable as far as day-to-day situations are concerned. Not so, however, when it is at the center of discussion itself. Often, even long texts on meaning do not explain its nature as such. In a preliminary way we may hold that *meaning is what we understand of a particular aspect of reality.*

This may be taken as a definition. But it is not a very explanatory one. We usually explain by means of words and strings of words. The most important terms in the context of meaning are: reality, thing, object, property, appearance, cognition, concept, representation, thinking, emotion, understanding and knowledge. These terms themselves indicate complex and highly interdependent issues. It is probably fair to say that they together represent as topics the majority of what philosophy is about. Here is obviously not the place to make even an attempt to address the many, often controversial views about them. I can only direct attention to the extensive treatment in the literature.[1] To avoid confusion, however, I make my basic comprehension of them in architecture the central issue of this and the next chapter, and elaborate further wherever it seems to be necessary.

To start, I will enlarge on the just given notion that meaning is what we understand of a particular aspect of reality. Meaning is intentional and implies action. And, meaning occurs when information is transferred between a giver and a receiver by means of a medium, such as speech in language or the built environment in architecture. The medium has a considerable impact on how meaning is communicated, influencing more or less its content. What and how the giver perceives, conceives, understands and means with regard to a given object is never exactly the same as what and how the receiver does.

Looking from the receiver's point of view, meaning is at the end of the process which we call *impression*. Looking from the giver's point of view, meaning is at the beginning of the process which we call *expression*. At the center of both is thinking with a large portion being inspiration (usually called imagination). The expression oriented thought of the giver searches for a form, a realization, to embed his or her understanding in a medium for communication which allows the receiver to derive understanding from impression oriented thought. It is important to stress the distinction between the two situations, especially also on their place in the design process.

As designers we synthesize tokens of understanding into a broader understanding and eventually select a solution for realization as expression of meaning. As observers and perhaps users we analyze the expression via impression, that is, explore and evaluate the various features of the design for meaning. The meaning embedded by the designer in expression is the ground for the meaning of the observer in impression. Because they are different and serve different functions, I often point out the distinction referring to *expressive meaning* or *impressive meaning*. And finally, as judgment and decision making is involved in a particular understanding toward meaning, we may say for both that *meaning as activity is selective understanding and as result it is selected understanding.*[2]

2.1 Things and things in themselves

Architectural design is concerned with things, that is, anything we encounter and work with in creating built environments, be they physical or mental, natural or artificial, causes or effects, processes or results. We change existing things into other things which we hope serve us well for our needs and desires. To do that requires understanding of what the things are as far as possible and what we like the changes to be. Here is, I believe, where meaning plays its fundamental role in architectural design.

Often, perhaps mostly, there is no obvious 'giver' in communication which things provide, although we say that "things mean". But things do not mean themselves. They are media which convey a given meaning. Unless there is a human being, such as a designer, embedding meaning in things, there is no identifiable source of it. But there is always meaning when we perceive and, therefore, a cause. For absolutely not identifiable sources of meaning we may postulate that the giver is nature or God.

Meaning is always about things, that is, objects under our consideration. The word thing, as the word meaning, is one of those broad terms with a multitude of applications and interpretations. We ourselves are things who encounter other things (though politeness has it that we should not refer to other people as things). My use of the term *object* implies anything which may be perceived or conceived and which, therefore, exists physically or mentally and may be referred to – a thing potentially considered. How do we relate to things and how do we know about them? These questions were already among the earliest ones asked in philosophy. It should be helpful to review what some of the thinkers, mostly in recent times, have proposed as answers. The selection of issues and commentaries by philosophers in the next chapters emerged from the relevance to architectural design, necessarily without intensive elaboration on the broader systematic importance of such views in philosophy itself.

At least since Plato issues of belief, knowledge, justification and truth have been at the center of philosophical thought. Also ideas on the dual nature of body and mind can be traced back to then. It was at the time of René Descartes, however, that understanding emerges as a fundamental issue in the search for certainty: How can we know things? How and how far can we understand? Is there a method to find truth generally and the trueness of things specifically? By contrasting his own corporeal being, as part of the material universe, with his incorporeal soul, as the substance of thinking, René Descartes opened the door to a flood of controversies in understanding reality. He writes in 1641:

> But what, then, am I? A thinking thing, it has been said. But what is a thinking thing? It is a thing that doubts, understands, conceives, affirms, denies, wills, refuses; that imagines also, and perceives.[3]

The issues he raises have become and still are to this day the most fundamental questions in philosophical inquiries about the nature of being and reality. The extremes in both directions may be taken as 'there exist only material things', the view of strongest materialism, or 'there exist only mental things', the view of strongest idealism. Accepting both, at least to some extent, is dualism. At its strongest, Cartesian dualism views our being as mental existence without physically extended substance and as bodily existence with physically extended substance – the mind being beyond the brain though in causal interaction with it.[4]

This position leads to many questions about how mental and physical entities relate to each other. The problem, also known as the mind-body problem, is alive today as ever and we will be confronted with it in various ways during our discussions. I believe in a crucial dualism, to be shown along our way, but not the kind that Descartes proposed.

A few decades after Descartes John Locke writes of ideas and representations. He holds that when we think about material entities we must employ mental entities, ideas, which represent the material entities. Locke uses the term *idea* for

> … whatsoever is the Object of Understanding, when a Man thinks, …[5]

There are two sources for objects of understanding:

> External Material things, as Objects of *SENSATION;* And the Operations of our own Minds within, as the Objects of *REFLECTION,* are, to me, the only Originals [origins], from whence all our *Ideas* take their beginnings.

Whereby,

> *External Objects furnish the Mind with the* Ideas *of sensible qualities*, … And the *Mind furnishes the Understanding with* Ideas *of its own Operations.*[6]

He views the nature of physical things and the workings of human minds as the objects and sources for understanding. The resulting representations he calls ideas. They are the mental equivalent to the physical nature of things.

How do sensuous experiences and rational thinking come together to yield understanding? The answer is *imagination*, our faculty to search for and connect events of cause and effect, aside from the more usually assumed connotation of providing fantasy. It is here where the empiricist thinkers of that period especially complement the rationalists. Thomas Hobbes writes already in 1651 that

> When man thinketh on anything whatsoever, His next Thought after, is not altogether so casual as it seems to be. Not every Thought to every Thought succeeds indifferently [no thought succeeds another independently]. But as we have no Imagination, whereof we have not formerly had Sense, in whole, or in parts; so we have no Transition from one Imagination to another, whereof we never had the like before in our Senses. The reason whereof is this. All Fancies [imagination processes] are motions within us, relics of those made in Sense … by coherence of the matter moved …

And,

> The Trayn of regulated Thoughts is of two kinds: One, when of an effect imagined, we seek the causes, or means that produce it … The other is, when imagining any thing whatsoever, we seek all the possible effects, that can by it be produced; that is to say, we imagine what we can do with it, when we have it. … In summe, the Discourse of the Mind, when it is governed by design, is nothing but *Seeking,* …

And,

> Sometimes man seeks what he has lost; … to find where, and when he had it; … This we call *Remembrance*, or Calling to mind …[7]

Imaginations are instances of thought convergence. As process they are associations and connections of thought remembered from former experience prompted by new circumstances. Locke derives from this understanding of imagination that, through ideas connecting in our mind, new and more complex ideas may come forth.

> In this faculty of repeating and joining together its *Ideas*, the Mind has great power in varying and multiplying the Objects of its Thought, infinitely beyond what *Sensation* or *Reflection* furnished it with; …[8]

The infinite possibilities which come out of the association of ideas requires control. Already Plato had warned in this respect about the potential for excesses, especially in the arts. Therefore, Locke points to the importance of judgment:

> For *Wit* lying most in the assemblage of *Ideas*, and putting those together with quickness and variety, wherein can be found any resemblance or congruity, thereby to make

> up pleasant Pictures, and agreeable Visions in the Fancy: J*udgment*, on the contrary, lies quite on the other side, in separating carefully, one from the other, *Ideas,* wherein it can be found the least difference, thereby to avoid being misled by Similitude, and by affinity to take one thing for another.[9]

We may draw from this view that our understanding arises from the relationships and associations of ideas which are raised in our mind. But what we believe to be true of such understanding must come through our judgment.

There is another contribution of Locke which has given a fundamental direction in how we may think to relate to the world. Our process toward understanding seeks to sort out in detail what our sensations provide. We try to grasp what properties of objects are. He writes that

> Whatever the Mind perceives in it self, or is the immediate object of Perception, Thought, or Understanding, that I call *Idea;* and the Power to produce any *Idea* in our Mind, I call *Quality* … Thus a Snow-ball having the power to produce in us the *Ideas of White, Cold* and *Round*, …, as they are in the Snow-ball, I call *Qualities*; and as they are Sensations, or Perceptions, in our Understandings, I call them *Ideas;* …[10]

Ideas are determined by the properties of what we encounter which he calls "qualities". Additional ideas, a kind of secondary ones, arise out of reflection of other ideas and their combination. We can only reflect on what we have earlier encountered and now remember. Therefore, also combined ideas can only be derived from once experienced properties. This view prompted David Hume, who was strongly influenced by Locke, to write that

> It seems a Proposition, which will not admit of much Dispute, that all our ideas are nothing but copies of our Impressions, or, in other Words, that 'tis impossible for us to *think* of anything, which we have not antecedently *felt*, either by our external or internal Senses.[11]

This is why for Hume all understanding is based on experience. "Impressions" are perceptions which are gained by the mind from involvement with the outside world. There is a causal relationship between object and subject which he calls "necessary connection", established by a "power" which we cannot sense but only know from the results it produces. He asks

> *What is the Nature of all our Reasonings concerning Matter of Fact?* the proper answer seems to be, that they are founded on the Relation of Cause and Effect. When again it is ask'd, *What is the Foundation of all our Reasonings and Conclusions concerning that Relation?* it may be repli'd in one word, EXPERIENCE. But if we still carry on our sifting and examining Humour, and ask, *What is the Foundation of all Conclusions from Experience?* this produces a new Question, which may be of more difficult Solution and Explication.[12]

There are limits to what things reveal and what our capacities to perceive and understand are. He is right when he adds that

> It must certainly be allow'd, that Nature has kept us at a great Distance from all her Secrets, and has afforded us only the Knowledge of a few superficial Qualities of Objects, while she conceals from us those Powers and Principles, on which the influence of these Objects entirely depends. Our Senses inform us of the Colour, Weight, and Consistence of Bread; but neither Sense nor Reason can ever inform us of those Qualities, which fit it for the Nourishment and Support of a human Body.[13]

Hume refers here to the dual nature of all things, one part observable by us and the other not – the latter being the nature of "things in themselves". Immanuel Kant makes this aspect in 1783 a major issue in his philosophy:

> … experience teaches us what exists and how it exists, but never that it must necessarily

exist so and not otherwise. Experience therefore can never teach us the nature of things in themselves.[14]

Whether there are *things in themselves* has not been settled, and probably never will be, as it is beyond our capacities to prove one way or another. I believe that we encounter, within a certain horizon, all of what there is, that is, we encounter holistically. But we cannot perceive *all* of what there is. We can perceive only what our nature allows us to perceive, the phenomena, what "appears" to us as Kant says; and that is is not all there is. Kant differentiates between phenomena of objects which are accessible by our senses and noumena which exist in the same thing but are not accessible (the thing in itself).[15] Even if we could perceive all, that is, get to know all, it would not mean that we understand all. This point has some relevance for terminological clarity. It is an unfortunate convention that we use in ordinary language 'to know' and 'to understand' as synonyms. They are related. But we may know information and not understand it. We understand only what we have conceptualized, at least to a certain extent. There is usually a transition from knowing to full understanding. We always get something to know before we understand it. Even more problematic is the frequent use of the term knowledge to indicate in depth understanding, whether it is recently acquired or lodged in our memory or stored in other devices, such as books or computers.

Information is the foundation for our understanding. Importantly, most of our understanding is belief, not certainty. There are overall very few propositions which we may judge with the highest degree of certainty. I don't know of any which are not mathematical, except the a priori condition that there is reality and we, including our thoughts, are part of it. I hold here a Kantian position and I believe that we understand only more or less what exists. Beyond are the things in themselves. By necessity we exist on an operational level with uncertainty as a fact of life and with tolerance sufficient for success. There is no question in my mind that there is reality, or we would not exist and not be able to think, and have no mental representations of it. Ludwig Wittgenstein says in 1953 about the dependence of representations on reality that

> An inner process stands in need of outward criteria.[16]

What something is, its content, and how it is accessible via our senses, its form, is reflected by the concept we develop of it. We encounter reality from which we draw these concepts. I can follow George E. Moore, one of the staunchest defender of strict Realism, when he writes in 1903 that

> The content of the thing is what we assert to exist, when we assert that the thing exists.[17]

But not so when he insists that

> … what is called content of a sensation is in very truth what I originally called it – the sensation's object.[18]

The "content of a sensation" is not "the sensation's object". The sensation's object is a thing. The content of sensation is neural signals which prompt my thoughts toward conceptualization. While the existence of anything beyond our mind has a content which we encounter in its form, we can only assert the content of the thing's representation in our mind, the content we can be aware of through our capacity to think in consciousness. We do not have the object in our mind but its representation. The content of sensation is the sensation's result being impressed on our mind. Maurice Merleau-Ponti writes in 1962 that

> Consciousness is being towards the thing through the intermediary of the body.[19]

Consciousness has intentionality. When we are conscious we are always conscious of something. We cannot relate to and conceptualize something which does not have any content. According to John Searle

> Intentionality is that property of many mental states and events by which they are directed

at or about or of objects and states of affairs in the world.[20]

When we are conscious we direct ourselves toward and are aware of objects, be they physical or mental. Sometimes consciousness and intentionality have been understood as synonyms. But this view is controversial together with that of the nature of consciousness itself. On the other hand, if we view intentionality as that part of consciousness, which is "directed at or about or of" in the sense of *active awareness of something,* we avoid this synonymy. As mentioned, if we are aware and perceive a physical thing, we obviously do not have the thing in our mind but its representation. Looking at a tree we do not have the tree in our mind but its representation, its neural equivalent. Nicholas Rescher writes about metaphysical realism and pragmatic objectivity that

> Realism has two indispensable and inseparable constituents—the one existential and ontological, the other cognitive and epistemic. The former maintains that there is a real world – a realm of mind-independent, objective physical reality. The latter maintains that we can to some extent secure adequate descriptive information about this mind-independent realm – that we can validate plausible claims about it. …
>
> … What is at issue here is a practice-enabling presupposition that experience is indeed objective. That what we *take* to be evidence indeed *is* evidence, that our sensations yield information about an order of existence outside the experiential realm itself, and that this experience is not just a mere phenomenon but represents the appearance of something extramental, belonging to an objectively self-subsisting order – all this is something that we must always *presuppose* in using experiential data as 'evidence' for how things stand in the world.[21]

And,

> … reality-as-we-think-of-it (= our reality) is the only reality we can deal with, and this is not mind-independent, but construed in mind-involving terms.[22]

When I touch a tree or when I see a window, I touch or see these things in their reality although I do not understand this reality in its entirety. My perception is real but I have no certainty how far the external reality and my internal reality, my mental representation, essentially agree. They certainly do not in their form, form understood as ways of existence. Trees and windows which we encounter are in their material form different from our representations of them in mental form. Material and mental forms occur in their particular reality.

We are reality and something we conceptualize or conceptualized from reality exists; similar to what others conceptualized before us from reality which existed then. But our concepts are relative to our capability of understanding the reality of the things. This position amounts to having aspects of external realism and conceptual relativism brought together – a representative realism. Searle brings the two positions together in writing that

> Properly understood, realism is not a thesis about how the world is in fact. We could be totally mistaken about how the world is in every detail and realism could still be true. *Realism is the view that there is a way that things are that is logically independent of all human representations. Realism does not say how things are but only that there is a way that they are.*

And,

> Let external realism be the view that: Reality exists independently of our representations of it. Let the relevant thesis of conceptual relativism be the view that: All representations of reality are made relative to some more or less arbitrarily selected set of concepts.

And,

> … the real world does not care how we describe it and it remains the same under the

various different descriptions we give it.[23]

What we sense of the world *is for real,* exists, and it is the ground of what we perceive. When we see a red cloth, our sensation and conception gives us the mental representation we call 'red cloth', whatever that thing in reality may be. Hitting with my toe and then seeing a hard stone tells me in mental representation what we call 'hardness' and 'stone'. That there is something like hardness and a stone is not in doubt. But hardness and stone are entirely human concepts, and we identify them by names. Both is our doing. Designing and assembling a building is using mental representations of physical things in our mind but in its fundamental essence the building is a thing in itself. It has the features we have given to it, *as we believe they are.* But we nor anyone else will ever understand the building in its full reality.

The ultimate ground for all our understanding and knowledge is the world, the reality external to us. We are connected with it via sensation, but according to Kant

> ... sensuous perception represents things not at all as they are, but only by the mode in which they affect our senses; and consequently by sensuous perception appearances only, and not things themselves, are given to the understanding for reflection. ...[24]

As this is such an important aspect for our understanding, let's look at two reinforcing explanations, one by Henry Putnam, the other by Sebastian Gardner.

> Immanuel Kant, writing two hundred years ago, told us that knowledge of the world is possible, but it does not go beyond experience. The words might have pleased Bishop Berkeley, who held that human knowledge does not go beyond *sensation,* but sensations are not what Kant meant by "experience". Kant's purpose, unlike Berkeley's, was not to deny the reality of matter, but rather to deny that things in themselves are possible objects of knowledge. What we can know — and this is the idea which Kant himself regarded as a kind of Copernican Revolution in philosophy — is never the thing in itself, but always the thing as represented. And the representation is never a mere copy; it always is a joint product of our interaction with the external world and the active powers of the mind. The world as we know it bears the stamp of our own conceptual activity.[25]

And,

> Copernicus explains the *apparent* movement of the sun in terms of the movement of the observer on the earth. Kant explains our knowledge of *apparently* independently constituted objects in terms of our mode of cognition. In both a phenomenon which had been regarded previously as having independent reality is redescribed as an appearance, dependent on the subject. In that respect both Kant and Copernicus break with common sense.

But,

> … there is reason for regarding objects as subject-dependent *only* to the extent that they are conceived in terms of the conditions under which objects are possible for us at all, i.e. only with respect to those of their features by virtue of which they conform to the structure of experience; we are justified in regarding as subject-dependent only whatever in objects pertains to the possibility of their being objects for us at all.[26]

Sensory experience and conceptual capacity thus allow us to know and understand the world, as far as we are able, and this happens through the appearance of things in our mind after we have encountered them in their physical reality and where they exist in their totality.

There is only one world and we are part of it. This – our being part of it – adds something very unique: understanding and meaning. Only through our experience of reality do things become understood. Only through our experience of them do they become meaningful.

2.2 Objects and concepts

We sense objects but understand them through concepts. The distinction between object and concept has been clearly expressed already in Scholasticism, the dominant philosophical direction during the Middle Ages. New understanding was mainly derived through dialectical approaches. A distinction was made between *objectum quod* and *objectum quo*.[27] The former is the object under consideration, as we encounter it in its existence. The latter is the object in our conceptual thinking about it, the way we understand it. Or today we may say that the object quo explains the object quod, at least to some extent. In understanding something, we represent what we believe its essence is in our mind. Though helpful as a definition, the differentiation of objectum quod and objectum quo is easily mixed up in discussion and it is, therefore, much better to use *thing* or *object* for the former and *concept* for the latter.

When using the terms *object* and *properties* we hint at concepts. *Concepts* are the results of understanding what objects and their properties are and do. They are thought constructs of what exists, that is, mental *representations*. Concepts have a crucial function in the analysis of other concepts via comparison. The term object is sometimes used to indicate mental items, that is, thought objects. Unless I mention otherwise, I mean with the term object physical things and with properties their physical properties. The counterparts of object properties in concepts should be called *attributes* or perhaps concept properties. They are our conceptualizations of properties, that is, what we think they are. We sense properties but conceptualize to understand them as attributes. To use the term attribute all the time when we refer to concepts would be the right thing to do. It would, however, often require us to think about the differentiation, which I just made, between properties and attributes, even when out of context we would not need to. Therefore, I stay with convention and use *property* for both objects and concepts, and use *attribute* only where it is important to emphasize conceptual, attributive nature.

Complex objects consist of multiple properties, so do their concepts. The color red on a wall is a singular property object. A red wall is a multiple property object with a red surface, a structure as space divider with its own multiple properties and a surface on the opposite side. The wall has physical dimensions. An object is anything which we consider by means of our senses; for example, a window we observe, a drawing of a window we look at or the written word 'window' we read. To all three we have access by way of our senses. For all three we develop mental representations which relate to each other via the *generic concept* of 'window'. Generic is a notion about which I will have to say more later. For now it should be taken as the quality of common features which objects of a category have.

There is only one way we can come to concepts and that is through our experience of objects and thinking about them, in short, *object thinking*. Kant writes, following Hume:

> There is no doubt whatever that all our cognition begins with experience; for how else should the cognitive faculty be awakened into exercise if not through objects that stimulate our senses and in part themselves produce presentations, …[28]

And,

> … there are two conditions under which alone the cognition of an object is possible: first, *intuition*, through which it is given, but only as appearance; second, *concept*, through which an object is thought that corresponds to this intuition.[29]

It is important to differentiate this use of the term appearance from the use in ordinary language which refers to the coming of an object into our presence so that we can observe it. To obtain a sensation-generated mental appearance in Kant's sense, first a physical appearance of the object or at least an equivalent communication must occur from which perception can originate.

In order for us to understand a particular object, every intuition, from sensation or through recall from memory, produces an appearance. Appearances are preliminary mental representations from which we develop and determine concepts through judgment. We may visualize the dependence of our minds on the world as shown in 2.1.

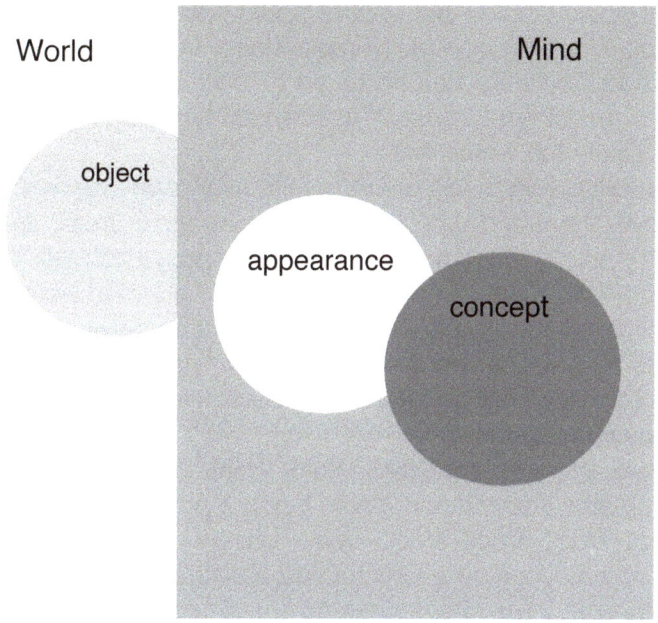

2.1 From object to concept by means of object thinking

As perceiving and thinking observers we conceptualize objects with regard to their properties. Looking at a particular door we understand it as an instantiation of the concept of door. Looking at a red painted hydrant we gain a primary concept of 'red'. This concept may reinforce the secondary concept of the relational property 'for fire fighting', if red color is repetitively used and commonly understood to indicate that purpose in conjunction with a hydrant. In other words, we can understand objects in comparison with existing concepts in our mind, which naturally leads to the question we we will have to address eventually, how we come to an original stock of concepts stored in our memory.

One aspect which, according to Kant, defies conceptualization is the pleasure or displeasure about an object. Kant largely neglects the issue in writing his First Critique but makes it a central theme in his Third, in which he writes that

> ... there is only one so-called sensation that can never become a concept of an object, and this is the feeling of pleasure and displeasure. This is merely subjective, whereas all other sensations can be used for cognition.[30]

True. Pleasure and displeasure cannot be a concept *of* an object. But emotion – feelings of pleasure or displeasure – *about* an object influences more or less our conceptualization through our judgments about it. Pleasure or displeasure about concepts is subjective, as dependent on individual judgment. It cannot be conceptualized by itself. But it influences our thinking and actions in conceptualization and thus becomes inseparably part of our understanding.

This view points back to the issue of properties versus attributes, properties of things in our understanding of them are *qualities* which we attribute to the things and are subject to judgment.

From this more comprehensive point of view, the term concept in 2.1 should be changed to understanding, which is broader than concepts. As we are, however, presently concerned with conceptualization (and the explanation of that change would require more elaboration than is helpful now) I leave it at that. We will return to this important aspect later in detail.

We develop new concepts by comparing presently gained experiences with concepts we already have in mind. In other words, existing concepts serve to classify appearances, our initial mental representations of objects. This use of concepts has a very special status in the process of understanding which we need to clarify. Before we get to this, however, it may help to look at the main distinction between the meaning of 'concept' in common language versus that in philosophy and also psychology. Ray Jackendoff writes that

> There is a fundamental tension in the ordinary language term *concept*. On one hand, it is something out there in the world: 'the Newtonian concept of mass' is something that is spoken of as though it exists independently of who actually knows or grasps it. Likewise, 'grasping a concept' evokes comparison to grasping a physical object, except that one does it with one's mind instead of one's hand. On the other hand, a concept [this concept is then] spoken of as an entity within one's head, a private entity, a product of the imagination that can be conveyed by means of language, gesture, drawing, or some other imperfect means of communication.[31]

We use, closer to our interest, the term concept to point to the drawing or model of a building, a physical representation of an idea, the representation being a *physical* object in its own right. But this is *not* how I use the term for the purposes in this text unless I especially point this out. My use of concept refers to the *mental* representation of an observed object or state of affairs of whatever kind, physical or mental. It may be, for example, the concept (mental comprehension) of a directly encountered object like a building, the concept of an activity, the concept of a representation of an object like a drawing or the concept of a recalled dream. How we come to such concepts is our present concern.

Concepts are derived from preliminary mental representations – via inner appearances as thought constructs of outer appearances – from what we believe particular parts of reality are. They are compared with and sorted under concepts we already understand. We understand through categorization. This is so whether we consider very simple or very complex situations, obviously with variations in effort accordingly. To regard something to be 'red' is comparing it with earlier sensations and understandings of things being red. Grant Gillett and John McMillan write:

> A concept ... involves the organization of aspects of a sensory presentation and the application of a category. Consider your concept of a triangle, if an experimenter told you to sort out a set of shapes into squares and triangles you would pick out the triangles on the basis of them possessing three sides.[32]

Therefore, resemblances play a crucial role in our understanding of the world. In fact, we could not coherently think without them. Henry Price writes:

> We cannot deny that something which may be called 'the recurrence of characteristics' is genuinely there. We must also admit that if it were not there, conceptual cognition could not exist. If the world were not like this, if there were no recurrence in it, it could be neither thought about nor spoken about. We could never have acquired any concepts; and even if we had them innately (without needing to acquire them) they could never have been applied to anything.[33]

Recurrence of at least some resemblance is the grounds of bringing intuitions under concepts. But now I must add a comment on how we originally acquire concepts to compare with. The very first concept of something, that is something we have not yet any knowledge about, can obviously not be acquired through conceptualization based on resemblance but only through intuition and 'understanding as such'. We can grasp resemblance of some occurrence of 'red' only after we have the concept of 'red' from an earlier occurrence already in our memory for recall. We must possess a cognition of something before we may have a re-cognition of it. In this very first exposure to the property 'red' we perceive it *ostensively* and learn to call it 'red'; the name given to it by convention. Learning by ostension is simply by acceptance. Words, for example, are originally given and accepted ostensively, that is, learned ostensively as symbolic references to something.[34]

An ostensive concept of red then is the first of the *specific concepts* of red I encounter and at the same time the first instance and exemplification of the *generic concept* of red in a classification of red objects. This means that generic concepts stem originally from specific concepts (without us knowing at this point that these concepts are specific in the sense of being part of a group of other specific concepts).[35] Specific concepts refer directly to the objects we consider and generic concepts indirectly to their classification. We may consider generic concepts as idealized prototypes of concepts. I believe that this is what Kant had in mind when he wrote about the formation of concepts:

> The capacity (receptivity) to acquire representations through the way we are affected by objects is called *sensibility*. Objects are therefore *given* to us by means of sensibility, and it alone affords us *intuitions*; but they are *thought* through the understanding, and from it arise *concepts*.[36]

So, concepts are what we understand because of input from sensation and memory (by means of combinatorial inference and reconceptualization) or from memory alone (which is comparatively rare). Most concepts are learned, that is, their properties are not fundamentally investigated with regard to their origin. In growing up we accept things as they are for a long time before we question them, if at all. Whatever be the case, we conceptualize by comparison. What is decisive here is regularity and similarity. We cannot recognize things unless they reoccur and have repetition of features.

2.3 Understanding and judgment

In our exploration of object and concept, I assumed without saying that object is cause and concept is effect. Let's consider in more detail the process in 2.2.

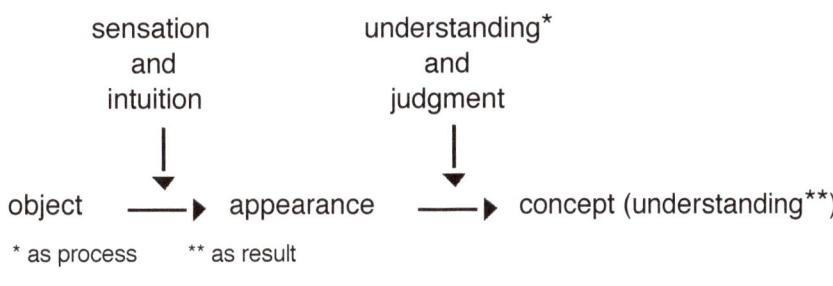

2.2 Judgment in conceptualization

Sensation is at the threshold between world and mind. It results in appearance of raw data in our mind. Thinking takes this information from appearance and compares it to what we already know and understand, the existing concepts in our memory, and develops additional concepts, additional understanding. Note: while it may appear that I use the term thinking only for the process of understanding and judgment, this is not so. Thinking as process and thoughts as its results are for me any neural activities which contribute to awareness and lead eventually to understanding as result.

It is important with regard to 2.2 and in general to differentiate between understanding* as process and understanding** as result. The latter resides in our memory. Additional concepts come to us through understanding as process which includes judgment to ascertain and sort out what they are in comparison with the existing concepts. Kant points out that

> The appearance depends upon the senses, but the judgment upon the understanding; ...[37]

To select, that is, to make a judgment on what an appearance is and which conceptual category it belongs to, we must have existing understanding to compare with. In other words, the process of understanding of the mind depends in part on its already existing understanding. In reference to what I said earlier, concepts being created are rarely completely new as memory usually contributes. Understanding never develops on a 'clean slate', except in early childhood.[38] 'New' concepts are nearly always combinations of features from present perceptions and from former perceptions remembered.

By now it should be clear that conceptualization is, while addressing great diversity, rather rule governed through ordering into categories. 'Red' may be considered a simple concept, a single quality, with a name given arbitrarily a long time ago.[39] The recognition of red, however, is not accidental. It is rule governed as being controlled by the same neural properties of sensation and understanding as the first time around. 'House' is a rather complex concept with a system of properties and their relationships about which we learn over a long period of time. Along the way most concepts develop hierarchically as being in a systems context with subsystems and components.

With regard to a given situation, our cognitive faculties allow us to perceive and categorize in various foci of detail, say, narrow or wide, which is not the same as simple or complex. We also perceive and categorize from different points of view and interest. This kind of considering something we call *aspectual*. We may see a house conceptually, for example, as a shelter with rooms for various functions, as a system of building construction or as a part of a neighborhood. This line of thought also reveals the crucial role language plays in the ways we classify reality.

Appearances, though we may think of them as wholes, consist of many parts. Even when only seeing and concentrating on the color of a wall, we cannot do that without in one way or another implicating, perhaps subconsciously, the overall environment. Impressions, as short as they may be, are usually based on sequences of intuitions which leave residual aspects in mind. Together with objects of direct interest we conceptualize their environments in the broadest sense including physical, historical, cultural and technical aspects.

The parts of appearances must 'come together' for us to grasp concepts as wholes. To accomplish this is one of the main functions of thinking. Kant writes:

> Synthesis in general is, ... the mere effect of the imagination, of a blind though indispensable function of the soul, without which we would have no cognition at all, but of which we are seldom even conscious. Yet to bring this synthesis *to concepts* is a function that pertains to the understanding, by means of which it first provides cognition in the proper sense.[40]

Kant uses the term imagination with a rather obscure notion, "a blind though indispensable function of the soul". My take: it is the capacity to recall earlier developed concepts from memory to be combined for new ones by themselves or with presently developed ones. It is inspiration.

Judgment in understanding is made on the basis of defining object features and making decisions about their fit into conceptual categories. This implies resemblance. Judgments take tokens of understanding and look for resemblance to decide whether they fall under an existing generic concept category in our memory.

We always should bear in mind that concepts exist as derivations from objects. This is why Kant writes, looking back to where cognition originates, that

> All cognition requires a concept, however imperfect and obscure it may be; but as far as its form is concerned the latter is always something general, and something that serves as a rule. ... However, it can be a rule of intuitions only if it represents the necessary reproduction of the manifold of intuitions, hence the synthetic unity in the consciousness of them. Thus in the perception of something outside of us the concept of body makes necessary the representation of extension, and with it that of impenetrability, of shape, etc.[41]

"Extension" means here manifestation of a concept in reality beyond our mind. The particular building, I may presently observe, is an extension, a physical realization, of a particular concept which, in turn, is a member of a set with the generic concept of 'building'. We should remember that an indefinite number of concepts already exist in our mind. They may play a role not only for judgment toward understanding but for specific concept development, such as in design during which we combine concepts from present observations with those from earlier ones.

During the process of design we employ also another kind of judgment. We develop alternative understandings and eventually grasp one – therefore my view of meaning as selected understanding. The preconditions for this activity are sufficient understanding of things and criteria for judgment on solutions for selection. We obviously want to understand as broadly and as deeply as we can to allow for possibilities of choice. In observation (impression) the selection is limited by what is given in the object under consideration. In design (expression) we have usually some choice, though constrained by what purpose and context require and provide. The judgment criteria themselves are understandings as well. They arise out of particular circumstances. Based on experience the criteria are goal oriented, forward looking. They are, as all understandings, subjective but not completely so as all our backgrounds have objective influences from the reality of the world we constantly are exposed to. They also are responsive to intersubjective discourse with fellow men. From our understanding of understanding we derive that there is, as far as our judgments go, no absolute objectivity nor absolute subjectivity. Things, which we consider, are for us objects and are objective by being the same to us under the same circumstances. Our perception and understanding of them, however, is subjective. *We are subjectively involved with an objective world.*

So, in design we arrive at meaning as understanding involving two kinds of judgment: conceptual judgment for understanding of our own design proposals from inspiration and evaluative judgment for selection of one particular alternative for expression. We must first understand what the alternatives are before we can reasonably select one (2.3).

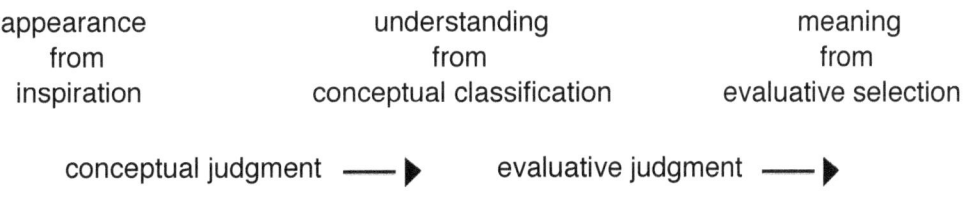

2.3 Judgment towards meaning in design

Appearance is here again the appearance in our mind. Inspiration is from memory and may be supported by sensation of present aspects, which is naturally the case in observation. Let's consider the very simple example of variously colored doors in the hallway of a classroom building: I was told that I should go to the classroom with the yellow door. Under these circumstances yellow is particularly meaningful to me and I make first a conceptual judgment about which door is yellow and then make an evaluative judgment and select it to enter. If I would pass by the classrooms without interest to look for a particular door, yellow would be just a color like any other, unless I may single it out as particularly to my liking, this now being also an evaluative judgment, shown as part of 2.3. If I am the color consultant for the building, I propose to myself a certain range of door colors through conceptual judgment and then choose for each door, perhaps in relation to other colors around (additional conceptual judgment), a color through evaluative judgment.

What about rules for the two kinds of judgment? The conceptual judgment, as mentioned earlier, is resemblance based. The evaluative judgment can be based on all kinds of reasons, such as cultural, monetary and physical ones. This means that there apply rules from these various fields at least as guideposts. There is also the possibility of simply aesthetic 'reason' on the basis of the object being more or less pleasant, an aspect we will look at later extensively.

The process from perception to meaning may look like a one dimensional sequence. It is, however, much more complex. Things have many features which are perceived in a kind of dialectic with iterative and parallel processing. Integration occurs with influence of many conceptualizations based on external sources and internal recall from memory. Underlying the whole process we discussed is the progression to that condition which Kant calls the "unity of the consciousness in the synthesis of the manifold of the representations" and "synthetic unity of apperception". In a nutshell, the process may be grasped by the notion "I think".[42] It is the integration activity which brings our representations together so that they may be compared and sorted out to form additional concepts. Generally, when we are conscious our basic status is thinking for concept generation.

Thoughts are in our minds. They are meaningful, if we are aware of them, even if they may mean nonsense. They may by extension be communicated through various corporeal media, such as speech, literature, radio, graphics, movies, dance and architecture. While thoughts are directly accessible to our intellect, everything else is only indirectly accessible to our reasoning via our senses. Therefore, our thoughts are certain to us as they are part of us, but everything else cannot be certain.

The process from perception of reality to understanding is at the center of Kant's interest and attitude. He named his position "transcendental idealism" – a problematic choice of wording of which he was aware. It can lead to confusion with other contemporary and later views called idealism.[43,44] I believe that 'mental representationalism' or, less awkward 'conceptualism', would better point out what we address here. While the objective world is independent of our perception of it, though some of it is continuously changed by us, this world is different in our understanding from what it is by itself. We perceive it modified by our sensible, intellectual and psychological idiosyncrasies.

Kant's views, which I largely make my own, are not easily grasped, especially in concentrated description, but also not in his wide ranging terminological diffusion.[45] The simple example of seeing a tree may help. The tree is there and I am here, both in reality. The physical process of sensing the tree is the ground for my mental representation of it. This representation, *cannot* exist independently from my encountering the tree. Imagining a tree, such as my dreaming of one or my drawing one, is not experiencing a tree but experiencing a dream or experiencing the drawing of a tree. They are two different conceptualizations of a tree and different from the one I develop right after sensing the physical tree from reality. In Bryan Magee's view

> … it is essential for us to be clear that what the transcendental idealist is saying is not that the empirical world does not 'really' exist: of course it exists. … The point is that the world of experience [what we hold this world to be] cannot exist independently of the experience.[46]

A crucial issue missing in all of this discussion, one which Kant addresses inadequately in connection with understanding, is the nature of feeling and how it influences the process of understanding and its results. It is the subject of Chapter 4.

As mentioned in connection with 2.2 the term understanding is used as verb (activity) and as noun (result). The process of understanding arrives at new concepts by comparison with existing ones and judgment. In impression, an understanding becomes meaningful to us because of our belief in its truth value for whatever reason. It is at that point active understanding which we select to be singled out to ourselves. In expression, we select, in a much stronger sense, an understanding and make it active as a meaning to be communicated beyond ourselves. In both modes, meanings are representations as all understandings are. In designing, the selection implies intention for representation in our mind and representation through architecture; actions about which we will have to say much more.

In this context it is helpful to compare design actions with speech acts. John Searle writes first about meaning in communication that

> A primary-meaning intention is an intention to represent; a communication intention is an intention that the hearer should know the representing intuition.

Then he mentions, contrasting speech acts and picture acts, that

> … in the standard speech situation the utterance both represents and communicates, and it is tempting (and, in general, correct) to construe a failure to communicate as a failure of the speech act; but with pictures the fact that the picture can represent a certain state of affairs is clearly independent of the question of whether it is ever used to communicate anything to anybody.[47]

As I will discuss later, language is in many other ways different from pictures or any other objects in representing and communicating.

2.4 Observable and relational properties

So far we addressed mostly the way we get to the understanding of physical objects by means of sensation. Their properties are the basis for corresponding representations in our mind, that is, concepts which serve for explanation. Even language, which is fully symbolic, comes to us in physical form which we sense, be it spoken or written.

All concepts and their properties are referential. They refer to the objects and their properties which we encounter. But there is more than reference to what we directly observe and sense. We are also prompted to think about related aspects. These indirectly, by reflection derived properties stand for what the observable properties mean to us beyond themselves, but in connection with them. Therefore, it makes sense to think about the directly encountered properties as *observable properties* and about the indirectly derived properties as *relational properties*. There are naturally also many unobservable properties in the encountered objects because most objects consist of multiple, spatially integrated properties. Hence, relational properties refer to hidden properties within observed objects and to properties in other objects or states of affairs. A door to a building has observable properties. Through them we are prompted to think that there is an interior space beyond and that there is the possibility to enter. Both are relational properties. The space of a classroom has among many other properties the crucial relational one of accommodating a group of children and, in a wider frame of reference, of providing an environment for education. The observable and relational nature is a feature of all objects having complexity, including architecture.

Note: All observable properties are physical or we could not observe them, which is a physical process. But relational properties are not physical though they may refer to physical properties within objects, presently encountered, or beyond such objects, that is, in other objects. This distinction is the reason that I do not contrast terminologically physical and relational properties but observable and relational properties. The contrast is not between physical and non-physical aspects, that is ontological, but between observable and relational, that is procedural. This view obviously shall not mean not to use the term physical where appropriate.

Relational properties are secondary, not in importance, but in the sequence of conceptualization. Our understanding of the relational properties is only possible through contemplation of the observable properties. We only call them properties of these objects because we are prompted by their observable ones, that is, to think about them. Again, regarding a door: after observation of it through sensation and perception we may think about its operability to accommodate passage of people or about its proportional fit within the overall facade.

Properties are never by themselves but part of objects. They are always on, in or about something, even if we believe that we consider them in isolation. Paint is not by itself. It is in a can or bucket, or belongs to a surface. Its appearance to us is influenced by the kind of light falling on it. If it is on a wall, we infer that it protects the wall and that a dirt spot may be easily removed because of it. If paint is used for writing on the surface, it has a very strong relational, nonphysical property: it establishes communication whose content, as such, has nothing to do with the paint. Here, the paint is instrumental as the medium of conveyance, which is an observable property with relational power. These, sometimes simple, sometimes complex, references have meaning for us. Full understanding and meaning, as far as possible, comes to us from conceptualizing the completeness of objects in their observable and relational nature, and in their interaction with other objects, most importantly people – all within context.

Thinking about the fountain in a museum courtyard, designed by Richard Meier, provides a simple example of such conceptualization (2.4 and 2.5). The fountain has easily observable features from which we derive the relational features. Its location and arrangement within the larger building geometries indicates a physical and social environment where a sip of water and perhaps a chat may be had. Embedded in the broader environment of the surrounding museum complex, the fountain's meaning arises from very specific characteristics.

Looking at parts of buildings we get to understand shapes, materials, walls, windows, roofs with overhangs, etc., as the results of perception and conceptualization. These objects have observable properties, such as rectangular, red, hard, rough, wet, acidic, etc. In evaluating these observable properties with regard to their influence on us and others, we come to relational properties, such as very large, well proportioned, delightful, highly disorganized, expensive, cheap, etc. With even further consideration we may come to relational properties, such as heavenly, organic, overpowering, faceless, depressing, dangerous, etc. And, we may derive even wider relational, often highly contextual properties, such as security, privacy, controllability, familiarity, conventionality, etc.

What I am addressing here is the fact that there arise usually many relational properties, often developing through multiple stages and yielding crucial insights. We arrive at them through emotion and reason; the nature and impact of their relationship to be discussed at length in Chapter 4.

Museum for Arts and Crafts, Frankfurt a. M.

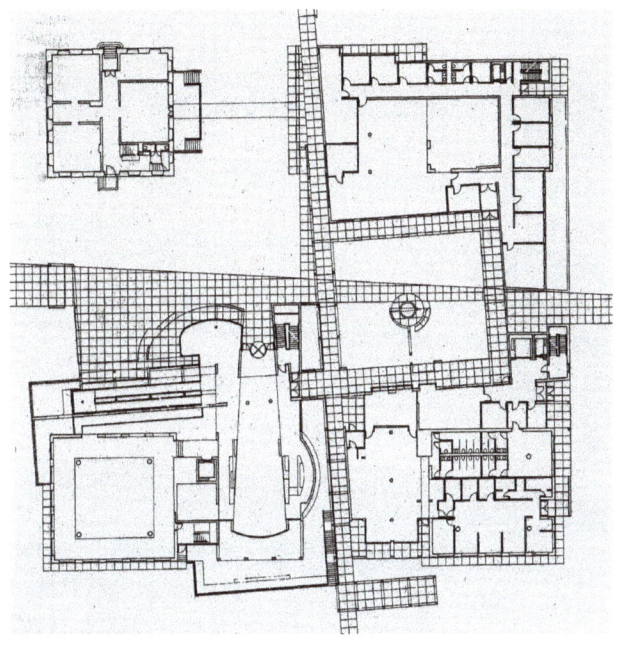

2.4 First floor plan with courtyard (© permission)

2.5 Fountain in courtyard

A housing project, Parkview Commons in San Francisco, may serve as the example to show complexity of motivation from relational properties, in part arisen from what we consider as functional, but also from many issues beyond what we usually as designers mean with this characterization (2.6 to 2.9).

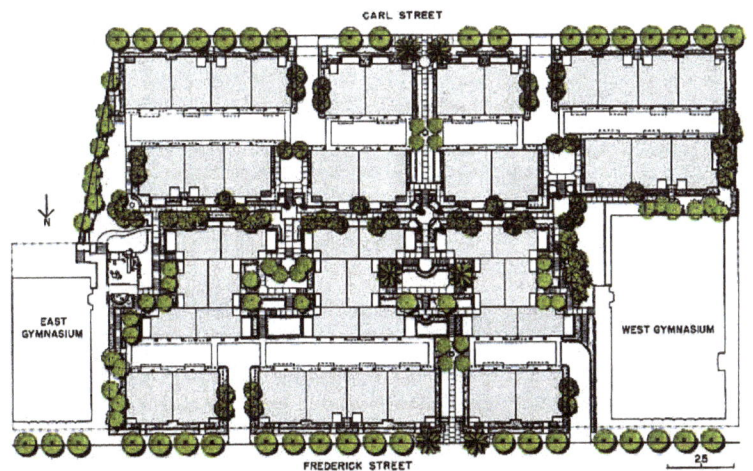

Parkview Commons, San Francisco

2.6 Site plan (© permission)

The project, designed by David Baker+Partners, has easy accessibility of all units on a sloped site with short distances to public transportation but also careful integration of private parking. It fits into the city's typical residential vernacular. Accommodation of highly varied income levels plays a crucial role. Apartment sizes from one-bedroom to four-bedroom are provided. Walk up flats have their own doors located at ground level. Compared to the courtyard fountain of the museum, meaning arises here from understanding many more and very diverse factors which combine to bring about the overall concept.

Parkview Commons, San Francisco

2.7 At Frederick Street, north elevation

2.8 Courtyard, south elevation

2.9 Access to garages

Although we are usually not aware of them in these terms, relational properties require a great deal of attention before design commences. Many of them lead to overriding motivations or constraints in finding and developing solutions. Historical aspects may be involved at a particular site, perhaps requiring preservation of existing substance and formal accommodation of what is being added. Local topography or other natural features may favor or even demand particular geometries. The ways how the cities on the old continents and then in the New World were structured over long periods of growth reflect the patterns of the cultural and commercial life of their communities. Two examples, the evolution of the urban patterns of Basel and Chicago, can make this clear (2.10 to 2.13).

Basel

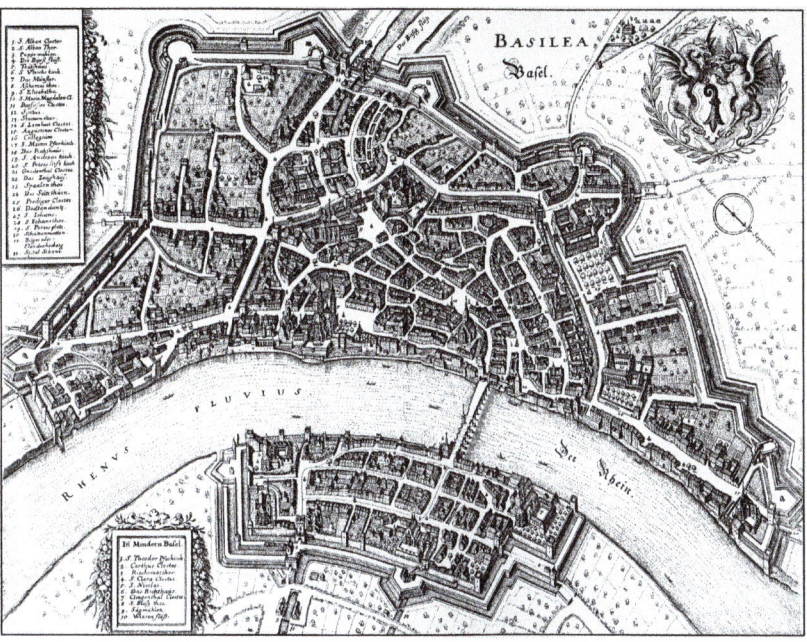

2.10 Bird's-eye view by Matthaeus Merian the Elder, 1642 (source)

Basel has its origins over two thousand years ago with Celtic and Roman settlements on the hill, overlooking the turn of the Rhine river northward, and in the narrow valley of a tributary southwest of it. The two orientations and the level differences favored from the beginning of urbanization rather informal street and plaza arrangements. During the Middle Ages Basel became a town with special governmental and religious privileges in this vital region of the Germanic empire. It was a prince-bishop's seat with a cathedral above the bluff at the river. The trades developed mainly in the valley of the tributary. Because of having built one of the first bridges over the Rhine in the 13th century it developed into a hub along the travel route from the south of the Alps to the north and the Low Countries. Crafts, commerce and the arts flourished. A temperate climate and good soil favored farming and vine growing in the surrounding areas. All of this made it a very prosperous place and even its present appearance is woven through with much of this cultural and enterprising heritage.

2.11 Freie Strasse toward market plaza

Chicago

2.12 Bird's-eye view by Poole Brothers, publishers, 1898 (source)

2.13 At Jackson and Dearborn

Chicago, after being a small non-native Western outpost since the late 1700s, exploded in population along with the enormous industrial and commercial developments starting in the early 1800s. A harbor was constructed in 1833. The population grew to about 300 000 by the time of the Great Fire of 1871. There was some planning before that time at least for a rectangular grid layout of streets which anticipated the Federal Land Ordinance of 1875, demanding the same for many other towns across the country. Major influences were the arrival of rail roads in 1848 and the incessant growth in manufacturing and commerce, making Chicago the "gateway city" between the continent's mainly industrial East and agricultural West. All of this demanded concentration in downtown. In the 1880s the first skyscrapers went up, made possible and practical by Elisha Otis' invention of highly effective safety devices for elevators three decades before. The first such buildings housed offices, but they were soon followed by apartment buildings, department stores, manufacturing facilities and warehouses, much helped also by advances in sanitation systems as well as electrical systems for power supply and artificial lighting.

The two urban developments show different relationships between environmental conditions and physical growth – 'environmental' understood broadly contextual from the given climate, landscape, culture, technology and economy. While one must be on guard against oversimplification, one can say that Basel grew rather organically with regard to its natural setting and with emphasis on historic preservation. In contrast, Chicago grew with emphasis on rational planning and industrial innovation. It is amazing how such fundamental background conditions reveal themselves in observable properties. Basel's traffic downtown is controlled today as it was centuries ago by narrow streets and features many pedestrian-only zones, whereas Chicago hums with cars and buses. Both cities developed distinct ways as centers of culture and the arts. Thus, relational properties of given situations influence the whole range from broad observable properties of urban development to more narrow ones of architectural design. They are at the roots of how cityscapes and building types in their great diversity come about.

All of this points to the very involved nature of how we come to meaning. An essentially undeterminable number of inputs from present and former conceptual experiences lets new conceptualizations evolve in our random memory machine, called brain – not at all like typical machines do by producing the same outputs in the same sequences again and again, but by connecting and rearranging particulars with lightning speed in highly varied and often unexpected combinations. It is the dialogue of observable and relational aspects which spurs in its neurological, rather mysterious fashion the evolution of what is eventually before us, usually as coherent entities of complex understanding.

All observable properties prompt in one way or another relational ones. When we are conscious we reflect what our mental representations including judgments tell us about them, about their origins and what they mean to us. For example, 'being good' is not the property of an instance of nature. It is our attribution to a relational property of a state of affairs. 'Number' is not the property of an instance of nature. It again is a relational property which we attribute to a state of affairs.[48]

How does the understanding of relational properties contribute to the development of design concepts? It provides the central criteria for our thinking about consequences of our decision making on using observable properties by thinking about cause and effect while we develop the forms of objects. I concluded that relational properties bring us to aspects beyond what we observe in present objects. But we conceptualize them in dependence of what is present. They are mental products derived from physical experience. We should remember Hume's and Kant's precepts that all our cognition begins with experience and this means by way of sensation – but with imaginative thinking in addition. And, all becomes part of our memory.

In architectural design, as in other teleological activities, we arrive at new concepts by thought and experimentation using content from memory, that is, understanding from earlier experiences in response to present requirements and conditions. We connect thoughts about reality to create new thoughts about it by means of inspiration. In addition, however, validation is necessary. Kant says clearly that

1. Whatever agrees with the formal conditions of experience (in accordance with intuition and concepts) is *possible*.
2. That which is connected with the material conditions of experience (of sensation) is *actual*.[49]

We develop concepts by reason, but we must show that they are viable in application. We must experience them in reality. Any concept to have utility must be validated via perceptual understanding of its implications derived from simulation of anticipated and observation of completed projects. This is why architectural history is such an important subject to study, be it related to decisions which were made because of sociological, technological, climatic or whatever design factors.

At first glance, what was just discussed may seem rather theoretical with some common sense mixed in. But there are at least two practical benefits from thinking it through. The first provides help in working out the distinction between the commonly used terms of reality and illusion, especially with regard to some postmodern tendencies to predict that simulacra will become eventually the only reality. Architecture cannot only be a dream world, an aspect which must not be confused with having dreams about architecture. Architecture is architecture because of its physical reality status with *all* its existential consequences. We will return to this issue later.

The second benefit, presently closer to our topic, is the practical help in grasping how relational properties influence observable ones. The realization of form results from the selection of observable properties of objects. Before we make choices, we look *for* what the objects and their properties are meant, that is, their relational properties. In impression we encounter observable properties and draw conclusions about related properties. But in expression for design we contemplate about relational properties and then search for corresponding observable properties. This is essentially so even when we kind of play around with observable aspects to fulfill relational demands. For example, for shading of a window in summer, but letting sunshine pass in winter, it is best to use an adjustable outside shading device (to keep solar radiation away from the window surface when we don't want it). The content of this understanding is a relational property. We have to grasp it before we can make a well informed choice in selecting the best kind of shading device and in selecting its physical properties (material, geometry, dimensions); many alternatives being available. The solar orientations of the facades are also relational properties for the shading devices. They are relational criteria. We have a similar situation when thinking about deciduous versus evergreen trees as shading devices.

There is usually a large variety of physical solutions available to satisfy relational demands. We act on the basis of knowing an existing stock of solutions which we believe will satisfy desired relational aspects. But we need to be aware that emotions enter the development process, especially when present relational understandings are insufficiently clear or when strong aesthetic preferences are given priority. Often we work with attempts of trial-and-error to keep our inspirations going and then narrow down the space of solutions. In any case, we let impressions from proposed solutions arise and let evaluations lead to eventual decisions.

So, physical properties of design solutions are answers to relational demands. In looking for these factors they can be found by asking the following questions which I formulate by paraphrasing and broadening what Amos Rapoport calls the three basic questions which best define the domain of environmental design research:[50]

1. Which social, psychological, physiological, cultural, economic, technological, material, climatic, etc. characteristics of individuals or groups or conditions influence which characteristics of built environments, and how?
2. Which characteristics of particular environments have which effects on individuals or groups? Also how and why?
3. What is mutually instrumental in these relations and interactions between people and environments, to bring them about and to sustain them?

My answer to 3 is in a nutshell: fundamentally expression based on impression, and within it the workings of meaning – quite an enterprise to elucidate, even when limited to a particular field as architectural design. There is obviously no nutshell answer possible for 1 and 2. Infinitely many questions lay embedded in what the world and our lives are about. Our answers will be incomplete. But we always live with partial answers – search for and exist with them.

From these questions we derive that a large part of architectural design is essentially environment-behavior research. Its inquiries together with those from many other fields fall in what we may view the *wide* domain of architectural design, obviously requiring the help from various disciplines outside architecture.[51] We may then view the act of planning and realization, the work toward expression in physical form, to be the *narrow* discipline of architectural design. To bridge the gap between the two has much to do with meaning based on understanding. Therefore, my emphasis in our discussion is on the understanding of understanding itself.

What I have explained in this section for the physical realm, using the terminology of observable and relational properties, has its parallel in using the concept of denotation and connotation in linguistic analysis. These two terms are used in ways which can lead to confusion unless clearly defined. Over the past 150 years many definitions, some going back to the Middle Ages, have been suggested. There is still controversy and different fields of inquiry define the terms variously. In short and rather generally, they are used to differentiate the two main components of direct and indirect reference in meaning. The American Heritage Dictionary notes about their usage that

> *Denote* and *connote* are often confused because both words have senses that entail signification. *Denote* means "to signify directly or literally" and describes the relation between the word and the thing it conventionally names. *Connote* means "to signify indirectly, suggest or imply" and describes the relation between the word and the images or associations it evokes. Thus, the word *river* denotes a moving body of water and may connote such things as the relentlessness of time and the changing nature of life.[52]

Beatriz Garza-Cuarón explains

> … the distinction between *denotation*, understood as the direct reference of a sign to an object, and *connotation*, understood as adjacent meaning, which is added to primary meaning. It is generally acknowledged that denotation is established through the subject of a proposition and points to a substance, and that connotation refers to the qualities [relational properties] that subject may possess, the actions it may perform, and so on.[53]

The "primary meaning" is primary in the sense of originally constitutive of meaning not in the sense of value judgment.

Denotation has simple meaning immediately remembered. Connotation has more elaborate meaning reflectively contemplated. Often denotation is simply what the name of something points to. Connotation is what a name or other denotation means beyond its own direct power of reference. Therefore, we may call denotation immediate meaning and connotation explanatory meaning. Denotations and connotations in language, be it spoken or written, are purely referential, be it in the impressive or expressive mode. Not so in the physical realm, including architecture. Here we derive both in the impressive mode directly from the corporeal object. When we see a house, we do not hear or read the word 'house'. Our perception results in a mental appearance as sign from which we conceptualize denotative and connotative understanding (2.14).

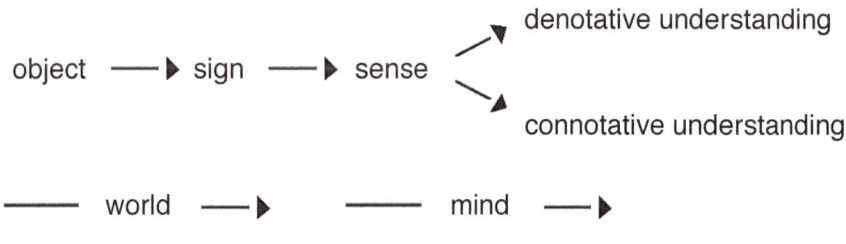

2.14 Denotative and connotative understanding

The encounter with a stair may serve as an example. We may conceptualize the denotative understanding of the observable property as 'connecting two floors' and the connotative understanding of relational properties as 'requires effort to climb' or 'fits well in its environment'. To observe people around or in a building helps us to understand whether or not the building has the necessary denotative and connotative aspects for their activities.

In the expressive mode of design we 'give' the object corporeal properties which are represented in a medium, such as drawings. Corporeal properties must be thought of and selected to prompt in observers and users the needed denotative and connotative understanding. In this sense denotative and connotative point in the same direction as observable and relational respectively. The more observable the properties are the usually more enriched will be the understanding of the designed object. Always imagination is involved as we cannot directly and completely translate ideas into observable properties.

In our designs only observable properties, and only a few, can be strongly expressed. They evoke through sensation strong denotative aspects in the observers. Hidden physical and other relational properties must be inferred, being connotative. In successful nonverbal communication, like successful design, the denotative and connotative aspects developed by designer and observer are similar. But we still denote and connote differently to some extent. Denotation and connotation require inspiration and, as said, imagination – all our thinking does to some extent. A major force for ideas in the design process is the playing off against each other of denotation and connotation. Their difference of semantic intensity plays an important role in the creativity of design and in the theory of signs to which we turn in the next chapter. I summarize in terms of our interest for meaning in design:

1. Denotation is factually strong representation derived from the reference to an object as it most directly and comprehensively appears to us in our mind and is so most readily remembered. Denotation refers to observable properties.
2. Connotation is conjecturally strong representation derived from the reference to an object. It refers to relational details which often prompt us to have 'a second look' at observable properties for further relational properties.

From what we discussed in general and from the examples it becomes quite clear that in linguistics no strict separation can be made between denotation and connotation. Daniel Chandler writes that

> … while theorists may find it analytically useful to distinguish connotation from denotation, in practice such meanings cannot be neatly separated.[54]

Because of the immediacy of denotation in observing reality, as in architecture, separation is easier achieved than in language. The concept of observable and relational properties supports this assumption.

In *How Buildings Mean* Nelson Goodman suggests that in architecture meaning exemplifies properties.[55] Exemplifications give emphasis and clarity to what they address. Through exemplification, observable properties are emphasized and in doing so become usually stronger in their reference to relational ones. Designers must, before they select properties for exemplification, which often includes amplification and even exaggeration, understand their implications for the overall nature of the project and this requires first to understand the properties themselves. This thought confirms, what we know instinctively, that we move in creative work with complexity – as in architectural design – from general aspects of the whole to details and then adjust the whole from understanding those details in depth. In the broader aspects of our interest here, Goodman's notion of exemplification reinforces my view that meaning is select understanding and that we are better careful what we put forward not to produce confusion. I am not speaking here against the use of ideas external to the main theme, such as decoration, but for careful primary integration in order not to overwhelm or delude the exemplification of the most important design factors.

Goodman is right when he says that architecture does not denote in the same way as a text does.[56] Architecture is not text. We denote by putting in words what we believe architecture consists of. But he does not say, what I think is crucial and must be highlighted, that it strongly connotes by pointing beyond itself to other properties that I label relational properties as part of the effect exemplification and denotation has on us. A door we see exemplifies the opening in a wall and connotes our possibility to enter or exit. The building in my neighborhood which exemplifies a set of classrooms and some other typical spaces connotes that children come here to learn, that our future is at stake here and my taxes are at work. This is why meaning in architecture so comprehensively becomes part of meaning in our lives and environments. We arrive at meaning through understanding of what we believe some state of affairs is and our behavior in action or reaction should be.

Denotation and connotation provide cues which stimulate and focus our awareness. Cues, in the flow of events, encourage judgment and action. We may say that cues and actions are connected by motivation. Perceiving a column while walking toward it gives me the cue to avoid it. Perceiving a chair gives me the cue that I may sit on it. Remembering that at northern latitudes the sun paths are low in winter and high in summer gives me the cues that I should maximize south orientation of windows and place overhangs above them as they work there well for shading; both actions helping energy conservation.

As part of understanding, cues come about through reference to relational properties of objects about which we learned from earlier experiences. They may point to mental or physical aspects. A gate in a fence refers to a welcoming of visitors and to the entry door of a house, reinforced by the view of a walkway between the two. The fence also refers to keeping unwelcome visitors out. A roof refers to the building it protects. A subway station refers to the trains which stop there from time to time. Generally, in observation many cues arise simultaneously but can only be thought about sequentially. Cues have often the effect of entailing additional cues. I agree with Aldo Rossi that

> The emergence of relations among things, more than things themselves, always gives rise to new meanings.[57]

The emergence of relations among things provides cues first for remembered meanings and then new ones. Complex relationships provide multiple cues. In thinking about two building entries, one in Taos, New Mexico, the other in Basel, Switzerland, we become aware of how differently physical relationships may provide denotations by which connotations and cues are prompted (2.15 and 2.16).

2.15 Adobe house entry, Taos, NM

The house in Taos is welcoming, simple, rural, informal and unadorned. The house in Basel is protective, elaborate, urban, formal and opulent. Looking at the entries for broader meaning we find that they do let arise particular understanding of details and differences. Aside from the obvious ones, such as the differences in material and configuration, they lead us to contemplate the difference in historical and cultural context, the difference in life style, representation and privacy of those who live or lived there.

2.16 Baroque house entry, Basel

The cues from objects and their properties are, like the meanings they prompt: mental constructs. When they arise from new relations during design they drive innovation. Such innovation may be simply by variation of spaces, not had before in a particular way, or, more fundamentally, by never before applied realization with truly new concepts. Simple innovation happens to some extent in every design. Architectural design always implies change because purpose and context are never the same. Strong innovation, however, brings into play unusual thoughts about given circumstances, sometimes leading also to unusual physical means of execution. Simple innovation is the every day concern of architectural design, such as working on housing floor plan variations in response to traditional design criteria. Strong innovation is paradigmatic advancement, often through pioneering efforts, such as when the solid masonry walls in multistory construction were replaced by steel skeletons or when the rigidly contained classrooms in school building were replaced by flexibly open ones.

2.5 Function and complexity

The world is full of complexity. Therefore, architectural objects are influenced by usually large numbers of design factors which influence our decisions. This complexity often generates conflicts. Many can be resolved during program development and before physical design begins, that is, by reconsidering and adjusting purposive and contextual aspects of the project.

At the center of early development is spatial fit in response to operational and organizational requirements. It is a process of geometric integration within the limits of desirable and affordable boundaries. A fundamental axiom invariably guides the design work: the exclusivity of locale or 'where one physical thing is another thing cannot be at the same time'. To solve the configurational problems is one of the more difficult but interesting tasks of the design process. Solutions must be sought by adjustments of spatial shapes and, when necessary, original demands.

Looming in the background of the whole design process is the long standing issue of function and form. Because of complexity, multiple functional demands arise which must be channeled toward an overall successful design resolution. Some spatial and material redundancy is inevitable which, in turn, provides operational variability. In this regard, Louis Sullivan's dictum should say 'Form ever follows function[s]' with emphasis on the plural.[58] There is rarely, if ever, a form – understood as realization – which is not influenced by several functional aspects; and they frequently need mutual accommodation.

There is another issue of Sullivan's aphorism which needs consideration and has fundamental consequences for how we view the position of function in our understanding. It has to do with the way he uses the term function. At least in conventional perception it indicates something like utilitarian 'property'. This leads to ambiguity and has not helped in the many interpretations and disputes. Function in general and in architecture does not define properties but indicates crucial linkages between them. It refers not to what the properties of objects *are* but points to their *relationships*, to their dependence or interdependence. Function in mathematics does not refer to the kind or value of what the members in the equation are nor to the outcome of the relationship. It simply points to the fact that there is a certain dependence or interdependence. The function of a stair is established by our understanding of the existing relationship between two floors. What the stair is or what we design it to be is the result of this function, not function itself. The function of a window is the window's relationship between inside and outside for the desired result of ventilation or daylighting to occur. The function of a whole building is the sum of its purposive, performance oriented relationships which it is supposed to accomplish in the given context, not the results of how the performance is physically achieved. We will discuss such criteria in detail later. What is important, however, to keep in mind for now, is the fact that functions don't have physical properties but are relational concepts that we use in the determination of such object properties to satisfy certain needs or desires. We arrive at them and define them in design out of understanding programmatic needs and desires which must be satisfied by physical properties.

Any realization in architecture is formed physical matter. This is in part why spatial or other conflicts occur and accommodation is required in response to multiple functional relationships. And it is why any absolutistic translation of "form ever follows function" fails in practice. Further, I believe, it helps to consider observable and relational properties together as the *mental content* of objects, *physically represented in form*. They are what makes objects for us significant. This understanding is a more explanatory view than what is usually understood by *function* and it locates it in broader context. Therefore, '"form follows function" should now be paraphrased as *'form follows content'* – being less catchy perhaps, but more to the point and more comprehensive.

There should be no doubt that when we design, we have functions in mind of what our designs should accomplish. But we never can fully predict and show their impact. It is not so as Stewart Brand writes that

> Sullivan's form-follows-function misled a century of architects into believing that they could really anticipate function. Churchill's ringing and-then-they-shape-us truncated the fuller cycle of reality. First we shape our buildings, then they shape us, then we shape them again – ad infinitum. Function reforms form, perpetually.[59]

"Reforming form" of an existing building has limits. It is certainly true that to elevate Sullivan's dictum to a kind of absolute necessity of expression led to many shortcomings of overall design. But we cannot design without anticipating functional relationships. A building *is for* something, not just *is*. That we often change it for other functions – adapt it, make it somewhat larger or smaller, etc. – is a matter of life and time.

When we design a project to fulfill a certain function, we give it certain properties enabling it to perform this function. We design a table to support things at a desired height, such as food, books or lamps. That tables can be used for all kinds of other imaginative happenings, such as a 'roof' for children to crawl underneath or as a surface to dance on it, simply indicates that things can be used for many originally unintended purposes. But there should be no doubt that we always design buildings for certain functions: relations with purposive intentions. Not much architecture would have come about, if it only were meant as 'walk-in sculptures' (and even that may be based on a certain function: our relationship with being inside). How far we are able to 'read' such functional relationships from the physical result of a particular design is a matter of functional conflict resolution and must not be a constraining demand but should simply be part of showing the way things work out. It is not difficult to find many examples of how functional relationships contributed to interesting design solutions.

In the second half of the 1800s rapid urbanization called for strongly increasing, concentrated administrative services. At the same time three major developments occurred which revolutionized office building design: steel framing, elevators and large sheet glass windows. Skeleton construction allowed nearly unobstructed floor plan layouts. Elevators made never before seen building heights possible; way beyond typical walk-ups. Large windows permitted daylight to penetrate deep into the interior. The Reliance Building in Chicago, designed by Charles Atwood of Daniel Burnham and Company in 1895 , is a prime example with functions taken care of (2.17 and 2.18).

Reliance Building (now Hotel Burnham), Chicago

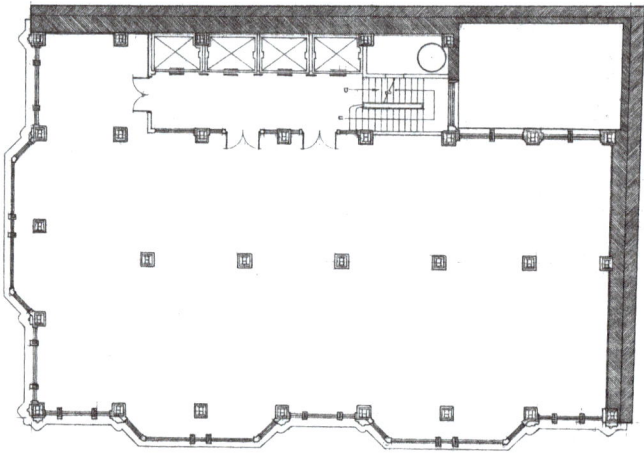

2.17 and 2.18 View south from North State Street and structural plan (source)

After World War II enormous demand for educational and research facilities brought about the rethinking of functional relationships. In school buildings it led to specialized spaces for instructional concentration and to media centers. In research facilities it led to the need for flexibility in service systems with, in part, clear separation of work and service areas. For both building types large structural spans and service integration was the answer. A good example is the Science Center at Harvard University, designed by Sert, Jackson and Associates (2.19 to 2.23). Prefabricated concrete beams with perforations facilitate variability, rearrangement and maintenance of service systems. They connect to shafts at the north side of the building. Efficient space utilization is achieved. Functional relationships are readily understood.

Science Center, Harvard University, Cambridge, MA

2.19 Prefabricated concrete (© permission)

2.20 From southeast

2.21 Courtyard

2.22 Hallway

2.23 Laboratory

In considering this development or others we may like to back up and ask: What are we referring to? To the overall function of an object and its relational aspects as building type? Or, to functions of a building component and how it relates to others? There is no question that we begin to arrive at meaning through relatively few aspects of the total of something. But only through aggregates of many detail meanings do we understand what homes, schools, restaurants, offices and theaters are. Two examples, the Heinrich Hübsch Trade School, by Heinz Mohl, and the Weatherhead School of Management, by Frank Gehry, illustrate the fact that we accumulate understanding of wider frameworks necessarily from many details (2.24 and 2.25).

2.24 Heinrich Hübsch Trade School, Karlsruhe Germany

2.25 Weatherhead School of Management, Case Western University, Cleveland

In the large trade school building a series of windows emphasizes a stairway which ties all floors visually (and factually) together. The size of the whole identifies the building easily as institutional. But it reveals itself as a school only by observation at the inside. Although the undulating roof-wall plays in most of Frank Gehry's buildings are dominant and obviously functional, especially aesthetically functional, they do not support any particular notion of building type. The exterior appearance of the School of Management gives hardly a clue of what its overall function as a college building is.

Nasar et al found in a 2005 study about revealing overall function in the expression of buildings that
> … people infer meanings from housing, restaurant, and small suburban-office exteriors; and this suggests strong commonalities in those inferences.

But,
> … some building types failed to express, in the exterior form, codes that convey to ordinary observers the function housed inside.

And,
> … one might argue that architectural form and function has a many-to-many relationship, or that certain functions are not distinguishable through architectural form.[60]

This is not surprising, considering the conflicts discussed earlier in this section. We readily recognize whether we are in a residential neighborhood or in a central business district. With regard to the rest of their quote: only part of any building's overall function can be perceived or inferred from exterior form. One must be careful, however, not to generalize their conclusion that
> Louis Sullivan's enduring maxim that "Form follows function" did not hold up in our study. … We conclude that, for the present, unbiased sample, form did not communicate function; and based on that we speculate that building form may detract from legibility and emotional security or satisfaction of people unfamiliar with cities or places.[61]

That Sullivan's dictum did not hold up for this study does not mean that it does not hold up in a broader sense. Sullivan writes about the expression of properties satisfying any function, not limiting his remarks to the overall building type function and certainly not only to exterior appearance. Sullivan did not say that form 'always communicates' function and certainly not 'comprehensively'. But every observable property of architecture points to functional relationship(s), a hall way to the connection of activity areas, a wall to the division of space, a roof to the protection from precipitation, a door to the allowance for entry or exit, or an elevator to vertical movement. Even the simulated windows in the entry facade of the Sainsbury Wing, National Gallery, London, designed by Venturi Scott Brown and Associates, have a function (3.43). They decoratively relate with neighboring buildings. *There is no architectural expression without a functional relation to design factors.* All what we encounter with interest, we want to understand. Whether ordinary or outstanding, function evokes meaning with more or less intensity. We comprehend buildings, neighborhoods and cities overall only through many meanings of particular understandings. Meanings communicate functions.

When I refer to meaning as understanding, I point also to the much broader view of function which includes ostensive associations once learned by adoption, like hearing from somebody that "this is City Hall" or "this is our high school". To become familiar with an expression attached to something, such as a name or an other abstract sign, is an understanding; here a meaning is given and accepted, rather than acquired by contemplation. We usually do not design buildings with intended expression of what happens in them. But we cannot completely avoid functional expression, even if we wanted to. We identify by whatever expression they 'make available' or sign they have attached to them. There are always functions legible, that is, relational properties derived from observable ones, even in the most abstract of buildings. This does not mean, however, that we necessarily can detect from exterior observation that the building has this or that overall function beyond the most basic of being shelter for some activity. But certain buildings, more than others, have very distinct features from siting, scale, volume, organization, facades, etc. which lend them, through our familiarity with these features, to building type recognition. They exhibit, in Ludwig Wittgenstein's words, "family resemblances".

We always experience a building from part to whole, even when we observe it as assembly of parts. This is so regarding its exterior or interior. Our understanding of it increases from experiencing ever more parts over time to the point at which we know more or less what its overall appearance is. What makes its understanding possible are the functional relations which are embedded informally or by design when the building is realized in physical properties. Depending on requirements of building type as well as specific programmatic desires and needs, there is extensive freedom in design formation. Properties of the stair in the mentioned high school were used as one of the main facade schemes. They could have been shown in other ways or not at all. More liberally, the roof forms that dominate the college administration and classroom building go far beyond what necessary properties require. The windows and columns at Tate Gallery have intended significance beyond their own building. The expressions of all three objects provide, in their very different ways, meaning for identification. Whether we may or may not have to be told what the overall functions of these buildings are is not as important as that their features will evoke in us meaning of them, being remembered and useful for their intended purpose.

In our discussion of form we need to consider the role of play to achieve aesthetically pleasing results. All designers use play to some extent and we shall discuss later its inevitability in the development of configuration. When it occurs strongly a priori, however, and controls the integration of design factors, then play seeks content and dominates form. What is implied here and throughout my account is a clear distinction between observable appearance, including shape, and form. Regarding design, form is the physical manifestation of design thinking, be it as images, models or buildings in reality. Form is realization, one part of it being shape. Shape is the geometry of form. When we work with shapes without taking into consideration at least the most important design factors of purpose and context, we work in the abstract except for aesthetic judgment as a design factor – which in fact the latter also is. As we will discuss further on, the possibilities with computerized shape making pose the danger of neglecting crucial functional relationships and design choices.

One must not be an opponent to free wheeling shapes in design to recognize the usually higher spatial efficiency of rectangularity in the aggregation and the usage of spaces, an important consideration in resource allocation for construction and operation; especially in small buildings and those with limited budgets. This shall not mean that less constrained geometries do not have advantages.[62] But the spatial redundancy they add, must be considered. That we are able to bring such shapes into being must not be their only or main justification. We will return to this issue later on as well.

A very different aspect addresses the advantages of spatial redundancy for potential changes in functional relationships. Over the past decades efforts have been made to design buildings which can accommodate future needs, as in variable dwellings, laboratories, hospitals, offices and schools. An apartment building of this type is the "Wohnregal" in Berlin, a seven floor infill object with highly variable floor plan arrangements. The only fixed points for the floor plans are vertical service connections.[63] More complex building types have elaborate utility cores and interstitial floors providing space for service installations and their adjustment. But there is in most buildings not enough foreseeable change to justify the typically high additional front-end costs for variability. It is obvious that we cannot design for all kinds of functional relationships in which buildings may find themselves because of changed circumstances. This shall not mean that space should not be provided for crucial change which can be expected. Louis Kahn's Richards Medical Laboratories, University of Pennsylvania, and the Harvard Science Building by Sert, Jackson and Associates are early examples of one resisting, the other accommodating change.

The design of the Richards Laboratories concentrates and exhibits function derived appearance of small laboratory spaces between utility towers, to the point that the latter inhibit spatial flexibility. Not so the Harvard Science Center (2.19 to 2.23) in which extended spatial layering of service space and work space is provided for accessibility and variability with service towers to one side of the large and open laboratory areas.

Also related to change are issues of recycling existing buildings. That a building, say originally designed as a church, can serve now as a restaurant is obviously not so because the building was designed for this function but because it was designed large enough for the assembly of many people. Different functions come into play to perform as a restaurant which requires re-distribution of space, additional mechanical and electrical installations, etc. The meaning of the interior refers to 'restaurant' while the exterior, which may allow only little change, will still refer to 'church'. The building itself as sign connoting it as church may require a linguistic sign explicitly denoting it as restaurant. Many forms exist which allow for functions and related content not thought about when initial design occurred. Multistory school buildings have been successfully turned into apartments, office buildings into hotels, warehouses into shops, etc. Usually sufficient redundancy of space is present and provides flexibility for redesign. The earlier in 2.17 shown, over a century old Reliance Office Building, Chicago, was recently turned into a hotel with restaurant spaces on the first two floors; similarly the Philadelphia Savings Fund Society Building, Philadelphia. There are many reasons, beyond economics, for the recycling of buildings, such as conservation of resources toward ecological sustainability or simply historic preservation of a community asset.[64]

When addressing complexity and function one cannot get around to recall Robert Venturi's so highly seminal *Complexity and Contradiction in Architecture*. He writes that

> ... architecture is necessarily complex and contradictory in its very inclusion of the traditional Vitruvian elements of commodity, firmness, and delight.[65]

I agree but only with regard to architecture as process not as result. Design factors arising out of the triad sometimes hinder, sometimes reinforce each other's influence on design development; a fact which makes it challenging but interesting. I view the relationships of these elements as providing freedom and constraint in design decisions. In architecture as result the relationship among commodity, firmness and delight are settled in one way or another. Contradiction ran its course. As never all of complexity can be perfectly balanced, ambiguity arises as inevitable by-product of understanding. Ambiguity is not contradiction. In addition, as stressed earlier, we never understand fully; especially regarding context. This is an aspect Vitruvius omitted in naming the triad, though it is somewhat implied in all three of its members. There is no reason, however, that we should by design and matter of course increase ambiguity beyond that which arises naturally. On the other hand, we have always to some extent the freedom to do so. In response to Venturi's

> I am for richness of meaning rather than clarity of meaning; ...[66]

I claim that clarity does not exclude richness. Clarity is, in fact, richness of a necessary kind. Clarity helps understanding.

Let's make sure we understand what we mean with ambiguity. The floor plan of Villa Savoy does not have contradictory features nor is it ambiguous because it contrasts a rounded form within a rectangular pattern of columns. The meaning of both forms can clearly be understood. Multiple meanings of something do not necessarily make it ambiguous. Ambiguity means that an understanding arises in us which makes it at least to some extent difficult to decide what it is or what it means to be. One important question should always be asked regarding ambiguity: in what respect? A few examples, two adjacent doors to the same room make the entry mildly ambiguous as far as our decision on the usage of the doors goes. A church interior which is a mix of many architectural styles is strongly ambiguous as far as our decision is concerned to place it overall historically; especially if no emphasis is given in any direction at all. A well balanced sour-sweet sauce is somewhat ambiguous because it is difficult to decide whether it is sour or sweet. A radical thought: anything having no meaning for us is not ambiguous. It does not exist.

The physical constraints which we encounter in translating content into form obviously influence our decision making on the systems and components of objects. As mentioned, conflicts develop. Denise Scott Brown regards this conflict situation as contributing to her and Robert Venturi's conception of Mannerism.

> Coming at a definition via consideration of patterns and systems, form-function relationships and a pulsating, supporting context, I would add that you break the rules because you can't follow the rules of all the systems all the time, or at the same time. For one thing, some will be in conflict.
>
> So conflict between systems is a condition that evokes Mannerism.[67]

She goes on by pointing to physical component and system conflicts in urban design which happen similar to those in architecture, but on a different scale.

To resolve conflicts of components and systems we have to interrupt or perhaps 'bend' the continuity of extensions which individual components and systems have and exhibit. This is not "breaking of the rules", however. It is discontinuance of one thing to make place for another. I would not characterize it as Mannerism.[68] It is not breaking the rules as it is making a difference out of necessity. Physically experiential discontinuities and differences of this kind do not produce contradiction nor ambiguity. They are usually well understood as inescapable features to make architectural solutions possible.

It is quite another thing when she refers to changes designers impose "because they were [or are] bored with the rules" in the Renaissance or in any other architectural epoch.[69] These rules were or are not necessities of physical integrity but rules of stylistic convention. The resulting conflicts were or are, deliberately or perhaps unconsciously, designer-made. This is, I assume, what Robert Venturi has in mind when he submits his

> … attempt at a definition of mannerism in architecture appropriate for now:
>
> Mannerism as Convention Tweaked – or as Modified Convention Acknowledging Ambiguity. Mannerism for architecture of our time that acknowledges conventional order rather than original expression but breaks the conventional order to accommodate complexity and contradiction and thereby engages ambiguity – engages ambiguity unambiguously.[70]

I don't understand what all that means. If it is to mean to be explanatory, I wonder whether there is not a simpler and more explicit way to say it; including an explanation of what is meant by the terms ambiguity (inconclusive signification?), contradiction (conflicting opposition?) and original expression (innovative appearance?). In commenting on examples Venturi mentions "incorrect/ambiguous pendentives" (St.Paul's Cathedral), "is it a facade or a tower?" (Hawksmoor's Christ Church), "of ambiguous beauty" (Church of the Jacobins), "aesthetic of chaos" (Tokyo). How is this complexity accommodated? Where is here contradiction? Why signifies a row of columns in the center of a nave not only beauty, but "ambiguous beauty"?[71] There is naturally the question how far we can deliberately break the rules of styles without excessively inhibiting necessary understanding. Tokyo's chaos (much is not chaotic there) or Las Vegas' strips (in repetition boring) are in my view not models to emulate.

To conclude. Our capacity to think comprises the whole process from sensations of reality, appearances of them in our mind, judgments of them for ordering into categories to placements of the developed understanding, that is, to concepts located in our memory. So, concepts are the result of our impressions from objects and their properties. We develop new concepts by rethinking those existing in our mind, usually prompted by additional impact from outside. This process is also at the core of design activities. We select suitable concepts for expression by means of associating properties with objects.

At the beginning of the chapter I pointed to the need of sorting out the roles of expression and impression in design. It should be understood that when I speak of the expression of an inanimate thing, like a building, I do not mean that it expresses in the sense humans and to some extent animals do but that it makes available content to be perceived through the form it has been given. The term expression is a metaphorical analogy similar to the one "a building speaks in a certain way" which is obviously not true. If a facade has a door, it makes available this fact for our perception. It does not exclaim "here is my door" but has that door directly available for the observer and user. Through design the designer defines physical properties which have content to be communicated. The perception of the door is the effect of a cause: the impression from an expression. I generalize that an impression must have an expression as its ground; a fact we will have to say more about.

Impression derived from the form of expression becomes meaning. Ralph Weber writes that
> The overall concept here is that meaning is not an intrinsic property of form; it is *inferred* by the beholder on the basis of concepts derived from cultural conventions, individual experience, and learning. On the basis of this determination it is possible to see that meaning can be both intersubjective and individual.[72]

What can be inferred exists not intrinsically but is associated with properties of form. The properties make, given by the designer to the form as medium, intersubjectivity possible. Forms are not meaningful on their own in a, by us, desired way. They let such meaning arise when those who design and observe them have related understanding in common. Meaning is more than self-reference to existence, such as a rectangle being a rectangle. A door is more than materials arranged in a rectangle. It is relational, referring to entry or exit. The form of the door is a property meant by whoever put it in the facade, that is, the designer and builder. Meaning is denotative and connotative.

Architecture, as everything else, cannot but evoke meaning whether it is ordinary or outstanding, whether we concentrate presently on a door only or experience over time most of a building. Impression transitions from physical form into mental form. Expression transitions from mental form into physical form. Both are influenced by context. We observe something, but then we search for what is 'behind' it. When we design we project and then observe what we have created. As all happens in space and time, our work develops within the continuity of part and whole. Like the door handle is part of a building, so the building is part of the landscape, rural or urban. All these events have meaning for us by being snapshots in the continuity of understanding observable and relational properties. We then judge and select.

We have no choice in selecting properties of objects which we perceive. They are given. We understand them through interpretation. On the other hand, we have, within the constraints of circumstances, choice in selecting properties for design. Each instance of impression or expression involves observable and relational properties. In fact, we can have impressions only from sensing observable properties and then derive associated relational ones. For expression, however, such as in design, we seek to understand relational properties of given circumstances and then select observable properties in response.

Function is a concept of relationships. It manifests its impact in the choice of object properties, in what happens among them, or among them and those of other objects. In the complexity of architectural design the impact of functional relationships can never be made fully explicit as not all physical properties of objects are observable and the response to multiple design factors requires physical accommodation.

The understanding of how we derive our meaning from objects is fundamental for understanding the process of design during which we propose meaning to be conveyed through things architectural.

3 Our World of Signs

From the foregoing we derive that we understand objects and states of affairs because through experiencing them we obtain information which we conceptualize. There is an additional view of understanding which helps us in perception and has important implications for efficiency in communication. It is the representation in form of *signs*. It obviously cannot replace the need for the described conceptualization. But thinking about objects and affairs as signs helps us to conceptualize in many ways more explicitly. It was most likely John Locke (1632-1704) who in modern times first referred to "Semeiotics" as the "Doctrine of Signs" and used "Sign" as the term for the representation of things.[1]

At the end of his essay on human understanding he suggests a three part division of what science needs to address: the nature of things, the right human conduct in the world of things, and the means by which knowledge of both can be attained and communicated. With regard to the latter he writes that

> The third Branch may be called [in Greek] *semeiotika*, or *the Doctrine of Signs*, the most usual whereof being Words, it is aptly enough termed also [in Greek] *logika*, *Logick*; the Business whereof, is to consider the Nature of Signs, the Mind makes use of for the understanding of Things, or conveying its Knowledge to others. For, since the Things, the Mind contemplates are none of them, besides it self, present to the Understanding, 'tis necessary that something else, as a Sign or Representation of the thing it considers, should be present to it: And these are *Ideas*. And because the Scene of *Ideas* that makes one Man's Thoughts cannot be laid open to the immediate View of another, nor laid up any where but in the Memory, a no very sure Repository: Therefore to communicate our Thoughts to one another, as well as record them for our own Use, Signs of our *Ideas* are also necessary.[2]

More strictly I suggest that signs are the communicative part of mental representations. We depend on this nature as it is the operational feature providing the content from sensation and appearance, the raw material for conceptualization. A sign is in this sense not a physical object. It is the result of discursive thought developed from external sources or recalled from memory. We obviously use the term also in day-to-day language by referring to material signs which is essentially anything we encounter in the physical world. Daniel Chandler writes:

> Whilst semiotics is often encountered in the form of textual analysis, it also involves philosophical theorising on the role of signs in the construction of reality. Semiotics involves studying representations and the processes involved in representational practices, and to semioticians, 'reality' always involves representation.[3]

Words, when their reference is remembered, are known to us as signs. Trees, when we have once understood the concept of tree, are known and remembered as signs. So do architectural aspects, when we have once understood their concept. *Understanding the material sign implies grasping its mental significance*. Unless it is obvious from context, I will especially indicate whether I refer to the physical or mental version of signs presently under discussion.

3.1 Signs and communication

While the term sign has been used in various ways for physical and mental constructs for a long time it was Charles Peirce (1839-1914) who made it the central focus in an approach to logic which he called, like Locke did for his views, a "doctrine of signs". Our consciousness draws its present understanding from the multitude of signs which we were exposed to and conceptualized since our birth. Our personal worlds of signs are what exists in our memory. We may say that they are the internal material for our thoughts. Peirce postulates that

> It seems a strange thing, when one comes to ponder over it, that a sign should leave its interpreter to supply a part of its meaning; but the explanation of the phenomenon lies in the fact that the entire universe – ... the universe which we are all accustomed with to refer to as "the truth" – that all this universe is perfused with signs, if it is not composed exclusively of signs.[4]

So, everything we encounter receives eventually a semiotic dimension. Although it may in this quote sound so, Peirce does not equate signs with objects. Signs are mental representations which are derived from objects. For Peirce three components are involved: the sign itself, the object to which the sign refers and the interpretant which is what the sign represents with regard to the object:

> A *Sign*, or *Representamen*, is a First which stands in such a genuine triadic relation to a Second, called its *Object*, as to be capable of determining a Third, called its *Interpretant*, ... The triadic relation is *genuine*, that is its three members are bound together by it in a way that does not consist in any complexus of dyadic relations. ... A *Sign* is a Representamen with a mental Interpretant. ... *thought* is the chief, if not the only, mode of representation.[5]

Carl Hausman explains that

> ... every thought is a sign. Now the essential nature of a sign [representamen] is that it mediates between its Object ... and its Meaning. ... the object and the interpretant being the two correlates of every sign. ... the object is the antecedent, the interpretant the consequent of the sign.[6]

Peirce's signs stand in a triadic relation: object, "representamen" and "interpretant". The mental equivalent of the object is the sign which gives rise to another thought, the interpretant. Often Peirce's triadic relationship has been depicted as a triangle, which leads easily to confusion.[7]

The object is the ground for the representamen and the interpretant. Without an object there is no representamen nor interpretant. Peirce's unfortunate choice of 'interpretant' could be taken as 'interpreter' of the object to produce the representamen. He clearly says, however, in the first quote that the *"... Representamen*, is a First [we encounter mentally] ... as to be capable of determining a Third, called its *Interpretant*, ...". It is as Hausman writes, as quoted, that "the object is the antecedent, the interpretant the consequent of the sign". From these remarks one can conclude, which I fully agree with, that the sign (the representamen) is between the object and the interpretant (I would call the latter interpretation). The sign "mediates" between the two. Roughly in our earlier used terms, representamen is appearance and interpretant is concept. Therefore, I believe a much clearer depiction of the triadic (not triangular) relationship, still in Peirce's terms, is

$$\text{object} \longrightarrow \text{representamen} \longrightarrow \text{interpretant}.$$

The object determines the representamen and then the representamen determines the interpretant. Both happens by perception and judgment. There are multiple instances of receiving information for representamens while we observe a building with sequential input, even when we only look at an image of it. The interpretants are also influenced by existing representamens in us, usually 'asking' for information and clarification. Representamen and interpretant are not stable until final decision is reached and ends the process. It is helpful to remember the nature of the Kantian appearance which we explained earlier as the raw, yet undetermined representation in need of conceptualization.[8]

By viewing the ongoing process, including preliminary representamens and interpretants, and the concept as final result, we can write the sequence simply as

$$\text{object} \longrightarrow \text{conceptualization} \longrightarrow \text{concept}.$$

At the end of the process there is a relatively stable interpretant. There is nothing more to interpret and the final representamen is the concept, the mental sign now being the accepted concept, which we more generally also call representation of the object. They are now synonyms. In terms of behavior we may label this sequence as

$$\text{stimulus} \longrightarrow \text{affection} \longrightarrow \text{response}.$$

Objects are, through whatever properties they have, more or less active stimuli. They evoke through our sensory system physical and mental responses, the latter being understanding and individual instances of meaning. We are stimulated by objects when we are conscious of them but at times also when we are only subconscious of them. In reverse direction, that is, when we have a concept in our mind, remembered or new, we refer to an object. The referenced object is the referent:

$$\text{concept} \longrightarrow \underset{\text{(signifying)}}{\text{referring}} \longrightarrow \underset{\text{(object)}}{\text{referent}}.$$

So, concepts are the interpreted representations. They are what we believe the properties of the object are. This is what we contemplate in the design process and use for developing physical representation. We develop a mental concept into its physical equivalent. A concept refers (signifies) to an object. *Referring* aspects to the relation between concept and referent is called reference. Sometimes, confusingly, the referent is called reference which needs to be sorted out from the present context.

In one of the above quotes Peirce mentions that "… *thought* is the chief, if not the only, mode of representation." True, but not only thoughts are representations. Physical things also represent other things. Words represent all kinds of things. Drawings in architectural design represent architecture. Therefore, I believe our common view of an object being a sign makes practical sense, because objects, as we talked about, have observable and relational properties which are represented in our mind. From this point of view, objects can be called signs. But we clearly should, if not evident from the context in which they are used, differentiate between physical signs and mental signs. And, we can conclude that all physical signs are understood by us as mental signs (eventually producing concepts).

All objects and states of affairs are for us potentially signifying entities, evoking understanding through communication – in the sense of 'an object means something to somebody'. There is no mental sign unless there is somebody who conceptualizes it from sensation. Every sign has its ground in materiality and, therefore, in reality. Signs may be intended, like someone's gesture or the design of a building. Or they may be corollary, producing unintended positive and negative effects. With anything as complex as architecture such side effects are unavoidable. We could not avoid producing them, even if we could predict the outcome of every design completely and to the finest detail.

If we come short of sufficient understanding, we need to develop available signs further or search for additional ones. Peirce holds that using belief and doubt in this process as guiding criteria for decision making will lead to a successful problem solution or abandonment. Belief is satisfactory and desirable. Doubt is unsatisfactory and undesirable. Peirce writes

> The opinion which is fated to be ultimately agreed to by all who investigate, is what we mean by the truth, and the object represented in this opinion is the real. That is the way I would explain reality.[9]

In the overall context of truth and reality, Peirce holds pragmatically that the real is what information and reasoning will eventually yield. But this absolute real is in an indefinite state. Therefore, this pragmatism goes too far for me. I hold that belief is real, true occurrence, but what I hold for the real is belief, being opinion accepted as truth – as meaning. This obviously implies uncertainty. In some instances, as in mathematics, we are referring by all human standards to the true and real. But in most instances this is not the case. In other words, signs refer to the truth of objects, that is, they refer to reality, be they simple things or complex states of affairs. To a large extent, however, they do so incompletely which we understand from the notion of things in themselves. There is no reason for distress, however. Nicolas Rescher writes very much in the tradition of Peirce that

> The circumstances that our hold on the truth is insecure no more indicates that truth should be consigned to limbo than the fact that our hold on life is insecure indicates that we should commit suicide.[10]

And,

> … the epistemic route is our only access-way to reality: only by *estimating* the truth can we validate claims about the real.[11]

But how can we tell that our truth-estimates make good on their promise?

> 'Because they are provided by methods which yield results that work. They emerge from the use of inquiry methods whose products can be implemented successfully in practice – with success monitored in the usual way of effective application and prediction.'[12]

I take "methods" to mean, in a general way, any suitable approach to a particular problem, whether used often or rarely. The emphasis, I think, is on results of "effective application and prediction". What naturally follows is the issue of validation.

> 'Be prepared to regard the best that can be done as good enough' is one of pragmatism's fundamental axioms. …

This commonsense axiom stems from a highly positive attitude. An example in the area of science is the use of statistically robust results as 'proof' for closeness to real occurrences.

> After all, estimation here is a matter of truth estimation and where the conditions for rational estimation are satisfied we are – *ipso facto* – rationally authorized to let that estimates stand surrogates to the truth. The very idea that the best we can do is not good enough for all relevant reasonable purposes is – so pragmatism and commonsense alike insist – simply absurd, a thing of unreasonable hyperbole.[13]

What is successful or not successful in "application and prediction" is as Hilary Putnam emphasizes not a matter of the subjective judgment of an individual but of a community of those who have experiences and make judgments. He quotes his own earlier writing in comments on Rescher's views:000

> According to the pragmatists, whether the subject be science or ethics, what we have are maxims and not algorithms; and maxims themselves require contextual interpretation. Furthermore, the problem of subjectivity was in the minds of pragmatists from the beginning. They insisted that when one human being in isolation tries to interpret even the best

maxims for himself and does not allow others to criticize the ways in which he or she interprets those maxims, or the way in which he or she applies them, then the kind of 'certainty' that results is always fatally tainted with subjectivity.[14]

In many endeavors and certainly in architecture it is not only a community of experts who are the judges but the general public.

When an object is actively signifying, be it a human being, an animal or an instrument, it is at that point engaged in giving a signal. Its sign nature is not only a byproduct of its existence but intended to presently draw attention by means of an explicit or encoded message. For example, a gesture by a person to communicate that a meeting is over and a buzzer in a school which indicates the end of a class period. Flashing advertising lights are signals. Music played consists of signals, though we usually do not call its sounds and melodies by this term. The activity of every signal has been conceptualized by a mind based on the potential understanding of the signal by the perceiver. The actively signifying object emphasizes the understanding which is embedded in the sensory nature of the sign. There are relatively few strong signals in architecture, its overall profusion with signs considered. Many signal devices are programmed to be activated electronically and automatically, such as for lighting and thermal controls.

Derived from all this I confirm the precept of "things in themselves" as being part of the ultimately true status of things and everything else being mental representation of truth, that is belief, perhaps strong belief. We have lived with this constraint for a long time and have learned to cope with it. I hold that we can decide reasonably and act well on this practical, though not infallible foundation. The world is "perfused with signs" as Peirce claimed. Whether he thought of physical signs or their mental equivalents he did not say. One thing is for sure: while the physical signs are the grounds for our mental ones, the latter provide our understanding and we act according to them. Consequently we design to some extent in uncertainty and accept this as part of our work. The world has succeeded in many ways and many wonderful things have come about on that premise, admittedly also failures.

3.2 Iconic, symbolic and indexical signs

According to Peirce there are three classes of signs: icons, indices and symbols. In common usage the terms sign and symbol have been used interchangeably. But they are not equivalents. All symbols are signs but not all signs are symbols. My following definitions abridge Peirce's very detailed descriptions with examples mixed in:[15]

- *Icons* represent their objects by means of *similarity*, though often with strong abstraction. They refer to features of the objects perceivable through sensation and, therefore, have directly explanatory content. Examples are pictorial traffic signs, portraits, descriptive speech, and drawings of architectural floor plans and elevations.
- *Symbols* represent their objects by means of *arbitrary* and usually exclusive notions, understood solely through convention. They are purely referential to something beyond themselves which they represent without similarity. Examples are words including names, numbers, letters, mathematical signs, the dove as the emblem for peace and the steeple representing the function of a building for worship.
- *Indices* represent their objects by emphasis of correspondence in *causal* relations. They are referential indicators with some actual, generally rather limited content. Indexes may point out an activity. Examples are smiles in connection with a thought, a level indicator of a thermometer or the digital numbers of a clock, the smoke from a fire, a bibliographic reference and

the activity reference of a critical path diagram for construction scheduling. Most signals are also indexical.

From the just mentioned examples we notice that they point to physical signs, which evoke mental signs of the three described kinds. From Peirce's quote above we take that signs are "representamen" and, as our use of 'representation', they are in the mental realm. The dependence of the mental sign on the physical counterpart in the object becomes very clear when we hear him point out that

The word sign will be used to denote an Object perceptible, or imaginable, ...[16]

with denotation referring to the substance of a physical object from which we derive the mental sign.

For us it is important to consider that the physical properties in architecture are the physical signs which attract our senses. In turn, the sensations cause, in highly concentrated fashion, the effects in the form of icons, symbols and indices in our minds. These forms are what we determine in conjunction with their content as part of the meaning of objects. When we talk about signs we really refer (1) to the content in impressions from whatever is present for understanding (as mental concept) or (2) to the content which we embed and communicate in expressions of design for understanding (again as mental concept).

Objects can rarely be attributed to strictly one of the three categories. In their complexity, however, usually one type dominates. The broader our focus of consideration, obviously, the typically higher sign diversity is present. In the sequence of events, we usually encounter an object as a whole. But one property typically stands out. Or a few do. Observing the object more closely and reflecting on it evokes in us a multifaceted sign or multiples of signs; often both. We may look about what surrounds us or we may only imagine or recall an environment. Let's think another time in this regard about the fountain in the courtyard of the museum in Frankfurt (2.4 and 2.5). People may become aware of the place because of a few strong signs among many others which are less eye-catching. Some objects are iconic and resemble others we have seen before, such as beams, columns, benches, fountains, etc. Especially designers may even suppose that the project because of its iconic overall whiteness is by the well known architect Richard Meier. The view of the fountain lets arise the feeling of coolness and the possibility for quenching thirst symbolically. That there are three children refers indexically to the fact that they are part of a group, so does the fact that the lady is talking with them as one person. That people enjoy to congregate around fountains is indexical reference to certain place qualities but also symbolic with regard to attractiveness of community and communication.

This simple example shows the general fact that in our observation of environments and what happens in them we focus on a spatially limited sign and perceive it as part of an overall sign with wider context. We look at an 'explicit' center and an 'implicit' field around it. Usually our interest in signs is essentially particular. But then we look at them to infer aspects beyond those from direct observation, that is, to relational properties, such as cultural, social, psychological or economical ones. Signs and our understanding of them give rise to frames of reference. We recognize school buildings because they are iconic, having forms similar to other schools, with classrooms, media centers and gymnasiums. They are symbolic because of standing for the importance of education. They are indexical because of having a certain size accommodating a large or small number of students. We may arrive at an exciting place, perhaps entering the Piazza del Campo in Siena or walking around Broadway in New York (3.1 and 3.2). That the piazza is formed by surrounding buildings makes it iconic in relation to other plazas. The main side is given by the facade of city hall which evokes symbolically government. The plaza provides space for people to gather. The size makes it indexical, being large enough even for yearly horse races which are held with much pageantry. As functions represent causal links, we often can derive indexical significance from asking: what is the object's function or consequence?

3.1 Piazza del Campo, Siena

3.2 Times Square, New York

The three very different objects, shown in 3.3 to 3.5 have clearly iconic references but also symbolic and indexical ones. The drawing in the sign referring to a stair is iconic as featuring resemblance. The word "stair" is symbolic. If there were an arrow, pointing toward the stair location, the sign would be also indexical. The school floor plan, designed by RB+B Architects, is iconic as it displays likeness of its geometric shapes. Having rectangles, it is iconic by similarity relation to all rectangles ever encountered. The seating in the spaces is iconic as showing other known geometric shapes (rows and circles). The arrangements are also symbolic as indicating various ways of communication. Symbolic also, though differently, are the names of the spaces, language being symbolic. And, they are indexical as they causally link the meaning of the labels with the spaces they indicate. The number of seats is indexical as it stands in causal relationship with class size. The items named in the critical path diagram by Jeremy Kemp are indexical as causally connected and informative about building processes and their connection. The abbreviated words and the numbers are obviously symbolic.[17]

3.3 Sign for Emergency Exit

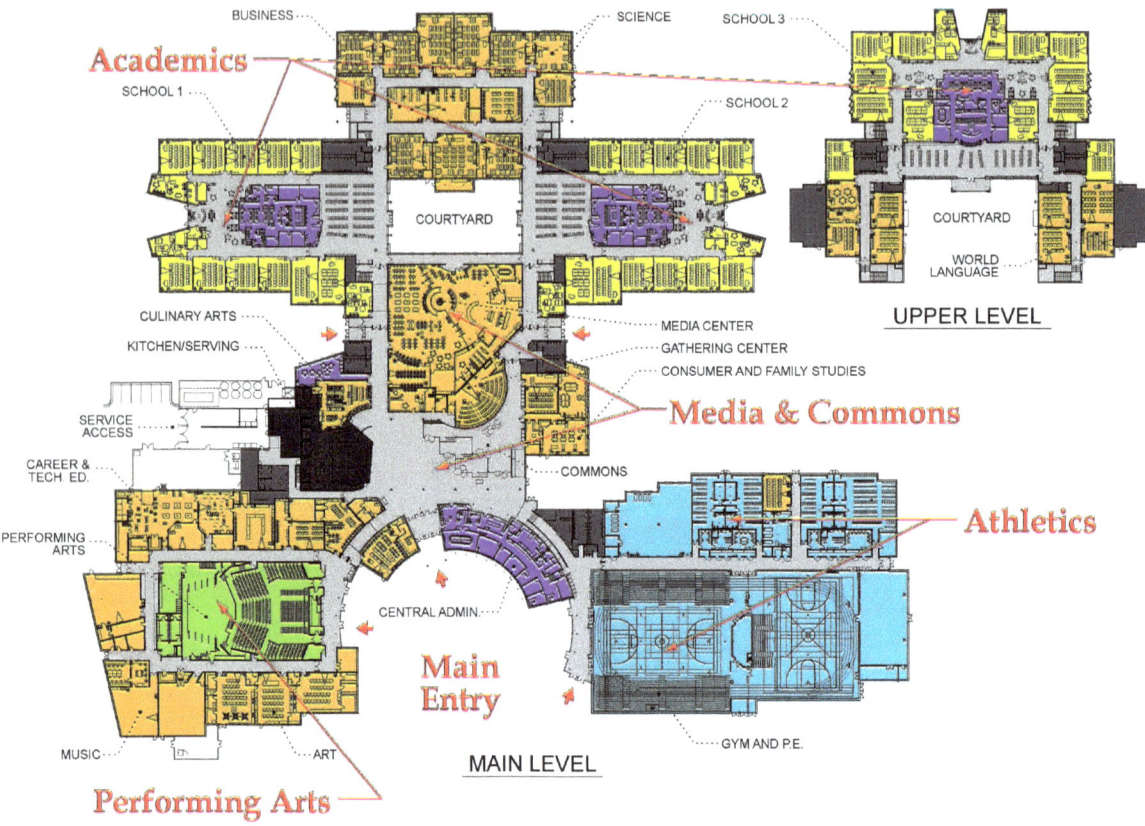

3.4 Fossil Ridge High School, Fort Collins, CO (© permission)

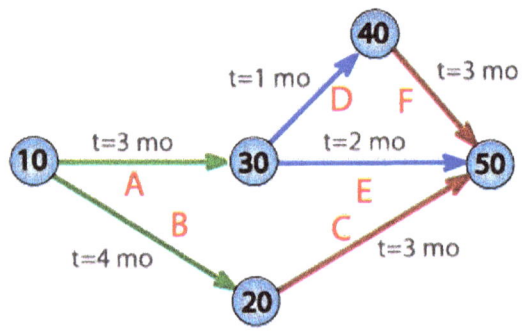

3.5 Critical path diagram (source) — PERT chart for a project with five milestones (10 through 50) and six activities (A through F). The project has two critical paths: activities B and C, or A, D, and F – giving a minimum project time of 7 months with fast tracking. Activity E is sub-critical, and has a float of 2 months.

Let us another time consider focus. The letter o in any word comes to us through one singular sensation. Most words we can similarly obtain as one sensation. Only when we read long words or phrases multiple sensations are required. We read a text. Also, we hear a single tone as one sensation. So it is even with musical accords. Only when we want to hear several tones and accords in sequence multiple sensations are required. We hear a melody. Words and texts are on different comprehensiveness levels, so are tones and melodies. Words and tones, even more texts and melodies evoke some relational ideas. In observing natural or manmade environments we encounter much more complex situations and circumstances. Even what we call details, unless they are at the simplest levels, are already composites and have typically individual functions. Parts and wholes are simultaneously present, requiring us to make successive decisions on focus among highly different components. Depending on the comprehensiveness of our desires and needs, we gain incomplete meanings unless we let them 'merge' over time. Not all we encounter obviously must or even can produce in us meaning and stays in the background as part of the whole. Peirce makes an interesting distinction when he talks about, as I take it, that signs are not quite meaning yet and even less originating objects when he writes that

> The object of a sign is one thing: its meaning is another. Its object is the thing or occasion, however indefinite, to which it is to be applied. Its meaning is the idea which it attaches to that object, whether by mere supposition, or as a command, or as an assertion.[18]

From this we can derive that signs cannot be carried to their full potential of meaning. A building facade has many components with properties which all are candidates for understanding but can only be carried to more or less development in perception and conceptualization. The first conclusion from this is that, in the process of impression from what is given, we must make decisions on what is most important of the typically many signs vying for attention, be they relatively weak or strong. Different people observing a given object perceive the same properties but do not, at least not exactly, conceptualize them in the same way and, therefore, come eventually to different meanings. This is in part why I stressed earlier that we have nearly always a multitude of understandings from which we select one as *our* meaning. On the other hand, often several understandings melt into one meaning. Observable and relational properties reinforce each other to evoke such combinations. The second conclusion is that we, in the process of expression in design, must take care when selecting signs as carriers of importance to be communicated. But importance is not necessarily obvious, not signifying itself strongly, often not at all or only at certain times. Many forms let their capacities show quite readily, such as the Y-shaped columns and the folded plate roof of the turbine building on a dam of the Rhine river near Basel, designed by Hans Hofmann (3.6). This and the next example show clearly that the iconic, symbolic and indexical signs of objects are interwoven following the ways we have discussed with regard to properties.

3.6 Power plant, Birsfelden near Basel

Many parts of forms are hidden or at least not readily observable for organizational or technical reasons, or perhaps because of aesthetic preferences. The Therme Vals, Switzerland, by Peter

Zumthor, has a structure of concrete and 60,000 locally quarried quartzite slabs which give the building in- and outside a highly unified appearance (3.7 to 3.9). There are windows, doors, stairs and lamps, and naturally water. Concentration is on bathing. Purpose, plan and space correspond intimately. In this building, people are typically not aware of the mechanical and electrical systems until someone controls them by adjusting a thermostat or a light switch, or people sense the presence in other ways (for example, through light reflection in the water). In many buildings exposure of such systems has become rather common, as in the earlier shown Harvard Science Center, with its visible and accessible mechanical, electrical and other service systems (2.19 to 2.23).

3.7 From southeast

3.8 Interior swimming pool

Therme Vals, Switzerland

3.9 Floor plan (© permission)

At times the term symbol is equated more broadly with signs as such. The main proponent of this direction is Ernst Cassirer (1874-1945), a historian and philosopher of culture. He views the world and our mental representations of it as thoroughly symbolic. In a short chapter "A Clue to the Nature of Man: the Symbol" he writes that

> … Between the receptor system and the effector system, which are to be found in all animal species, we find in man a third link which we may describe as the symbolic system. …
>
> … No longer in a merely physical universe, man lives in a symbolic universe. Language, myth, art, and religion are parts of this universe. They are the varied threads which weave

> the symbolic net, the tangled web of human experience. All human progress in thought and experience refines upon and strengthens this net. No longer can man confront reality immediately; he cannot see it, as it were, face to face. Physical reality seems to recede in proportion as man's symbolic activity advances. Instead of dealing with the things themselves man is in a sense constantly conversing with himself. ...
>
> ... Hence, instead of defining man as an animal rationale, we should define him as an animal symbolicum.[19]

For Cassirer sensation and sign are much closer related than in what we discussed above by clearly distinguishing between physical signs and mental signs. He does not address this distinction at all; although he acknowledges that particulars "must be given as such". He claims that the task of content is solely to signify:

> It is not the case ... that the symbolic signs which we encounter in language, myth, and art first 'are' and then, beyond this 'being', achieve a certain meaning; their being arises from their signification. Their content subsists purely and wholly in the function of signification. Here consciousness, in order to apprehend the whole in the particular, no longer requires the stimulus of the particular itself, which must be given as such; here consciousness *creates* definite concrete sensory contents as an expression for definite complexes of meaning.[20]

But it is our conscious mind which creates content from sensations of form, that is, understanding and meaning. We conceptualize representations, which are signs in our mind. When physical signs evoke mental signs, our capacity to think, our capacity to understand, works with appearances, early mental representations, to develop understandings from which we derive meaning through judgment. I do not believe that there is a "symbolic function of consciousness".[21] Our thinking, enabled through consciousness, sorts out the mental content it has created from sensation with regard to having iconic, symbolic or indexical nature. As content itself, these three categories are constructs of our mind. We, in reflection about objects, commonly (and not correctly) associate the terminology with objects directly by saying that they 'are iconic, symbolic or indexical'. From contrasting the sign theories of Peirce and Cassirer I believe that the former's triad of sign categories is a very meaningful division of mental sign content as derived from the variety of physical forms we encounter. In ordering the world through semiotics we are not becoming beings who understand only symbolically but stay rational beings – thinking beyond what we perceive – using the triadic semiotics to evaluate and categorize understanding.

There is a fundamental difference between the communicative nature of language and that of the objective world. Language is purely symbolic, even when it describes non-symbolic aspects. It is always only referential in this sense. The objective world can be symbolic, iconic or indexical – understood by us through contemplation before we refer to it by language. To affirm: when we talk here about content of the observable, physical world (objects, occurrences) and content of language, we talk about thought content that our thinking provides. As language is purely referential, it requires reconstitution of its referenced content from memory (a kind of imagination). We may not be aware of this process at all, if we are capable to remember easily and well. The objective world, on the other hand, prompts us at least in part through its physical, observable properties to directly think in terms of content (what something existentially is), the other part being the relational properties, inferred by us indirectly. Accordingly, the processes of thinking about the content of the objective world and the content of language vary considerably, about which I will have to say much more later when we extensively contrast meaning in language and in architecture.

In this context another aspect requires mentioning: language does not interpret. I believe that it is not so, as Emile Beneviste emphasizes, that
> Every semiology of a nonlinguistic system must use language as an intermediary, and thus can only exist in and through the semiology of language. ... language is the interpreting system of all other systems, linguistic and nonlinguistic.[22]

Thinking interprets. Language only *refers* to what thinking interprets or points to what is to be interpreted. Architecture or architectural design does not interpret. Thinking interprets to what architecture and our representation of it, architectural design, refer. Only humans interpret rationally from impressions and for expressions. Language and corporeal systems, including architecture, are used as means of communicating interpretations. Claude Lévi-Strauss points out that
> ... language is the semiotic system par excellence; it cannot but signify, and exists only through signification.[23]

This is true. But in so doing, it is still only a tool, though arguably the most flexible and available one we have to communicate.

Peirce's view of signs and their dynamic behavior enhances our understanding of conceptualization. The components of the world are not naturally organized in iconic, symbolic and indexical categories. But these categories are concepts which are particularly useful in how we see the world, shape it and communicate about it.

3.3 Semantics, pragmatics and syntactics

The three branches of semiotics which deal with signs as components and systems of communication are called semantics, pragmatics and syntactics.[24] The following descriptions are based on the definitions by Charles Morris of 1938 and additional understanding since then.[25]
- *Semantics* refers to the content of meaning which the sign nature of objects with their observable and relational properties evokes in us, that is, specific understanding of denotative and connotative aspects.
- *Pragmatics* refers to the interrelationships of signs and their users, that is, why and how beings interpret and produce signs in given circumstances.
- *Syntactics* refers to the relationships, rules and patterns of components or systems of signs, that is, the formative characteristics of parts in relation to each other and toward wholes.

While this threefold differentiation has grown out of linguistics and behavioral science, we benefit from it in the world of all signs. Signs in architecture arise from our perception of its physical components and systems. The semantic aspects of architecture are what this present study is mainly about. But to give projects the meanings, which we think they should have, we must understand from where they originate and why they come about. The pragmatic aspects lead us to the implications in practice, especially communication. The syntactic aspects let us understand how this formally happens. All three obviously have to do with the relationships of our minds and the world of which we are in one sense part, but which is in another sense beyond us. *In design development we are using semantics which arise out of pragmatics to bring about realization by means of syntactics.*

Pragmatics surely entered architecture, though informally practiced for a long time, in the guise of environmental psychology of the 1960s and through developments in sociology. Amos Rapoport, who has done a great deal of work in cross-cultural studies, emphasizes in 1989 the need for more work in the pragmatics of the built environment:

> Generally, in semiotics, meaning has been regarded as a relatively unimportant, special, and utilitarian form of significance. Yet meaning, as those associational, sociocultural qualities encoded into environmental elements, characteristics, or attributes, would seem to be precisely the most interesting question. Another major problem, therefore, with semiotic analysis is that it has tended to concentrate on the *syntactic* level, that is, the most abstract. There has been some, although not enough, attention paid to the *semantic* – but hardly any at all to the *pragmatic*. Yet it is by examining which elements function in what ways in concrete situations, how they influence emotions, attitudes, preferences, and behavior, that they can best be understood and studied.[26]

I agree with his last sentence but believe the rest is overstated. I hold that it is not possible to work in architecture on one of the three levels without getting involved with the other two. Every designer, for better or worse, addresses all three on a daily basis; how well is a different matter. Every design poses problems of semantics, pragmatics and syntactics; requiring decisions accordingly. Without at least informal understanding of all three in the design process no good buildings could have and can come about. Most matters of syntax are not "abstract" but are very much oriented toward physical solutions in response to design criteria. But I believe that pragmatics should be more explicitly part of our efforts in the design process. It is an objective which all who are involved with built environments need to support.

Since the 1960s a great deal of work has been done as outcome of the 'environment and behavior movement'. The best source for documented studies are the yearly proceedings of the Environmental Design Research Association.[27] The link of pragmatics to semantics is probably best summarized by Herbert Blumer in 1969 in what he calls "symbolic interactionism", which I, based on earlier comments, would rather call semiotic interactionism:

> The first premise is that human beings act toward things [objects and people] on the basis of the meanings that the things have for them. ... The second premise is that the meaning of such things is derived from, or arises out of, the social interaction that one has with one's fellows. The third premise is that these meanings are handled in, and modified through, an interpretive process used by the person in dealing with the things he encounters.[28]

I could not agree more. Many of the properties in the built environment are culture based, often with long traditions. They come about through the ways people understand themselves and their world, and develop its environments accordingly. These properties are nonphysical content, over time given to and derived from physical form. They evoke meaning, because they inform. Forms are bearers of content. In short, they are signs. But meaning is not intrinsic and interpretation plays a critical role.

Many cues come from codes, such as cultural, ethical, behavioral and political rules, often arrived at through long conventions. In the terminology of environmental design research the associated activities are therefore called encoding and decoding. Rapoport writes that

> If the design of the environment is seen partly as a process of encoding information, then the users can be seen as decoding it. If the code is not shared or understood, the environment does not communicate.[29]

In view of what I said earlier, the latter sentence does not quite convey what happens. Environments do not 'communicate' or 'not communicate'. People do by encoding or decoding. Environments are only material means to do so according to their particular physical properties. All environments are more or less understood, as all of them let us derive cues. Some 'communicate' based on given human codes, others through their very own nature.

Syntactics in architectural design addresses organization, coordination, morphology and connectivity. It evolves from the programming phase and gains increasingly detailed physical expression during the design development:
1. Organization, based on programmatic demands, sets priorities and interrelationships of components and subsystems within the system as a whole. Influential factors are requirements of building types, single versus multiple occupancy utilization, public versus private spaces, accessibility and adjacency valuations, primary versus service functions, site geometries, horizontal versus vertical project dimensions, entry and exit arrangements, etc.
2. Coordination is concerned with combination and fit on any level of scale including functional considerations and correspondence in all three spatial dimensions, and suitable sequences in time of construction. A major factor is the increasing prefabrication of building components and the role computers play in their sizing and production, not only for repetitive but also individualized realizations. While there will be always, hopefully, the influence from local site and environmental factors, we are increasingly in a global market also for architecture and its design.
3. Morphology manages and manifests the change from organizational and coordinative models into constructional form. It takes into consideration all subsystems, such as load bearing structure, external and internal walls, mechanical and electrical distribution, wherever they occur in the overall building fabric. It represents the spatial needs for physical substance and infrastructure while shaping spaces for the purposes of utilization.
4. Connectivity is how the physical components relate and attach to each other in detail within the three-dimensionality of construction. More broadly, however, it also refers to the ways the construct of form allows interrelationships of movement and communication, indoors and outdoors and from one to the other.

Every project must address these formative aspects. There is a hierarchy of dominance from organization to connectivity but all four are highly interdependent and adjustments are made back and forth. Syntactics in architecture can probably best be characterized as the methods and practices of systems integration in space and time from initial design through physical realization. What happens in the four areas just described, can be demonstrated on any architectural project. Every set of design and construction documents is more or less an extensive effort in showing syntactic relationships and details. As an example I show a small project, the Provincial Office Building, Flin Flon, Manitoba, by IKOY Partnership (3.10 to 3.14). It exhibits the design development through

Town Hall, Flin Flon, Canada
(© permissions)

3.10 Main entry facade

particular clarity in component assembly. Rarely have I seen a building whose appearance lets us so readily understand how it 'came together'. It belongs to a category of construction which has become known over the past decades as 'high-tech', with the Centre Pompidou and the Hongkong & Shanghai Bank perhaps its most prominent instances.

Town Hall, Flin Flon, Canada

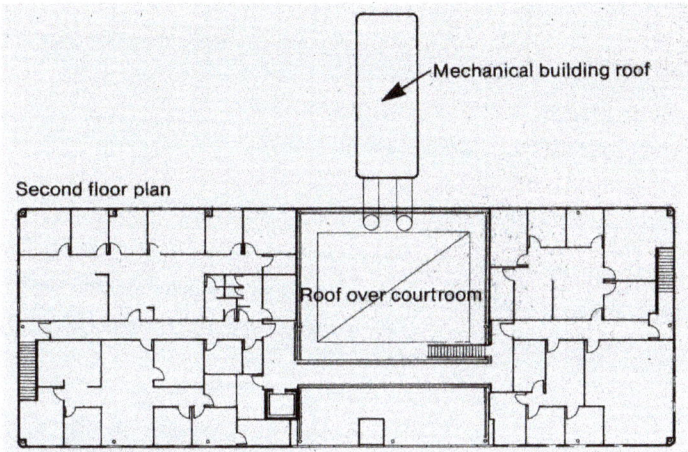

3.11 Second floor plan

3.12 Hall and elevator tower

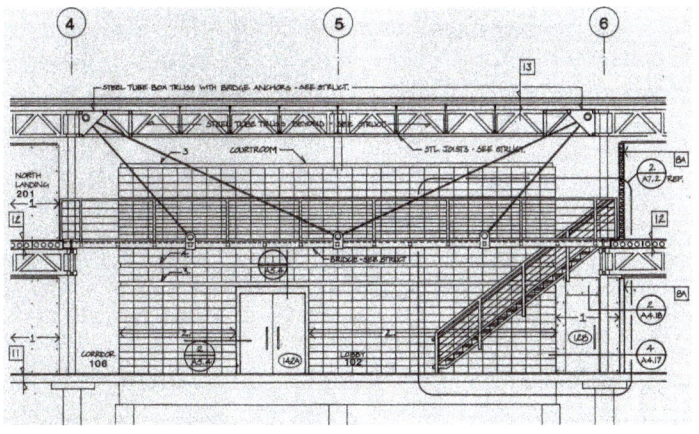

3.13 Section of entry hall

3.14 Bridge over entry hall

The nearly unlimited variety of possible choices gives designers in conjunction with purpose and context a great deal of discretion for physical expression. From this fact and from the listed aspects it is quite clear that syntactics in architecture are different from those in linguistics. While both are rule based, the rules cannot be transferred from one realm into the other, and make talk about text in architecture not more than an analogy. Regarding language we talk about a comparatively narrow set of components, spoken or written, with quite similar physical characteristics in highly varied arrangements. They not directly relate to the physical environments. They only refer to them, are not actually part of them. Architecture, on the other hand, has an essentially endless variation of physical components which are to a large extent self-referential. But it has also a very physically influential context to consider in which to fit the components physically. Built architecture becomes part of its context in reality and changes it in doing so.

This leads to one aspect which needs to be emphasized and influences our further discussion on pragmatics and syntactics. Syntax in language comprises the structure and connectivity of sentences. As all sentences physically are combinations of words, which are 'connected' by spaces, the words are not influenced by the connections. Further, the words and the sentences are physically of the same 'material', that is, letters which are not influenced by syntax. Very different in architecture where material plays a central role in what the components and their connection details are. Adjacent connection details are necessarily interdependent. So, aspects of pragmatics and syntactics influence architectural form much more fundamentally than linguistic form. We will return to these issues in Chapter 7.

In a general way it must be acknowledged that environment-behavior research, which has a major role to play in pragmatics, has been criticized for not having been able to span the so-called 'applicability gap' from theory to practice for sufficient influence on design. This view has some justification. But knowledge and understanding in a new field often takes considerable time to be absorbed and to show impact, especially when much of it has to be derived from matters in other areas. This is not different from concerns which gain emerging relevance, such as new construction methods, requirements for energy efficiency and sustainability, introduction of computers in design practice, etc.

In addition, that environment-behavior studies and, especially, pragmatics in architecture cannot be envisioned as a scientific enterprise to produce very generally applicable rules, has to do with the incredibly diverse demands of community, site, climate, occupancy, economics, etc. which the design of architecture has to combine into a few strongly deciding influences for one overall solution, that is, with only a rather small number of main properties to be emphasized – while at the same time having to satisfy the demand for a pleasing aesthetic of experience.

With regard to environment-behavior studies the case has been made that meaning arises from the influence of culture on environment. Keith Diaz Moore writes

> If culture-environment studies have informed us of anything, they have revealed that meaning is integrally related to a given setting. Culture-environment relations can be viewed as producing meaning; meaning resulting from the negotiation amongst the multiple dimensions of the culture-environment nexus.[30]

Culture has been variously described. I view it as the manifestation of lifestyle in a society's behavior and in what it produces over the history of this society's existence. In other words, we observe culture from temporary and lasting manmade environments. Meaning arises. As actors in society, we think meaning and translate it into forms to manifest it. Linda Groat rightly speaks of the "architect-as-cultivator".[31] Whenever we undertake anything of public consequence we are cultivators – not only as architects, but as human beings, and for better or worse. We are sometimes "architect-as-technicians", other times "architect-as-artists", sometimes empiricists, sometimes rationalists, all in one. Meaning is whatever understanding we select out of our own mental complexity in relation to the complexity of the world which we experience under present circumstances. With regard to the overall picture: culture exists in whatever situation we find ourselves.

By understanding what exists and changing it by design we inevitably contribute to it presently and for the future. Understanding of what exists must lead to understanding of the direction change should be pursued – an aspect which requires value judgments beyond those on architectural design in a narrow sense.

So, the question is: what do we cultivate? We have global technologies, and increasingly global designers, but also local circumstances. This leads not to the elimination of the local but to its hybridization. The local is to be interpreted by taking into account the universal. This partial leveling is not completely new to us, as our needs and desires always had common roots in the intellectual and bodily capacities of human beings in general, but also in having our own personalities. To clarify the notion of the local versus the universal is perhaps best done by thinking about what we encounter and use as local signs versus universal signs, what they mean to us and why they inspire us.

A critical regionalism is to be found in the relative power of context, in the present uniqueness of place. In 1951 Martin Heidegger tells us in *Building Dwelling Thinking* that we should think in terms of "Raum" (room beyond physical space) with the connotation that

> Boundary is not that at which something stops but, as the Greeks recognized, boundary is that from which something *begins its essence*.

This essence is the being of something through what it is and where it is – "Dasein" (being there) as he often names it. Bounded space as place is architecture. But this implies not only what is within the boundaries but also without, the local influenced by the global. It is as he suggests that

> ... Room is essentially the room made, fit into its boundaries. That made room is always bestowed and hence matched, that is, gathered due to a place [situated], ... *Accordingly, the rooms receive their essence from place and not from "space"*.[32]

And therefore,

> Man's relation to places and of places to rooms is based on dwelling. The relation of man and room is nothing else than the essentially thought dwelling. ...
>
> When we, in this way, think about the relation of place and space, but also about the relation of man and space, then a light falls on the essence of the things which are places and which we call buildings.
>
> ... As building brings forth places, the joining of their rooms brings necessarily with it space as spatium and extensio in the thingly assembly of buildings. But building never forms "the" space. Neither directly nor indirectly. Nevertheless, because it brings forth things as places, building is closer to the essence and the origin of spatial understanding than geometry and mathematics.[33]

What we design as architectural spaces must receive its main essence in most instances not from shape making but from forming what place implies, that is, internal and external conditions.

By designing we are not first creating architectural space, we first think for what it is meant. Wherever a project is to be located we find design factors which become active when we seek means for realization of purpose; may they have historical, social, technical, economic or environmental origins – enhancing freedom or enforcing constraint. The project must be influenced by what exists around the site, how people enjoy to gather there, what kind of construction fits the local program, how affordability makes it possible and how climate affects its appearance. Meaning must be looked for, even when familiar. It cannot be found in a so-called autonomy of architecture but in the service of architecture as places to dwell in Heideggerian comprehensiveness.

Lewis Mumford writes in 1967 that

> The philosophic problem of the general and the particular has its counterpart in architecture [as well as in other designed things]; and during the last century that problem has shaped

> itself more and more into the question of what weight should be given to the universal imprint of the machine [including the computer] and the local imprint of the region and the community.[34]

It is clear that architecture to be responsive today needs to adopt a comprehensive functionalism – one which connects all that is needed as purposive content to influence built form with an overall aesthetic as balance.[35]

Information on pragmatics is widely spread over the whole field of architectural practice. Building regulations address demands for safety and security, for lighting and air quality, etc. Then there are the very detailed guidelines and related literature on barrier-free design.[36] Less formally and quite market oriented, a wealth of pragmatics-related experiences have improved building product utility and quality over decades. We must only think about how kitchen and bathroom equipment has changed because of studies on behavior and ergonomics by architects and other researchers in practice and in industry. Most comprehensively, building type studies contain a wealth of pragmatics-oriented information.[37]

The best way to provide strong input from pragmatics is through involvement of environment-behavior researchers in design development, especially when highly specialized understanding is necessary. It is standard practice to have consultants for structural, electrical and environmental control systems on projects of any considerable size and complexity. It should also become so for the field of pragmatics from areas, such as psychology, sociology, medicine, communication and ergonomics; not only for hospital and manufacturing projects in which it is already routine today.

Not enough post-occupancy evaluations are performed. They must not all be based on extensive statistical analysis, though this gives the strongest basis for evaluation to those who want in depth information. It should become customary that each designer conducts post-occupancy interviews with clients after they had a chance to experience their project for a sufficient time. This is part of learning about the effectiveness of architecture from the impressions of others, not only for potential adjustment of what has been built but for informed development of expressions in future projects. Herman Hertzberger's *Lessons for Students in Architecture* is perhaps the most wide ranging and pertinent document on informal pragmatics. Based mostly on his own projects, he addresses many building types from overall to detailed design. The title of the studies could be changed to 'Lessons for Designers' as we never finish learning in the complex and constantly evolving field of architecture.[38] Examples, 3.15 to 3.21, by Hertzberger and by Steidle+Partner, show two approaches with the same objective of pragmatics: community interaction. Hertzberger writes about the 'in-between' as transition from public to private space:

> The threshold provides the key to the transition and connection between areas with divergent territorial claims and, as a place in its own right, it constitutes, essentially, the spatial conditions for the meeting and dialog between areas of different orders. … We are concerned here with the encounter and reconciliation between street on the one hand and a private domain on the other.[39]

And more directly, he comments on the courtyard of the LiMa Housing project in Berlin and the results of involvement by the people who live there:

> … [it] is conceived as a public open space with six pedestrian routes, including connections with both the street and the neighboring courtyard. … The centre of the courtyard is marked by the large segmented sand-pit, which was decorated with mosaics along the curved sides by the families themselves. … [this] area with which the inhabitants themselves are involved and where individual marks are put down for themselves and for each other is appropriated jointly, and is turned into a communal space.[40]

LIMA Housing, Berlin

3.16 View from the street

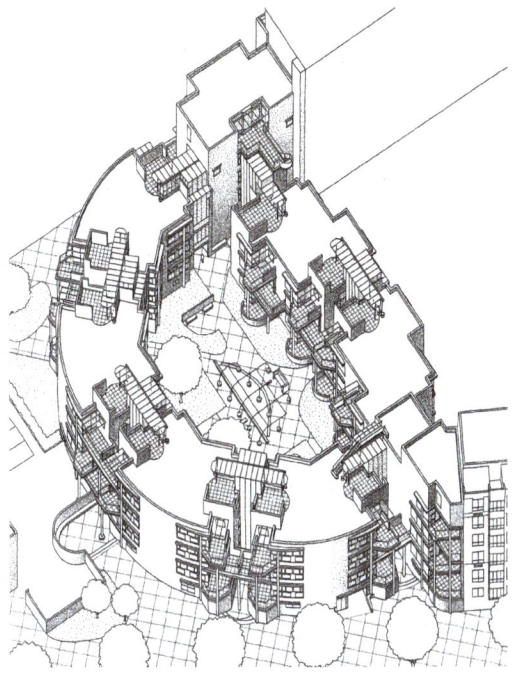
3.15 Bird's eye view (© permission)

3.17 In the courtyard

The Munich "Integrated Housing" project, by Steidle+Partner, has its name from the effort of the city to develop, through an architectural competition, a demonstration project with over hundred apartments for a mixed population of all ages, income levels, and some for people with physical challenges. Ten three-story units with one to four bedroom apartments are distributed in a park-like setting with the first floor levels reserved for barrier-free living. One building contains a facility for common use. Quiet access roads lead to parking spurs directly adjacent to the entrances. This project is today considered a prototype for many others. And this not least because of interviews which were conducted with those who live there.[41]

Integrated Housing, München-Nymphenburg, Germany

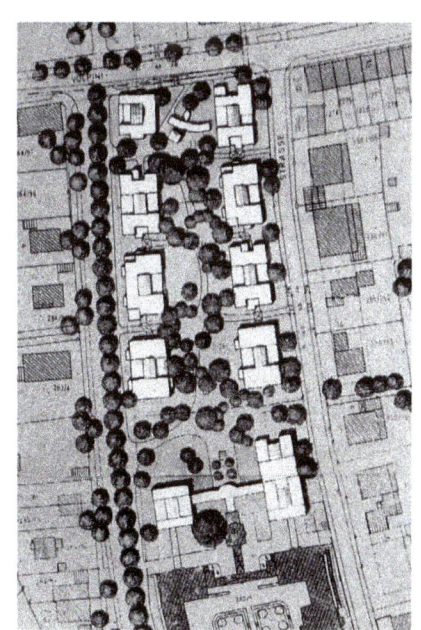

3.18 Site plan (© permission)

65

Integrated Housing
München-Nymphenburg, Germany

3.19 From south into spinal courtyard

3.20 From west toward common facilities

3.21 Entry area to housing with parking

Particularly rich sources for studying pragmatics and their follow-up in syntactics are, in addition to the mentioned recent building types studies, the developments over the past century of spatial arrangements and technical means to support socio-cultural and behavioral outcomes, be they related to residential, administrative, educational, recreational or industrial settings. Let's consider what happened with residential floor plans in general and kitchen layouts in particular. The comparatively largest developments took place from the earliest tenements – simply with rows of rooms on corridors and without inside water supply, privies and bathrooms – to the early modern apartments in the 1920s. And since then many more changes occurred in two of the main functional areas of dwelling: food preparation and dining, and personal care. Peter Faller writes that

Today the immediate adjacency of cooking and eating belongs to the few essential functional concentrations of dwelling floor plans. For this, however, the conflict of the bourgeois ideas of dwelling had to be overcome, whereby the dwell-in-kitchen in a residence must not be observable at all, and the kitchen of the working class, in which cooking, eating and residing features are in the most imaginable unity. ...

Today this question ... is not anymore a question of class or money but one of desires for individual living and the possibility of its realization in given overall circumstances.[42]

Often dining area and general dwelling area have no separation anymore at all. A similar adjacency adjustment occurred in the personal care area, often with a guest restroom close to the dwelling entry and a bathroom adjacent to bedrooms. Comparable developments occurred based on the desire to have private areas with bedrooms doubling for retreat and work of individuals during daytime.

Kitchen layouts themselves have undergone major changes. Behavioral studies in kitchens have clearly established a triangular relationship between food storage (refrigerator), cleaning (sink) and cooking (range) with work areas in-between and no triangular leg measuring more than 9 ft. 3.22 by the Kohler Company shows that there is a strong interrelationship between behavioral patterns and technical advances – inevitably the case in all well developed building types and their components.

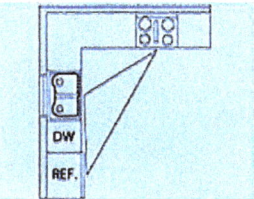 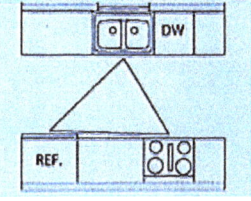 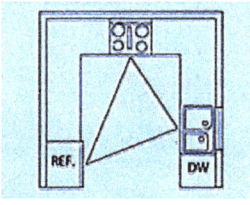

3.22 Kitchen triangles
(© permission)

One of the most important indicators whether meaningful organizational relationships have been achieved is the inclusion of furniture in floor plans as shown in 3.23, by Fundel, Holste, Kermann, Priesemeister, von Mann. See also 3.4.

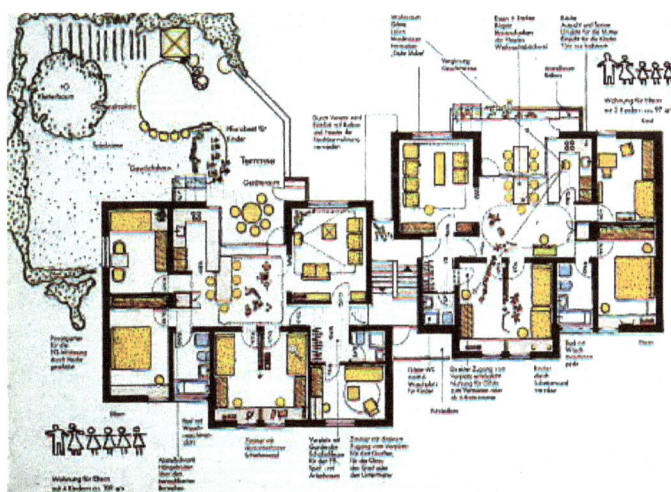

3.23 Apartment with furniture layout
(© permission)

Overall, many innovations took place over the past decades in facilities for education, administration, research and health care. Here pragmatics, coming out of intensive programming, are translated into functional relationships of physical service components. Most building types, because of increased understanding in pragmatics and of technical advances, have considerably changed during the past decades. The design of office buildings, for example, has undergone adjustments in response to the changes of how people interact in corporate structures. Schemes with individual offices strung along corridors have given way mainly to open office landscapes which are highly flexible in workplace arrangements. Innovations of indoor climate and lighting controls as well as electronic communication systems supported these efforts. The underfloor distribution of services in the Kloeckner Building, Bremen, Germany, pioneered by Hentrich-Petschnigg & Partner in 1977, is one example for the translation of pragmatics into technical innovation (3.24 and 3.25). Much of what is evident from the examples shown in my account can be traced to environment-people interdependence and interaction studies.

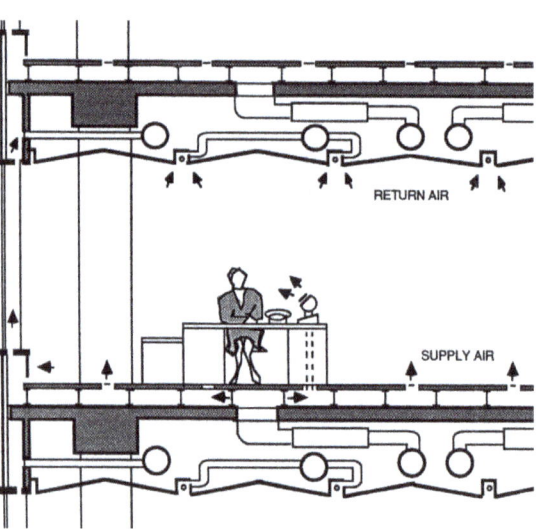

Kloeckner Building, Bremen, Germany

3.24 and 3.25 Underfloor services supply systems with extensions to desktop

There is a crucial connection of pragmatics with semantics and syntax also in architecture which Cassirer pointed out more generally in the quote given some eleven pages earlier. His view of over six decades ago that "no longer can man confront reality immediately; he cannot see it, as it were, face to face" should remind us even more today that we have increasingly media between ourselves and things; some of these media being very complex. Only few of our bodily activities are anymore in direct contact with the world. The world is for us a world of signs which we experience and understand in a Kantian way, according to our capacities, that is, through interpretation. Taken this as a given, Cassirer points to a troubling phenomenon of our times: the remoteness of ourselves from what actually happens in spite of the enormous frequency of our contacts and communications. Our ever more extensive and speedy information systems, including virtual reality creations, allow us to dream worlds which tend to exaggerate what material formations can accomplish environmentally and economically for sound and enjoyable living. This view is obviously not intended to speak against progress and innovation but to plead for the use of our instruments in ways which allow us to stay in meaningful control of them, rather than being controlled by them.

It helps here to return another time to sensory aspects of signs. We encounter in a typical day a huge variety of them. Most are images, many are sounds and touches, and there are smells and tastes. When we produce objects, we produce physical signs for those who perceive them, including ourselves. Our design documents are objects, but they are representations of ultimately anticipated objects. They are material in nature, compared to our mental representations, carrying information between mind and world, uniting in realization formative aspects of both. How they represent content very much depends on the characteristics of signification tied up with their material properties. Their ways of manifestation affect not only perception but also the ways we conceptualize.

Drawing by hand versus generating computer images, for example, results in two different ways of decision making. With hand drawings the medium is under exclusive control by the one who draws. This is still largely so in using the computer as a drawing tool. In cases of advanced simulation, however, using virtual reality programs, some control is 'prefabricated' by the code programmer. The impression/expression cycle of design is influenced step by step by what is given in the program. It is questionable, at least, whether computer programs can be developed to be, in combination with the user's decision making, as creatively sensitive as the conventional approach. What speaks for them, naturally, is the nearly instantaneous access to large data bases with many kinds of relevant information. Warning is warranted, however, because of their intoxicating and overpowering tendencies. Robert Innis writes that

> Modern digital technologies, because they reside on a formal, articulate, and abstract base, which is semiotically opaque to most users, nevertheless gives rise to a peculiar 'transparency effect'. By this I mean that we can radically shift the outcomes of the instruments without concomitant somatic or intellectual input, although it is clear that the code can prevent the realizations of one's merely arbitrary desires and that those who can write the code are 'in the long run' those who control the effects. This, however, from a semiotic point of view is problematic, since 'making possible' a semiotic effect, no matter how technically sophisticated, does not validate or valorize that effect in any sense of the term.[43]

This is not only problematic from a semiotic point of view. Good computer codes are able to provide combinatorial fit of properties and provide quickly solutions for decision making. But they may short circuit the thinking process and deprive it from maturing through consideration of potential alternatives, a crucial part of the gestation process in design. What is at work in the latter is imagination, bringing together the manifold of intuition in the necessary unity of apperception.[44] This is a disadvantage in the use of computing among its many advantages. We are a long way from being able to simulate by machines what the mind can accomplish through imagination, if that ever will be possible.

Similarly, a disadvantage or at least danger exists in the abstraction that occurs in the use of hypermedia when on cues ready-made components make up a desired concept, however fine-grained the input may be. Media memories provide highly developed outputs, and with it deliver highly deceptive immediacy, but what happens between the input and output is largely remote and inaccessible. David Bolter and Richard Grusin write

> … the logic of hypermediacy is to represent the desire for transparent immediacy by sublimating it, by turning it into a fascination with the medium.

And, the

> … new digital media oscillate between immediacy and hypermediacy, between transparency and opacity.[45]

This is obviously the fundamental problem all artificial intelligence faces in simulating mental processes, perceptual or conceptual. How far the sensitivity, cultivation and discrimination of the human mind can be matched and traded off with the responsiveness, multifariousness and selectiveness of hypermedia is not clear at all. More will have to be said later on this issue.

All mental representations are abstractions, helping us to grasp the structure and other essential features of what we encounter. They go through a reduction of information, compared to the originals they stand for. Successful conceptualization maintains coherence and clarity in spite of such reduction. The reduction is always more or less balanced by the addition and integration of earlier representations from our memory. The computer does not have access to our mind, at least so far. We must 'feed' it accordingly in a way it is able to 'grasp'. This process and its results are equivalent to adding aspects of our present design thinking to evolving drawings or scale models, thus enriching them. Experience from observation of the outcomes of our conceptions is the key to future successful abstractions, be it about joining two pieces of wood, giving the right measurements to steps for climbing a stair, laying out spatial arrangements for way finding in a complex building or generating multimedia impacts to enhance being in architectural settings.

What does all this have to do with aspects of semantics, syntactics and pragmatics of meaning in design? I think a great deal. When aspects of semantics, pragmatics and syntactics in design are more and more replaced, not only supplemented, by aspects of 'dream worlds', we face the possibility of a coerced transformation of ourselves brought on by such atypical environments over which individuals have little or no control anymore – especially not designers who may now know no better anymore. Disney Lands and Las Vegas type cities and architectures are then not only examples of learning about "complexity and contradiction" but impoverished ends of creativity.

If this would become common occurrence, then Jean Baudrillard's utopia of three decades ago would come closer to reality than we can think of today. Evolving from Marxist analysis, structuralism and McLuhan's work he develops an extreme position on the relationship of signification and value:

> *Referential value is annihilated, giving the structural play of value the upper hand.* The structural dimension becomes autonomous by excluding the referential dimension, and is instituted upon the death of reference. The systems of reference for production, signification, the affect, substance and history, all this equivalency to a 'real' content, loading the sign with the burden of 'utility', with gravity – its form of representative equivalence – all this is over with. Now the other stage of value has the upper hand, a total relativity, general commutation, combination and simulation – simulation, in the sense that, from now on, signs are exchanged against each other rather than against the real ... The emancipation of the sign: remove this 'archaic' obligation to designate something and it finally becomes free, indifferent and totally indeterminate, in the structural or combinatory play which succeeds the previous rule of determinate equivalence.[46]

And,

> Neither Saussure nor Marx had any presentiment of all this: they were still in the golden age of the dialectic of the sign and the real, ... Their dialectic is in shreds, and the real has died of the shock of value acquiring this fantastic autonomy. Determinacy is dead, indeterminacy holds sway.[47]

And,

> A kind of unintentional parody hovers over everything, a tactical simulation, a consummate aesthetic enjoyment, is attached to the indefinable play of reading and the rules of the game. Traveling signs, media, fashion and models, the blind but brilliant ambience of simulacra.[48]

Postmodern manifestoes, such as Baudrillard's, make for stimulating general reading. But they must also make us think about what may happen and what our position should be, as designers and as those who live in our designs. We may consider that such simulacra fantasies have their forerunners in the overly enthusiastic modernist manifestoes during the first third of the past century. But they are more dangerous than those were, because their ultimate success would be to make out of designers simulacra activists. Peter Eisenman writes:

> A sign begins to replicate or, in Jean Baudrillard's term, "simulate" once the reality it represents is dead. When there is no longer a distinction between representation and reality, when reality is only simulation, then representation loses it's a priori source of significance, and it, too, becomes a simulation.[49]

Simulation of what? When reality is dead, representation and simulation of it represent and simulate what it is dead. When there is no reality, no representation and simulation is possible. When there is no architectural reality, there is no representation of architecture. Otherwise truth would be simulacrum – a nonsense. The assumption of a time, now or in the near future, "when reality is only simulation" produces, perhaps enticing, but ill founded rhetoric, such as

> Seeing is believing, as the proverb would have it – but now literally so: seeing is the only believing. The truth still seduces, but invisibility is no longer its favourite stratagem. We have abandoned the metaphysical perception of the universe that made us long for the reality behind appearances. When the contract on this essentialism expired, all we had left was the image, the sign. From that moment onwards, the truth lay in the image itself and must hence also be sought there. Truth no longer seduces through image, but as image. And that is quite a different matter. Once the arbitrary relation between image and meaning, between signifier and signified, was discovered, the way was open for total manipulation and fictionalisation of the image. In these times, the signifier has supplanted the signified, the representation has usurped the original, the semblance has displaced the essence, and verisimilitude has ousted truth. Deprived of its former metaphysical certainties, the eye, that actively searching, documenting organ, has taken on an immeasurable importance.[50]

Seeing alone is not believing, but sensation. In whatever we encounter and do there is truth behind it, though we cannot understand it fully. What we see, hear, touch, etc. has a reality. There is no sign without signifying something, the signified – be it physical or spiritual. A sign, by definition, signifies beyond itself, to a truth, though at times a mistaken one, for sure an incomplete one. Representation represents something. Understanding, and with it meaning, implies thinking in addition to sensation. As long as we can be conscious, essentialism does not expire. Essence is in everything existing, as trivial as it may be. Every sign, every communication, has an essence, right or wrong, understood or not, or it would not exist. This is so with architecture as with anything else. The invisible in architecture is what is the signified, thought and understood beyond the signifier, the observable. The invisible, the unobservable, is the relational.

Michael Hays writes with reference, I assume, to the Baudrillard/Eisenman connection that

> We must signify the fact that we can no longer signify; we must represent through architecture the impossibility of architectural representation, and an autonomous architecture does just that.[51]

No architecture can jump over its own shadow, whatever autonomy is ascribed to it. For our foreseeable future, I believe optimistically that people, as long as they live and build objects to occupy, will represent in their mind and communication what they believe these objects are. Nature leaves no choice but to derive meaning from objects and to embed meaning in objects.

The just given quotes describe not, as it may seem, an inevitable liberation of the semantic from real life – even less one which we can make by choice. With all the many changes life may have in store for us and future generations, we cannot disassociate ourselves from our physical being and that of the world. Our mentality is intimately tied to it. Nor is the mental and with it the semantic, in its form we are addressing here, autonomous in relation to other things we encounter in reality, including our community with other individuals. The semantic exists only in its syntactic expression and can be explained only in reference to reality which is occurrence, materiality, use, behavior, etc. and is part of causality in space and time.

Our thoughts about life and culture for architectural expression are not fundamentally different from our thoughts for expression in language. But architectural design, very differently, must embed its concerns into built environments with three-dimensional materiality. In addressing the relationships of human needs or desires pragmatics and syntactics in architecture are constrained by this physicality. On the other hand, language is referential and it does so indirectly by words and phrases. Though highly flexible, its basic means are very repetitive (words from a rather small set of letters). Architecture, even in its design stage, is to a large extent direct and self-explanatory. In spite of generic similarities among many of its components and systems, it is quite non-repetitive, and this not only from project to project but also within projects. While architecture's long history makes it rich with traditions its pragmatics must respond to always different purposes and contexts which determine its syntactics. Strong cultural changes and technological adjustments exert major influences, amplified by enormous advances in information and communication. This makes for rich variety and causes architecture as medium to have a highly developmental nature.

3.4 Interpretation and metaphor

In our quest for meaning we are aware that understanding has limitations. Our access to truth is incomplete and subjective. Therefore, we may well view understanding as interpretation, having some uncertainty. Much of our thinking, as discussed, goes beyond what we immediately observe. Often we use metaphors to explain and to communicate such thoughts. We use them to clarify impressions and expressions. Metaphors obviously have been mainly used with language as medium. There is a long history of writing about their use in prose and poetry. But they are also quite common in other media, such as music, dance, painting, sculpture and architecture. While there are similarities of their nature and performance compared with language, there are important differences. First about language.

Metaphors have been used for a long time, even before Aristotle. It was he, however, who probably explained their nature first, by saying that

Metaphor consists in giving the thing a name that belongs to something else; ...[52]

And,

... a good metaphor implies an intuitive perception of similarity in dissimilars.[53]

For one of the recent writers on metaphors, Ivor Richards, there are two associated thoughts which bring forth another thought.

... when we use a metaphor we have two thoughts of different things active together and supported by a single word, or phrase, whose meaning is a resultant of their interaction.[54]

Two meanings result in another meaning. Metaphors are more than saying something stylistically different. They produce something new.

Metaphors have dual concept status (3.26). The first concept, C_b, is the basic reference to something. The second concept, C_d, is a declarative reference which challenges us to rethink C_b. It points out and explains in a specifically metaphorical way. For example, 'The roof is the hat of the house'. Here, C_b is 'the roof' and C_d is 'the hat'.

$$C_b \text{ is } C_d$$

basic concept   declarative concept

3.26 The conventional form of metaphor

The 'of the house' indicates to what the metaphor relates and is typically omitted when understood from the overall context in which the metaphor is used. One can infer from 'roof' that it belongs to a building.

The metaphor 'The roof is a hat' can be understood in two ways. Literally it makes nonsense. Metaphorically it makes sense. The metaphor is C_b and C_d together because the declarative expression C_d must have a basis C_b which additionally is targeted by C_d for interpretation producing another, ensuing concept C_e, the result of metaphorical understanding. C_b and C_d by themselves are not metaphorical, but together they are.

A distinction is generally made between metaphors and similes with metaphors referring to 'C_b *is* C_d' and similes referring to 'C_b *is like* or *is as* C_d'. Both associate the concepts of C_b and C_d to produce a concept C_e. I side with those who believe that the effects of the *is* and *is like* are essentially the same with a difference in form of expression only. The *is*-form is implicitly and the *is like*-form or *is as*-form is explicitly metaphoric. There is, in my view, essentially no difference between 'The roof *is* a hat' and 'The roof *is like* a hat'; except the latter reinforces the similarity aspect on which both forms are based. The *is*-form is in fact indicating equality, but this is a false equality which is understood as such in our mind by the otherness of the declarative concept (hat) in comparison with the basic concept (roof). While the metaphorical relationship includes aspects of similarity it does obviously not indicate equality. The *is*-form is, not in fact but in effect, nothing but a short form of the *is like*-form. When we express all *is*-forms as *is like*-forms all logical unintelligibility disappears, because we exchange equality by similarity. We move from stating a nonsensical identity to stating an interpreted comparison with regard to resemblance which, however, can only be a partial one.

Although metaphors are literally not true, what they say is understandable. The metaphor 'This man is a wolf' is not true but is perfectly understandable. It may, depending on circumstances, point to the awful eating habits of this person or the ways he hunts down people for business purposes, whereby 'hunting' hints at another metaphorical meaning. Adrian Snodgrass and Richard Coyne write:

> Metaphor is an assertion of simultaneous identity and difference, unintelligible by the modes of strict logic or in terms of representation, but not to the modes of understanding that operate in our everyday encounter with language and with the things of the lived-world.[55]

I do not agree with the first part of this sentence but very much with the second. 'This man is a wolf' is not an assertion of identity. It is an attribution of a partial similarity associated because of a particular context. Is it "unintelligible by the modes of strict logic and in terms of representation"? It is, but we are usually aware that, when we speak metaphorically, strict logic does not apply. Consider 'The floor plan is a fish'. It is obviously not true as given. A floor plan cannot be a fish but some of it, its shape, can be similar to that of a fish.

There may be poetic or perhaps other reasons to make the distinction between the *is*-form and the *is like*-form. In differentiating, one can say that all similes are metaphors but not all metaphors are similes. 'Life is tough' is a metaphor and cannot be expressed as a simile without additional phrasing. The category of metaphor is primary and, therefore, I will use in our discussion also the term metaphor when they have linguistically simile or simile-like character. At least for architectural applications of metaphor I find the differentiation rather irrelevant.

This line of thought brings up a crucial issue about the way we think versus the way we express what we think. The latter is governed by grammatical rules which are necessary to guide our expressions to avoid misconstruction. Strictly taken, 'the roof is a hat' is nonsense, whereas 'the roof is like a hat' is not. But metaphorically speaking both mean the same as we make the connection in either way. This shows that to a large extent we do not reason in our mind grammatically but associatively in direct fashion. When we think, in our example, we simply bring together 'roof' and 'hat', and then infer the relationship. We engage object thinking.

There are thinkers who believe that all interpretations are metaphorical. Snodgrass and Coyne write that

> At all levels of understanding, from simple perception through to the interpretation of texts, we are constantly interpreting things by way of projection of meaning, that has the structure of metaphor.

And a little further,

> The operation of the hermeneutical circle of metaphoricity is not instrumental. It is not something we can choose to use or not, in the manner of a tool. It is, rather, embedded in thought and action; and no thought or action would be possible without it.[56]

They refer to a passage by Heidegger who writes about interpretation that

> We can call the development of understanding interpretation. In it the understanding appropriates what has been understood in an understanding way. In the interpretation the understanding does not become something else, but itself.

And, about the result of understanding *as* interpretation:

> What has been carefully taken apart with regard to its in-order-to [be in a certain way], which is the *explicitly* understood, has the structure of *something as something*.[57]

"Something as something" is something with certain properties. What something is interpreted to be and is believed to be, is given in form of a statement. According to Heidegger, statements have three-fold significance: to point out the existence of something, to predicate by explanation of properties and to communicate the two for participation in understanding.[58] When Heidegger talks of "something as something", he refers to something interpreted, that is, a thing understood as representation. The aim of a metaphor, however, is the interpretation of a representation as something *else*, in the sense of an alternative representation – explained in a certain context by means of something different – though having some similarities. To see a roof as being sloped is not metaphorical, but to see it as a hat is so. We always perceive and understand something by seeing-as, seeing it as what we believe it is, holding it for a fact. Heidegger does not mention the term metaphor in this context and rightly so. He elaborates only on the representation theory of things.

If all representations would be metaphorical, there would be no need to talk about a difference between metaphorical and anything else representational. Every explanation would be metaphorical including, for example, 'this table surface is a rectangle' which is a representational statement of understanding, an expression of explicit meaning, not a metaphor. It does not evoke anything beyond making us aware of a geometrical feature of the table. In a metaphor we compare something with something different which prompts us to refer to an understanding which one of the two alone does not have and only the two together in a unique way provide. Every metaphor uses interpretation as we ask for understanding. But not every interpretation is a metaphor.

As metaphors are a way of explanation, it is not surprising that they play an important role in communication. Earl Mac Cormac writes that
> The meaning of metaphors results from the semantical aspects of communication, the context in cultural settings, and the creation of new concepts.[59]

In fact, we are so accustomed to think, to speak, to write and discuss our thoughts in metaphors that we are often not aware that we use them.

As with all understanding, metaphorical meaning is in our head and nowhere else. When we think about architecture metaphorically, we choose architectural properties so that others may develop the meaning of our meant metaphors in their own minds. This indicates, strictly speaking, that there are no physical metaphors, including architectural ones; only physical aspects to which we may relate by thinking metaphorically. In other words, the manifestation of metaphors is through linguistic or other physical expressions, including architectural forms.

Metaphors are highly context-dependent as their explanatory power arises from interpretation and happens always with regard to objects in particular circumstances. Wayne Booth writes that
> What any metaphor *says* or *means* or *does* will always be to some degree alterable by altering its context.[60]

The present circumstances are not only influencing the objects to which we relate metaphors but also the process of their perception and understanding. 'He is as tough as a nail' may refer to positive or negative qualities. In sports it may refer to an athlete reaching an especially high performance level. In politics it may refer to a leader guiding his country through difficult times. In family affairs it may refer to a parent being unjustly harsh with his children. In an architectural environment: 'This house is my castle' may refer to ownership, to a place of safety, to a style of living, etc. 'The roof is a hat' would most likely be used in reference to requirements of protection against environmental influences, such as rain or snow, perhaps also with regard to hat-like appearance. The basic and the declarative components are context-dependent.[61] So is their relationship and with it the resultant metaphor. It is not so, as Donald Davidson writes, that
> The central mistake ... is the idea that a metaphor has, in addition to its literal sense or meaning, another sense or meaning.[62]

He is right with regard to the fact that the basic expression and the declarative expression are the only components given and the only ones which evoke in us meaning directly. But they would not make sense to be used by us for a metaphor, were it not for the *additional meaning* which results from their relationship in a particular environment. It is true that metaphors do not describe or display anything beyond what they literally express but they make us think about something we would not have thought about without their specific dual concept expressiveness. This is why I emphasized at the beginning of this section the dual component nature of metaphors. Obviously it is false that the roof is a 'hat' and my house is a 'castle' taken as what these expressions literally mean to us. But it is exactly this falseness, or whatever the effect of the juxtaposition in fact is, which gives them their power toward meaning "in addition". Davidson says that
> The common error is to fasten on the contents of the thoughts a metaphor provokes and to read these contents into the metaphor itself. No doubt metaphors often make us notice aspects of things we did not notice before; no doubt they bring surprising analogies and similarities to our attention; ... The issue does not lie here but in the question of how the metaphor is related to what it makes us see.[63]

Not so. Both issues belong to the same aspect. "... the metaphor is related to what it makes us see [understand]" through its declarative power of its additional, comparative meaning.

Referring metaphorically to protection, 'the roof is a hat' contains two connections, one explicit and one implicit. The first is "C_b is C_d" (making the connection between 'roof' and 'hat'), the second is "$C_d \longrightarrow C_e$" (making the connection between 'hat' and 'protection'). Both are necessary for the result, the metaphorical thought based on nonliteral, additional interpretation. Therefore, the complete form of metaphor, I suggest, includes its result.

$$C_b \quad \text{is} \quad C_d \longrightarrow C_e$$

basic concept   ensuing concept
declarative concept

object $\longrightarrow$ conceptualization $\longrightarrow$ concept

3.27   The comprehensive form of metaphor

Josef Stern is right, if I understand him correctly, and agrees with what Heidegger says about interpretation that

> ... strictly speaking, there are no literal or metaphoric *expressions* per se (except as terms of art); there are only literal and metaphoric *interpretations* of expressions.[64]

When we refer to 'metaphoric expressions', we refer to a string of expressions with interest in the ensuing interpretations (C_e). The process is not metaphorically successful unless this ensuing concept emerges. From this point of view the concepts C_e could be called metaphorically derived concepts. And, it should go without saying that, for a metaphor to work, the originator and the perceiver must understand its basic and declarative concepts, and their context. The early stage of the process prompts in us meanings which we understand traditionally. But through these constituents and from their generally unusual juxtaposition in a particular context additional meanings arise as result.

In architectural design, metaphors are used to enhance the understanding of physical expression. Over the centuries this has probably been nowhere more apparent than in buildings for government and religion. Aspects of power and faith find metaphoric expression. The buildings are usually not only large and richly decorated, their centering in the communities is thought to support their importance, in addition to being reached conveniently. Returning to the bird's-eye view of Basel shows this clearly (2.10). The cathedral is located prominently on the hill above the Rhine river. Another church and city hall are in the valley of a tributary, wrapping around the hill. The main commercial activities still take place in the valley today. In front of all three landmarks sizable plazas enhance their importance, providing subtle symbolic expressions we rarely think about anymore as such (3.28). Of modern buildings with this enhancement, the Lever House, by Gordon Bunshaft of SOM, and the Seagram Building, by Mies van der Rohe and Philip Johnson, come to mind (3.29, 4.4 and 4.5). Across from each other at Park Avenue, the Lever House features a court like space on street level, with its office tower sideways above, and the Seagram Building has a large open plaza with the office tower centered away from the street. At a place of very valuable land and with its elegant bronze metal and similarly colored glass facade, the Seagram Building brings architecture and luxuriousness together to especially convey the idea of corporate wealth and power.

This line of thought coincides with what I mentioned about symbolism in regard to the Piazza in Siena and Times Square in New York (3.1 and 3.2). Often symbolic aspects are closely linked with metaphors. A piece of land or the realization of a building symbolize financial or political implications, the latter being inferred also from context. When we say 'This building is powerful' we operationalize the symbolic aspect as the declarative part of a metaphor in reference to the basic concept of 'this building', resulting in the ensuing concept of finances or politics. 'Hat' stands symbolically for 'protection'. In 'The roof is a hat' it is operationalized to lead to the inference of 'protection' from 'roof'. *The symbol function is to refer to something. The metaphor function is to explain something.*

3.28 Marktplatz, Basel   3.29 Seagram Plaza and Lever House, New York

In figuring out what metaphors mean – stronger than through symbols alone – intermediate thoughts occur. To get to the ensuing concept, connotations of the basic and the declarative concept develop and are associated, often subconsciously. It helps to make them explicit as they are design factors, that is, functional aspects which we usually describe as relational properties.

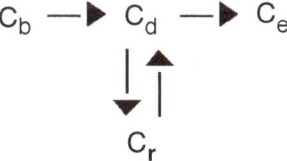

whereby C_r indicates relational concepts (connotations)

3.30 The concepts in the overall metaphoric process

An example, now related to the design process, should make this clear. A council chamber for a city hall is demanded as a room of certain size. The designer views the situation in terms of the metaphor "this room is for assembly" with 'room' being the basic and 'assembly' the declarative concept. He comes up with 'room with circular seating' as ensuing concept. The crucial, relational concept of 'assembly' is 'communication'. The underlying premise, that is, the basic concept of 'room of certain size' does not disappear completely. It is obviously still understood as condition (room, size, etc.) for the new concept, the room with circular seating. The basic concept, spelled out in language by words, is in the reality of architecture what we consider the building type or component type. It is transformed into the ensuing concept – from being generic into being specific – here by means of metaphor. 3.31 shows the sequence of events which I just explained in relation to 3.30.

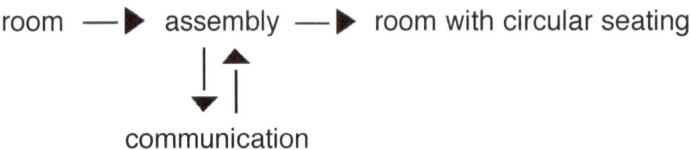

3.31 The metaphoric process in the design of a city council chamber

The juxtaposition of the basic and declarative concepts is the metaphorically motivating force. The council chamber in the Town Hall of Rødovre, Denmark, by Arne Jacobson, shows such a room arrangement (3.32 and 3.33). The separation of the council chamber from the office wing emphasizes its visual importance for the public. This separation is itself metaphoric, as the giving of importance through that separation is a declarative concept, derived from a physical, observable property – the giving of importance metaphorically indicated through connotation of the role the citizenry plays for the government in a democracy. A similar scheme, even reinforced by the from outside visible circular building shape, is at Toronto City Hall, by Viljo Revell, where the council chamber is centered between the two curved, high-rise administration towers embracing the chamber (3.34 and 3.35).

In the expressive mode of design, we start with the rather neutral concept 'room', associate it with the rich concept of 'assembly' (communication facilitated by people facing each other) and replace the concept 'room' for the concept 'room with circular seating'. The use of metaphor generally does not lead to a change of the basic concept. But It leads to a change of thinking toward

Town Hall, Rødovre, Denmark

3.32 Administrative building with chamber wing (© permission)

3.33 Council chamber, interior

a similar concept prompted by the declarative concept. The reasoning for the basic concept is reevaluated because of a metaphoric idea. The metaphor in design is a powerful motivator toward potential change, not only a vehicle of explanation. The use of metaphors amounts in the design process to the search for design alternatives for a given understanding. An original meaning, which perhaps was formulated only as a programmatic demand by a client, is used as the basis for another meaning by the designer and given explanatory metaphoric expression in physical realization.

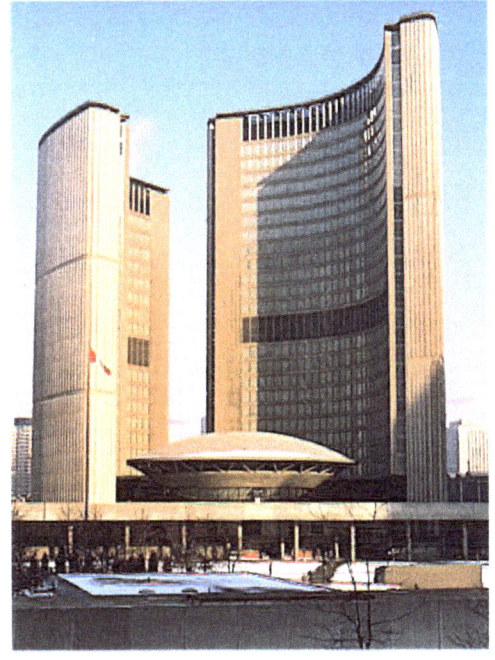

City Hall, Toronto, Canada

3.34 Administration towers and chamber

3.35 Council chamber interior (© permission)

When we or others are in the impressive mode of observation, we start by perceiving the circular room and infer that it is for the purpose of assembly because of its metaphorical reference to communication (3.36).

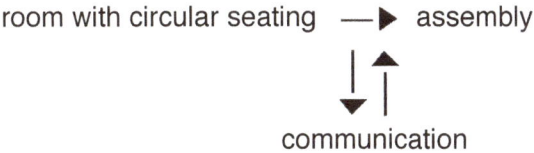

3.36 The metaphoric process in the observation of a city council chamber

By comparing the two processes of metaphoric expression and impression we find a kind of reversal but not a quite symmetrical one. In the expressive mode we start, as designers, with something which we have to define by means of properties. We do that by 'communication' in the assembly room example and derive from it that a circular shape is best suited. In the impressive mode we and other observers start with something which has existing, defined properties, here it is a room with circular seating, then think about its meaning which is the relational concept of communication.

Observers often ask for explanations and that is especially the time when the metaphoric thinking of the designer comes into the open. Two examples, Hans Scharoun's Philharmonic Hall in Berlin and Reima Pietilä's Kaleva Church in Tampere, here shown as drawings by Anthony Antoniades (3.37 and 3.38). In the music hall 'the seating is arranged like vineyards' (see section). The metaphoric result is the understanding of 'valley surrounded by hills', most vineyards in Germany covering hills. To be grasped in this way the observer must, as mentioned, understand the connection directly or, at least indirectly, by being prompted verbally, to take the observation in this way. If not, the metaphor may still be involved, as the designer simply may have used it to generate ideas. Either way metaphoric likeness is at work. The Kaleva Church sanctuary floor plan is 'like a fish', calling to mind a sign of Christianity, the symbol of early membership in faith.[65] Here, both metaphoric likeness and symbolic reference are at work.

3.37 Philharmonic Hall (section), Berlin
(© permission)

3.38 Kaleva Church (floor plan), Tampere, Finland
(© permission)

These lengthy explanations may seem to make the use of metaphors in architectural design a rather complicated affair. It seems so only, however, because to describe the process, which necessarily has to be done in language, is tedious. But our processing of thoughts is much more efficient than our modes to describe them. In our assembly room example our thoughts simply connect 'room' and 'assembly' to come up with 'circular room'.

Many times the premises for an original and basic understanding, is reevaluated because of metaphoric ideas. Therefore, the metaphor in design may become a motivator of expressive change rather than a vehicle of explanation only; and in so doing it becomes perhaps an instrument for aesthetic choice and enjoyment. At other times metaphors creep into focus subconsciously. As the declarative concepts of metaphors nearly always point to aspects beyond architecture, typically to easily grasped daily and natural, but also often to sociological, religious and even political matters, they tell something about the metaphysical outlook of those who suggest them.

Two examples whose metaphoric meaning point in similar directions, airplane and seagull, but with very different functional bases of transportation facility and sun screen respectively, are Eero Saarinen's TWA Building at Kennedy Air Port in New York and Santiago Calatrava's brise soleil at the Milwaukee Art Museum (3.39 and 3.40). Being highly innovative and in very prominent locations, these buildings achieved landmark status. They are also strongly iconic, therefore easily remembered. The same is the case with Scharoun's philharmonic hall and Pietilä's church.

3.39 TWA Building, Kennedy Airport, New York

3.40 Milwaukee Art Museum, Milwaukee

If a metaphor is to be more than a vehicle for his or her own idea generation, the designer must select component concepts which are understood similarly by others who encounter them. Towards the strong end of a metaphoric scale of buildings, one most likely will find the Sydney Opera House, by Jørn Utzon. Most people assume that its striking appearance looks like a set of 'shells or sails'. A less direct visual connection belongs to the design of the Netherlands National Building in Prague, by Frank Gehry. Its corner towers have become known as 'Fred and Ginger', the famous dancing couple. Such nicknaming of unusual buildings combines reflection of declarative metaphoricity and popular fabulation.[66]

Obviously, the further we move away with the declarative concept of the metaphor from the basic concept the greater is the risk of not being understood or wrongly so. But, at times, the greater is the potential of being innovative. This remark should not imply, however, that innovation is valuable as such. Peter Eisenman's sculptural shapes at the Wexner Center of Art, Ohio State University, are quite unusual and highly self-referential until one knows that they refer to a fortress like building, called "Armory", which once stood on the site. Therefore, these forms should best be called iconic and only mildly metaphoric; depending wether they are understood as resembling shapes of the former building or not (3.41 and 3.42). The Armory itself was highly metaphoric as it looked like a castle of centuries ago.

Ohio State University, Columbus OH

3.41 and 3.42   Armory (demolished) and the Wexner Center for the Arts
(© permissions)

Overall, metaphors have great significance for architecture as they are a necessary part of how we connect as designers with the world and our clients, and they with us psychologically, behaviorally, technically, economically, etc. Let's think about a few more, whereby the words in marks are the metaphorically indicative ones. These trees 'shield' against the wind. This building is a 'beehive'. This hotel 'feels' like a 'prison' but its location made it a 'gold mine'. The floor plan really 'works' in spite of being 'straight forward'. We designed a 'gang' kitchen and did it so well that it is this woman's 'paradise'. Some air duct distribution systems are 'spider like'. Many office buildings have 'curtain' walls. This company displays construction sequences as 'decision trees'. As usual, there is considerable difference in the metaphorical intensity of these examples. Most are literally not true. Some refer to physical, others to mental declarative concepts. Examining the metaphor 'This building is a beehive', we compare the building by reference to what a beehive is: compact, divided in many little and perhaps uniform spaces, full of busy activities all the time, etc. The basic, rather neutral, concept of building is associated with the concept of combining these properties.

When we think metaphorically of a building, we typically attribute to its properties the power of an intention. For example, when we say that a building 'calls for attention', the building does nothing except that 'we are drawn to it' (metaphorically). When we speak of a particular place as 'heavenly space', we may understand it in reference to a church as 'God's dwelling' or in reference to any secular space simply as 'spiritually uplifting', and so on. Depending on one's view, 'dwelling' may be more than a metaphor when the sanctuary in one's faith is where God is present, always or at least in worship. For the believer, God's dwelling is not only a metaphor but mystery become reality. But with these examples and those of the previous paragraph we are mostly back in the mode of descriptive, that is language and architecture related metaphors, not purely architectural ones.

There are metaphors about which we don't think anymore metaphorically. The faked shutters at street-side windows of typical suburban homes nearly everywhere in North America were once metaphors referring to a shading function which the really hinged shutters long ago had and in Europe still have – not being metaphors but true signs of their function as adjustable shading devices. Today, the 'shutters' are simply decorative color patches. They are now 'dead' metaphors in the sense that nobody thinks about them anymore as metaphors. In contrast, two free standing columns at the entry of housing estates are living metaphors as they still indicate gateway functions, although the gates themselves were never installed. Very much alive as metaphors are the decorative pilasters and windows at the Piccadilly Square side of the National Museum's Sainsbury Wing in London, by Venturi Scott Brown and Associates, referring to what some of the columns, pilasters and windows of neighboring buildings in fact are: load bearing and letting light pass respectively (3.43).

3.43 Sainsbury Wing, National Gallery, London (© permission)

From this discussion we can derive that most if not all architectural metaphors are iconic in nature with their basic and declarative concepts collapsed into referentially strong signs. Iconic signs, as discussed, refer through some similarity to an ancestral entity. This prompts recall of the earlier mentioned aspect that metaphors are based on partial likeness, whether this is true or not. The closer the likenesses of the basic and declarative concepts are, the more they approach to be 'the real thing' and the stronger is their explanatory power; but also, of course, the less they are anymore metaphors.

Metaphors have at times become influential architectural paradigms, such as 'The house is a machine for living in', 'Less is more', 'Less is a bore' and 'Architecture is text'. They contribute to the development of styles – style taken as the form in which individuals or cultures pattern their expressions and so communicate by means of similarities often over long periods of time. Architectural metaphors play a crucial role in remembering history in the life of people and whole nations. Few cities show this better than Berlin with sites like the Kaiser-Wilhelm-Memorial Church, modified by Egon Eiermann, the Jewish Museum, by Daniel Libeskind, and the Reichstag Building, restored by Foster+Partners, buildings which are only a few miles apart (3.44 to 3.46). To leave the prominently located church as bombed out is a metaphorical approach to very directly remind us of the horrors brought upon this city during World War II. The zigzag plan and twisted spaces of the museum remind us of emigration and holocaust. In the parliament building, light falls into the plenary chamber from a glass dome through which visitors on the roof can look into the chamber below, implying metaphorically and here even literally that people are 'above' their governmental representatives.

3.44 Kaiser Wilhelm Memorial Church, Berlin

3.45 Jewish Museum, Berlin

3.46 Reichstag Building, Berlin

We are in the design process oriented toward goals. We reach them through what properties give us, what they are, and what we think in terms of function, in terms of relations between these properties. We talk here about goals related to accomplishments of something needed or desired, being of physical nature and aesthetic attainment. Yes, the aesthetic is a function. Toward these ends, thinking is often enhanced by metaphors which inspire and enrich design creativity, design thinking.

We return to what Aristotle said about metaphors implying "an intuitive perception of similarity in dissimilars". Objects of similarity in practice feature iconic quality (roof and hat in 'the roof is a hat' have in a certain way resemblance). But here similarity ends. Protection, the ensuing concept with additional meaning, is not similar to roof or hat. The similarity nature does usually not apply, or only mildly so, to what the targeted and to-be-explained, ensuing object is supposed to be. The reference is symbolic, not or only mildly iconic.

To summarize. In looking at metaphors we moved from considering linguistic to nonlinguistic expressions, from the descriptive to the observable. Although they have a similar conceptual effect, there is a crucial difference in how the descriptive and the observable are developed in practice. In linguistic constructs, including the language *about* architecture, metaphoric expressions are given in two parts (basic and declarative concepts) from which we infer a third (ensuing concept). In the reality of objects, including the reality *of* architecture, metaphoric expressions are physical expressions, simple or complex, from which we perceive first the basic and then the associated, the declarative concepts. From them *together* we derive the ensuing concept to complete the metaphoric process. That a roof as hat connotes protection, a hill-like seating connotes vineyards, a fish shaped floor plan connotes Christian faith is contained in the single expression of the dual nature of the observable, metaphorically evoking physical form. In impression we start with the perceivable form of the given object and in expression we end up with a designed form in the projected object.

This section ends with a note of caution. The definition of the term icon has been stretched in recent years beyond the aspect of resemblance toward that of landmark. As mentioned, metaphors function through some features of resemblance. But, in addition, they are intended to point through them to non-iconic aspects for reasons of explanation. The Kaleva Church floor plan is iconic (resembling fish shape) and metaphoric by letting arise the concept of nourishing Christian faith (pointing to the miraculous feeding of thousands with fish at Lake Galilee). That a building is unusual or outstanding, that it is a landmark, does not make it an icon. I cannot follow the selection of Ricardo Bofill's Les Espaces d'Abraxas in Marne-La-Vallée as "an icon of low-cost housing" and Frank Lloyd Wright's Guggenheim Museum as "the first example of the iconic icon" in Charles Jencks' *The Iconic Building* (3.47 and 3.48).[67] What is iconically "low-cost" in the former and an "iconic icon" in the latter? To what do they refer by means of resemblance? There is a communication problem of trivia when "anything can be an icon", as Jencks claims.[68] The inflation of the word shows in his reference to the AT&T Building in New York, by Philip Johnson, as an icon of change (away from flat-topped office building) and to the Institut du Monde Arabe in Paris, by Jean Nouvel, which, with its "High-Tech virtuosity" on the facade, produced "an instant icon of an Arab world meeting the Western challenge".[69] Through this misuse, the content of the word has become so shallow that it can be used in nearly every situation because on such levels of discourse we can construct relationships from anything to anything. If novelty becomes the defining quality of the iconic, we have terminological confusion.[70] In the context of his "iconic", Jencks generalizes in reference to one work by Renzo Piano that "Function stymies form".[71] He does that without balancing his remarks by mentioning any of Piano's many other, excellent

3.47 Les Espaces d'Abraxas, Noisy-le Grand, France (© permission)   3.48 Guggenheim Museum, New York

buildings in which function enhances form, such as in the museums in Houston, Chicago and Riehen near Basel (3.49). Piano's museum in Riehen is contextually well placed in the landscape with walls of local sandstone. Its filigree, daylight filtering roof unobtrusively functions in support of viewing exhibitions. The confusion of icon with landmark or milestone is the result of the incessant search for word coinage with 'pregnant' meaning during the recent decades. It is 'iconic-speak' by hijacking and distorting the meaning of icon. There is meaning in sense and in nonsense. Let's be aware of what we prefer.

3.49 Beyeler Museum, Riehen near Basel

3.5 Unity of content and form

There is an important concept which, I believe, ties together the many aspects we have considered so far and is very helpful for our further discussion. It is the way how we consider content and form do belong to each other. Content brings about form. It is what we conceptualize from and associate with form. It brings about its properties. With form, we should always remember,

I mean realization which we can observe and through which we communicate. As the physical sign of content it is accessible by sensation. The interdependence of content and form is total. But we are not able to determine content completely; nor form. First, because the whole of content is the thing in itself to which we have not complete access and second, although we encounter its form completely, we can only observe it aspectually.

During the early 1900s, when Peirce formulated his mature ideas in semiotics out of his pragmatic positions, the Swiss Ferdinand de Saussure (1857-1913) developed his concept of signs related to linguistics (3.50).[72]

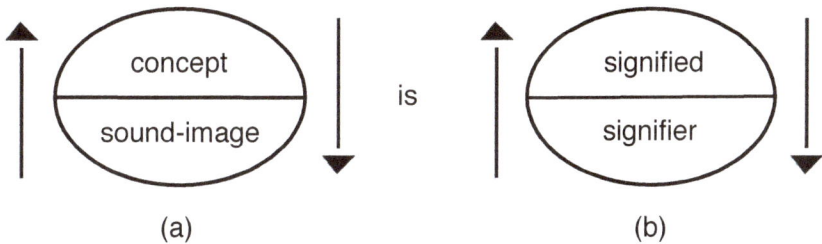

3.50 Juxtaposition of De Saussure's two linguistic sign representations

Though sparsely documented, the work became highly influential in structuralist approaches to psychology, anthropology, literature and philosophy with the premise that regularities in mental experiences and physical expressions correlate and that a systematic understanding of parts to wholes is fundamental. De Saussure proposed to view language as a system of signs (words or phrases) with each linguistic sign consisting of a semantic component and a phonetic component: the signified and the signifier. The signified is the concept and the signifier is the sound-image of the sign.[73]

The arrows indicate that the upper and lower parts are "intimately united" in spite of the dividing line. The signified, the concept, is to what the sign belongs, what it identifies. The signifier, the "sound-image", is what makes the signified known to us through our senses. It is its form, its physical realization.[74] The sentences of our language consist of nouns, verbs, adjectives, adverbs and function words, such as prepositions and conjunctions. The first four of these components carry major sign characteristics, that is, they refer to concepts and their attributes, the mental equivalents of objects and their properties. They provide our main understanding and meaning. Function words (the, of, to, for, but, either … or, etc.) have only little meaning but help to provide the connective structure of syntax.

The crucial difference between language and architecture exists not only in the nature of the signified and the signifier, but also in the way they relate.[75] In language the relation is symbolic and originally arbitrary. The spoken and written words were given at some time as names and were from then on adhered to by convention. "Eau" in French and "water" in English are not similar. But they point to the same thing. They are purely referential. Not so with signs in architecture (and other physical reality) where we mean without words. What we observe (what is signified) or what we design (what we signify) is with regard to its realization to some extent self-referential. When we look at a window we perceive its features directly. We do not think about it prompted by a symbolic sign, its name in language. Because of resemblance relations, the representation in our mind is iconic. And, strictly taken, it is also indexical because of causative relationships. When we design a window and place it into a facade, we show features as we assume they should be. We design them because of causative aspects. In addition, what we look at or design is referential beyond itself. Seeing a window brings to us thoughts about daylight transmission and the possibility of ventilation. Although this is somewhat true also after we only imagine a window, caused by language reference, the basic sign natures are very different – physically direct versus mentally indirect.

Therefore, we must carefully look at the status of concept in De Saussure's linguistic sign in comparison to what we mean with concepts in architecture. Let's pursue another time this line of thought because it has strong implications for what follows. Words are referential entities. They are names of concepts of things we are familiar with, if we know the language. The form of words is either sound or script and is intimately tied to the concept.[76] But these concepts are rather general. They are what we imagine when hearing or reading the linguistic expression. When we speak the words "water" or "building", the words are linguistic signs and the ways I write them or speak them does not influence what we perceive them to be in reality, that is, beyond their reference. Words are symbols not icons. Somewhat of an exception is phonetic imitation of natural phenomena in poetry reading or emphases in singing of verbal expressions. Here the meaning of words slightly influences their realized and communicated form. In architecture, other than with words, we conceptualize all material objects from direct sensation of accessible, exactly given reality. What we sense is fundamentally influenced by the object, not its name. We compare what we intuit with what we find similarly as concepts in our mind. We do not simply refer to these concepts but form a new one from what we perceive.

The signified/signifier distinction as shown in 3.50 is helpful in contrasting what we call concept of a physical object and what De Saussure calls "concept" of a linguistic statement. In looking at a physical object we intuit a preliminary sign (an appearance) which relates to what and how the object is, its content and form, completely unified. We can come to content only in and through its form. At this point of perception we do not have a concept yet of what we observe but it has its potential in what we perceive. The content *of* the form is the content *in* the form. The appearance is the mental 'raw material' of conceptualization. Differently in language where the form of the sound image or written image (word, sentence) is not the concept. It only refers to a concept, is its name, although it is intimately related to it, as De Saussure says. With regard to the physical object: as it is the total unity of content and form, the signified is at the same instance the signifier and this is so also in its representation in our mind which we call concept: 3.51. The arrow indicates the translation from the physical object – as unity of content and form – to the mental concept.

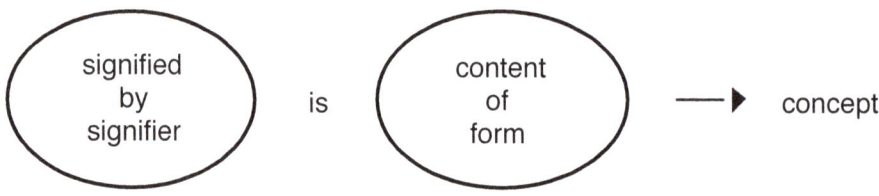

3.51 From physical, nonlinguistic signs (objects) to mental signs (concepts)

My use of *form* is, as mentioned before, not in the sense Plato uses the term, essentially pointing to universality, like the idea of the 'horseness' of a horse or the 'houseness' of a house. Though the idea of something is implied in what I call form, it is for me foremost how something is and how it is accessible to us in its existence. A form is necessarily so because of its essence. In short, form is instrumental for us to understand content. It is the content's physical manifestation.[77] In reference to this inseparable association of content and form it makes sense to talk in short of *content-form unity.*

What we can sense is matter which, when first represented in our mind, yields a form of appearance which we pragmatically call also, as it is grounded in and is attributed by us to the physical object, the form of the object. Therefore, I hold that form is what we grasp as the appearance from the physical existence of something which allows us to be informed about its content. Kant writes:

> I call that in the appearance which corresponds to sensation its matter, but that which allows the manifold of appearance to be intuited as ordered in certain relations I call the form of appearance.[78]

Every original appearance comes to us via sensation in a form and this form is given a priori, that is, before conceptualization. It has its ground in the totality of what is given in the object. What we call 'physical form' (the form of the object) cannot exist by itself. It exists only because observable properties and their relational properties are its content.[79] With this point of view I am in agreement with Georg Hegel when he writes about art that

> … through a determinate content also a corresponding form is determined.[80]

I believe, however, this is so not only for art but for every observable thing.

Where does form come from? As said, from the object's properties. For the result of impression we can explain it with Kant's "the manifold of appearance … ordered in certain relations". It is the ideas we get of what we believe something we perceive is and does. We observe, analyze and judge.

For the result of expression, that is in the development of design, we conceive ideas of what we believe something might be and might do. We also observe, analyze and judge in a preparatory way but then select and synthesize properties, and judge toward a "manifold of appearance … ordered in certain relations". In other words, these relations require physical properties to become existential in objects. The properties are purposive and contextual, and arise out of the realization of the manifold; aspects about which we will have to say much more.

The term *form* is very broadly used, probably as much as *meaning*. In fact, its profusion happened much earlier because the terminology of meaning entered the realm of philosophical discourse in a major way only about a century ago. The two terms are being used so many times without even the most rudimentary definitions that they often give way to ambiguity of understanding. This prompts Adrian Forty to conclude his revealing chapter on "Form" that

> In a sense, 'form' is a concept that has outlived its usefulness. People talk of form all the time, but they rarely talk about it; as a term it has become frozen, no longer in active development, and with little curiosity as to what purpose it might serve. Ask this question, and it may lose some of its seeming naturalness and neutrality.[81]

But he is not completely sure, or only "in a sense" so. When form is used with a clear definition it makes sense and I hope that I provide one for our purposes. *Form is the observable manifestation of content.*

There is correspondence of signified and signifier in every sign. I believe it is so intense with all signs of physical things because content and form are wholly interdependent. The physical object is content embedded in its material form. Look at any physical object around you and you can only understand it because its form reveals some of its content, some of its existential essence. Kant makes this very clear when he says, and I agree, that

> ... in the case of the perception of something outside of us the concept of body makes necessary the representation of extension, and with it that of impenetrability, of shape, etc.[82]

I like to emphasize "representation of extension" as it is crucial for us to grasp that perception of what something is comes to us via sensation of how it is. We can only indirectly understand what something is. How something is, its extension, is the form of its realization, its observable properties. Whatever 'content-form' is in reality determines what we conceptualize it to be in our mind. We think and describe in mental representation as if we were knowing and understanding the corporeal properties of objects representing content. There is obviously more to physical signs, as mentioned earlier. Beyond being physical they point to other objects and states of affairs. A window is not only self-referential to its own physicality but refers to the potential opening in the wall through which fresh air may pass. We experience comprehensive object thinking.

So, concept is mental representation in content-form unity. Form is much more than shape. It is the eventual realization of all parts of an object's content into a perceivable manifold of properties, be they programmatic, functional, organizational, geometric, material, behavioral, etc. From this follows that we must be careful in using terminology like 'formal concept' or 'conceptual form'. There is no concept which is only formal. Concept implies content. And, that I say "perceivable" has its reason in the fact that not all parts of what things consist of can be observed. Many things, objects and affairs, are physically quite opaque in the sense that we can observe only part of them. And, as I believe in things in themselves, there is more to content than what we understand through their perceivable form.

The separation of content and form is nothing but a conceptual construct to let us discuss and grasp the nature of the parts in their unity. This unity always exists whether we talk about objects in the material or the mental realm. But a transition occurs between the two realms. Physical objects are in the material realm and this is so for any occurrence we have access to by way of sensation, be it a dance, a movie or a building. Their conceptualizations, however, are in the mental realm. It looks as if corporeal form is in the foreground and content, its co-constituent, is behind it. In the transition the form recedes and content takes the foreground. We cannot but sense form and we cannot but conceptualize content. This is how I believe an object's content-form unity is carried over into its mental concept, from material nature into mental nature. And the process is in reverse order when we project form from content. Here we contemplate about attributes of concepts from memory and from present reality, then (re)arrange them in designing them, allocating properties of physical objects in association with the program and its context.

Content-form unity implies that content influences form. But form may also influence content. What does that mean? Anyone who designs and plays with alternatives finds that this is so. When we select form first, because of whatever reason or for no reason (if this is possible at all), it influences content. This is procedurally similar as when we are in the mode of impression. Then, form is a given and we observe it and conceptualize its content. For example, the air volume, the geometric shape, the surface absorption, etc. of a concert hall, that is, its acoustically relevant physical properties (form) influence the qualitative perception of sound and, because of it, to some extent the musical expression (content). Here, form determines content. On the other hand, when we start with musical expression and sound (content), translate it into desired volume, shape, absorption, etc. and allocate properties (form) accordingly, content determines form. Therefore, in prospective design, content determines form. Or, we desire to have sun shading (content) on the fenestration of a south facade. We add an overhang (form). When we want to know which overhang we need, we must start with the desired quality of shading to determine the geometry of the overhang (content determines form). When we play with facade articulation first, we better watch out because it determines shading (form determines content).

In suggesting Sullivan's famous dictum "form ever follows function" to be viewed as 'form follows content' I believe that form and content are united with mutual functional relationship indicated. In other words, the importance of function is only being the relationship that leads to form from content, not being form itself, or in playful occasion being the relationship that leads to content from form. It is not property but expectation and power of what property may or does accomplish (as explained earlier). This discussion brings us to visualize the procedural aspects surrounding content-form unity in its reciprocating nature:

$$\text{content} \leftrightarrows \text{form}$$

The arrow to the left points toward perception of content from form (observation). The arrow to the right points to conception of form from content (design). Content and form influence each other mutually as cause and effect.

The activity which underlies and motivates the content and form dialog is obviously the whole process of thinking from sensation to understanding or understanding to realization. We may view it as a dual component undertaking of *content thinking* and *form thinking* in enduring unity and correspondence – in general and so in architecture. A special kind of form thinking aside from the realm of this object related unity is *language thinking* about which I have to say a great deal later.

Content-form unity is not a value judgment, a decision on whether we like or dislike something. It is a *fact*. Form arises out of content or, in reverse, content manifests itself – in the only way possible – through its form. We should view content in design as the intentional equivalent of form which comprises everything we associate with it; be it ability, accommodation, friendliness, organization, might, preference, proportion, spirituality, or material aspects, such as brick, shading, etc. and, in the broadest sense: all the related properties an object as thing in itself may have. With content-form unity in architecture cannot only be meant that the physical exterior must reflect the interior, although this is usually to some extent the case. Content is ideation translated into realization of form. There should be no doubt that there is content in what occurs out in the world and that there is content in what occurs in our mind.

Concepts are the abstracts of objects which we develop according to our capacities to perceive and understand. We sense the objects with their content and, unless we misconstrue them, at least some of this worldly content is being reflected in our mental representation. We would not have any concepts of the world, including ourselves, if such content would not carry over; not as identity but equivalency. I agree with John McDowell:

> In a particular experience in which one is not misled, what one takes in is that things are thus and so. That things are thus and so is the content of the experience, and it can also be the content of judgment: it becomes the content of a judgment if the subject decides to take the experience at face value. So it is conceptual content. But that things are thus and so is also, if one is not misled, an aspect of the layout of the world: it is how things are. Thus the idea of conceptually structured operations of receptivity puts us in a position to speak of experience as openness to the layout of reality. Experience enables the layout of reality itself to exert a rational influence on what a subject thinks.[83]

It is in content-form unity, similar to the value-image unity of a coin, where a particular idea and its manifestation correspond to each other, both being present by necessity. Unless the world has 'reasonableness', that is content which can be reasoned, our reasoning cannot come to an understanding and absorb worldly content. Evan Fales writes:

> To grasp the 'whatness' or nature of the phenomena is necessary if empirical thought is to have any determinate content at all. Whether we call such preconceptual grasping or noticing thought or not is perhaps a matter of little consequence. It is, in any event, an act

> in which the given is most primitively given to us; and it is an act upon whose possibility conceptual and prepositional thought depends.[84]

The "primitively given" is the originating appearance of the given. Looking back to what is given by understanding and judgment, Fales says that

> … what cannot in the relevant way be conceived to be false must have a special kind of transparency or clarity – and that judgment, if it is to produce knowledge, must not stray beyond what is transparent and clear. So, even if human conceptual powers are limited, that does not preclude there being items that can be grasped by our judging faculty in a fashion adequate for knowledge of them.[85]

There is a crucial aspect of content-form unity which we may think of as internal structural relationships. It will help to return to the analogy with language. Words are, as De Saussure noted about language, part of a wider environment of text. From a general point of view, objects never occur in isolation. We have architectural objects in a wider natural and manmade environment of other physical objects. The equivalent in architecture for word is building component or building unit. De Saussure asserts that

> Language is a system of interdependent terms in which the value of each term results solely from the simultaneous presence of the others, …[86]

I agree, except I don't believe that the "solely" applies. De Saussure's view echoes what Gottlob Frege writes at about the same time that

> … never ask for the meaning of a word in isolation, but only in the context of a proposition …[87]

Words are meaningful through their being in context, in addition to their meaning as such.

Values in language certainly depend largely on the simultaneous presence of other words. I take here "value" as pointing to resultant meaning. Additions of words, if not confused, increase understanding. In the process they influence each other in the sense that the whole is different from what the individual words as such contribute. Their value also depends on who uses the language and who perceives it. Judgment plays a role. But the value does not "solely" result "from simultaneous presence of the others". Words evoke individual understanding even by themselves. Their value is in the "property of standing for an idea".[88] And, values are contextually influenced. "Water" means something as a term by itself referring at least to a generic concept. But we understand it in a much more pointed way when we use it, for example, in the context of "the water in this swimming pool", especially on a hot afternoon.

This is similarly so for building components. Windows are as individual parts a less meaningful concept than as components of walls or roofs. Wider contextual aspects play a role, perhaps through the experience of windows first from outside and then from inside of a building, perhaps at daytime or at night. From this discussion we can conclude that the value of meaning is what the components are but it is inevitably and highly increased by the environment in which the components happen to be.

What is signified physically in a word as verbal sign does not change in combination with others. What changes is what we understand, not what is signified.[89] This is not so with building components in context. They reflect to some extent their environment physically and as physical signs. They even differ in relation to our own positioning to them in space and time. In other words, our conceptualization generated by words in context is purely mental (with perhaps minor impacts of inflection or gesturing) whereas our conceptualizations from building components are physically first and then mentally influenced by wider context. Not even included here is another more or less influential factor given by the physical connectivity of building components, which is in case of word components completely abstract because there are voids between words.

I used the work by Peirce and De Saussure as a background for our discussion of semantics and syntactics in architecture mainly because of the elucidation we can draw from it on the sign nature of architecture but also because of the often ambiguously used assertion that architecture is text without text being defined. There are, as we have seen, some similarities but reference to them without explanations is misleading. *Architecture is not text*. We do not 'speak' nor 'read' architecture in reference only. We encounter and experience it in three dimensional physicality and self-reference, whereby the observable properties are in addition relational beyond themselves, at times iconically (an open door is a hole in the wall), at times symbolically (an open door may indicate welcome). With the short remarks in these paragraphs we only touched preliminarily at the helpful but often overrated analogy of language and architecture. We will return to it in the second to last chapter.

To conclude. We live in a world of signs which are around us and in us. Expressions are the content of physical signs which we derive from mental ones. Impressions are the content of mental signs which we derive from physical ones. All signs are representations because this is the only way we can make sense of them. Semiotics helps us to order our understanding. Signs can be iconic, symbolic or indexical. Often these characteristics overlap. In the wider realm of understanding is another triad which helps us to bring about and understand the structure of what we think and communicate: semantics, pragmatics and syntactics. All of this is beneficial to our grasping what the world is, how we live in it and how we change it. Eventually all our understanding relates to parts of the world, large or small, existing in content-form unity.

An example for the dual aspect of content-form unity in design is in the perception and conception of architectural space. When we conceive space we search for content: first for relational properties (what is to happen within the space?) and then for observable properties (how to construct the space?). This is the way we understand and develop form. But when we perceive space we intuit form: first observable properties and then the relational properties which we infer from the observable. This is the way we discover and understand content. During the iterative process of design we alternate between conception and perception by attending to relational and observable properties.

Content-form unity is a central concept. The properties of content are what we encounter. They constitute the form. But form as realization is not only physical matter. It is what the terms Gestalt (noun) and 'gestalten' (verb) comprehensively imply in form of observable properties, given by the total of all present and historical influences. Content-form unity implies that "the medium is the message".[90] Form in its unity with content serves us as medium. It is what we sense, see, hear, touch, etc. This is the way we have access to anything in reality. Our attention to a medium makes it an object being observed by us. With the assumption that "the medium is the message" is true, all of the message is contained in the medium. This naturally does not guarantee that we fully understand the message.

The 'physical' properties of objects after we have perceived them are really mental representations and the physical content-form of what we perceive is really mental content-form. But there is the physical world from where we intuit it. This is why we also speak of forms 'out there', beyond our minds. In impression we start with this physical form to find mental content. In expression we start with mental content to find physical form. In the former we start with content-form unity. In the latter we end with it.

We say: architecture communicates. But this is not quite so. All that it does, it does simply through its existence because of those who brought and bring it about. We communicate through architecture as signs – signs as media. Architecture as signs has been with us since the first primitive hut was built and could be found because of its appearance. It was not Renaissance, not Mannerism, not 'Billboardism'. It was a sign in form of a hut, had some complexity and evoked perhaps some ambiguity. It certainly broke convention compared to what was before to live in, the caves. It was modern for its time. Architecture has meaning for us because of what it is and because of what it points to beyond itself. A door at the ground level of a building facade 'tells' us that it has the purposive and physical properties in its content-form to let us and others pass from outside to inside or inside to outside. The expression of the door cannot communicate all the content which makes its form what it is. There is gravity and friction, tolerance between moveable and fixed parts, hinges to hold it in place, a handle to open and close it, a special color perhaps to differentiate it, etc. This simple example may stand for the enormously complex content embedded in the sign nature of components and even more of whole buildings.

Only a relatively small number of functional design factors can find reflection in form. But some of the more important ones inevitably will. And another factor, whether we are aware of it or not, has always a strong impact. It is the aesthetic which is the decisive component in the judgment on our own designs and in the judgment of others experiencing them. The aesthetic has major functional impact and is, therefore, the subject of the next chapter.

4 The Aesthetics of Experience

What we call 'aesthetic experience' arises from how objects and states of affairs affect us through emotion and reason. We have the tendency to view emotion and its resultant feelings as rather mysterious compared with what we call reason. This attitude comes to us largely from centuries of western intellectual heritage. We have been taught that the ways we view the world and act in it is determined mainly by reason and that emotion is a rather separate capacity; reason supposedly being responsible for understanding. I think this is a mistake which has its roots in not adequately defining the roles of emotion and reason, especially through the lack of grasping their interdependence.[1]

Often, especially in day-to-day reference, emotion and feeling are considered synonymous and used interchangeably. Sometimes feeling is considered the ground of emotion, other times the result of it. Emotions are reactions which may have their origins outside or inside us. They challenge our understandings from conceptualization and usually alter them. This fundamental position at least, I think, is in accordance with recent and presently emerging research. The role which emotion and feeling play in the formation of understanding and with it meaning, especially through what is implied by the term aesthetic, is of particular interest in our endeavor.

4.1 Emotions and feelings

What follows entails a shift from the inadequate positions which I believe most philosophers have taken on the importance of emotion in the process toward understanding; Baruch Spinoza, William James and John Dewey being historically the most important exceptions. Our explanation of understanding based so heavily on rationality will have to change, including my own neglect of emotion and feeling in the previous chapters. This does not invalidate what we found there but enlarges on it. Over the past century, especially since the 1960s, considerable physiological and psychological, theoretical and experimental research evolved showing that emotion affects results of understanding fundamentally. Preliminarily and rather generally I suggest to view emotion as part of the process to understanding and feeling as result of emotion.

For the scientific background in this section I am heavily indebted to work by Antonio Damasio and Joseph LeDoux, among others.[2] More recently an area of research addresses similar issues from a perspective called "emotional intelligence".[3] I find this a confusing notion as intelligence is not emotional. Intelligence is the capacity to understand complexity and to solve problems. The results, however, it produces are influenced by emotion and feeling.

All stimuli which we encounter from the outside world become known to us through sensation, that is, through our body. This is the *only* way the world affects us. Stimuli, such as sound, light, heat, odor, weight, pull and resistance, cause responses of our body and eventually influence the brain through thinking and understanding. Around 1670 Baruch Spinoza had already the fundamental insight that

> The human mind is capable of perceiving a great many things, and this capacity will vary in proportion to the variety of states which its body can assume.

And very pointedly,

> The human mind does not perceive any external body as actually existing except through the ideas of the affections of its own body.[4]

In other words, our mind can gain *original* thoughts only through external effects on us, that is by the means our body has available. In turn, these effects evoke reactions in us. This *us* operates during perception in world-to-mind direction which often prompts us to react in mind-to-world direction.

All our experience of the world starts with sensation and leads eventually to understanding. Emotion is part of the whole process and arises in two ways of interest: (1) We are bodily affected via sensation from outside. Nerve signals to the brain influence its present neurological state. This emotion results into more or less bodily reaction, such as gesture, smile, outcry, fighting or fleeing, and into feelings, such as satisfaction, joy, enthusiasm, fondness, embarrassment, dissatisfaction, disgust, hate or fear. From this externalization emotion has its name. In common language it is understood very much in what the etymology of the term tells us. From Latin: *ex* for out and *movere* for move.[5] This naturally refers to the outward reaction associated with emotion as mentioned above (gesture, smile, etc.). But we associate more with emotion than this etymology indicates. It is comprehensively engaged in our body-mind activities. (2) We are affected by and react to memories of concepts and feelings from earlier experiences, consciously or subconsciously. What is referred to under (1) is rarely, if ever, experienced alone because memories are always present and interact with new information. In this category also belongs emotion and feeling aroused by thinking alone, that is, without external stimulation, such as in dreaming and daydreaming.[6]

I use the term 'feeling' to mean the result of emotion, not as a synonym for sensation. We progress from sensation to emotion to feeling whereby conceptualization provides the underlying process along the way. In the broadest sense: emotion is 'e-motion', electro-neural transmission in our body, because of external sensation or internal sensitivity. It stimulates 'reactions', such as conceptualization including judgment, feeling, volition and productivity.[7]

All of this obviously amounts to a view which presupposes for understanding more than the input mode of conceptualization and raises a crucial and loaded question. Where, when and how does emotion arise? Many of the answers given have been rather controversial. I will eventually suggest an answer which, I believe, will serve our purposes. As preparation I give a short commentary on recent thinking about emotion and feeling; expositions which I find most convincing.

Experiences of sensation are the ground for all earlier and new understandings, and the body-mind relationship is broader based than we have traditionally assumed. Antonio Damasio, a neurologist, summarizes this complex situation in very accessible terms:

> What do we gain by considering the mind in the perspective of the body, as opposed to considering the mind in the perspective of just the brain? The answer is that we gain a rationale for the mind that we would not discover if we considered the mind only in the perspective of the brain. The mind exists for the body, is engaged in telling the story of the body's multifarious events, and uses that story to optimize the life of the organism. ... The brain's body-furnished, body-minded mind is a servant of the whole body.[8]

Our brain in order to understand relates to what happens to the whole body in many different ways. We think with emotion playing one part and reason another. How they relate is of essence, especially with regard to their sequence. Earlier in his account, Damasio clearly differentiates emotion from feeling and gives emotion, not feeling, first place in the course of perception when he writes that

> We have emotions first and feelings after because evolution came up with emotions first and feelings later. Emotions are built from simple reactions that easily promote the survival of an organism and thus could easily prevail in evolution.[9]

This means that we are not starting with a blank slate as far as any of our present thinking and understanding is concerned. Emotion, at least to some extent, influences how we reason. Feelings follow. Why? We have memories short term, long term and extremely long term; the latter inborn from evolution. Their content is based on emotional and rational experiences. As our present experiences start with sensation, emotion is the first (re)action of our thought process. The still today counterintuitive view that emotions are first and feelings second goes back to William James who wrote in 1884 that

> Common sense says, we lose our fortune, are sorry and weep; we meet a bear, are frightened and run; we are insulted by a rival, are angry and strike. The hypothesis here to be defended says that this order of sequence is incorrect, that the one mental state is not immediately induced by the other, that the bodily manifestations must first be interposed between, and that the more rational statement is that we feel sorry because we cry, angry because we strike, afraid because we tremble and not that we cry, strike, or tremble, because we are sorry, angry or fearful as the case may be.[10,11]

Our body-mind entity must somehow 'know' why to react in this way. Remembered experiences of emotion and reason, especially those acquired from evolution, enable *instinct*, the capacity of inborn responsiveness and impulse.

In common language we say that we feel sensations. But in reality this is not the case. What Damasio calls "simple reactions" are the results of sensation which the nerves signal to the brain where "emotions are build". Often we are not aware of emotions. Only if emotions are strong enough, we become aware of the feelings they evoke. When emotions trigger strong bodily responses we register related feelings because the latter require a relatively long time to fully develop.[12] Other responses develop over prolonged periods of emotions because of reasoning in feedback mode.

As long as we are alive we have at least low level emotions and feelings of which we are usually not conscious. Damasio calls the latter "background feelings", the "feeling of life itself".[13] Our breathing, for example, is motivated largely by subconscious emotion and the emotional level is usually too weak for conscious feeling. I use 'subconscious' in two ways: (1) For an unintentional contribution to my mental state which comes by way of memory from an earlier had experience and influences my behavior but may or may not now come forth as part of my conscious mental state. 'Instinctive' is in this regard a synonymous term. Breathing is a subconscious, evolutionarily acquired instinctive behavior. (2) For a mental state which is not conscious but also not unconscious. Being unconscious is the state of complete unawareness. Brain activity is random without intentionality. Nothing can be remembered. When we dream we are not unconscious. We are subconscious, as our capacity of intentionality makes us aware of remembered experiences in our memory. We may or may not remember, however, dream experiences after awakening into consciousness. Sleepwalkers are in a subconscious not unconscious state. A sleepwalker has subconscious awareness or could not walk up a stair nor find a door. When people use 'unconscious' they often mean 'subconscious'.[14]

James was right but there is one important aspect to consider. Unless there is some kind of appraisal, here an instinctive one, action as he suggests would have no basis. Subconscious appraisal has its roots in evolutionary memory or other remembered experiences, perhaps including instruction. Magda Arnold writes:

> How, then, can emotion be distinguished from sense perception? Both perception and emotion have an object; but in emotion the object is known in a particular way. To perceive or apprehend something means that I know what it is like as a thing, … that I appraise it as desirable or undesirable, valuable or harmful for me, so that I am drawn toward it or repelled by it.

And,

> The appraisal that arouses an emotion is not abstract; it is not a result of reflection. It is immediate and indeliberate. If we see somebody stab at our eye with his finger, we avoid the thread instantly, even though we may know that he does not intend to hurt or even touch us.[15]

Appraisal may or may not be "a result of reflection". Appraisal is judgment. Here, in our present discussion: without reflection it is subconscious and instinctive, based on earlier had concepts and feelings.

Emotion obviously also occurs in chains of events and not only from external sensation. Richard and Bernice Lazarus (1994) emphasize the crucial role of reason for emotion as twofold:

> First, since emotions are aroused by an evaluative judgment – what we refer to as an appraisal – about the significance of what is happening for our well-being, we will never be able to understand how emotions come about without examining the reasoning behind them.
>
> Second, to view emotion as irrational [as sometimes happens] is a way of denigrating emotions as not to be trusted when, in reality, emotion is an important resource that helps us survive and flourish. It is probably not going too far to say that reason may hold our emotions in check, but often in constructive ways the emotions hold reason in check. There is somewhat of a balance between them. If not, there lies madness.[16]

It is emotion and reason together which make our lives livable, interesting and, when in balance, enjoyable. The quote first addresses emotion following judgment but then acknowledges that it also influences reason.

Here is not the space even to attempt a further discussion of the vast amount of literature on research of the mind and the many positions taken, contrasting emotion and reason. But one problem creeps up very clearly: the confusion in the definition of what emotion is as such. On the basis of a fair amount of the literature I define for our purposes by answering my earlier posed question of "Where, when and how does emotion arise?" Emotion, because of outer sensation, produces reason. And reason produces inner sensation and emotion. These latter emotions arise from our iterative relationship with remembered historical and present experiences. There is, I believe, no reason without emotion and we may well consider thinking to be fundamentally and physically emotion of our brain. As thinking uses judgment on the way to conceptualization, that is evaluation, appraisal has psychological and physiological effects. *Emotion is not a parallel process to thinking but part of it, happening together with reason.*

From this position it is clear that thinking is more than conceptualization, though conceptualization is its central task. Emotion is part of all the processing the brain does from perception to understanding to memory. We exist as we are because we think emotionally. We think evaluatively and, therefore, qualitatively. Many emotions are considered physiological and, when light, they may bring on an increase in heart beat, or when strong, may trigger us to run away or become frozen in place. The physiological and psychological components are part of the interdependence within our body-mind existence, the difference of their being not so much in basic nature but in our categorical and terminological constructs. There are no meaningful feelings which come about because of emotions alone. They come about through the combined *emotion-and-reason* process. Mark Johnson writes that

> An identifiable, meaningful experience is neither *merely* emotional, nor *merely* practical, nor *merely* intellectual. Rather, it is all of these at once and together. We call it *emotional*, after the fact, when we wish to stress the felt quality of its emotional valence. We call it *practical* when we wish to profile its outcome and the interest it might serve. We call it *intellectual* when we are interested primarily in the distinctions, associations, and connections of thoughts that arise through the course of the experience.[17]

I believe this does not require, however, as he writes, at least not completely, to

> ... reject the classical representational theory of the mind, replacing it with an account of embodied meaning that emerges as structures of organism-environment interactions or transactions.[18]

We are highly interrelated and interactive subjects vis-à-vis the other worldly objects with the emotion-reason process leading to representations, that is understanding and meaning in our subjective minds. The paradigm of representations does not imply a dualistic mind/body ontology but the individuality and to some extent authority of the human being in the world surrounding it. All it indicates is that our thinking bodies understand the world beyond us differently from what it is in reality.

From this discussion the chain of events to understanding, now including emotion, can be shown as in 4.1. It traces the iterative paths of thinking as process from sensation to understanding and meaning as result, supported by memory, with instinctive and reflective appraisals. What we usually call mental states are the activities through which the brain works – here more explicitly understood as *emotion-and-reason* process. The results are concepts and feelings which together are called understanding.

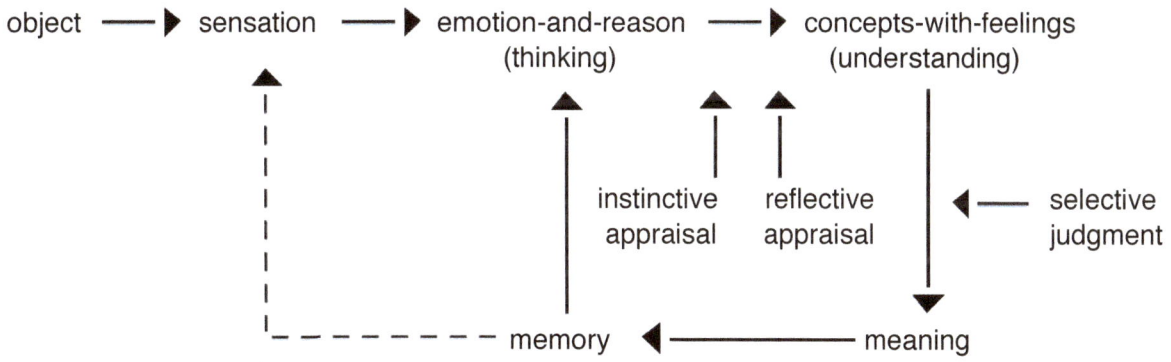

4.1 The Emotion-and-Reason Process

The emotion-and-reason process could also be called emotion-and-thought process as thought traditionally points toward reason. Or, as I associate emotion and reason overall with thinking, I believe that simply the designation of 'thought-process' could be used. I want to emphasize, however, the two involved components of emotion and reason. The mental is physical as form. It is the physical, neural arrangement of thought in our brain. Gestures, spoken and written words, drawings, playing with a ball, etc., that is, anything we do with our body, are indications of the mental in the realm beyond our brain or – more explicitly – our thinking body.

Thinking is more than reasoning. It is reasoning because of emotion. *There is no reason without emotion and no emotion without reason in the process of thinking.*[19]

An important aspect in the discussions of philosophical but also of other inquiries about mental states is often overlooked and may lead to confusion: the distinction between process and result while using for both identical names. For example, the term feeling is used for a process or for its result. Let's make this clear in considering the emotion-and-reason process as shown in 4.1. We may view concepts and feelings as results of the process but should realize that they are evolving parts of the ongoing process of understanding. Everything is in flux and additional input from sensations, memories, reappraisals and selective judgments keep change going. In short, I take emotion-and-reason as the technical term of our brain's process which leads to concepts and feelings as intermediate and final results; with 'final' indicating the end of a particular consideration. Mental states like fear and joy are results of our emotion-and-reason processes. Mood belongs in this category as well. Moods can be long lasting, they are more like what Damasio calls "background feelings" and we may view them as presuppositions of new perceptions coming into play.

The emotion-and-reason process is a dual facetted convergence and is continuously interactive with what we call memory. Some of the great discoveries in neurological research over the past decades have determined what is called the plasticity of the brain.[20] The brain's maturation process is not only developmental during our growing up but reconstructive during all of our lifetime. We learn by adjustment of neurons in the brain and through changes in their connections. Such changes take also place in relation to our sensorimotor activities, a crucial aspect when we consider that all our goal-oriented mental activities find expression in activities with physical output, be it work or leisure related. Our brain structure is in constant flux and it is well understood that frequent exposure to variation enhances brain plasticity and, with it, creativity.[21]

On this basis we can easily grasp that there is no "emotional mode" as such in which the brain 'engages'. When the brain is active, it is reasoning *based* on emotion. Every change in mental state is change of emotion and reason, and has mind-body consequences which may or may not be strong enough to be felt. In other words, much of this process is subconscious, especially so in the early stages of an episode and in quickly developing short episodes. They often are not remembered. Strong episodes, however, may leave strong feelings and remembrances, and can play a major role in living through and assessing later experiences.

The concept of the thinking body has its ground in the presence of evolutionary and individual memories, which provide instinctive appraisals by help of emotion (understanding without conscious conceptualization). But in the chain of events of our mental process, emotion is also very much the result of conceptualization based on reflective appraisals which then lead to feelings as bodily reaction. From this point of view, we could speak of emotion-and-reason process or reason-and-emotion process. I stay with the former terminology because I believe that thoughts are always initiated by an emotional causation, although overall thought, including reason, is what typically determines feeling. We think emotionally. Strong or weak feeling may result as bodily reaction which may or may not be observable.[22]

So, our emotion-and-reason process is controlled by instinctive and reflective appraisals, that is, by appraisals based on former and reinforced by present experiences. Appraisals are judgments, subconscious or conscious. The process is iterative with loops of various durations, often with episodes as short as milliseconds. Therefore, we are mostly not aware of its progression, only of its results along the way. This is where consciousness comes in as a concept. Consciousness is for me the awareness of 'what my brain comes up with' from sensation, new thought and memory or even from memory alone. John Searle writes that

> Consciousness is by its very essence qualitative, subjective, and unified. ... It is absolutely essential to understand that consciousness is not divisible in the way that physical objects are; rather, consciousness always comes in discrete units of unified conscious fields.[23]

Kant, as we may remember, talks in this regard of the "synthetic unity of apperception". The manifold of intuitions from sensation comes together as complex representation.[24] We have only a general impression, which we often simply call a 'feeling' of things, unless we pause and think about in detail where it comes from. But this overall impression is an important aspect and is usually more or less carried into the dynamics of thought about details.

On the other hand the very search for understanding, especially also in architectural design, requires to observe and develop qualities by combining properties on various subsystem levels. Whatever we encounter in reality or through inspiration, we do so as a whole. But there is always complexity in what we focus on and even more in what surrounds it. This indicates that there is much hidden and if we want explanations, we may have to look beyond what the general quality of something is. Again the relational nature of our enterprise plays a crucial role. Relational properties may simply determine that the spaces in the particular circumstances of a project are best arranged in one sequence and not in another. Or that the energy simulation of a project suggests this choice of facade details versus others. Or that my investigations about a certain site makes it more advantageous for the purposes of one contemplated building rather than an other. All kinds of cultural, social, physical or otherwise contextual factors enter consideration. Clients, consultants and contractors of projects may ask questions about influences by factors the designer has not thought about, leading perhaps to in depth investigations, unexpected results and altered design responses. We may characterize such aspects as *the hidden, but to be explored meaning of design*.

Often we have no power to keep such meaning from intruding. Usually we should embrace it to enrich our design work. The case can be made that most emotional aspects of the emotion-reason process are due to relational properties. They are what adds 'life dimensions' to our experiences. To illustrate the point: Most photographs of architecture are taken by avoiding to show people or other 'functional' objects. That is a mistake. Not that relational aspects are missing entirely. Every perception is in one way or another subject to such influences. But showing for what architecture is built, that is, the relationships to life's activities which are expressively revealing, enriches its understanding and meaning. People in an architectural setting manifest in large part its relational properties.

The emotion-and-reason process is not a one-way development (see again 4.1). There is an important path from intuitive understanding to conscious appraisal, leading often to further action. Joseph LeDoux writes:

> While many animals get through life mostly on emotional automatic pilot, those animals that can readily switch from automatic pilot to willful control have a tremendous advantage. This advantage depends on the wedding of emotional and cognitive [rational] functions. ... cognition also contributes to emotion by giving us the ability to make decisions about what kind of action should occur next, given the situation in which we find ourselves now. One of the reasons that cognition is so useful a part of the mental arsenal is that it allows this shift from *reaction* to *action*.[25]

This shift from "reaction to action" moves us from impression to expression in design, that is, from analysis to synthesis. Along the way a memory based creative input takes place via conscious appraisal, usually supported by additional input. Not shown in figure 4.1 is another important aspect, namely motivation. It should be obvious that motivation occurs in any ongoing mental process or it would cease. Motivation is maintained and heightened when appraisal modes exert strong impact during observation and design.

This perhaps somewhat tedious discussion, and it will continue for a bit, has its justification in the answer, which I give preliminarily, to the question "What is the utility and value of the emotional component in the process toward understanding?". *The utility and value of emotion is to furnish the feeling of pleasure or displeasure about the conceptualization with which it is associated and is the basis for decision making as far as we have freedom to do so.*

To reinforce practical understanding, let's look at a few examples. Sitting outside on a cool day exposed to sunshine stimulates an emotion which produces feeling of well-being. Viewing a sunset stimulates an emotion to produce feelings of pleasure. These feelings are mainly due to external stimulation but reason and memory may contribute consciously or subconsciously. We may remember the company of a dear friend in sharing a sunset years ago. The process may or may not produce a reaction of public display. Looking at a building will produce sensation, and eventually concepts and feelings. Experiencing an outstanding building, such as Le Corbusier's Chapel at Ronchamp, will evoke strong motivation to understand through concepts and feelings from every glance we may have at it, outside or inside. It is as Damasio writes:

> We can feel our emotions, and we know we feel them. The fabric of our minds and our behavior is woven around continuous cycles of emotions followed by feelings that become known and beget new emotions, a running polyphony that underscores and punctuates specific thoughts in our minds and actions in our behavior.[26]

Emotion-reason aspects feed on each other. Intermediate concepts and feelings result along the way. Sensation and memory provide the motivation to start the development and to keep it going. Memory keeps track of intermediate steps so we may get a relatively comprehensive impression. The process is the feedback loop from understanding (4.1). Its results are new concepts and new feelings – together new understanding.

While sensation may happen anywhere in the body, the processing center is in the brain with its billions of neurons in a small space. Here the iteration toward understanding can occur incredibly fast between various functional areas for vision, hearing, language comprehension, speech control, etc., always in connection with memory which provides continuity and stability. Meaningful life in human terms is not possible without memory. Emotions occur along the process of conceptualization. They drive it. There is more to emotions than the manifestation of feelings: emotions help us decide what we select and hold as valid and preferred conceptualizations.

The signals from sensation transmitted by the nervous system bring about emotional excitation in the brain. This is, as said, the only way we perceive the world beyond us. Jeffrey Gray writes that

> The whole of the perceived world, extending to its most substantial features (solidity, three-dimensional extension, etc.), is a construct of the brain. There must be a good fit between this constructed model and the real external world 'out there', otherwise our efforts to interact with the real world would not be the spectacular success that they are. There must also be a good fit between the constructs of the world made by each and every other human brain, otherwise we would not agree as often as we do in our modes of interacting with the world. Nonetheless, the only direct contact we have with the real external world is by way of our [largely] unconscious sensorimotor action systems.[27]

The decision making part for these systems is the brain. My insert in the last sentence refers to the fact that we are often not, but at other times we are, conscious of our sensorimotor actions. When we draw we often do not think about our hand which does it, but other times we consciously control it because of various kinds of reasons. Sometimes we undertake consciously strong mental and physical efforts to continue processes which started subconsciously, for example, when lifestyle preferences, of which we are not aware, instinctively arise and become major, to be contemplated design factors. Contextual prompting often triggers such reactions.

The emotion-and-reason process results in concepts and feelings at the same time but variably strong, depending on the perceived object. Although there are distinct functional areas in the brain with which we perform particular tasks, they are more or less interrelated and interactive. Importantly, considerable parallel processing takes place which allows us to accomplish various tasks at the same time, such as seeing while walking and judging while drawing – all with feeling while conceptualizing. It helps also here to consider more closely the process with regard to impression and expression. 4.1 shows that impression motivates us to acquire concepts and associated feelings. They together require judgment for making decisions on values, be they personal, social, religious, economic, political, etc. Will for expression motivates us to bring forth concepts, influenced by what we remember and what is present, again judged with feelings associated. *The foundation for expression is in impression* because without the understanding of what is remembered and of what is present – what is purposive and contextual – we would have nothing to work with. *To gain new understanding we must build on available understanding.*

When we judge an understanding, we submit it to the emotion-reason process for appraisal and perhaps change. In the impressive mode of observation we end the process when we believe that we have reached the truth conditions as far as we are able to attain them. We may or may not like the conditions. But this is the case with existing conditions. We take and judge them as they are. In the expressive mode of design we end the process when we believe that we have reached desirable truth conditions which we select from the potentially very many available. We usually try to make judgments derived from the rational aspects of the process. But we know that this is not completely possible. We can never escape our being emotional animals.

There are considerable differences of emotional impact, obviously because of the nature of the objects we consider. Meeting a bear is a different occurrence than sitting exposed to the sun. Reading a dramatic story is a different occurrence than looking at a fine building. Fear, satisfaction, empathy and joy follow our judgments of these various affairs. They come out of our instinctive and reflective appraisal activities. The differences of understanding arise from the differences in our experiences, that is, from the differences in the objects and the different ways we perceive them physiologically and psychologically. This is similarly so at the end of the design process when we judge what we have produced with pleasure or displeasure. Appraisals make us *feel* what we think conceptually.

As mentioned, many appraisals are procedurally so weak that we don't feel reactions. But all observations go through judgment because we require it for conceptualization. Looking at the sign '2' and then at a 'yellow' surface most of us will say that the '2' requires more conceptualization than the 'yellow'; typically the '2' being more referential and 'yellow' being more self-referential. Low levels of judgment are involved as both are easily conceptualized for categorical understanding. For both the emotional aspect is low unless one has a strong preference for or aversion against yellow, or one associates with '2' the meaning of a strong experience.

Now consider the Venezuela Pavilion, by Carlos Villanueva, at the Montreal World Exhibition of 1967 (4.2). Here we have a more complex situation and it brings on more intense appraisals.

The pavilion has strong color contrasts and geometries which support each other visually. The entry is another conceptually strong element. Most people feel with subconscious emotional reaction that color supports shape; even more so if the colors, as here, may be consciously perceived to stand for sun, sea and vitality associated with the country which the exhibition in the pavilion represents. The effervescent illumination in the tunnel between the two main parts of the United Airlines Terminal at Chicago's O'Hare airport (4.3), by Helmut Jahn, supports the idea of being moved from one place to another in anticipation or remembrance of flying. The curvilinear shapes with variations in light intensity and color, together with the narrowness but length of the space, reinforce 'coming and going'. Here we have a metaphor strongly supported by emotion, a frequent occurrence. The emotion created is part of the declarative concept of metaphor.

4.2 Venezuela Pavilion, World Exhibition 1967, Montreal

4.3 Tunnel, United Air Lines Terminal, O'Hare, Airport, Chicago

Looking at these rather simple examples we may ask the fundamental question: where do our preferences, we call aesthetic, come from? After consideration of much of what has been written about aesthetics, I believe it is impossibly to explain *how* in essence our preferences come about. The *why* is another story. We identify the components of emotion and reason as instrumental in the process toward preference – with properties of objects as origins – but the nature of the dialectic between the subject and the object, between us and the world, is largely obscured and, I believe, will remain so. This in mind, let's consider two other examples which will bring us further in sorting out aspects of rather personal choices: Ludwig Mies' Seagram Office Building in New York and Herman Hertzberger's Home for the Elderly in Almere, Netherlands – two of the buildings to which I reacted years ago and still react with especially strong aesthetic notions (4.4 to 4.7). Not many buildings in recent times evoke aesthetic responses with regard to so few concentrated aspects as the Seagram Building – impressions of quiet elegance from superb proportions and exquisite materials. These qualities are an outcome of properties given by a designer who channeled for decades his emotion and reason toward the perfection of what proportion and materials combined can yield. Half a century later, we still can comprehend, if not the process leading to it, then the satisfaction from its result. While captivated by its seductive serenity, however, we should not overlook its aloofness.

Seagram Building, New York

4.4 and 4.5 View from Lever House and facade detail

The Almere Home, on the other hand, lets us sympathize with its necessary aspects of life as part of being aesthetic – impressions of nurture from environmental comfort and supportive community. Its setting incorporates the individuality of people and their circumstances into the relative diversity of a common scheme. If there ever was planning from inside-out as aesthetic principle, we find it here, in the massing, the hall ways, the dwellings, the solarium balconies and the courtyard. What an aesthetic contribution exterior sun shading can make beyond mere comfort control.

De Overloop, Home for Elderly, Almere, Netherlands

4.6 and 4.7 Overview and courtyard

There is an interesting dimension of the emotion-reason process in connection with resemblance and repetition. It was first described by Israel Waynbaum in 1907:

> Everything new and unknown will have a strong tendency to affect us and to evoke an emotion of variable intensity. ... when no cognitive representation exists, perception instead follows ... to transform itself into an emotion before generating cognition. From this phenomenon arises the pleasure of traveling; at such times we feel we are doubly alive, and everything is beautiful and interesting. ...[28]

However, the more we are acquainted with things the more a dulling effect occurs:

> Since humans are almost always prescient, perception routinely loses its affective qualities and more frequently addresses the cognitive elements directly.[29]

This is why I said earlier that we often will not be aware of emotions involved. They are dulled when experiences are often reoccurring in similar ways (dulling not meant negatively per se).

> But if cognition is the least bit lacking, the affective elements of perception will reappear. *The affectivity of perception is therefore inversely related to prior knowledge.*[30]

When we encounter objects with high degrees of similarity, perceptions are quickly conceptualized and understanding easily develops. So does associated meaning. We become easily familiar with what we experience. But if repetition of similarity is high, we eventually may get bored. Endless repetitions of the same housing units or office buildings are examples. On the other hand, unfamiliarity and variation catch our attention and search for understanding them motivates us. This tendency to a considerable part drives design in search of novelty. Novelty raises interest. We all are familiar with architecture being described as 'exceptional', 'dramatic', 'dynamic', 'daring', 'chaotic', or being simply 'different'. The entry roof to the Culture and Convention Center in Luzern, designed by Jean Nouvel, can certainly be considered to be stunning if not daring (4.8).

4.8 Culture and Convention Center, Luzern

Extremes, however, may be counterproductive. If differentiation for differentiation's sake makes comprehension difficult, understanding may be confused or even unattainable, even when a certain uniqueness effect may be the result. This is, among others, the case in recent Daniel Libeskind's designs, such as in the Denver Art Museum (4.9), and even more so in Will Alsop's 'anything goes'-design of the Sharp Center for Design, Ontario College of Art, Toronto (4.10). Architecture needs more than self-reflective collage which coerces purpose and alienates content. There is a productive balance to be struck for every project. Eventually we have to ask ourselves: Can we justify to build anything we like because it can be constructed? If yes, the two just given examples may be 'just fine'. So may be as well, on a very different level, the Hotel Inntel in Zaandam, Netherlands, by WAM Architects (4.11).

4.9 Denver Art Museum, Denver

4.10 Sharp Center for Design, Toronto
(© permission)

4.11 Hotel Inntel, Zaandam, Amsterdam
(© permission)

When we are not familiar with aspects of unavoidable objects we encounter, we develop the interest to understand them. Norbert Schwarz, echoing Waynbaum, writes that

107

> When facing a problematic situation, we are usually motivated to do something about it. Any attempt to change the situation, however, initially requires careful assessment of its features, an analysis of their causal links, detailed explorations of possible mechanisms of change, and an anticipation of the potential outcomes of any action that might be initiated. …
>
> Conversely, when we face a benign situation that poses no particular problem, we may see little need to engage in detailed analyses and may rely on our usual routines and preexisting knowledge structures, which served us well in the past.[31]

These are aspects any problem solver, any researcher is faced with when looking for answers to particular questions. And, this is so when we are engaged in design which in this regard can be considered a research activity. For example, problematic building sites often bring forward more interesting designs than those without such challenges. Or, in highly complex projects we may find relatively simple solutions by working through architectural design efforts rather then relying on the enormous advances which present building technologies offer us as costly answers. Strong environmental control of building interiors by excessive mechanical systems made it possible for a long time to neglect simpler energy conscious design solutions. On the other hand we have rarely, if ever, circumstances in which all design factors can be fully satisfied. Compromises must be developed in positive direction. To make the necessary value judgments among the design factors involves emotion as well as reason and this is what, I believe, aesthetic responsiveness and responsibility is about.

4.2 Aspects of beauty

There is perhaps no more puzzling quality in the relationship of emotion and reason than that which through the ages has been called beauty. Early thoughts about it go back at least to Homer and Pythagoras. We need to consider, however, that beauty in ancient Greece (kalon) had not the narrow notion we have of it today. It included aspects of purity, regularity, appropriateness, rationality, suitability and especially goodness, all being aspects of virtue. In short, every aspect which pleases.[32] And, art (techne) was much broader than what we understand by the term today. It meant craft, that is, skillful production as means to an end.[33] Beauty was not as institutionalized in art to the extent of today. For all which follows in this chapter we should be aware, when art is mentioned, whether the original notion of art as techne and craft is meant or the modern, narrower notion of art as institutionalized activity, beginning in the Renaissance.

By the time of Plato (ca. 428-ca.348 BC) mainly three views of beauty existed, though they often were not referred to by this name:

> the mathematical theory of the Pythagoreans (that beauty depends on measure, proportion, order and harmony); the subjectivist theory of the Sophists (that it depends on the pleasures of eye and ear); and the functional theory of Socrates (that the beauty of things resides in their suitability for the tasks they are to perform).[34]

Plato accepted the first, opposed the second to a large extent, broadened the base of the third and added his own great contribution: an ultimately idealistic base for any view of beauty. In one of Plato's early writings, a dialogue between Hippias and Socrates, the latter rhetorically lets an unknown inquirer ask the difficult questions about beauty.

> "How, if you please, do you know, Socrates," said he, "what sort of things are beautiful and ugly? For, come now, could you tell me what the beautiful is?"[35]

Two questions are asked: one regarding the nature of beautiful things, another regarding the nature of the beautiful itself – presumably different issues. After a long winding discussion essentially on whether beauty is a property of the things we call beautiful or is appearance only (which we like or not like), the question of what the nature of the beautiful is remains unanswered, and Socrates invokes questions of causal relationships of the beautiful with the useful and the suitable and especially the good. The dialogue, highly stimulating but mainly about raising questions, ends inconclusively with Socrates saying to Hippias

> ... I think I know the meaning of the proverb "beautiful things are difficult".[36]

The search for the answers to questions about beauty is puzzling and elusive.

Plato himself seems undecided. He thinks that one comes to know beauty through experience from as different characteristics as the physicality of objects and the structure of institutions, with goodness and its enjoyment as the central criteria.[37] Beauty is for Plato essentially an absolute value, hence important for all aspects of life and culture, the ultimate object of love to be approached; more by reason, however, than emotion. That emotions should be avoided or controlled as much as possible, as they may cause trouble, is an early acknowledgment of linking beauty with emotion.

Socrates' later views that the beautiful and the good are intimately related is probably best described in the writing of Xenophon, a younger contemporary. Aristippus asks whether he knew any beautiful things.

> "I know a great many," said Socrates. "Are they all like one another?" continued Aristippus.
> "Not in the least," answered Socrates, "for they are very different from one another." ...

Beauty is not a fixed quality from object to object, consideration to consideration.

> "You answer me," said Aristippus, "as you answered me before, when I asked you whether you knew any good thing." "And do you think," replied Socrates, "that the good and the beautiful are different? Know you not that the things that are beautiful are good likewise in the same sense? It would be false to say of virtue that in certain occasions it is beautiful, and in others good. When we speak of men of honour we join the two qualities, and call them excellent and good. In our bodies beauty and goodness relate always to the same end. In a word, all things that are of any use in the world are esteemed beautiful and good, with regard to the subject for which they are proper."
>
> ...
>
> Thus we see that when Socrates said that beautiful houses were the most convenient, he taught plainly enough in what manner we ought to build them, and he reasoned thus: "Ought not he who builds a house to study chiefly how to make it most pleasant and most convenient?" This proposition being granted, he pursued: "Is it not a pleasure to have a house that is cool in summer and warm in winter? And does not this happen in buildings that front towards the south? ..."[38]

In this view all beautiful things have something in common, as different as they may be. They have the essential form of beauty, its ideal form – like the idea of being hard is a characteristic of stone, steel, glass, etc. and the idea of being government is a characteristic of legislatures, courts, police, etc. We should think of ideal beauty as archetype, as absolute beauty with every other beauty being relative. How do we have to understand this?

> ...; but beauty absolute, separate, simple, and everlasting, which without diminution and without increase, or any change, is imparted to the ever-growing and perishing beauties of all other things. He who from these ascending under the influence of true love, begins to perceive that beauty, is not far from the end. And the true order of going, or being led by another, to the things of love, is to begin from the beauties of earth and mount upwards for the sake of that other beauty, using these as steps only, and from one going on to two, and

from two to all fair forms, and from fair forms to fair practices, and from fair practices to fair notions, until from fair notions he arrives at the notion of absolute beauty, and at last knows what the essence of beauty is.[39]

Accordingly, as beauty manifests itself daily in many ways, we increasingly know about beauty as effect and ideal. But this is not the same as to understand "what the essence of beauty is". Monroe Beardsley writes in reference to Plato's Symposium, Republic and Phaedo that

… besides the changing beauties of the many concrete things in the world, there must be one Beauty that appears in them all. This is the essential Form of Beauty, absolute Beauty, not seen with the eyes but grasped conceptually by the "mind alone".[40]

From this point of view, beauty is part of things and there is a category of beauty to which all beautiful things belong, though they are otherwise very different.

Eventually, while there is mention of physical arrangements as a quality of beauty, like proportion and symmetry, for Plato is at center the relationship of beauty and the good. So he sides with Socrates' suggestion. He emphasizes the correspondence of the physical and the spiritual as well as the moral.

Everything that is good is fair [beautiful], and the fair is not without proportion, and the animal [living creature] which is to be fair [beautiful] must have due proportion. Now we perceive lesser symmetries or proportions and reason about them, but of the highest and greatest we take no heed; for there is no proportion or disproportion more productive of health and disease, and virtue and vice, than that between soul and body.[41]

William Knight summarizes the essence of Plato's teaching on beauty:

In every beautiful object two things are conjoined – the sensible phenomenon (the form), and the idea which it embodies, and which underlies the form. The one is individual, and concrete; the other general, and abstract. The former is visible, and transient; the latter invisible, and permanent. The chief use of the lower is to lead on, and lead up to the higher; … Beauty which cannot appear or disappear, but which always is, always was, and always will be, at the very core of things, and at the center of the universe.[42]

Form and idea (content) are conjoined in every object, not only in those we call beautiful. Knight means here with form, as I do, the physical realization of an idea.

Aristotle (384-322 BC) had a rich heritage to work with. All the important aspects of aesthetics, in which beauty is embedded, had been touched on. But he made many contributions on his own by building on these often puzzling and unsettled ideas. Much more than Plato he tried to define beauty in practical terms. He does not subscribe to Plato's ideal forms. He clearly states that

The chief forms of beauty are order and symmetry and definiteness, which the mathematical sciences demonstrate in a special degree. And since these (e.g. order and definiteness) are obviously causes of many things, evidently these sciences must treat this sort of causative principle also (i.e. the beautiful) as in some sense a cause.[43]

For Aristotle beauty is a cause. It motivates and is fundamental to the art of Ancient Greece in the sense of capacity and action to make things; and make them well. Symmetry has a broader meaning than what we associate with it today. It is the union and conformity of parts within a whole.[44] Art and with it the creation of the beautiful is the result of reasoning, in architecture as in any other activity:

Now since architecture is an art and is essentially a reasoned state of capacity to make, and there is neither any art that is not such a state nor any such state that is not an art, art is identical with a state of capacity to make, involving a true course of reasoning.[45]

One of the main features of art to be achieved is mimesis: imitation as representation of what exists and might become. To achieve excellence in mimesis constitutes beauty. In this sense all art is re-creation as abstraction of reality. Abstraction implies appraisal and selection which has ethical dimensions. So, mimesis is more than what we in common language usually grasp with imitation.

Plato in the *Republic* (Books III and X) and in the *Sophist* makes a distinction between narrations, which he views to be art's closest imitations of reality, and appearances, which he views to be more or less exaggerated with often dangerous interpretations. In a dialogue in which Socrates is only an observer he lets a Stranger rhetorically lead the conversation:

> … I can discern two divisions of the imitative art, but I am not as yet able to see in which of them the desired form is to be found. …
>
> One is the art of likeness-making; – generally a likeness of anything is made by producing a copy which is executed according to the proportions of the original, similar in length and breadth and depth, each thing receiving also its appropriate colour. …
>
> And may we not, as I did just now, call that part of the imitative art which is concerned with making such images the art of likeness making? …
>
> And what shall we call those resemblances of the beautiful, which [make] appear such owing to the unfavorable position of the spectator, whereas if a person had the power of getting a correct view of works of such magnitude, they would appear not even like that to which they profess to be like? May we not call these "appearances," since they appear only and are not really like? …
>
> There is a great deal of this kind of thing in painting, and in all imitation. …
>
> And may we not fairly call the sort of art, which produces an appearance and not an image, phantastic art? …
>
> These are the two kinds of image making – the art of making likenesses, and [the art of making] phantastic [compositions, which is] the art of making appearances?[46]

The Stranger essentially refers to objectivity versus subjectivity in representation or, perhaps even more, to what its content of truth is. Here is the basis for Plato's distrust of some of the arts and their potential for not only overemphasis but falsification.

Imitation plays for Aristotle a different role. For him, excellence in mimesis constitutes beauty of a special kind. It emphasizes, perhaps even exaggerates, the important features of communication for increased understanding. There is freedom in the ways of imitations because of what they relate to and how they come about:

> They differ, …, from one another in three respects – the medium, the objects, the manner or mode of imitation, being in each case distinct.[47]

Aristotle refers mainly to poetry. But his comment holds for all fields in which imitation is practiced. Especially the latter points to an ethical dimension in our work. Imitation is more than copying or fantasizing appearance. It is to depict the truth as far as possible. Referring to Plato, but for me even more applicable to Aristotle, Stephen Halliwell writes that

> … it is reasonable here to recognize overlapping and connected criteria – the "what?" the "how?" and the "what for?" – of the beauty of representation, and this nexus of considerations entitles us to speak in terms of a concept of ethical form. On this account, the beauty of a mimetic work (visual or otherwise …) depends not on straightforward, one-to-one correspondence to a (putative) model but on a complex relationship in which a certain kind of purposiveness … must be taken into account, and in which mimetic imaging turns from a technical into an ethical activity.[48]

Objectivity is derived from reality. At the same time, with regard to mimesis as representation in art and, for that matter, in anything else, we should be aware that representation is subjective. In short, *representation is subjective with an objective ground*. This should mean for architecture to let its forms express as far as possible important functional origins and relationships, but to let at the same time aesthetic freedom play a considerable role in design and realization.

The only extensive treatise on architecture and its beauty which survived Antiquity is that of the Roman architect and engineer Vitruvius (ca. 75 – ca. 25 BC). His *De architectura* addresses the art of building in ten books of chapter length (hence today's title *The Ten Books of Architecture*). In introductory remarks about the variety of buildings he writes:
> All these must be built with due reference to durability, convenience, and beauty. … beauty [will be assured] when the appearance of the work is pleasing and in good taste, and when its members are in due proportion according to correct principles of symmetry.[49]

As I mentioned earlier, symmetry had at that time a much broader meaning than now. This view is reinforced in another translation of the latter sentence:
> Beauty is produced by the pleasing appearance and good taste of the whole, and by the dimensions of all the parts being duly proportioned to each other.[50]

We clearly have here beauty as the subjective effect from objective causes. Appearance brings about subjective judgments. Proportions of architecture, evoking beauty in us, are to be derived from those of the well shaped human body which Vitruvius extensively describes.[51] He even claims that
> … the Doric column, as used in buildings, began to exhibit the proportions, strength, and beauty of the body of man.[52]

Since that time, pleasing proportions have been derived or claimed to have been derived from the 'Vitruvian Man', all the way to Le Corbusier's *Modulor*.

The most astonishing aspect of Vitruvius' work is how comprehensively it addresses the many elements which contribute to the overall quality of architecture we judge as being beautiful. His writings are the first record which survives from a practicing architect. We may well consider him to be the first functionalist. But, although he posits proportions in quantifiable magnitudes as the central criteria for architectural coordination and composition, he leaves the door open for deviations to achieve additional choices with pleasing impressions.[53]

To bring order and harmony of parts into wholes is a central aspect of beauty in Late Antiquity and the Middle Ages. The earliest comprehensive and explicit account is by Plotinus (204-270) a Greek-Roman Neoplatonist philosopher. Beauty evolves from perceiving things but
> … minds that lift themselves above the realm of sense to a higher order are aware of beauty in the conduct of life, in actions, in character, in the pursuits of the intellect; and there is the beauty of the virtues.

A distinctive characteristic of ideal forms is unity. He writes that
> Only a compound can be beautiful, … Yet beauty in an aggregate demands beauty in details; it cannot be constructed out of ugliness; its law must run throughout.[54]

And,
> … where the Ideal-Form has entered, it has grouped and coordinated what from a diversity of parts was to become a unity: it has rallied confusion into co-operation: it has made the sum one harmonious coherence: for the Idea is a unity and what it moulds must come to unity as far as multiplicity may.

Therefore, the unity of ideal form, its beauty, is the correspondence of the parts within their whole:
> ... Thus, for an illustration, there is the beauty, conferred by craftsmanship, of all a house

> with all its parts, and the beauty which some natural quality may give to a single stone. This, then, is how the material thing becomes beautiful – by communicating in the thought that flows from the Divine.[55]

The ultimate grounds of beauty are in ideas which are intellectual and of divine inspiration. Therefore, he writes that

> ... the Soul will come first to the Intellectual-Principle and survey all the beautiful Ideas in the Supreme and will avow that this is Beauty, that the Ideas are Beauty.[56]

Beauty is order in variety which is another explanation for unity. It is through "the Intellectual-Principle" that we can perceive it via sensation or conceive it via memory. Beauty is the ideal form internalized from what exists beyond us "by thought that flows from the Devine". But what is the Soul's contribution itself? – this is an issue we eventually must address.

During the Middle Ages and at least in the Western tradition, beauty was ever more thought about in theological context. Religious themes dominated in painting, sculpture and architecture. By the time of Augustine of Hippo (354-430), the neoplatonist turned church father of the spreading Christian faith, beauty is fully lodged in God's existence and everything beautiful has its source in it. The absolute good and perfection of God is the ideal of beauty. Art – still for a long time mainly understood as the general making of things – draws inspiration from this source:

> The artist is not like God, though he draws his creative power from God. God creates ex nihilo, by means of his wisdom; the artist creates in and by means of material.[57]

Augustine's view draws art fully into the philosophy of his faith. We may consider this to be perhaps the first claimed institutionalization of art – among others to come. It is crucial to keep in mind that, while raised as a child in the Christian faith, he fell a way from it and lived a hedonistic fifteen years during his early and highly successful career as a philosophy professor and rhetorician. After his conversion he entered the priesthood to become eventually the most important and seminal thinker of the rapidly developing church. The contrasts of his life's experiences led him into the unique position of contemplating more than anybody before him about the tensions which the perception of an objective world brings to the understanding of a subjective mind.

He tells a story of asking an imaginary craftsman about his work on the arrangements in a building facade and about his thoughts on what beauty is.

> ... if I inquire of an architect [artifice], who has just built one arch, why he is at pains to make the one on the other side its exact equivalent, he will answer, I believe, that it is to have the parts of the building corresponding in every way to their opposite numbers. ... he will say that this is how it should be, that this is beautiful, that this is what pleases the eye of the beholder.
>
> ... but I will not give up prodding the man, who has eyes inside him and can see the invisible, to tell me why these things please ... And my first question will be whether these things are beautiful because they delight, or delight because they are beautiful. Here he will undoubtedly answer that they delight because they are beautiful.[58]

The last two sentences succinctly state one of the still most controversial issues in aesthetics. Prompting further, the story leads to an understanding that the reason for the enjoyment is harmony and unity. Augustine tells that

> Then he [the craftsman] needs to be told himself: "How have you come to know this Unity, in accordance with which you make a judgment on bodies? After all, if you could not see her, you would not be able to make the judgment that they [the arches] do not fully realize her; ... since with these eyes you only see bodily things."
>
> So therefore it is with the mind that we see her. ... she is not contained in a place, ... and there is nowhere that her writ does not run.[59]

The answer that "things delight because they are beautiful" is not confirmed by Augustine himself. He states a few paragraphs hence that

> ... what a body looks like never lies. Because it does not have any will.

And,

> ... the eyes themselves do not deceive either. For the only thing that they can report back to the spirit is how they are affected. ... So the eye has acted correctly; that is what it was made for, after all – to have just that capacity.[60]

What our eyes see and what the mind comes up with are different. The view of a body which is objective, as given, is judged on the basis of a concept beyond what we actually see, which makes the result subjective. Human concepts of unity and judgments are fallible and cannot be assumed to be absolute but relative. There can be deception when the mind accepts as objective what the eyes see. He asserts:

> For it [the mind] is trying to understand things of the flesh and see things of the spirit, which cannot be done.[61]

Although Augustine does not say so explicitly, I believe, he means that what we sense and what we judge is in effect not the same. We judge mental representations. He adheres, especially under the influence of Plotinus, to the widely accepted views from Greece. Order is fundamental and this implies number, proportion, rhythm, harmony and, especially, unity from small pieces to the whole universe, God's ordered universe, because

> There is nothing, after all, that is in order which is not also beautiful. And as the apostle says: All order is from God (Romans 13:1).[62]

The beautiful has order. This also implies reason as nothing can be brought into order without thoughts and judgment. Every time we deem something to be large or small, good or bad, beautiful or ugly, etc. we make a judgment. Augustine emphasizes that judgment is based on reason when he writes that

> True equality ... and unity itself are not to be observed by the eyes in our heads, nor by the sense but only by the mind's understanding of them.[63]

And,

> ... I judge that those correspondences I perceive with the eyes are all the better the nearer they approach, within the limits of their nature, those I understand with the intellect. But why these should be as they are, nobody can say, ...[64]

He gives great value to equality and unity. Valuation, however, arises out of judgment. Equality should not be viewed simply as repetitive sameness but as modularity and sameness within categories of components to foster variation with combinability for fit. Equality also has value because of resemblance which we remember. We enjoy what is familiar to us, unless it is repeated to often.

There is a law, according to Augustine, on which we base our judgments. It arises out of the equalities in geometries and measurements. He gives examples of the squareness of paving stones and the equal lengths of steps which even ants as well as elephants take.

> This law, ..., governing all the arts, is altogether unchanging, while the human mind, to which has been granted a sight of it, can undergo the changes and chances of error; hence it is sufficiently clear that this law is above our minds and that its name is Truth.[65]

It is the truth of reality which is for the older Augustine the absolute and universally present reality – the wellspring of beauty, God. At the end of his *Confessions* he writes, considering his earlier life:

> I was so fallen and blinded that I could not discern the light of virtue and of beauty which must be embraced for its own sake, which the eye of flesh cannot see, and only the inner vision can see.[66]

The "inner vision" is our mind and for Augustine it is also the faith which is necessary to see the beauty of God. All beauty in this world is for him relative to this ultimate and ideal Beauty – as enjoyed by the neoplatonic Christian.

Thomas Aquinas (c.1225-1274), one of the main philosophers of the Middle Ages, and no less pious than Augustine, sides more with Aristotle. He derives beauty from contemplating the form of things as God gives them to us in nature. This implies conceptualization of what things are and what they are for:

> Beauty and goodness in a thing are identical fundamentally; for they are based upon the same thing, namely, the form; and consequently goodness is praised as beauty. But they differ logically, for goodness properly relates to the appetite (goodness being what all things desire); and therefore it has the aspect of an end (the appetite being a kind of movement towards a thing). On the other hand, beauty relates to the cognitive faculty; for beautiful things are those which please when seen. Hence beauty consists in due proportion; for the senses delight in things duly proportioned, …[67]

The good and the beautiful are conceptually different. Goodness is a function to an end. Beauty has an effect on us as an affect. But they have the same source, the form which arises out of their essence. There is influence because our liking of what is good affects our view about what we then call beautiful. We call things beautiful because their appearance *and* their being good are pleasant. Aquinas gives three conditions to qualify for being beautiful. They are

> … "integrity" or "perfection," since those things which are impaired are by the very fact ugly; due "proportion" or "harmony"; and lastly, "brightness" or "clarity," whence things are called beautiful which have a bright color.[68]

He emphasizes very interestingly, all still in the context of Christian doctrine about God the Father, the Son and the Spirit, here with regard to the Son perhaps in reference to the awfulness of the crucifixion:

> Hence we see that an image is said to be beautiful, if it perfectly represents even an ugly thing.[69]

The very possibility that ugliness can be attractive is for me a major reason that I hold beauty not to be a property of something but an affect on us because of our experience and judgment. We will return to this issue at various instances. In this regard we need also consider that in one sense something may be ugly but in another beautiful.

In the Renaissance the theological-metaphysical bond broke open. Still, religious institutions played a strongly supportive but sometimes also a restrictive role by enforcing narrow interpretations of established Church dogmas. A similar role of resistance happened also later by fundamentalist Protestantism. But overall, the concept of beauty became more explicitly approached and the arts became more self-consciously 'artistic' in the modern sense, even self-referential, as the individual human being became more and more the center of interest and inquiry. Marsilio Ficino (1433-99) writes that

> … the appearance and shape of a well-proportioned man agrees most clearly with that concept of mankind which our soul catches and retains from the author of everything.

Earlier in the same study he writes about the

> …composite of all the Forms and Ideas we call in Latin a *mundus,* and in Greek, a *cosmos,* that is, *Orderliness.* The attractiveness of this *Orderliness* is Beauty.[70]

These are themes following Plato, whose works Ficino translated into Latin. He also wrote a book on platonic theology. His themes were enlightenment and advancement, but also restriction of propagating bodily sensuality, living toward idealism rather than realism. This is also the time of Alberti, Leonardo, Michelangelo, Dürer, Luther and Columbus. Theories in painting, building and many other fields developed out of very practical inquiries and the emancipation of reason. Leon Battista Alberti (1404-1472) wrote about beauty, echoing Plotinus and the Ancients:

> Beauty is the reasoned harmony of all the parts within a body, so that nothing can be added, taken away, or altered, but for the worse.[71]

And, with emphasis on reason:

> When you make judgments on beauty, you do not follow mere fancy, but the workings of a reasoned faculty that is inborn in the mind.[72]

Beauty is a property of the whole, grasped through thought about what is perceived. The process includes judgment. We achieve beauty by making favorable arrangements and then judgments about what we have attained.

Again, now considering results: is beauty lodged in what we judge or is it in the result of judgment, the result in our mind? Alberti seemed to favor the former by saying

> … I believe, that beauty is some inherent property, to be found suffused all through the body of that which may be called beautiful; whereas ornament, rather than being inherent, has the character of something attached or additional.[73]

His "inherent" refers to what is part of something by its nature. What Alberti had in mind were rules of building derived from nature, as given in what materials were and could be used for, what numbers and proportions accomplished in various ways according to tasks, what history could provide in what Vitruvius and others had written, and what he was surrounded with and could visit as the legacy of Greek, Roman and Tuscan art and architecture. Joseph Rykwert is right when he emphasizes that Alberti makes a distinction between beauty and ornament, as we clearly can derive from the last quote above. But is beauty a question of overall framework versus individual expression? Is ornament not part of beauty? Rykwert writes that

> … beauty is the overall intellectual and primary framework – the essential idea – while ornament is the phenomenon – the individual expression and embellishment of the frame.[74]

For Alberti, beauty arises out of the qualities of what is necessarily built, if designed and done well. It arises from required concerns of design, based on purpose, context and realization. Ornament is in our discretion. It is what we may add to make things appear more varied and pleasant, and may contribute to beauty as well. Alberti's "inherent" versus "attached" is an important distinction to which we will return in the more detailed discussion of ornament.

The 15th and 16th centuries were extremely productive in the arts, in fact to such an extent that they allowed broad segments of secular society to participate. No new theories, however, developed on beauty beyond what Antiquity and the Middle Ages had established and reformulated. Reason was more emphasized as the driving force of most if not all endeavors. Exploration and experimentation became fundamental aspects of art. Albrecht Dürer (1471-1528) depicts in his *The Painter's Manual* the method of how to transfer what he sees of a lady's body through a frame with a transparent grid of squares unto a piece of paper with a similar grid on it. But even after a prolific output of drawings, etchings and paintings with scenes from nature, daily life and biblical stories, and also after writing manuals on painting and human proportions, his findings on beauty are for him a disappointment:

> What, however, beauty is, that I don't know.[75]

Three centuries later Johann Wolfgang Goethe (1739-1832) gives a wise answer in the discourse with an imagined person searching for answers:

> "Can you tell me what beauty might be?" he [the person] called out.
> "Maybe not!' I uttered, 'but I can show you." …[76]

'As far as you can appreciate', one might add, as the answer points to the subjectively arrived nature of what we call beauty.

Monroe Beardsley writes that the giants of early modern philosophy Descartes, Spinoza and Leibniz did not directly enlighten aspects of beauty, nor did Hobbes and Locke.[77] But I believe, from their seminal thoughts about the correspondence between the world of things and the world of our mind, many empiricist and rationalistic approaches emerged from which we still benefit so profusely today also in aesthetics.

Descartes writes that what we get through the senses is often obscure and confused, and that we need to limit ourselves to the clear and distinct ideas.[78] There was uneasiness about 'confused' perception; confused in the sense of difficult to explain – if at all possible to explain. Gottfried Wilhelm Leibniz (1646-1716), as much a rationalist as Descartes, describes the dilemma:

> When I am able to recognize a thing among others, without being able to say in what its differences or characteristics consist, the knowledge is confused. Sometimes indeed we may know clearly, that is without being in the slightest doubt, that a poem or a picture is well or badly done because there is in it an "I know not what" which satisfies or shocks us. Such knowledge is not yet distinct. It is when I am able to explain the peculiarities which a thing has, that the knowledge is called distinct.[79]

This uneasiness existed and exists similarly among many who thought about beauty over the centuries and think about it today. We cannot explain beauty as such. It is an "I know not what". We may know what produces it through our perception and judgment but do not understand it completely. *We cannot explain feelings about beauty only propose facts about what causes them*.

Matters of the beautiful were discussed in British philosophy especially beginning with the 3rd Earl of Shaftesbury (1671-1713), a pupil of Locke. In his views about taste, which is mainly acquired by education, he emphasized the concept of an "inward eye":

> No sooner the Eye opens upon *Figures*, the Ear to *Sounds*, than straight *the Beautiful* results, and *Grace* and *Harmony* are known and acknowledg'd. No sooner are Actions view'd, no sooner the *human Affections* and *Passions* discerenʼd (and they are most of 'em as soon discerne'd as felt) than straight *an inward Eye* distinguishes, and sees *the Fair* and *Shapely*, *the Amiable* and *Admirable*, apart from *the Deform'd*, *the Foul*, *the Odious*, or *the Despicable*.[80]

This "inward eye", not further defined but supposedly developed, is the ability to concern oneself with matters of beauty and associated judgments, a major theme in the 18th century. In Shaftesbury it is an elitist aspect of virtue and character:

> The Taste of beauty, and the *Relish* of what is decent, just, and amiable, perfects the *Character* of the Gentleman, and the Philosopher. And the Study of such a Taste or *Relish* will ever be the great Employment and Concern of him, who covets as well to be *wise* and *good*, as *agreeable* and *polite*.[81]

For Shaftesbury beauty and morality are closely related. So it is for Francis Hutcheson (1694-1746) who, however, adds an important dimension: the differentiation of absolute and relative beauty.

> Beauty is either Original, or Comparative; or, if any like the Terms better, Absolute, or Relative: Only let it be noted, that by Absolute or Original Beauty, is not understood any Quality suppos'd to be in the Object, that should of itself be beautiful, without relation to any Mind which perceives it: For Beauty, like other Names of sensible Ideas, properly denotes the Perception of some Mind; … were there no Mind with a Sense of Beauty to contemplate Objects, I see not how they could be call'd beautiful.[82]

Only through a present mind it is possible to grasp and sort out what is beautiful, as

> Let it be observ'd, ..., the Word Beauty is taken for the Idea rais'd in us, and a Sense of Beauty for our Power of receiving this Idea.[83]

Hutcheson, as Shaftesbury, clearly places beauty as a *result* of sensation in our mind. It is an "internal sense" or "internal sensation", expressions John Locke had already used with regard to thinking in general.[84] The distinction of "absolute" and "relative" may well be considered as a neoplatonic interpretation of the contemplated ideal and the observable real. Further, there is in mimesis

> Comparative or Relative Beauty ... in Objects, commonly considered as Imitations or Resemblances of something else.[85]

"Internal sense" and "internal sensation" is here a process *and* result by means of a "Sense of Beauty". The result is a special understanding according to the receptivity of the individual.

It is David Hume (1711-76) who describes the uniqueness of every mind clearly when he writes that

> All sentiment is right; because sentiment has a reference to nothing beyond itself, and is always real, wherever a man is conscious of it. But all determinations of the understanding are not right; because they have a reference to something beyond themselves, to wit, real matter of fact; and are not always conformable to that standard. Among a thousand different opinions which different men may entertain of the same subject, there is one, and but one, that is just and true; and the only difficulty is to fix and ascertain it. ...

We "fix and ascertain" individually and subjectively, and this is why

> ... Beauty is no quality in things themselves: It exists merely in the mind which contemplates them; and each mind perceives a different beauty.[86]

I very much agree. Hume's view implies a denying position in the never ending questioning about whether there exist properties of beauty intrinsic to objects. Beauty, and more comprehensively, all aesthetic notions that we attribute because of pleasure or displeasure, are in our minds not in objects. The folk wisdom 'beauty is in the eye of the beholder' has it quite right though we should broaden it and say 'beauty and any other aesthetic notion is in the mind of the beholder'. There are properties in the objects which are the ground for our aesthetic – our feeling of pleasure or displeasure about something. But these properties are not 'aesthetic' in any sense of intrinsic or permanent.[87] This is why styles in architecture and sometimes whole cultures change, based on changing desires of appearance. For Hume beauty is broadly based and cannot be defined as such. He writes that

> The order and convenience of a palace are no less essential to its beauty, than its mere figure and appearance. ... from considering that beauty like wit, cannot be defin'd, but is discern'd only by the taste or sensation, we may conclude, that beauty is nothing but form, which produces pleasure, ...[88]

Hume's "form" is not whatever the realization of the object is, although it is related to it. Although it has its ground in the apparent qualities of the object, it is that form which through realization *in our mind* brings about pleasure. Beauty has for Hume various sources but their effect is always the same. There is only *one* beauty. With regard to visible sensation, and we have no reasons to believe that this should not hold for sensation in general, he writes:

> ... the beauty of all visible objects causes a pleasure pretty much the same, tho' it be sometimes deriv'd from the mere *species* and appearance of the objects; sometimes from sympathy, and an idea of their utility.[89]

With regard to "sympathy", I find it helpful to think about affection, responsiveness, even empathy. Sympathy is a fundamental kind of imagination. It arises out of emotions which impact us during conceptualization; though it may be rather automatic because of earlier related experiences. It is a reactive result from feelings of beauty. Examples are the response to understanding the grounds of observing pleasure of others and, architecture oriented, the pleasure from perceiving favorable functional features in combination with all other aspects of a building. But utility can also more directly affect us as pleasant and be thus beautiful, for example, from the comfort of sitting on a chair in addition to its visual appearance. The aesthetic of experiences goes beyond those from vision and sound, such as from eating or even walking. In short, *what we judge to be pleasing is beautiful*, from whatever the feeling originates and however we feel it.

It is only natural, out of this context, that the question of conformity of judgment about beauty should come up and whether there can be wide spread agreement about it. We find it perhaps most elaborately in Hume's wide range of writing on sensation, reflection, passion, etc. We may summarize from his thoughts that there is often agreement among those with ability to judge, but there are variations among those able to judge carefully, and likely even more in the general public. With regard to possible standards of taste Hume takes a rather noncommittal position. At one point he writes:

> The general principles of taste are uniform in human nature …

But at an other:

> … a certain diversity of judgment is unavoidable, and we seek in vain for a standard, by which we can reconcile the contrary sentiments.
>
> … preferences are innocent and unavoidable, and can never reasonably be the object of dispute, because there is no standard, by which they can be decided.[90]

That we have appreciation of and frequently agreement about beauty in things and happenings, that is, taste, is obvious. But that does not mean that there are generally valid principles of taste to which we can adhere to and simply make judgments accordingly. This would mean that judgments on beauty would be like the more objective judgments about properties on the way to reasoned conceptualization which, I believe, is not the case.

4.3 Aesthetics and the aesthetic

Aesthetic experience is part of our path to understanding. Again, a remark on terminology is in order. The Ancient Greek adjective *aisthetikos*, from which our terms aesthetic and aesthetics originate, did not have our rather narrow meaning nor was it particularly related to the arts. It was quite generally associated with *sense perception*.[91] Since the 18th century, however, *aesthetics* has been especially related to the qualities of being beautiful and with the fields which study these aspects throughout history. *Aesthetic*, sometimes *aesthetical*, is generally used as an adjective, often of an activity, such as aesthetic experience, aesthetic appreciation, aesthetic evaluation, etc. Once in a while one finds 'aesthetic' also used as the singular of aesthetics pointing towards a quality of being beautiful. Differently and in concurrence with the ending of the last section, *I use the term aesthetic for that component of meaning which arises from judgment about pleasure or displeasure in the understanding of any object or state of affairs.*

This view, especially given in such a condensed version but with far reaching implications, raises questions and needs elaboration which again can best be done interwoven with quotes from influential thinkers on aesthetic issues in general and beauty in particular.[92] My account is roughly in historical sequence, highlighting only what I believe is crucial for our purposes. It will become abundantly clear what I mean with *the aesthetic* in detail, especially with regard to understanding and the beautiful. Throughout the long history of aesthetics there are two controversial themes which play overlapping roles. One is concerned with the fundamental issue of what the aesthetic is. The other is concerned with how it comes about.

It may come as a surprise that in our foregoing discussion I did not include 'aesthetic quality' as one of the causes of meaning in things. The reason is that I consider the aesthetic to be not a cause but an effect from our experience of objects – an outcome developing subjectively along the way to any understanding and meaning. The aesthetic (noun) is a part of our mental state resulting from the emotion-reason process. Understanding as mental state is aesthetic (adjective). The selection of an understanding for meaning is founded in part on aesthetic judgment, that is, judgment on liking or disliking of what an object is and does, including how it looks, smells, etc. The aesthetic is a correlate outcome of causes that provide meaning. While it is not wrong to talk about 'aesthetic meaning', one must be careful in not viewing it as a property of a physical object. Aesthetic meaning happens in our mind as all meaning does.

An unfortunate development occurred over the past two and one half centuries by the increasing use of 'aesthetic' and 'beautiful' as synonyms. This led over the whole history of recent aesthetics to confusion. It is also in part to blame for the push to locate the aesthetic of experience in the confines of art as institution rather than to take it as natural occurrence in the realm of everyday understanding and communication.

It was Alexander Gottlieb Baumgarten (1714-62) who proposed aesthetics as a discipline of philosophy in terms of "a science of sensory cognition" with a narrow focus on beauty. In other words, he tried to embed beauty as part of a scientific framework of understanding. The modern use of the term aesthetic has its origin in his efforts. His *Aesthetica,* published in the 1750s, tries to establish an autonomy of aesthetics as a discipline with irreducibility of its findings in a world that was increasingly dominated by the rational aspects of the emerging scientific and industrial revolution. He writes:

> Aesthetics (as theory of the free arts, as logic of the lower [fundamental] cognitive faculties, as art of the beautiful thought and as art of the intuitive cognition equivalent to that of rational thought) is the science of sensual cognition.[93]

And,

> The aim of Aesthetics is the perfection (the bringing of perfection) of sensual cognition as such. With this, however, beauty is meant. Correspondingly, the imperfection of sensory cognition as such, that is the ugliness, is to be avoided.[94]

The original text of his book is in Latin in which he gave the theory of his "scientia cognitionis sensitivae" the name "Aesthetica". Baumgarten connected quite a range of connotations with this term as we see in the parenthesis of the first quote. Although he does *not* say that the aesthetic *is* the beautiful, his close association of the two has been increasingly taken in this way.[95]

Baumgarten's interest was to establish a field of inquiry toward "sensual cognition" in contrast to rational cognition. He so uses the term cognition in the dual sense of being sensual and rational for which I use understanding, combining both.[96] But I stay with cognition when being in close connection with his writing. He viewed the faculties of sensual cognition to be "lower", in a "natural aesthetic" state, deriving cognition immediately, not reflected, not conceptualized. The field's aim was to bring perfection to sensuous cognition. The coming about of this perfection is beauty. The coming about of imperfection is ugliness. He lists three main issues that determine the general framework as the objective of the new science:

> The general beauty of sensual cognition is 1) the harmony of thoughts, … that is the correspondence of thoughts toward unity, which comes into appearance, … Ugly things can

> be thought as being beautiful and beautiful ones as being ugly. ... 2) the harmony of order ... particularly in the conformity with itself and its conformity with the related matters, as far as it comes into appearance. Therefore, we speak of the beauty of order and disposition. ... 3) the harmony of means of expression among themselves, ... as far as it comes into appearance. ...[97]

And,

> Out of the richness, the magnitude, the truth, the clarity and certainty, and the lively movement of cognition arises the perfection of any kind of cognition. This is so when these qualities harmonize in one representation, ... When these qualities appear [in harmony], they bring forth the beauty of sensual cognition ...[98]

This harmony is the result of imagination, the making of internal sense from impressions and external sense for expressions by finding what properties of objects are and can do in creative fit. Baumgarten extends this state of mind into "the art of beautiful thought", into the reality of qualifying things by calling them "aesthetic objects":

> The beauty of sensual cognition and the fineness of the aesthetic objects themselves represent composed perfections, that is, such which are generally valid. ...[99]

Baumgarten makes here a distinction between the cognitions in the mind (beauty) and qualities in the objects (fineness). But he also points to their connection and interdependence as "composed [composite] perfections". To my knowledge he did not clearly explain how the sensuous and the rational cognitions are interrelated, though he must have been aware of the issue. One indication is given in his view of the "natural aesthetic", supplemented by the "artificial aesthetic", being fundamental for all "higher cognitions" driving our human endeavors, including all the sciences and the arts.[100] He gives obviously sensation a more direct role in cognition than most others who have tried to enlighten us on the process and who view sensation as the basis for cognition but not as cognition itself; among them Kant who thought highly of Baumgarten and used his *Metaphysica* as text in his own teaching.

In his critique *The Baumgarten Corruption* Robert Dixon blames Baumgarten's confusion of the term *aesthetic* for the supposedly poor state of discourse in matters aesthetic:

> ... What Baumgarten corrupted was the Greek meaning of sense and sensible. *aesthetic*, that which is perceivable, as opposed to conceivable; of the senses, as opposed to reason. Now, of course, this meaning is precisely the meaning that matters when sorting out sense from nonsense in our ideas about art and beauty, but is in no way confined to such questions.[101]

And,

> When Baumgarten corrupted this Greek word he inadvertently un-named the elementary idea of sensible and obscured it with the sticky questions of What is art? And What is beautiful?[102]

And,

> The Baumgarten corruption of aesthetic takes a matter-of-fact Greek descriptive label for an elemental distinction in human knowledge, and turns it into a buzz word for a system of belief that confuses the perception of beauty with the cultivation of art appreciation.[103]

I agree. Baumgarten twisted the meaning of the Greek term aesthetic, which points to general perception, to become "sensual cognition" with the connotation of "beautiful thought", and then suggested it as a "theory of the free arts". His views succeeded on this corrupted basis, as Dixon says. In addition, Dixon aims to make the case

> (1) that the sensible and the reasonable are inextricably linked, and (2) that the cognitive role of the sensible is primary.[104]

No question that (1) is the case. And, regarding (2), the sensible is primary in the sense that it provides the foundation for all of perception. Dixon's further interest is to show that the confusion of the terms eventually resulted in the present situation of art, as an institutional enterprise, in contrast to art as broadly based, everyday activity creating things and communicating through them; an aspect whose discussion goes beyond our present context.

Baumgarten is quite aware of the limitations which a "science" of aesthetics was to face. He writes that some of the perfections and imperfections of sensual cognition are

> ... so hidden that they remain for us in the dark altogether or we can view them only in our thoughts, ...[105]

He qualifies this view by writing that

> The sensual cognition is ... the whole of representation below the threshold of strictly logical distinction.[106]

As discussed in the previous section, I firmly believe in emotionally influenced thinking with conceptualization and feeling as the components of eventual understanding. Baumgarten has much to tell us in this respect. He ran into problems, however, with his intention to develop for aesthetics a separate "science ... of the intuitive cognition equivalent to that of rational thought" instead of emphasizing the interdependence of conceptualization and feeling in overall understanding within one science that has this understanding as central objective. Immanuel Kant saw clearly the potential problem Baumgarten's use of the term aesthetic may bring forth when he wrote in 1781 that

> The Germans are the only ones who now employ the word "aesthetics" [Aesthetik] to designate that which others call the critique of taste. The ground for this is a failed hope, held by the excellent analyst Baumgarten, of bringing the critical estimation of the beautiful under principles of reason, and elevate its rules to a science. But this effort is futile. For the putative rules or criteria are merely empirical as far as their sources are concerned, and can therefore never serve as a priori rules according to which our judgments of taste must be directed, ... For this reason it is advisable again to desist from the use of this term and to save it for that doctrine which is true science (whereby one would come closer to the language and the sense of the ancients, among whom the division of cognition into άισθητα και νοητα was very well known).[107]

The three words in Greek mean essentially 'percept and concept'. What Kant seems to emphasize is to save the term aesthetic for use in connection with its original meaning of perception and for the scientific inquiry into it, not 'mixed up' with beauty in the very strong sense which Baumgarten intended. A few years later, however, Kant softened his position by relating the term in a special way to our appreciation of beauty.

In the *Critique of the Power of Judgment*, Kant associates the aesthetic clearly with the representation of things, not the things as such, when he writes in the *First Introduction*:

> The expression an "aesthetic *kind of representation"* is entirely unambiguous if we understand by it the relation of the representation to an object, as an appearance, for the cognition of the object; for then the expression of the *aesthetic* signifies that the form of sensibility (how the subject is affected) necessarily adheres to such a representation and that this is unavoidably carried over to the object (but only as a phenomenon).[108]

The carrying "over to the object (but only as a phenomenon)" clearly shows Kant's view of the distinction between the aesthetic as impact on our mind and the perceived properties in things and states of affairs, which produce the impact. In the first paragraph of the *Critique of the Power of Judgment* he writes:

> In order to decide whether or not something is beautiful, we do not relate the representation by means of understanding to the object for cognition, but rather relate it by means of the imagination (perhaps combined with the understanding) to the subject and its feeling of pleasure or displeasure. The judgment of taste is therefore not a cognitive judgment, hence not a logical one, but is rather aesthetic, by which is understood one whose determining ground *cannot* be *other than subjective*. Any relation of representation, however, even that of sensation, can be objective (in which case it signifies what is real in an empirical representation): but not the relation to the feeling of pleasure and displeasure, by means of which nothing at all in the object is designated, but in which the subject feels itself as it is affected by the representation.[109]

This paragraph contains, highly concentrated, much of Kant's foundational thoughts on judgment of perception. The following is an abridgment, which conveys what is important for us, I hope, in somewhat easier comprehensible language: When we decide about whether something is beautiful or ugly, we make a judgment about whether it gives us pleasure or displeasure. This judgment is not by cognition but imagination, not logical but aesthetic, and therefore subjective. Aesthetic simply relates to the question whether we are pleased or displeased about the appearance of something. The feeling of pleasure and displeasure which has its ground in the representation in our mind does not refer directly to anything in the object but to the feeling of the subject (the observer), that is, the affect from representation. In the extreme, something which is as object usually thought to be ugly may be judged by us to be beautiful.

In other words, the aesthetic of experience and judgment is not about anything 'aesthetic' in object properties but about whether and how strongly feelings of pleasure and displeasure arise in us from such properties. The aesthetic does not come from 'aesthetic' properties, though we expediently but inaccurately call those properties so which we hold particularly influential regarding beauty. *There are no aesthetic properties. There are only properties which affect our judgment with regard to an object. The aesthetic evolves from our mind.* Therefore, this position may be called *radically subjectivist.*[110]

My point of view, especially as expressed in the last sentences, may well be contrasted to that of Frank Sibley who writes in 1965 that

> (i) Aesthetic qualities are dependent upon non-aesthetic ones for their existence. ... (ii) The non-aesthetic qualities of a thing determine its aesthetic qualities. ... Aesthetic qualities are "emergent". ... (iii) In addition to being able to state the general truth that aesthetic qualities depend on and result from non-aesthetic characteristics, we can state particular truths about individual objects – for example, that these particular non-aesthetic qualities of this object (described as fully as one wishes) give it *some* aesthetic property rather than none, and that what they give it is, say, *grace* or *balance*.[111]

Sibley uses "quality", "characteristic" and "property" as synonyms. I usually stay with "property" to avoid ambiguity for reasons explained in the second paragraph of Chapter 2.2. What he calls "aesthetic qualities" are in my view the outcomes of our judgments about properties. They are relational properties, associated by us, which I earlier defined as attributes. A facade, for example, has certain proportions because of its overall dimensions, the sizes of windows and the pieces of wall between them, etc. The proportions and the materials are physically existing properties and are part of the object. But whether we are pleased or displeased with the proportions or materials is derived from subjective judgment. Proportion (an attributed or relational property), say, the Golden Section, has by itself no beauty and aesthetic. An observer is required to judge it to be so. 4.12 shows an example. The division of the window at left is according to the Golden Ratio. The one at right has 'a' increased by 15 percent within the same overall width.

I prefer the proportion at right, having 'more tension', an attributed, relational property. The addition to the Kunsthalle Karlsruhe, by Heinz Mohl, shows great sensitivity in allocating proportion (4.13). The side versus middle parts of the windows in the old building are in width having or are approaching Golden Ratio proportions. But this is not so in the new building. Even with the vertical inversion of the new versus old window shapes, pleasant harmony of the two facades is achieved.[112]

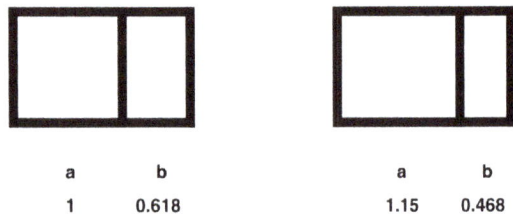

4.12 Golden Section and slight deviation

4.13 Kunsthalle Extension, Karlsruhe Germany (© permission)

For differentiation in aesthetics, that is where judgment plays a deciding role about quality, I use the term *qualities*. How strongly influential qualities are aesthetically is not so much what they are objectively as properties but how we judge them regarding pleasure or displeasure. This aspect carries over into language. Words that refer to pleasure or displeasure have aesthetic meaning. Aesthetic qualities are usually defined by polar dualities, such as pleasant/unpleasant, beautiful/ugly, orderly/messy, tasty/tasteless, etc. In reference to Sibley's points (i) and (ii): as there are, in my view, no aesthetic properties precludes that there are non-aesthetic properties on which they are supposedly dependent.[113] There are no aesthetic properties, only aesthetic values. Properties are objective. Values are subjective interpretations of them, implying judgments. Qualities, including Sibley's "aesthetic qualities", are relational properties and are dispositional, because they require our presence and involvement with them. What we have here is a category change from thing-possessed materiality to human-generated mentality. The observable properties in an object are more or less relevant for the effect on our mind. What arises in our mind are obviously not properties but our interpretations of and our reactions to them. What Sibley mentions to be "*some* aesthetic property …, say, *grace* or *balance*" are explanations of judgment. Aesthetic aspects are not observable properties. Rudolf Makkreel (1990) writes:

> … when I say "This rose is beautiful" the amplification obviously differs from that contained in the proposition "This rose is red". The latter can be said to involve the synthesis of two empirical concepts. By contrast, the predicate "beautiful" adds to my appreciation of the rose merely the consciousness that I feel pleasure about it. Beauty is not something that

can be connected to the rose as one of its qualities [observable properties]. There is no act of synthesis that expands the concept of rose. Nor can the apprehension of the rose and the pleasure be merged. The former is directed at the object, the latter at the subject.[114]

Properties are the cause for the aesthetic of experience and are, as said, not aesthetic or non-aesthetic themselves. Their aesthetic significance is their eventual effect. In fact, there is no beauty but what we make it to be individually or collectively. There is nothing beautiful, unless we deem it to be so.

From time to time it has been claimed that in order to have an 'aesthetic experience' one must adopt an aesthetic attitude. But we do not aim at something aesthetically but experience its result. We put ourselves in a mood of observing or designing properties of something and judge related pleasure or displeasure. This may include aiming at something because we had a pleasant experience with it. But this is simply remembering an earlier instance of the same kind of process. There exists no aesthetic for us unless we have experienced it ourselves, which shall not mean that we don't know of experiences of others similar to ours. It helps here to ask about the position of beauty's occurrence in the chain of cause and effect. If beauty were what causes pleasure, it would occur before pleasure. Is that so? No, because unless there is pleasure there is no beauty.[115] Beauty is simply the name we give to a subsequent state of mind.

John Dewey (1958) puts the aesthetic of experience clearly within the context of all experiences we have:

> ... the esthetic is no intruder in experience from without, whether by the way of idle luxury or transcendent ideality, ... it is the clarified and intensified development of traits that belong to every normally complete experience. This fact I take to be the only secure basis upon which esthetic theory can build.[116]

Every experience is derived from an object which then prompts us to react aesthetically, though we may, because of its everydayness not be particularly aware of it. This is best understood from the commonness of nature's beauty that we experience but of which we are not always aware. Experience of the aesthetic, to be understood and felt requires attention and receptiveness. But it is not a mysterious attitude. We must simply allow it to 'sink in'. Then we also will be aware of the fact that understanding is not only influenced by the aesthetic but is actually part of it. The aesthetic is part of the meaning of something.

It may be noticed that I talk of 'the aesthetic of experience' rather than, what is often simply used, 'aesthetic experience'.[117] The aesthetic of experience, as a state of mind, is not an activity. The aesthetic is the outcome of judgment about an experience. It is value related and must await the completion of some increments of perceptual and conceptual occurrences, if not the end of their full sequence. In addition, every experience as result is more than 'aesthetic experience' can indicate. In other words, there is no such experience by itself, not as activity nor as result. It is always part of a holistic one and contributes importantly. *Every experience has an aesthetic dimension.*[118] There is the world from which we derive pleasure or displeasure, resulting in states of mind we call aesthetic. From this point of view I believe that there is nothing called art as such but only more or less properties in anything that we may call artistic, given consciously or not, to evoke in us the aesthetic of experience accordingly. This shall obviously not mean that art and what we understand it to be has to vanish but that it is not a realm for itself except as an institution of activities, among an indefinite number of less explicit others, that have aesthetic concerns.

John Dewey called his pragmatic book on aesthetics *Art as Experience*. He could as well have called it the 'Aesthetics of every Experience', as he is right in pointing out that everything we encounter triggers in us more or less what we call the aesthetic of experience or simply the aesthetic. I do not address art in my account to any extent. It provides often heightened occasions for the aesthetic of experience. On the other hand, there is no reason to believe that what we feel as the aesthetic of art is different from the aesthetic we feel from anything else. Susan Langer writes

> ... a work of art does not point us to a meaning beyond its own presence. What is expressed cannot be grasped apart from the sensuous or poetic form that expresses it. In a work of art we have the direct presentation of feeling.[119]

Like everything else a work of art points us more or less to a meaning beyond its own presence. Even when highly abstract it points at least to stylistic tendency and aesthetic appreciation. The portrait of a person may point to the appearance, for me becoming a meaning, of that person in addition to possibly other aspects of the work. We have representation. Whose feeling is involved? It is the 'embedded feeling' of the artist given as partial content represented by the work's properties and in part re-felt by me. My feeling arises from the exposure to the work. So, there is the artist's feeling, my feeling and a medium in between. Feelings are in people and other animate creatures, not in things which cannot feel. When I present a gift it represents my feeling. The gift is not a feeling, it is a sign of it. It indicates the feeling by what is presented. A feeling is a "direct presentation" only in ourselves and in others by themselves.

Every state of mind is the result of an experience of conceptualization and feeling in combination. Our eventual state of mind is understanding, including the aesthetic. From this point of view I stand with Roger Scruton who titled a whole book *The Aesthetic Understanding*. He writes at the beginning of his account with regard to Kant and Hegel that

> Both philosophers were convinced, … that aesthetic judgment is no arbitrary addendum to human capacities, but a consequence of rationality, a bridge between the sensuous and the intellectual, and an indispensable means of access to the world of ideas.[120]

The aesthetic judgment is a subjective "consequence of rationality" after the process of conceptualization. What we conceptualize as content is judged on whether we like it or not. And then "aesthetic understanding" happens whether we are aware of it or not. As all understanding has an aesthetic component, I avoid the terminology of "aesthetic understanding". There is absolutely nothing aesthetic by itself. There is always something which causes it to arise in us.

The process to all understanding, shown in 4.1, can be shown simplified with perception and conception being the emotion-reason process and understanding (including aesthetic) being the concept-with-feeling result (4.14). We must remember, however, that the aesthetic is not a component which at the end of the process arrives and prompts our judgment on whether we like an object or not. The object is usually complex and our understanding requires multiple observations which eventually coalesce into a more or less complete whole. Each step along the way has its own aesthetic judgment and aesthetic result. As this iterative process is so common, we become only aware of it when, depending on circumstances, we must make a special effort to look at many aspects of the complexity and, thereupon, are reasonably satisfied to have sufficiently comprehended the whole.

object ▶ sensation ▶ perception and conception ▶ understanding (including aesthetic)

4.14 The path to understanding including aesthetic influence

To confirm that emotional and rational influences are at work more or less in all expressions and impressions one needs only perceive any present object or think about any earlier experienced object. Simply look around you or recall from memory, and reflect on what we just discussed. The result of your understanding will always show that an aesthetic component is involved.

Kant's view in matters of beauty and aesthetics, a necessary extension of his critiques on pure and practical reason, has formed a crucial background for anyone who has since contemplated related aspects. All the basic questions are asked by that time. But the answers are controversial and proliferated since Kant by the extensive broadening and specialization as reflected in the increase of museum collections of art, the rise of art criticism, the detection of aesthetic values in education, manufacturing, commerce, fashion, etc., even politics.

Throughout the history of inquiries about the beautiful, the arts were deemed to be a special place for it. But this relationship intensified with the investigations of Baumgarten, Kant and especially Georg F. Hegel (1770-1831). The latter stakes out his positions on beauty with particular regard to the arts; arts viewed in the modern, organized sense (architecture, sculpture, painting, music, literature, theater, etc.). At the beginning of his lectures on aesthetics he states that

> These lectures are devoted to *Aesthetics*. Their topic is the wide *realm of beauty*, more precisely *art*, and particularly the *fine arts*. For this topic, though, the name *Aesthetics* is not quite right, because *'Aesthetics'* more exactly signifies the science of sensation, of *feeling*, ... the feelings of pleasure, admiration, fear, pity and so on.[121]

Hegel acknowledges that aesthetics are broad in scope but shies away from looking into the possibility of common features of the aesthetic in all we encounter or bring forth. Aesthetics in the arts is what interests him and what he addresses. He asserts, not found in Kant, that

> ... the beauty of art is higher than nature. The beauty of art is beauty *born and reborn out of the spirit,* and the higher the spirit and its productions stand than nature and its appearances the higher also is the beauty of art than the beauty of nature.[122]

He separates here 'apples and oranges', that is, "beauty of art" versus "beauty of nature", and then asserts on this basis that "the beauty of art" is higher. He does not give a proof for this and I believe nobody can. Yes, "beauty of art is beauty born and reborn out of the spirit". So is all other beauty. He claims that

> Art ... and its works, as sprung from and begotten by the spirit, are of mental nature themselves, even so their representation assumes the appearance of sensuousness and suffuses the sensuous with spirit.[123]

Works of art are spiritual, though by necessity they come in sensual form to be communicated. For him, beauty is in sensuous form and impacts us on that account. But it does so because of *what* the form expresses, that is, the content of the object, the rationale of the concept. He writes that

> If now indeed the beautiful is to be grasped in its essence and its concept, this can happen only by means of conceptual thought, through which the logical-metaphysical nature of the *idea overall* and the particular *idea of the beautiful* enters our thinking consciousness.[124]

Therefore,

> ... the idea and its appearance, the reputation and the excellence of art, according to its conceptual reality, will depend on the degree of fervor and unity into which idea and appearance are combined as to seem one and the same.[125]

I agree, although not quite with his last sentence. The unity of idea and appearance of an object, its content and its form, does not have to be combined "to seem one and the same". They are inevitably so. The form of a tree can only have the content (the concept) of tree. The form of a house can only have the content of house (or it is not the form of a house). A church turned into a restaurant will have features (content, concept) of a restaurant, though some church-like features may remain. A form which does not express much definable content is abstract and self-referential, as mentioned earlier. On the other hand, I do not know any better justification for my views about the total content-form unity of objects and the aesthetic necessarily arising out of it – though not only in art but in anything we encounter – than when Hegel writes that

> All that exists is only truth as far as it is an existence of the idea.[126]

Truth (reality) is existence (form) of its idea (content). For Hegel the idea reveals itself in the unity of the concept and its reality, its experiential form. But then he advocates the extreme that

> Beauty defines itself through the *luminance* of the idea.[127]

Not only, but through our judgment of the object overall, luminous or otherwise. And then he even claims that

> ... reason always remains finite, one-sided and untrue. In contrast beauty is in itself *infinite* and free.[128]

This view makes beauty fully independent and does not acknowledge that beauty depends on our necessarily subjective, but reasoned judgment. The aesthetic and what we call beauty is not independent in general and especially not from objects we relate to because of the nature and necessity of judgment as part of our emotional and rational being. Beauty is not "free".

Hegel's aesthetics is heavily indebted to Kant's, not least for contrasting his own views. For him, nature with its material reality has its beauty but the ultimate beauty expressed is that of the idea given by the spirit, never more than through the arts. But for Kant, beauty arises not out of the idea of the object alone but from the play of imagination while perceiving the object and the related judgment of feelings of pleasure or displeasure. For Hegel beauty is grounded primarily in the ideality of objects, for Kant primarily in the feeling about appearance because of objective and subjective influences.

That the unity of concept and appearance should be considered the idea of beauty was even before Hegel expressed by Friedrich Schiller (1759-1805), who deemed that the search for the beautiful brings the sensuous and the rational together through exposure to the arts and related education. Through art, reality and ideality may become one. In his letters *On the Aesthetic Education of Man,* he longs for an imperative:

> Beauty ought to let itself to be revealed as a necessary condition of humanity.[129]

We might progress in three stages:

> Man in his physical condition suffers merely the power of nature; he rids himself of this power in the aesthetic condition, and he controls it in the moral condition.[130]

He adds an important dimension which has proven itself not least in architectural development. His findings show the lively connection between, what I earlier described, the interplay between impressions of observation and expressions of design:

> The sensuous impulse wants to be determined, it wants to receive its object; the formative impulse wants itself to determine, it wants to bring forth its object. Therefore the impulse of play wants to receive as it itself would have brought forth and bring forth as its sensuousness wants to receive.[131]

This line of thought is very much an extension into that field of aesthetics to which Kant pointed with his notion of imagination in concept development. For Schiller the impulse of play is a fundamental part of human nature:

> For, eventually to say it, man plays only where he is man in the full meaning of the word, and he is entirely man only where he plays.[132]

In connection with Kant, Hegel and Schiller, one of their contemporaries needs mentioning: Arthur Schopenhauer (1788-1860). His position is grounded in Kant's view of things in themselves, in what things are beyond what is observable. But he goes beyond Kant by claiming that we can approach things in themselves through experiencing the aesthetic, especially through the arts. After explaining his dual view of the world as *Ideas* being objects for us subjects, and as *Will* being manifested in the objects, he summarizes that

> In accordance with this knowledge we called the world as idea, both as a whole and in its parts, the objectification of will, which therefore means the will become object, i.e., idea. Further, we remember that this objectification of will was found to have many definite grades, in which, with gradually increasing distinctness and completeness, the nature of will appears in the idea, that is to say, presents itself as object.[133]

Will is desire, urge, motivation but also origin. It is energy in all its possible states. From this point of view it is easy to understand why Schopenhauer conflates will and thing in itself as fundamental conditions of being. After elaboration on Kant's concept of things in themselves and Plato's concept of Ideas he finds that

> ... the will is for us [in effect] the thing-in-itself ...

And,

> ... we find that Kant's thing-in-itself, and Plato's Idea, ..., these two great obscure paradoxes of the two greatest philosophers of the West are not indeed identical, but yet very closely related, ...[134]

Eventually, Schopenhauer points to where deepest immersion in contemplation occurs, where pure essence is revealed and satisfaction is whole. He contrasts this state with instances of science for which never comprehensive resolution is possible.

> All these, of which the common name is science, proceed according to the principle of sufficient reason in its different forms, and their theme is always the phenomenon, its laws, connections, and the relations which result from them. But what kind of knowledge is concerned with that which is outside and independent of all relations that which alone is really essential to the world, the true content of its phenomena, that which is subject to no change, and therefore is known with equal truth for all time, in a word, the *Ideas*, which are the direct and adequate objectivity of the thing-in-itself, the will? We answer, *Art*, the work of genius. It repeats or reproduces the eternal Ideas grasped through pure contemplation, the essential and abiding in all the phenomena of the world; and according to what the material is in which it reproduces, it is sculpture or painting, poetry or music. Its one source is the knowledge of Ideas; its one aim the communication of this knowledge.[135]

This is perhaps the most radical claim ever given to the arts, giving them a singular privileged position as a means to deepest understanding and contributing strongly to art as institution. Schopenhauer envisions the understanding of pure "*Ideas*, which are the direct and adequate objectivity of the thing in-itself, the will ..." to be the foundation of "*Art*, the work of genius". This is a position I strongly oppose believing that the aesthetic is evoked in us more or less by everything we encounter and judge. It lets us reflect on what content may be in its unity with form and how far we can understand it. While I enjoy the arts and believe they can give us many ways of reaching deeper understanding than otherwise had, I do not believe that it can break the barriers to the nature of things in themselves better than science. We can never reach the level of Platonic Ideas, the absolute of anything. There are simply limits in understanding. Somewhere along the way belief or maybe even faith must take over, if we want to cross the barriers. Schopenhauer does not spend a word on emotion in this immediate context (which one should expect). On the other hand, will is intentional, and is actively involved in everything we are doing, also in art, and we may concede that will is emotional, while often instinctive, especially in the fundamental and comprehensive role in which Schopenhauer sees it.[136]

The views discussed from Plato to Schopenhauer provide a broad base from which many diverse positions emerge during the 19th and 20th century. The fundamentals, as far as we are concerned, are laid out. This by no means shall indicate that great contributions have not been made by thinkers like Karl Marx, Friedrich Nietzsche, John Dewey, Benedetto Croce, George Santayana, Robin Collingwood, Monroe Beardsley, Clive Bell, Rudolf Arnheim, Roger Scruton, Arthur Danto, Umberto Eco, Paul Guyer, Mary Mothersill and many others.[137] It is not the place here, however, to discuss these various positions but reference will be given to them, when for us pertinent.

In summary, I emphasize another time the difference between the beautiful and the aesthetic: Beauty does not exist without an object because a subject must experience an object to feel pleasure. Beauty and pleasure have their ground in our intentionality, our awareness of an object, even if it is only in a dream. They are affective response to our sensuous exposure of the object and are psychological in nature. Beauty does not exist without an observer because if there is no subject, there is no feeling, and without feeling there is no beauty. *More broadly, the aesthetic is any instance of state of mind between the extremes of pleasure and displeasure because of the encounter with an object, a state of affairs.* This means for architecture – arguably the least institutionalized and the most practical of the arts – to find what constitutes the aesthetic in and for the present setting, being pleasant or not. Architecture is not mainly art to look at. It is lived-in art and, therefore, more than any other art impacted and constrained by the forces of environment, history, urbanization, commerce, technology, finance, etc. and this in times of rising mass production and consumption. The positioning of art vis-à-vis all these other demands in architecture underlies stronger than in any other field the debates of aesthetic concerns.

4.4 Objects and 'their' aesthetics

At least since Shaftesbury and Hutcheson the issue of value judgment on aesthetics from the experience of an object has been explicitly raised.[138] Kant made it an important aspect in his aesthetics when writing that

> *Taste* is the faculty for judging an object or a kind of representation through a satisfaction or dissatisfaction *without any interest.* The object of such a satisfaction is called *beautiful.*[139]

And,

> ... the subjective aspect in a representation *which cannot become an element of cognition at all* is the *pleasure* or *displeasure* connected with it; ...[140]

And,

> That is *beautiful* which pleases universally without concept.[141]

Kant claims that we decide about the beautiful not by means of understanding – which is for him only the result of conceptualization – but "by means of imagination (perhaps combined with understanding)".[142] The qualification in parenthesis points toward a potential impact of understanding depending on circumstances, but he does not elaborate on how the "perhaps combined with understanding" works and comes about. Kant is naturally aware that many objects are conceptually connected with interest which influences our judgment. He writes that

> There are two kinds of beauty: free beauty and merely adherent beauty. The first presupposes no concept of what the object ought to be; the second does presuppose such an object and the perfection of the object in accordance with it. The first are called (self-subsisting) beauties of this or that thing; the latter, as adhering to a concept (conditioned beauty), are ascribed to objects that stand under the concept of a particular end.[143]

This dual track view is the main reason for my opposition to parts of Kant's aesthetic theory. He reserves the terms understanding and also cognition only for the process and result of conceptualization. I do not. And, I do not believe in free beauty. Kant explains on the same page that "In the judging of a free beauty (according to mere form) the judgment of taste is pure." I believe there is nothing like "mere form", except as platonic ideal. All forms have content of interest, as abstract as they may be (nothing is absolutely abstract, if it exists). We can describe a Piet Mondrian painting as 'abstract'. But its geometric configuration is content. Or the material of which an abstract sculpture is made has a conceptual content of what it is physically. Every form represents (through properties), even if it does represent only itself.

One of the problems that we easily overlook in analysis is the fact that we usually are, even in apparently simple cases, concerned with complex issues and circumstances in which components always are together with others in wide or narrow context. This is strongly the case in architecture and needs to be kept in mind not only for what we observe as such but for judgment about it. Therefore, the aesthetic of experience also occurs usually in complex circumstances.

Emotional and rational influences do not happen separately.[144] Representation happens in our mind which contains memory, the store house of earlier experienced content-form unities. Thoughts from memory interact with the thought structure of representation. While our sensations may be without interest, our emotions and reasons in dealing with them are not. We are never starting with a tabula rasa mind, not even as children. Our evolution as a species saw to that. Earlier experiences, even when we do not explicitly acknowledge their remembrance, are the background of our emotions and reasons. Their influences on judgment are inevitable and difficult to sort out. Our approach to form is part reactive, instinctive, and part teleological, goal-oriented, therefore with interests. Friedrich Nietzsche makes this point bluntly with regard to aesthetics, though perhaps stronger than many of us would, when he writes:

> Against Kant. Naturally I am also connected with the beautiful which pleases me through *an interest*. But this is not nakedly apparent. The expression of happiness, perfection, stillness, even the silence and the letting-itself-to-be-judged of the art work, they all speak to our *instincts*. – In the end I experience as "beautiful" only what complies with an ideal ("*the happiness*") of my own instincts ...[145]

We must also remember that, according to Kant, and I agree, understanding presupposes imagination to bring about concepts. Imagination ties the whole process together. It is the play of thoughts which requires judgment to complete the process of understanding. Disinterestedness would require pure judgment of appearance of form without any contemplation of content. But such truncation is not possible.

Based on Kant's view of "free" (disinterested) beauty and "adherent" (interested) beauty many proposals as to their individual and combined pleasantness have been advanced. Recently Paul Guyer, Robert Wicks and others speak of one pleasure derived from an object's form and another from its function which we combine into overall pleasure.[146] This constellation serves as well as any to explain more thoroughly my disagreement with Kant on his "free" versus "adherent". The former would be absolute, unconditioned. The latter is relative, conditioned, usually multi-grounded. To be possible at all, beauty is adherent, causatively connected with something. Our interest may be strong or weak depending on the object, its circumstances and our understanding. But it always exists.

I don't believe that there is any mental representation which is not conditioned and beauty is a reaction caused by understanding the representation – instinctively and reflectively. Instinctively caused does not mean free, as instinct has an existing, subconscious background. Further, we cannot stop intentionality, which is our directedness toward objects, without conceiving content after perceiving form. Let's assume I know nothing about how seashells come about and exist (purpose, function, etc.). When I find one which I appraise as very beautiful: is my feeling about it a disinterested aesthetic, here free beauty? No, because various kinds of associations come to mind, such as circles, undulations, proportions and colors, resulting in desires. Beauty and every shade of the aesthetic of experience has its grounding in what is observed and what is remembered from precedents. Whether we want or not, we cannot be disinterested, as long as intentionality lasts. Maybe a better term for disinterestedness would be detachment. We never can detach ourselves completely from associative aspects. Sensation comes to us through perceiving form but always with content, in whatever way we end up understanding it.

From all of this I derive that every process of understanding including its aesthetic component is entangled with interest. Anything observed or designed cannot belong in the category of disinterestedness; even less, anything so strongly purposive, as architecture. I find my view reinforced when Arnold Berleant writes that

> I contend that modern aesthetics, insofar as it is grounded on disinterestedness and related notions, is obsolescent if not altogether obsolete. It cannot adequately account for much in the contemporary development of the arts, for the aesthetic appeal of the natural world, or for the aesthetic manifestations of industrial cultures. The aesthetics of disinterestedness offers an escape from those domains rather than an enlivening understanding of how art works. …

He sees disinterestedness among the notions which

> … in aesthetics lead to serious pitfalls. One is the transformation of experience into an intellectual puzzle that compromises the perceptual immediacy at the heart of aesthetic. Another is the tendency to fragment the aesthetic situation into separate elements, typically the beholder on one side and the art object on the other, elements that then need to be related and reconciled. Such a division has created many of the "problems" that dog much philosophical aesthetics, among them problems concerning emotion, representation, expression, and the like. Characterizing appreciation as ideally contemplative is misleading and unnecessary. An activist, participatory sense of aesthetic appreciation does not exclude an attitude of thoughtful, receptive regard when that is conjoined with intense, focussed attention to the ongoing course of experience.[147]

Disinterestedness is a helpful concept for the discussion and sorting out of what happens. But it is an ideal which is not achievable. Even purely decorative embellishment attached to architecture is designed and observed with interest, in one way or another. But Roland Hepburn writes in response to Berleant that

> … with aesthetic appreciation of nature: we suspend our utility-dealings with nature, suspend equally our pleasure-seeking recreational encounter with it, and disinterestedly appreciate nature's own qualities.[148]

With regard to any appreciation, we may be able to push back to some extent our "utility-dealing" and "pleasure-seeking" for concentrating on what is at hand. But we never can completely suspend them. Even through deepest contemplation of anything, we cannot suspend our being from worldly relationships. While we encounter and observe reality, we understand it aesthetically as representation in our mind. We do not suddenly have, being part of an experience, a second mind because we contemplate 'a piece of art', nature or whatever. This does not exclude that we experience on various intensity levels.[149]

The rejection of aesthetic disinterestedness implies that there is no unencumbered judgment. Interest influences aesthetic judgment by way of reason. In other words, we cannot prevent reason from influencing emotion on the way to understanding. Nor can we, as earlier discussed, prevent emotion from influencing reason to do so. Emotion and reason are interdependent. They play off each other incrementally, but we cannot determine how. This aspect reinforces the broader view that there cannot be fully objective judgment overall as emotion is potentially even more subjective than reason.

The content-form unity brings forth one beauty or ugliness for every chosen or given frame of reference. Sorting out how much individual properties contribute is a process of breaking the frame of reference into smaller increments and letting their intuitions evoke aesthetics accordingly. In other words, when we perceive an object, we have sequential impressions. Any experience has a duration, though it may be rather short; sometimes so short that we may believe it is instantaneous. We should take into account that during the emotion-reason process understanding coalesces at high speed over the short distances in our brain. Therefore, during contemplation of the object the tokens of understanding develop with their judgments occurring often before sensation has completely finished. The aesthetic aspects arise along the way of the process. But the aesthetic of a whole is not simply a sum of the aesthetics of its parts. I appreciate Berleant's concern given in the second quote. Mutual influences occur which cannot be completely traced and assessed. This is, however, a part of our inability to grasp experience in full. Still, we know from many encounters that *aesthetic appreciation is holistic*, however far we may understand the experience.

The emotion-reason process is based on representation of the object in our mind. Therefore, our judgments are not judgments on the object directly but indirectly by way of its representation. The representation is influenced by more than the form of the object, because it is in unity with the content, and it is impossible to restrict our mind to sense only and not to allow it to think about what was sensed. Our perception relates to form and our conception to content but our judgment relates to them together. When we say 'I like this form', even when we may not like the material of which it is made, we make two interrelated judgments. Moreover, there is context as part of content about which we will have to say considerably more, especially with regard to architecture. It influences the appearance of the content-form unity at the time of perception. For example, inevitable and perhaps undesirable light or sound influence the understanding of a building and sometimes the happenings in it.

Examining the sequence of occurrences in 4.1 and 4.14 yields helpful explanations of the process. Our experiences relate to the essence of the object in all its perceivable manifestations. Therefore and in reference to the comprehensive Greek meaning of perception, we may as well confirm naming those results of the experience which are the intermediate or ending feelings of our mind and body as to pleasure or displeasure about an object: *the aesthetic*.

There is an important observation which Mary Mothersill makes and which we may review here to advantage. She writes that the following proposition needs no argument but is commonplace derived from experience and observation:

(1) Beauty is a kind of good, a 'positive' value.
(2) Beauty is linked with pleasure: what we take to be beautiful we enjoy. The converse does not hold, since we enjoy things that we do not think beautiful or even seemly.[150]

I agree with most what she says about beauty, but not with the qualifying ending of the second claim. My main reason for the exception is derived from our earlier discussion and my view that the aesthetic, including beauty, is a state of the mind in reaction to perception: *beauty is not cause but effect*. Beauty is not only "linked" with pleasure. It is effect as *affect,* different from individual to individual, often even varies over time for the same individual. Beauty is a "value" as Mothersill says and I agree. It is an effect we judge. Objects have properties and values, the latter being subjectively given by us through judgment because of properties. Whether "The converse does not hold" is true depends on the definition of beauty. For me *what is pleasant is beautiful*. It has the value of being so, at least with regard to the particular phenomenon under consideration. As beauty is value, result of pleasure, it is pleasure-dependent. There is only one pleasure, though it comes from different perceptions and in variations of intensity, depending on properties of the cause. "The converse does not hold" is only true if beauty is an innate property of things, which I do not believe. I have not found anything which I enjoy which is not beautiful as a value and that is all which beautiful implies. What I enjoy is beautiful by definition. This does not only apply for the beautiful as high value but for the whole range of the aesthetic from beautiful to ugly. What I do not enjoy is for me not beautiful, perhaps even ugly.

The problem with the term beauty in aesthetics has been its wrongly attributed status as property, material or mental, of objects instead of value, which arises out of our judgment. We associate values with things, not so much for what they are but for what they mean to us, though the latter follows from the former subjectively. This is also the reason that we may call something beautiful, whether it is considered a piece of art (in the narrow sense) or not. Judgment on pleasure as value, aesthetic judgment, may relate to anything, an artifact, a dream or whatever, even a horrible occurrence; for example, in the quality of a theater performance.

Beauty as effect of a particular object may change slowly or quickly while the properties on which that judgment was based do not. I mentioned earlier the example of the Golden Section. Our being affected changed. Another example, we may be pleased by looking at exceptionally well arranged food on a plate in front of us and call it beautiful because of our judgment on its visual appearance and the pleasure we derive from it. This value may lose its 'power' because of another affect, giving displeasure, when we find that the food is overly salty. Here the complexity of affects from various properties influences the overall effect; obviously a common occurrence in any complex situation, such as in architecture. The pleasure about a building may change considerably from experiencing its exterior to experiencing its interior. From this line of thought we derive that beauty and ugliness usually arrive out of complexity, sometimes being only temporary and always dispositional, in the sense that they are qualities dependent on the presence of pleasure or displeasure respectively. I am also in agreement with Mothersill that

> ... there are no serious laws of taste and that, without laws, the conception of principles (or criteria) assumes an unattractively arbitrary aspect. There is the added fact that those who believe there must be principles have not been able to say what they are, ...[151]

But this does not mean, and history shows many examples, that during certain times principles of taste have not been proposed, and accepted, even enforced, and endured as socially, ideologically or religiously necessary. Beauty is always an effect from impression not a 'material' for expression. There is nothing like ready-made beauty to be applied. In design as in general life, we test properties, and through their impression on us judge them as to their aesthetic value. If we like them and they fit, we let them contribute in projecting realization and expression.

An insufficiently treated aspect in the aesthetics of architectural design is the extent of how we physically interact with our immediate environments and how representation and interpretation may be influenced by the multiplicity of meaning. What is considered to be the aesthetic is largely dominated by visual judgment to the point that it usually has control status. It does not help when accompanying texts are only descriptive rather than analytic. For example, there is often an uneasy relationship between building physics or ergonomics and what is claimed for positive aesthetics.

Form contains always more than visual qualities. It represents the totality of physical appearance, though often dominated by certain particulars. The aesthetic of hearing, touch, smell, taste and associated ergonomic issues require consideration. An example may help. Paul Goldberger wrote in connection with retrospectives of Mies van der Rohe's work in 2001: "His only real interest was in physical form, and he was fanatical in his search for ways to perfect it."[152] Visual perfection that is. But Mies' "Less is more" is simply not enough. His Lake Shore Drive Apartments in Chicago are not comfortable to live in, or were not when built, especially during very cold temperatures outside (5.18). Sitting in his famous lounge chair for a while gives an understanding of his neglect of comfort in favor of look.[153] The aesthetic is relative to our present and overall physical and mental experiences.

While most of our communication with our environments is visual, there are the other senses which contribute strongly to our experiences. Kenneth Frampton writes that

> One has in mind a whole range of complementary sensory perceptions which are registered by the labile body; the intensity of light, darkness, heat and cold; the feeling of humidity; the aroma of material; the almost palpable presence of masonry as the body senses its own confinement; the momentum of an induced gait and the relative inertia of the body as it traverses the floor; the echoing resonance of our own footfall.[154]

These eminently sensory perceptions are part of what we encounter as consequences of form. We may believe them to be on the fringes of what we call aesthetic effects but they often become crucial in our experience of physical environments. Sometimes our understanding of them is highly aesthetic and we like or dislike them without further analysis. All attempts to isolate the aesthetic as a single feature of an object fail. Marston Fitch writes that

> ... a fundamental weakness in most discussions of architectural esthetics is a failure to relate it to its matrix of experiential reality. Our whole literature suffers from this conceptual limitation since it tends to divorce the esthetic process from the rest of experience, as though it were an abstract problem in pure logic. Thus we persist in discussing buildings as though their esthetic impact upon us were an exclusively visual phenomenon. And this leads to serious misconceptions as to the actual relationship between the building and its human occupants.[155]

Understanding as meaning is the result of engaging our whole being. We get not only acquainted with the object but become familiar with it. What we are talking about here is in part directed toward efforts in a field which Richard Shusterman has called *somaesthetics,* somatic aesthetics, that is, aesthetics of the well-being and appearance of the human body with all its senses. He writes:

> ... somaesthetics seems to cut across the whole range of aesthetic genres. This is because it treats the body not only as an *object* of aesthetic value and creation, but also as a crucial sensory *medium* for enhancing our dealings with all other aesthetic objects and also with matters not standardly aesthetic.[156]

Concern about our body in this respect improves sensory perception and related conceptualization, and broadens our basis for environmental design. The result is an appreciation of all design qualities and with it enhancement of form toward comprehensive experience. At any time of our being, consciously and subconsciously, we experience the world and ourselves somaesthetically, based on all we may sense and feel. Sometimes it helps to refer to negatives to imply that there exist also opposites. In this direction, somaesthetics may be crucial in assessing lack of lighting, glare of a light source, noise interference, stuffiness because of insufficient ventilation, drafty air movement, prolonged confinement in a windowless space, poor color combination, etc. Positively, I perhaps cannot better exemplify the wide range of felt experiences but by telling about a cold winter day in Taos Pueblo and observing there a resident who was warmed by the sun and the reradiating adobe wall while observing and contemplating contently what happened around him (4.15 and 4.16). To such broader meaning also belongs the bodily enjoyment of a concert in Scharoun's Philharmonic Hall, Berlin, with spatial impressions lingering from the approach through its crossing stairs in the foyer, or savoring the fragrance and expectation while being surrounded by eclecticism in Heinrich von Ferstel's Café Central, Vienna (4.17 and 4.18).

4.15 and 4.16 Taos Pueblo, New Mexico

4.17 Philharmonic Hall, Berlin, foyer   4.18 Café Central, Vienna

To conclude. Taking into account our present terminological situation I try to be as clear as possible in my use of the terms aesthetic and beauty. My explanations throughout this book and in short below are not definitions of *what* the aesthetic and beauty are as such, as I believe this is not possible. I believe that the closest we can get to what they are is by explanations of *how* they are implicated in states of consciousness and meaning:

1. Representations in our mind are the substance of understanding. They evoke in us the aesthetic, the feeling of pleasure or displeasure.
2. As representations come in content-form unity, the two parts of understanding which arise from emotion and reason come to us interdependently. We can understand content only by means of its form. This may be why the aesthetic of experience has been associated mainly with form alone, which I believe is untenable.
3. As all of meaning, the aesthetic is not a property of objects or affairs but has its ground only in them. The aesthetic of something arises out of the impact its properties have positively or negatively on our judgment about it.
4. Beauty is that aesthetic which gives us pleasure. Ugliness is that aesthetic which gives us displeasure.
5. The aesthetic arises from content and form. Even minimal content has physical, financial, ethical, etc. implications. Therefore, judgments and the aesthetics of experience cannot be disinterested. The whole range of instances from beauty to ugliness cannot be "pure" or "free" but only "adherent" to aspects associated with the object.
6. The aesthetic comes about because of what we believe the properties of objects are and do. Experiencing it as result from decisions on properties, which we and others make, is crucial guidance in future design work with practical and ethical dimensions.
7. Pleasure or displeasure as indication of the aesthetic influence on understanding, which an object evokes in us, is often qualified by associating connotations from emotional or behavioral circumstances, comfort conditions, or even material properties, such as exciting, uplifting, cool, soft, rhythmic, challenging, morose, unsettling, vulgar, hard, brutal and forbidding. Many of these expressions are obviously meant metaphorically.
8. As all our understanding of things beyond us, that is, from objects and their surroundings, comes to us via physical sensation, that is somaesthetically, its combined physiological and psychological effect is a crucial part of our overall feeling of pleasure or displeasure.
9. My comprehensiveness of the aesthetic, as discussed here, denies that there is, on one hand, a pragmatic and, on the other, an aesthetic approach to architecture. To arrive at the aesthetic of architecture or anything else we judge what we encounter in unity. If this would not be so, one might agree with Karsten Harries that
    > ... on the aesthetic approach the beauty of a building has to appear as something added on to what necessity dictates, as decoration in a broad sense. The tensions that result from this mingling of pragmatic and aesthetic concerns all but rule out the aesthetic completeness.[157]
10. We judge what we encounter at a particular time as completeness and in unity which lets arise one related aesthetic, even if it concerns one part of a building only. Against Ruskin, Pevsner and many others with a different view of completeness I claim that decoration does not make a building into architecture, although it may among other things enhance its aesthetic appeal, as will be discussed in the next chapter. Peter Zumthor has it right when he said recently:
    > I think the chance of finding beauty is higher if you don't work on it directly. Beauty in architecture is driven by practicality. ... If you do what you should, then at the end there is something which you can't explain maybe, but if you are lucky, it has to do with life.[158]

We better be lucky, because architecture always has to do with life.

From this chapter we can derive that all mental concepts are influenced by aesthetic judgment to become comprehensively understanding.[159] Overall, this view seems narrow, as it clearly limits where the aesthetic has its place and what it does, that is, only in and through the mental realm. But it seems also broad because it ties the aesthetic to the wide range of meaning which has its ground in matters corporeal and incorporeal, way beyond what is called art. What I call the aesthetic is a corollary of perception and conception in our mind. It is a dynamic and pragmatic consequence of experiencing judgments while observing things and designing things. William James writes about the pragmatic method that

> ... only an attitude of orientation, is what the pragmatic method means. *The attitude of looking away from first things, principles, 'categories,' supposed necessities; and of looking towards last things, fruits, consequences, facts.*[160]

True, in the process of making we look toward what we want to achieve. But in doing so we cannot attempt "looking away from first things". In design we look towards ends and utility, we define purpose, but this happens in context, in what we have available to achieve what we want, what we want first things to become. The comprehensiveness in our mind is supported by what we may call pragmatic aesthetics.

This chapter includes very few pictorial illustrations. Can one discuss issues of aesthetics and beauty independent from sensory stimulation? No, one cannot. And I do not think we have done that in the past pages. Each of us reading their content remembers experiences of the aesthetic. In whatever we do, we live by nature aesthetically. Any visual representation of architecture on these pages, or for that matter any other sensory experience, can be taken to prove the point. Sense and feel the chair you sit on or the space surrounding you. Or remember the buildings you walked toward this morning. Did they provide for pleasant or unpleasant experiences?

Architecture is highly complex in space, time and causation. It is a multistage setting for our perceptions and conceptions with ever changing forms appearing as we experience it in depth. Through this multiplicity, content through form gains center stage with unity in variety, not necessarily balanced but to a large extent coherent. In Schopenhauerian terms we may say: in consciousness, there is will to understand and to mean, and, with it, will to experience the aesthetic. We may add what the phenomenologist Maurice Merleau-Ponti states bluntly that

> Because we are in the world, we are condemned to meaning …
>
> ... To say that there exists rationality is to say that perspectives blend, perceptions confirm each other, a meaning emerges.[161]

We cannot escape meaning and our feelings with it. Meaning and its aesthetics are always part of conscious living.

5 Type, Style and Ornament

This chapter is in many ways a continuation of our discussion on aesthetics. For its foundation, however, we need to address in more detail the importance of resemblance for conceptualization. Every process of understanding yields a specific concept which we judge in regard to its generic features, that is, its commonality with other concepts. As we discussed earlier, there are two steps in conceptualization: sensible comprehension from intuition, the result of which is what Kant calls appearance, and conceptual classification based on resemblance. Both come into play continuously while we are conscious. From childhood on and as long as we are able to think, the process of understanding adds to our memory more and more specific concepts by referring to generic concepts. Classification based on conceptualization is a major tool of understanding and communication for all what we do. In our present concern it is also part of the way to come to types and styles.

5.1 Concepts and resemblances

There is a philosophical debate, documented in a sizable body of literature, which looks at implications of resemblance in terms of *particulars* and *universals*. I will not address the related issues beyond a short description of what I see this means in our context.[1] A particular is viewed as a separate and limited, therefore, distinctly individual item, something singled out. There are particulars within larger particulars depending on how broadly the frame of reference is defined. In other words, objects are made up of more or less particulars but can, as unified manifolds, be considered particulars themselves. Particulars are also called individuals. If any particulars are similar to particulars within or in other objects, though not identical, they are in addition considered universals. You and I, are individuals, having our own properties. But we are also universals, having in common similar properties; the most obvious being humans. We have, as Wittgenstein says, "family resemblances".[2] I believe my approach in explaining concepts by means of resemblances in connection with specific and generic aspects, rather than by means of particulars and universals, covers the field more clearly, especially for our purposes.

When the intuition of an object is being developed our understanding with the help of memory provides a specific concept which in part also belongs to a generic one. The specific properties, be they physical or relational, allow us to grasp wider contextual complexity in the analysis of perceptions and in the synthesis of conceptions, such as in design. Complex concepts are combinations of simpler ones. They are representations of objects with their properties. The classification of features depends on the comprehensiveness of the frame of reference we select which, in turn, is derived from the physical and intellectual environment one presently is concerned with. We may visualize this notion geometrically as nestled or sometimes as overlapping frames of reference.

As a simple example the generic and specific properties of a particular type of window may be verbally given in a dual column format:

generic	specific
operability	sliding
glass type	double pane
frame type	wood*
wood*	oak
color	red*
red*	bluish red
shape	square*
square*	2 ft x 2 ft
area	2 ft x 2 ft
. . . .	. . . .

The items with asterisks show as specifics as well as generics. The last two items in the columns show an example of a specific concept belonging to different generics. The items in the generic property column may for other objects be much more abstract than in a corporeal object like a window, such as for objects of organizational or social structures. Two generic examples are 'important' and 'pleasant'. Specifics which may belong to them respectively are 'unconditional' and 'most beautiful'. All complex objects have both specific and generic properties. And, to repeat, properties may be observable or relational. 'Sliding', in the window example, is specific and belongs to the generic group of 'operability'. As a relational property (possibility to slide) it depends on some observable property of the window frame, such as a certain edge shape and perhaps a certain hardware.

Now let's look at a wider context. A building, we may look at, has a roof, walls, windows, enclosed spaces, etc. similar to other buildings. These common features let us bring individual cognitions under the concept of building. That a certain building may have an arched entry door is a relatively rare feature of the concept of door; but 'door' as such is an extremely common feature. The arched door falls under the generic concept of arches and falls under the generic concept of doors. In contrast, a house and a neighboring house are individuations of the generic concept of house. Similar features do not imply complete identity. Individuation can arise from differences among similarities.

There is an essentially indefinite number of resemblances among objects and, therefore, also among their concepts. The more often they occur in our experiences the more familiar we are with them. Each particular concept, PC, has properties which are resemblances and properties which are not resemblances in relation to other members of a set:

PC = a, b, c, d, e, f ... z.
     resemblance   no resemblance

In an example for windows we may have six specific concepts (5.1). Each has various properties of which only those which have resemblances are identified. Other properties which have no resemblances within the domain of the six objects, therefore point to the outside of it, are marked collectively with z. There are very few completely unrelated properties and, if we would find them, they would be strange to us and would require, if they are crucial, original conceptualization. Using this, for simplicity rather limited, group of properties and being identified by the letters, as defined, the set of *single resemblance*s, SR, shows

SR = 2 c; 4 s; 3 al; 2 wo; 6 gl; 3 w; 2 b ... z.

The features with the higher numbers are most likely dominating in the conceptualization, such as glass (gl) and sliding type (s); not a surprise, as glass and frame dominate windows existentially. If however, weighting of importance of the characteristics is applied (not shown here), the result will be quite different. An example would be to hold the color for more important than the material. Other weighting may relate to times of crucial consideration, such as for shape and size during daytime versus nighttime appearance or utilization.

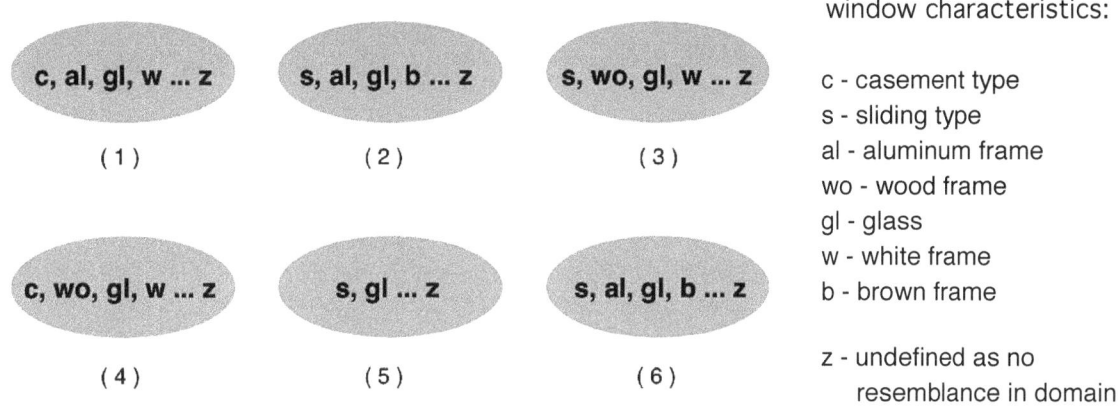

window characteristics:

c - casement type
s - sliding type
al - aluminum frame
wo - wood frame
gl - glass
w - white frame
b - brown frame

z - undefined as no resemblance in domain

Note: Every window by its very nature must have glass. One kind of window (5) is shown without a frame being a frameless sliding type.

5.1 Particular concepts and their properties

There are not only singular resemblances but also *cluster resemblances*, CR. Their listing, partial only, yields several semblance combinations, even in this simple example:

CR = 2 s, al, b; 1 c, wo, w; 3 al, gl; 2 wo, gl; 3 gl, w; 2 gl, b; ... z.

Interrelationships within the cluster combinations or between clusters and individual properties may exist and yield variations. The window frames of casement versus sliding windows may vary from each other because of interdependency of glass versus framing dimensions or because of how the frames appear (casement without overlap, sliding with overlap), etc. And then there are all the presently undefined combinations because of resemblances beyond the domain we are involved with, such as in neighborhood buildings.

As single resemblance is derived from all properties which occur in the set of particular concepts, it provides in abstraction (indicated by capital notation) and without weighting, the most rudimentary form of the total *generic concept* set, GC:

$GC_{1,2,3,4,5,6}$ = C; S; AL; WO; GL; W; B.

If only number (3) and (5) in Figure 5.1 should be members of the encountered set, its generic set would be

$GC_{3,5}$ = S; WO; GL; W

and for (1) and (5) it would be

$GC_{1,5}$ = C; S; AL; GL; W.

In encountering present objects, concepts come individually forth to allow discrimination and ordering for classification. It is an act of understanding to where each feature of the object belongs. The description of this rather simple example shows the enormous combinatorial framework within which we can classify properties through similarity relationships. The more objects of similar kinds we experience, the more extensive and detailed our stock of generic concepts is, although there obviously is a capacity limit which our individual memories have. Generic concepts exist in our memory, abstracted from specific ones, and increase in number over many years through further conceptualizations.

Looking at three rather diverse examples we find properties with and without resemblances, all in reference to the generic concept of entry: (1) One gets to the nave of the 12th century cloister church of Maulbronn, South Germany, from a plaza through an open narthex as transition; (2) The approach to a combined entry of a dentist's home and practice, by Kurt Brandle, also in South Germany, is via landscaping, breezeway and common entry hall. (3) The entry wall to the office building on 333 West Wacker Drive, Chicago, by Kohn Pedersen Fox, features a triple hinged door arrangement flanked by two revolving doors (5.2 to 5.4).

5.2 Maulbronn Abbey, Germany

5.3 Wöhrle Residence and Clinic, Weil am Rhein, Germany

5.4 333 Wacker Drive, Office Building, Chicago

These three examples show several concepts within the category of entries. One is observable in all three examples, our understanding of entry as the transition from outside to inside. All three provide some protective cover against inclement weather. Both concepts are particularly evident at Maulbronn where the transitional space also allows to collect one's thought before approaching a place of worship, to meet perhaps other worshippers before entering and to serve for overflow from the church at special occasions. The doors, usually the central component of an entry, are a nestled concept within the larger one. Resemblance of doors is observable at the residence and office building entries. It is only inferable at the monastery entry, but will reveal itself with the approach toward the narthex opening. This is a relational property (expected door) becoming observable. Two resemblances of door operations within an object is given by repetition of the three hinged units and the two revolving units at the office building entry, the hinged doors being more suitable to the physically challenged, when automated. The latter again is a relational concept, revealing itself only during operation.

Two single conceptual aspects at the residence entry which fall under 'z' (undefined resemblance) are the connection under roof cover from the entrance at right to a garage access at left (not visible) and the possibility to look at the entry from a window on the home's first floor. These two features are *relational* qualities made possible by physical properties of the design. There are other relational resemblances among all three. The most prominent of them is probably the inevitable expectation of finding some kind of interior space beyond the entries. What can be easily appreciated from this discussion is the enormous amount and complexity of conceptual processing our brain is capable of, and this in an extremely short time. What the examples also clearly show again is that all physical properties, which we observe and utilize, have relational consequences. *Everything we encounter has physical, observable properties, or we could not encounter it, and has relational properties, whether we think about them or not in a particular case.*

This dual nature of conceptualization is a profound feature of communication. We know that other people with whom we are in contact have experience with resemblance as well and, therefore, we are able to communicate with them about observable and relational properties. Charles Baylis writes:

> The existence of communicable knowledge requires shared meanings. Such knowledge, in its simplest form, is knowledge of the common characters exhibited by various objects and events. In the more advanced form of scientific knowledge it is knowledge of the interrelations of these characters in all their possible instances.[3]

When we walk toward a door, we conceptualize the physical properties of its door handle – shape at least and perhaps material – so that we may grasp it. But we typically do not conceptualize its relational properties, how it is fitting to our hand or how it contributes to the door closure, unless we become especially aware, perhaps because something unexpected occurs. This observation points to an important aspect: most relational properties are in the 'background' of our consciousness. Of most we become aware only when we are prompted; in our example, when we have a problem turning the door knob because of its less favorable shape compared to an easier graspable lever handle or because of the resistance of the door when locked. Relational properties often require more intensive thought input than observable ones. This raises an interesting point. We derive the relational aspects from directly observable ones. Is this relationship interrelational? David Lewis writes that

> … what is had by X relative to Y is not a property of X. It is a property of the pair (X,Y) – on my account, any relation is a property of pairs (or triples, or whatnot) that instantiates it.[4]

Generally, the activation part in relationships is not equivalent; often not even similar. For example, our visual relationship to a door. The door and our eyes are the involved parts with properties (capacities) to reflect and to sense light respectively. As far as understanding and meaning in architecture go, the observing side is the more active one, as being intentional. When we say that 'we perceive something which points beyond itself to something else', having a relational property, it is us who conceptualize the 'pointing'. But there is usually an interrelationship because the process of perception is iterative. After gaining understanding from sensation by the object 'giving' us information, we contemplate and then, when needed, return for more in depth sensation. In the observation of architecture we encounter physical properties first and then think about their relations. Differently in the design process. Here relational aspects and not aspects of form initiate the process. *In design we typically think about relational properties first and then search for suitable physical (observable and unobservable) choices.*

Particular concepts may be viewed to consist of complex or singular properties, depending on where we set the boundaries of the domain under consideration. Singular ones are only theoretically viable, as reality has never one property only. Properties are together with other properties. The minimum we conceptualize of every property is its physical nature and at least one relational property. The color red is a physical property of an object or it could not exist for us to be perceived. It has at least one relational aspect, such as reinforcing our impression of control by means of pressing a red panic button or simply being an aesthetic choice. And, there are contextual relationships. Everything is in some context. 'Red' reflects light in a certain wavelength, which makes it visible to us. This observable property is dispositional, that is, it depends on the availability of light and our being there to perceive it. Another observable property is being part of an other component, such as a steel surface of a fire hydrant. A basic aspect of these relationships is what we may call a 'condition of adjacency'. Every property is surrounded by at least one other property and both relate to each other physically by shape, temperature, adhesion, etc. The relational property of pointing elsewhere, such as red does to firefighting, is a functional one. So are many others, such as the paint protecting the steel of the hydrant.

Multiple observable and relational fit conditions of properties are what allows us to bind together complexity of understanding. They are the syntax which ties together semantic tokens into larger wholes. For David Hume the fit conditions are made possible by "resemblance", "contiguity" and "causation",

> … and as these are the only ties of our thoughts, they are really *to us* the cement of the universe, and all the operations of the mind must, in a great measure, depend on them.[5]

When we look at a floor plan and a section of a project, and envision the eventual realization of the building, we find that they were conceived together in give-and-take fashion and we understand them now through the reciprocation of their components in resemblance, contiguity and causation, tying all together in our mind. Proper correspondence of observable and relational properties is the prerequisite for syntax in architecture to succeed.

Many efforts have been undertaken in recent decades to gain an understanding of conceptualization. How do all these billions of large and small tokens come together in this small wobbly mass in our head, and produce in never resting fashion what we think that we see, hear, smell, taste or touch? The systems of the brain are sometimes referred to as architectures of the mind. They include more or less characteristics like tree structures, vectors in space, connectivity, modularity and composition. While I find these terms helpful for discourse about mental input/output and its representations from and for the worldly things, I consider them not enlightening in how our mind internally works. This is not to say that I believe that activities in conceptualization of the mind itself are not crucial, such as for experimentation in children's mental development or finding cures for diseases of the mind. As to the physicality of the brain-mind-consciousness existence I am simply happy to consider it an amorphous mass of information nodes which has the capacity to connect in lightning speed out of the billions of nodes those which fit, so that we may gain understanding and meaning through judgment.

The kinds of exercises as described on the past pages are tedious and not what we typically perform explicitly, but they help us here to demonstrate the infinite variability and complexity through which appearance and understanding come about. It never can mean that we itemize and list everything, though sometimes we do part of it extensively for practical purposes of analysis and communication. We use the split of observable form and relational content as categorization for innumerable subject classifications. As reference, for example, we sort a spatial program into functional needs and area requirements. As form we arrange floor plan adjacencies and geometries. We bring together and fit on the basis of observable and relational similarities. Such activities are a major part of our design efforts. We should again remember that form is more than shape. It is realization, here as design scheme developed from references to desired, preliminary attributes. Obviously another part of realization, with its own aspects of classifications, occurs during the construction phase.

Let us now observe an existing object rather than one we bring about through design and construction. Looking at a column, we experience its form. It may be round or square, wide or narrow, high or low, red or blue, etc.; all of this belonging to property classifications. To get at meaning we search for content by means of appearance what something is and does. To get at content we think about functions; not usually about many of them but in sufficient depth. The column accepts loads to bear, provides needed floor-to-ceiling height and spatial variability, allows demountable walls to be relocated, etc. All of these features belong to content property classifications, here because of functional relationships. We should keep in mind that what we presently observe is a member of a class which may have its similar counterparts in many other places. Classification is a mental construct which has no boundaries. As long as our memory has properties to compare with, it is able to classify.

Although similarity is, as Nelson Goodman pointed out, not something we can fashion into a tool for exact measurements, it is a necessary means in understanding and communication. Then it may well be as he concedes after warning about too much of similarity's allegedly very strong powers for understanding, which he thinks it does not possess:

> If statements of similarity ... cannot be trusted in the philosopher's study, they are still serviceable in the streets.[6]

Architecture and its design make certainly the case for the service rendered by aspects of similarity, be it in observation or projection.

It is important to consider that generic concepts change, though not as often as specific ones which by definition are highly individualized and change from instance to instance. But when generic concepts change they may have widespread and strong impact. When they change, potentially all related particular ones change also as their structural essence is what generics are about. In architecture such paradigmatic changes often are initiated from the outside. An example is the impact which the reforms of educational concepts had over the years on the generic planning concepts of school buildings. Here, generic concept changes in one field, education, brought about generic concept changes in another, architecture. At times, singular powerful events may trigger such changes. The arrival of the elevator and the automobile are strong examples, the elevator providing the impetus for the generic concept and feasibility of high-rise buildings making possible high-density urbanization, and the automobile providing the impetus for the generic concept and feasibility of individualized speedy travel with enormous impact on many aspects of such urbanization, also in connection with suburban low-density development.

Every design solution is a manifestation of more or less explicit concepts and their characteristics, that is, specific concepts with their generic ancestors embedded. Design representations accomplish this in various ways, from the simplest and very preliminary sketch with little detail to the built design with all its experiential corporeality, prescribed by verbal specifications, scaled drawings and models, computerized images, etc. Like the possession of a generic concept itself, so is its manifestation a matter of degree. Only parts of reality can ever become observable. Therefore, we better also think about the unobservables parts, whose features can only be inferred, mostly from functional relationships.

My present use of the term concept has been mainly limited to criteria which determine mental representations of material objects. Anything we mentally conceive is a concept, however we may be able to come to it and represent it.[7] As generic concepts, though being very important for understanding, are in the background and we rarely talk about them in practice, compared with specific concepts which we encounter and experience front end, I use from now on *concept* only for the latter. Whenever a generic concept is meant, but not evident, I will mention it.

5.2 Type and objectivity

Closely related to what we have discussed about resemblance is the nature of *type*. Type is defined in various ways. Broadly taken, it is synonymous with kind, sort, character (typeface), classification, categorization and obviously typology. Very confusingly, typology or type is sometimes used to signify 'singular' type as an entity in a set of one. There are no such individual types. Type or typology always refers to multiple occurrences of what is typical in associated resemblances. Even character implies this aspect. Any of the letters in an alphabet was an archetype when used the first time. All its following instantiations exhibit now the type feature. *To be a type signifies association of a specific object in a classification with other specific objects which have at least some resemblance in common and therefore have membership in a typology.* In the following I use the term type in this way.

This explanation naturally points to how we arrive at results of explicit understanding. We learn as infants about type long before we can form words. We learn to understand the reoccurrence of our mother's face and voice, the milk bottle, her touching our head, etc. These repetitive appearances of the same object or state of affairs, similar though never exactly the same, become for us typical. The central issue of type for understanding is recognition. We may say that the phenomenon of resemblance is based on conceptualization of repetition. Obviously there is no recognition without repetition.

Types are not "vague", as has occasionally been asserted.[8] Types always have specific properties which are more or less similar to those of members in the same classification. They also have specificity of other properties which may be quite different (dissimilar) from those which make for their immediate type membership – providing design freedom among otherwise type related solutions of a problem. If all properties among each set of objects are the same we have identical objects. They are replications and usually mass-produced by machines. But rarely, if ever, are there absolutely identical mental representations coming about, even of identical objects, because of various influences of surrounding contexts, differences in aspectual positioning from object to object and our subjectivity in the ways we come to understanding. Whatever objects and particular designs represent, they are always combinations of specific properties. On the other hand and in the totality of things, all objects and their properties belong to typologies. Virtually everything known to us has some kind of similarity with something else.

Classifications in architecture have been with us since the books of Vitruvius, in fact since organized building commenced. But the first who refers to types was probably Leon Battista Alberti when he writes about 1450:

> If we wish to give an accurate account of the various types of buildings ... and of their constituent elements, our whole method of investigation must open and begin here, by considering human variety in greater detail; since building's arose on man's account, and for his needs they vary; so that they may be dealt with more clearly by distinguishing their individual characteristics.[9]

In this one sentence we have a juxtaposition of most aspects which are at play: individual characteristics, human variety and needs, types of buildings but also their constituent elements, that is, component types. The affinity to nature, to which Alberti refers throughout his treatise, could be added. Often occupied with churchly matters, it is surprising that he makes no mention whatsoever of divine origins, although many have viewed his frequent references to nature as implication of the divine. It is amazing how far Alberti went into details of building type studies, not only to describe groupings of spaces but functional relations among them.[10]

That type as concept – if not by that name – is understood long before Alberti's time is evident from the rules and repetition of how temples and churches, castles, theaters, residences, palaces, baths, etc., are built since Antiquity, and how even whole towns are laid out. The monastic architecture in the Middle Ages is a prime example of building types. Their component types were developed and controlled by the particular religious orders. The earlier mentioned abbey at Maulbronn, Germany, has an overall layout typical for the Cistercian order to which it belonged, though variations were made in response to local purposes and contexts. There are several types of vaulting, each type chosen with regard to structural requirements, functional importance and, more broadly, aesthetic interest (5.5 and 5.6). Profuse modular resemblances of vaulting support spatial continuity in each part of the complex.

Abbey Maulbronn, Germany

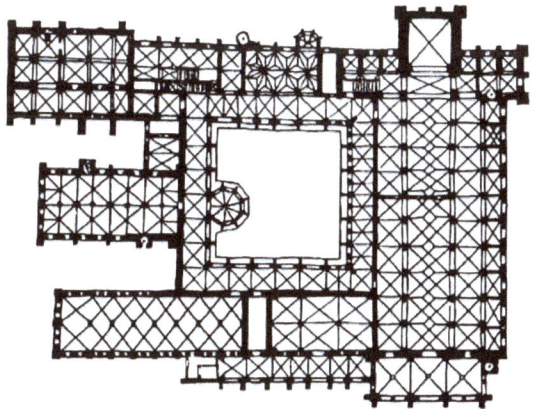

5.5 Reflected ceiling plan with vaulting

5.6 Narthex

Johannes Gutenberg's invention of mechanical printing made possible the wide spread of books also for architecture. Many were less well theoretically founded typologies than Alberti's or

Andrea Palladio's. But they were successful 'pattern' books of building types, of the Tuscan, Doric, Ionic, Corinthian and Composite column orders, of many kinds of ornaments, etc. Sebastiano Serlio's books on rules in architecture came out in Dutch, French and German translations soon after they were published in Italy in the 1540s.[11] Joseph Furttenbach, a merchant, prolific writer and city architect of Ulm, who as a young man visited Italy for a decade, begins in 1635 to publish a series of books which addressed schools, hostels, barracks, prisons and hospitals.[12] His descriptions concentrate on functional aspects.

In 1751 the term type is traced by Denis Diderot explicitly to its Greek roots and then defined as

> ... the copy, image or resemblance of some models. ... Types are not simple conformities or analogies that nature makes between two otherwise different things, nor are they arbitrary images that are founded only on a casual resemblance between one thing and another. It is additionally necessary that God particularly intended to make a type and expressly declared that type is in fact a type.[13]

Type is still also understood as "figure", "shadow", "representation" and "ideas of God" from whom supposedly all things derive.[14] Types imply resemblance to an origin or principle. Remnants of this view, though transformed, are reflected in architecture to this day. Anthony Vidler writes that

> The idea of type has, since the late eighteenth century, informed the production of architecture in two different ways. First, by rooting architecture in a notion of first principles, either in nature or industrial production, it has provided an ontology, so to speak, for the legitimacy of design in an age which has largely discarded the ancient theory of imitation and absolute beauty. Second, when assimilated to the emerging theories of typology in the natural sciences it has provided a ready basis for the generation of entirely new species of building demanded so insistently by the rising consumption and production society.[15]

In 1771 Jacques Blondel classified buildings according to their characteristics:

> All the various kinds of productions which belong to architecture should carry the imprint of the particular purpose of each building, all must have a character which determines their general form, and which announces the building for what it is.[16]

While he does not use the term type, it is implied in his use of "genre" and in the description of the programmatic characteristics various categories of building should have. A generation later J. N. L Durand (1760-1834) classified building types extensively according to their utility as houses, apartments, schools, theaters, etc. Durand asks rhetorically:

> Without doubt the grandeur, the magnificence, the variety, the effect and the character which one observes in buildings have so many beauties, so many causes of pleasure which we find in their observation. But what is the need to go after all this? If one arranges a building in a way suitable to its intended use, will it not make sense that it differs from another building with another use? Will it not naturally have a character, and furthermore its own character?[17]

He develops a catalogue of architectural elements which were to serve with relatively minor variations for all kinds of building tasks. The result is a dual task of design process: use of types for overall organization and use of types for construction components as an additive and combinatorial approach of ever more refinement:

> Durand subdivided architecture, or rather, built it up, out of combinations of basic irreducible elements. These elements – walls, columns, openings – were to be combined to form intermediate units – porches, stairs, halls, and so on – and these again built up into complete ensembles, which in their turn formed towns.[18]

Durand's central design concept is purposive arrangements ("dispositions") for which the understanding of needs and desires in the building program are the determinants. Appropriateness ("convenance") and economy are to guide the composition of given building elements for reasonable disposition with the result of "grandeur" and "caractère".[19] He uses rectangular grids for the dimensional coordination of wall and column placement (5.7). In effect, Durand emphasizes the need for formal expression to represent functional aspects, though in a moderately historicist way, and anticipates Louis Sullivan's dictum on function by nearly a century.

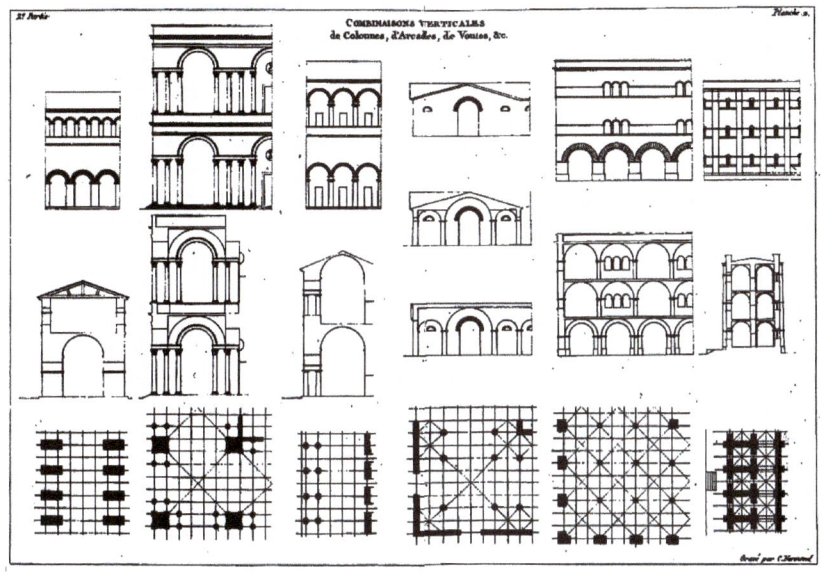

5.7 Grid Coordination of Building Components by J. N. L. Durand (source)

But it is A.-C. Quatremère de Quincy (1755-1849) who, another generation later and after a long personal path, away from a rather rigid, historicist position, uses the term 'type' broadly and with an environmental and truly historical foundation. He brakes away from Marc-Antoine Laugier's and other theoretician's "primitive hut" as the sole origin of all architecture. Laugier, not an architect but a Jesuit priest, had claimed in 1753 that

> … by imitating the natural process, art was born. All the splendors of architecture ever conceived have been modeled on the little rustic hut I have just described. It is by approaching the simplicity of the first model that fundamental mistakes are avoided and true perfection is achieved. …
>
> … I therefore come to this conclusion: in an architectural order only the column, the entablature and the pediment may form an essential part of its composition. If each of these parts is suitably placed and suitably formed, nothing else need be added to make the work perfect.[20]

Well, were design as simple. Laugier is a 'romantic rationalist', if someone like this exists. His essay had wide distribution. It is clearly written and easily understood also by laypeople, but misleading through its claim that only a very few kinds of building components, derived from nature, were necessary for architectural projects.[21] Differently, Quatremère's type has the connotation of origin, not single sourced, but related to the location and other living conditions of hunters, pastoral tribes and farmers. This view perhaps can be best derived from his remarks on the central role antecedents play in a very broad sense:

> In every country, the art of regular building is born of a preexisting source. Everything must

> have an antecedent. Nothing, in any genre, comes from nothing, and this must apply to all of the inventions of man.[22]

If nothing comes from nothing, with which I fully agree, then something carries over from what is before to what comes about. The generic connection of architecture's origin is for Quatremère the environmental need for shelter but it is also grounded in wider societal circumstances; not like Laugier's solely natural origins. Quatremère's type is an early anthropology based derivation. Sylvia Lavin writes that

> For Quatremère, the problem of relationship between primitive hut and modern architecture was none other than the process of the transformation of type, a conceptual metamorphosis required each and every time a building was designed. As a result, architecture's past type became the key to its future and most importantly to its public legibility.

And,

> ... while type revealed the historical dimension of all architecture, it did not, in de Quatremère's view, produce architecture that was inherently historicist.[23]

The historical dimension does not have to produce "historicist" architecture in the sense of the widely used book of Durand and in the sense of the typical classicist architectural realizations which came about in the eighteenth and nineteenth centuries. Quatremère also strongly differentiates between type and model:

> The word 'type' presents less the image of a thing to copy or imitate completely than the idea of an element which ought itself to serve as a rule for the model. ... The model as understood in the practical execution of art, is an object that should be repeated as it is, while the type is an object after which each [artist] can conceive of works that might not resemble each other.[24]

True, the concept of type implies idea as origin and "antecedent". But we must be careful in interpreting what he means by "the type is an object after which each [artist] can conceive of works that might not resemble each other". He is right when he warns that resemblance in type is not simply copying. But type is for him in part something typical and in part something beyond this typical. The indication becomes very clear when he writes that the principle of type is

> ... like a sort of nucleus about which are collected, and to which are coordinated in time, the developments and variations of forms to which the object is susceptible.[25]

Type as "nucleus" of "variations of forms to which the object is susceptible" implies repetition of resemblance within building categories and often in building components across many building projects, and according to use, giving them their individual expression, although they belong to categories. There is individual variety within overall similarity. For example, schools are different from one to another but they have common functions and physical features. They are generically related.

Quatremère is at the threshold of bringing together in type what is on the one hand character recognized because of historical precedent, and on the other character imposed because of present circumstances; both conceptualizations based on resemblances. Type represents an essential property of form but form of the same type usually varies from realization to realization. It is character, about which he writes a long chapter in the *Encyclopédie Méthodique*, which brings about the deviation within members of a class of type. In reference to Quatremère, Aldo Rossi writes with an outlook for our time that

> ... no type can be identified with only one form, even if all architectural forms are reducible to types. The process of reduction [to find typical features] is a necessary, logical operation, and it is impossible to talk about problems of form without this presupposition.

And,

> Type is thus a constant and manifests itself with character of necessity; but even so it is predetermined [through the existence of the object]; it reacts dialectically with technique, function and style, as well as with both the collective and the individual moment of the architectural artifact.[26]

The main continuation of Quatremère's thoughts is undertaken by Gottfried Semper who in his inaugural lecture at the University of Dresden in 1834 says that

> … Architecture has its antecedents for the representation of an idea not readily given in the gestalts and formal appearances of nature, but it is based on undeterminable but nevertheless secure and firm laws, (which seem to be in accord with the fundamental laws of nature,) after which it orders and combines all spatial needs of the human conditions with prompting and sensitive artistry.[27]

That implies that there are precedents, but not a priory and readily given to be copied because there are only "undeterminable ... laws" which echoes an earlier remark by Quatremère in 1800 that

> There are two ways of imitating Greek architecture; one consists in imitating the style; the other in grasping the principles and the spirit.

And,

> The right way to imitate the good *Greek architecture* consists in penetrating the spirit, find the reasons, expand the principles, develop its means, discover the hidden routes through which it affects our souls, …[28]

This means not to copy its formal approaches, but to imitate its essence. In a letter to the editor Vieweg, regarding a future book on his theories, Semper writes that it should be helpful

> … to produce a survey of architecture by selecting from the infinite amount of subject matter what is related, grouping it in families, and tracing what has been selected and combined back to origins and elements.[29]

There is naturally somewhat of a contradiction. If architecture's laws are "undeterminable", it is more than difficult to find and select "what is related, grouping it into families". Nevertheless, Semper proposes four archetypes, "elements" as he called them, instead of the three Laugier proposed (column, entablature, pediment): foundation (Terrassenmauern), wall, roof and hearth. They have, even more than Quatremère's types, a grounding in cultural, environmental and behavioral necessities, especially the hearth which he sees as having strong symbolic significance in any society.

> Before men thought of erecting tents, fences, or huts, they gathered around the open flame, which kept them warm and dry and where they prepared their simple meals. The hearth is the germ, the embryo, of all social institutions. The first sign of gathering, of settlement and rest after long wanderings and the hardship of chase, is still the set of fire and the lighting of the crackling flame. From early times on, the hearth became a place of worship; …[30]

Perhaps more important, Semper's elements have a more generic and even symbolic base, than Quatremère's; thus they could stand for a much more diverse typology of cultural concepts, design aspects, construction systems and building materials. But regarding Quatremère or Semper, we must take their elements not as the literal components which they name, but as indicating originating motives or themes. Both were in search of a theoretical base for the enormous technological advances which took place during the ongoing industrial revolution and which influenced how buildings were to be designed and constructed. Modern building technologies began to impact aesthetic considerations explicitly. Semper found the favorite example for his archetypes in the hearth, structure and wall fabric of the Caraib hut which he had seen in 1851 at London's Crystal Palace exhibition (5.8 and 5.9).

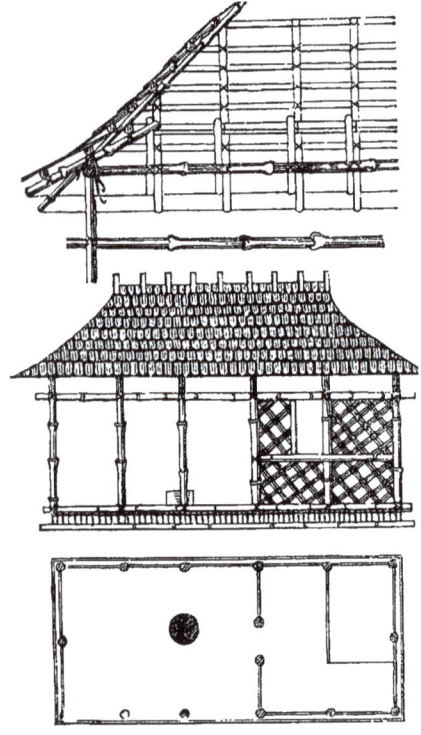

5.8 Caraib Hut (source)

5.9 Crystal Palace, center transept and north tower (source)

It is hard to imagine that the Caraib hut located within the Crystal Palace, by Joseph Paxton, should not have prompted Semper to contemplate resemblances. On very different levels of technical advancement hut and palace exhibit type development for repetitive production and assembly. One is made of precut bamboo columns, beams and rafters tied together by ropes, the other of manufactured steel columns, girders and beams bolted together. One has a woven fabric of organic material as infill between bamboo structure. The other has framed glass panes hung between steel structure. We must consider here that Semper lives at that time in London and is often at the exhibits, being charged with the arrangement of four exhibition stands. But strange enough, in a long treatise *Science, Industry and Art* with extensive discussions about especially stylistic aspects of the exhibits, all he has to say about the Crystal Palace as a place and building, housing the exhibits, are a few paragraphs on its possible reuse as a place for large exhibitions, art and industrial studios, and lecture halls.[31] That his attitude toward the building is positive, however, is clear from a newspaper article on the exhibition in which he calls it

... a glorious work – this enormous and airy and yet strong building, a wonderful triumph! [32]

Semper looks at these exhibits for his motifs of foundation, wall, roof and hearth, and he associates with them stone, textile, wood and ceramic. He clearly understands the correspondence between two groups of typologies, one referring to building components, the other to building materials. He sums up his overall view of type in a long and loaded sentence which appears at various times with slight variations in his large amount of writing:

Just as nature in her variety is yet simple and sparse in her motives, renewing continually the same forms by modifying them a thousandfold according to the graduated scale of

> development and the different conditions of existence, developing parts in different ways, shortening some and lengthening others – in the same way the technical arts are also based on certain prototypical forms (*Urformen*) conditioned by a primordial idea, which always reappear and yet allow infinite variations conditioned by more closely determining circumstances.[33]

Mari Hvattum rightly observes that

> Semper redefined the notion of type and comparison from the mechanistic model of Durand – which used form as a basis for comparison – to an organic model, comparing according to functional and structural relationships.[34]

Semper obviously gained from Durand's extensive analytical studies of type which, however, resulted in a rather prescriptive approach to design. His view, likely helped by Quatremère, is founded on a more forward looking attitude with subtle differences in the diversity of type: as component types even developed for particular projects. The Crystal Palace, as he could see, is the first very large, mainly off-site fabricated building with such components. Some prefabricated components for building types had been manufactured and shipped since the late 1700s.[35]

The second half of the 19th century was marked by a mix of architectural movements from gothic, baroque and classicist revivals to arts and crafts as well as early modernist developments. Hermann Muthesius who studied in England the Arts and Crafts Movement helped in 1907 to found the Deutsche Werkbund, an organization of architects, industrial designers and artists especially concerned with the emerging mass production in manufacturing and building. Most of its members supported what they called "Sachlichkeit", supposedly functional objectivity. Muthesius expressed in 1911 probably with more emphasis than anybody else that

> If any of the arts, it is architecture which strives toward the typical. Only in doing so can it find its fulfillment.[36]

This was necessarily so long before he made this comment as architecture is more utilitarian than any of the other arts in the modern sense, serving needs and desires which are on very basic levels similar throughout cultures and times. Much of the discussion was at that time driven by the calls for strong building activity in response to the enormous increases of population, especially in European and American cities, and by the opportunity to satisfy the requirements through the advances in technology. Developments of type brought about the mass production of goods made possible through the substitution of manual labor by machines powered with steam and electricity, but also by the simple fact that differentiation has limits. This is the case in various ways under democratic and less free market oriented regimes. Even capitalism, which provides the largest variety of goods ever produced – most of them mass-produced – is at the same time a potent leveler of desires. Our suburban sprawl made possible by automobiles is only one example.

Therefore, it is a natural condition that things repeat themselves in what we perceive as types. Everything that comes about has to some extent a precedent. This tendency underlies all our cognitive and creative efforts. While the desire to differentiate is a basic human trait, it varies within rather narrow boundaries for individuals and societies; therefore, the results have resemblances. We all have to eat, sleep, take care of our health, need to know things, enjoy ourselves, go from place to place, etc., which calls for similar features of related products.

The modern movement of the first half of the twentieth century shifts attention rhetorically from type to function. But it cannot get away from type because function is tied to type. Functional relationships determine what we want objects 'to do' for us. All objects are types. Schools are types, so are classrooms, their walls, doors, windows, lamps, etc. Bricks, used to build the walls, are of a type. When Louis Kahn asks brick "What do you want brick?" and brick answers "I like an arch." then brick answers what, as type, its capacity is to accomplish – a functional relationship. In addition to their resemblance features, objects become understood by us as types through their functional relationships, that is, for what they are typically useful.

Function is a rather empty term until it is filled with specific content, that is, until it marks the interrelationship between purposive and contextual aspects with those of realization and its form. The so-called Modernists are essentially not wrong with their basic axiom concerning function. They were often wrong – and this is not different in today's architecture – in not letting purpose and context fully guide realization. 'Fully' indicates here as far as possible the weighted reconciliation of all design factors; and this includes aesthetic judgment. It means to let a generic type manifest itself in a specific, broadly satisfying realization. I think it is an oversimplification in hindsight when Brent Brolin, in an account with otherwise many helpful facts and observations, writes that

> The public never embraced modernism, a fact modernists passed off as a "failure to understand". But the style was not rejected because of a simple misunderstanding, or, as some postmodernists claimed, because its symbolism was obscure and unfamiliar. Anyone could tell that modern buildings looked like factories; the symbolic vocabulary fairly screamed out its origins. Modernism was rejected by the majority of people because they did not like the way it looked.[37]

There is not a general rejection of modernist architecture but mainly dissatisfaction with the excesses of mass production in the 1960s and 1970s, often with seemingly endless repetition of similar objects on the same site, generating boredom. Type as natural principle in repetitive production is unavoidable in a mass society. But at the same time a great variety of types are developed and available. Mixing them at the same place avoids the just mentioned problem. To reduce excesses is not only a matter of balancing economic constraints with aesthetic preferences, but contextually responsive planning. Dislike of certain designs can be found before and after the period called Modernism.

We not only deduce types from what we encounter by necessity but also establish them on our own by creating resemblances. Karen Franck is right in writing that

> Without types of some kind we could not survive; at the same time, the particular kinds of types we create have significant implications for the kinds of lives we lead.[38]

And they have signifying implications for what we mean in design. Rafael Moneo emphasizes the dual utility of types in our field when he writes that

> Architecture ... – the world of objects created by architecture – is not only described by types, it is also produced by them. ... The design process is a way of bringing the elements of a typology – the idea of a formal structure – into the precise state that characterizes the single work.[39]

The individual work we bring forth is a unique combination of membership in types; sometimes of many, other times of only a few.

During the design process we derive from purpose, context and realization the design factors, largely functional relationships which are mostly satisfied by means of component typologies. But there are broad types and there are narrow types as to the inclusion of components and properties. Through the continuum from broad to narrow types it is then quite understandable that Quatremère writes:

> ... the type, ..., is an object after which each [artist] can conceive of works that might not resemble each other.[40]

But it may be also confusing. What he says here is, I think, that these objects may resemble each other generically; not overall. There are usually many component types assembled into overall buildings which do "not resemble each other" in other respects. For example, the Kimbell Art Museum in Fort Worth, by Louis Kahn, brings forth its uniqueness – outside and inside – by the specific type character of its concrete roof barrels (5.10 and 5.11). They give its architecture a thematic rhythm by means of similarity but with variations.

Kimbell Art Museum, Fort Worth, TX

5.10 and 5.11 Northwest corner and north gallery (© permissions)

Type development is even more the rule in so-called high-tech architecture projects. The Hong Kong & Shanghai Bank in Hongkong, by Foster+Partners, consists of many component types, most of them in large numbers of units. This made production lines possible in several countries far away from the building site (5.12 to 5.14).

More broadly viewed, our modern buildings consist of a great variety of more or less typical components. Essentially all use components which are mass-produced for the general, off-the-shelf market. All buildings require doors, windows, various kinds of repetitive mechanical, plumbing and electrical equipment, etc.

Hongkong-Shanghai Bank, Hongkong
(© permissions)

5.12 Tower structure with service modules

155

Hongkong-Shanghai Bank, Hongkong

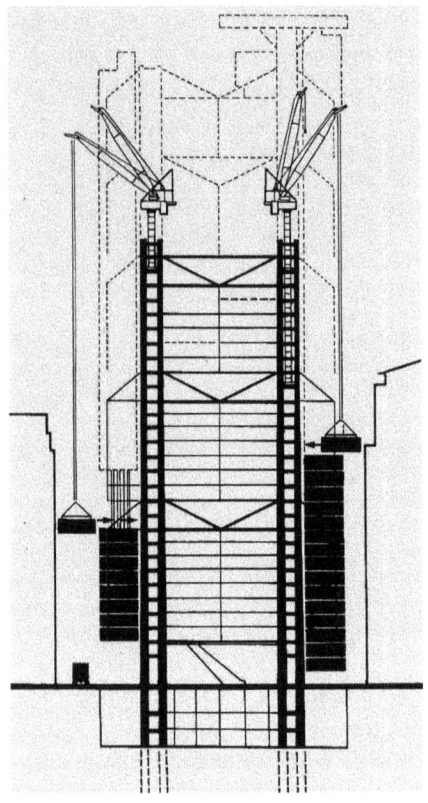

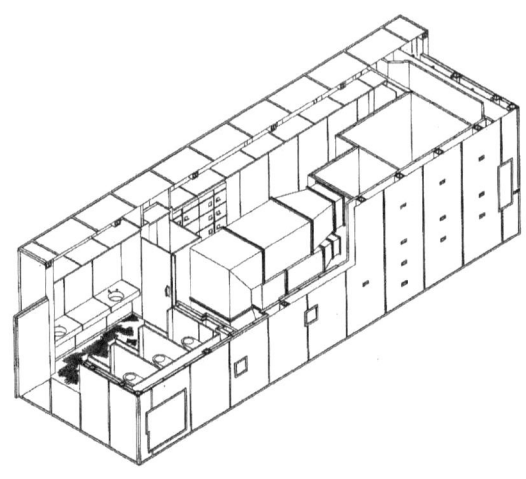

5.13 and 5.14 Service module assembly into the structure on site and service module

Other interesting, rarely mentioned causes of type development in the broader realm of urban design and architecture arise from the normative influences of society, such as from cultural preferences, economic constraints or safety requirements. We also use type resemblances on a daily basis to communicate our thoughts in orderly fashion. So we do in design by arranging physical things in orderly ways. This includes as background and foundation for design: social behavior typologies, organizational typologies, spatial typologies, building construction typologies, dimensional coordination typologies, color typologies and so on. In this wider context, for example, family types influence housing floor plan arrangements. From neighborhood developments to plumbing installations, type permeates all manmade environments.

To summarize. The manifestation of type is always derived historically. We can only know of a type after it has occurred; only after resemblance of a concept exists. Repetition gives resemblance in one way or another and gives rise to a new grouping in typology. Even imagination is a repetition. Something cannot come from nothing. Like anything 'new', new types may come about because of never before encountered purposive demands on a project or because of realizing conventional demands in different ways. But both demands and responses do not come 'out of the blue'. They are variations of resemblance. Societal and technological developments, especially over the past two centuries, brought on enormous new demands in the ways we live, work, educate, provide food, take care of the ill, have vacations, etc. and in the ways we build in response. These demands and the responses become types through repetition which makes many aspects of design very efficient. We do not have to reconceptualize all objects and designs with which we dealt before. We easily remember types. When we understand what the members of a certain typology have in common – let's say of classrooms, what goes on in them, what their typical dimensions are and which window orientations and sizes provide good daylighting – we are able to apply such understanding in a present project, though the environmental conditions and many details may be quite different from previous school projects. Because of many other building and component types we have experienced, we have a wealth of more or less connected aspects in memory from which we may draw for variation. In Aldo Rossi's words:

> A design pursues this fabric of connections, memories, images, yet knowing that in the end it will have to be definitive about this or that solution; on the other hand, the original, whether in its true or presumed state, will be an obscure object which is identified with its copy.[41]

Whereby we should take "copy" liberally, that is, not being identical but with some resemblance. All "connections, memories, images", concepts and beliefs come to us from memory. They come to us sometimes instantly or after some contemplation, now refreshed, though they may have been there a long time. Other times they come to us indirectly when we recognize them stored in books or in computers, sometimes in documented classifications.

Mass production by means of types must not mean mass production of whole buildings, although there is always the temptation to pursue this tendency when many units with similar overall requirements are needed, especially under stringent economic conditions. But there is no justification, for the shear endless repetitions once proposed by Le Corbusier and Hilberseimer. Modernism paid a high price for having been broadly associated with such directions. Bruno Taut advocated in 1929:

> The same constructions for the same requirements, for which exceptions should only be made in the case of special requirements. ...

And,

> *The aim of Architecture is the creation of the perfect, and therefore also beautiful, efficiency.*[42]

We must not take this as absolute. There are usually multiple solutions to solve problems. There can be great variety even with high efficiency and mass production, especially in a worldwide market.

There are typologies at which we arrive quite naturally because of reoccurrence of functional requirements and building procedures. For others we search purposively because of economic advantages or aesthetic preferences. In fact, we never can design anything without obeying to some extent type producing criteria. Nothing which we design is ever completely new. There are always constraints, such as climate conditions, safety requirements and organizational aspects. Purpose provides focus for orientation toward results. Context provides the background and means toward realization. Our understanding of types helps us to define what is necessarily normative and what is not. Here I appreciate the value of Christopher Alexander's "pattern languages", not as ready-made rules but as examples of type application from which we can think to make our own variations according to present circumstances. Types are grounded in the objectivity of comparison. Not so styles, to which we turn now. Styles arise out of the subjectivity of choice.

5.3 Style and subjectivity

The concept of style, though it had not this name for a long time, has been understood since Antiquity. Perhaps the simplest notion may be given in the dual aspect of 'activities and their results of doing something in a certain manner'. Style had nothing necessarily to do with art as understood today, but with the way anything is done and comes into being, such as through the art of cooking, the art of fighting, the art of oratory and the various arts of making artifacts. In one of the latter is the origin of its name: the stylus, the instrument to engrave wax and metal plates, came to stand for the result of using it – a style.[43,44]

Style today is understood as the result of choices to create particular themes of expression. Before globalization, locality and history influenced and limited choices profoundly. Things were done in certain styles. This was the case whether we talk about styles of societies or those of individuals. The 'Norddeutsche Backsteingotik' in the 13th to 15th centuries used the regional structural building material, brick, for the largest buildings of its time and area. Often conventions played a strong role. This was already well understood by Quatremère when he wrote in 1825 that

> *Style*, ..., becomes synonymous with *character*, proper manner or distinctive physiognomy which belongs to each work, each author, each genre, each school, each country, each epoch, etc.[45]

With this early modern definition of style a relationship is implied but not yet clearly demarcated. It is what we should consider as collective style in response to the given conditions of one particular cultural epoch, the Zeitgeist, the esprit of a present society, reflected in what it produces and in how it lives with the environment thus created. Then we can consider what the personal styles are in response to and in support of such given and developing environments. Collective styles and personal styles are obviously highly interdependent. Collective styles come about through transformation of personal styles and personal styles are influenced by collective styles. The relationship is not symmetrical. Collective styles are comparatively broad in location and duration, while personal styles are narrowly focused and more short-lived.

Personal style in artistic endeavors did not gain great prominence until the increasing institutionalization of art. In the 15th century, together with the general assertion of the individual being, intellectualization and systematization occurred also in painting and architecture, as exemplified in the theories and methods of Alberti, Da Vinci, Dürer and many others. This development can at least in part be ascribed to the elevation of the position of artists in society versus those of 'mere' artisans.[46] It helped lead eventually, nearly three centuries later, to Baumgarten's and Kant's philosophical foundation of modern aesthetics, and to latter's definition of genius:

> ... genius ... is a *talent* for producing that for which no determinate rule can be given, not a predisposition of skill for that which can be learned in accordance with some rule, consequently that *originality* must be its primary characteristic.[47]

Genius, however, does not work in a vacuum but in its epoch and environment. And – for genius or not – there is, especially in architectural design, a dialectic at work of the demands given in functional requirements and the subjective responses from aesthetic preferences, resulting in our choices of particular properties. Karl Friedrich Schinkel (1781-1841) wrote:

> As purposiveness is the fundamental principle of all building, the best possible representation of the ideal of purposiveness, that is the character or the physiognomy of a building, determines its value as art.[48]

To achieve the "ideal of purposiveness" would be the absolute fulfillment of purpose. But this is never possible. The best possible solution must do. It gives the building its character and, according to Schinkel, its value as art, value from beauty. Beyond, however, Schinkel's differentiation of purpose (Zweck) versus purposiveness (Zweckmässigkeit) points to the divergence between verbal and 'materialized' rhetoric in architecture, always and inevitably encountered. While most of Schinkel's building layouts certainly come, for their time, close to the "ideal of purposiveness", their exterior appearances are dominated by neoclassicist and, for some time, neogothic themes.

With regard to historical context we should remember that his buildings reflect the Zeitgeist which was dominated by the Greek idealism of Winckelmann, Lessing then Goethe and Schiller, and finally Fichte, Schelling and Hegel, to mention only the German line of major figures in neo-classical thinking, having parallels in England and France (5.15). But in 1836, toward the end of his career, Schinkel comes closer to expressing overall purposiveness also on the exterior, in the "physiognomy of a building". His Building Academy very much shows features which anticipate 20th century functionalism by purposively expressing utility in structure and facade (5.16).

5.15 Altes Museum, Berlin, 1830
     etching by Friedrich A. Thiele

5.16 Bauakademie, Berlin, 1836
     painting by Eduard Gaertner

Around Schinkel's time, August W.N. Pugin (1812-1852) wrote about purpose that
> It will be readily admitted, that the great test of Architectural beauty is the fitness of the design to the purpose for which it is intended, and that the style of a building should so correspond wtih its use that the spectator may at once perceive the purpose for which it was erected.[49]

Ideas about architectural beauty from functional appearance were part of the controversy about styles long before Sullivan. Style nearly always reflects to some extent purpose and use. Purposiveness as a topic gained its currency, at least in part, through Kant's aesthetics – his "adherent beauty" is purpose related – and played a considerable role in the discussions of architectural theory and practice throughout the 19th century, though with variations in terminology. Expressions, such as 'organic nature', 'inherent laws', 'matter-of-factness', 'objective practicality', are found throughout much of the texts on architecture. Gottfried Semper claims that architecture gains organic properties, if its designs follow laws of nature. He generalizes, but means it for his own work, when he writes that
> One calls the forms of architecture organic, if they arise from a true basic idea and if with their formation the laws and the inner spiritual necessity evolve through which nature creates only the good and the beautiful, and even uses the ugly itself as necessary element for the harmony of the whole.[50]

And,
> Style means giving emphasis and artistic significance to the basic idea...[51]

The question naturally is what is "the inner spiritual necessity" and the "basic idea". Do the ideas not have to arise, at least to a large part, from what is purposive – needed and desired – and contextual, and eventually become subject to our judgment? Then style will give organic expression to these basic ideas as result of architectural design and realization.

Hermann Muthesius wrote in 1902 with regard to the long "battle of styles" during the 19th century – styles with Greek, Roman, Romanesque, Gothic, Baroque and whatever elements, one even called Art Nouveau – that

> If we would be successful for now to ban the concept of style altogether, if the architect would at first adhere always clearly to what the special kind of task demands of him, then we were on the track to an art of the present, not far away from the fitting new style. Would he only contemplate that in a department store one above everything else wants to sell, in a dwelling to dwell, in a museum to exhibit, in a school to teach, and would he just seek, in the basic arrangement, in the structure, in the configuration of rooms, in the pattern of windows, of doors, of sources for heating and lighting, to do only justice to the arising requirements in all details, then we would be already on the way to that strict matter-of-factness [Sachlichkeit] which we have come to recognize as the basic feature of modern sensibility.[52]

He naturally asks for nothing else but a style to his own liking with emphasis on letting functional relationships show. His advocacy for "Building-Art" instead of "Style-Architecture" is for a less decorative style, not for no style at all. Style is unavoidable when we make decisions of preference.

So, we have on one hand the understanding of style as cultural development of the time and on the other the understanding of style as preference of individuals in positions of influence – influence because of creative talents and, not to forget, powers of decision making. Personal styles played and still play a crucial role in the evolution and fluctuation of collective cultural styles. Palladio and Michelangelo come to mind for Italian Renaissance, Neumann and von Hildebrandt for German Baroque, Wright and Gropius for Modernism, Venturi and Graves in reaction to it. Personal styles result from efforts to break away from collective formations as more or less extensive variations of them. There is no complete autonomy of designers because there is no unconstrained freedom of anyone in society.

Something features a style because of belonging to a developed or adopted type of some distinction. 5.17 by Paul Righini shows two sets of residences in the area of Cape Town, South Africa. In spite of considerable differences, they show clearly family resemblances of type associated as style with Georgian and Victorian cultural heritage. If the properties of a Greek temple would have only occurred once and not also in other temples, we would not associate them with a style.

5.17 Georgian and Victorian Residences, Cape Town, South Africa
 (© permission)

In whatever way they come, styles, like types, have normative aspects. Something 'has' style not through a one time distinction from everything else but through reoccurrence of its uniqueness through similarities. Style provides across a number of works, on an individual or societal level, repetitive features, a theme. Here is its main connection with the concept of type.

Arguably one of the most prominent and cohesive stylistic developments during the 20th century is represented by the glass walled apartment and office towers, designed by Mies van der Rohe (5.18). This approach changed from a rather individual approach into a broad one by a host of followers as infamously showing in the Prairie Shores Apartments in Chicago, by Loeble, Schlossman and Bennett (5.19).[53] A similar development, though out of different economic and technical motivation, was the enormous use of prefabricated concrete components for housing in Western Europe during the 1960s and 70s, even more so in Eastern Europe and the Soviet Union. A few well developed sites, such as Bellahøj near Kopenhagen, showed early possibilities in 1958 (5.20).

5.18 860-880 Lake Shore Drive, Chicago

5.19 Prairie Shore Apartments, Chicago

5.20 Bellahøj Housing, Kopenhagen

Unfortunately, type sometimes controlled style through the economics of repetition and even because of politics, such as at Thamesmead near London and, obviously much worse, at the Karl Marx Allee in Berlin (5.21 and 5.22). We should not forget, however, that excellent projects using similar techniques came about during the same time, one example being the Rietholz Apartments, Zollikerberg near Zürich, by Hubacher and Issler (5.23 and 5.24).

5.21 Thamesmead near London

5.22 Karl Marx Allee (Stalin Allee), Berlin

5.23 and 5.24 Rietholz Apartments, Zollikerberg near Zürich

So, styles are trends, pursued broadly by the design community or narrowly by individual designers. Recently, most typical of the latter approach is Frank Gehry's curvilinear way of shape making. It is associated with 'his' style because of its particular distinctiveness applied to various building types. It is part of the wider movement of non-rectangularity, not only in floor plans but frequently also in elevation, so prominent now also in the work of Zaha Hadid, Coop Himmelblau and others. It is interesting to look at evidence of early stylistic tendencies in two buildings by Gehry and Hadid, located a few steps apart on the premises of the Vitra Company in Weil am Rhein, Germany, and to compare them with more recent projects of the same designers (5.25 to

5.28). The rhetorical, but legitimate question may be asked: why make things simple when they can be done complicated? And less rhetorical: how far can we go in such directions?

5.25 Chair Museum, Vitra Company
      Weil am Rhein, Germany

5.26 Weatherhead School of Management
      Case Western University, Cleveland

5.27 Former Fire Station, Vitra Company
      Weil am Rhein, Germany

5.28 Guangzhou Opera House
      Guangzhou, China (© permission)

Styles exist through distinctions by manner of reoccurrence. Architectural styles as historical, functional, technical and aesthetic classifications have their common grounds in the uniqueness of their common features, their types. But style is not type. The grounds for type are objective, those of style are subjective, whether of societies or individuals. *Style comes about by the selection and use of preferred type*.

What is the utility of style? As so many other mental constructs, such as languages, numbers, types, metaphors, etc., styles are for us one part of the framework to understand and organize the world. We, as individuals or societies, delimit through inclusion and exclusion of properties, often without much thought or even subconsciously. We then perceive the resulting repetitiveness as style. Styles of activities and things are conceptual and derived from impressions or selected for expressions. But they are not conceptual in the sense of deriving attributes from or selecting attributes for general understanding (as typologies are for conceptualization). They are impressive or expressive in how concepts are chosen and combined in deliberate ways. *Styles are subjectively emphasized forms of meaning*.

5.4 Configuration and ornamentation

Form and style are determined by *configuration* in response to the influence of design factors. I include aesthetic preference as a design factor. Every object has a basic configuration of its form which influences the quality of our perception and conception. But there is an indefinite number of other configurations possible and it is often and, especially in highly complex circumstances, even impossible or at times even undesirable to find the best configuration – whatever we believe to be best. To arrive at it we use *ornamentation*.

This in-a-nutshell view needs explanation, especially with regard to terminology. Ornamentation and decoration are often considered being synonymous. This results in terminological confusion. Ornamentation and decoration are related. They are configuration. How do they differ? We have two kinds of ornamentation:

1) ornamentation as *amplification* of form derived through extension from *inside* its object, and
2) ornamentation as *decoration* of form through addition from *outside* its object.

With inside and outside I mean here the locations of cause. Both kinds of ornamentation are aesthetic in the sense of being based on judgment about pleasure and displeasure but have not only different origins but also different impacts.

It should help to give some thought to the origins of the term ornamentation. The Greek roots give ornamentation – ornament as result – a much broader and more important meaning than decoration alone. Its origin is in *cosmos,* in contrast to chaos, with connotations of universe, order, and arrangement.[54] Kent Bloomer (2000) writes that we can

> … separate out ornament from the other two [universe and order] by imagining it to be like a force that unites and transforms conflicting worldly elements.[55]

This is more than what decoration in today's understanding is about. But decoration is now the common understanding to which ornament refers.[56] This is a crucial shortcoming and also not justified from architectural practice. In fact, *ornamentation as configuration never lost its inevitability in the design process and its results.* Vitruvius wrote a short chapter on "the ornaments of the orders", in which he describes how ornament was developed in connection with construction.[57] Alberti's understanding of ornaments is much broader than we usually take it today and one which I endorse fully. He writes that

> The pleasure to be found in objects of great beauty and ornament is produced either by invention and the working of the intellect, or by the hand of the craftsman, or it is imbued naturally in the objects themselves. … These three must be applied to each part of the building, according to its respective use and role.[58]

His "imbued naturally" refers to ornament's inevitable natural occurrence as part of the development process. When speaking about ornament, he addresses more than decoration, though decoration is certainly one of the kinds of ornamentation. There is more to ornament than what in Venturi et al's "decorated shed" is applied independently of the systems of space and structure.[59] Bloomer finds, after a short overview of the long cultural history of ornament, that it has power to unify expression:

> The visual achievement of combining and uniting the expressions of utility and the expressions of adhering things from the world at large [culture, art, technology, etc.] is an act of mediation that occurs *within* the limited and transitional space of ornament.[60]

I would omit "visual" because ornamentation is the mediating force through which much more than visual aspects are combined and united.

As ornamentation is today viewed often synonymous with decoration its dual function needs articulation. I introduced above for reasons of clarity for ornamentation, arising out of the object, the term *amplification*. But decoration should be in no way considered to be a less valuable form of ornamentation than amplification. Or in a kind of contrast, amplification should not be mistaken as a 'nobler' form of ornamentation than decoration. Both can stand in their own right for important phenomena in not only architectural but broader cultural expressions.[61]

My uncommon use of the term amplification for one of the two kinds of ornamentation needs some further clarification. In architecture we should view amplification as the physically inevitable adjustment process for spatial fit in the formation of complex design solutions, bringing together the building components. The components are in response to cultural, social, constructional and aesthetic design factors influential in every building. So, amplification is in fact the geometric means to the fulfillment of these needs and desires. We seek combination and fit through variation. This understanding of configuration has, in turn, consequences not only for spatial aspects. It may influence the choice and details of structural systems, environmental controls, site accommodation, etc., sometimes to the point of fundamental decisions, all for achieving favorable results of fit through more or less redundancy of space and material. We may consider the deliberateness, which is to some extent necessary, as poetics of the tectonic in the broadest sense. It follows that there are infinite possibilities of arrangements in configuration, not only through decoration as adornment added but also through amplification of what we are working with. Amplification and decoration, together with the large variety of the given purposive and contextual design factors, are what makes for much of architecture's diversity. All architecture has configurational amplification, be it in floor plans and interiors of a straightforward Romanesque or an intricate Baroque church (5.29 to 5.32), be it as noticeable from the variations in Mies van der Rohe's Weissenhof Apartment House or as easily apparent from the twists and turns in Antoni Gaudí's Casa Milà (5.33 and 5.34), or be it in the arrangements of a school building or in that of a concert hall.

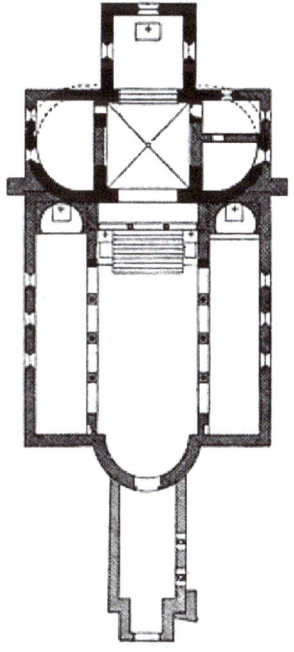 

5.29 and 5.30 St. Georg Church, Abbey of Reichenau, near Konstanz, Germany, floor plan (source) and interior

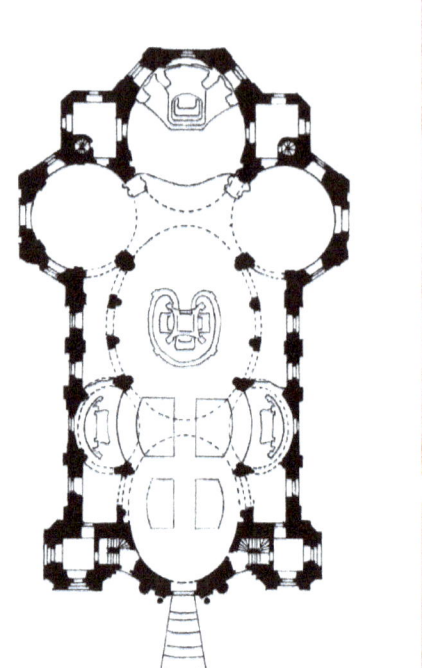

5.31 and 5.32 Vierzehnheiligen Pilgrimage Church, near Bamberg, Germany, floor plan (source) and interior

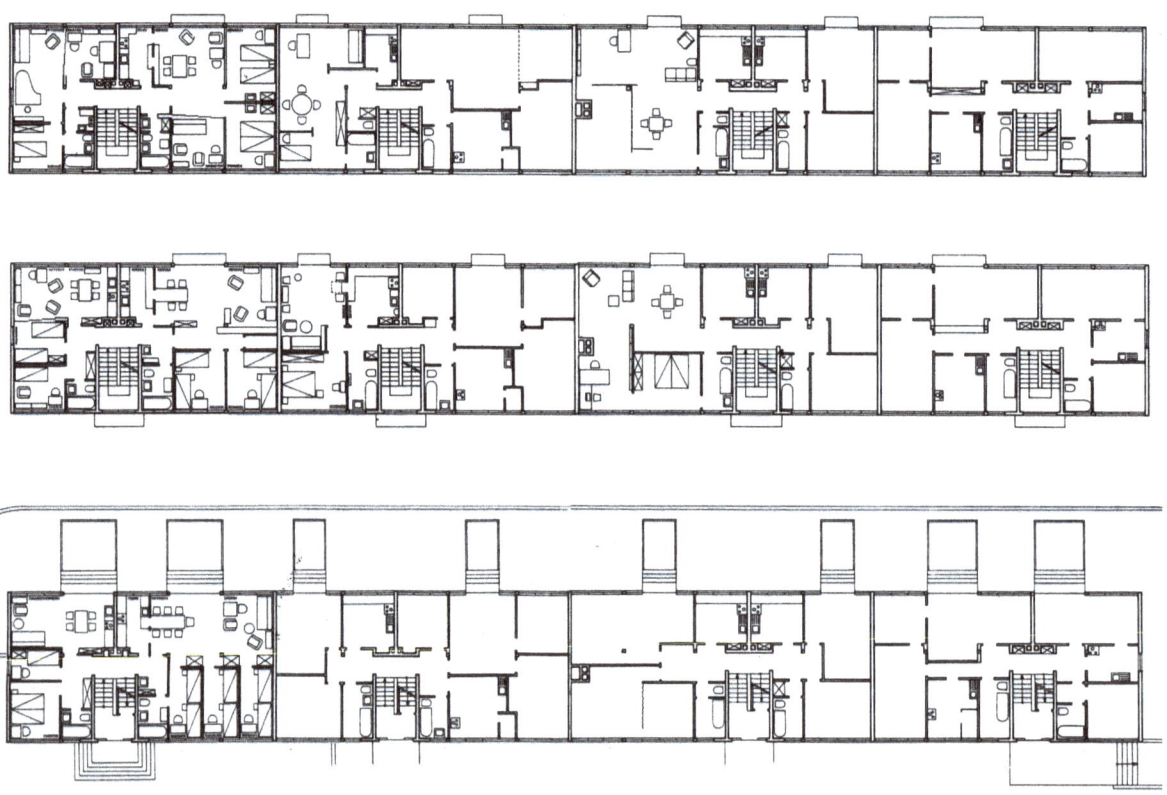

5.33 Apartment Building at Weissenhof Siedlung, Stuttgart, floor plan variations (© permission)

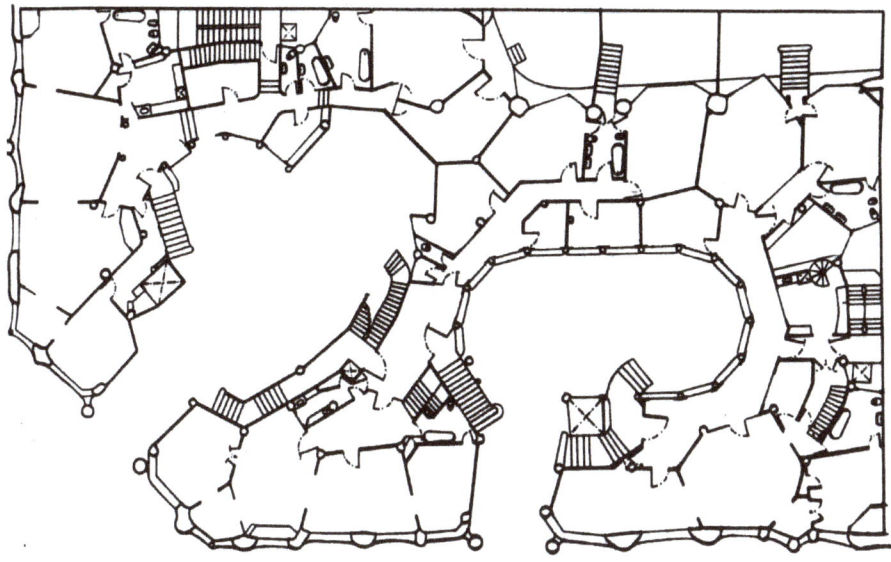

5.34 Casa Milá, Barcelona, entry level floor plan (© permission)

The examples show the dependence of functional relationships on configurational possibilities. Amplification obviously influences the spatial layout and efficiency of buildings. A measure of amplification efficiency is the floor area ratio of primary space versus secondary space, such as the area ratio of classroom versus hallway space in a school.

Amplification occurs not only in floor plans but also in sections and in every other aspect where combination and fitting occurs in design and construction, and, not surprisingly, it entails essentially all physical aspects of architecture. The use of the same or dominant building material throughout a project can be viewed as a theme of amplification. Material properties have 'fit' properties which influence component and system configuration. Amplification in structural systems can be traced throughout architectural history. The courageous experimentations of the Gothic cathedral builders provide very striking examples (5.35).

5.35 Beauvais Cathedral, France, structural system
(© permission)

With regard to a much more recent time, I agree with Michael Ramage who finds ornament – ornamental amplification – in the structural designs of Luigi Nervi. He writes that

> Architects constantly make decisions that involve ornament, whether they be integral to the structure or applied elements. Modernism championed an aesthetic of stripped down ornament, but not one devoid of ornament. Ornament arises in many ways, and not all are equal. The ornament of Pier Luigi Nervi, for example, is one of specificity and structure. His works are celebrated because of the consideration he gave for each structural member, but the structure of his sports halls remains ornamental. It is not a crime.[62]

The last sentence is obviously in contradiction to Adolf Loos' famous dictum. The structural system of the Palazzetto dello Sport, built for the 1960 Olympic Games in Rome, and many other buildings engineered by Nervi, innovate ornamentally while satisfying structural requirements (5.36). They are elegant, often filigreed, if not as playful perhaps as in Santiago Calatrava's work (5.37 and 3.40). In Calatrava's creations it is at times quite obvious how ornamentation and metaphor join to play; sometimes overplay.

5.36 Palazzetto dello Sport, Rome structure of roof (© permission)

5.37 Auditorio de Tenerife, Santa Cruz, Tenerife (source)

What is the case for particular materials happens broadly to the fit of multiple components and subsystems with various functions, often hidden behind suspended ceilings or in vertical shafts, or brought in the open with high-tech expressions, such as in the earlier shown Harvard Science Center (2.19 to 2.23) but emphasized the first time very strongly on the exterior of the Centre Pompidou in Paris by Renzo Piano and Richard Rogers (5.38 to 5.40). It has become quite common that some of the service systems, such as ducts, pipes and wiring, are left exposed. Amplification into open space not only reveals the initial building functions but also how they change over the life of the building. Amplification can be used to bring about diversity, as we have seen, but it can also be used to unify in various ways. The continuous tile pattern at the walls behind kitchen counters helps to unify spatial impression. Rowhouses with series of repetitive measurements establish a rhythm.

5.38 Plaza and west facade

Centre Pompidou, Paris

5.39 Detail of ceiling air diffuser

5.40 East facade

Amplified control can be used to advantage in unifying the physical process of building, especially through repetitive dimensioning in whole floor plans and elevations. This kind of co-ordination has profound consequences for the production and appearance of buildings. The Katsura Imperial Villa in Kyoto, finished in 1658, is an early and perhaps the most prominent example of modular coordination in Japanese architecture (5.41 and 5.42). The unifying power of modularity is apparent outside and inside. The approaches used during the 1960s and 70s in the Consortium of Local Authorities Special Program (CLASP) in England (5.43 and 5.44), in the School Construction Systems Development (SCSD) in California (5.45 to 5.47) and in the expansion of German construction for higher education, such as in the Marburg Project, are various examples of ways modular coordination principles can be applied, from structural systems to laboratory equipment, not least in support of controlled amplification.[63]

Katsura Imperial Villa, Kyoto

5.41 Main building, exterior

5.42 Main building, interior (source)

CLASP System

5.43 Secondary Modern School Tuxford, Nottinghamshire
(© permission)

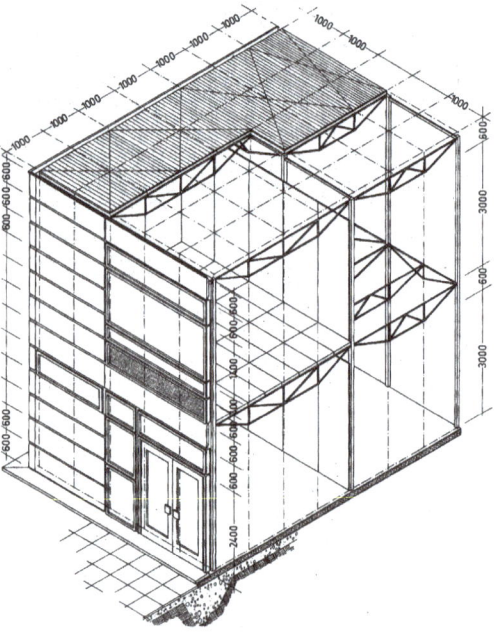

5.44 Modular coordination
(source)

SCSD System

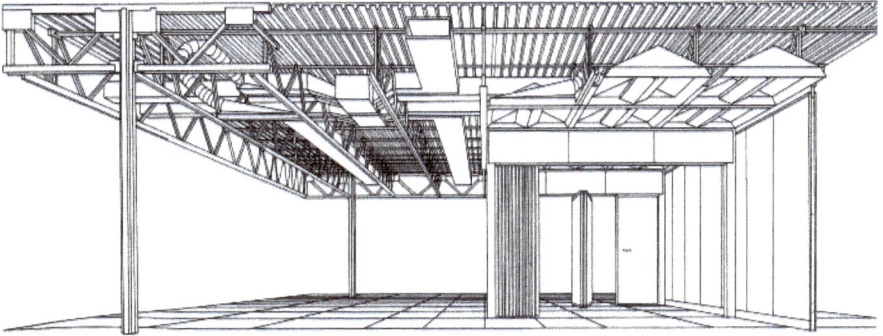

5.45 Modular coordination (© permission)

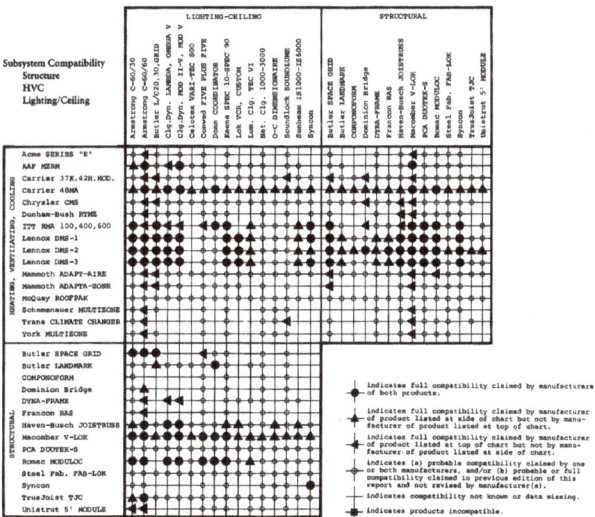

5.46 Subsystems compatibility: structure, HVAC, lighting/ceiling (© permission)

5.47 High School, Barrington near Chicago
(use of SCSD systems components beyond California)

That ornamentation as amplification is often configuration for purpose in context can easily be derived from the diversity of three examples among the many available. A housing development in Darmstadt, Germany, by Rüdiger Kramm and Manfred Meyer, shows housing with outside-inside

171

amplification from the main road to a secondary road, access passages, stair wells, and playgrounds. The central courtyard even has small garden plots (5.48 to 5.51). Design freedom within the constraints of the particular program articulates overlapping transitions of public, semi-public and private space.

Apartments at Bessunger Strasse, Darmstadt, Germany

5.48 Access from Bessunger Strasse

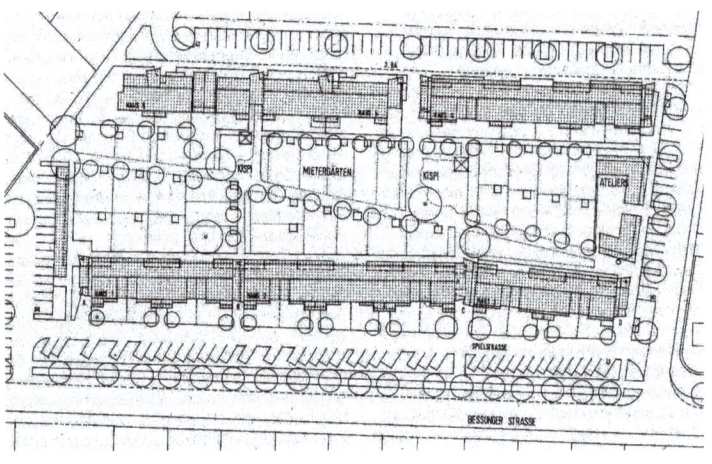

5.49 Site plan (© permission)

5.50 View into center courtyard

5.51 Gardening plots and view back toward access

The library of the Catholic University, Eichstätt, Germany, by Behnisch & Partner, features on a wide open site a central approach with star-like distribution of spaces. The design takes advantage of combining non-rectilinear and rectilinear forms. Diffusion of daylight throughout ties inside and outside uniquely together (5.52 to 5.55). We have here a highly articulated geometric response maximizing visual access to the surrounding rural environment. Another example is the highly varied amplification within a particular building type which is achieved in John Portman and Associates' atriums of large hotels with attractive central spaces.[64] All of these examples show functional configuration paired with aesthetic innovation; some by overall amplification, others by amplification in detail.

5.52 View from southwest (© permission)

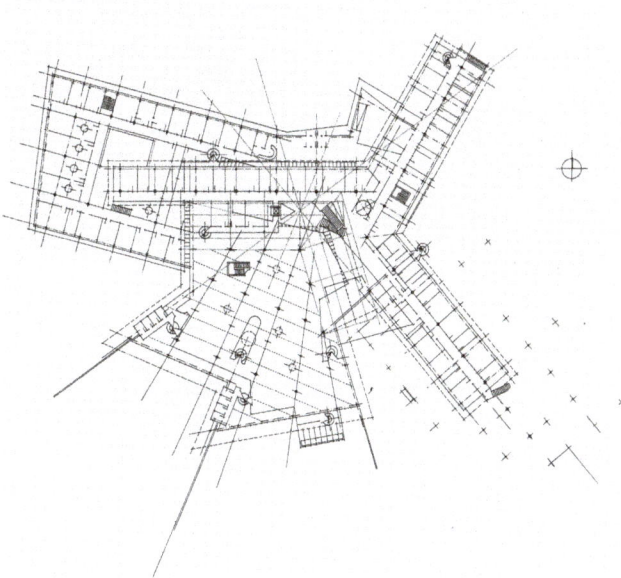

5.53 Structural grids and stair locations (© permission)

Central Library, Catholic University, Eichstätt, Germany

5.54 Central Stairs

5.55 View into south wing

Site context usually influences a project's configuration fundamentally and early in the design process, be it because of the site's topography, the existence of buildings or other objects on it, the access and egress requirements to and from it, or the surrounding urban fabric of which it is part. One of the parking structures at the University of Michigan, by Luckenbach Ziegelman, is layered into its slopping site, connects through a bridge arrangement with the main buildings it serves and in doing so signifies a large gate to the university's main campus on whose northern edge it is located (5.56 and 5.57). It is a result of relational, even metaphorical and certainly strong physical amplification. A substantial tree on the corner of a small site in a town near Tokyo was one of the reasons for amplifying a small apartment building around it (5.58).

Glen Avenue Parking Garage, University of Michigan, Ann Arbor, MI

5.56 View from northeast

5.57 View from southeast

5.58 Apartment house near Tokyo

For changing our discussion from amplification to decoration, we return to Gottfried Semper's thoughts. There is an interesting position for comparison with his theories of ornament and style.[65] Karl Bötticher, a contemporary of Semper, had introduced through his work on Greek art and architecture the terms "Tektonik, Kernform und Kunstform" – tectonic structure, core-form and art-form – all manifested in the unity of a given instance of architecture. Bötticher writes that

> The realization of each part can be considered to have come into existence by two elements: the core-form and the art-form. The core-form of each part is the mechanically necessary,

statically serving construct. The art-form, on the other hand, has only the characteristic of explaining the function. This characteristic gives sense not only to the very nature of each part but also to the relationship to adjacent parts, ... ; and as all parts are already brought together mechanically into a static unity, so do the corresponding symbols connect all parts to one inseparable organism. Therefore, this explaining characteristic is like a shell, a symbolic attribution of it – *decoratio*, ... It arises in the moment at which the mechanical construct of the part is conceptualized; the thought regarding both [core- and art-form] is one, they come about at the same moment.[66]

Bötticher speaks, regarding art-form, of "decoratio". But his meaning points in the direction of what I refer to as configurational amplification.[67] For him art-form evolves from its core-form. It is appearance of how something arises out of what it is. As mentioned, this is a natural and inevitable occurrence. The unity of core-and art-form is present – though usually not consciously perceived – in everything which physically exists. It can be observed strongly, for example, at the exterior walls and the interior columns of the Cathedral of Siena where black and white marble slabs are layered to form patterns: "*decoratio*" configurationally integrated (5.59 and 5.60).

Siena Cathedral

5.59 West facade, south facade, bell tower   5.60 Nave, central aisle (© permission)

Semper, too, seeks to explain decoration as something more than simply added because of subjective desire when he writes that

> The harmony of the tectonic work of art with the general law of nature is this work's embellishment (Schmuck), and where man embellishes, he emphasizes more or less consciously a law of nature in the object which he embellishes.[68]

Again, what are the laws of nature which he means? Unless they are well defined, they can only be vaguely emphasized. Unless one accepts Semper's "dressing" principle (Bekleidungsprinzip) in architecture as natural law, one has a hard time to understand what embellishment as ornament in his buildings means. In fact, he opens here the door to all kinds of views about ornament which in no small part contribute to the controversy about styles during the second half of the 19th century. His Dresden Opera House is one of the strongest examples of dressing as design principle, overall and in detail (5.61). We probably need to take his "Tektonik" with "embellishment", one and one-half centuries and many diverse developments later, as the realization of architecture out of purpose and influenced by context, the later to be taken comprehensively as what culturally and physically exists in the present circumstances, and with the combination of amplification and decoration viewed as being part of purpose.

Where ornamentation as amplification ends and ornamentation as decoration begins is fluid – Semper's work being a prime example. The progression from amplification to decoration is already discernible in the classical column orders: evolution from the Doric to the Ionic to the Corinthian capitals (5.62).[69] Instances of such progression occur during any physical formation we are involved with, that is, for any answer to need or desire through satisfaction. The columns at the entry of the Basel Art Museum show amplification of the column capitals extended into decoration depicting aspects of local cultural events, in this case the masks of pipers and drummers (5.63 and 5.64).

5.61 Semper Oper, Dresden (source)

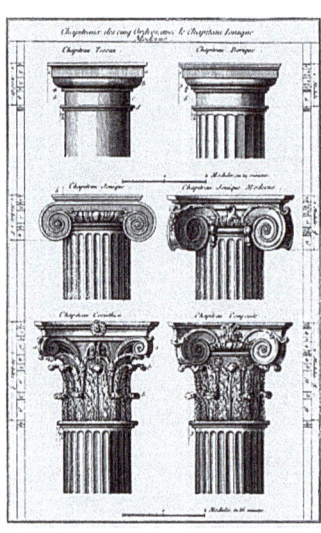

5.62 The Classical Column Orders (source)

5.63 Column, Basel Art Museum

5.64 'Gugge' music band, Fasnacht (Mardi Gras), Basel

Compared to columns, we find usually much more ornamental flux in accommodating complexities from selecting facade or floor plan geometries – with the choices based on but also beyond utilitarian needs. The work of Henry Van de Velde and Victor Horta comes to mind and perhaps even more the biomorphism of Antoni Gaudi and the more recent playfulness of Friedensreich Hundertwasser (5.65 to 5.66).

5.65 Casa Milà, Barcelona (© permission)

5.66 Hundertwasser Haus, Vienna

Even simple modernist examples can support these thoughts, such as the Bauhaus dormitory facade in Dessau, by Walter Gropius (5.67). After the decision to include balconies was made, they had to be realized in one way or another. The solution is minimal ornamentation. Is it amplified? Is it decorative? I think it is both.

5.67 Bauhaus Dormitory, Dessau

Usually the function of decoration, in the strictest sense, is highly aesthetic, that is, with the function simply to please. But often it is although used to inform. Like amplification, it always belongs to an object, to a building in case of architecture. Rather than being formative of the object itself to any large extent, it is an addition to it; often using the object's surface as a substrate.

The materials which conform to this view are paint, plaster, mosaic and other types of cover in various colors, patterns and textures. But it may also have a stronger purpose on its own, such as being a curtain or a sculpture. So, decoration may range from highly abstract to highly explicit. An example for the former is coloring of a surface without any signage. One for the latter is a relief attached to a wall telling a story. The Byzantine mosaics in the church of San Vitale, Ravenna, decorate by giving in part biblical information. The plaster arabesques and calligraphies at the Alhambra Castle, are similarly decorative and narrative (5.68 and 5.69).

5.68 San Vitale Church, Ravenna, Italy

5.69 Alhambra Castle, Granada, Spain

A vivid example for using colored surface protection, here on wood, is the Bulguksa Temple in Kyongju, Korea (5.70). Every time colors of paint or of any other surface material is consciously used, we may consider it as decoration. Other examples are the facade of an apartment high-rise building in Miami (5.71), the elevator shaft enclosure in the Neue Staatsgalerie, Stuttgart, by

5.70 Bulguksa Temple, South Korea

5.71 Apartments near Miami, FL

James Sterling, and a mechanical room in a building of the Steel Case Company in Grand Rapids, Michigan. Here, colors reinforce the differences among building components and also help to categorize them (5.72 and 5.73).

5.72 Neue Staatsgalerie, Stuttgart, Germany
      elevator shaft and enclosure

5.73 Steel Case Building, Grand Rapids, MI
      mechanical room

Even small details can benefit from decorative highlighting as is the case with the red suspension rod of a stair landing in the Town Hall of Rødovre, Denmark, by Arne Jacobson (5.74) and the fire fighting equipment in the stairwell of the Science Center, Harvard University, by Luis Sert (5.75). These simple but colorful contrasts let us often forget their protective and informative utility.

5.74 Town Hall, Rødovre, Denmark
      red rod for suspension of stair

5.75 Harvard Science Center, Cambridge, MA
      orange pipes of fire fighting equipment

Extremes of decoration are reached by John Outram's prolific colorations in support of metaphoric propositions, whether easily understood or needing explication (5.76 and 5.77). The main space at Duncan Hall, Rice University, TX, has coloration for

... scripting of surface applied to a scripting of space. It is applied, above all, to the great

'picture-planes' of the floor and ceiling that are 'enframed' by the columns and beams of the 'Architectural Order'. Their inscription with an iconic 'text' turns a 'view' into a vision.[70]
Horizontal 'layering' of the columns by color contrasts the freely given floor and ceiling patterns. The exterior reflects the interior through continuation of richly colored columns with brick patterns. This extension relates to the appearance similarly found at many older buildings on this neo-classical campus.

5.76 and 5.77 Duncan Hall, Rice University, Houston, TX (© permissions)

A few thoughts in connection with the physical properties of color are in order here. White is the combination of wavelengths which produces a physiological balance of perception which we consider as absence of color. The actual colorlessness is true black from which we receive no light for sensation and, therefore, no color. Everything in between of the two we consider to be color. Color was added to architectural forms as far back as we know of them as designed artifacts. Otherwise color has always been a visually important property of natural materials. It can be used to differentiate between components, to single out, or to equalize, also to unify. Color differences support the perception of shapes, that is, rooms, walls and ceilings, columns, etc. In doing so, they increase the experience of depth. What we see are either originating or reflecting light sources. As most objects can only reflect light which falls on them, their perceived color depends on the light source which illuminates them and on their own reflectance characteristics. Therefore, the selection and location of light sources strongly influences our visual experiences of objects. The choice of colors is largely subjective and evokes a particular aesthetic through emotional meaning. It becomes more explicitly meaningful when a certain understanding is connected with it. The redness of a fire hydrant or a telephone booth highlights functional meanings.

About the fluidity between amplification and decoration we may be reminded by the large corner column of an apartment building in Berlin, by Aldo Rossi, and the bell tower as a 'gate' to Saint John's Monastery Church, Collegeville, Minnesota, by Marcel Breuer (5.78 and 5.79). The column is exaggerated beyond load bearing capacity, emphasizing the corner. The bell tower has symbolic and ornamental aspects developed out of a sign function. The fenestration in the church facade can be considered to be more decorative than amplified. The framing of concrete around the small window components supports aesthetically the solidity of the overall scheme.

5.78 Apartment House, Berlin

5.79 Saint Johns' Abbey Collegeville, MN

5.80 and 5.81 Schullin Jewelry Store and Wienzeile 38 at Nashmarkt, Vienna

One of the designers who has brought amplification and decoration into fabulous mix is Hans Hollein. In one of his early engagements (1972) he used provocatively a delicate crack and decorative hole above the entry of a small jewelry store at Vienna's posh Graben shopping street, not far from the Nashmarkt area where highly ornamented buildings by Otto Wagner and others from around 1900 can be found (5.80 and 5.81). Hollein's designs of the Köhlergasse School in Vienna, located on a very tight urban site, and even more the Haas House with shops and restaurants, on a prominent site across from the Stephan's Cathedral in the center of Vienna, benefit greatly from ornamental diversity of both kinds (5.82 to 5.85). Even closer to ornamental 'autonomy' toward decoration, Frank Gehry lets hallways deliberately 'flow' to accommodate the surrounding, functionally primary spaces, such as in the Weatherhead School of Management at

Case Western Reserve University, Cleveland (5.86 to 5.88). These organizational patterns have their correspondence in Gehry's undulating wall and roof shapes which have, through "family resemblance", become his icons at many places around the world.

5.82 View toward main entry

Haas House Shops and Restaurants, Vienna

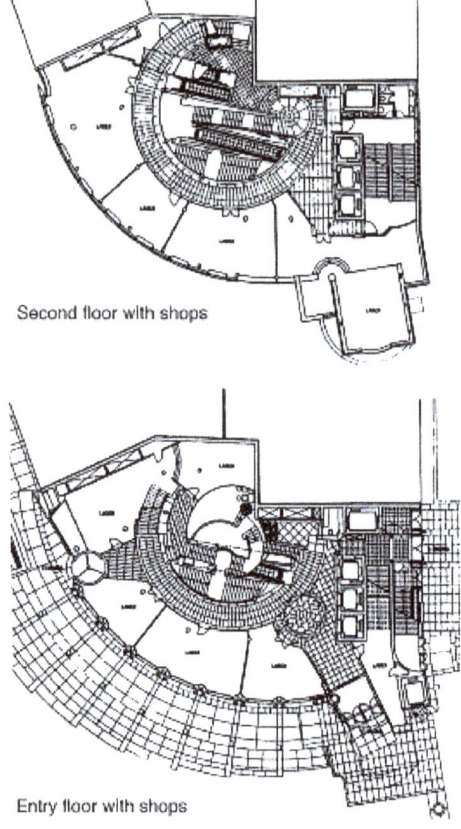

Second floor with shops

Entry floor with shops

5.83 Floor plans (© permission)

5.84 Shops and stairs

5.85 Details at stair landing

The architect Owen Jones differentiated between decorated construction and constructed decoration. He writes in 1856 that

Construction should be decorated. Decoration should never be purposely constructed.[71]

I assume that Jones means "decoration should never be purposely constructed" for its own sake. True, we cannot do that. Decoration is always part of something which it decorates. But we purposely 'construct' it when we apply it to whatever it belongs, on a surface or as other addition without architectural necessity. Amplification is necessary in one way or another, decoration is not.

5.86 Southwest facade

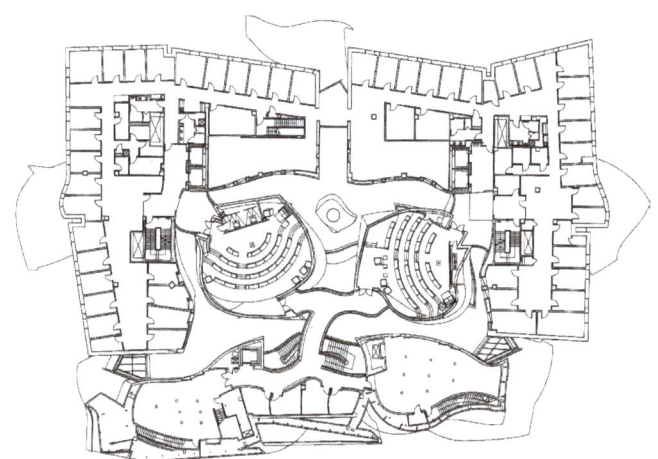

Second level

**Weatherhead School of Management
Case Western University, Cleveland**
(see also 1.5, 1.6 and 5.26)

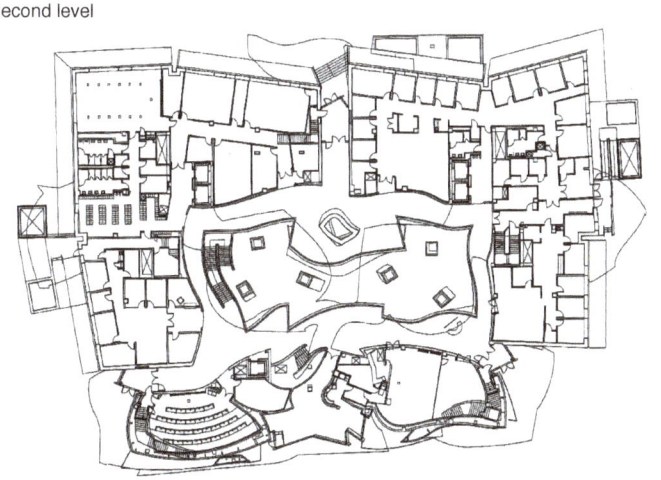

Ground level   5.87 Floor plans (© permission)   5.88 Lower level

Style and ornament allow for deliberateness. But they are never completely free. Any alternative chosen among amplifications in architecture is tied to the functions of their object. Any alternative chosen among decorations, though not tied up with utility directly, must at least obey the conditions of being an addition to a utilitarian thing. The decoration of a facade is confined by the strictures of the facade, such as dimension, geometry and construction method.

Karsten Harries defines in connection with the polemic distinction between ornament and art by Adolf Loos:

> ... I shall call decoration that articulates a communal ethos *ornament* and decoration that we experience primarily as an aesthetic addition to building *decoration*.[72]

I cannot see value in this differentiation. For example, the interior of most Baroque churches is loaded with decoration (see 7.29 and 7.30). Ornament as decoration was at that time part of the "communal ethos", an expression of religious exuberance, willed by the church as organization.

All of present ornamentation and of any other epoch reflects part of a particular culture. The dual nature of ornament, as amplification and decoration, can be traced back to the beginning of civilization when people started to erect buildings, even tents, rather than made do under the open sky or in caves. Formalization beyond environmental necessity was soon also culturally desired, as influenced by the spirit of communities. With the arrival of highly developed societies, be they Mesopotamian, Egyptian, Aegean, Indus or Mayan, codification occurred embedded in the given communal structures. Amplification (in part) and decoration (in full) are realizations based on aesthetic preferences, including societal judgments through acts of its members, collectively or individually.

Broadly viewed, icons and symbols, rhythms and proportions, geometries and massing, even textures and colors become media of style and ornamentation. Often it has been suggested that Modernism is devoid of ornamentation, sacrificed for the expression of function. This is not so, although Modernism reduced decoration and to some extent amplification. The polemic by Loos in *Ornament and Crime* does not apply as usually understood. No architecture can exist without ornament, that is, ornament develops *by necessity* in one way or another. Loos writes in 1930:

> From a thirty years struggle I have emerged as a victor: I have liberated humanity from superfluous ornament.[73]

He says "superfluous ornament" and may mean that there is ornament which is not superfluous. He obviously attacked the overload of decorative ornament, especially the eclecticism of the 19th century but also the excesses of contemporary Art Nouveau. The best known building he designed, the commercial and residential building on Vienna's Michaelerplatz (called Loos Haus), is certainly not completely without ornamentation. It is certainly not without spatial and facade amplification but also not without some decoration: the lower part of the building has rather strongly patterned marble gladding (5.89). There is much more to ornament than what Loos implies. The elegant office building at 333 West Wacker Drive in Chicago, by Kohn Pedersen Fox Associates, has gladding similar to the Loos Haus but also a highly decorative treatment of stainless steel air grilles and guardrails (5.90). The hole in the basement wall of the Staatsgalerie, Stuttgart, by James Sterling, is 'pure' decoration, "purposely constructed" (5.91).

When looking at the Loos Haus another aspect related to configuration comes to mind: the ways components contribute to proportional balance. As mentioned earlier, proportions are preferences being subject to change with aesthetic judgment over time. There is, for me, a certain uneasiness in how Loos emphasizes the height of the lower, the gladded part in relation to the building's total height. The large fenestration is in response to the business function of the ground floor requiring high spaces. The effect is somewhat softened at the side facades where he introduces strong horizontality in this lower portion. The example clearly shows that proportion is influenced by amplification and decoration. It may not be surprising that I find even buildings by Oswald Maria Ungers (an extremist of minimalism) strongly influenced by ornamentation, sometimes not positively. Square windows are a feature in most of his designs. In a Berlin apartment building, which he designed, they are stylistic decoration neglecting functional configuration for the spaces they serve (5.92). All windows are of the same size, even in the courtyard, whether there are living rooms, kitchens, bathrooms or bedrooms behind them.

5.89 Loos Haus, Vienna

5.90 333 Wacker Drive, Chicago

5.91 Neue Staatsgalerie, Stuttgart

5.92 Apartment house, Berlin

From all of this we may well derive that the 'death' of ornament never occurred. Nor will it ever occur as long as human beings are productive and do so by creating environments which please. As mentioned, the purging of ornament in modern architecture never happened, at least not to the extent often claimed. Particulars of ornament determine particular styles. As they provide what is beyond pure necessity, they determine the wider realms of culture in which architecture finds itself in a given epoch. Letting for a moment style substitute for ornament, because of their close relationship, it is as Hermann Broch argues:

> For style is surely not something which limits itself to building or the fine arts. Style is something which permeates alike all expressions in the life of an epoch. It would be incongruous to consider the artist as an exception, as someone who leads a special existence within the style and produces it, while the others remain excluded.[74]

In anything we do – so in design – the drive toward style and with it ornament is inevitable. The drive is reinforced by our human desire of variety. There is a place for sameness and a place for variety. We need both to understand – one to recognize what something is because of former similar experiences, the other to differentiate something from something else and to gain comprehension of what is new. Too much sameness produces boredom. Too much variety produces chaos. Where we want to come down in-between relies on aesthetic judgment: what is pleasant versus what is unpleasant, taken again in its broadest sense, as we have discussed. We apply ornament much more often than we may believe we do. We cannot design without variation. Every design individuality is in part due to ornamentation, be it amplification or decoration.

Never has the difference between amplification and decoration, but also their close relationship, become more evident to me than in the striking juxtaposition of two buildings in downtown Portland, Oregon. They can be viewed from the same place in the middle of a park between them. One strongly exhibits ornamentation as amplification, the other strongly ornamentation as decoration. The Multnomah County Justice Center in Portland, by Zimmer Gunsul Frasca, shows in its facades the layering of the internal organization for lobbies, prison cells, terraced recreation area and police offices (5.94). The Portland Building, by Michael Graves, shows colored bas-relief type packaging which forces the window pattern to conform to it rather than to the needs of the interior (5.93).

5.93 and 5.94 Portland Building and Multnomah County Justice Center, Portland OR

All of our life is involved with types, in general and in architecture. Our whole thinking process is enmeshed with type-structured information from our memory. When we respond to demands of purpose and context we become creative. As long as these creative acts are relatively minor variations from earlier experiences, common understanding stays largely in tact. When we become highly creative, especially when we not only are forced by circumstances to innovate but do so because of playful aesthetic motivation, common understanding may be impeded. This can probably nowhere be better observed than in abstract painting and sculpture in which strong creativity is the main driving force. In architecture we are less autonomous because we are not at liberty to ignore given purpose and context. They inevitably influence, sometimes dominate, our judgment. The more we remove ourselves as designers from their constraints the more we enter the realm where architecture becomes self-referential. In the extreme it would become non-relational beyond itself, that is, fully autonomous. If we could reach the latter, I believe, we would be at the point where we cannot speak of architecture anymore but of sculpture we walk around and perhaps in. Some recent projects approach this status, though not entirely, which is not possible. When the making of spectacular shapes is the main driving motivation, architecture is not the fundamental reason for realization, but its occasion. The result is largely amplification turned into decoration.

Prime examples of such extremism are the Akron Art Museum by Coop Himmelblau and the CCTV Tower in Beijing by the Office of Metropolitan Architecture (5.95 and 5.96). Himmelblau's design intentions articulate that

> The team attempts to generate asymmetrical structures that strive for freedom from the constrained formalism of a given style. They create "open-planned, open-minded, open-ended" designs, made up of complex, undefined spaces.[75]

Hm. Is this what architecture should be? What is the reason for "complex, undefined spaces" and what are "open-planned, open-minded, open-ended" designs?

5.95 Akron Art Museum, Akron, OH

5.96 CCTV Headquarters, Beijing (© permission)

Venturi et al claim in *Learning from Las Vegas* that

> Ironically, the Modern architecture of today, while rejecting explicit symbolism and frivolous appliqué ornament, has distorted the whole building into one big ornament. In substituting "articulation" for decoration, it has become a duck.[76]

At any time and also today architecture could not and cannot do without symbolism and ornament. Articulation has been and is necessary to bring them about. Modern architecture did not "become a duck" because articulation was substituted for decoration.

The contrasting of "duck" versus "decorated shed" brought on much lively and helpful discussion over four decades (5.97). But it can confuse the issues. Buildings of both kinds, duck or decorated shed, require articulation for configuration. That decoration is added to a shed, making it a "decorated shed", does not negate the necessity of ornamentation as amplification, which is in part the outcome of every building's functional design. The definition of the duck and decorated shed contrast is given by Venturi et al as

> 1. Where the architectural systems of space, structure, and program are submerged and distorted by an overall symbolic form. This kind of building-becoming-sculpture we call the *duck* in honor of the duck-shaped drive-in, "The Long Island Duckling," illustrated in *God's Own Junkyard* by Peter Blake.
>
> 2. Where systems and structure are directly at the service of program, and ornament is applied independently of them. This we call the *decorated shed*.
>
> The duck is the special building that *is* a symbol; the decorated shed is the conventional shelter that *applies* symbols. We maintain that both kinds of architecture are valid – Chartres is a duck (although it is a decorated shed as well), and the Palazzo Farnese is a decorated shed – but we think that the duck is seldom relevant today, although it pervades Modern architecture.[77]

5.97 Duck and Decorated Shed (© permission)

The duck in 5.97 refers through its own form to the restaurant function of the building. The reference is more iconic than symbolic, as it points to what you may eat there. The "eat" sign in front of the shed or on the shed is purely symbolic, being language. The ornamentation of the decorated shed facade is perhaps aesthetically relevant but not crucial as informative sign. It could be on any other building type. This is different with iconic nature as at a McDonald's restaurant, because of resemblance with other McDonald's. Chartres Cathedral is symbolic, because its floor plan refers to the suffering of Christ and to the community of Christians. And it is iconic, because it has resemblance with many typical functional features in other churches. It is a symbolically and iconically amplified 'duck', and a beautifully decorated 'shed'. Every building is made mainly of components with the nature of type and most buildings overall belong to a category of building type, being to some extent iconic because of resemblance. In addition, many buildings have symbolic features. "Ducks" (or "duck" features) are still highly relevant as there are still many architects around who build by having a crucial modern and modernist outlook of the positive kind – iconic, symbolic and perhaps metaphoric. All what we call architecture is ornamented, that is, amplified and usually more or less decorated. Therefore, most buildings are not ducks nor decorated sheds but both.

Most of what has been discussed here about type, style and ornament in architecture also holds true in the larger context of urban environments. Buildings and the voids between them are the reciprocal components of urban form and we experience the whole, as Kevin Lynch suggests, in the multitude of paths, nodes, edges, landmarks and districts.[78] A crucial part of architectural experience is determined by the envelopes which contain the interior spaces of buildings and by the exterior spaces between them. It is our staying in and moving through the extensions and sequences of these exterior spaces which make for urban experience. There is, however, a crucial difference in magnitude: the influence of distance as perceived by us in the succession of time and space. Not that we do not have some of this phenomenon within and around individual architectures as well – all our perceptions are in succession. But in the urban fabric, compared with individual objects, the present succession of time and space is heightened by the longer periods within historical and social diversity. Such diversity has often developed over many centuries and cultural epochs.

Manifestation of ornament in single buildings and in their assembly is to a large extent manifestation of power, be it religious, political or economic, often all three kinds together. To study ornament is to study the ups and downs of the powers of individuals and societies. Often the individual is suppressed in favor of the common. But also the reverse occurs. Today, for example, many urban centers suffer from large scale structures which dominate whole urban areas and stifle positive pedestrian experiences through monumental abstraction. Although we go up in buildings and can experience much from above, most of what we perceive and enjoy of urban quality is from lower levels. Therefore, it is especially important to provide relief through urban spaces with human scale and easily observable configuration especially on the ground levels of buildings. Also, for a long time, the emphasis on front versus side and back facades has played a major role in decisions on expression. More recently it has been recognized that backyards (and side yards) must not be 'backwards' at all but can enhance even tight urban fabrics immensely, an aspect that is missing in Lynch's and many other urban studies. Good design should not imply that buildings have 'ginger-bread' sides and lesser ones otherwise, but variations because of interior and exterior factors. Here, the interplay of private and public realms can play a very positive role.

To conclude. From this discussion we derive that type, style and ornament are crucial aspects of the understanding generally and of meaning in architecture particularly. Design is driven by the objectivity of type and the subjectivity of style. To a large extent: type is content and style is form. Type is *wha*t, style is *how*. Style may be taken as the manner of doing something, how something is made or how it performs. This cannot mean, obviously, that how something is done is independent from what it is. Form and content are interdependent, as I emphasized earlier.[79] We cannot design a building or a chair in a certain style without influencing its essence, its type. Style is more than decoration. It influences overall configuration. The differences between gothic and baroque architecture are not only in appearance. They have different cultural, sociological and functional foundations which influenced what was built and how it was built. From this complexity configurations develop to which we now, for reasons of function and aesthetics, refer to comprehensively as ornament: amplification and decoration.

Each design factor influences the fit of parts to arrive at a desired whole. Variability, and with it flexibility, is provided by the possibilities of ornamentation which we control, though only in part. Our judgment on design factors of objects is about the function of their associated physical properties. We come to judgment through our experiences and estimations of their values during the development process and at its end. Put differently, configuration as activity and realization as outcome arise from the necessity to fulfill purpose in context but are to some extent deliberately, aesthetically chosen ornamentation.

6 Cause and Effect in Design

There are fundamental conditions which make existence possible and perceptible. Everything occurs in space, time and causality. Everything is part of our worldwide system, having interdependencies with other systems outside and within. Kant argued that space and time are not things in themselves but are part of our experience of things. Space and time are not experienced as objects. But they are two of the most universal conditions one may think of and are absolutely necessary for the experience of objects. Kant writes:

> Space is a necessary representation, *a priori*, which is the ground of all outer intuitions. One can never represent that there is no space, although one can very well think that there are no objects to be encountered in it. It is therefore … an *a priori* representation that necessarily grounds outer appearances.[1]

And,

> Time is the *a priori* formal condition of all appearances in general. … and indeed the immediate condition of the inner intuition (of our souls), and thereby also the mediate condition of outer appearances. If I can say *a priori*: all outer appearances are in space and determined *a priori* according to the relations of space, so from the principle of inner sense I can say …: all appearances in general, i.e., all objects of the senses, are in time, and necessarily stand in relations of time.[2]

And,

> In the same way, …, that time is the *a priori* sensible condition of the possibility of continuous progress of that which exists to that which follows it, the understanding, …, is the *a priori* condition of the possibility of a continuous determination of all positions for the appearances in this time, through the series of causes and effects, …[3]

Space and time are givens. Without them there would be no cause and effect relationships. We can gain experience, knowledge and understanding only in the framework of time and space and causality. Arthur Schopenhauer (1788-1860) points out that

> … causality is the true point of transition, and therefore the *condition of all experience*. As such it does not have its origin in experience, but precedes it; for it is only through the category of causality that we recognize objects as *real*, that is *having effects* upon us, and the fact that we are unconscious of the inference we make here should not be seen as a difficulty, any more than the unconscious inference that we make from a body's shading to its shape.[4]

Time, space and causality are meant here as the quintessential reference settings in which things occur. This is true also for objects of thought that 'materialize' in designs and eventually in buildings. We simply cannot perceive, think and understand anything without it being in time, space and causality, that is, in instances of them. In the widest context, I believe that time, space and causality have no beginning and no end of instantiations, at least not from any practical point of view.

When we want to know why a particular meaning about an object developed in our mind, we ask for the properties of the object which, together with our intentionality, became instrumental for our understanding. We ask for causes in the cause-effect relationship between the world and our mind. While we are in this world our mind cannot avoid being influenced by it in so many ways. But it should be made clear from the outset of our discussion about causation that it is relational and we cannot observe it directly but only through its result, that is, change which is experienced by our mind because of conceptualization of an external event or reconceptualization as an internal event. All changes imply events. In other words, we cannot determine causes and effects without understanding change, the difference between the present state of objects and their former state.

6.1 Cause, effect, change and event

Causation is part of the way we conceptualize the world; the mind obviously being part of the overall universe as well. To simplify again our discussion terminologically, I will use from now on *world* as comprising everything beyond myself, corporeal and mental, and *mind* as comprising what belongs to my thoughts. This leaves my body in which my thoughts dwell. It is part of the world as it exists and acts in it. But at the same time it is part of and contains my mind which cannot exist without it. Whether I refer to my physicality or my mentality will become clear in context or will be especially mentioned.

All effects imply change – in the present context change as addition or deletion of concepts to or from our mind, or as adjustment of those already existing in that part of our mind we call memory. There is, in addition to this cause-effect relationship, the one which belongs to change in the world itself, the change of material objects and their properties, which eventually effects change in our mind. Both kinds of cause-effect relationships obviously play an important role also for meaning in architecture.

In asking about cause and effect we refer to how being happens and why; issues which exercised minds for thousands of years. The background in terms of common sense is rather well understood but the many concepts put forward are philosophically controversial. I again will try to limit the discussion to what is necessary for our purpose and must refer for broader study to the extensive literature.[5] Fundamentally I hold that, as far as we can conceptualize, every effect has a cause and every effect has the potential to become a cause of another effect, and so on. This obviously should not be taken in the sense that causes can be their own effects. There are always two or more objects or at least parts of the same object involved and their change always happens over time from cause to effect by some kind of influence.

David Hume whose work serves as point of departure for many modern theories on causation, writes in 1740:

> It is evident, that all reasonings concerning *matter of fact* are founded on the relation of cause and effect, and that we can never infer the existence of one object from another, unless they be connected together [be related], either mediately or immediately.[6]

Bringing in the notion of event, which adds the dimension of time, he explains in 1748:

> All events seem entirely loose and separate. One event follows another; but we never can observe a tie between them. They seem *conjoined*, but never *connected*.

And with regard to objects,

> … if the first object had not been [as cause], the second never had existed [as effect].[7]

This sounds rather clear-cut but implies a great deal and raises a host of questions. Hume describes a puzzling situation: it is evident that all reasoning about objects depends on the relation of cause and effect, that is, objects need to be somehow associated but, while they seem to be conjoined, they are never connected. What is this "connected"? And what is here the "mediately or immediately". Kant states the general law of causation in two versions of which the latter expands on the former:

> Everything that happens presupposes something which it follows in accordance with a rule.

And,

> All alterations occur in accordance with the law of the connection of cause and effect.[8]

Guyer and Wood write in this regard that

> Kant, …, argues that a genuine necessary connection between events is required for their objective succession in time, and that the concept of causality in which this connection is expressed is imposed on experience by our own thought as an indispensable condition of its possibility. The human understanding, therefore, is the true lawgiver of nature, and the successes of modern science are due to its conduct of its inquiries in accordance with a plan whose ground lies *a priori* in the structure of human thought. … the validity of the causal principle is to be restricted to the world as it appears under the conditions of our experience of it.[9]

What all of this implies is the fact that every causation, that is, every change from cause to effect happens within space and over time in the course of our understanding.

Causation is an a priori part of human understanding but causal relationships can be discovered only posteriori, that is, we grasp them only after they manifest themselves in our mind based on the perception of reality. Nicolas Rescher writes that

> Reality is viewed as the causal source and basis of appearances, the originator, and determiner of the phenomena of our cognitively relevant experience. "The real world" is seen as causally operative both in serving as external moulder of thought and as constituting the ultimate arbiter of the adequacy of our theorizing.[10]

By necessity we cannot other than think and understand the world as being and happening through causation. According to G.E.M. Anscombe:

> The concept of necessity, as it is connected with causation, can be explained as follows: a cause *C* is a necessitating cause of an effect *E when* (I mean: on the occasion when) if *C* occurs it is certain to cause *E* unless something prevents it.[11]

In the broadest view everything 'hangs' together with something else in a cause-effect relationship. There is nothing completely by itself. How far this is true in reality is not accessible to us but we conceptualize reality in this way and have found the concept workable, if not always satisfactory in its applications and results. We may not blame, however, the concept for such failings but rather our inadequacies in understanding the complexity of the world and making judgments on it. Considering everything we are surrounded by and involved with, reality is a concept because we perceive and understand it in a certain way. We view causality as relations among its parts. Many parts influence each other. As we are also part of this universe, reality influences us. John Searle puts it well when he writes:

> Part of our notion of the way the world really is, is that its being the way it is causes us to perceive it as being that way. Causes are part of reality and yet the concept of reality is itself a causal concept.[12]

If reality is a concept, which I believe so with Searle, then it is a mental construct. But concepts, though they are mental, can be what they are only because there is a reality to which they belong. The world as such is not a mental construct. It physically exists. And, therefore, in reference to Kant, every causation and our conceptualization of it – as change from cause to effect – happens within space and over time.

Causation is for us of strong practical interest as it gives the framework for asking about objects with their properties and relationships. When we want to understand what and how objects are, we conclude from observation of what happens. While it is true that we grasp causal relationships only after they manifest themselves in our mind, it is also the case that we can predict causation with some certainty out of such experiences. Charles Peirce asserted pragmatically that

> In order to ascertain the meaning of an intellectual conception we should consider what practical consequences might conceivably result by necessity from the truth of that conception; and the sum of these consequences will constitute the entire meaning of the conception.[13]

In other words, the understanding of an anticipated concept is what our thoughts will yield about the results from the application of the concept; "by necessity from the truth of that conception", that is, *from its realization*.

We can conclude that at a certain time our perception causes us to view the world in a certain way, resulting in a particular understanding, a meaning. If this meaning results in certain needs or desires or both, and we become motivated (effect becomes cause), we develop further meaning by projecting design solutions which, when realized, bring forth architecture. This progression contains in detail many cause and effect occurrences. In a nutshell, we have

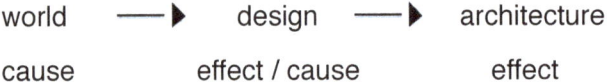

           world   ⟶   design   ⟶   architecture.

           cause   effect / cause   effect

We experience this process in architecture, as in any other causation, as change between events. In fact, part of the design process is, whether we are aware of it or not, observing existing conditions including changes and related events in the world surrounding us, and projecting changes toward events we desire.

Change refers to transformation or exchange. It implies the prospective difference of status of an object from an earlier status. It is a fundamental condition of the world and our lives. But in the time spans and local horizons we are concerned with, there is also much 'permanence' which provides us crucial histories of continuity. Many objects are for us now what they were some time ago – mountains more than cities, cities more than buildings, buildings more than cars, and so on. We may consider and label them as events of long standing, whose overall status as objects has not changed appreciably as to our present focus of interest and timeframe. Parts of our built environment may be considered so, others not. One may think of the life of old towns versus that of shopping strips. I agree with philosophers who consider physical objects as events and view built environments as events. Charles Broad wrote in 1923 that

> A thing … is simply a long event.[14]

Causes bring about events. Therefore, causal chains are series of events with change from event to event. While all physical matter is subject to time in progression, so it is subject to change in progression. When change is so small that we cannot observe it, or it is hidden otherwise from us, we call that physical matter a permanent thing. Bertrand Russell calls this state "quasi-permanence".[15] Much of architecture is quasi-permanent but much of it is changing rather rapidly. We understand architectural history as relatively slow changes of the built environment. On the other hand, operational changes are more rapid, examples being facades with adjustable shading devices, classroom spaces with moveable walls, renovations of whole building functions, etc.

Therefore, care must be taken in the use of terminology. Events are usually occurrences indicating the status of cause or effect at points in time. But they are also attributed, as derived from the just given quotes, for the duration from beginning to end of causal relationships, from beginning to end of change; that is, for two points in time. The relatively long term event 'building as result' is the lifetime existence of that so identified object. It is the effect of earlier causes, which brought about events collectively called 'building as process'. Whether we mean event as point in time or ongoing must be derived from context. In every instance of causation the pertaining causes, effects, changes and their events are reciprocally related. None of them occurs without the other.

The originating cause in design is the motivation, conceptualization and physical intervention of the designer; intervention taken as working with what exists, modifying it by adding to or subtracting from it. Intervention and change has always to do with existing things that become, are changed into, 'new' things. This answers in part the question: where do changes come from in relation to objects? They are typically externally caused, that is, from *cause-objects* which have an impact on targeted *effect-objects*. Note that we carry over the terminology of the mental construct of causation (cause and effect) into the existing world of objects. Material objects are often targeted by minds with physical action following; the sequence pointing to purposiveness. I say 'often' because not all causation is by volition. Unwilled causation happens in the destruction of a window by a storm or its irradiation by the sun, that is, through nonhuman intervention; or even by a 'non-occurrence', such as through absentmindedness of drivers in car accidents and, in architecture, through neglect of important design factors.

If causation occurs among objects, as when bodies collide, we may call it *external causation*. The cause-object and the effect-object are not the same. If causation happens within the domain of an object, we may call it *internal causation*. Concrete hardens after mixing because of internal reactions. The cause-object and the effect-object are the same, though the cause properties and the effect properties are not the same. A property cannot change itself; property assumed as not further reducible in its given state. The color red cannot change itself into something else. In such differentiations one must be careful with what one considers object and what property.

There are two main groups of cause-objects and effect-objects: physical and mental. Both provide poles for causation, as *cause-events* and *effect-events*. A building or a tree, physical entities, can be causes or effects. So can mental entities, such as reasons or desires. In general, if something happened because I caused it to happen as verified by me or others – though never with complete confidence in our understanding of how and what happened – we are justified to believe that this something happened in reality, as far as we can understand reality. This is the basis of my pragmatic view of causation. There is correspondence between what we call causation and what happened, observed by us in reality.

6.2 World and mind in causation

We develop much of our understanding of the world by means of causality. We can explain by it many pertinent aspects of complexity, based on the assumption that the complexity of representations in our mind parallels the complexity of the world. Still, our capacity to understand complexity and to predict its consequences is rather limited. Therefore, the better we can clarify aspects and relationships, the better we can look back and forth along chains of events for information which also can be useful for design. There are four types of causation and they are most helpfully named in relation to our world-mind dichotomy:
1) world-to-world;
2) world-to-mind;
3) mind-to-world;
4) mind-to-mind.

World-to-world causation refers to the physical influence of physical objects on other physical objects. When one automobile hits another, both are damaged more or less. When I open a window, the position of my arm changes to change the position of the window sash. Within a given building size, a spatial increase for one room will call for a decrease in another or others. There are of course many associated subchanges with their own cause and effect relationships, such as energy exchanges between the colliding cars, muscle activities in my body because of the arm's movement, friction in the hinges of the window being opened and building program reevaluation with regard to needs or desires.

World-to-mind causation refers to any sensory influence of the world on our body with representation of it in our mind. *Mind-to-world causation* refers to our mind's influence on the world by means of our body's activity. Although mind and body are highly interdependent, in fact unified, we may consider for both directions the body to be intermediary effect-cause event. *Mind-to-mind causation* refers, strictly taken, to direct influence between minds. As I do not believe in telepathy, I do not believe mind-to-mind causation to be possible. At best the case can be made to consider mind-to-mind a useful concept with the 'to' being a physical medium, such as language, providing the most direct and variable way of communication.

We must keep in mind in all of this discussion that whenever minds are involved with intentionality, the mind's attention to worldly things is first for directedness and then aboutness. Also we must not forget that our minds, as mentioned, are part of our bodies and our bodies are part of the world. Our minds are part of the world's overall reality. I will further discuss these four views of causation after a few more general remarks.

All four models refer to the beginning and end points of causes and effects with media in-between whose involvement is also causative. Many other causations may occur; some important for the main one, others not. Putting a door into a wall changes the wall from being a permanent barrier to being open at times. The cause-object is the intention to place the door (a cause-event in mind-to-world direction). The action to install the door follows. Intention and action change in the progress of things, that is, they 'disappear', which is change, as their task is fulfilled. The door goes not away, however. It is a permanent event, while the other two are temporary events, as far as our time frame is concerned. With regard to effect-events quite obviously the wall changes, it has now a door. Another effect-event, though a quite different one, is the new location of the door; different from wherever it was before, such as in the factory where it was produced. Here we have a change of one environmental event into another, from a 'here-location' to a 'there-location'. Another example of change is that from 'controllable' to 'uncontrollable' event with regard to what is desired or may happen inevitably. To clarify, when we talk about event changes, we refer to status conditions as resultant changes.

From the examples we get an idea of the complexity in conceptualizing causation in detail, with the many real or potential 'side' effects not even addressed. We are generally only interested in the cause-event and the effect-event overall. But we must watch out for important consequences of what happens in-between. This may not only inhibit or enhance what we are after in our particular design effort but may lead to aspects we have not thought of, obviously with meanings on their own. For example, the door in the facade may have a desirable or undesirable influence on planning the landscaping in front of the facade.

We know from experiences that similar causes under similar circumstances yield similar effects. Note that I use 'similar' (again) and not 'same'. Hume is not precise when he postulates in his early writing that

> The same cause always produces the same effect, and the same effect never arises but from the same cause. This principle we derive from experience, ...[16]

Experience does not show that. We cannot isolate singular causation, at least not on this earth, to the point that there would be no causal interference by something else. Air friction, for example, interferes variously with the free fall of bodies caused by gravity. A building is cause when seen. Light causes our eyes to see it. Depending on the nature of the light source, we see the building accordingly. Depending on our position in relation to the building, we see it accordingly. The effect of the building being seen is modified by contextual causes. Hume recognizes this in an abstract, written somewhat latter, when he qualifies:

> We conclude, that like causes, in like circumstances, will always produce like effects.[17]

The 'in like circumstances' is a crucial insert.[18] Strictly taken, no events in practice are ever exactly the same as others. Neither are instances of regularity. Nevertheless, reasonably close similarities allow us to infer 'approximate' laws of causation which, in turn, help us to predict repeat occurrence and performance. Therefore, in determining cause from effect we proceed under the assumption of regularity. This is why we can make decisions with confidence; having had experiences E happening because of causes C. But as total regularity is not the case, we always decide with some uncertainty, of which we are only too well aware from design and construction.

Without regularity and repetition, objects and our perceptions of them would trigger chaos in our understanding and meaning, with indeterminable difficulties. The underlying relationships of properties would be unpredictable. This is why rules have evolved and are important, not only to achieve change but also to prevent it. Remember our discussions on conceptualization and typology. Design completely without constraints cannot be realized as architecture. It would be, if it could be realized, confusing and irresponsible.

So, we explain causation to a large extent as construct for understanding regularity and for gaining confidence in conceptualization. This implies relatively limited frames of reference and amounts of detail. On the other hand, regularity in broad application results in endless repetition and leads to boredom and perhaps disorientation. The sprawling suburbs of large cities with their repetition of tract housing show what I mean. The challenge in the development of every design and the chance for successful meaning exists in finding the balance of change and regularity, movement and fixation, necessity and desirability, even ambiguity and clarity. Some ambiguity is not only inevitable but desirable as Robert Venturi has forcefully argued.[19] To probe for tolerance and to strike a reasonable balance is part of making design an exciting enterprise.

To conclude this introductory discussion, we can say that design is essentially intervention in existing chains of events; objects and states of affairs considered as events. We operate in causatively positive or negative modes, that is, we cause changes to happen or not to happen. If we 'cause' them not to happen, we allow other related causes to effect changes with their conditions. All intervention happens under natural laws which we must observe and heed to avoid problems. Having freedom within constraint poses one of the main challenges in design with responsibility.

World-to-world causation

World-to-world causation provides the best occasion to observe that, as Hume says, everything is conjoint, hangs together. Causes always entail effects (or there is no causation). But they are not isolated pairs. They are part of causal chains. That means that effect-objects become cause-objects in the sequences of events. The wall and door example implied this aspect already. 6.1 is an example which makes it even more explicit. The reading on a thermostat calls for cooling from an air-conditioning system. The air entering the room cools the space and with it has an effect on the sensing of the thermostat. Air enters the space (effect-event, ee) after being cooled and transported to the room. Its influence on the room air (cause-event, ce) makes the thermostat read the temperature (effect-event). When the desired set temperature of the thermostat is reached, it sends a signal (cause-event) to the cooling system which receives the signal (effect-event) to stop the cooling equipment to supply additional air (cause-event).

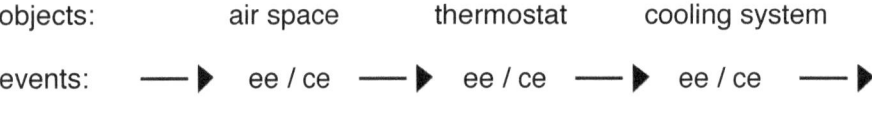

6.1 Causation in world-to-world direction

Airspace, thermostat, etc. in 6.1 are the physical components with the dual nature of serving as effect-objects and cause-objects, and being effect-events and cause-events. This is also the case when we look at a facade which is influenced as an effect-event by receiving solar radiation and a cause-event in reradiating part of the energy in the visible range enabling an effect-event of sensation in our eyes.

    The sequence in 6.1 shows only the three main objects of particular interest. Several other causations with their own events occur, such as what happens with the air and what is active to run the cooling equipment. Two objects in a chain, one following the other, constitute direct causation. More than two in a chain constitute in addition one or more intermediate causations depending on where the cause and event poles, that is, the selected beginning and end of causation, are positioned. This is the case in design very profusely, such as in the chains of events of arranging spaces to fulfill certain functional requirements and of allocating the many necessary physical systems and components. It is naturally up to us to analyze what happens between cause and event poles, say, defined by a client, and to understand what is implied in selecting the range between poles. Insufficient determination of and communication about the meaning of causation is a major detriment to successful design solutions.

    Effect-objects are obviously effected. But cause-objects are affected also by their very activity of causing, changing themselves, such as by loss of substance or by transformation because of external reactions, often by both. External reactions may also be caused by effect-objects because of the way how they were changed. The surrounding environment may react to the new properties of the objects which the effects represent. If this happens, the status of effect-objects more or less changes into cause-objects. An automobile being hit is reactive by being resistive but also perhaps by moving into an unpredictable direction. A thermostat is reactive, causing indirectly via electrical signal the change of the air temperature. Another very different example is the change that occurs in the pursuit of a design following an increase of our psychological or technical understanding from the analysis of potential solutions rather than accepting a readily achieved solution. We react by making better educated judgments. Reactions to impressions from our own design expressions and those of others have the tendency to change our views in decision making.

    In our thermostat example we have a delay between the initial effect on the thermostat by cool air entering the space, say at 55 F, until the leaving room air reaches the set temperature, say at 70 F. Only then the thermostat triggers the cause-event of a signal to the air-conditioning equipment to control the fan for pushing less cool air through the ducts. In fact, the incremental rise of temperatures in the thermostat is a sequence of effect-events up to the set temperature, at which point it becomes a cause-event. History obviously provides us with countless examples of long time 'lags' between cause having effect and effect being cause, particularly in architecture. Centuries have gone by until we enjoy today, and in our ways, the architecture of the Middle Ages. Buildings have come about (as effects) often long before they provide causes for uncounted experiences of their observers and users.

There are also causes which prevent effects. A large room (as a cause-object) will hold a large crowd of people and prevent crowding or even overflow. Hinges hold a window from falling down. Are changes involved? Yes. For the room, if design provided originally a smaller room, a kind of internal, reactive program change happened because of the anticipated number of people to be accommodated. For the window, the hinges accept pressure to counteract gravity which is reactive change because of the windows weight. One of the most frequent of preventive causations occurs because of the fact that 'something cannot be where something else is'. Where I sit, nobody else can. We may call it the exclusivity status of space occupancy, which has strong implications for space allocation and organization in design problems. Prevention may be causative, even if it does not imply present action and change. There is usually a sign at the entry door to an elevator saying "Do not use elevator in case of fire – Use stairs". A physical cause-event, a sign, warns for the case of fire not to enter but walk the close-by stairs, potentially causing an omitted physical effect-event (entering the elevator) by causing instead another physical effect-event (walking the stairs).

What we have discussed is most easily grasped in *world-to-world* direction, one physical object influencing another. Grasping as much as possible of all relevant causation in a system (we never can do so completely) is helped by the other three cause directions which involve the mind operationally.. Our mind is obviously involved also in world-to-world direction because without its involvement we would not be able to perceive or understand anything.

World-to-mind causation

In considering *world-to-mind* causation we analyze the relationships between a physical cause-event and a mental effect-event (6.2). Three constituents coexist: 1) a perceivable world, 2) a receptive mind, which implies our intentionality, and usually 3) a medium or media between the world and our body-mind to provide the link for sensation to happen (not shown). These media are part of the world. It makes sense to single them out as they play often a crucial role in modifying sensation. They double as effect-event and cause-event. After sensation causes perception the initial change of the mind yields appearance. Then understanding occurs which in turn brings about addition to and adjustment of the mind's memory (not shown). Every impression we have of the world, be it of a building, a movement, a sound, a smell, or whatever, is a world-to-mind causation.

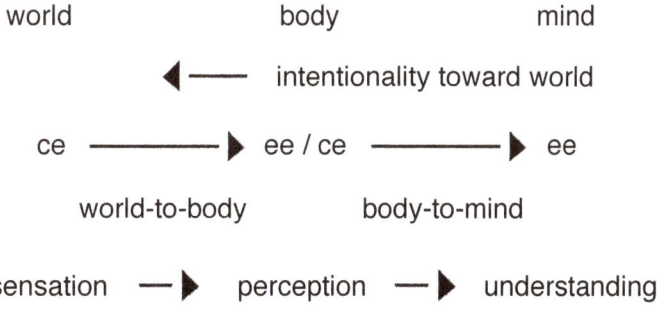

6.2 World-to-mind causation in observation

Intentionality provides our directedness toward objects external to our mind. It does not take the place of a physical link but through its result of awareness provides the necessary condition for perception and understanding to come about. There may or may not be links active as media. Our body may be immediately adjacent to an object of interest. Our mind's understanding that we sit on a chair does not require a link to it beyond or body. We feel the chair directly. But looking at a building requires the radiation of reflected light from the building as external physical link. We have two intermediate causations: from building to sensation (via light) and from sensation to mind (via understanding). The latter yields the shift from the physical into the mental realm with sensation on the 'world side' of the body and understanding on the 'mind side'; whereby we may consider the body doubling as cause-event and effect-event, being a thinking body, a physical and mental body in unity.

If volition is the originating instance of intentionality with attention directed toward an object, we may view its role as the 'active' cause and the object's role as the 'passive' cause. If the object is the originating instance to prompt our intentionality because it poses an occurrence calling for attention, we may view the object's role as 'active' cause and the intentionality's role as 'passive', at least initially. In either way, intentionality is the crucial state of a conscious mind to perceive. The change then, the effect, occurs because of representation in the mind.

Are physical things always causative to be understood by us? First, from what I said earlier it should be clear that I believe so. Those objects, broadly taken also as happenings which we perceive directly or by means of instruments, are manifest to us or we would not know of them. Therefore, they are causative, if perhaps only in a weak sense. Second, it is not so that we perceive and understand objects as they appear to us as representations of physical properties only but they are also always bearers of relational meaning beyond what they are themselves – whether we are aware of it or not. Much of this additional meaning is due to many objects being in a state of purposive causation. In our case, much meaning is given in form of properties by the designer; meaning which is conceptualized upon perception of the observer. The purposive opening of a south oriented facade to absorb solar radiation, when desired, and its protection by shading devices, when not desired, is meaning embedded at the time the facade was designed and constructed physically. It is meaning conceptualized by the designer and reconceptualized by the observer.

What happens in world-to-mind direction is transfer of energy (in light, sound, air, pressure etc.) toward sensation out of which informational content arises because of understanding. It is not a medium of transfer (usually present) which is the main cause of what we understand, although it is instrumental and it has inevitably some modifying influence. The main causes are the existence of the object and our intentionality toward the object. Sensation is effect-to-cause event for information transfer. Max Kistler writes on informational causes that

> Information is no intrinsic property of physical processes, but is well determined only within the background of a reference frame which is fixed by the observer.[20]

Information does not provide understanding. It is neutral. It is the effect of information on thinking which provides understanding, change of existing memorized understanding, caused in the mind of the observer (receiver).

When we talk about causation we typically refer to one instance, such as cause C brings about the effect E. This singularity is a limitation we impose for easier comprehension. In reality single causation does not exist as such. It is one instance of the occurrences in causal space with many more or less powerful events happening in a web of ever changing order. In addition, singular effects may be the result of multiple causes and singular causes may have multiple effects through complex causation. We tend to evaluate for high relative strength of causes to produce effects as they are typically the ones which yield the most information on why and how change comes about. But we must be careful not to overlook others which may not appear to possess high impact potential but may turn out to have. Potential long term impacts fall into this category – especially in areas with long object life spans, such as in architecture. Pollution of various kinds has had such unforeseen impacts.

Another time related consideration needs sorting out: causal space is directional as being progressive in time. Each cause is an event with unique identity in time. So is every effect. When we look at one event, we 'fix' it in time for consideration and do so with all others involved. Therefore, what is crucial for assessment is not only the relative strength of causal events – design factors for our purpose – but their position relative to each other in time. Events, considered rather minor in strength, may play a highly influential or even decisive role because of their time position in causal chains. Anyone who has looked at critical path diagrams of construction sequences knows of such conditions (3.5).[21] In most building processes critical time positions exist, such as for design input of building systems data by structural or mechanical consultants and for construction site delivery of products by vendors.

When we talked earlier about physical objects we came to the understanding that properties are what distinguishes objects from each other and that these properties are influenced by properties of other objects. Objects are always in an environment of objects which have more or less strong interrelationships with them. We can enlighten this aspect in view of causation. There are *intrinsic properties* of objects which fundamentally differentiate them from other objects. They are its inherent nature. Water, for example, is intrinsically H_2O. But it has one of three 'associated' properties: it is in gaseous, fluid or solid state in dependence on the influence of heat and pressure. All physical objects have this multiple nature. Each is distinct because of its existential intrinsicality, and its causal particularity and potential. There are no physical objects which are not influenced externally, as they exist in physical environments with particular properties, such as heat, pressure, sound or motion, which are potentially causative. There is a parallel in us beings with intrinsic characteristics and with environmentally influenced, causally dependent responsiveness. Things, if they react, do so in response to their own nature and to the nature of existing external conditions.

Usually explanation of cause to understand change in architecture depends on what we consider an object to be in given circumstances and in steady state, that is, not changing as far as our perception goes. For example, during a sunny and windy day, a building, observed by us, is thought to be in steady state. In many respects this is not so. The building endures dynamic thermal and pressure impacts, resulting in expansions and deformations. But this does not effect our perception of it (unless the building exhibits cracks or even falls down because of the impacts). But perhaps its visual appearance may not be in steady state as result of changing solar exposure, being external cause. If the building has adjustable external shading devices, operated automatically or by its occupants, then there is not only a change of appearance but a reactive physical change of the building structure itself. Another change of understanding very different from all others may be caused by a change of our mental attitude, such as from a different level of available information about the object, or from a change in how we judge our experience as felt, that is, by emotion. In generalizing this somewhat tedious discussion we may conclude that it is crucial for understanding to carefully differentiate between internally and externally caused changes of objects in chains of events, and whether changes are genuine changes of objects with world-to-mind consequences or are due to relational aspects, subjectively caused by our mental attitude. Often, out of the latter, mind-to-world causation arises in reaction to conceptual and aesthetic judgment.

Mind-to-world causation

What happens in *mind-to-world* direction is not simply a reversal of what happens in world-to-mind direction. Here, mental events provide specific understanding which results in change of the physical world (6.3). Motivation, inspiration and imagination are the causes. But they do not cause physical change directly, only physical actions do. Design thinking from impression is different from design thinking for expression. Both are based on understanding but the latter is more open ended. It is more creative, less reconstructive. At the intersection of mind and world the body doubles again for effect-event and cause-event, now in reverse direction, but in a very different mode of operation: it does what the mind tells it to do. The mind means the body to act toward solving problems.

Another important difference exists in the results from the design process: *simulations*, the intermediate results of physically representing the anticipated built environment in form of drawings, scaled models, computerized depictions, etc. They serve as intermediate objects in world-to-world mode toward changing the corporeality. Intentionality directed toward the world is now a precondition not only necessary for receiving impressions from the world (world-to-mind), so that we know about what exists, but for adjusting our emergent understanding toward the realization of the project.

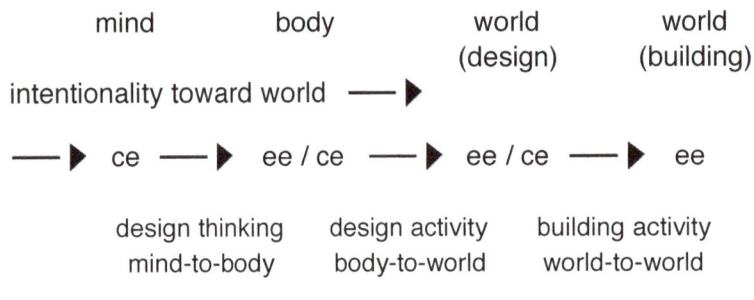

6.3 Mind-to-world causation in design

Understanding is a refinement process with iterative steps. This is the case in observation as well as in design. In both a back and forth between the directions of world-to-mind and mind-to-world occurs. Each of these iterations produces incrementally advanced impressions and expressions. In observation the motivational thrust is toward achieving eventually an understanding of the object which I characterized earlier as impressive meaning. The content of our intermediate and final impressions is immediately and automatically deposited in our memory (6.4). This capacity of our mind is crucial for building up impressions.

In design the motivational thrust is toward eventually achieving an understanding for the project's expression which I characterized earlier as expressive meaning. The expressive content of the intermediate impressions, now of the design progress, again is crucially deposited in our memory. But it is also actively used and deposited as content in the result of the physical design process, the simulated form of the object (6.5). We can postulate: *There is no expression in architectural design without impressions from its evolving stages of progression.*

6.4 and 6.5 show the incremental advances of impression (from observation) and expression (for design). We may think of three realms in world and mind relations: the object space in which corporeality exists, the space of understanding in which mental representations develop and the

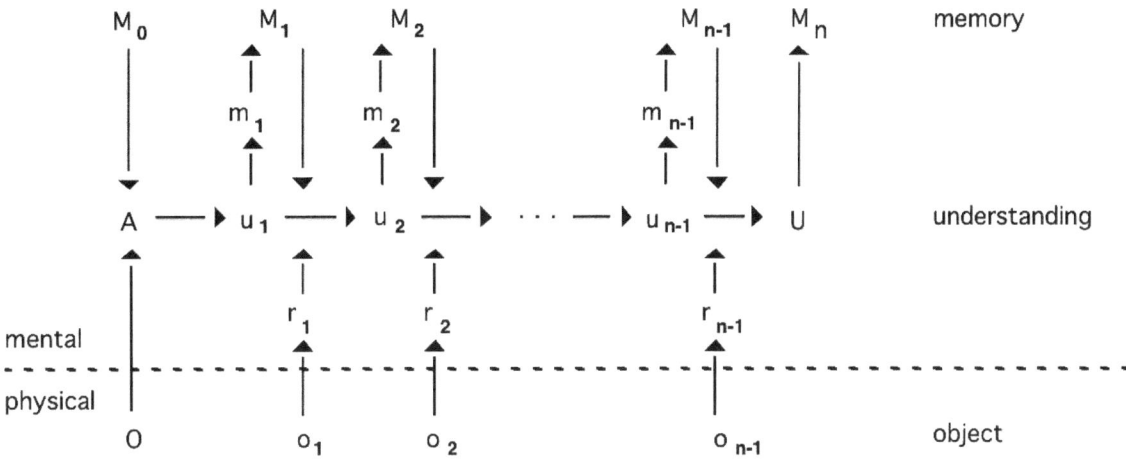

6.4 Cause-effect chain of events in the process of impression (observation)

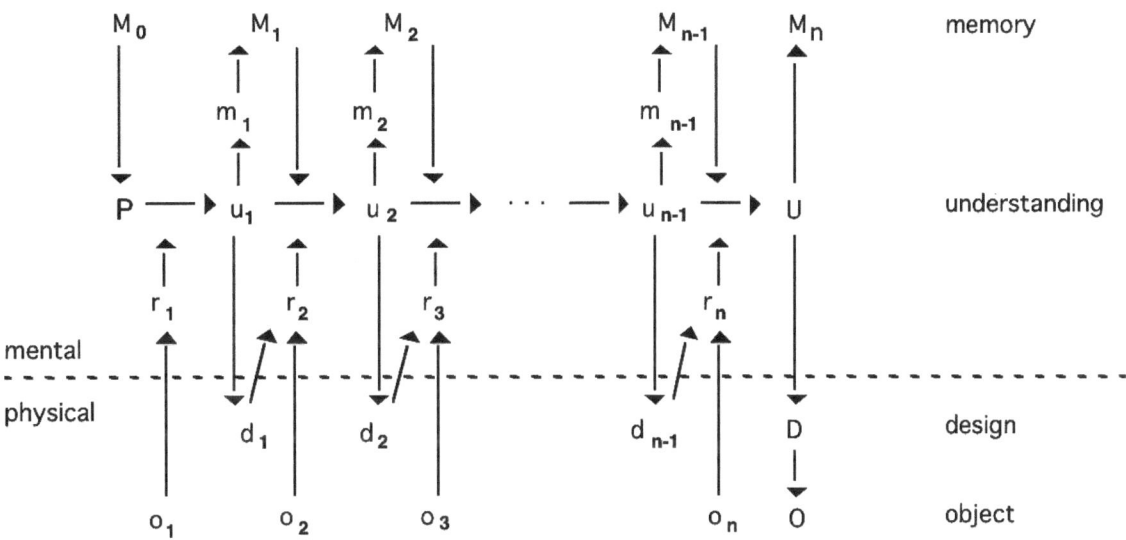

6.5 Cause-effect chain of events in the process of expression (design)

memory space in which the representations accumulate. The latter two exist in the brain. O indicates cause-object. o indicates additional input from the object space, the world, either as further information from the originating object (O) or from other objects, such as environmental conditions. r indicates representations of objective information as modifiers in the process of understanding. A indicates appearance (not yet understood representation). U indicates eventual understanding from developing understanding u. M indicates content of memory from earlier stored understandings. The memory is never empty and we cannot conceptualize without using our capacity to think which is fed from its fundamental content. It stores understanding of learning from early childhood on. m indicates the memory increments from presently developed understanding.

In the chain of events in 6.4 and 6.5 every effect-object also serves as cause-object for the next event. Each is also a potential target for external influence from other objects in context. Note that 'object' can be any occurrence. Each understanding *(u)* including the initial one derived from original appearance, stands for effect-objects serving as causes for the next step in the process.

In 6.5, P indicates the initial program with basic ideas about the anticipated object. It is constituted by input from the designer's memory *(M)*, that is, from earlier stored understanding, and from external, object related resources *(o)*, for example, information from the client. Incremental input from the memory and from the object space allows us to develop intermediate understanding *(u)*. Again, *m* indicates the results from presently developed understandings and *r* intermediate representations. Incremental design solutions (d) are deposited in drawings, models, computer simulations, etc. *D* is the final design and *O* the completed physical object which joins the existing environment.

This process operates on four levels: the memory space in which the representations accumulate, the space of understanding in which mental representations develop, the design space with the physical simulation of understanding and the object space in which resources and constructs eventually exist in reality.

The cause-effect schema shown for critical path in 3.5 is a chain of events not only for world-to-mind impressions but also for mind-to-world expressions. We project from the understanding of impressions toward expressions which are events, such as in design. Therefore, critical paths methods can also be used in complex time sequences of design processes, not only in projecting physical work processes.

Despite enormous increases in the knowledge of neurological processes, we are far from understanding how our brain connects what we call facts so that they become coherent wholes. We probably never will understand fully. We understand, however, increasingly in what mental events result, and this is what counts for us. An example is the production of a drawing as the expression of design in response to events in the mind. What is the cause of the expression? There is never a single one. We operate within a web of causal chains with an indeterminable number of events of which always several or many are constitutive in particular cases.

The most important causes are the ones which provide eventually the main content of the expression. They often arise in chains of events quite far back which indicates what is called the 'transitive' nature of causes (causes which are effective via intermediate causation). There are naturally many secondary causes, from the opinion of others about our project to the awareness of changing lighting exposure of the drawing we work on. Some may seem to be trivial and are so. But many are obviously not and influence more or less our imagination. The influences of computer graphics, for example, on what we design and bring into being have for many designers become not only highly instrumental but to some extent deterministic, especially because of the easily accessible, stored and 'prefabricated' information available.

Finally, a simple example about color perception and color use may further enlighten us about the world-to-mind versus mind-to-world directions and the asymmetry involved. Attributing 'red' when looking at a wall is due to finding the mental representation of what we call 'red' in our memory. But, referring to design expression, whatever 'red' is in my mind and however strong my desire might be to have it on a wall cannot make red color to go and stay there. Understanding cannot influence reality directly, only physical action can. In a different vain, the decision to use 'red' may be spontaneous, having no traceable history, therefore being instinctive or arbitrary. But often it does have a history related to the communication of understanding. To paint fire fighting equipment red or select blue tiles for the bottom of a swimming pool makes sense. However motivated, mental events are always causative on the world indirectly via the action of our bodies, such as our voices speaking, our hands drawing with pencils or our feet carrying us from one place to another.

Mind-to-mind causation

Mind-to-mind causation, as mentioned, does not exist unless one believes in telepathy. More liberally and restricted to language, it may be viewed as a combination of the mind-to-world and world-to-mind concepts with the "world" in-between replaced by the 'least physical' medium: written or spoken words. The focus is on the advantage of language as the most direct, variable and indispensable way of communication about something including architecture.

Expression can cause impression only by constituting itself into form, that is in physical realization. When language is the realization, it is so because it brings physicality to words, as simple signs. They are usually sufficient because of our capacity to derive relational understanding. "EXIT" signs for emergency guidance out of a building are an example. In this sense we can consider language as part of design, at least as a supporting component. Important here is the societal understanding of the giving and receiving minds. Alfred Schutz writes that

> I apprehend the lived experiences of another only through signitive-symbolic representation, regarding either his body or some cultural artifact he produced as a "field of expression" ... for those experiences.[22]

He addresses the general context of social behavior. Communication through design is naturally part of it. The "cultural artifacts" are in our case the objects of architecture; here in the form of language as objects, linguistic signs. Again as stressed before, minds of givers and receivers of meaning are subjectively involved. It is misleading to call such meaning "objective" as Schutz does in his phenomenological investigations.[23] Words or any other media are objective, but not their meanings (as given or received subjectively). Therefore, even if a design medium would perfectly reflect the subjective meaning of the designer, the meaning of the observer can never be exactly the same.

We must not belittle, however, that the meaning developed by the observer comes usually close to that developed by the designer. This is what we hope to achieve in communication every day and it is a measure of our success. While I can sympathize with Jacques Derrida's lamentation about our concepts of meaning – being essentially unworkable toward ultimate understanding of reality, our grasp of things being always an undefinable "Other" – I believe that we must be careful not to use this problem as an excuse in architectural design or in general. Although with some uncertainty, we make determinative decisions. Derrida's views have been terribly misused during the recent decades, often as a tool for rhetorical obfuscation, leading to confusion.[24] Mark Wigley, for example, writes that

> ... decisions are always made, not in spite of an unavoidable indeterminacy but on the very basis of it. There is an undecidability built into every decision. And this argument is not simply applied to the idea of a building, as the sense of determination can never be separated from the sense of a building.[25]

Not undecidability but uncertainty is part of our decisions. Meaning from mind-to-mind for decision making, necessarily somewhat subjective, requires clarity to minimize the potential of factual failure.

6.3 Powers of preference

Design is a teleologically oriented activity. We set goals to be achieved. Then we seek means to arrive at these ends. Design consists of chains of events coming about through successive action and interaction. In the course of all complex processes, so in design, all four of the discussed concepts – world-to-world, world-to-mind, mind-to-world and mind-to-mind – occur in a mix depending on what is involved.

Design is intentional by volition which implies power. It is action for something to happen. Action is an event of change from one state into another caused by somebody, an agent. Intentionality is an event itself, starting before action occurs. John Mackie interprets the teleological descriptions of human actions as causal accounts:

> … if A does B because he intends (or wants or desires) to bring about G and believes that his doing B would lead to G, there is not only A's belief about efficient causation between his doing B and the occurrence of G, there is also an objective relation of efficient causation between A's intending (or wanting or desiring) this, his believing that, and his doing of B.[26]

A is the cause-event, B is the intermediate action-event and G is the eventual effect-event. One part of explaining actions is giving reasons for it. According to Rowland Stout:

> … it should be accepted that teleological explanation is supposed to be a kind of causal explanation in as much as it is supposed to say something informative about the causal process resulting in the thing to be explained.[27]

In architectural design, teleological explanation is the description about what is necessary to realize the project, including objectives to be achieved, resources to be allocated and actions to be completed. Implied is the program statement about the project and the employment of design professionals and others required. This work represents not only the anticipated result but also provides its justification.

> Teleological explanation is causal explanation in terms of a practical justification. If there is anything in nature which can be explained teleologically, then whether or not such a thing is justified causally influences whether or not it happens. It happens because it should happen.[28]

Still on grounds of teleological explanation, we may paraphrase for our purpose in saying slightly weaker that *in design something likely will happen because we believe it should happen.*

So, teleological views have significance when we search for causes of design results, but also about how we understand the whole design process. When we anticipate a design result we represent it in our mind and search for possible causes that may bring it about. We contemplate change. This is in a broader context very much in line with what we mentioned earlier with regard to motivation and empathy. To make reasonable decisions on change we need to know what exists in detail. We set up a tentative result as a goal to find design factors that promise fulfillment. In other words, we look back from needed or desired effects to what may cause them. We use then these causes to simulate toward generation and fulfillment of what is needed and desired, as close to satisfaction as possible. We look from the ends to the means we may have available. This is not backward causation. What happens in reality is always understood on the basis of forward causation. The proof whether something works out is obviously in the future – in the results of the final design and ultimately in its realization. In other words, we look for hypotheses, that is, educated guesses, which may help to yield what we want. We return another time to Charles Peirce. He writes, in looking forward, that

> A hypothesis …, has to be adopted, which is likely in itself, and renders the facts likely. This step of adopting a hypothesis as being suggested by the facts, is what I call *abduction*. I reckon it as a form of inference, …[29]

Usually an

> … abductive suggestion comes to us like a flash. It is an act of insight, although of extremely fallible *insight*. It is true that the different elements of the hypothesis were in our minds before; but it is the idea of putting together what we had never before dreamed of putting together which flashes the new suggestion before our contemplation.[30]

The process of design is a sequence of many hypothetical steps and incremental advances which bring about the project. Because there are always some unknowns or at least uncertainties involved, the results are in part based on conjecture. On the other hand, architecture can rely on many pragmatic approaches supported by a wealth of historical precedents and experiences. Design activities are learning processes in search of information about projected effects. They prompt past understanding and combine it with information on present conditions to yield causes for new solutions. This is why approaching architecture from the past to the present in form of detailed case studies is so crucial as experience for future design work. The looking back from assumed ends to potential means to achieve them is at the roots of inspirational meaning during the whole iteration process.

6.6 shows the executive loop of the iteration process. It is repetitive in such a way that it returns to preliminary results for further improvement until a point of satisfaction or failure is reached.

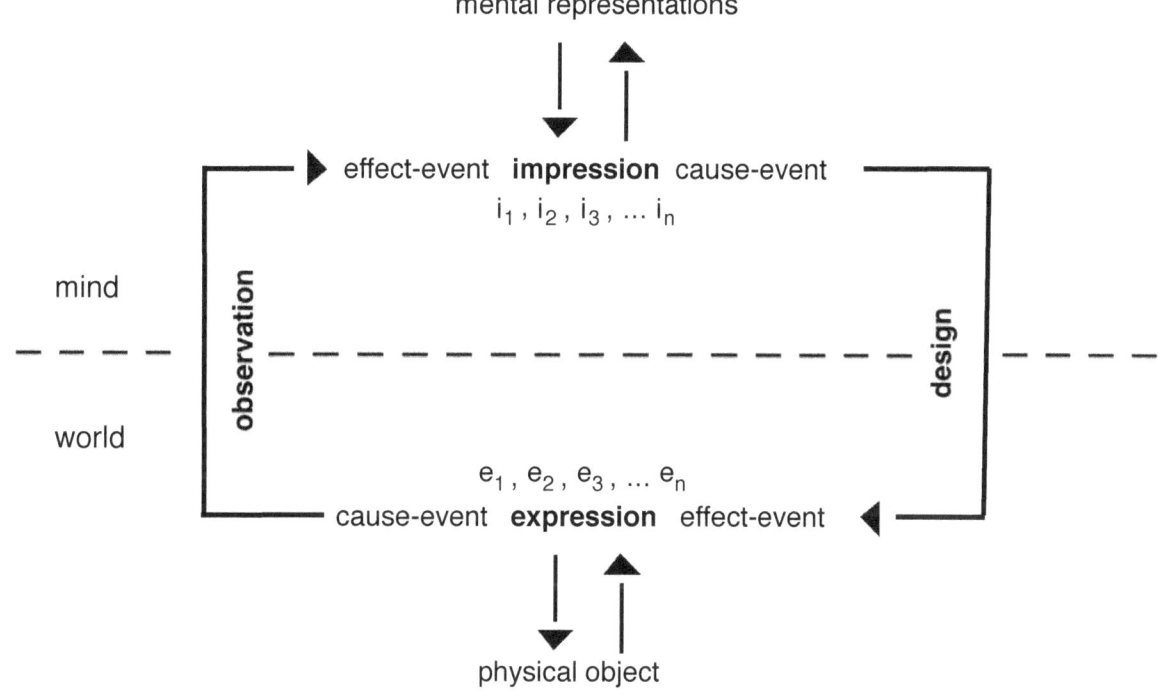

6.6 Iterations in design progression

The process starts with an observation as early input from present circumstances: program, site and other context. This is shown at left, the world-to-mind part of the loop. This initial impression receives further input from memory, that is, from expressions based on past experiences (note that nothing starts ever from nothing). A preliminary expression develops and is realized in a design medium (drawing, model, etc.), shown at the right as the mind-to-world part of the loop. Now judgment occurs whether the expression is satisfactory, based on this expression's world-to-mind impression. If it is not satisfactory, another expression is developed by further input from mental space, often in combination with additional external input. In later iterations, aspects of construction and economics increasingly play a role. Every conceptual input must be satisfied by a physical equivalent. The changes keep the dynamics of design progress in play from first intention to final overall scheme.

The loop combines the processes shown in 6.4 and 6.5. The point to make again is that expressions are the foundation for impressions and then impressions are the foundation for expressions. The design iteration is known in architectural lingo somewhat pessimistically as 'trial-and-error' process. Optimistically we should call it 'trial-and-success' process or, more neutrally, 'trial-and-possibility' process. Judgment on the potential of proposed changes to achieve the anticipated expressions is obviously involved. Every design process and its results are a learning process also of decision making for future solutions.

Every iteration in the design process is caused by thought input from owner, user, designer, consultant, contractor or any other contributor to the project. The design is a moving target in the sense of change during this evolution in large and small increments. These inputs – design factors in terms of activities – should be considered meaning of content which shapes the overall form from inception to realization with much accommodation in-between. Many of the factors are given and often not in our control. All produce sub-causes and sub-effects requiring sub-judgments which influence the progress. From a behavioral point of view William Child provides a highly appropriate model also for the design process from impression to expression:

> Now the properties of a belief [impression] are explained by properties of associated representation. ... If S believes that p and desires that q, then S stands in the *Belief* relation to an internal representation R_1, and stands in the *Desire* relation to an internal representation R_2; R_1 has syntactic properties which mirror the content p, and R_2 has syntactic properties which mirror the content q; and R_1 and R_2 causally combine to bring about S's physical movements.[31]

What here are called "syntactic properties" are the formative aspects of the content-form unity in design. In other words, the content p has the representational form R_1 and q has the representational form R_2. The state of affairs p of an object is desired to be changed into the state of affairs q of this object. R_1 is the present impression (from perception) of what p is and R_2 is the future impression (as projection) of what q should be. The associated *Belief* and *Desire* we experience related to R_1 and R_2 with their syntactic properties reflecting p and q are what we call semantic aspects – the meanings we experience along the design process. Here it is helpful to return to the concept of event which implies guidance from environmental clues. Every piece of architecture is an event which keeps on giving. Let's look at the results of two very different examples which show why their designs have moved from p to q.

The Neue Staatsgalerie Stuttgart, by James Sterling, is one of the great museums in Germany. It is a 'lasting' event as well in other respects. At the edge of a downtown park with buildings for the performing arts, it serves as a link to the hills above, full of housing. Pedestrians walk a half circular ramp over the museum, viewing the sculpture court below, which serves in part for daylighting interior exhibit spaces; all affording a unique way of experiencing exterior and interior in short order (6.7 to 6.9).

Neue Staatsgalerie, Stuttgart

6.7 Exterior pedestrian ramp above roof and courtyard
(© permission)

Neue Staatsgalerie, Stuttgart

6.8 Beginning of pedestrian ramp at right

6.9 View from upper to lower courtyard and ramp

Of a very different scale and nature is the momentous civic event of Washington, DC, based on the design by Pierre l'Enfant (6.10 and 6.11). The vision of how the constitutional powers of democracy are reflected in its plan and collocation of governmental landmarks causes daily reminders and understanding of what the people need to know as citizens. The guiding inspiration for the city's layout was not natural topography but an imposed rectangular grid of streets, broken by contrasting diagonals and large open spaces, emphasizing monumental architecture at end points.

Washington, DC

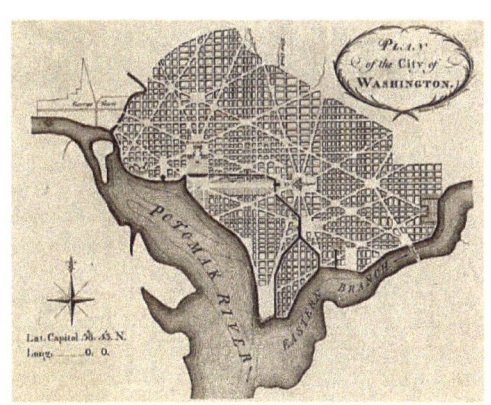

6.10 Pierre L'Enfant's Plan of Washington
(source)

6.11 View from Capitol Building toward National Mall and Washington Monument (source)

Causality plays a crucial role in our understanding of decision making. Decisions made or not made are causes or 'non-causes' of mental nature. In order to become effective, they require some kind of physical 'follow-up' as direct activity of the decision maker or communication by the decision maker for somebody else to act. The cause or 'non-cause' possibilities are fundamental for what happens in particular chains of events as actions or their omissions toward results. Of interest here is the view that certain assumptions of cause can be considered as counterfactual. Already Hume referred to that possibility.[32] Two simple examples, if a certain column would not exist, it could not support a load or if there would not be a chair, I would not be able to sit on it.

Action to advocate can often be strengthened by reference to definite or potential consequences from non-action. Counterfactual statements are the circumstantial foundation for such reference. Using our, by now well worn example of an exterior shading device: the device causes reflection of solar radiation before it reaches the window surface. In counterfactual terms: the omission of the device causes non-prevention. The consequence: increased solar heat gains with potential discomfort for occupants or higher cooling loads with larger equipment sizing and increased energy consumption.

As said, if a cause-event does not occur, an effect-event will not occur either. This sounds trivial but it opens up a line of thought which can be very helpful for concerns in design. We can extend this view into the issue of alternatives. If we make a decision for one strategy versus another, we preclude not only what could have happened in the latter but for any related events which could have happened evolving from it. This is why decisions in the early design stage and even more in the programming stage are so crucial, and feedback from all decision makers is never as important as at that time (6.12). To change directions later, including backtracking, is increasingly more time consuming and expensive. But it is occasionally not avoidable. Not to change, despite good reasons to do so, may lead to design defects of various kinds, often with results of poor meaning in expression.

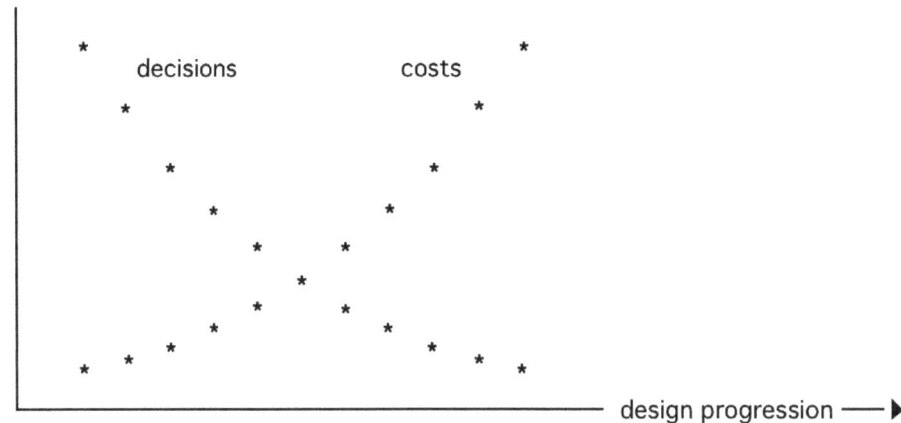

6.12 Impact on costs when design decisions are made

While in progress, even when we feel to be on a successful track, it is crucial from time to time to trace backward and check what happened; like in running a movie backwards to see what happened and what we may have missed. The impact of the side effects must be viewed in relation to the benefits which may be obtained toward an overall result. In complex situations, trade-offs are rarely avoidable. From time to time during the design process we must return to forks in the path we took, rethink our judgments on the basis of feedback from present selections and probe alternative paths for their potentials.

Since human beings emerged from primitive subsistence in nature, they developed the gift of providing for the future based on remembered experiences from the past. The ability to understand beyond the physical needs of the present started to empower individuals and cohorts to differentiate among alternatives. Subconsciously first, then ever more aware of relational aspects and their potential for purposive and enduring achievements, understanding became meaningful for simple day-to-day tasks as well as for comprehensive and complex interrelationships and undertakings. Hierarchies and organizations arose in families and communities with equivalent physical manifestations. The stories of civilizations are contained in the relational features of artifacts they left behind, including architecture.

To repeat, meaning is what we select as our understanding of a particularity on the basis of judgment which gives importance of one understanding over others. In observation we have little control over that to which our understanding is exposed. On the other hand, in design we have such control to a large extent and we can select and communicate understandings from the usually many developing. As there are typically many design factors influential, we make decisions on which to emphasize, depending on the freedom which given circumstances allow.

Meaning has a dimension which we grasp intuitively as urge or need toward expression of understanding. We give it power on our own or in behalf of clients. There are many kinds of factors from economics, ethics, politics, artistry, etc. Many are derived from the present context and we usually consider them to be purposive. Some factors reinforce each other. Some clash. Their resultants are imposed as meanings on the physical media which convey them, similar to ideas which words communicate. When we observe existing architecture, we perceive such meanings as given by others. When we design, we give them ourselves. Paul Frankl wrote a century ago about the role of intention that

> It is the practical and material certainty of purpose that determines the building program and hence the spatial form, but only intention gives to purpose its artistic character.[33]

It is true that intention is necessary to undertake anything. Nothing is ever accomplished without it, except by accident. But in architecture, purpose and intention aim at more than "artistic character"; the latter being only part of what design projects are about. Architecture, depending on particular circumstances, must satisfy various needs and desires which requires resources and control of them. It is only through intention, in part *power of meaning*, that design comes about. It is cultural and historical expression in general, as much as it is particular expression by individuals. This naturally raises the question about our abilities to exert influence on the world, as individuals and as a profession. Fate has it that we are always positioned at a place and a time, that is, in a certain context. Today, we are members of a society which is increasingly global in its outlook but we design architecture for local development, wherever that may be.

With this dual aspect of global and local in mind, we must ask where our responsibilities and motivations are to participate in changing the world by design, as far as this is possible. It requires ethical assessments and, whether we act on them or not, the results are in some form advocacy or neglect. There is no question that our profession throughout history has been by and large in the employ of politically and economically powerful elites. Architectural history books show mostly monuments of the power of individuals or institutions, at least up to the turn to the 20th century. One of the great, largely unacknowledged merits of Modernism has been to alert us to the broader obligations which the design professions have for all people. Despite the hyperbole which most manifestos of the first half of the past century represent, many of them contain more than a kernel of empathy for physical response to the call for social justice.[34]

This movement and the advances in democratic governance worldwide have led to a broadening of professional and general public involvement with regard to all building types. In Europe – with few exceptions – public projects are subject to open architectural competitions, which produce usually highly varied results, and extensive community comment and input. This is similarly so in urban planning. Often superior solutions are the result.[35] There is not enough of such an approach in the United States, not even for large, publicly financed projects. One result is, across the country, inadequately sustained involvement of federal and state governments in new, high quality affordable housing. The consequence is rising struggles of not-for-profit organizations in providing shelter.

This line of thought raises the issue of how far architecture as an enterprise can and should play a role in advocacy with regard to societal conditions and if so, on which level of context it may be most successful. Architecture is 'social' by definition. It is made by and for people. The 'by and for' must mean inclusion of communities and especially prospective users in project development and decision making. Richard Hatch wrote in 1984, and it is as valid today as then, that

> Social architecture defines three principle strategies for carrying out its difficult task. These strategies reflect the complex character of architecture as process, form, and content. Each is called upon to make a specific contribution to critical awareness and rich human needs. In the realm of process, we will consider new meaning for *participation*. Form will be called upon to provide *rational transparency*. Content will be discussed as *the structure of experience*. Together they posit a radical alteration in the relationship between people and the built world.[36]

With "social architecture" socioeconomic awareness and participatory decision making is implied. Content is more than "the structure of experience". It is the essence and purpose of any object and state of affairs designed and experienced as form influenced by context, the latter having its own wide and narrow, more or less influential content. There is no question that meaning in architectural design entails an ethical stance, though not in every instance, as not every instance relates to a social issue. But where the understanding and decision making about common welfare is at stake, selection of meaning and its physical realization must positively relate to public concerns.

One way to find content is through the practice which Schneekloth and Sibley call Placemaking. Professionals help people to make explicit the relationships among each other and in their particular situations.

> The first task is to open space for dialogue about place and placemaking through developing a relationship with the place of constituencies. This act of making a *dialogic space* is probably the most important activity of professional placemakers and others who wish to work on places, ...
>
> The second task is the dialectical work of confirmation and interrogation, which occur in the dialogic space. *Confirmation* is the activity which looks at the context of work [on placemaking] with an appreciative attitude in order to understand what is, and what has been, taking place. ... Equally important is the *interrogation* of that context, which consists of asking questions and problematizing the work through disciplined and critical perspectives. ...
>
> The third task of the professional placemaker is facilitating the *framing of action*. The ongoing, iterative, and dialectical acts of confirmation and interrogation reveal the opportunities and constraints for action. ...[37]

Dialogic space is the locus where thought generation occurs through social interaction, especially conversation. Interrogation and confirmation are aimed at understanding what the particulars of the context are from which present needs and desires arise. Framing of action lays the foundation for answers to these conditions. What is meant here with placemaking is empowerment for defining and envisioning what a project in a given situation should become.

These thoughts are echoed by John Anderson who wrote in 2001 for the introduction of a pamphlet on community design that

> The bedrock of community livability is community design – design that takes into account and deliberately reflects the aspirations and goals of the community for life, work, learning, play, and growth. Defined thus, "design" is far more than a "product." It's both a way of looking at challenges and problems and discovering opportunities.[38]

How far advocacy can go beyond affirmation of honest business behavior obviously is determined by the circumstances. Typical involvements are participation in community design center activities, promotion of open design competitions with public design critiques, membership in planning and design review commissions as well as on boards of not-for-profit corporations. Most of such activities address economic and political issues. The vision statement from the website of the Pratt Institute Center for Community and Environmental Development (PICCED), Brooklyn NY, exemplifies well the mission of community design centers:

> *Equity and justice*: We want to see "shared prosperity," a more equal sharing of the benefits of development. We want all people to have the things necessary for what Franklin Roosevelt called "freedom from want" (a decent home, sufficient income for a good quality of life, health care, etc).
>
> *Sustainable development*: We aim for development that provides a healthy environment and quality open space for all communities, that minimizes environmental harms and shares those burdens fairly, and that preserves natural resources for future generations.
>
> *Community voice/power*: People living and working in neighborhoods, especially disenfranchised ones, should have meaningful voice and power in shaping the future of their community.[39]

Innovative solutions usually arise from local situations. One of the best examples is the earlier mentioned Parkview Commons in San Francisco (2.6 to 2.9). After overcoming of many obstacles, it was possible to offer through innovative cooperation of many public and private entities high quality living to low- and moderate income households in a desirable neighborhood:

> Residents of Parkview Commons purchase their dwellings but lease the land under them for a nominal amount. To offset this subsidy, the city in turn holds a second mortgage on the property with a lien in the amount of the difference between the sale price and the market value. To ensure long-term affordability and to eliminate speculation and windfall profits, the city obtained the right to purchase the property under an option for four years and a right of refusal for as long as the owners have the home.[40]

Of the 114 units on the three-acre site, 72 contain three- or four-bedrooms.

Meaning relates to power in many ways. It is referential to material and intellectual importance. Thomas Markus writes that

> Power has to do ultimately with resources. Since these are finite the only freedom is to divide them in different proportions. It is the cake-slicing operation – more here is less there – so beloved of operational research scientists in their zero-sum games. Its results are seen in hierarchical structures, control, surveillance, decision processes and in differential consumption. In the design and the use of buildings, power can be evenly distributed, or concentrated so as to create great asymmetries.[41]

Many of the hierarchies of power have been long standing. Others are recent. Some only come to the fore at the time of defining and setting the purpose for the project or even when the project is already in development. Every project has its own mix of them. They fall into two categories: 1) External power hierarchies because of economics, politics, religion, family relationships, prestige, desires for historic preservation and ecological concerns, etc. 2) Internal power hierarchies because of spatial adjacency and sequencing, way finding, building systems and physics, security and related controls, etc. They are design factors which call for physical representation in the project and for functional expression. Large differences exist in power intensity. Rarely neutral, the powers usually reinforce or counter each other. Their influences can be seen from municipal master plans and how their flexibility is used, from where and how projects are located, from the prominence and size of projects, from facade proportioning and use of materials, from organizational patterns and spatial adjacencies, from seating arrangements in spaces, etc.

To understand power implications as designers, we must know, as far as possible, who has power and whether such power in particular instances is meant to be unconditional, propositional, normative, discursive or whatever. And, we must see power not only as political or economic phenomenon but as source of understanding of relevance, practicality and preference. Whole city plans and infrastructures have emerged through the influences of particular powers. The image building through corporate office towers, the kind of commercial promotion in shopping centers, the quality of informational media centers in education, the increase in museum construction, the neglect of public versus individual means of transportation, the demise of once prosperous city centers with the simultaneous rise of the suburbs, the green movement in relation to environmental degradation, etc., they all are manifestations of power at work – positively or negatively (6.13 to 6.16). And, we can add that design in architecture has power, especially because of providing the unified and physical foundation for meaning to be communicated.

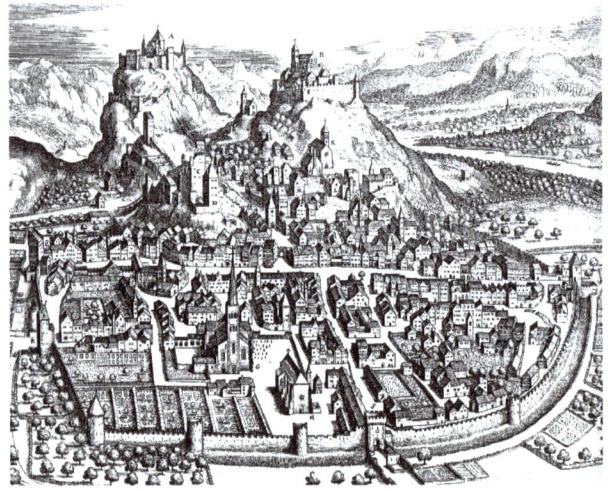

6.13 Expressions of power by government, religion and community, but also landscape. City of Sitten, Switzerland (source)

6.14 Expression of power by commerce, trade and transportation. Manhattan with Wall Street, New York City

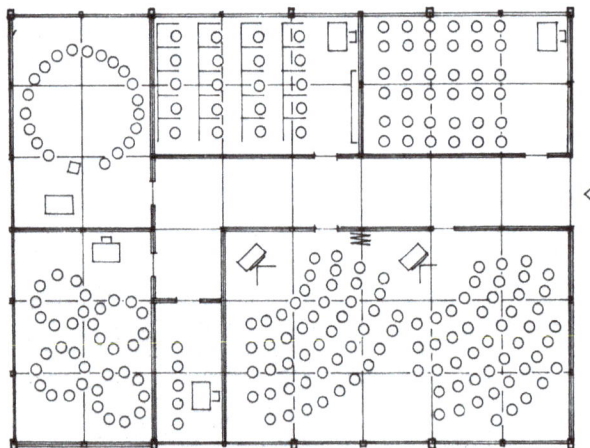

6.15 Power relationships expressed by classroom seating for information exchange

6.16 Information overload from power of expressions in advertising, here in Japan

As designers we find ourselves in the web of powers related to particular projects. For a general orientation we may use the two questions which Anthony King posed at the beginning of essays on architecture and society:

> What can we understand about a society by examining its buildings and physical environments?
>
> What can we understand about buildings and environments by examining the society in which they exist?[42]

We can obviously gain by thinking from the directions of both questions. Answers to the second, however, are for us the more fundamental ones, as every design task is sociological by addressing individual and collective human needs and desires. We must find answers to particular purposes and contexts of manmade environments in the broader framework of nature and humanity. Answers to the first question support those to the second as existing manmade physical environments including buildings are among the main records of social development showing how we have come to where we are today. They let us understand how designers in other times and circumstances have provided solutions for satisfying needs and desires, and they may inspire patterns for present societies in their environments.

Design efforts and solutions come essentially about in every project because 1) a genuine need exists for it to be built; 2) a client has the needs and desires as well as the resources to develop the project; 3) a designer is willing and capable to do the job; 3) a site with favorable location is available; 4) a well defined, though preliminary program has been put together; 5) the site's size, geometry and topography can accommodate the program; etc. Each of these items, and many others could be added, represents causative power arising from intellectual and material origins. Side issues feed into them. All together these conditions cause sometimes difficult, from project to project different, but often interesting dynamics of design resolution. The better we understand the necessity and influence of individual causes exerting power the better we are able to channel them to formulate progress.

The positioning of needs versus desires is important as it clarifies a project's nature and helps in sorting out the roles of all concerned, including roles in decision making. The classic relationship is triadic with client, designer and project in a given overall context. Depending on the project, clients are individuals or groups representing commercial and not-for-profit enterprises including governmental entities. Project progress comes mostly through decisions of individual designers but, with increasing project size and complexity, professionals for various requirements are involved. The needs and desires are obviously similar for client and designer. The obligation and task of the designer is to satisfy the client's demands. The client is mainly oriented toward the product but the designer toward the product and the process to achieve it. The more the client is versed in matters of design and construction, the usually smaller are differences. But they never completely disappear because of the never quite similar nature of projects and the personal approaches which clients and designers take in relation to the particulars involved.

I refer back to the discussion of configuration as amplification toward the end of the previous chapter. In working with design factors toward formal solutions, we engage in configuration more or less to achieve what we may call fit; whereby fit must be understood as observable and relational – for purpose, context and realization. In terms of content-form unity, we let form determine content to some extent, that is, form itself becomes a design factor and cause for allowing necessary fit to occur. There are usually redundancies involved which, when positively employed, are highly beneficial. We commit ourselves locally to some of the 'nonessential' to achieve overall the essential. This is a different "needs versus desires" concept than the one applied in purposive programming. The need (and perhaps desire) for configuration in this sense is a unique power the designer understands and applies. It is aesthetically dispositional which is the reason that I associate it with ornament. It poses for the designer, especially because clients and the public cannot easily relate to it, fundamental ethical challenges in its use. The process of architectural design is fundamentally a balancing of design factor impacts within a given overall limit. When successful these powers of design conceptualization and aesthetic discretion result in what we may call judicious realization.

Configuration in the design process is an inevitable physical accommodation within the project for solving conflicts among design factors. It is also the natural ground from which the designer draws freedom and inspiration for particular expression in the project, consciously or not. When applied far beyond its need, however, configuration becomes self-serving and costly, at times even distorting the projects original intent. *In terms of content-form unity of a project, ornamentation far beyond need results in form excessively determining content.*

Therefore, where and how far configuration beyond necessity may happen in a particular project or in overall practice is obviously a value judgment by the designer and well informed clients. Excessive configuration, even when thematically developed from the internal design factors of the project, is close to decoration, though with different origin than from what we usually associate with decoration, that is, purely aesthetic embellishment.

Configuration in the design of architectural form, and with it content, is to a large extent an enterprise of tradeoffs. We experience this most readily when working on the configuration of floor plans within the limits of a given area total. Form goes beyond shape, however, and embraces all of realization, observable and relational. An example of trade-off for the latter: what we spend financially on one part of a project is not available for another or others. Therefore, we need to study the diverse occurrences in the causation of particulars and how they combine to overall solutions. What is equally important is to trace the processes, especially the decisions with their marks they leave on the design results. Result, appearance and meaning in design are not obtained by us simply as a gift. They come about through our 'causing' of causes, that is, searching, selecting, combining and adjusting of resources through knowledge and understanding. It is to our disadvantage and may haunt us eventually when we neglect the dynamics of understanding and evaluation in cause-effect histories.

This view is in accord with what we mentioned early on that properties are not only what we typically associate with them, the substance of what something is, but also about what that something brings beyond itself. Design factors are not 'static'. They are functionally endowed and empowered through the intent of design over the lifetime of the building. And, there is always the complication from having several highly influential design factors calling for successful compromise. On the other hand, we have in the process considerable control on their influences, to the point of neglecting one or the other of them altogether.

It is generally detrimental in a particular project to single out a priori a single factor as the main determinant to be addressed. This eliminates from the start the chance for a reasonably holistic understanding and leads in the extreme to the exclusion of other highly relevant determinants. I am not talking here against the emphasis of showing the impact of certain design factors in the expression of architecture. Such emphasis is simply unavoidable. I point to distinctiveness accomplished by neglect of design factors which enrich necessary experience.

The exemplary villain in recent times is, as mentioned earlier, Mies van der Rohe, not only through neglecting crucial design factors in his own buildings but also through his influence on many followers. The direction Mies took was based on the mistaken idea that the aesthetic is a visual 'property' of things and all else had to be subordinated. But the aesthetic is a value based judgment in our consideration of a manifold of properties. Paul Rudolph was right when he wrote over four decades ago that

> All problems can never be solved, indeed it is characteristic of the 20th century that architects are highly selective in determining which problems they want to solve. Mies, for instance, makes wonderful buildings only because he ignores many aspects of a building.[43]

Mies has been a great master in what he addressed. At the same time he was a powerful master of neglect. Now, architects have always been "selective in determining which problems to solve". But this view must not be used to take license for neglect of crucial aspects, such as environmental comfort and energy conservation, for which Mies did not care sufficiently and for which many designers still do not today. The issue here is balancing factors toward overall satisfactory solutions, the most demanding aspect of successful design.[44]

The most powerful ornamentation results when abstract form is developed at the outset for the overall project and is set as a given to dominate all other design factors. Here, form mainly as shape is the major design factor. Another time Oswald Mathias Ungers may serve as an example of one who has driven this attitude in the power of design to an extreme by claiming that

> The only value of architecture is for me architecture. It is free of purpose.[45]

I assume that he means 'free of purpose beyond itself' which obviously cannot be so because even his buildings serve purposes and cannot completely neglect their function and environment. He echoes Eisenman's thoughts of the 1970s about the autonomy of architecture or Aldo Rossi's which found physical expression through formal abstraction, using memories as background. Although memories can contribute extensively, architectural design cannot be based on remembrance while neglecting other presence. Rafael Moneo (1978) alleges, somewhat exaggerated but in the right direction, that

> Rossi's types communicate only with themselves and their ideal context. They become only mute reminders of a more or less perfect past, a past that may or may not even have existed.[46]

All of us have memories, long or short term, and some of these memories participate inevitably in conceptualization for design. What is unique regarding Rossi is the emphasis on rather isolated types as heritage from cities of the past. In his designs and those of other minimalists an extreme tendency exists to reduce design input to very few types or to emphasize certain types strongly over all others. As mentioned, regarding Mies van der Rohe, this may lead to expressive strength but also to deficiency in communicative and functional performance. There is no unconditional existence of anything in this world. Therefore, to speak of autonomous architecture also can only mean relative autonomy, more or less depending on prevailing circumstances. If we mean by autonomous architecture that the designer may have complete freedom in decision making, we kid ourselves. Eisenman writes in the 1980s about the need to let architecture be "autonomous" and "arbitrary":

> As long as architecture is primarily a device designated for use and for shelter – that is, as long as it has origins in programmatic functions – it will always constitute an effect. But once this 'self-evident' characteristic of architecture is dismissed and architecture is seen as having no a priori origins – whether functional, divine, or natural – alternative fictions for the origin can be proposed: for example, one that is *arbitrary*, one that has no external value derived from meaning, truths or timelessness.[47]

I have not seen any architecture realized that does not have some "a priory origins" and none without some "functional" ones; not even with Eisenman as designer. In parts of architecture arbitrariness may have its place, be even inevitable. Decorative features may go in this direction. But an 'arbitrary architecture' overall in a project is not possible. Arbitrariness and autonomy mean independence. Somebody show me an instance of a fully arbitrary or autonomous architectural object which exists in reality – not only in rhetoric about it – and I will be an instant believer in such a possibility. We talk here about full occurrence, not partial occurrence, because about the latter we don't have to argue, it being not in question. Nothing is ever fully independent, at least as far as we human beings and our world is concerned.[48]

Since Eisenman wrote these sentences, the fallacious thinking that an autonomous architecture is possible has never completely subsided. It has its roots in the belief that creative genius to the exclusion of contextual limitations should be given the power to generate design solutions and has supposedly received support over the past decade from the enormous possibilities computers offer to drive conceptual design processes. But these processes cannot, or at least not yet, replace our mind's configurative flexibility and always differentiating value system in the decision making for every new project. They miss to facilitate the central component of aesthetic judgment which is posterior to design projection and is influenced by the subjectively weighted inclusion of all relevant design factors. Andrew Vande Moere writes in a text titled "Form Follows Data" that the Dutch Pavilion at the World Expo 2000 is an example of

> ... how analytical data can be literally translated into an architectural program and formality, shaping perpetual daily activities, or layering the essential features of a country as a human-scale information visualization.[49]

This is nothing new, however. Information is always more or less fundamental to design, though is today usually enhanced by the power of digital data bases. Form does not "literally" follow data but uses the content of data to occasion physical solutions. The text's term "analytical" points to the need of eventual synthesis. Both cannot be completely data driven. As mentioned, design is enhanced by digital data bases. But it requires project oriented human input, unless we accept a completely robotic culture with inadequate aesthetic judgments.

To summarize. Cause results into effect through change. Change to occur requires power. Causations, especially those as complex as in architectural design and its realizations, have many origins which motivate physical or mental powers. Some are very forceful and rather easily observed. Others are rather subtle, even subliminal. The influences of power reveal themselves in the outcome of expressions, understood as meaning. As creative beings we live from the power of making judgments. We may even speak of an aesthetic dialectic of content and form guiding the power of design.

6.4 Purpose, context and realization

During our previous discussion we have mentioned *purpose, context* and *realization* of a project as its central aspects to bring it about. We did not elaborate in sufficient detail. This is the task of the present section with the understanding that it is best to proceed in terms of design factors which characterize these three constituents. Experience from comprehensive design processes shows that design factors are interdependent and must be flexible to allow for give-and-take in influence. The following list shows 1) purposive design factors which are brought together for programming and tradeoffs of needs and desires; 2) contextual design factors which are derived from present circumstances and evaluated with regard to potential impact on program and design; and 3) design factors of realization which are derived from preferences and conditions posed by clients, designers, consultants and public entities for physical site development, construction and operation.

Looking at this complexity, we find that, while we can typically point to causes separately, we cannot clearly separate effects with regard to the influence from these causes. In other words, *causes in architectural design have combined effects* while they, as mentioned earlier, compete as design factors for influence. If we reduce our frame of reference to very detailed levels, we may come close to one-to-one relationships of cause and effect but rarely fully, if ever, as we can observe, for example, in mathematics. Meaning in design, therefore, is our understanding of inter-dependent design features. We can describe the features but must be aware of their being tied up in mutual relationships. The decisions about which factors may dominate and which may play lesser roles ultimately determine content and form of a particular project.

One of the best ways to study complexity is in its increasing manifestations over time. It is interesting, for example, to study the floor plans of Christian churches over the centuries with juxtaposing dogmatic, liturgical, sociological and architectural design factors: from worship in homes around a table during the early centuries to the cathedrals in cruciform with altar and clergy in the east oriented choir of the Middle Ages to the diversity of multi-polar worship spaces of modern times. Or, it is revealing to trace the development of spatial arrangements in residential environments because of technical advances. This is very obvious from the role indoor plumbing and energy supply systems played for the layout and equipment of kitchens and bathrooms during the past two centuries, in addition to socio-cultural changes.

Crucial to consider, as indicated earlier, is the fact that design factors, depending on nature and importance, come into play at different times during the emerging project. Their sequence from one project to the next is never the same, even if they are for the same building type. Various design factors are sometimes not even known at the beginning of a project, be it that they have been neglected or that they come to the fore only because of changing requirements of the project itself. The change of building configuration or main building orientation because of un-anticipated site utilization is an example.

It is obviously not possible to list all factors which may influence designs; not even for particular designs, unless we go to very limited frames of reference. Every substantive term we may utter in association with architecture has the potential of becoming a design factor. This must not deter us, however, from the search and documentation of particular design factors for projects under consideration. This is a causatively fundamental activity for understanding of a project throughout its development. Perhaps the best way to get at design factors is by asking questions, such as What are the available resources for the project physically and financially? What makes a project possible in this or that direction? What constrains or enhances it? Which properties determine the experience we want to provide? Can we order for a particular project, at least in a preliminary way, factors with regard to importance and time of impact in the design process?

What we want to achieve are objects which serve our purposes. Observable and relational properties are causatively involved. The correspondence of design factors and properties is helped by the fact that names identify activities, even if quite trivially. For example, light is causative because of what light is and does. Orientation is causative because of what orientation is and does. Costs are causative because of what costs are and do.

Design Factors of Purpose arise from needs or desires we anticipate a designed object to fulfill. They are the reasons why the object is created in the first place and are the basis for what context and realization must provide. They often require definition by experts from fields outside architecture. They usually comprise
- Building type functions (residential, educational, commercial, administrative, manufacturing, etc.),
- Occupancy patterns and scheduling in response to building types,

- Spatial requirements (sizes, heights, organizational patterns, etc.),
- Interior environmental conditions (thermal, electrical, luminous, acoustical),
- Physiological and psychological conditions (general and particular human comfort requirements, privacy and community aspects, decision making hierarchies, etc.),
- Building life cycle expectation (physically, economically),
- Ecological criteria (conservation, sustainability),
- Construction and life cycle costs,
- Completion schedules,
- Aesthetic preferences.

. . . .

Design Factors of Context arise from the existing, physical and nonphysical conditions in a particular situation and have impact on purpose and realization. They often also require definition by experts from other fields. They usually comprise
- Site, neighborhood and community relationships (historical, sociological, political, physical, etc.),
- Site conditions (geometry, topography, soil conditions, vegetation, etc.),
- Micro climate of site (solar impact, wind directions and velocities, temperatures and humidity, precipitation),
- Economic parameters (public or private funding, interest rates, taxes, etc.),
- Pedestrian, bicycle and automobile traffic patterns around the site,
- External building services (water, sewer, gas, electricity, etc.),
- Building codes and other regulations,
- Construction and life cycle costs.

. . . .

Design Factors of Realization arise from the factors that play a role in the physical implementation of the project, how it comes into being and how it operates. They often call for the adjustment of purpose and always influence context. They usually comprise
- Site development (access, topography, solar exposure, existing structures and vegetation, etc.)
- Building geometries (programmatic dimensions, massing, desired set backs, etc.),
- Building materials (types and availability, site production versus prefabrication, etc.)
- Structural and envelope systems (wall versus skeleton, infill, fenestration, earthquake stability, etc.)
- Mechanical and electrical systems (HVAC, sanitary, electrical, communication, etc.)
- Construction costs,
- Building codes and other regulations,
- Completion schedules,
- Management and labor relations.

. . . .

Looking at these descriptions it becomes quite clear that there is not only interdependence but also overlap in the sense that many factors are applicable in two or even all three of the categories. Some under context may be easily understood to be applicable under purpose. Solar radiation, for example, a crucial factor of context, may be proscribed as highly desirable for the purpose of energy conservation. A preference or even need for single floor design (purpose) may preclude development on a tight site (context). A material used in neighboring buildings may appear as a condition (purpose, context) for a material choice (realization).

The three categories are not equivalent at all in the way they influence our understanding. And, as it may superficially appear, they should not be viewed operationally as representing the sequence of a three step design framework. Some design factors are present in every project, such as spatial demands and structural integrity. Others are only building type dependent, such as certain building codes. Again others develop only during the design process and changing circumstances. For example, purposive aspects may still arise at a time we may rather think of realization and aspects of realization may become relevant already early in establishing those of purpose. While the ongoing task of the designer is to keep the process 'on track', openness to arising concerns along the way is equally important. To make the design process viable, setting of limits on inclusion and accommodation is naturally an aspect of every project. Eventually, the triple input from purpose, context and realization coalesces into a single design solution which provides the grounds for meaning, overall and in parts. Physical realization of any sizable architectural project has, at least since the Renaissance, two phases of implementation: 1) from design thinking to physical design (scaled representation with material description) and 2) from physical design to physical object. While the second step informs the first in every detail, it is in the first that meaning is largely determined for embedding in the eventual object.

6.17 summarizes what we just discussed and also shows content as input and form as output. What is called form is the physical realization derived from the design factors of purpose, context and realization. This is why I emphasize that the final result, the form, is in unity with content. Context is mentioned twice, first as source of design factors, second as the environment of form. Every form has its setting in an environment which is the context as changed from the previous one by the presence of the object. Something which comes into being changes the present environment. Realization is mentioned three times, first as source of design factors, second as the implementation process and third as constituted form.

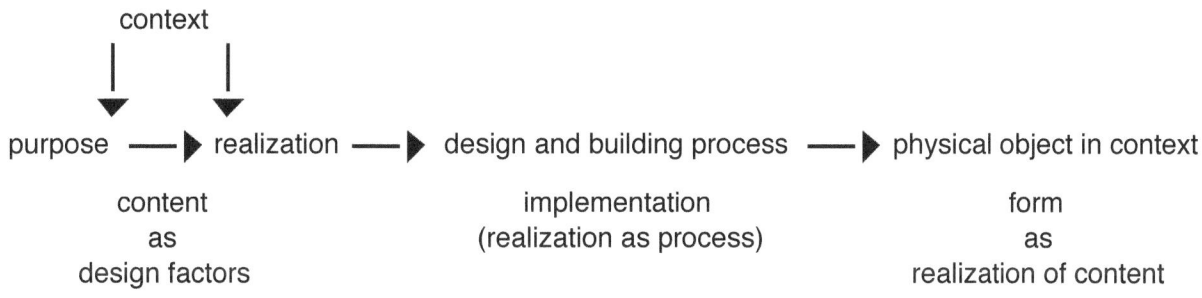

6.17 Process from content to form

The influence of context on content and form of an object is broader than usually assumed. As there are physical and nonphysical aspects to be considered and viewed in their interdependence, from the topography and microclimate of a site to the cultural and economic environment of the project, I view the relationship of context and form more comprehensively than Christopher Alexander who writes that

> … every design problem begins with an effort to achieve fitness between two entities: the form in question and its context. The form is the solution to the problem; the context defines the problem. In other words, when we speak of design, the real object of discussion is not the form alone, but the ensemble comprising the form and its context. Good fit is a desired property of this ensemble which relates to some particular division of the ensemble into form and context.[50]

True, "the real object of discussion" is "the ensemble of form and its context". But not alone, as design does not start with form and its context. It starts with purpose and then "context defines the problem" in part. In part only, because realization also does. We start with content and good design needs to yield fitness and form as result, fitness being the unity of purpose and realization in context – all in content-form unity. In other words, *form is the physical manifestation of purpose, modified by context and realization.* All three contribute design factors to result into form (6.18). While trade-offs are inevitable, successful design requires that at least the main design factors of all three categories are reflected in the eventual form, be they observable in the final result or not. Contextual properties need to be considered in design or poor fit ensues and perhaps undesirable compensation must take place. For example, poor consideration of solar orientation requires compensation by high energy consumption of mechanical systems. When we talk about fit we must keep in mind that we refer way beyond geometric fit to overall suitability and performance.

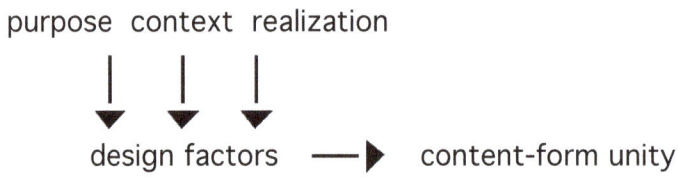

6.18 The sources of content in form

As mentioned, many design factors are unconditionally given and unavoidable. Others can be chosen. Every project has the former and usually the latter. The choice of certain design factors often determines and sometimes calls for others. Design factors are members in chains of causation. The required floor areas of spaces are design factors in the configuration of plans in detail and overall. They also determine the dimensions for ceiling spans. But for the spans we have considerable choice among various structural and material systems. These systems then often become themselves influential, technically and aesthetically. Zoning regulations for a particular site are mandatory but exemptions may be allowed when it can be demonstrated that the same or better results can be achieved with an alternative approach. Generally we think of design factor application as forward progression, goal oriented. But often we move sideways toward unusual possibilities or even back toward earlier missed or neglected ones. Design imagination combined with design experience is necessary to operate in this highly diverse give-and-take enterprise.

As long as in our thoughts any of the design factors is active, the content of the project is not stable, at least in parts. Only when an overall solution is decided upon the design is finalized in its content-form unity and the iterative process from impression to expression ends. The design factors are at this point considered definite causes of the object's form. This does not guarantee, however, any particular quality of the object's existence and performance. Quality is here not a matter of procedural structure but of successful judgment and choice. Again, we must be aware that, with only rare exceptions, the process to the achieved solution is multifaceted and many properties are not directly observable. This makes tracing the evolution of most projects in detail difficult for anyone not closely involved with their development. But the main design factors which influenced the designer nearly always show, which greatly enhances understanding and especially complex meaning.

Programming for purpose

Purpose is responsive to needs and desires, then determinative, though we adjust its demands in relation to given freedoms and constraints. The activity to clarify purpose during the first phase of the comprehensive design process is called *architectural programming* and the resultant document is called an *architectural brief.* As gathering, ordering and documenting of information, it is preparatory work for design development and always raises the general understanding of the project considerably beyond the listing of spatial requirements. Mainly drawn from owner and context information, the program describes the results which must be achieved qualitatively and quantitatively. It provides the foundation for preliminary decision making. Successful programming is "problem seeking" so that the information can be supplemented and clarified, and the design process can begin to either solve problems or avoid them. As such programming is a rich source for the identification of design factors, it is helpful to sketch here some of its aspects. William Peña and Steven Parshall write:

> Programming precedes design just as analysis precedes synthesis. The separation of the two is imperative and prevents trial-and-error design alternatives. Separation is central to an understanding of a rational architectural process, which leads to good buildings and satisfied clients.

The five steps of programming are

> (1) establish goals, (2) collect and analyze facts, (3) uncover and test concepts, (4) determine needs, and (5) state the problem. The first three are primarily the search for pertinent information. The fourth is a qualification test. The last step is distilling what has been found.[51]

Somewhat in contrast, Robert Hershberger writes that

> Architectural Programming is the first stage of the architectural design process in which the relevant values of the client, user, architect, and society are identified; important project goals are articulated; facts about the projects are uncovered; and facility needs are made explicit.[52]

Formal programming precedes the main design efforts and the design process builds on its results. But programming and design are not as separated as Peña and Parshall mention. In many projects it is communicatively efficient and creatively advantageous to have at least the main designer as a participant in programming. Furthermore, problem seeking does not come to an end when the formal phase of programming ends.

Design is not an activity of isolated steps. While it is a problem solving process, at times it causes collateral problems in solving the most pressing ones. Detrimental impact on the environment from not sufficiently thought through design decisions is an example. Identification of such impact is part of comprehensive problem seeking. On the other hand, some problems have a positive edge in that they prompt the search for better solutions. Our inability, for example, not to find an easy answer in the site planning for a difficult topography may lead with additional efforts to an innovative and more exciting arrangement than a less challenging topography might have called for. There are always new aspects to consider while design is in development, but the more design factor information we can gather early on and understand its implications, the more readily we can address design proper which is creative propositioning of physical schemes out of design factor influence and conflict resolution.

Peña's step 5, problem statements, and there may be many from overall to detail, are in the crossover zone from programming into physical design. Whether we consider them already as part of the design process is irrelevant. More important is that at this point, issues of purpose have been clarified and, if necessary, revised. Tentative solutions may be envisioned and discussed. Preliminary holistic meaning evolves. This is early project oriented design thinking. Importantly, problem statements serve as records of foundation when looking back from present solutions of the design process and from the final product.

Not surprisingly, what Peña and Parshall list under goals, facts and concepts (steps 1-3) are design factors: interaction/privacy, hierarchy of values, security, transportation/parking, efficiency, behavioral patterns, organizational structure, communications, physical comfort, way finding, projected image, neighbors' interest, etc. These items essentially represent questions calling for informative answers. As often in categorization, we find strong overlap of these steps and their grouping may only be considered a loose order of listing.

Eduard White views programming for architectural design in terms of cause and effect relationships. The program, as a statement of requirements, must be based on facts.

> In gathering the facts in a given design problem, a key issue is that of relevance. A fact is only relevant to programming and design if it is part of a chain of events or cause-effect relationships that lead to an effect or consequence that we judge as important.
>
> In architectural design we are faced with both natural and man-made facts. All may be viewed as 'if ... then' situations.[53]

These cause-effect relationships must be based also on facts from many other fields which have influence on particular projects. Therefore, especially for complex projects, programming teams include not only clients and architects but various consultants, such as engineers, psychologists, physicians and educators. Depending on building type, input by the general public may play a pivotal role. The process of putting information into interrelationships for obtaining performance criteria amounts to pre-coordination of the design and construction process. Properties of the site, environmental concerns, building functions, project delivery times, economic constraints, etc. are juxtaposed and discussed with reference to experiences from earlier projects. The formulation of purpose is the common base for understanding and meaning. Critical needs versus desirable features are assessed. Issues of privacy and security are raised. A 'down-to-earth' activity like comparing initial building costs versus life-cycle costs may guide initial decision making toward providing high flexibility for facilitating alterations because of potentially changing functions. Or, highly prefabricated building systems may be discussed as alternatives to more conventional construction processes for reasons of more predictable construction quality or for fast track scheduling. Design will be strongly impacted by following one or the other of such programmatic directions concerned with realization.

Well put together, the information package from programming amounts to a detailed document of communication for all concerned, beyond being just a list of an owner's basic needs and desires. For example, adjacency matrices, when developed from broadly based interaction analyses, become meaningful indicators for spatial proximity arrangements. 6.19 shows in template form the visualization of adjacency priorities for spaces A through F, resulting in a bubble diagram for design.

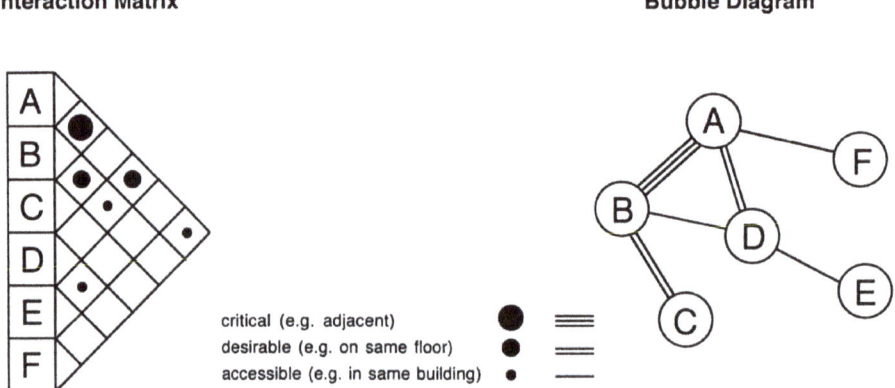

6.19 From adjacency requirements to bubble diagrams (after Peña and Parshall[54])

Up to about the middle of the past century the purposive design factors of projects were established rather informally in the discussions between clients and designers during the programming stage with occasional input of consultants on particular issues for which clients and designers had insufficient backgrounds. With the increasing complexity of projects and the inevitable need for specialized knowledge, not only a more formalized process developed, as just discussed, but also a new field of inquiry emerged, called Environmental Design. It addresses in a broad sense the issues of pragmatics which we mentioned earlier, that is, how we use and respond to signs in environments in which we find ourselves.[55]

Sociologists and psychologists joined architects and planners to broaden the theoretical base for physical design. Perhaps the most comprehensive account of these developments is given in Jon Lang's *Creating Architectural Theory* of 1987.[56] There is also an abundance of literature in specialty areas of architecture with input from various sciences; for example, on the diversity of housing because of demographic changes or on the innovation in medical facilities because of changing health care.

Environment-behavior research has been criticized for not having been able to bridge the 'applicability gap' to sufficiently influence design. This view is justified, but only to some extent. This is a relatively young field and new knowledge often takes considerable time to be absorbed. The rather gradual acceptance is not different from other fields which have increasingly gained and still gain relevance, such as new construction methods, introduction of computers in design practice, approaches to energy efficiency and other sustainability measures, etc.

That pragmatics and all other types of environment-behavior studies cannot just be seen as a scientific enterprise to produce generally applicable rules has to do with the incredibly diverse demands the design of architecture has to combine and satisfy in ever different circumstances of community, site, climate, occupancy, economics, etc.; not the least also the demands for aesthetics as pleasant experiences. There is no question, however, that a great deal of environment-behavior information is available and is being used. Information with which designers work has emerged, and still does, from research or simply from informal understanding of environment and people relations, and from building guidelines and regulations, including safety, lighting and air quality codes, and ergonomic and accessibility standards. Much of it is also found in building type studies and building products development.

The success of problem seeking depends, in addition to general experience, on *performance simulation* and *post-occupancy evaluation*. The design process is essentially a form of simulation with adjustments on the basis of analysis and judgment. The propositions we put forward in simulation are usually based on former experiences we had and perhaps on those of others. Full scale mockups, when affordable, are preferable and come closest to the real thing. But this approach has obviously limits in comprehensiveness and size. Therefore, the more complex and specialized our projects are, the more we need the help of others who know more about certain contextually relevant issues than we as architects do, such as anthropologists, psychologists, sociologists, pedagogues, and engineers.

Whether demands for a project are rather typical or unusual, well documented post-occupancy evaluations represent a wealth of knowledge about architecture which had until recently not a good tradition in knowledge management. Results of POEs help, beyond satisfying the curiosity of designers about their success, two very practical purposes: they serve as basis for improvement in the performance of the presently evaluated object and increase the understanding for the design of future projects. They provide important background for facilities management, especially in the early period of occupancy. The evaluation process in the overall building process is shown in 6.20. After being occupied, the building's performance is measured and studied with regard to the prescribed specifications.

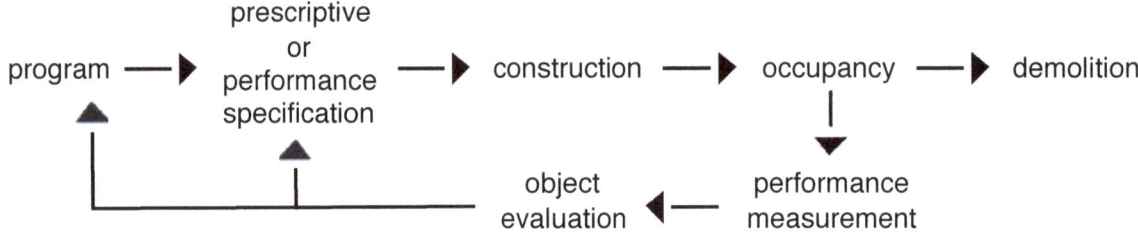

6.20 Specification and evaluation in the overall building process

One of the most important issues in POE is how performance is assessed. The performance criteria, which serve as goals to be achieved, arise from requirements and expectations every architectural project as building type needs to address, and from those which particular circumstances require. The mix may range from a project's response to location and site all the way to its operation in support of the occupant's physiological and psychological well-being. What has been listed as design factors of purpose, context and realization applies here, now taken as criteria for achievements to be more or less met. These performance criteria and the results of evaluation relate to three interest groups: owners/users, designers and managers of the building. The nature of these target groups determines the ways information is solicited and used. A variety of methods and intensities are applied depending on project type, data requirement and resource availability.[57]

Post-occupancy evaluations have been used to assess all kinds of buildings, but most often for office, educational and retirement facilities. Margaret Calkins writes about POEs of the latter:

> As structured hindsight, the review and critique of the design and operation of senior living communities can be extremely beneficial. Upon completion and after a period of stabilization, there is a unique opportunity to review the design team's assumptions about how environments will be used and assess whether design, operational or social goals have been met.
>
> . . .
>
> Post-occupancy evaluations can be a time-saving resource for providers and designers contemplating new construction, offering lessons learned to avoid repetition of often costly mistakes and to improve the state of the art.[58]

There is a progression of intensity and expense of POEs from being indicative to diagnostic.[59] Indicative POEs are done to observe and assess strengths and weaknesses of the performance of buildings. They usually consist of walk-throughs and interviews with operations personnel. Diagnostic POE's require additional efforts for using elaborate measurement techniques. They collect environmental data and occupant feedback, thus allowing for detailed documentation and statistical analysis of functional and operational concerns.

Architectural objects are physically and operationally integrated entities. Their unity is given by the contribution its components make collectively. According to Hartkopf, Loftness and Mill, there are six components: spatial, thermal, air quality, acoustical, visual and building integrity. They address the physical substance and environmental quality of the facility.[60] People and community aspects arise out of these physical aspects of the built environment: physiological, psychological, sociological and economic. Indicators, such as comfort, safety, privacy, security, organizational flexibility, work patterns, etc., are also part of these categories. Some of the components we can measure rather exactly. Others cannot be directly measured but require assessment through personal judgments, usually from occupant questionnaires with large enough sampling.

It has been claimed that most results from POEs confirm what common sense can tell us. This is to some extent correct, but only for rather basic levels. While common sense gives us some indication that something is this or that, it gives us little explicit information about why it is so. Common sense feedback alone is usually much less than what even a minimally structured approach can provide. Post-occupancy evaluations are not done often enough.

As mentioned, the performance of buildings gives us cues for management and for improvements in those still to be designed. For example, way finding, as a result of floor plan organization and visual prompting, is part of a building's quality. Judgment about how easy it is to find what we are looking for is the result of simple post-occupancy evaluation. So is judgment about working in an office which allows the adjustment of a shading device to control daylight before it enters the space. More broadly taken, the overall aesthetic evoked by an object is the result of its physiological and psychological influences on us. Building evaluations of any kind give owners and designers some of the best and most concentrated insights on how people think about buildings and what we should not miss to consider already in the programming stage of a project.

Returning to the discussion of the design process, it should be noted that performance oriented approaches can also take on developmental functions. Formulations of this type emerged in the 1960s, especially as part of the earlier discussed systems and prefabrication approach to a series of educational facilities in California.[61] Not exact design solutions were specified but goals to be achieved (6.20).[62] Performance specifications leave the building contractor and the building industry freedom to come up with innovative solutions rather than to comply with strict adherence to prescriptive specifications of the designer. Ezra Ehrenkrantz writes that

> When you use a prescriptive specification, the opportunity to have new products developed to do the job more effectively disappears, as do the opportunities to use existing alternate products. The concept of specifying by performance provides for new ways to meet a given set of criteria, and opens new opportunities for ingenuity and innovation in the development of new methods and technology, and potentially for new ways to meet the basic user requirements.[63]

The performance specification concept is applied to obtain high quality overall objects or subsystem details by making the basis of input as open as possible. The interface coordination of project components needs special attention, however, especially when a multitude of different contractors and manufacturers are involved (see 5.45 to 5.47). Successful submissions can only be expected when the design team issues well-defined criteria of required performance and evaluation with enough flexibility built-in to accommodate aesthetic preferences.

Realization in context

The classification of design factors according to their origins of program, context and realization is helpful and the design process, by and large, relates to them in this order. Therefore, one might expect that I discuss now context in detail and then realization. A fundamental issue, however, leads me not to do so. When purpose motivates us to design we program needs and desires on a relatively general level. This accomplished, we look to what exists in our horizon and lends itself to our undertaking and satisfaction. We look at the context of the project. Different from purpose, which is essentially goal oriented, context refers to what exists. Context in its totality includes everything from which we draw the physical and nonphysical design factors that we find in the present circumstances into which the project is to be located and designed. In this broadness we may view it synonymous with given reality pertaining to the project. We look for opportunities and constraints which influence our objectives and with them realization. In other words, we identify and assess resources and obstacles for design development.[64]

Therefore, I find it useful to discuss design factors of context in connection with those of realization. I believe that there is no reasonable way of discussing context without realization, as it focuses us on particulars through which realization comes about. It is no accident that we juxtapose here terminologically realization and reality. Design implementation realizes part of reality anew, more or less depending on the project's purpose and the present, contextual setting. Realization reforms reality. At the beginning context influences purposes to some extent on the basis of our earlier experiences. But its major influences happen during the realization of design. *Purpose is fulfilled by its realization in context.*

The fulfillment of purpose, the satisfaction of needs and desires, results in the change of present conditions. Depending on the project and the frame of reference (context), change may range from very local to rather comprehensive. It makes sense to consider any given reality as a system of subsystems and components which are more or less in change and never completely in balance. Design activities are undertaken to eliminate or at least reduce intolerable or undesirable imbalances. On the other hand, any design realization introduces new imbalances, be they physical or relational, and, if too large, they must be counteracted. Needs and desires themselves should be perceived as imbalances. The genuine need for building a school indicates an imbalance in the educational system. The construction of a large building in an already crowded area introduces additional traffic of various kinds which may call for appropriate intervention, obviously being a change itself. The present efforts in design toward sustainability are based on the recognition of major local and global imbalances in our environment, neglected for too long. No doubt, corrective efforts will introduce their own imbalances which need amelioration.

These dynamics prompt us to look at contexts as states of affairs, constantly changing because of their own dynamic nature and human intervention. The more we can take advantage of these situations, the more successful our designs are. This is probably from no other aspect easier understood than from the activity flow in buildings. It is the flow of energy contained in its infinite variations of forms. Life's processes, such as the preparation of food in a kitchen, the presentation in a lecture hall or the daylight penetrating windows, manifest such energy flows. The configuration of a building's fabric, such as spatial arrangements, cross sections, facade geometries and equipment locations, but also material choices, ventilation air flow rates and acoustic enhancements by loudspeaker systems, are design responses.

There is a special kind of realization which inevitably occurs: self-realization. As designers we are acting to influence reality. We are the intellects and motivators who drive many changes. Even with best efforts as agents, we are not quite neutral. We have egos which weigh need versus desire. Self-realization is a necessary force for motivation and manifests itself in the physical realization of objects. In excess, it overpowers some of the other crucial aspects of realization and may create imbalances in the system. We know that not all imbalances can find nor should find complete resolution. But acceptable levels of accommodation must be reached between general realization and self-realization. As process, we may view this issue as the private dialog of the designer with the requirements of the project. For this matter, the client and other involved players, such as contractors, can be considered 'requirements of the project'. There are many physical and relational issues which we can resolve with our capacity of relative design freedom. Self-realization is a powerful component in the overall aesthetic of the result.

This discussion points to the central constitutive role which context plays as a wider concept than we normally assume, not only as environment into which physical things are placed but as environment from which we understand given circumstances and take things to start out with. An example is the level of project financing a client is willing to provide. Another is the required time frame for the projects completion. Again another is our status of experience from former projects of similar kind. It is in our context, present or still evolving, from which we together with others bring forth the factors for our designs. This requires alertness. *Unless we are observers who grasp well, we cannot be designers who express well.*

Contextually understood, all properties have global and local dimensions. This is increasingly so because of the enormous overall growth in worldwide interdependence, communication and transportation. The globalization of architecture is a response to the globalization of life and technology in general, a process that started centuries ago. Educational facilities, banks, shopping malls, factories, transport terminals, etc., even residential buildings, are within their building type categories quite similar worldwide. But differences exist. Each locale has idiosyncrasies of place because of present cultures and traditions, and certainly because of variations in climate. Therefore, design factors of global and local origins typically lead to hybridization of understanding and meaning. The result is local differentiation within global trends. There is and isn't an 'international style'. *Modern* is what we make out of our resources today, whatever they are and from wherever they come – not what a style called Modernism was some eighty years ago.

We naturally have to ask in each case what the peculiarities of place are. They are on the one hand given by the natural environment of location and climate. On the other hand they are increasingly given through manmade interventions and their infrastructure, whether in urban or rural settings. Earlier influences from purposive design factors are embedded and we need to consider this history as part of context. History derived from the physical environment often provides a great deal of relational aspects, though tempered by time. How far they should be reflected in present developments is often more a question of general aesthetic judgment than necessity. How far if at all, for example, should a historic structure on a site compromise the development on the same site of an additional project which comes with strong design factors of its own? Or, how far may a former structure, once present on that site and still remembered, influence what is now contemplated?

The obviously strongest source for relational factors are the life styles of present communities and individuals. Here, all what we said earlier about behavioral, social and cultural aspects applies. This points to the crucial dimensions which overall historical trends provide for developments in planning and architecture. I will use the remainder of this chapter to explain with a few examples from recent urban and suburban history how contextual diversity influences realization fundamentally. All of these objects naturally also show the more narrow architectural aspects of project realization derived from building types, construction systems and material choices.

Toward the latter part of the 19th century it was widely understood that measures needed to be taken for guiding physical development from socially conscious viewpoints. In architecture, more and more information on building types was collected and published. Such records had their foundation in similar features among projects. The first building codes were introduced which not only established minimum safety standards for structural integrity but, together with increased understanding of hygienic living conditions, mandated the ready access to fresh air and natural lighting for every habitable space. Water supply and drainage systems in buildings replaced outhouses, the new systems having traps in dirty water lines to prevent foul air from entering interiors.

To accommodate large densities, apartment and office buildings sprang up, many of them high-rise, made possible by the invention of the elevator. To educate all children was not only a desire anymore but a necessity for a society which increasingly depended not on physical labor but on productive thinking. Many schools had to be built. Places for specialized study and training supplemented the relatively few universities. Concert halls and museums, which had been mainly places enjoyed by cultural elites and the well-to-do, now became accessible to a broader public. The concentrations of places for manufacture and commerce were made possible by mechanized transportation of people and goods. All of this was to have fundamental consequences for the livability and infrastructure of cities and neighborhoods.

There is no question that the enormous technological and industrial advancement in general had a profound impact on what architecture physically could accomplish. But what architectural developments mainly drove was the changing cultural outlook of societies, locally and now ever more globally informed. This was especially made possible through the nearly instantaneous communication over long distances by telegraph and telephone. Private vehicles and public streetcars or trains made commuting possible between crowded centers of cities and their fringes. Worldwide travel came into the reach of many. What happened on one continent could be transferred rather easily to another. The ever more powerful combination of finance, commerce, fashion and advertising brought on heightened awareness especially for consumption by all segments of population. Purpose, as formulation of needs and desires, became overtly programmatic for the physical realization in context. And with that, the concept of function – as correspondence of purpose and realization – was identified, named and applied based on the concept of causation.

These were the conditions out of which emerged what is now called Modernism in architecture. We should not fail to appreciate that many explicit functional relationships had their roots in sincere efforts to bring about architecture more responsive to human needs.[65] Although often criticized today for its excesses, it shows many achievements in broad consideration of social aspects, especially in the design of housing projects. An early example is Pullman Town on the south side of Chicago in 1881 (6.21 and 6.22). George Pullman, the paternalistic founder and owner of the company which produced the elegant railroad sleeping cars, created adjacent to the factory a model company town with housing for workers, church, market house, hotel and many other amenities. Stanley Buder writes that

> To Pullman aesthetics had a virtue and function of its own which he called the "commercial value of beauty". ... Pullman firmly believed an aesthetic town setting would have a dramatic and lasting impression on a community, "ennobling and refining" it.[66]

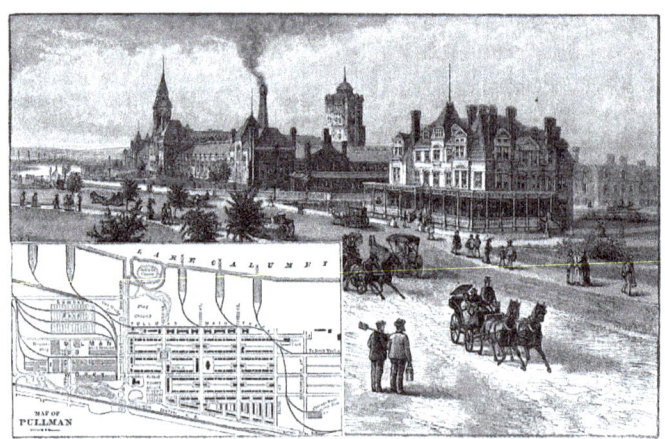

Pullman Town near Chicago

6.21 Plan of Pullman with Palace Car factory and hotel (source)   6.22 Townhouses (source)

There is no question that for Pullman, the shrewd businessman who thus became landlord for his employees, aesthetics implies here more than "commercial value of beauty", that is, value of an environmentally and socially positive setting. Altruism needed not to exclude self-interest. I use this extraordinary achievement here as an example in contrast to the vastness of housing which sprung up on a speculative basis and with little regard to human wellbeing in all large cities of North America and Europe.

After World War I beneficial criteria for livable housing conditions were more explicitly formulated and applied on a rather wide scale. Social-democratic governments brought forth housing estates such as Freidorf Muttenz near Basel in 1921, Hoek van Holland in 1927, Sandleiten in Vienna in 1928, Siemenstadt in Berlin in1930, among many others. Sandleiten was the largest of the social housing projects of the 1920s in Vienna, Austria. Still fully in use, it features amenities, such as kindergarten, central laundry, bathhouse, library, pharmacy, shops for work and sales, even a movie theater. Publicly financed by the city, it was built on the basis of an architectural competition, won by Emil Hoppe, Otto Schönthal and Franz Matuschek (6.23 to 6.25).

Sandleiten Housing, Vienna

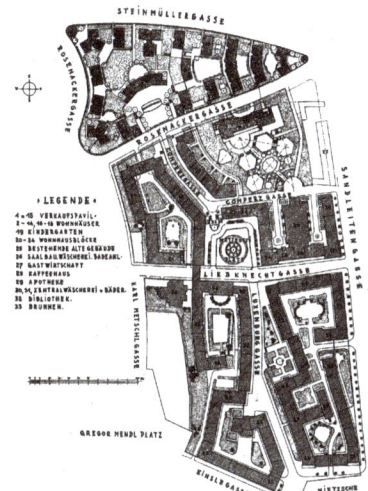

6.23 Site Plan with housing, shops, etc. (source)

6.24 Library with apartments above   6.25 Rosenacker section

This is also the time when the great masters of Modernism did their work: Sullivan, Wright, Gropius, Le Corbusier, van der Rohe, Saarinen, Scharoun, Kahn, Aalto and many more. They greatly vary in the ways they chose to integrate as many as possible design factors and single out certain factors for emphasis. There is some commonness of an "International Style" but also

231

much difference, not least from responding to local context. One commonness derives from the inevitability of response to building functions. There is no building in Antiquity, in the Baroque or today which does not display some functional relations. There is no 'post-functionalism' as much as there is no 'post-modernism'. We cannot prevent functional considerations from influencing the appearance of architectural objects and their aesthetics. Function and aesthetic are inevitable as cause and effect, be they experienced from a landmark building in town or from a barn out in the fields. There is no 'post' for modern as modern means by definition *at present*. Purpose, context and realization are always part of a present time – a modern time that is.

Looking at the vast developments in planning and architecture over the past half century one finds a multitude of trends. After World War II pent-up demand for building, not the least because of large increases in population, are answered by unprecedented construction activities with the help of advanced mechanization. The realization of projects is now strongly influenced by the new possibilities which mass production and transportation of building components offer – very much along with what happened overall in manufacturing for an ever more consumption oriented society, particularly in Europe, North America and Japan. This obviously favors building types which are repetitive, such as homes, apartments, office buildings, shopping centers and educational facilities.[67] In housing, some of the most influential early developments were the Levittowns near New York and near Philadelphia from 1947 to 1958, the satellite towns, such as Vällingby near Stockholm, Tapiola near Helsinki and Reston near Washington in the 1950s and 1960s, with master planning of the latter by Conklin Rossant (6.26 to 6.31). The Levittown developments show how strongly by this time the automobile influenced urban planning (6.26 and 6.27). The reliance on cars for driving to work, to schools, to shopping and recreation became a way of life, especially so in North America. It still is one of the major contextual factors shaping our environment. Not quite as much in Europe and the rest of the developed world where mass transportation played and still plays a more important part even in areas with relatively low population densities.

Levittown, Pennsylvania

6.26 Aerial view, about 1959 (source)

6.27 Typical street scape (© permission)

The last quarter of the 20th century brought many excellent housing projects with further improvements in living conditions of individuals and communities (see again examples 2.6 to 2.9, 5.23 and 5.24, 5.48 to 5.51). But there were also incidents of careless planning and mass production causing major problems in and around cities, due to insufficient concerns for social and environmental conditions. Two of the worst failures: Pruitt-Igoe Housing in St. Louis, an isolated, never fully occupied place with few amenities, built 1954 and demolished 1972, and Embarcadero Freeway in San Francisco, which separated downtown from the Bay, built 1959 and demolished 1991 (6.32 and 6.33).

Vällingby near Stockholm

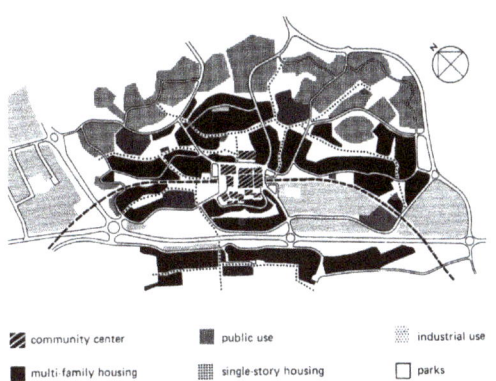

6.28 City center with train route (© permission)

6.29 Center Plaza above train station

Reston, Virginia

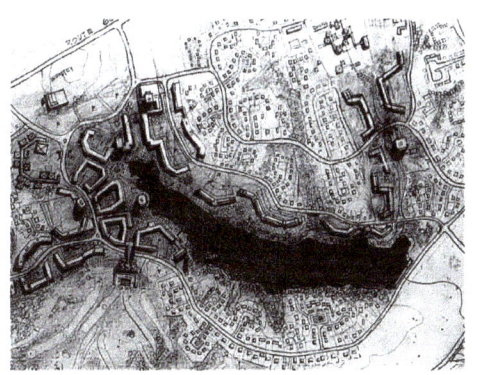

6.30 Master plan with Lake Ann (source)

6.31 Lake Ann with plaza in foreground (© permission)

6.32 Pruitt-Igoe Housing (source)

6.33 Embarcadero Freeway (© permission)

More explicit understanding of the interrelationships between cultural, economical and ecological conditions was needed. Writers like Jane Jacobs, Peter Blake, Herbert Gans, Kevin Lynch, Ian McHarg, Christopher Alexander, Constance Perin and Oscar Newman called for change and provided the background for possible redirection.[68] They could build on what historians and critics of technology like Lewis Mumford and Reyner Banham observed and analyzed. There was a new awakening about design issues with regard to what architectural environments, socially, organizationally and spatially represent. At the center were interests in design methods and environmental design research which spawned major publications by Christopher Jones, Christopher Alexander, Gary Moore, Amos Rapoport and others; in addition to the earlier mentioned, yearly series of EDRA volumes.[69] The result was a better understanding of complexity of building in response to the enormous demands of a highly diverse society and the beginning digital information revolution.

While all this happened, however, a shift began with post-structuralist tendencies, anticipated in some architectural projects, such as Le Corbusier's Chapel in Ronchamp. Structuralism which developed in the 1950s can explain much of so-called Modernism including functionalist tendencies. Reaction to it spurred Post-structuralism, a name which has much more explanatory power than what is the more often used term Postmodernism. John Lye writes that

> Post-structuralism is marked by a rejection of totalizing, essentialist, foundationalist concepts:
> - a *totalizing* concept puts all phenomena under one explanatory concept ...
> - an *essentialist* concept suggests that there is a reality which exists independent of, beneath or beyond, language and ideology ...
> - a *foundationalist* concept suggests that signifying systems are stable and unproblematic representations of a world of fact which is isomorphic with human thought.[70]

I agree with rejection of the first claim, not with rejection of the second and in part only with rejection of the third. As our world view is perspectival it cannot be totalizing. But all our concepts are essentialist, derived from a reality which exists at least in part "independent of, beneath or beyond, language and ideology" and, therefore, can only in part be influenced by us. There are things by themselves. If this were not so, we could potentially understand reality completely without the need at all to refer to the representational nature of our world view. What we conceptualize is often problematic but more often not. It is foundationalist in the sense not of an absolute truth "whose signifying systems are stable" but of a relative one with which mankind has lived and arguably thrived for a rather long time.

Postmodernism is best viewed as the initial phase of post-structuralism but is a buzzword for all kinds of movements over the past half century. Merriam-Webster Dictionary defines Postmodernism as

> ... being any of various movements in reaction to modernism that are typically characterized by a return to traditional materials and forms (as in architecture) or by ironic self-reference and absurdity (as in literature) ... or being a theory that involves a radical reappraisal of modern assumptions about culture, identity, history, or language.[71]

Out of these tensions – with related literature strongly impacting architecture – grew what is called Deconstruction.[72] Diane Ghirardo writes that

> The architecture produced in the name of Deconstruction attempts to embrace notions of fragmentation, dispersion and discontinuity through formal means.

And, in reference to the role of architects associated with the movement,

> ... the formal exercises offer little toward the construction of a theory different from that of Modernism, and even less to rethinking the role of the architect – and this despite dramatic

> social and economic changes since the late 1960s. Indeed, in their absolute indifference to issues of context, their exaltation of the role of the architect as form-giver and interpreter of society, it is difficult to discern significant departures from dogmatic Modernism except in the particularities of form.[73]

I agree. But "absolute indifference to issues of context" is not possible in architectural design, even under the narrowest of definitions.

There is a place for deconstruction in architecture as it is for any intellectual activity. Deconstruction in this sense is analysis of what exists and is eventually used for constructing in our thoughts something new, either by change of itself or by change through addition. *We analyze in order to synthesize.* We take apart, we "destruct", to speak with Heidegger, what is "at hand", so that we can speak or design constructively. If we design, we cannot stop at deconstruction as it is at best informative fragmentation of what exists. The result of what we deconstruct may be new to us, because we have not thought of it enough in detail. But it is not yet design. In 2003 Anthony Vidler asked whether what was 1988 called "Deconstructivism" has come of age:

> Has a tendency that was never entirely unified now attained the status of a movement? Stylistic evidence, if such can be adduced in a modernist context, would argue against this supposition. Even the most tenacious periodizer and style hunter would find it difficult to identify a single mode of expression among these architects; labels such as "late modern" and "neoavant-garde" fall short of serious characterization, and they resist being incorporated into a generalized postmodernism. If a movement may be identified, it would be, like all modern movements in the twentieth century, based on principle – on a common theoretical stance.[74]

Deconstruction cannot create style in the sense of "a common theoretical stance" because style is a matter of synthesis not analysis. 'Deconstructive design' is an oxymoron. Deconstruction in Heidegger's sense is part of the means to get to what we want but is not what we want itself; certainly not in architecture. It points to the process of finding the content from which form follows; form being much more than shape.

When shape making is the driving paradigm of design we develop surface architecture. We suspend content to a large extent. But eventually it must fully enter into our negotiations with form. There is an air of the virtual to such beginnings. It lends us a freedom fraught with dangers which are heightened by the increasing perfection of digital representation techniques. At a time when support of sustainability should be in everyone's mind, shape making a priori is not a viable approach. Fortunately, there is much architecture being practiced which has little to do with supposedly deconstructivist tendencies and approaches design more comprehensively.

To conclude. Design ideas, which are essentially expressive meaning, result either from needs or desires. They develop from many causes, such as cultural preferences and codes, historical precedents, functional requirements, ordering principles, political mandates, material and technical resources, and climate conditions.[75] The design ideas become active in any of the three areas of the highly interrelated design framework of purpose, context and realization. Every architectural form is the physical effect of ideas as design factors. Their explication enlightens the content of form. As human beings we understand content by and large implicitly. As designers we seek to understand it explicitly, so that we may utilize this understanding in future designs and their expressions. Design is in process a dialectic of understanding with actions caused in world-to-mind and mind-to-world directions. The effects are not objective, though they are based on objective reality. We are subjective. We never sense nor understand fully. In world-to-mind causation the world changes our mind via impression. In mind-to-world causation our mind changes the world via expression. The design factors of purpose, context and realization vary with every project in what they are and in how they activate in combination. All outcomes of design are eventually the confluence from this triadic source into the duality of the project's content-form unity. All of it is conceived by us in the framework of causation. Certain is that every effect has a cause and, while not all causes can be understood, trying to understand as many as possible enlightens meaning and decision making in architecture.

7 Language, Meaning and Design Narratives

Our progression to this point has shown that we draw inspiration and insight for design from many sources of information about the world of reality. In observation we perceive first a whole, however wide our frame of reference is, then explain it through details and how they interrelate. We define how something is by arriving at what it is – analysis. In design, however, we conceive the whole programmatically, which is formally quite abstract, then select physical components and connect them within frameworks. We define the what of something new by arriving at the how of it – synthesis. In other words design development requires formation, that is, fitting parts together. We activate the content of something to find its form through a kind of dialectic.

At the end of this chapter an operational content-form dichotomy emerges which I believe is the best way to communicate understanding to ourselves and others, here about architectural design. Understanding communicated is meaning. As I emphasized before, meaning is subjective because understanding is subjective. Meanings about architecture vary among designers; probably even more between designers and non-designers. This obliges us to communicate as well as we can what we believe is objectively the case in the formation of our designs. Communication by means of content-from dialectic can greatly benefit from understanding the nature of language – it being the most widely used means of communication and explanation. Therefore, the relationship of language to physical reality is the next item of discussion, with architecture considered as being part of physical reality.

7.1 Language and thought

It is probably safe to say that there is nothing which dominated philosophical exploration during the second half of the 20th century more than the phenomenon and function of language in connection with meaning, sometimes to the point that language as such was taken as meaning. Philosophers talk about the "linguistic turn" in their field. Architecture is influenced by this turn – as all of human undertaking – through association and analogy. The related literature in philosophy and even in architecture is extensive and controversial.[1]

The main reasons for this strong movement is the assumption that our consciousness of the world is insufficiently served by what we can obtain through the earlier philosophical models and that linguistic structures have certain generative capacities which we cannot avoid, even if we wanted to. Although the beginnings of this view go back about two centuries, it became part of a broader movement called structuralism, especially in anthropology and sociology, then arguably even more so in post-structuralism, including what has become known as deconstruction.

This is obviously not the place to go into an extended discussion of how language relates to reality in general. I refer to the just mentioned literature. Still, before we get to issues of language and architecture directly, it helps to address some issues in this broader framework which are particularly pertinent to architecture.

While we can have thoughts without words, they may overwhelm us when experienced and used in complexity. This is, in part, why nature gave us language, so that thought, which is content, may have a form to remember and communicate with. Probably the first who saw this necessity clearly was John Locke who wrote that

> Having shown the original of our ideas, and taken a view of their several sorts; considered the difference between the simple and the complex; and observed how the complex ones are divided into those of modes, substances, and relations – all which, I think, is necessary to be done by any one who would acquaint himself thoroughly with the progress of the mind, in its apprehension and knowledge of things – …
>
> … I find that there is so close a connexion between ideas and WORDS, and our abstract ideas and general words have so constant a relation one to another, that it is impossible to speak clearly and distinctly of our knowledge, which all consists in propositions, without considering, first, the nature, use, and signification of Language; …[2]

We may add that thought cannot become effective in the world beyond us unless it is manifested in physical existence and representation. The most common means to this end is language.

As outcome of early in depth studies of languages, but also in response to strict idealism in the 1830s, Wilhelm von Humboldt claimed that every language, as an "inner structure", shapes our experiences and views, and with them our cultures. He went as far as to say that

> For man to be able to actually understand a single word, not only receive it as a purely sensuous affection, but really understand it as an articulated sound referring to a concept, he already has to have the language completely and with its framework in himself.[3]

This would mean that we cannot understand individual words, at least not with their ultimate potential. But what about a child who learns to speak or somebody who learns a second language? We certainly can understand part of a language. Perhaps even more radically, he writes the now famous sentences:

> Language is the formative [bildende] organ of the thought. The intellectual activity, throughout mental, throughout internal, and in a way passing without trace, becomes through the sound of speech external and perceptible for the senses. Therefore, it and language are one and inseparable.[4]

Do I not think about some experience, when I am at a loss of words? "Formative" as used here is usually understood as meaning 'constitutive'. But we must be careful not to view "das bildende Organ" as to mean to be constitutive only. It also can mean forming in the sense of just the shaping of something. True, when "perceptible to the senses" intellectual content (thought) and language are inseparable. But not so the "intellectual activity" by which we arrive at the content. Language is formative when it transforms into physical form, as sound or word, what already *exists* in mental form, as thought. There is no rationally spoken or written language content without first being thought.

Humboldt views words as sensory signs. They play an active role.

> The sensory designation of the units, into which certain portions of thinking are united, in order to be contrasted as parts to other parts of a greater whole, to be put as objects in front of the subject, is called in the broadest sense of the word: language.[5]

Thinking is reflective. Its partial results, externalized by sensory forms of languages, serve for rethinking. In this way, form (language), in part, influences content (thought) which already has been thought. There is no question that language has an influence on our thinking but not because it is constitutive of it, but because of its versatility as the most comprehensively applicable structure of signs for ordering and communicating information in reference to objects and states of affairs, and because it is such an important mirror for reflective thinking. I believe that thinking does not imply language necessarily and this applies also to thinking in relation to design, about which much will have to be said.

Over a century later, Martin Heidegger after his 'linguistic turn' writes, motivated by Friedrich Hölderlin's poetry and perhaps Humboldt's thoughts, that

> Language serves for communicating. As equipment for this it is a 'gift' ['Gut']. But the essence of language is not exhausted by the fact of being a means of communication. With this determination we do not meet its authentic essence but only one consequence of its essence is set forth. Language is not only a piece of equipment that man possesses alongside many others. Instead, it is language first of all that provides the possibility of standing amidst the openness of entities. Only where language is, there is world, ...[6]

I disagree. It is not "language alone that first provides …". Language to be perceived or conceived requires thinking. It is the conscious and thinking being who, often with the help of language, but not necessarily so, stands "amidst the openness of entities" – with understanding more or less him- or herself and other entities, and perhaps describing this understanding. There is no "openness of entities" for us human beings without thinking. True "… where language is, there is world." But not "only". When we look at a circle or a door, we do not conceptualize the word circle or door. We conceptualize the direct sensation of a corporeal entity. If I draw a circle and show it to you, both of us do not need the word 'circle', not for understanding nor for conveying the associated meaning, unless we communicate about it verbally. Language is not fundamentally constitutive of anything. It represents what is given in thought. Therefore, the limits of language cannot be the limits of what we perceive or conceive of the world because what we understand of the world is much broader than what language can characterize. In one of his later works, *On the Way to Language*, Heidegger even claims that

> The thing is a thing only where the word is found for the thing. Only in this way *is* it. Accordingly we must emphasize: there *is* no thing where the word, that is the name, is missing. Only the word supplies being to the thing. ...
>
> Something only *is*, where the appropriate and also relevant word names something as existent and in this way establishes the particular being as such. ...
>
> Language is the house of being.[7, 8]

Being is not supplied by what words are but words refer to, namely objects and properties. To successfully refer to properties, they must exist, at least as content in our memory. To understand that they exist, and what we believe they are, we have to think, and then perhaps speak or write about them. This view obviously shall not mean that language is not part of our being.

The essential activity of language is to combine and articulate sounds and letters into verbal forms. For both an essence – content of thought – must exist. In impressions *from* sound or word, language is the ground for thought toward understanding the original thought which was constitutive for that particular formation in language. In expressions *by* sound or word, thought is the ground for the formation in language. In Wittgensteinian manner I say: whereof one cannot think, one cannot understand nor speak.[9]

Language is the most common medium to externalize our thinking in communications. This capacity of language is very important for life processes in general, so also for architectural design. Thinking does not preclude that many words and sentences have become to us so familiar that it seems they occur to us quasi simultaneously with our non-verbal thinking. In this sense word and thought seem to have become one. Here, language seems to have crossed the threshold from being *instrumental for* to being *integral with* thought. It is like with a musician hearing the tone A' when somebody talks about the tone A'. Or, it is like understanding that we will pass from one space into another when somebody tells us that we should use "this door, please". It may seem that language 'produces' thought. But this is not so. Language, as signs, prompts earlier thoughts to be retrieved from memory. These thoughts had to be thought first at least once, and usually many times, to become 'automatic'. Such occurrences do not make language constitutive of thinking. They only prompt it more quickly.

Signs are the ways how we communicate with each other for understanding. Jürgen Habermas writes, and I agree, that

> Language is not conceived as a means for transmitting subjective contents but as a medium in which the participants intersubjectively share an understanding of a given matter. The sign *x* is not a tool that an individual can use, and with which *S* gives *A* to understand something by prompting her to recognize his meaning or intention; rather, the sign *x* is an element of a repertoire used in common that permits the participants to understand the same matter in the same way.[10]

The sign *x*, say the word 'door', is not a subjective entity of yours or mine. It is a common signifier which you or I derive from impression or select for expression to communicate our mutual understanding. We sense from the sign the same matter, but subjectively interpreted. The end of the quote "understand in the same way" is somewhat misleading. We understand procedurally in the same way, but the results are only more or less the same. Representations in our minds of the same impressions differ more or less, though usually without negative consequences; but not always.

For communication, content is in search of language. This content exists or we need to think it first. We use the signs of language to communicate our meaning and hope that the recipient's meaning will be close to ours, but, as said, it is never exactly the same. We communicate from subject to subject. So it is with communication in architecture. We may replace in the quote from Habermas "language" with architecture or architectural design, and it still holds.

These thoughts lead to another issue of communication in connection with the linguistic turn, namely that *meaning determines reference*.[11] I believe that this notion applies but only in a certain way, and that is not based on the view that language determines understanding in such a fundamental way as Humboldt, Heidegger and others suggest. The view that meaning determines reference does not require the linguistic turn. It does not arise from precedence of language over thought. It simply arises out of the natural order that rational beings try to evaluate and select carefully the means by which they can best communicate a particular understanding. It is our choice to mean something – in language, design or otherwise. We select our referents for communication because of what we think about them.

For this highly consequential aspect, which needs discussion in the comparison of reference of language versus architecture or any other physical matter, I give another time my definitions of relevant terms:

- Meaning is our particular understanding of something. It is its significance.
- Reference is the action and form of referring to this something. It is its signifier.
- Referent is the object to which we refer. It is the signified.

Meaning of expression determines selectively reference, the signifier. Our understanding becomes embedded in the sign, the form of the reference, the expression. This understanding is derived from analysis of the *anticipated* referent and not from any implicitness in language or any other referential entity. In other words, we determine reference based on the quasi impressive meaning from the properties of the assumed object, be it a named or a physical entity.

As meaning is subjective we do not have certainty how close meaning and reference come to what the object, the referent, is in a particular case and context. Mankind has lived and decided with this handicap since people have communicated, sometimes more and sometimes less successfully. There is usually interest in as stable as possible communication from giver to receiver. This is achieved the closer the reference comes to signify the meaning of the giver and the closer to that meaning the reference is understood by the receiver. The reference and the referent as such are objective entities.

Language has rather uneven flexibility in serving as reference, depending on the subject matter. Certain words refer to rather general concepts; others to more specific ones. For example, water. Depending on our thinking about water in a particular context of time and place, we may choose as reference H_2O, rain, flood, Niagara Falls, 'this lake on which we sailed yesterday', etc. When an individual word is insufficient we use a sequence of words as signifier.

Communication *about* architecture operates under the same conditions. We are still in the realm of language. Communication *by means of* architecture, however, is very different because not language serves as reference but architecture itself which we understand as observable and relational properties. This difference has profound implications which we will explore in the next section.

A watershed in philosophy's turn toward intensified studies of language was the work of Gottlob Frege (1848-1925). Not because of the work itself, which is very significant, but because of the inspiration it provides to this day. One of the issues which is crucial for language and any other aspect of representation, including architecture, is his differentiation of sense and reference. The title of his paper "Über Sinn und Bedeutung" has been sometimes confusingly translated as "Sense and Meaning" (sense and meaning are usually understood as synonyms). Perhaps "Sense and Reference" is best because "Bedeutung" points to the object, the referent. Even better might be "Sense and Signification".[12] Another suggestion for clarification was made by Bertrand Russell "Meaning and Denotation", but it did not catch on.

Names which we give an object have as expressions no related thought content about the object. They are symbolic. The names 'water', 'school' or 'spirit' do not directly tell me anything about what water, school or spirit are. They simply indicate or denote. We associate with the three names, however, properties, such as water is a liquid, school is a place for learning and spirit is mental. Such connotations explain denotations. Propositions are the content of connotations, the meaning of denotations. We have encountered denotation and connotation before in our discussion of observable and relational properties (Chapter 2.4). I address them here another time because they help in the present context to show the difference between the processes of observation and design (7.1). From observation of an object we connote its meaning (sense) and denote through language its name (reference). For design we are given a denoting name (referring to a problem) and select connoted meaning (propositions), then develop the physical object (properties). We observe a building, understand its meaning to be a school named 'school'. But we design what is named 'school' by searching for its meaning and design the building accordingly. We then can refer to what exists as design, what the building is and does (by reference, the word 'school', to the referent, the school building).

In linguistic (descriptive) circumstances, denotations (references as names) are symbolic. So are connotations (senses as propositions). In nonlinguistic (physical) circumstances, including architecture, the duality of denotation and connotation does not apply in the same way, they coincide. We directly encounter the physical objects. They may be the actual buildings or their physical representations in form of drawings, models, etc. We understand them iconically as we conceptualize them by means of resemblances. But when we verbally communicate about physical objects, including architecture, we are back again in a purely symbolic environment with its denotations and connotations.

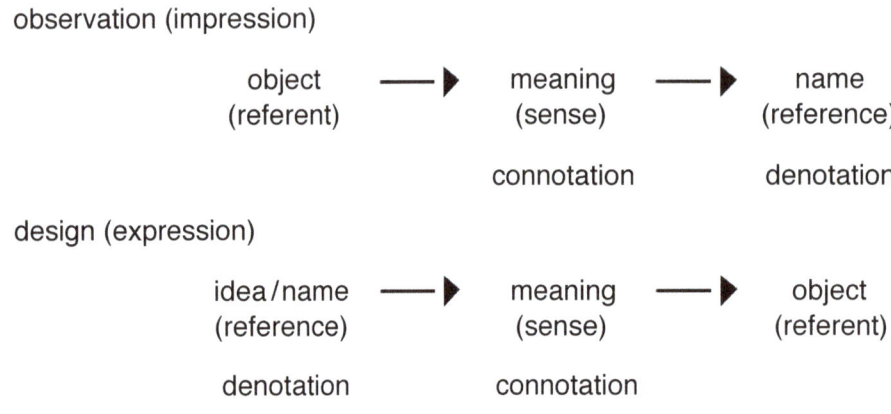

7.1 Denotation and connotation in observation and design

One of the most important thinkers about the relationships of language and reality in general, but especially so for purposes in architecture, is Ludwig Wittgenstein. He published in 1922, his *Tractatus* in which he claims that every meaningful sentence must have an exact logical structure. Every sentence is made up of truth-functional (logical) concatenations of names (words). The sentences give a logical picture of states of affairs which have the same structure as the sentences. This view is known as his "picture theory of meaning". As an extension of Bertrand Russell's logical atomism, Wittgenstein viewed the world as a totality of so-called atomic facts, made up of simple objects. Quotes from parts 1 and 2 of the book explain:

> The world is the totality of facts, not things. ... We make ourselves pictures of facts. ... The picture is a model of reality. To the objects correspond in the picture the elements of the picture. ... What the picture represents is its sense.[13]

Here, ordinary objects, such as tables or chairs, are elementary units in logic. They are the meanings of names which relate to real world objects. Wittgenstein does not explain the connection of names with their real world objects and how the connections come about. Dale Jacquette writes:

> ... Wittgenstein's conviction that there must be an exact parallelism, isomorphism, mirroring, picturing, or representing of the world in language at some level of analysis between any logically possible language and any logically possible world is the central thesis of his picture theory of meaning.[14]

In language, names stand for things in existence. They provide, in language, the main part of 'picturing' what the state of affairs is. Concatenations of words, among them the names, are propositions. Semiotic meaning is hidden in their sign nature. Therefore, signs require interpretation. Wittgenstein recognizes that all of this is somewhat difficult to absorb and explains that

> The essential nature of the propositional sign becomes very clear when we imagine it made up of spatial objects (such as tables, chairs, books) instead of written signs.[15]

Wittgenstein then goes on to explain in detail the relationships of propositions and pictures. This is a powerful view of language as representation of reality. Less than a decade later, however, Wittgenstein embarks on a journey that leads to his other main work, *The Philosophical Investigations,* concluding that the approach that he described earlier, this strictly logical arrangement in propositions, is in error and that, indeed, other types of arrangements must and can meet many different requirements. Important again is the issue of naming, but now very differently. Wittgenstein finds that naming of objects, though fundamental, is only a preparation. The names help us to communicate but they alone make for a very inflexible system. What very much counts in language are "language-games". The structure of sentences is highly variable. Words and parts of sentences make their contributions according to the locations and relationships in the particular structure of the language-game but also in response to countless external and internal, environmental and individualistic factors. This means the contributions are contextually influenced and interdependent.

> But how many kinds of sentences are there? Say assertion, question, command? – There are *countless* different kinds: countless kinds of use of what we call "symbols", "words", "sentences". And this multiplicity is not something fixed, given once for all; but new types of language, new language games, as we may say, come into existence, and others become obsolete and get forgotten. ...
>
> Here the term "language-*game*" is meant to bring into prominence the fact that the *speaking* of language is part of an activity, or a form of life.
>
> Review the multiplicity of language-games in the following examples, and in others:
>
> Giving orders, and obeying orders –
>
> Describing the appearance of an object, or giving its measurements –
>
> Constructing an object from a description (a drawing) –
>
> Reporting an event –
>
> Speculating about the event –
>
> Forming and testing a hypothesis –
> .... [16]

The cultural and temporal diversity of life forms is reflected in the language-games. The name "language-game" may sound strange at first encounter. But it is a very good summary expression for Wittgenstein's belief how language works. One of the most important of Wittgenstein's insights is his assertions that

> For a *large* class of cases – though not for all – in which we employ the word "meaning" it can be defined thus: the meaning of a word is its use in the language.
>
> And the *meaning* of a name is sometimes explained by pointing to its *bearer*.[17]

Here is the notion that a meaning may be understood from what its referent is. I think this is usually so. To use a meaning in language, its referent must exist. In reverse order, meaning can be derived from language by naming. This is verbal communication at work. A word, if known and meaningful, has a useful content and that is its referential power. A word has a form – letters written, sounds spoken. This is naturally due to the semiotic character of words. Closely connected with this view is the question about how we understand. As discussed, we come to understanding by means of the emotion-and-reason process. It is the process of explaining the nature of something to ourselves and involves concepts and feelings. Therefore, Wittgenstein says that

> "The meaning of a word is what is explained by the explanation of the meaning." i.e.: if you want to understand the use of the word "meaning", look for what are called "explanations of meaning".[18]

To take for the meaning of a word its use is a very pragmatic approach – an impression one gets when reading Wittgenstein on meaning. The pragmatic psychologist William James, whom Wittgenstein cites several times, seems never to be far away.

It is common to all language-games that they are made of words or word sequences. But there are other similarities. Looking at them

> ... we see a complicated network of similarities overlapping and criss-crossing: sometimes overall similarities, sometimes similarities of detail.
>
> I can think of no better expression to characterize these similarities than "family resemblances"; for the various resemblances between members of a family; ...[19]

Components of language-games, even whole language-games, have more or less similar features, like family members have. Colors are an example. The words red, green, blue belong to a group that has family resemblance. We view them as a category. There is a word family for 'red': red, reddish, burgundy, bloody, etc. There are word combinations, more or less close to 'red': tomato-red, red like a lobster, red pine, red heat, red-handed, etc., many with metaphorical meaning. Or, we find family resemblances in whole phrases, such as 'Upon his arrival they rolled out for him the red carpet (in fact or metaphorically)' and 'This issue raises for me a red flag'.

In language about architecture, for example, we may look at 'stair': stair, staircase, steps, stairway, etc.; and, straight stair, circular stair, steep stair, etc.; and, upstairs, stair tower, stairs as exits, etc. We see the family resemblance of these expressions in various uses. In a wider context, we may think of perceptions of spaces. They all have family resemblances, such as in dimensions and proportions. Or, lighting types in spaces have family resemblances. So have the activities occurring in spaces. Sometimes such resemblances are permanent, sometimes dynamic, most often physical, but also referential, and again at times metaphorical.

All games, language-games or other games, have rules. Without them they could not be played. Games without rules produce chaos. But rules must only provide a framework of order within which a somewhat limited freedom may unfold. Even chance may have its chances. Rules exist to be followed. In language-games, they typically have long traditions and are understood as being reasonable. They are essential parts of a technique:

> To obey a rule, to make a report, to give an order, to play a game of chess, are *customs* (uses, institutions).
>
> To understand a sentence means to understand a language. To understand a language means to be master of a technique.[20]

Rules have an aspect of agreement. They typically evolve from agreement. Even, when we cannot follow them 'blindly', we should come as close as possible to agreement with them. There is judgment involved regarding freedom and constraint.

Rules are subject to interpretation. But the interpretation is still a rule. Very importantly, following rules is not a private matter; nor is much of communication. What happens in the public realm, whether spoken, written, designed, built or otherwise, is not a private matter. Nearly everything that has to do with how we communicate has social dimensions, that is, impacts and consequences in the public domain, therefore, requires value judgments. This is why Wittgenstein asserts that

> An 'inner process' stands in need of outward criteria.[21]

The quote is part of his discussion about the privacy of thought and language. We must control our inner process, in our case thinking about design, by inner but also outer public criteria which can only come from careful observation of the prevailing context in all its environmental and human complexity.

Much of what we call 'use' happens in the public domain. While thinking is a process in our private minds, it has mostly to do with the world. Our communication of thinking, be it through language or wordless signs is a more or less public affair. Grant Gillett and John McMillan write, associating a concept of use with its meaning, that

> ..., we could say, with Wittgenstein, that the criterion of understanding is correct use of the concept and that, in the general run of things, correct use is a publicly accessible fact about the thinker.[22]

It is "a publicly accessible fact about the thinker" whether she or he is the thinker who caused the use of the concept or the thinker who was affected by it. In other words, only when both sides in a communication understand its meaning and implications is it successful in the sense hoped for; though the understanding is never exactly the same. This points toward the need for responsibility to make concepts as clear as we can to avoid problems, at least as far as basic properties and their functions are concerned. Part of this responsibility in design, as in all else we do, has obviously a profoundly ethical dimension.

What especially can we learn from Wittgenstein? 1) Throughout all of his later writings it is clear that he confirms the totally referential nature of language. We encountered this view first, though more narrowly, in De Saussure's "signifier and signified". 2) Wittgenstein prompts us to look at the use of meaning when we want to know what it is. His writings, especially his later ones, suggest to look at language from an as practical as possible point of view. Language helps us to explain for ourselves and others what we believe things are. Language is always about things, about states of affairs. We then look at meaning as the result of a particular understanding of reality. 3) He points to understanding and meaning as result of process, not process itself. This confirms my view that meaning is the result of personal impression; the result of analyzing a given expression and, in the design process, a proposition for a further developed expression. Meaning is not a priori given. It is derived understanding. 4) Language consists of "language-games" with rules, however highly flexible. To some extent this is true in design also but the rules are much more rigid as we work with physical components which must physically connect, not with voids between words which allow for highly open combinations to bring about understanding and meaning. 5) His notion of "family resemblances" is a powerful metaphor for the grounds of conceptualization, also in architecture. Often architectural resemblances are stronger than those in linguistic expressions because of being highly self-referential in the physical realm with material and geometry playing directly interpreting roles. 6) In pointing out that language and what it produces in meaning is publicly grounded and has eventually its impact beyond our subjective musings, he lets us grasp that language (and with it meaning) is mostly a social event, even when it occurs in our private mind. I derive from this view in part my resistance against the view that a fully autonomous architecture is possible. 7) Wittgenstein made for his *Tractatus* a kind of linguistic turn from the then prevalent philosophical thinking and another major adjustment for his *Philosophical Investigations*. But his turn is not at all like those of Humboldt and Heidegger. And certainly not like those of others who to this day reify language as the central paradigm in philosophical thought, giving even foundation to the claim that architecture is text. Wittgenstein's views can help us clarify our views about thinking with language and thinking without it.

Our living requires activities of our brain which I call *content thinking* and *form thinking*. The brain provides and makes intelligible to us by means of thinking the content and form of what we communicate by means of written or spoken words and sentences. When we are conscious, our brain thinks content, combining present understandings and earlier ones from our memory, and then selects form for what is presently needed as linguistic expression for ourselves or others. While recent research on the mind has made enormous progress on where in the brain thinking for various subject areas occurs, we have no detailed understanding how neural interactions unify content and form aspects toward eventual impressions and expressions. We know, however, from observing the results of impressions and expressions that some subject areas imply more, some others less, some none at all, what can be called *language thinking*, that is, thinking which aims at linguistic formulation.

Language thinking is unique – a one of a kind of form thinking. It is in search of expressions to formulate content of thought. It does not exist by itself but is associated with object related thinking, such as law thinking, poetry thinking, traffic thinking, football thinking or design thinking.

All thinking is more than language thinking, as important as the latter is. Language thinking always goes beyond itself and supports thinking about something.

One of the wider functions of thinking is to order and manifest verbally much of the content from the uncountable kinds of content thinking in which we are engaged. Some of these kinds of content thinking are strongly associated with language thinking, such as poetry thinking. Others are not, such as design thinking which is very directly associated with physical objects. That language is intermittently or even finally used for descriptions of design does not change this distinction.

This view of language thinking must not be confused with what was proposed as "Language of Thought" by Jerry Fodor in 1975.[23] Murat Aydede writes that

> The Language of Thought Hypothesis is so-called because … token mental representations are like sentences in a language in that they have a syntactically and semantically regimented constituent structure. Put differently, the mental representations that are the direct "objects" of attitudes are structurally complex symbols whose complexity lends itself to a syntactic and semantic analysis. This is also why the LOT is sometimes called *Mentalese*.

The thinking processes

> … are causally sensitive to the syntactic/formal structure of representations defined by this combinatorial syntax.[24]

Fodor proposes that the mind is modular and that these modules make it possible to enter into causal relations with external objects. These relations and others which occur among tokens in the mind can only be symbolic and language like; therefore the term "language of thought".

Here is the connection to our interest. Mentalese produces what are called mental representations related to the appearance of physical objects and uses these representations to produce additional ones. It is Mentalese of the individual mind, linked to the world and fed with content from past and present experiences. In other words, it is dependent on the world of impressions to be able to produce expressions. In this sense my language thinking is the same as what Fodor suggests. But in another crucial aspect it is not.

What I would call Mentalese does not create content, it describes and rearranges it. Content may come from outside via sensation and content thinking, joined or not joined by language thinking, depending on what is sensed and what is recalled from memory. This process leads to mental conceptualization. If externalized by speaking or writing, the physical result is language, linguistic expression. The syntactic and semantic thought functions, necessarily interdependent, give linguistic expressions their unique procedural and communicative formation. They can address in highly flexible and, very important, rather explicit fashion many content areas. They provide a variable system, called language, which is commonly practiced across cultures, and worldwide applicable through translations. These language properties have crucial advantages also for architecture in ways we will have more to say ahead. As language thinking for external expression, Mentalese does not determine content but does have influence through its structural properties on *how* we understand content. We cannot have thoughts *of* things, only *about* things, as far as they can be understood by us.

Language thinking participates in our mental process only when we are engaged with impression from or with expression through the form of language. If we are engaged with design, our thinking process is design thinking toward design expression. Language may or may not be used during this process, such as in a secondary, discursive or specifying function. While I sympathize with the wish to broaden the meaning of the term language in "language of thought", "language-like thinking" and similar expressions to refer to the operation of thinking, I find them misleading, if more is understood by them than an analogy to natural language. The neural processes in our mind are the signs *of something going on* which we call thinking. But they are not explicit signs *standing for something* just to be exhibited. Thinking to be represented externally needs an explicit physical medium.

So, there is language thinking but not linguistic thinking, that is, thinking for language but not thinking as language. Similarly, there is vision thinking, that is, thinking because of vision, but not visual thinking. And, there is no visual memory but memory which contains neural arrangements derived from visual sensation. We see the word 'water' as symbol and see water in reality. The understanding and meaning of both exists as separate neural states in our mind. But we perceive and conceive both iconically, from their physical state as word and as matter, because we remember similarities from earlier experiences.

Neural processes in our mind are what we call thinking. They are not useful representations of anything until they gel as understanding, the results of thinking. Thought is what we thought about something, that is, past tense. This is what "mental representation" means throughout our discussion. To be communicated, thought requires an external medium. Natural languages are in essence *external* to our mind, though we learn them and deposit neural equivalents in our memory for reconstitution. They represent through verbal formulation our object related thinking, which is also neural. To repeat, language itself does not produce content but lends itself to structuring and conveying it.

In a nutshell: Content thinking provides understanding and meaning. It creates new meaning through conceptualization and reconceptualization. Language itself is the physical manifestation, the form, of content managed by language thinking. Design thinking or other content thinking addresses design or other content with or without the use of language.

I cite here a helpful list of what John Searle calls default positions onto which one holds unless convincing arguments arise and prompt us to change them:
- There is a real world that exists independently of us, independently of our experiences, our thoughts, our language.
- We have direct perceptual access to that world through our senses, especially touch and vision.
- Words in our language, words like *rabbit* or *tree*, typically have reasonably clear meanings. Because of their meanings, they can be used to refer to and talk about real objects in the world.
- Our statements are typically true or false depending on whether they correspond to how things are, that is, to the facts of the world.[25]

For our immediate interest I add:
- Language in combination with thought is an extremely powerful instrument. That it can select, order and prompt other thought is itself an achievement of thought. But language does not constitute thought. *Language does not think. We think language.*
- Language is the most commonly used medium to represent the world in communication, and it does so symbolically. And there are other media. One of them is architectural design, which represents foremost iconically and sometimes symbolically.
- As discussed earlier, emotion is part of thinking. Therefore the result of thinking always includes feeling whether we are aware of it or not.
- Our emotion-and-reason process consists of content thinking and form thinking. If the form is to be language, language thinking formulates results of content thinking. The result is in content-form unity. A simple example, water. Our meaning about this wet stuff arises out of content thinking. The formulation of the word 'water' arises out of language thinking.

Natural languages presuppose language thinking which processes and connects by means of syntax the simple and complex semantic components of content thinking. So one role of language thinking is to correspond with a natural language in whatever structure it may have, that is, to provide translation in directions from world-to-mind and mind-to-world, prompted by language as a unique medium of communication. Its other role, often utilized, is to structure and organize information from content thinking, of which there are uncountable kinds, one of them being design thinking.

My use of the term design thinking is narrower than that of Peter Rowe whose book with the same title addresses the various frameworks in the process of design overall.[26] He describes many of the approaches which developed over the past century, such as creativity from association; mental imaging with sensations and feeling; intending and focusing through mental acts; holistic organization of information; problem solving based on purpose; studies of replicable patterns in physical behavior from stimulus-response models; and generate-and-test procedures. While there have been given emphases to some of these methods, emerging generally from positions of particular researchers, I believe that in practice they all apply more or less. They manage the design process by 1) thinking about need and desire understood as purpose; 2) thinking about what exists in available environments and resources understood as context; 3) thinking about what might come out of them through change; 4) thinking whether the change with its new understanding produces value and for whom; and 5) thinking about ways by which particular architectural and planning concerns can best be realized. These kinds of thinking are not unique to architectural design. But architecture and its complex processes depend arguably more than many other endeavors on them.

7.2 Language *of* and language *about* architecture

With regard to all of the last section we must clearly differentiate language *of* architecture from language *about* architecture. Language *of* architecture, if meant to be more than a general analogy, is supposed to be instrumental like verbal language is in speaking or writing. Attempts to develop such a language have not been successful. The reason is that the translation processes from the mental realms to the physical realms, that is, from thought to language and from thought to design, are very different. To lay the foundation for this view I first address language *about* architecture and then contrast the differences between language thinking and design thinking in their semantic and syntactic features. This shall not mean that studies about "Language of Architecture" did not help to better understand architecture in directions not primary to these studies. In fact, finding and evaluating the difficulties of making a language of architecture operational close to that of natural language is an important result of that work. 7.2 depicts the situation for our two basic modes of impression and expression with language about architecture as outcome.

In the impressive mode we encounter an object, in our case architecture, develop a mental representation and possibly make a description, which as far as the nature of language goes is symbolic. In the expressive mode we conceptualize the design factors, develop from them a design representation whose nature is in part iconic and in part symbolic, given in drawings, scale models, labeling, etc. This representation eventually serves the realization of the building. We also may verbally describe the intermediate and final solutions in general and by means of specifications which feed into the design process. They, being in language, are symbolic. In terms of properties: architectural design has in part iconic, non-relational properties which are immediately present and self-referential, and in part symbolic, relational properties which are referential to aspects beyond the present object. Language is only symbolic, only referential to any properties.

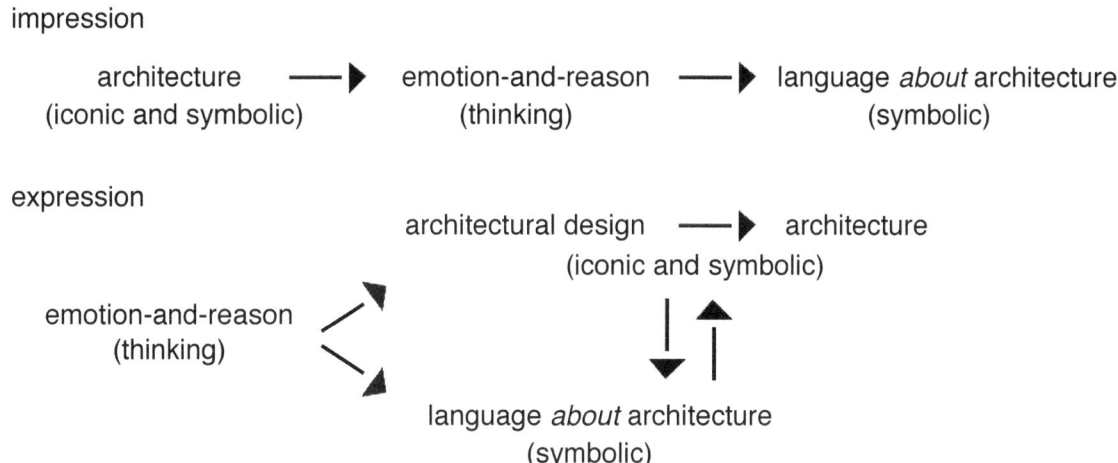

7.2 Language *about* architecture

The expressive mode in 7.2 shows two paths of thinking, the upper directed toward design of architecture, the lower toward language about architecture. The former implies the full-fledged design process. The latter is, when related to the same project, an accompanying verbal commentary. The impressive mode is similar to the latter. It starts, however, with existing architecture. All verbal references to objects in architectural history and criticism as well as post-occupancy analysis are of this kind. The architectural program related input in the mode for expression (not shown) is language about architecture from pre-design activities. Descriptions of the clients requirements and the brief on programming are examples.

For design the expressive mode is obviously at the core of our interest. In the translation from thought to architectural design we move from neurological abstraction to physical representation. In the translation from thought to language about architecture we move via neurological activity to verbal representation. When both address a presently anticipated project they run parallel and, though not structurally translatable into each other, are mutually beneficial for understanding. Using this parallelism is the main justification for intensively studying architectural history and theory, and with it the dialectic of thinking and language in architecture. While history and theory are largely lodged in the impressive mode of 7.2, their connection to the expressive mode is obvious – impressions being based on expressions.

The syntactic aspects of architecture and architectural design are much more complex than those of language. They demand very specific fit and connectivity requirements compared to the rather general ones in language (grammar). In the use of language, we learn to bring together a rather small number of relatively simple sounds and letters to form words and sentences with associated meaning. The meaning of most words is flexible in response to the combination with other words and the overall context of the application. The success of communication depends on the mental capacities and efforts of giver and receiver in using the language and its flexibility. For example, the term 'house', in context with other terms, is used to refer to many different situations, such as 'this house there', 'to house many people', 'we have a housing problem', 'the housing of this equipment', 'the house of parliament was in session', 'this household includes many', etc. In architecture and its design we are concerned with physical substances, dimensions and connections. We have to work with a large number of rather complex elements and systems. Often the elements and systems are quite rigid, not like words which can accommodate various conditions. This complexity is further increased by the arrangement of elements in three dimensional space; sometimes in multiple layers. Architecture is environmentally, that is, physically influenced and influential. We are in it or around it and have perspectival perceptions of it depending on our positions in space. In addition, at the time of observation of a building or at the time of a design being considered, much information is simultaneously present, assembled, integrated; whereas language is more incremental, linear in direction and successive in time. That we encounter architecture also sequentially over the time we spent with it is true but we still experience it simultaneously as an integrated entity.

All of this leads to the conclusion that developing and using a language *of* architecture has foundational problems. We cannot get far in search of attempts which genuinely apply language as a system to structure architectural synthesis. Most publications which bring "architecture" and "language" together in their titles address only semantic aspects, not syntactic ones in the sense architecture requires. Therefore, the claim "Architecture is text" is an analogy, but a rather weak one, as it explains little beyond the fact that architecture has properties and qualities which lend themselves to develop narratives. All objects more or less do.

The most concentrated and most developed attempt in using language explicitly toward the process of design evolution is still, I believe, Christopher Alexander's pattern language. He claims that

> … as in the case of natural languages, the pattern language is *generative*. It not only tells us the rules of arrangement, but shows us how to construct arrangements – as many as we want – which satisfy the rules.[27]

If this were so, I would have to drop or revise what I mentioned above. His pattern language is not "generative" as "in the case of natural language". It does not originate, and it cannot do so as language because not even language does so for itself. Only thinking does in language and design. His pattern language, however, is helpful in searching and organizing information to increase understanding for design and, therefore, is of interest to us. Alexander explains that

> … every pattern we define must be formulated in the form of a rule which establishes a relationship between a context, a system of forces which arises in that context, and a configuration which allows these forces to resolve themselves in that context.
> It has the following generic form:
> Context —▶ System of forces —▶ Configuration.[28]

Design does not start out with context. It starts with purpose as shown in the previous chapter. And, design is not to a large degree an activity of using patterns as a rule; patterns understood as models for the repetitive making of things. Design, while it may use patterns, goes far beyond them. The design factors of purpose, context and realization determine in give-and-take fashion and with us in control the form as hopefully positive arrangements.

The sequence from Context to Configuration is not as simple as Alexander, for example, presents in "the outline of a pattern language for a farmhouse in the Bernese Oberland" in central Switzerland (7.3):

> NORTH SOUTH AXIS
> WEST FACING ENTRANCE DOWN THE SLOPE
> TWO FLOORS
> HAY LOFT AT THE BACK
> BEDROOMS IN FRONT
> GARDEN TO THE SOUTH
> PITCHED ROOF
> HALF-HIPPED END

BALCONY TOWARD THE GARDEN
CARVED ORNAMENTS

Each of these patterns is a field of relationships which can take an infinite variety of specific forms. And, in addition, each one is expressed in the form of a rule, which tells the farmer who is making his house just what to do.[29]

His list contains simply names and partial descriptions of components or properties which are typical for many other buildings including other farmhouses, such as in the southern Black Forest farmhouse (7.4). There are very few relationships given which could serve as connection rules. Nothing is said about the topological organization of items and their physical connections, for example, how the "NORTH SOUTH AXIS" influences the assembly or how the "WEST FACING ENTRANCE DOWN THE SLOPE" and the "HAY LOFT AT THE BACK" or the "BEDROOMS IN FRONT" and the "BALCONY TO THE GARDEN" relate to each other, or where the living room is located, or where the animals are housed and how their location relates to the hay loft.

7.3 Berner farmhouse, Switzerland (© permission)

7.4 Schwarzwälder farmhouse, Germany

The syntactic relationships must be resolved in building to construct anything reasonably called 'patterns' which is very different from how syntactic relationships in natural language are resolved. It is especially in geometric fit and technical connectivity where the analogy of natural language and architectural 'language' (or pattern 'language') breaks down. The only aspect which has anything to do with a "rule" is that these components and properties are commonly found in Bernese Oberland and Black Forest farm houses among many others.[30] But beyond that they provide very little "which tells the farmer who is making his house just what to do". They are typical program items which, when used, necessarily create patterns of some similarity and, therefore, of meaning. They are the outcome of functional relationships, whether in schools or offices, or in any other building type. The same items can give rise to a great variety of arrangements. Repetition out of tradition is at work here, rather than necessarily compelling patterns. Many other arrangements with the same components are thinkable and actually found.

Alexander's pattern language is essentially a framework for referring to similarities of objects, components and properties, and some of their organizational structure. It is analytical and motivational, thus very helpful in the design process, as it provides background information for potential synthesis. The latter amounts in design to a highly varied, purpose and context dependent and, because of repetitive similarities, somewhat pattern-driven enterprise. In addition, overall aesthetic preferences provide for great variety. This is naturally so with all building type groupings and related functional analyses.

Many efforts have been undertaken to apply in very close analogy the semantic and syntactic characteristics of language to the morphological aspects of architecture. Günther Fischer identifies four "syntactic dimensions": form, function, space and construction, and then adds a variety of reference, value and expression codes.[31] He views forms as geometric shapes and essentially reduces the other syntactic dimensions also to geometry. The result is four layers of volumetric syntax for which he mentions the need for "synchronization" but does not develop any rules for them. He sees the integration of the syntax aspects as the main problem.

> From the fact that the syntax of the architectural language has fourfold polarity arises the relative instability of architectural systems and the periodic decline of styles: stability is much more difficult to achieve than in spoken language.[32]

His semantic dimensions are "reference", "rank (of importance)", "expression" and "relevance". He gives them descriptively but with few details of relationships. They appear like another layer of structure in addition to the syntactic one.

The infinite observable and relational variety of architectural components and properties, dependent on physically present historical, cultural, social and constructional conditions, cannot, as in language, be pressed into the schema of a rather limited, though highly combinable, number of elements, the semantics of which come solely from reference.

I refer here to this study, because it shows clearly that architecture cannot be considered as being a comprehensively 'open' system as language is. Attempts in such directions by means of reasonably open and modularly coordinated prefabrication systems have been successful within some building types, such as schools, but they still lack universality beyond.[33] At most, parts of overall architectural objects, particular subsystems, can be achieved to be combinatorially open, that is, have extensive repetitive connectivity of all components within the domain of the subsystem. The most advanced developments of this type have been the earlier mentioned Clasp System in Great Britain, the SCSD System in the United States and the Marburg University Building System in Germany. More limited subsystems, such as structural concrete and steel frameworks, suspended ceilings, demountable walls, plumbing installations, and kitchen cabinetry, have found wide application and are today to a large extent common in the building industry.[34]

Intensive research efforts using informed spatial patterns toward well functioning design have become known as studies in Space Syntax.[35] John Peponis writes that

> In principle, what space syntax adds to more traditional models of location, distribution and circulation is sensitivity to physical configuration on the ground. At the risk of both simplifying and overstating, we might say that syntax does not only ask whether a connection is available and what the capacity of the connection might be, but also what is the shape of the route, how at every step, it intersects all other potential routes, how it features within the global pattern of the spatial fabric, how it is spatially defined along the way, how it acts as an interface to local conditions.[36]

Space is endless in all directions. For practical purposes, we differentiate two kinds of space on our planet: filled or empty, occupied or unoccupied. The former is filled with dense material, the other with air. The two complement each other. In architecture, solid forms determine the voids in between. In design, we organize these forms to form voids, architectural space, according to functional needs and desires of cultural, social, constructional and general aesthetic aspects.[37] It is the human dimensions – not only those of individuals but all those of their activities as community – which form architectural and urban spaces. In Chapter 5.4 I pointed to this expressiveness as configuration, the physical fit according to purpose and context, being part of overall architectural ornamentation of space.

In the 1980s, Bill Hillier initiated the theory of Space Syntax which addresses configuration and uses functional criteria for computation of preferences in architectural and urban space formation. He writes:

> Encountering, congregating, avoiding, interacting, dwelling, conferring are not attributes of individuals, but patterns, or configurations, formed by groups or collections of people. They depend on an engineered pattern of co-presence, and indeed co-absence. Very few of the purposes for which we build buildings and environments are not 'people configurations' in this sense. We should therefore in principle expect that the relation between people and space, if there is one, will be found at the level of the configuration of space rather than the individual space.[38]

So far the work on space syntax is mostly "configurational analysis" of horizontal patterns of space in architectural and urban environments producing graphic and computed information of movement and connectivity. One result is explication of spatial relationships by means of visibility polygons (isovists) derived from many points in space and overlaid to create a density graph (7.5).

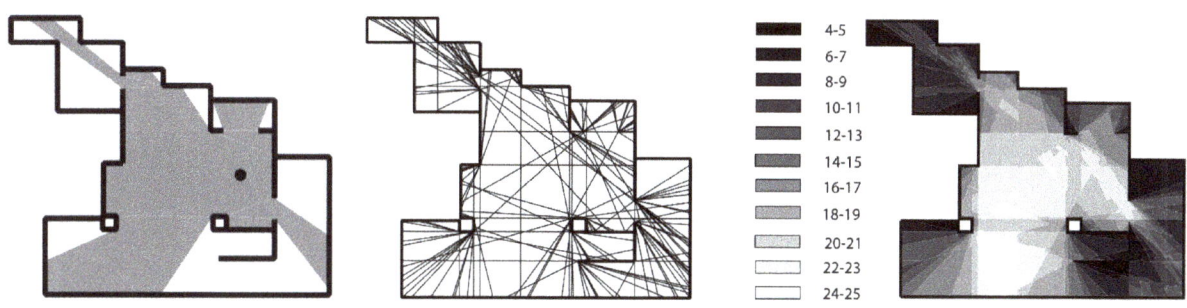

7.5 Plan with visualization of spatial relationships using space syntax analysis. The lighter the result (at right) the stronger is the visual communication from space to space (© permission)

Even on this relatively simple but for architecture so fundamentally formative level of syntactic relations, that is, in the connectivity of spatial sequences and adjacencies, the crucial differences between linguistic structure and architectural structure become very obvious. As emphasized before, language assembly is based on purely referential components and mental coherence. Architecture assembly is based on physical components and corporeal coherences, which naturally also have relational aspects. This is why Hillier views the process of design as testing of conjectures with configurational analysis as the vehicle:

> ... through spatial configuration culturally determined patterns are embedded in the material and spatial 'objectivity' of buildings. ...

He speaks of the non-discursivity of configuration which

> ... means that we do not know how to talk about it. ...[39]

True, we cannot talk about how we come to configuration as thinking process as we do not know (yet) how elements of thought find each other and connect in our mind to larger assemblies of thought. But we are aware of the elements and become aware of the assemblies, both represented by what we call properties and objects respectively. We are aware of *what* we think but not aware of *how* we think. We can be aware of what configuration as result of effect is, and what its causes are, although we do not know and cannot talk about what it essentially is as thinking process beyond its neurological indication.

When we get in the design process to form conjecture we never start with 'a clean slate'. We have internalized background information about the project in the narrow sense from the programming phase and in the broader sense from previous projects and general studies in architecture. Procedurally, configuration is at the center of the design process and it is much more encompassing than arrangements which space syntax addresses. After a discussion of the analysis-synthesis paradigm and Alexander's work, Hillier writes that

> A design conjecture is not simply a conjectural form but a formal conjecture embodying a functional conjecture. The formal conjecture in effect comes to us already replete with a functional prediction which offers a solution to the problem posed by the brief.[40]

But then he suggests that

> Architects design form, but hope for function. The most difficult aspect of prediction from an architectural conjecture is the prediction of function from form. It is only in existing buildings that function as well as form can be seen. By an empirical appeal to cases, then, function, the key unknown in the design process, can become part of the predictive reasoning about forms which characterize the design process.[41]

Function is not "the unknown in the design process". It must be known as we test form conjectures with dependence on functions of design factors. While we work with form, we are informed by functions as far as we have knowledge of them, thought about them before hand. Every designer, worth his client's trust, is able to predetermine functions for the anticipated building type and program specifics, at least the basic ones. So "prediction of function from form" is not a viable paradigm for design – though understanding of function from form is crucial for observers and users of existing buildings, and certainly for designers as background knowledge for future projects. Prediction of function from form would be highly chancy and inefficient procedurally, which shall obviously not indicate that we always produce optimal solutions. As architects, I hope, we never neglect analyzing purpose and context for indications of function in design. This view does not exclude early, even quite abstract play with shapes. But that is not yet project oriented design to any acceptable extent. Design starts when purposive and contextual design factors with their functional interrelationships come into play. In other words, conjecture has its foundation to a large extent in function.

We have configurative freedom within the limitations which context and realization represent. The design factors, which are the operational components of content, must eventually bring about one resolution of form. As mentioned earlier, this activity is one of the most demanding in the configuration process. Being conformation, it is the main synthesis aspect of design. The assessments of the design factors and their influences toward the overall design solution end in rational but also emotional judgments, therefore are essentially aesthetic (in the sense I defined it) and demand major responsibility. All of this process is very different from how verbal text comes about and what it constitutes.

That there cannot be a language like 'language *of* architecture' is expressed, in a nutshell, by Roger Scruton who writes that

> If it were true that architecture were a language (or, perhaps, a series of languages), then we should know how to understand every building, and the human significance of architecture would be no longer in question. Moreover, this significance would be seen as an intrinsic property of buildings, and not as some external or fortuitous relation.[42]

Such intrinsic nature is what strong supporters of the 'language *of* architecture' paradigm need to claim. If it would be the case, the signifying power of architecture in the way language signifies would not be in question. On the other hand, I don't think that anybody doubts that "the human significance of architecture would be [or is] in question" in any case. But if we could put architecture together like we put language together and read its significance similarly, we could learn architecture like speaking and writing – which obviously is not the case. We understand through architecture in a very different way than through language. Language is about something else, not about itself, it has no physical properties beyond being written or spoken. Architecture directly encountered, however, is in the first instance about itself, has physical properties, though also refers to something else out of this material being. Again, architectural design is materially constitutive and referential beyond itself but language is only referential.

The problem of using the wording of architectural language or architectural text is shown well in an article by William Whyte on how buildings mean. After describing some of the concerns, similar to mine, that he has with using the terms 'architectural language' and 'architecture is text' he writes that

> This is not to suggest that buildings cannot be understood as texts. The problem is that buildings are a particular sort of text – one that does not yield readily to the process of reading. For one thing, the very materiality of architecture differentiates it from other types of text.[43]

He does not explain in detail how "buildings are a particular sort of text". The use of architectural language and architectural text, unless clearly qualified as analogy only, is simply misleading and complicates the already difficult inquiry about meaning even further. He proposes to look for meaning related to transpositions:

> As a building is planned, built, inhabited, and interpreted, so its meaning changes. The underlying logic of each medium shapes the way in which its message is created and understood. This suggests that the proper role of the historian is to trace these transpositions. Buildings, then, can be used as a historical source, but only if the historian takes account of the particular problems that they present.[44]

What we call meaning of buildings changes during their evolution and that may be of interest for historical and procedural reasons. After they come into use, however, buildings are relatively fixed entities, unless we change them physically. Whyte uses transposition here to indicate change of the object. But he also has in mind a very different idea:

> When Eero Saarinen was commissioned to build the TWA terminal in New York, his self-declared aim was to "express the drama and specialness and excitement of travel." Yet his audience soon understood the building in other terms. They compared it to a bird in flight. The building had not changed, but its meaning had. It was a shift that Saarinen accepted pragmatically. "The fact that to some people it looked like a bird in flight was really coincidental," he commented. "That was the last thing we ever thought about. Now, that doesn't mean that one doesn't have the right to see it that way or to explain it to laymen in those terms, especially because laymen are usually more literally than visually inclined."[45]

Here transposition is not used with regard to differences in status of the object but to differences of view between designer and observer. True, "the building had not changed", but the meaning of observers was simply different. People differ in meanings about objects. This point prompts me to reiterate what happens to meaning while it is communicated. Meaning is the result of emotional and rational understanding of the designer during the project's evolution and is, because of the choice of properties, embedded in the building as medium. The choice of the medium is part of the designer's meaning. Through perception and conception it is re-understood by the observer as her or his meaning. Part of this is that every meaning is necessarily influenced more or less by its medium because every communication requires physical transmission with syntax.

If one defines that any means of communication is language, than architecture obviously qualifies as language. Everything in corporeal form has a content which evokes more or less understanding in us. But this is too broad a definition to have any real value. When it is asserted that "architecture *is* language", coming about and constructed like linguistic text, problems arise, as discussed. Finally it should be emphasized that very different from the relational properties of language, the relational properties of architecture arise out of its physically observable properties and are, out of this dependence, more directly and observably context related than those of language.

Language *about* architecture, in contrast to language *of* architecture, covers a broad spectrum of descriptive and interpretive approaches from simple communications on day-to-day architectural issues to extensive descriptions of aesthetic aspects. It is text for the benefit of architecture and its design. Most of the work on architectural theory, history, criticism, even the writing of architectural programs and specifications is language *about* architecture. So is this book. Essentially all what is written in studies which contain in their titles in one way or another 'language of architecture' are in fact *about* architecture and have misleading titles as they do not address the nature of architecture as a language, there being nothing like that.[46]

On the other hand, we can take advantage of the descriptive and explanatory power of language which makes it the best medium of discourse on architectural realization, whether its concern is existing buildings or prospective designs. Thomas Markus and Deborah Cameron write on language issues in architecture that

> Using language – speaking and understanding it – is a defining ability of human beings, woven into all human activity. It is therefore inevitable that it should be deeply implicated in the design, production and use of buildings. Building legislation, design guide lines, competition and other briefs, architectural criticism, teaching and scholarly material, and the media all produce their characteristic texts. When these prescribe what is to be built then, in a sense, they can be said to 'design' the eventual building. When they describe what is already built they are formative of our judgment and responses.[47]

Note the mitigating quote marks around 'design', indicating essentially the supportive rather than substantive nature of language. This becomes additionally clear when they write that

> Treating architecture as a language has the unfortunate effect of obscuring the role played by actual language, speech and writing, in shaping our understanding of the built environment. It is that relationship between buildings and language – an interactive rather than analogical one – which is our central concern ...[48]

It is my concern as well, though perhaps a more narrow one which has to draw from a wide array of resources: *how can language facilitate to bring forth meaning from or for architectural design?*

With this question in mind we connect to our earlier discussion on the sign nature of language. When we ask 'what does the word mean?', we cannot expect a highly exact definition. Whatever we refer to by a word, let's say 'building', has become associated with this term through convention. While the term does not explain, it acquired meaning because of its use at many occasions. The term does not only point to its referent, but also to what has been 'absorbed' into the word, typically a general concept. We do not have to rethink every time in detail, when we use a common word, what it refers to. Alan Gardiner writes that

> ... every word is a heritage from the past, and has derived its meaning from application to a countless number of particulars differing among themselves either much or little. When now I utter such a word, I throw at the listener's head the entire residue of all its previous applications. Indeed, how could I do otherwise?[49]

This is the same when we use language to describe architecture. Not so, however, when we observe or when we design architecture. For explicating this difference it helps to hear another time De Saussure. He held that signifier and the signified of linguistic signs are two parts of unified wholes. But,

> The bond between the signifier and the signified is arbitrary. Since I mean by sign the whole that results from the associating of the signifier and the signified, I can simply say: *the linguistic sign is arbitrary.*[50]

The original association of signifier and signified is chosen, not necessitated. It is a *symbolic* sign. This is not so regarding the long time usage of the sign itself. While originally arbitrary, the usage is now customary by convention. This may be easily understood from the fact that in different languages very different signifiers refer to the same signified. The signifier 'maison' in French refers to the same signified as the signifier 'house' in English. They are two different terms, at first arbitrarily given, referring to the same object. In realized architecture, however, designed or built, we encounter the real thing, a physical truth condition, not a verbal reference. The signifier in language, the word, is made up as a combination of characters from an alphabet with the set of characters in kind and number unchangeable. The words evoke no meaning beyond referring. On the other hand, the signifiers in nonlinguistic situations are, case by case, made up from properties with which we associate content and meaning themselves. Perhaps more than any of the other reasons we have given earlier, this fact provides, in a nutshell, the foundation why 'architecture as text' cannot serve directly as structural framework for architectural design.

When we encounter a building in physical reality, our mental representation of it is not arbitrary. It has objective grounding. The representation is obviously not identical with what we encounter. But the representation definitely has features of similarity (iconic information), although, we are only able to express and communicate the features of similarity through explanatory language or other representations external to our mind, such as drawings or scale models.

In language thinking we search for words which match as closely as possible what our descriptive expression should be. In design thinking we search for solutions which match as closely as possible what our physical expression should be. Being based iconically, design thinking has often also elements which refer symbolically and indexically. This triadic aspect in our understanding has its correspondence in the physical representation of drawings, models, etc., very much like having impressions from observation of existing architecture. Design thinking is content thinking not language thinking, though we may use the latter to communicate it verbally.

From all of this we can derive that meaning in architecture, as all meaning immediately related to physical things, is meaning not mediated by words. It becomes attached to words only when formulated in language for communication to others, sometimes also 'communicated' to ourselves when we talk to ourselves. Language conveys thought. It is one of two very fundamental categories of communication, the other being the direct sensing of things. Both are physical. Communication is a physical process.

This makes language obviously crucial for communication. But it is also the best classifying instrument for our thinking process. It has categorizing capacity far beyond any other communication device including design. One reason is its referential nature which keeps it positioned one step away from whatever it stands for, be that physical or mental. The other is its simple, universal materiality and 'smallness' of its basic components with very broad to very narrow information content. Its concentrated power as signs is simply stunning, ranging from one letter for parking, to a few letters and numbers for a chemical notation, and to an incredibly small number of different words for telling a whole story. This makes language in many respects a highly efficient medium.

To grasp fully the advantages of verbal description, compared to physical depiction, we need to look in more detail at the kinds of sentences which explicate concepts. Sentences can be individual words or groups of words. The latter typically provide more opportunity for increased content. The semantic efficiency of single words or multitudes of words may also be increased because of contextual aspects present when particular language is employed. In language such context can be explained quite easily and often with very few referential expressions. For example, the single expression 'entry' has a very large number of extensions from a simple and unprotected opening in a wall of a hut to the grand and sheltered access of an important building. To make clear what is meant we can apply the 'pinpointing' and highly flexible power which is inherent in language. A few words on context are usually enough to reinforce what is primarily meant. The simplicity of the additive and linear nature of language can accomplish this task in very short time frames.

Multiple expressions in language can either add up to more elaborate detailing of content within the same concept or in bringing together various other concepts generally without any or little syntactic connection. 'This window is made of wood frame, glass pane, steel hardware, etc.' and 'Windows provide views of outside, including playgrounds, fresh air, daylight, solar heating from south orientation, etc.' are examples respectively. This bringing together of many separate concepts in very small 'space' makes verbal description very efficient.

On the other hand, the referential, indirect nature of language of being symbolic for something else is a communicative inefficiency which our more direct encounters with physical depictions, such as drawings, models, computer simulations, photographs, etc., and, obviously, built reality, do not have. There is much truth in the saying that "a picture is worth a thousand words". The picture or reality of a window shows me its details directly without my thinking what it is by means of reference. It shows also necessarily its geometry, its color, more or less of its context in the building, etc.; all through one effort and experience on my part. Nonverbal meaning related to physical things provides immediately multifaceted richness of reality itself.

To conclude. Every word we think and understand evokes in us a meaning. Several words logically associated amount to a meaningful long or short text. Examples are references to observable referents, such as roof, facade, window, garden, floor plan, green, sloped landscape, etc., but also relational referents, such as comfortable, joyful, accessible, affordable, style, great beauty, etc., or, both together, such as the metaphor 'house like a beehive'. Whether we gain impression or give expression, language helps us to make thoughts explicit in ways nonverbal forms cannot provide at all or only less efficiently. While we design, crucial links of essence may manifest themselves through verbalization. We conceptualize, classify, systematize by verbal referencing an activity of which we rarely have a record because we proceed as quickly as we can to designed results.

It is in the 'space' between impression and expression where thinking plays its major role. It is here where the small or large tokens of understanding from the emotion-reason process evolve, be it on the way from given form toward impression as observation or from hypothetical content to expression as design. Together they amount to the main part of all our thinking because nearly all our thinking leads to either impression or expression from external or internal sources, or both. Often verbalization as explication of thought is helpful for ordering what belongs together but also for efficiently prioritizing properties before physical design commences. The process is not just relating words to their equivalents in reality. It is a discourse during which semantic aspects of design are born through sequences of analysis and synthesis. Here we find and apply properties and eventually concepts for design solutions with program and context contributing toward realization. While we may formulate our understanding in language, we need to carefully look at how our verbalization corresponds with reality.

As mentioned, language usually provides large semantic flexibility in developing the meaning of concepts. Not so architecture which is much more deterministic. The word 'door' in language can have this or that interpretation and is preliminarily rather generic until further described in detail and context. But despite its initial indeterminacy language can be put to use in explaining architecture which, as such, only provides us meaning without words.

Written language helps us to visually break open the given comprehensiveness of the built or projected assemblage into 'decomposition' by using linguistic description as meaning with words. This may sound as something we should routinely do when we experience architecture or design it. True, we approach it doing so subconsciously by content thinking in whatever way we are engaged with things, even in simply walking through a building. The explicitness of meaning with words derived from meaning without words can enhance the design process from preliminary solutions to dialectically well considered ones and potentially lead to results with properties and relationships otherwise not found. Using language in this way is not a 'linguistic turn' of architecture equivalent to that in philosophy. But if broadly applied, it yields many practicable answers. It provides especially answers to questions which the postmodern lingo in architecture has posed and is a step in the direction, to use Jürgen Habermas' words, toward working on the unfinished business of modernity.

Together the advantages of descriptively indirect and physically direct communication provide the comprehensive basis from which we can develop design narratives with content-form correspondence. Before we get to them, however, a few comments on the measurement of qualities in meaning.

7.3 'Measurements' of meaning

Considerable efforts have been made to enlighten meaning by what may best be viewed as 'the measurement of meaning', based on results from questioning observers or users. Charles Osgood et al published in 1957 a book with this title. It was seminal for the development of various models to measure meaning, most often using statistical analysis based on semantic difference scales between polar adjectives, representing 'meaning dimensions', such as "large-small", "diverse-monotonous", "loose-inflexible", "intentional-unintentional", "pleasant-unpleasant", "clumsy-elegant", "oppressive-liberating", even "artistic-inartistic", "functional-nonfunctional" and "meaningful-meaningless". Martin Krampen writes:

> Subjects are confronted with stimulus material, which can be either verbal or nonverbal, and mark a particular scale between a polar pair [of adjectives], presumably in accordance with some kind of internal reaction towards the stimulus material.[51]

I find the application of semantic scales, if their polar adjectives can be well understood by those who answer questionnaires, helpful for elucidating detailed aspects in the analysis of existing architectural objects. I emphasize 'well understood'. I do not count the three pairs, mentioned above, "artistic-inartistic", "functional-nonfunctional" and "meaningful-meaningless", suitable as being well understood, at least not without further explanation to what the adjectives refer in detail (which is generally not done). Well defined semantic differences may also help in directing discussions, though being less formal than 'measurement' implies, for example, between clients and designers.

Various models using semantic differences in architecture have been used from the 1960s through the 1980s.[52]

One may ask why more recently only very few evaluations have been undertaken by means of them. The main reason is the difficulty in handling overall complexity because of the interdependence of the many factors influencing architectural design (semantic difference scales address single dimensions at a time). The diversity of models allows only for few comparative results, making it difficult to draw unbiased guidance for the design process. David Canter raised already in 1975 important criticisms of semantic difference scales:

> First, the sets of dimensions revealed overlap to the degree that it seems plausible that within the limits of the procedure and methodology currently employed, little will be revealed. Secondly, the assumptions underlying the methodologies employed are now seriously questioned. In particular it is being asked whether the search for *independent* dimensions is psychologically valid. Many of the reactions we have to buildings appear to be interrelated.
> As a consequence, forcing on the analysis an orthogonal structure may be an injustice.[53]

With all the advances in engineering and technology we have achieved high standards of building construction and comfort conditions which we can physically, individually and rather objectively measure. Not so with dimensions of psychological and aesthetic aspects which semantic difference studies mainly address. Results are derived from very personal preferences, ever more when idiosyncrasies of designs are hyped to extremes. The more it is crucial for designers to study 'what decisions produce which outcomes', what content can be derived from form as result. This is a matter of understanding well particular built environments by individual laypersons and designers.

Other analyses, such as sorting type methods, have been developed as well. As is the case with most semantic difference applications, they were used for the assessment of building exteriors by architects and non-architects. The best summary discussions with examples of these and similar methods are by Martin Krampen and Linda Groat.[54] Such studies either address the affects which objects have on the opinion of subjects, that is, the impact of chosen attributes, or they cluster objects in relation to judgments derived from integrated multi-attribute affects of objects for some kind of classification, such as environmental taxonomies or architectural styles. They are not aimed at and do not generate understanding of what in the objects causes the affects to arise; the understanding which is fundamentally important for input in the design process. They assess, on the basis of given design expressions, impressions as derived meaning, which then can serve for further interpretation. In contrast, the early design process aims at developing content for expression. Content is the essence of form and must be developed and adopted, hopefully in balanced response to needs and desires, before realization of form may occur. Unless we understand, we cannot mean, that is, select an understanding for manifestation in a suitable form and environment.

From these observations we may draw the conclusion that meaning has a substantive and an evaluative component. The substantive aspect is as Hershberger writes

> … represented in the human organism as a percept, concept, idea, image or whatever.

And the evaluative aspect (for decision making)

> … consists of internal responses to the already internal representation.[55]

The more we move from the substantive toward the evaluative, the more our contributing impetus is not the object directly but our mind, though on the basis of what we conceptualized the object to be. Meaning stems never only from one or the other. There cannot be an evaluative aspect without a substantive aspect and there is no effect from a cause without some subsequent judgment, as rudimentary and perhaps subconsciously it may occur to us. My emphasis is on elucidating cause without ignoring that its effect as mental representation is to some extent subjective, like all manmade representations.

The present study is not about measurement of meaning and its qualitative judgment. It is not, for example, about whether something is more or less beautiful or ugly, interesting or boring, good or bad, welcoming or forbidding, bold or timid, clear or ambiguous, simple or complex, etc., that is, about judging on the basis of scaling and statistical analysis by means of polar adjectives, as Hershberger used extensively.[56] The present study is about what meaning in architecture *is*, about what it is based on and how we come to it – why and how it is evoked in us.

It is important to keep in mind that there is no way to separate design factors of things fully into categories, such as functional, ethical, aesthetic or by what else one may label them. This shall not mean that we cannot differentiate some properties of things or particular details of things more than others; details being properties and multiples of properties. But we must be aware that properties are, as mentioned earlier, never by themselves. They are together with other properties in ways that they influence each other more or less. It also does not mean that we cannot or should not make judgments using bipolar adjectives, for example, beautiful versus ugly. Making judgments is our way of life. Even if we wanted to, we cannot avoid them. But we must be aware of the limitations within which we operate.

At least I question whether measurements on the basis of statistical analysis using bipolar scales with extremes, such as most beautiful to most ugly, yield results which can be generalized. All judgments are value-laden depending on our idiosyncrasies and the entanglements among properties. These conditions apply on whatever level of whole or part we make judgments. All judgments are subjective which, however, is no excuse not to search for objectivity, especially where it is so very important: in environments of intersubjectivity for which architecture plays a crucial communicative role and in which we are all involved. With our judgment capacities burdened by constraints, common sense goes a long way toward reasonably objective and meaningful decision making. In other words, we design architecture never for ourselves alone but for the community of others who are also involved, at least as observers and consumers. We must provide descriptions of existing and prospective architectural designs which allow for open and critical discourse, and provide the foundation for intersubjective consensus, resulting in guidance toward positive decision making as Jürgen Habermas advocates in his "theory of communicative action".[57] After all, architecture is a society forming enterprise, with all of society having a stake in its development and judgment. There is no reason, for example, that all public and private projects over a certain size should not be exhibited in our municipal libraries for public reviews and comments. The experiencing and discussion of architecture is as much a public concern, or should be, as the quality of the air surrounding us. In fact, the two are more than metaphorically interrelated as we begin to understand from the issues of environmental sustainability.

To make communication by means of architecture successful, I agree with Robert Hershberger who writes that

> If architects wish to create specific meaning in the physical environment for those who will use it, indeed, to have their buildings used as intended, they must develop a better understanding of how physical forms are attributed with meaning by layman – the potential user.[58]

This understanding attributed by laymen depends foremost on how we as designers understand meaning and how we incorporate it in our designs. In perhaps the most direct way we may ask: where does the expression of architecture come from and how are we able to explain it for ourselves and others? This understanding and what we do with it is at the core of this present work.⁵⁹ Therefore, my interest is in the ways we approach identification of properties and their impact as far as we can. All of the present study has this main objective and I believe that what I call 'the dialectical narrative of meaning', based on well understood property identification, is the most accessible and practicable approach to what meaning in architecture is about.

7.4 Design narratives

We defined the design process as an iterative progression with future oriented input. We are now at the point where we need to look at how content and form behave in this progression, and how we best can make emerging meaning explicit.

From form to content and from content to form

From our notion that meaning has its ground in our understanding and judging of signs in particular situations, we can postulate that meaning is what our mind 'gives' us when we experience whatever we are involved with. When engaged with design, we look with purpose at what exists, that is, the context and its resources to be used physically and relationally. Together, purpose and context represent the motivating content. We derive all in the mode of impressive meaning. Then we progress from this content and its form to new content and its form based on imaginative transformation of what is directly available, and what is additionally acquired and incorporated. The overall content is eventually the result of activity by all design factors which become active in a project, be they preconditions or conditions which arise during the process. The synthesis of their effects as progression from content to form brings with it the explicitness of design. This happens in the mode of expression. Considering design practice, we let the *what* of the program, that is given by need or desire, determine the *how* of a new entity, the design. We may characterize this externalization process of design as *expressions from impressions* with as many iterations of the two as we deem necessary for a satisfying result.

It is rather difficult to comprehend what essentially happens leading to what I densely described in the past paragraph. Allowing for some repetitiousness with what I just said and also discussed before especially regarding causation in design (Section 6) the following should help to show the process in detail:

1. Impression is based on expression and expression is based on impression.⁶⁰
2. Expression is design modified impression made explicit by means of form.
3. The process of making explicit by means of form we call design development.
4. The willful action of making explicit and of developing impression and expression in design is what we call creativity. This implies that understanding from perception and conceptualization is to some extent an act driven by informed imagination.⁶¹
5. The world beyond us presents itself to us as expressions. Our inner world is for us understanding of impressions from earlier met expressions. It is the basis for new understanding. In other words, we arrive at new understanding through the combination of new external information and existing information already in our mind.
6. The motivating information comes in form of needs and desires, which are translated into performance requirements. Project relevance and categorical fit is required to allow for creative motivation to develop successfully.⁶²
7. The information includes content, such as the client's requirements, consultant's input, building

type organization, site conditions, material and process considerations, etc., and naturally the designer's specific interests and knowledge.[63]
8. The design thinking process is the iteration of impression and expression. 7.6 shows an abridgment of 6.4 through 6.6 for our present concern. Impression and expression then expression and impression become cause and effect respectively. If attempts are successful, the process may stop at any satisfactory expression. If not, we have to begin again or abandon the whole process.

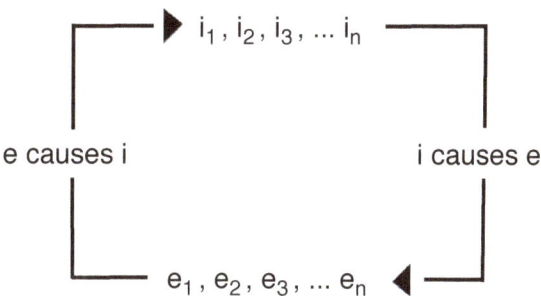

7.6 Design thinking as causation of impressions (i) and expressions (e)

9. During the process our expressions as designers, in whatever form they may be, are the basis for further impressions by ourselves.
10. Whenever we stop with a successful design process, the result is an expression of the project as planned. The perception of others of the object leads to their impression of it.
11. The process we call design thinking is an activity of understanding. The impressive and expressive thought at any point along and at the end is a result of understanding. Again, this is why I define meaning as select understanding.
12. The step from understanding to meaning implies judgment of value. In design we project content, and thus create form (expression). Impression from expression provides the basis for judgment and choice.

This description has a clearly experiential basis and does not attempt to explain the workings of our mind beyond its provision of results which we judge. Bernard Tschumi writes that

> The paradigm of the architect passed down to us through the modern period is that of the form-giver, the creator of hierarchical and symbolic structures characterized, on the one hand, by their unity of parts and, on the other, by the transparency of form to meaning.[64]

"The paradigm of the architect passed down to us through the modern period" is more "than that of the form-giver". It is based on "the transparency of form to meaning" which the architects of that period wanted to show through crucial functional relationships as part of their architecture's appearance – more or less, as we know, and not fundamentally different from today's successful architecture. Form reflects meaning of whatever content it has, good or bad. Where else should meaning come from, if not from the content we search for, evaluate and embed in form (including functional relationships), which others then understand as meaning of this form?

Although content and form are intimately unified, one reflecting the other, we may suppose that the task of content is semantic and the task of form is syntactic. The syntactic is determined by the semantic because the syntactic has to serve the semantic. The semantic is derived from various sources (purpose, context, realization) and is manifested through the syntactics of the form properties which we select. 7.7 shows the way the design factors of content activate the evolution of the object.

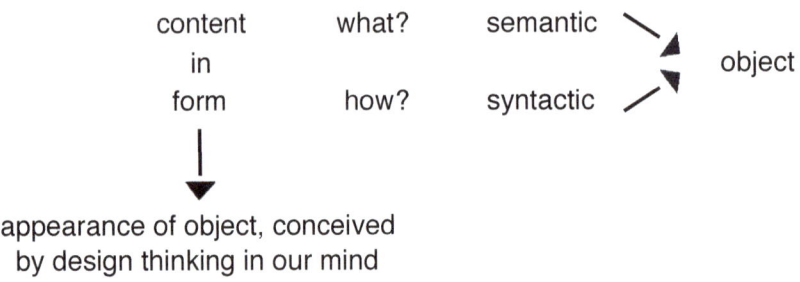

7.7 The semantic and syntactic aspects of designed objects

While design progresses from impression to expression meaning is embedded in every iterative cycle. We want to know into what meanings evolve and how they manifest themselves. From what we talked about in contrasting language and architectural design, and from the highly complex nature of architecture, it should not be surprising that we find a narrative approach linking the aspects of content and form as the most appropriate structure for the explication of meaning. There is no other approach I know which is as comprehensive, explicit, flexible and dialectical.

We understand through object analysis. We observe backward from form to content:

impression: content ◀—— form .

We create through object synthesis. We design forward from content to form:

expression: content ——▶ form .

I take now this simple dual aspect as the foundation of what I call *design narratives*. They look in both ways using decomposition for analysis and composition for synthesis. We analyze results with intention to understand what brought them about, that is, we analyze the circumstances and propositions which are foundational and constitutive for the design process. *There is no synthesis without analysis*. In other words, we look at parts to understand the whole. In conceptualizing components we lay the basis for their possible change and combination in our mind and in reality.

Design narratives look for and describe design factors influential toward understanding and realization. They address in multiple frames of reference particular aspects of the object with wide or narrow focus and reveal the discourse between content and form of an architectural object. Therefore, they are more or less comprehensive but never exhaustive. We can never fully describe in language what exists in physical reality.

Each moment in the understanding of a building component evokes an episode of meaning in the sequence of experiencing the whole. This is so whether we are in the modes of conception for design or perception from observation. It also is so whether we consider the large frame of reference in a spatial arrangement or the narrow one of a detail in focus. We may compare moving through and inhabiting architecture with reading phrases and words of text. Every building, simple or complex, provides such experiences. Museums can serve as particularly strong examples as shown in Sophia Psarra's *Architecture and Narrative*.[65] Her study of the patterns for various alterations on the fourth and fifth floors of the Museum of Modern Art in New York reveals the interrelationships of meaning and spatial arrangements (7.8).

Viewing and movement possibilities change depending on wall and door locations. Glenn Lowry writes on the occasion of the latest redevelopment of the museum that

By locating objects and people in time as well as in space, the Museum is constantly mapping

relationships between works of art and their viewers, so that the space of the Museum becomes a site of narration where many individual stories can be developed and realized.[66]
In a sense the museum exhibits become details of its architecture, so do the people visiting it as they reflect through their behavior in part how the museum is laid out and the objects arranged in it, how it has profuseness of daylighting or concentrations of artificial light, how it provides opportunities of viewing and contemplating, etc.

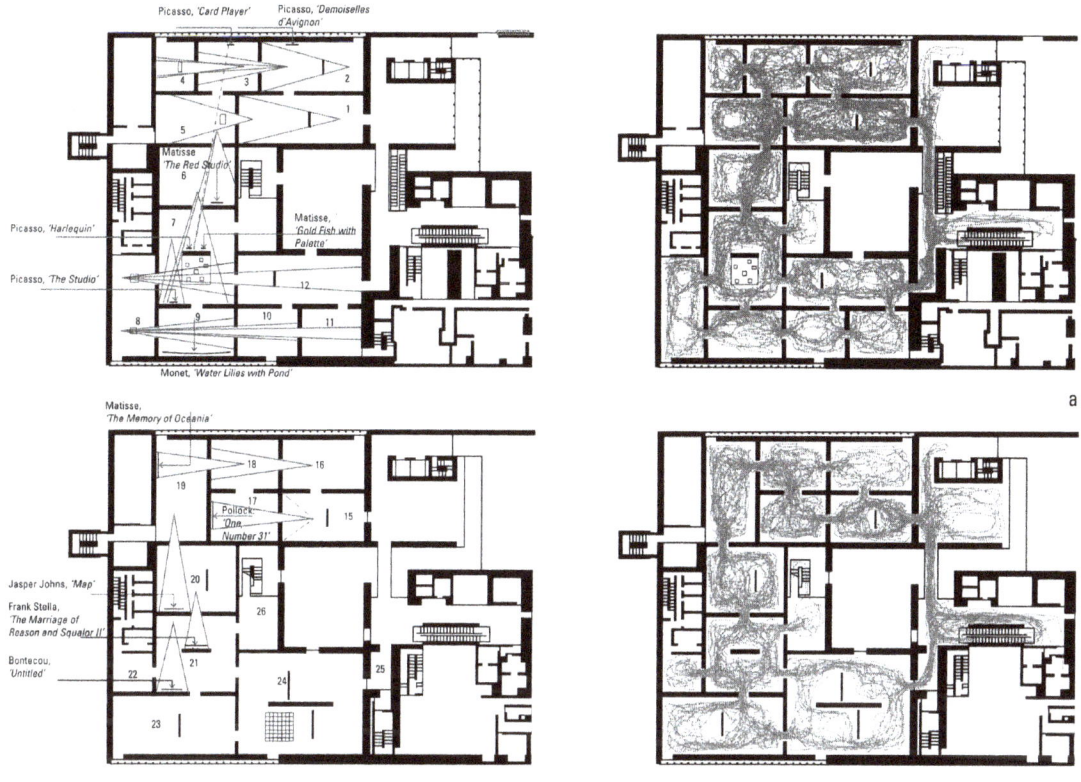

7.8 Visual access in space and related pedestrian traffic
Museum of Modern Art, New York (© permission)

In every instance of conscious life at residences, schools, museums or wherever, we experience tokens of meaning which, when called out to ourselves or communicated to others, are design narratives. They are recounts of something existing or at least planned; here about architecture.[67] Psarra writes that

> Narrative enters architecture in many ways, from the conceptual 'messages' it is made to stand for to the illustration of a design through models, drawings and other representational forms. This aspect of architectural expression, what the design *speaks of*, is relevant to narrative as representation.[68]

My use of narrative is to describe verbally how an architectural design is and what it does through its existence. What the "design speaks of" is what we perceive and conceive. Content is mental and functional. It is represented by form which is physical and spatial. There is no form ever without content. The description of the dialogue between content and form of any architectural object, in development or existence, in detail or overall, provides the foundation of the textual narratives. It is under this premise that I use the term narrative.

A Stair in the Roth Residence, Weil am Rhein

For the first example of a design narrative I use a simple object: the stairway in a residential setting, Roth Medical Clinic and Residence, Weil am Rhein, Germany (7.9 to 7.11).

Stair in Roth Residence, Weil am Rhein, Germany

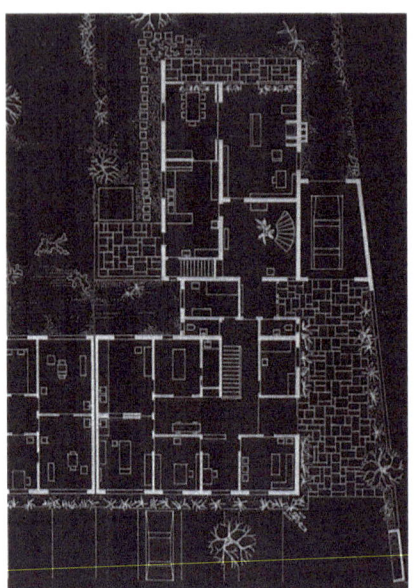

7.9 and 7.10 View of stair and first floor plan

Content		Form
relational		observable
connecting first and second floor of a one family residence	◀—▶	stair in residential entry hall
indicating up- and downstairs	◀—▶	articulation for upper and lower arrival points in two story space
enhancing smooth traffic flow	◀—▶	circular shape within rectangular shape of generous dimensions
providing for comfortable and safe movement especially for children	◀—▶	steps with risers of 7 inch and various tread width, handrail height of 34 inch with intermediate height handrails
representing and emphasizing sculptural asset	◀—▶	spiral structure contrasting with material and colors of spatial enclosure
enhancing visual importance of main object	◀—▶	little articulation of walls and only single, but highly diffuse daylighting source
suggesting lightness	◀—▶	open risers allowing visual transparency and light penetration
complementing materials of other objects in same space	◀—▶	red oak as main material being the same as door and trim, and having similar color as marble floor
providing ample space for other objects and movement of people	◀—▶	spaciousness under stair, around it and in its open center
fitting stylistically with baroque furniture	◀—▶	round contours of stair in diffuse light being reflected from flat painted walls and ceiling
. . . .		. . . .

7.11 Design narrative of the stair

As the stair is in a building which I designed its analysis is informed by my own design efforts. This means that it has a broader background than an analysis by someone who is only an observer. Let's assume as frame of reference the view of the stair in its immediate environment as depicted in the photograph and the floor plan. The stair is in the hall, shown in the middle of the drawing. Out of reasons I mentioned, we look at form and contemplate content and then narrate causatively from content toward form (design thinking). But our interest is not only to find *where form comes from,* in the direction from content to form, but also in the other direction, *how form influences content*. The development of the narratives is inspired by this duality, indicated by the double-pointed arrows of the narrative. Some of the descriptions may appear redundant or trivial but they are not so for demonstration purposes. They may seem to be more so for designers compared with laypersons who are not as acquainted with contemplating architecture.

Even looking through the narrative of this rather simple example, we find a great deal of design factor interdependence. Sometimes an item on the content side relates to more than one on the form side and vice versa. Design factors often enhance each other. On the content side of our stair example the interdependence of "enhancing smooth traffic flow", "representing and emphasizing sculptural asset" and "suggesting lightness" enhance each other, so do on the form side "circular shape ..." and "spaciousness under the stair, around it and in its open center".

On the other hand, there are only few projects which do not begin with conflicts of design factors or develop them along the way. For example, desires of building owners clash with available finances, building regulations prevent anticipated site utilization or proposed spaces cannot accommodate required functions. They must be discussed by clients and designers, as openly as possible, especially with regard to adjustments, potential trade-offs, and even incompatibilities. These interdependences are the reason that the design process is to some extent, in Horst Rittel's words, wicked in the sense of baffling, puzzling or fiendish, therefore, in part requiring the highly iterative approach to design.[69] Usually, when we change one aspect, we more or less will need to change another or others within the domain of the whole. Such conflicts are not easily traced in looking back without documentation. They must be, if not minor, be resolved before completion of the project. Their understanding is after the fact mainly of value for tracing the history of progress and decision making.

The derivation of meaning from design analysis is largely thoughts about underlying properties of form and is not simply a description of the manifest aspects of its appearance. The design factors are evident from both columns of the narrative. The double arrows indicate functional relationships between them. We break the unity of content and form apart to identify and analyze them. Although they belong to the same aspects, there is a categorical difference between them. *Content is described by relational aspects, that is, what the object does beyond how it is: essence, connotation and intension. Form is described by observable properties, that is, how the object is: existence, denotation and extension*. Both descriptions are representative thought constructs. Due to language as the medium, the senses of descriptions on the content and form sides are sometimes quite similar and care is needed to differentiate. This is not surprising as they are derived from content-from unity. Examples are the pair "connecting first and second floor of a one family residence ◄—▶ stair in residential entry hall" and the pair "providing ample space for other objects ... ◄—▶ spaciousness under stair ...".

No effort was made to prioritize the items in the sequence of listing which would indicate scaling design factors according to importance. Their inclusion obviously indicates relevance. Several are simply indispensable. To rank them, however, does not bring, at least in this case, any advantage. The narratives on the form side are usually longer, as we refer by them to realization and often to context. Sometimes the relevance of context is implicitly understood from already given form items. For example, in the seventh item on the form side, reference is made only to "open risers allowing visual transparency and light penetration". In the second to last item reference is made to "spaciousness under the stair ... and its open center". In both, reference is made to the form of the stair itself not to the wider environment around the stair. But it is implied that a light source exists and ample space is available.

The descriptions show that while every object is in a context, it is only more or less formatively dependent on it. Fundamentally, space is necessary to locate anything anywhere. But a space of sufficient size may accommodate an undefined number of stair geometries (see the third item in the form listing). An important point emerges from this observation: realization occurs by objects requiring space within wider space. Close or very close correspondence of the two spatial shapes may be achieved. But often this is not the case and redundancy of space exists. This provides configurational design freedom for alternatives in giving expression and meaning.

In impression, as mentioned earlier, causes cannot be chosen. They are given and to be understood from their effects. We encounter things as they are, although we have some latitude how we approach them. We may walk around a building but the building stays the same. In expression, many causes can be chosen, but others cannot, such as given by purpose or context. Although there is generally flexibility in developing purpose, taking into account context and selecting means of realization, there are obviously constraints.

An effect may arise from one of various causes. The circular form of the stair in the rectangular space was my response of a 'soft' geometry following the desire by the owner for a form fitting with baroque furniture and the choice of diffuse lighting conditions (large window with translucent not clear glass). Often a particular cause may follow from the effect of another. The circular form of the stair in the rectangular space was a choice. After this decision, the remaining 'open' space, as an effect, causes traffic patterns over which we now have little control. Or, the oak material for the steps was a choice whose effect causes the need for a certain thickness of material. Also in our example, code requirements are unavoidable causes, such as the requirement of handrails and the maximum rise of steps. Successful design strongly depends on thinking through such causal chains and their effects which, when listed, make design narratives informative in depth.

There are certainly variations or perhaps rather different alternatives to this approach to get at design factors. The two column content-form dialog could, for example, be a continuous description of evidence (of the realized form), as is typically used for accounts in architectural history and criticism. My impetus again comes from the fact that the content-form unity is exactly that: unity. The two column dialog is a device to foster and structure thinking and documenting. It helps to find design factor impacts and shows the semantic role which object properties play in our professional engagement as observers and designers. It is quite obvious that what is suggested here is not what people ordinarily do when experiencing environments. We, however, analyze to understand about explicit cause and effect relationships. Typical beholders do not look for causes and effects. They are exposed to causation, as designers are, but they do not need to reflect on them with similar intensity.

Another aspect that needs mentioning: the design factors of purpose, context and realization are not static because of interdependence in various ways and over time. A client's need or desire may change rather rapidly and, therefore, the design factors of purpose change. Or when technology advances during design or changes later the realizations and renovations may be influenced by their costs. Narratives may change accordingly.

From this discussion we conclude that it is the dialogue between physical form and mental content which advances our understanding of what the world means to us. In architectural design, as in any other worldly enterprise, we work with reality. Our output is physical in drawings, models, etc. and eventually built environments. In the formative stages of understanding and meaning, however, the variability and flexibility of language is more helpful than any other approach to order our thinking. In addition, architectural design narratives are the spoken or written record of the content-form dialog about existing or proposed objects, an important resource for remembering.

The significance of design factors and their effect on meaning may weigh in at many points along design development; more or less according to circumstantial conditions but also to designer preferences. Design factors and changes of factors often appear unexpectedly. One change in design factors may precipitate another one, such as a change in building orientation may result in unwelcome solar gains of a facade which otherwise might have had little exposure to the sun. The diversity in meaning of architectural design is endless as the diversity of design factors is endless. This fact has its ground in the uncountable abundance and variability of things, relationships and happenings embedded in the infinity of space and time. Every meaning, however, evolves from one instance of theme, location and focus, such as an assembly of buildings or the detail of a facade.

This line of thinking leads to a crucial aspect in the emergence of meaning, which we may call the *prominence of uniqueness*. Looking at the many and highly varied approaches to meaning of the past century, be they founded in semiotics, arise out of analyses in similarity or reveal themselves in patterns of cultural, behavioral, historical, technical and other environmental aspects, we find that all inform us about the singularity of situations in space, time and causality. All of these approaches are helpful to sharpen our awareness and enlighten us about the central importance of difference, of particularity. All our meaning evolves in our mind from the given circumstances with which we happen to be confronted in the reality of special presence.

While meaning as select understanding eventually must give specific answers to questions our whole cognitive apparatus is engaged together with our memory to conceptualize what our senses perceive. We pose questions to focus our thinking and narration. They can be gleaned from case studies like those given here. A listing of questions may look like this:
- What are the background facts which contribute to understanding of the object, such as history, culture, politics and economics?
- What are the criteria qualifying the object as a particular building type?
- What are the observable and relational design factors which influenced purpose, context and realization?
- Which sensations of the object are experienced and to what effect?
- What are especially prominent features of external and internal aspects?
- By what is the inside reflected by the outside?
- What are the main impressions from the object during the time observed?
- What qualifies as cause and what as effect in the sequence of events?
- Which harmonies are especially noticeable and which conflicts had to be resolved?
- What is common and what uncommon in the experiences encountered?
- What can we derive from the precedents of the presently contemplated object?
   . . . .

Such questions are incomplete and often rather general. But the answers have to be specific to make the analysis meaningful and applicable. As mentioned earlier, for sorting out particular meanings from their overall circumstances one needs to set frames of reference. The focus may range from the broadness of a cityscape to the detail of a door handle. In common occurrences we set frames of reference instinctively. To make them in design as explicit as possible is a practical condition for discussions of complexity. We must realize that meanings are nested within meanings. Their regionalism will vary according to needs and opportunities of elucidation, that is, broadly and narrowly focused observations will follow each other depending on personal interest and causal impact.

The meanings of the following two examples evolve from their narratives on content and form similar to the prototype given for the stair. They are more elaborate as the objects are larger and more complex.

The Philharmonic Hall, Berlin

The concert hall complex in Berlin, 'Die Philharmonie' by Hans Scharoun, is the project in which one of the directions of what we call Modernism found its culmination (7.12 to 7.17). Designed at about the same time, it is comparable in architectural importance to Le Cobusier's small Chapel at Ronchamp. Both lead very differently to an abundance of meaning which never can be fully described to do justice. This became readily clear from developing a narrative about this masterwork (7.18).

7.12 East elevation of both halls

7.13 West elevation with main entry

7.14 Main foyer, connecting both halls

7.15 Main hall

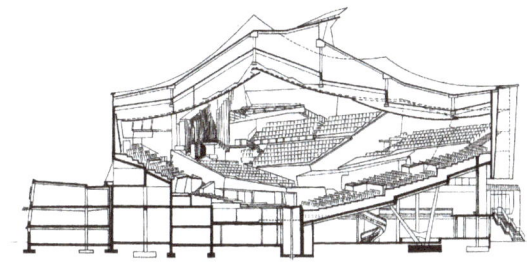

7.16 South-north section (© permission)

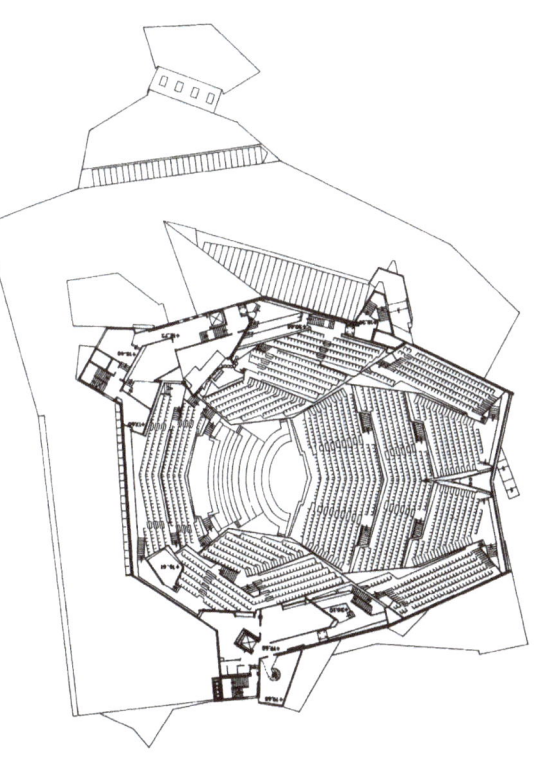

7.17 Main hall floor plan (entry roof shown at top)
(© permission)

The Philharmonie as it exists today came about in two phases. The first part, the main hall completed in 1963, was the result of a competition in 1956 and was planned originally for a different site. Three years later it was decided to locate it as part of the cultural hub, which Scharoun had proposed for the southern edge of Berlin's large central park, the Tiergarten. A second, a chamber music hall was added in 1987 by his pupil and associate Edgar Wisniewski designed according to Scharoun's first overall plan.[70]

Content		Form
One of the most important cultural assets of Berlin. Home of one of world's best orchestras.	◄──►	Prominent location. First building of cultural center with museums and national library. Close to Potsdamer Platz commercial district.
Place for all kinds of musical performances.	◄──►	One hall for large and one hall for small scale performances, and auxiliary spaces.
Historical circumstances of site: built on land bordered to the East by "Berlin Wall", where now location of busy traffic route. Reminder of Berlin's long period of uncertainty. Today, therefore, arguably ambiguous main entry orientations.	◄──►	Main entry orientations away from Potsdamer Platz commercial and entertainment center, but calming vehicular traffic via secondary access loop with view toward Cultural center area.
Priority for pedestrian pedestrian movement on site.	◄──►	Loop of walkways around whole complex. Public bus and taxi stops at main entry. Underground train station nearby. Some surface parking on site but not interfering with pedestrian traffic. Underground parking in neighboring buildings.
Arrival with expectation. Ready access to all building functions.	◄──►	Approach through two main entrances, away from main traffic, into spacious, highly varied foyer which connects both halls. Easy access to ticket booths, coat checking and restrooms. Wrap-around extensions of foyer, partially under the halls, with many stairs and balconies for dispersed access to hall entrances. Four elevators at well placed locations.
Musical happenings visually and psychologically at 'center'.	◄──►	Location of stages toward center of the halls with seats surrounding stages.
Enhancement of sense of community but with share of individual identity.	◄──►	Musicians surrounded by audience. Many seating orientations so that members of audience may see face to face. Many small groups of audience seating.
High quality of sound distribution to each member of audience.	◄──►	Very geometrically diverse wall and ceiling components of the halls. Rather short distances between audience and musicians.
Concentration and diffusion for enhancements of attentiveness and relaxation.	◄──►	Contrasts for visual focusing and visual meandering given by space, structure and envelope components, material and color diversity, and lighting variation. Examples: apexes of ceilings and suspension of reflectors and lamps concentrated above stages, foyers as highly open multistory webs providing differentiated vistas.
Inside 'reflected' outside.	◄──►	Exterior tent-like roof shapes of halls and foyers emulating what they enclose. The hall floor structures are part of the sloping foyer ceilings.
Freedom in formal approach to most of the main building components.	◄──►	Structural, wall and stair components mainly of reinforced concrete. Halls with additional interior shell of convex plaster ceiling and often tilted wood wall paneling.
Unity in all its diversity.	◄──►	Alike but distinctive shapes of halls, same type and color of their cladding, and same lean roof edge detail support strong effect of unity.
Ample space for intermission activities.	◄──►	Large peripheral foyers for auxiliary activities such as strolling, socializing, enjoying refreshments, viewing exhibits, and passage to restroom facilities.
Privacy but easy accessibility of spaces for musicians and administration.	◄──►	Musician's foyer directly behind stage with adjacent practice rooms, accessible also from extended public foyer and separate entrance. Similar access to administrative office on floor above.
. . . .		. . . .

7.18 Design narrative of the Berlin Philharmonic Hall

The Biomedical Science Research Building, University of Michigan, Ann Arbor

Coming from the inside of the main University of Michigan campus, this state-of-the-art research facility is the first building one encounters at the edge of the sprawling Medical Center complex. Designed by Polshek Partnership, now Ennead Architects, it was completed in 2006.[71] Located along the north side of the curved transition of Huron Street to Washtenaw Avenue, the main extension of the building is east-west and is distanced from the busy road by the 300-seat auditorium set piece. The complex contains overall 472,000 sq ft (7.19 to 7.25).

A full-height sky-lit atrium is the central access space between the main, south oriented office wing and the west and north oriented laboratory blocks. The ground floor of the atrium features areas for casual encounters, exhibits and scheduled events, and serves as foyer for the auditorium. Bridges span the atrium, connecting offices and labs which provide space for research in areas, such as molecular imaging, nanotechnology, regenerative medicine and gerontology. The elevator banks at each end of the atrium provide vertical transportation.

7.19 View from southeast

7.20 View from southwest

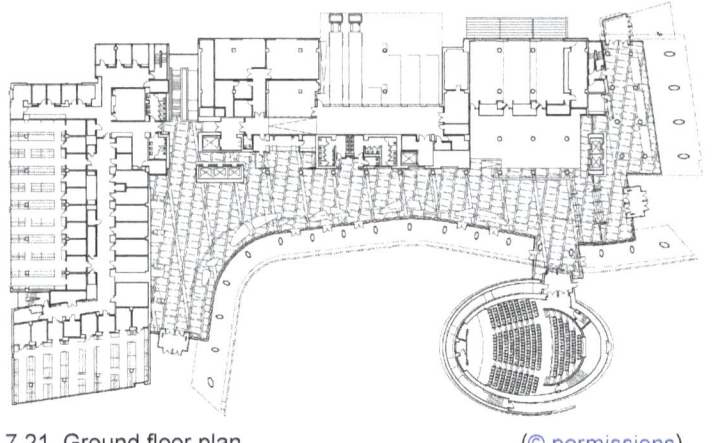

7.21 Ground floor plan (© permissions)

7.23 View from west into atrium

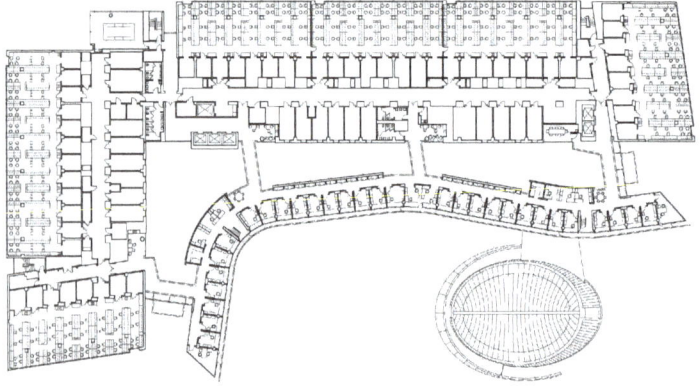

7.22 Typical upper floor plan

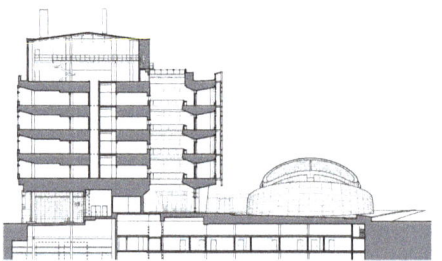

7.24 North-south section

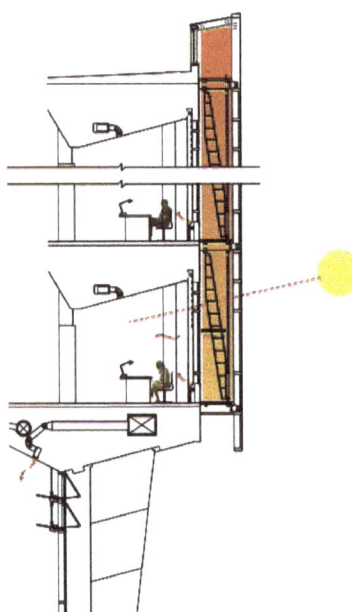

7.25 Vented facade under winter and summer conditions

Content		Form
Enhancement of university's great reputation as institution. Attraction for world's biomedical scientists: aesthetically and operationally.	◄──►	Outstanding appearance with state of the art facilities on prominent site. Ample space for labs, offices, vivarium, break rooms, conference and seminar rooms, auditorium.
Expression of reverence for scientific exploration. Enhancement of scientist's individual ways of working but with promotion of collegial and cross-disciplinary interaction.	◄──►	Central and open atrium of singular and unifying nature with verticality of space and quality of lighting to inspire occupants and visitors alike. Realization of new parti and paradigm for laboratory building. Promotion of serendipitous encounters through the creation of destinations such as meeting rooms, lounges and rest rooms at circulation crossroads, eddy spaces, staircases and corridors.
State-of-the-art laboratories.	◄──►	Neighborhood clusters. Flexibility in spatial organization and operational services. Abundance of natural lighting.
Accommodation and expression of programmatic functions.	◄──►	Distinction of laboratory blocks and office 'ribbon'. Material contrasts: double glazed curtain wall envelope at offices and terra-cotta wall surfaces at laboratory and vivarium blocks. Auditorium set piece.
Favorable support functions: atrium, auditorium, seminar rooms, elevators.	◄──►	Large, ground level floor area of atrium for events and conferences. Direct access of auditorium and seminar rooms from atrium space. Placement of elevator access without disruption of main atrium space.
Unifying medical school and academic campuses. Advancement of community spirit.	◄──►	New 'front door' to medical school. Atrium as semi-public event space. Material palette complementing other buildings on campus. Curtain wall technology emblematic of scientific methods used by scientists. Building rationalizes grade level changes.
Reinforcement of the campus plan's logic. Promotion pedestrian traffic around and through building. Liberal transparency and access.	◄──►	Response to multiple site considerations including pathways and continuity with adjacent green space. Creation of gateway building by extending lawn from Palmer Field to site. Multiple points of entry on all sides of building. ADA accessibility despite elevation changes. Single columns at office wing braced back to lab wings maximize visual transparency and access.
Favorable scale in context.	◄──►	Reduction in overall massing: relocation of parking, pull back of building from street, devices to mitigate large floor-to-floor heights (metal channels to divide façade into smaller units, clear story windows, etc.)
Sustainability and low impact on the environment.	◄──►	Energy conservation strategies throughout. East-west elongation of building to take advantage of solar exposure. Active south oriented curtain wall façade at offices with single-glazed exterior wall separated from insulated glazed wall by open space, metal grates and continuous louvers, providing chimney ventilation effect, shading and daylight control. Terra-cotta and stainless steel panel façades at laboratories as rain screen with minimal air infiltration and no thermal bridges. Daylighting of offices and atrium space. Compact massing of laboratory/vivarium blocks. Zoning of mechanical services according to programmatic functions.
....		....

7.26 Design narrative of the Biomedical Science Research Building, University of Michigan (by Todd Schliemann and Susan Strauss, Ennead Architects)

To conclude: Meaning is our understanding of how things are around us, how others understand them and how we may change them through design. Language helps us to formulate and communicate meaning. It is our text about the world in whatever frame of reference we encounter and describe. To be considered in all of this are the necessarily changing ways we have perspectives, physically and mentally. With regard to architecture the positioning of its components relative to our present position is rather temporal. We stand at one moment in front of a building affording us one perspective. Next we may walk around it or inside, giving us another perspective, though often associated with the former. Our understanding changes and perhaps with it what we retained. This is why meanings are never exactly the same, even when we experience the same thing again. Memories overlap and blend. Meanings have histories. But some are quite stable. Thinking about former experiences of architectural sequences confirms this. I have perhaps the strongest remembrance of such occurrence from an approach to the Wies, a South Bavarian pilgrimage church, by Dominikus Zimmermann (7.27 to 7.30). One must not be especially religious to appreciate the significance of passing the signs on the way, approaching the church with a cloudy sky above, then being surprised by the radiance of the interior.

Wies Pilgrimage Church, Bavaria

7.27 A sign on the way

7.28 At the church

7.29 and 7.30 Views towards chancel with altar and detail at ceiling

It is quite clear from the shown narratives that they consist of descriptions which range from wide to narrow focus. Each point in their sequence provides its theme of meaning. Because only some design factors, that is, usually the more important ones, can strongly influence the eventual design solution, certain aspects emerge as dominating also in narratives. In this sense narratives track reality closely. After all, narratives reference reality. Language can be in certain ways more appropriate for characterizing objects compared to the ways other more physical representations can, such as simulations through images or scaled models. This is why we write material and performance specifications, or use text in architectural analysis and history.

Another example, a theme of sun protection and daylight utilization dominates the overall outside and inside of the TVA office complex in Chattanooga, Tennessee, by Caudill Rowlett Scott and The Architects Collaborative (7.31 to 7.33). If we would develop a narrative of this building, we would see the extraordinary power of language in supplementing of what is directly sensed from its reality. We would describe the many relational properties and their influences on each other in detail; difficult to do without verbal representation. Also, the readily observed duality of whole and parts in this and other buildings can only be well explained by means of language.

Tennessee Valley Authority Building
Chattanooga TN

7.31 West elevation with atrium articulation

7.32 Courtyard between building wings

7.33 Atrium

Narratives, whether we write them down or simply think them through, structure our thinking about reality. We usually produce them from understanding past occurrences. But they often are part of anticipating what may happen in the future. A little boy or girl at the entry of a Japanese kindergarten has already indications of the day's joy from camaraderie (7.34). He or she narrates about what may come. We may think about making the expectations of these and other children possible through our narratives and physical solutions. While we design we think about progression by weaving the narrative of an evolving architecture.

7.34 Expectations at a Japanese kindergarten

Every one of the many diverse examples in this book, be they mentioned only or illustrated, could be made object of content-form narration. In whatever way, exemplification manifests content through form. Nature gave us vision as the preferred sense to begin comprehending why something is what it is. There is more to things, however, than what we see and narration can prompt us to go further, especially by means of relational thinking. It is not a linguistic accident that the term sense applies to sensation of appearance and to sensibility of understanding. And, there should be no doubt that meaning is the necessary particularization of what we believe to observe or intend to design. Architectural design narratives are meanings assembled for explanation and communication.

8 Meaning as Zeitgeist

From what we addressed, it should be clear that I believe that there is complete unity of content and form in all physical objects as far as our understanding is concerned. Following Kant, I believe that all understanding begins with experience, that is, from the perception of forms. Our intentionality finds properties, the contents of the forms. Usually we derive and define properties of present or anticipated designs rather narrowly. There are broader aspects, however, which further can enlighten us. They happen through *Zeitgeist* – the understanding of a particular time of being and life. It is part of the overall context of that time. On one hand architecture is an expression of such times, on the other it influences what happens and supports continuity. While Zeitgeist is the prevailing spirit of a given time it builds on earlier times. So does architecture which stands in tradition and provides an enduring record of history.

Surveying the past century, we have a rather quickening succession of Zeitgeist tendencies. A comprehensive analysis of its recent cultural influences on architecture still has to evolve. But pieces can be found in what thinkers like Reyner Banham, Lewis Mumford, Siegfried Gideon, Jane Jacobs, Kevin Lynch, Vincent Scully, Christian Norberg-Schulz, Roger Scruton, Robert Venturi, Kenneth Frampton, Charles Jencks and Thomas Markus have written. This leaves us to ask: where are we now? More pointedly: what do the present, broader tendencies portend as meanings for today's architecture?

The present time is more diffuse than any other ever was. On one side we have highly consumption oriented, largely democratic societies, driven by free market forces with strong tensions between common and individual needs and desires. On the other we have a rising challenge by the dynamics of developing nations with large population increases and basic demands. All of this plays out in the globally connected environment of manufacture, trade, finance and resource utilization. Enormous wealth contrasts with enormous poverty. Life styles and population pressures impact the natural environment in unprecedented magnitudes. Resultant stress is evident.

Accepting these facts as the present background of cultural, social and economic circumstances, I believe that our work in architecture is now fundamentally influenced by

1. a great diversity in views about what content in architectural design should be, that is, about understanding which design factors need to become effective and require preference over many others which are also present;
2. a world wide market for participation in architectural design and development, strongly driven by emerging technology, commerce and communication;
3. a powerful shift of the architectural design and engineering process from a generally iterative and fragmented mode of operation, as it always has been, to an iterative and highly integrative mode, made possible through the enormous advances in computerized representation, manipulation and transfer of information which also influences profoundly manufacturing processes for construction;
4. a long overdue trend toward responsiveness to sustainability in all phases of architecture from inception to demolition.

Aspects 3 and 4 need elaboration on the background which aspects 1 and 2 provide. If we want to know what the meanings are and should be in today's world of design, we again must ask what the content is which determines form. As always it can only come from the purpose by which design is driven, from the context in which it finds itself and from the realization by which it comes into existence. An overall aspect emerges: it appears possible that complexities, never thought about before in architecture, can be accommodated. But constraints in resource utilization of the physical environment evolve and must be reflected in what we decide.

8.1 Virtuality and reality

During the last third of the past century a rethinking about fundamental positions in design occurred, in part arising from the unease with the results of architectural Modernism and in part from the influences of new movements in philosophy, anthropology, psychology and sociology. It is not the place here to trace these influences, which followed in rapid succession, but also ran often in parallel. I can only refer to the abundance of recent literature about them in architectural theory and criticism.[1] One aspect many have in common is the preoccupation with appearance over performance in the meaning of architecture. As pointed out before, there is a fundamental need to address functional relationships. What happened and is still ongoing is an emphasis on stylistic differentiation and diversity to which the "battle of styles" during the 19th century compares rather mildly. A helpful survey for contemplating the dialectic between overall culture and architectural developments leading into the 21st century is Diane Ghirardo's *Architecture after Modernism*.[2] It describes the time when structuralist precepts in search for universal grounding were undermined by various tendencies of designers to assert their right to highly subjective and self-referential aesthetic choices.

The situation now may be characterized as the search for approaches which allow to exploit more intensive potentials of *virtuality* in design. Not that virtuality is new as an element of design. Its etymology includes pointing toward "essential qualities or facts" and is in this sense close to what meaning entails:

> virtual: ...The meaning of "being something in essence or fact, though not in name" is first recorded 1650s, probably via sense of "capable of producing a certain effect" (early 15c.).
> ... virtually: early 15c., "as far as essential qualities or facts are concerned;" from virtual. Sense of "in effect, as good as" is recorded from c.1600.[3]

Perhaps derived from the latter, virtuality has more recently taken to indicate computer-generated simulation and appearance. This sense of

> ... "not physically existing but made to appear by software" is attested from 1959.[4]

Representation in any medium has to some extent the status of being virtual and simulated by abstracting the real. Computer application, especially visualization facilitates representation immensely, especially through its efficiency in near real time production.

With the availability of ever more advanced software and hardware for computer-aided design in architecture, and in connection with post-structuralist views, especially in philosophy, tendencies developed to ascribe to 'virtual architecture' an air of autonomy beyond representational status. Based on the nearly unlimited geometrical modeling possibilities by computers in designing and the emergence of very advanced, computer guided manufacturing capacities, many designers assume that shape making should have preference in decisions on form making. Such shapes are in search of form and do not simulate comprehensively. They must eventually be translated into some kind of physical realization, if deemed to become architecture. A study, emphasizing hypersurfaces, called *The Möbius House Study* shows such a representation while neglecting reference to any purposive design factors beyond geometric manipulation and color indication. Stephen Perrella and Rebecca Carpenter write that

> Hypersurface theory and the Möbius House study argue that if the constituting or governing structures of form are considered separately from a lived program, then 'animate' form will exist only in the realm of materiality. What is most significant about the work of Deleuze and Guattari is that they offer a means to evacuate such dualities.[5]

Whatever the merits of hypersurface or other philosophical theories are, they are not needed to show that "considered separately from a lived program, then 'animate' form will exist only in the realm of materiality". They are not needed "to evacuate such dualities" of program (content) and form because content and form *always* exist in unity, for better or worse. Within that unity, however, we assume a duality for our understanding which we then can explicate in connection with purpose, context and realization.

Various present developments in architectural theory neglect or even deny such understanding. Not that shape making is not crucial. Architectures throughout history attest to that and I hope the previous chapters of my account do so as well. To claim a priori status for such developments, however, is another matter and highly problematic, not the least in relation to today's worldwide circumstances. Literature which documents and discusses the tendencies is widely available.[6] Here, a few comments with regard to recent positions taken must suffice.

There is more to experience of the aesthetic than from visual appearance. The problem which I see with the worlds described in most of the so-called virtual architecture approaches is how the human being is served in its bodily dependence on the physical objects which architecture must provide. How is the virtual reality, sometimes even hailed as "simulacrum", made up of "hypersurfaces", capable to serve the residential, educational, medical, infrastructural, administrative needs and desires, even in only parts of buildings and cities? The value of virtual reality is in its extraordinarily dynamic memory and representation capacities of physical realities, no less but also no more. Strictly and honestly taken, there is no virtual architecture, only architecture simulated by means of virtual modeling. There are no "sentient" or "intelligent" buildings. There is only human ingenuity ever more broadly translated into programs of digital machines to the point that machines and buildings as machines become responsive to the mentioned needs and desires, though within constraints – never with their own judgments, even less with their own emotions.

Derrick de Kerckhove writes with regard to "searching for the principles of web architecture" that

> We are no longer operating with only two spaces, physical space and mental space, but have added a third zone of exploration: digital space, cyber space, virtual space, call it what you like. Physical, mental and virtual spaces make up distinct areas of human activity that not only naturally have different possible superimpositions, and definitely many points of contact, but also many significant differences.[7]

I dispute this characterization of the virtual as having its own space. There is no equivalence in importance of "physical space", "mental space" and "virtual space". Virtual reality is nothing but representation into which concepts of the physical and the mental have been merged. It is today arguably the most advanced technique of coordination and visualization, made possible by the means of electronic media. As sophisticated as it may be, its reality is not more than representation of observable and relational properties. Although very different in space, time and causation, its existence is comparable to that of language making mental reality possible to be manifested by the physical means of speaking and writing. The virtual is *result of thought* which eventually happens to reveal itself in a medium: in brain waves, in images on paper or computer, in objects like architecture. It is essential mental content which becomes informative when communicated through its medium. Architecture is not enough to be shape. It must find a purposive physical form to inform. Virtual architecture is at best highly intellectual and graphically appealing design representation by means of computer. This is a great deal but not enough for indicating a realm as fundamentally important as physicality and mentality.

Jennifer Whyte writes that

> ... virtual reality has been described as an interactive, spatial, real-time medium:
> - *interaction is not the same as action.* Embodiment in virtual reality is problematic and at least partial. ...
> - *virtual space is not the same as place.* Virtual reality is not fully spatial; it is a 2½D medium and subject to optical distortions. ...
> - *real-time is not the same as time.* The pace at which we experience virtual worlds is quite different to the pace at which we experience the real world. ...[8]

I agree. Any representation – virtual reality being a representation – falls short of simulating comprehensively the reality it represents. It can only represent part of reality's content. The "2½" in White's quote points to this limitation all representations by nature have. When the virtual is accepted essentially as reality it becomes dangerous as any other simulation is dangerous when taken as reality of what it depicts, because then it is taken as truth rather than a path to truth which crucially requires judgment on every step along the way and, in architecture, requires physical realization as proof.

Communication is the flow of informational content between manifestations in either mind-to-world or world-to-mind direction. Eventually, the virtual needs the real (for proof) at least as much as the real needs the virtual (for representation). Impression needs expression and expression needs impression ever more closely derived from physical feasibility. And in connection with earlier comments, virtual architecture, computer modeled and computer manifested architectural content, is not in anyway autonomous. Being purposive, it is contingent on features of context and realization. And, it ceases to be virtual when it becomes part of the real world, when content and form become content-form unity of the object as architecture in reality – not withstanding that architecture may at times itself be used to simulate virtual worlds as other media may also do in their own ways.

This line of thinking rests on my belief, against Descartes, that the mental is the result of the capacity of our whole-body enterprise, the whole body viewed as extension of the brain, to produce sensation and thought with emotion related to any content of form. As our whole-body enterprise is all physical and the physical can only produce anything physical, the mental is essentially physical. I count the mental among those physical things we cannot sense as such, only through their influence on us and our reactions. I believe that energy fundamentally has the same status. It may very well be assumed that the mental is energy in this very sense. This has a speculative tune to it and we must acknowledge that there are simply things we cannot understand in their absolutely basic existence. Mentality and energy in their fundamental nature are mysterious, with implications which we also only understand in part. By tradition we differentiate between mind and body, our mentality and physicality. There is no reason to change this tradition as it has many instrumental advantages for understanding and communication. But the originating and real unity must not be forgotten as it has far-reaching consequences for our views of culture, science and technology, and obviously philosophy and theology – and virtuality.

The virtual is obviously not without power and enhances motivation. This is why we are what we are and bring about objects, among them architecture. This implies what Giovanna Borradori calls "nontechnical interpretation of virtuality". Referring to Nietzsche she writes that

> Diametrically opposed to the rationalist conception of space, Nietzsche's idea of space is

> that of an immanent field of forces. If space is conceived as a field, entities and forms are not simply contained by it but produced by the very differential that constitutes the relation between them.[9]

Space as a field of forces does not exclude space with physical dimension, finite or infinite. The mental has motivations and powers to produce forces which produce results in physical space. We do not have, however, any evidence of the mental occupying space. Only its media do, as small or large they may be. This is why it is better to talk of virtual realm than of virtual space, that is, a realm in which simulation of reality by means of computers is produced and experienced.

As the virtual is not independent – it relates to reality – it is understandable that I resist Eisenman when he agrees with De Kerckhove in claiming that

> Virtuality is one part of an evolving architectural value system, … Modernism is a past in relation to these the new architectural values created by the virtual. In this context, the investigation of the virtual and its theorization become important.[10]

If we take virtuality as part of our value system, we take what we are supposed to judge as part of the values we hold. Virtuality is part of representational reality. Every value system is used by humans who judge. Virtuality is not a value system or part of it unless we endow it with an internal capacity to judge itself or, for that matter, other things. Those capacities, however, would not be abilities of genuine judgment but automation, based on artificial intelligence provided by us. The virtual so far, whether in our mind or in a machine as extension of our mind, has always only content of representation of reality and is not part of a value system, but object to be judged by those who have value systems, that is, by us. Again, an instance of virtuality, as instance of representational reality, cannot judge itself. All rhetoric about it, sometimes implying its autonomy, cannot change this fact. Finding jungle as a useful metaphor for the conditions of virtual space, Eisenman suggests that

> ... the jungle represents a metaphor for the conditions of virtual space. We must understand what kinds of human behavior will exist in the jungle, as opposed to the human in the labyrinth. This means that new rationalities must be formulated, adapted to the type of time-space relationship experienced in the jungle. We must not limit ourselves simply to producing new spatial relationships and images for them.[11]

When things which we have not considered come along, we must not adopt them because they come along but because we judge them to be of value. Eisenman does not say what he thinks we should seek beyond that "we should not limit ourselves" and what the new rationalities are which "must be formulated". Why even "must" we in the first place? Change, based on behavior which "exists in the jungle", would eventually not only bring chaos but catastrophe, a term virtualists sometimes too lightly and dangerously evoke. It would bring conditions and consequences which Eisenman knows as well as anyone.[12] As architects whose responsibility it is to design, that is, to plan part of the future, it is our obligation to judge virtuality as architects always have judged simulations of reality. To understand how the virtual inhabits the real, the mental inhabits the physical, we must evaluate the virtual, that is, its content, and judge this essence or we will lose control for better or worse – a gamble. This is why in architecture we program, design and judge before we build.

There is a tendency in our time to make architecture appear more complex than it already is. That complexities, contradictions and ambiguities in architecture exist is not new. To strongly remind us of that is Robert Venturi's great merit, writing that

> Architecture is form and substance – abstract *and* concrete – and its meaning derives from its interior characteristics and its particular context. An architectural element is perceived as form *and* structure, texture *and* material. These oscillating relationships, complex and

contradictory, are the source of ambiguity and tension characteristic to the medium of architecture.[13]

This is not only characteristic to the medium of architecture but any medium addressing strong complexity. Highly various issues and materials come together. Otherness produces sometimes contradiction which cannot be completely resolved, often producing ambiguity. This must not mean, however, that we should make architecture or any other medium by design more complex and ambiguous than what it becomes and is as a matter of course.

In addition, since Venturi wrote these sentences, various kinds of other rather obscure factors have been postulated to motivate opaque design approaches and decisions. Concepts like Derrida's "trace" and Deleuze's "fold" are used to philosophically underpin such approaches.[14] Unconstrained shape making is usually justified by reference to such supposedly "deep structures" of philosophical thought when reference to a practical design criterion would be of much more interest. Whole essays are written to justify such work with sheer endless word strings that can be taken this way or that way, nowhere exacting, such as in a section titled "Folding and other catastrophes for architecture" by Greg Lynn:

> Despite the differences between these practices, they share a sensibility that resists cracking or breaking in response to external pressures. These tactics and strategies are all *compliant* to, *complicated* by and *complicit* with external forces in manners which are: submissive, suppliant, adaptable, contingent, responsive, fluent, and yielding through involvement and incorporation.[15]

Not a word about what these external pressures are and where they come from. Context is not explained. No wonder that important design factors like solar orientation and neighborhood fit are neglected, not to speak of practical considerations toward comprehensive form-giving, such as organizational requirements. An explicit realization of 'folding' is the Rebstockpark Masterplan by Eisenman Architects (8.1). Peter Eisenman refers in its description to Gilles Deleuze (in quotes):

> 'Leibnitz [in *Le Pli*] turned his back on Cartesian rationalism, on the notion of effective space and argued that in the labyrinth of the continuous the smallest element is not the point but the fold.' ... The continual variation is characterised through the agency of the fold: 'No longer is an object defined by essential form.' He calls this idea of an object, an 'object event.'
>
> The idea of an event is critical to the discussion of singularity. ... Singularity is always other, always different. Singularity is an individuality no longer able to belong to the realm of multiple as formerly defined. For singularity does not mean that a thing is simply unique. Singularity refers to the possibility in a repetition or a multiple for one copy to be different from another copy. The difference lies not so much in form, in size or in shape as in the distinction of a *this* thing from any other like thing. Singularity resides in this 'otherness' of the *time* of such a *this* thing; not so much in its form or space.[16]

Unless the announcement that "the continual variation is characterised through the agency of the fold" is followed by a clear definition of what is meant by "the fold" the claim is empty. Our perception and understanding can only come from form of the object which always is "essential" because of being the only manifestation of essence. Singularity is unique through its difference from other singularities, which for architecture, as for all other physical objects, can only mean otherness of form and perhaps in time; not at all an undefinable 'otherness'. Although singularity implies otherness the latter can only be partial, as earlier addressed. If a thing has no resemblance with anything else at all, it is totally unique and cannot be understood from memory but only through present sensations – a difficult, possibly even frightening, but fortunately rare experience.

Every object becomes an event for those who encounter and perceive it. One can only guess that folding here means change of expressions by the designer with impressions accordingly by the observer in an "object event". The singularities of the individual objects in Eisenman's scheme of the Rebstock settlement arise out of slight variations of non-rectangularity in otherwise rather conventional block and courtyard arrangements. They are variations of type. The "otherness" within type in architecture is for the built object fixed, for an observer subjectively experienced in the course of time.[17]

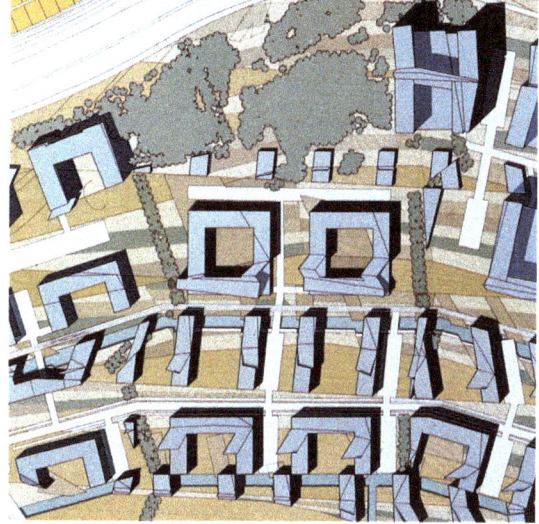

8.1 Rebstockpark, Frankfurt am Main, Germany, 1990 partial site plan (© permission)

Architectural design is presently too often confused by being based on confusing philosophy. In addition, inventing unfamiliar and catchy terms is a preoccupation of 'deconstructionist' and 'post-deconstructionist' philosophers and some architectural theorists; for example, "Hypersurface" in a text by Stephen Perrella:

> As a verb, hypersurface considers ways in which the realm of representation (read images) and the realm of instrumentality (read forms) are respectively becoming deconstructed and deterritorialized into new image form-intensity. Hypersurfaces are an interweaving and subsequent unlocking of culturally-instituted dualities. Hypersurface theory is not a subjective invention, …

Not a word about how these ways of deconstruction and deterritorialization are initiated and work, and what the resulting "culturally-instituted dualities" are. Further

> 'Hyper' implies human agency reconfigured by digital culture, and 'surface' is the enfolding of substances into differentiated topologies. The term hypersurface is not a concept that contains meaning, but is an event; one with a material dimension.[18]

The first sentence of this quote gives a definition of hypersurface, of which perhaps a dozen others are given on five pages. But the second sentence denies that it is a concept with meaning; rather being an event. Does an event with material dimension not have a concept for us? With meaning? And so the text goes on and on with references not explained by relevance to the given context. It ends with the presentation of Bernard Tschumi's model of a Zurich Department Store with the usually curved ramps to parking, an object that "reveals an attempt to express the dance of consumer-to-object, object-to-consumer"; a meager example for whatever a 'hypersurface' derived solution is in relation to this rather straightforward project.

On the more practical level of shape making, often the term "topological architecture" is evoked as the fundamental essence for deriving surfaces from mathematics about continuous deformation, that is, rubber-like stretching. This may be a valid approach in the use of certain types of construction materials but a constraint surely not acceptable for architecture to be realized in response to a wider variety of purposes and contexts.[19]

A central issue for the practicality of shape making is how its suitability and performance are evaluated against which criteria. Rivka Oxman writes that

> Typological knowledge is one of the foundational principles of modern architectural education [and practice]. According to Colquhoun (1989) it is precisely through the persistence of earlier forms that the system can convey meaning. These forms, or types, interact with the tasks presented to architecture, in any moment of history, to form the entire system.
>
> Models and processes of digital design may provide a different orientation to design exploration and creativity. Instead of a conventional holistic typological problem definition including context and explicit functional programs, definitions of digital models such as 'formation by animation' or 'parametric design' can serve as a starting point for design exploration. Such orientations are explicitly anti-typological.[20]

This approach would mean that we move from "anti-typological", that is, nonfunctional shape to find utilization and would inevitably neglect to consider potentially necessary design factors because of non-definition of a guiding prototype, a preliminary whole with performance criteria. Such an approach has its possibilities for the few kinds of projects where multi-functionality is of little or no concern. However arrived at, conventionally or digitally, architecture of any complexity and practicality is by nature topological (form and place related) and, at least in the development stage, spatially transformational, but also broadly typological.

The office interiors of Zentralsparkasse at Favoritenstrasse in Vienna, by Günther Domenig, is an early realization of what has become known since the 1990s as architectural hypersurfaces, but built in 1975 without the help of extensive computer modeling – a result of freely flowing, rather random spatial variations based on subjectively chosen 'transformational events' within necessarily limited object boundaries, and without elaborate theoretical underpinnings (8.2).

8.2 Zentralsparkasse at Favoritenstrasse, Vienna

Perhaps best exemplified is the falling in love with shape making by the text accompanying the illustration of "Batwing", by the Tom Wiscombe Project Team (8.3):

> Batwing is part of a larger body of work concerned with creating coherent relationships between building systems through geometric and atmospheric means. The aim is to move toward a higher-order emergent wholeness in architecture while still maintaining a performative discreteness of systems.
>
> The language of the piece consciously looks to automotive and aerospace design in terms

of fluidity and integration of systems as well as processes of construction. These disciplines have flourished through the feedback of design sensibility and extreme shaping environments, a process which is of profound interest to our office.[21]

"Automotive and aerospace design in terms of fluidity and integration of systems" was never a good place to look for the very basis of architectural design, not even as "a machine to inhabit" – during Le Cobusier's early years and certainly not today. "Wholeness in architecture" requires definition of purpose and context before building systems may be selected and emerge as part of realization; be they of the Batwing type or others.

8.3 From the Batwing Project (© permission)

As should have become clear from my approach to meaning, I firmly believe that philosophical thinking can strongly enhance our view of architectural problem solving. But we must avoid trying to translate philosophical concepts or any other, for that matter, into architectural concepts without understanding and criticizing them and their implications explicitly. Great danger arises when such concepts are used as primary influences without balancing them with the other concepts which always exist and are relevant for a present project.

The various kinds of computerized representation techniques available today and still to come are excellent tools to visualize and coordinate geometric aspects of architecture better and quicker than designers ever have been able to accomplish. The possibilities to be programmed also for random surfacing can produce unknown imagery with the potential for evoking fantasy. This is for certain projects of advantage, but it is not a paradigm shift as is sometimes claimed.[22] *While computers can produce imagery, they cannot produce imagination.* That occurs in our head. I agree with Frank Gehry when for him, according to Mildred Friedman,

> ... the computer is a tool, not a partner – an instrument for catching a curve, not for inventing it.[23]

By their very nature and *on their own*, computers lack the critical capacities of acquiring, processing and evaluating all the kinds of information for balanced judgment in design. In other words, they cannot simulate and judge architecture in its totality. Only human beings can. Architectural design serves more than the processing of information. Design and building as process should be viewed as sequential instantiations of the object changing over time in a cause-effect environment. Referring to my view of content-form unity, architectural objects exist of interdependent mental, functional, procedural, structural and material properties. This requires at first more than shape-related virtual modeling. It requires critical thought.

Even Andrew Benjamin, whose writing is not easily accessed, is explicit on the inseparability of form and function. He writes that

> ... it is not as though bringing form into consideration is to add on a hitherto missing element. Form is not an addition to function or function present in addition to form. ...
>
> ... Forms function. Consequently form has to be understood as the enacted presence of a specific function in a given location.[24]

Functions influence form. But what are they? Through their relations they bring into reality what content in its great diversity demands. Function indicates an active and activating relationship – here between content and form. This is why I believe architecture would be in trouble, if it would be true, as he claims toward the end of his account, that

> Perhaps the most important shift that has occurred with architectural theory is – to use a generalized formulation – the move from a concern with meaning to a concern with form.
>
> ... On the one hand there is a return to a consideration of the object as an architectural object. On the other, central to that return, is a consideration of form not as a static entity but as that which is produced.[25]

If there is a "concern with form", realized in architecture, there must be meaning, or the concern is empty. Meaning is inevitably a result of design factor influences on form. They are its required or chosen content. We cannot design architecture without meaning something. Context – that is the coexistence out of which the object arises and on which it depends – often influences this meaning dynamically. There was never a turning away from the object as an architectural object and a turning away from meaning. To observe that one must only examine the enormous output in building over the past decades. And, architectural form, which was rarely produced without consideration of its aesthetic qualities, was never and is not today "a static entity", at least not as far as its impacts on life in and around it is concerned. Architectural objects and their forms – with their realizing power over time – are always influential on the understanding and behavior of us beings.

Much what is presently considered avant-garde architecture and is reflected in the design studios of architecture schools shows a tendency of a priori shape making. Often it has reached the status of a laissez-faire: anything goes as long as it can be physically built – or perhaps not even that. But let's be clear. That something can be built does not imply the justification to do so, especially when the tectonic is twisted, the law of gravity and other natural laws are neglected, and functional relationships are fit into form rather than the other way around. When what buildings are for becomes incidental to how they appear, self-reference becomes paramount and understanding impoverished. Decoration, deliberate embellishment, takes over amplification and response to basic requirements. But the point seems to be reached when shape making cannot further outdo itself and signs begin to appear that such projects seem to encounter resistance. The controversies about the recent schemes for the Victoria and Albert Museum addition and the World Trade Center redevelopment are signs of discontent.

Talking in 1991 about the metaphorical architectonics in the thinking of Descartes, Kant, Hegel and Heidegger, Jacques Derrida jumps to the future of real architecture and prognosticates that

> ..., if I were forced to stop here and to say what the architecture of the next millennium should be, I would say: in its type, it should be neither an architecture of the subject nor an architecture of Dasein. But then, perhaps, it will have to give up its name of architecture, which has been linked to these different, but somehow continuous ways of thinking. Indeed, perhaps it is already losing its name, perhaps architecture is already becoming foreign to its name.

In conclusion of his thoughts he offers:

> At that moment, architecture will have perhaps lost its name, its unity; it will perhaps become a stranger to itself, foreign to itself. And that will be good. Perhaps this has already begun today. Perhaps architecture will ... move from anyone to anything.[26]

This is naturally the move to endless difference, and with it indifference to present meaning. It is willful confusion. If adhered to, it leads to the view of what John Silber calls "architecture of the absurd".[27] Then not only particular forms of architectural objects become willfully confused with regard to what they represent but, with them, the public is sold incomprehensible, if not bogus, verbal meaning. Then one may find in an otherwise helpful book on *Designing the Sustainable School* this text accompanying a drawing of a high school:

> Though the campus program necessitates expansive energy-intensive indoor spaces, such as the 950-seat theater and adjacent lobby, the campus exceeded energy performance criteria by 20 percent. Designers achieved such efficiency while maintaining connection elements with the community, including a two-story glass lobby and portal windows offering passersby a visual path into the life of the facility.[28]

Nothing is said about what the energy performance criteria were, how energy efficiency is achieved during seasonal cycles or what all the decoration, structural and otherwise, does to embodied energy of the building components in this strongly 'shape generated' school.

Considering the realization of architecture, we are not in a world of language which describes and is referential. We consider a world of building which does not describe but is. That it is iconic, sometimes symbolic, at times even metaphoric, is an important but secondary issue. Language is symbolic as such. Heidegger's Dasein (Being there) is for architecture engaged and manifest existence. Derrida's deconstruction cannot exist as architecture as it is endlessly postponed. Built architecture is more than built dreaming, though we can certainly dream about what it might be. It is certainly more than 'différance'. Architecture is about the presence of thingness. Not about playing only but constructing. Derrida writes that

> From the moment there is meaning there are nothing but signs. *We think only in signs.* Which amounts to ruining the notion of the sign at the very moment when, as in Nietzsche, its exigency is recognized in the absoluteness of its right.[29]

True, meanings are mental signs, if that is what Derrida means. All our understanding is representation. But there is necessarily architectural reality, to which design thinking refers. We build foremost not signs but their reality which signifies by means of our mental power. We make judgments about our mental signs of what we build. Architecture is a medium of meaning. That "we think only in signs", that we represent mentally, does not ruin the notion of signs of architecture as dependent on physical reality.

When Charles Jencks claims that there is a new paradigm emerging since the 1970s I agree with him.[30] This is not a unique situation considering architectural history which always has been responsive to social, cultural and technological changes. The question is whether we have in architecture to refer, as he so readily does, to chaos theory, fractal geometries, blobs, folds, etc. and even to complexities that "emerge as a surprise to the designer from the belly of a computer" as a priori and originating determination of design development.[31] I answer with his elsewhere used warning "beware of orthodoxies". He suggests that

> We do not live in a cosmos, as was represented in Greek, Christian or Modern architecture, but in a cosmogenesis, a process of unfolding and sudden emergence, a surprisingly creative universe. This is one of the great insights of our time to be celebrated in architecture as in all arts.[32]

Even when we assume he is right, which one may doubt considering change at least since the Renaissance, one must question whether architecture should arise from "sudden emergence";

emergent from the belly of a computer or not. Architecture will serve anytime best when considering human needs first and comprehensively, instead of attempting to a priori reflect cosmogenic imponderabilities. This position does not deny our obligation, as designers or general public, to take into account contextual change as broadly encompassing as I mentioned, but it points toward the fact that human nature depends on order and stability, especially in the midst of chaos and indeterminacy. Architecture needs to mediate between life and adversity, not reinforce the latter through its forms which always means through its content. It cannot avoid complexity, contradiction and configuration. But randomness and waste, though never completely avoidable, must not be a desirable and guiding outlook.

As at various points earlier and in this section the relationships of architecture and text have been raised, explicitly and implicitly, I conclude here with an important issue which Karsten Harries addresses regarding today's position of theory in architecture. He is making his comments in a chapter of *Relearning from Las Vegas*, and in reference to recent architectural works.

> Words serve to augment the meaning of a building not just or even primarily in the form of conspicuous signs but as called forth by thoughtfully placed markers that invite the knowing to engage in playful theorizing. The inventiveness of such plays lets us appreciate the architectural significance of such work.[33]

I appreciate it when architectural works stimulate discourse in whatever ways. Explanations why certain paths were taken in their design help our understanding. But questions arise when elaborate 'theories' are put forth to back up decisions with no further reason than 'to be different' while neglecting or suppressing crucial aspects which otherwise would arise out of a project's purpose and context as a matter of course. Architecture has expression. Caution is indicated when theories are associated to explain what an object is supposed to be beyond what it is and to what it is related. For one, the importance of metaphors, earlier discussed, is not in question. They must not be used, however, to mask otherwise fuzzy design thinking.

Harries attributes to Georg Hegel the belief that "Theory is to return to art a voice it has lost".[34] He derives his view from Hegel's introduction to *Lectures on Aesthetics*:

> ... Art is and remains for us, as to its highest purpose, a thing of the past. ... What is now aroused in us by works of art is not only immediate enjoyment but also our judgment by which we make the content of the work, the means of its presentation, as well as the appropriateness and inappropriateness of both, subject of our thinking consideration. Therefore, the *science* of art is in our time even more a necessity than at the times when art as art by itself gave full satisfaction.[35]

Whether judgment entered the realm of art so decisively during his time, as Hegel asserts, is questionable. One may safely assume that it was always and variously part of the appreciation of art – as it is part of any human endeavor. Kant, for sure, made it a generation earlier central to his aesthetics. Anyway, Hegel took this consideration to call for the need of a science of art. It is a proposition he develops throughout his *Lectures on Aesthetics*. Harries writes:

> Theory here does not mean theorizing that in some fashion serves the production of architecture, for example, by analyzing the pressing problems some buildings should address or the means, materials, and technologies available to the builder ... But to really speak to us moderns, even the greatest works of the past need to be illuminated by texts that allow us to understand how they once satisfied what Hegel took to be the highest function of all art: to provide, like religion and philosophy, not so much physical as spiritual shelter ...
>
> ... Appropriate to our spiritual situation is an understanding of the work of art as a source of a purely aesthetic pleasure that leaves our deepest spiritual need unsatisfied. With the loss of its former ethical function, the work of architecture comes to be understood as well-

built, functional building to which a pleasing aesthetic component has been added. This may sound like a recasting of the Vitruvian architecture = firmness + commodity + delight. But what gives delight, the aesthetic component, now no longer attempts nor has the power to provide that spiritual shelter that the temple and the cathedral once offered.[36]

But theory must not be held away from the production of architecture, of which the crucial first phase is design. I hope this is clear from what I have said. What about "not analyzing the pressing problems some buildings should address"? The ethical function of architecture has not been lost, though it often is today – as it was at other times – insufficiently taken into account. "The temple and the cathedral" are and were never the only "spiritual shelter". All well-built homes, schools, museums, etc. are today, as in former times, spiritual as well as physical shelters. Hegel ends the paragraph from which Harries took the above quote by saying that

> Art invites us to thinking consideration, and this not for creating art again, but for scientific understanding of what art might be [was die Kunst sei].[37]

This sentence is important because it points to what art – for us architecture in particular – in part should mean: "scientific understanding", that is, with practical consequences. It points to analysis, obviously to be followed by synthesis. It points to broader theory building. But the aim of analysis is understanding of what is at hand: the circumstances of the architectural project, situated in its time and subjected to theoretical influences. It is not so that "the aesthetic component, now no longer attempts nor has the power to provide spiritual shelter", also not in Hegel's view. Hegel speaks, see above, of "immediate enjoyment" which comes from the aesthetic as the effect of any pleasing object properties. Nonetheless he speaks of the loss of "a satisfaction which was at least through religion strongly entwined with art".[38] But "firmness + commodity + delight" is still valid and we must see it as three parts of a unity. Delight is the aesthetic from the result of firmness and commodity with the latter two understood in our wider modern complexity as purpose, context and realization. Not to forget: ornament, when added, is part of purposive content. Aesthetic judgment had at the times of Vitruvius and Hegel and today spiritual, that is rational *and* emotional, grounding.

We must be careful not to conflate theory with text. Earlier I discussed why I believe in language about architecture, not of architecture, as architecture is not text. I claim that we need to resist the terminology of 'an architecture of the built word', beyond occasional metaphoric allusions, because as a theoretical construct it leads to a priori justification rather than to flexible understanding from scientific inquiry. Architecture also is not an art of "the painted word" as Tom Wolfe once characterized an episode of painting.[39] It must be guided by thoughts about quite explicit and present conditions. A school as a building is not a school because it is called so, comparable to Robert Rauschenberg's assertion that painting is a portrait because "I say so".[40]

I learned from *Complexity and Contradiction in Architecture*, among much else, that each design project requires not predetermined attention but freedom to become what it needs to be and, at least to some extent, what we want it to be. This means that it may come about with general as well as subjective principles but not through preempting crucial functional aspects. The aesthetic arises necessarily out of the object, as pleasure or displeasure, depending on what the object is and how we feel about it.

8.2 Complexity and inclusion

To design is to mean and the process how we arrive at design in part determines the meaning. Today's complexity of architectural design requires more than ever the input from many individuals, all with their own ways of developing and contributing information. Therefore, it is a major challenge how to manage the information exchange comprehensively and efficiently, and to make the various approaches compatible for influence toward integrated solutions. Design collaboration progresses as an iterative sequence of proposals and evaluations with input by consultants when needed. The designer manages the development and decision process, asking for help along the way from experts in the various specialty areas. The latter inevitably increases from early to late stages of the process because of the need of detailed knowledge in engineering and construction for the project's physical realization. The decision, however, on which solution to ultimately advance is by the designer with consent of the client.

Eventually, ever larger computational power can sustain broadly based computer supported collaborative work (CSCW) by parallel processing in the various domains of a project, producing feedback about the impact of all design factors and showing changes dynamically as consequences of what individuals or the team decide and project. At the center is initially a prototype which is supplied by the designer derived from preliminary understanding of purpose, context and, to a lesser extent, realization.[41] Already at this early stage, aesthetic idiosyncrasies play a crucial role. Placing a particular prototype for modeling implies judgment based on knowledge and intuition. In the future, when software and extensive data bases on particular building types will be available, even prototype selection can be achieved at this early stage by computerized and automatic integration and judgment.

It is sometimes claimed for 'virtual architecture' that it not only provides habitats for life's happenings but generates such happenings through realizations and activities on its own. How far this will be possible, if ever, is an open question. At the center is the paradigm of self-organization, that is, automatic self-adjustment in relation to contextual freedoms and constraints. Such behavior can, for example, be observed in ant and bee populations. Here and in much of nature it is instinctive. But architecture is not a natural and biological system. It is artificial even when programmed as flexible as possible. If fully automatic self-adjustment in the process of architectural creation should come about, an equivalent to the instinctive behavior of nature including reactions to freedoms and constraints, would have to be found. Neil Leach writes with regard to a self-organizing digital program for structural configurations by Kristina Shea that

> The computer is being used not as a tool of representation [only], but as a generative instrument that is part of the design process itself. In other words, at the most radical level, the computer has redefined the role of the architect. No longer is the architect the demiurgic form-maker of the past. The architect has been recast as the controller of processes, who oversees the 'formation' of architecture.[42]

His use of "generative" requires qualification. The computer can generate in the sense of replication but not in the sense of fundamental origination. At best, and appropriately constrained, it can yield useful production. This production occurs during self-adjustment within clearly defined limits. Shea herself writes that

> Generating new forms while also having instantaneous feedback on their performance from different perspectives (space usage, structural, thermal, lighting, fabrication, etc) would not only spark the imagination in terms of deriving new forms, but guide it towards new forms that reflect rather than contradict real design constraints.[43]

Decisions on such forms can then be made by comparing the performance and effectiveness of various systems – a positively meaningful, as well informed, approach.

The result of the interactive collaboration is a designer-generated 3d computer model with attached verbal and numerical background data which can be easily updated and serves as the basis for the construction documents. 8.4 shows the idealized framework of the CSCW, located in the worldwide space of Industry Foundation Classes (IFC) which is increasingly filled with information on uniformly coded building systems and components.[44]

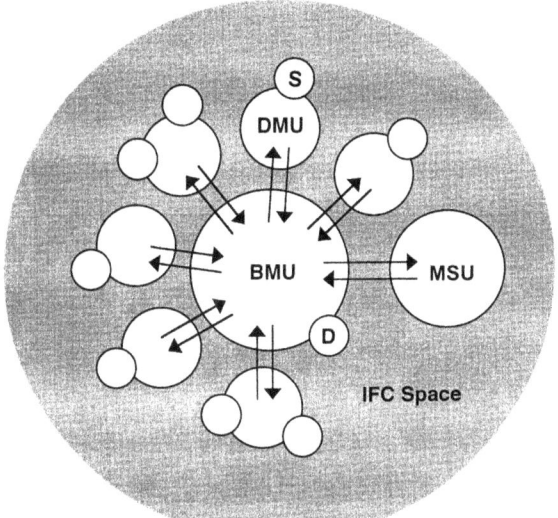

8.4 Computer-supported co-operative work (CSCW)

Interactive CSCW for design and construction requires in my view the following main operational components and capacities:

1. The Building Modeling Unit (BMU), in which the prototype is modeled by one of the commercial architectural 2D/3D computer applications, serves for developing current derivatives and eventually the final version of the project representation. It is the common work space in which all inputs from domain specific modeling, such as structural engineering and construction scheduling, influence current models through integration. The essential coordinating tool is geometry but verbal and numerical input needs to be attached as qualitative and quantitative supplements. The final model version provides what is conventionally known as the construction documents and is the basis for as-built documents after project completion.
2. The Modeling Storage Unit (MSU) stores the history of the project, including prototypes and interim derivatives. Also Information may be collected in it on design factors and on building type precedents for reference and comparison. Ideally this memory contains all the types which have some category relationship with the project type presently considered. The unit contains a usually very large data base.
3. Domain Modeling Units (DMU) provide input for all specialities, such as spatial geometries, structural and environmental systems, building and life cycle costs, construction processes and facilities management. They are used and controlled by the domain specialists (S) and run likely, at least for the near future, on digital programs different from those of the BMU.
4. Translation Units (implied as part of the double arrows) are the input and output mechanisms between the BMU and the particular DMUs. They are needed as the DMU results usually differ in format from what is compatible with the application which produces the project in the BMU. This lack of compatibility has been the subject of extensive efforts during the past two decades in the development of advanced Building Information Modeling (BIM) and is discussed below with reference to CSCW.
5. There often are also inputs from domain specialists which are not arrived at nor documented in a computerized format, such as cultural or psychological criteria. They require adjustment of

the building model by the designer (D). Adjustments for preferences of architectural appearance also are of this kind.

The designer controls the overall process, including what is simulated in the BMU, and prompts specialists about input needs. In most projects, especially the larger and more complex ones, a building model manager will be required as part of the project team. Additional expenses for all these activities will be more than offset by savings from the reduction in other work, such as drafting and data search. There is a frequent need for communication among the owner, client, designer and specialists about what happens often rather quickly in the BMU.

At the heart of all recent CSCW efforts is Building Information Modeling (BIM). The most extensive and complete description of its methods and applications so far is in Charles Eastman et al *BIM Handbook*.[45] Building information modeling has naturally occurred long before it was known under this name, even in predesign activities and along all building design stages. Conventional calculations provided simulations for energy consumption or daylighting assessment based on building massing and envelope design. What makes most of the presently developing BIM methods so compelling is the connection of the extensive and ever more comprehensive domain specific computations together with computer-aided architectural design applications (CAAD) by way of the industry-wide uniform codifications of building components, the Industry Foundation Classes (IFC). The result is enhancement of design solutions through immediate input from all architectural domains in predesign, design, specification, construction, occupation and eventual disposal with updating of the emerging proposals according to any present changes, large or small.

The IFC format has a nonproprietary, object-oriented file structure into which geometric and descriptive data of any building product, such as wall panels, windows, lighting fixtures and air-conditioning equipment, are fitted. It is the main response to overcome the coordination obstacles in the many areas of building design, construction and operation. The wide acceptance of the IFC approach will contribute strongly to the 'open' building systems approaches of the 1960s and 70s in which exchangeability of prefabricated components was sought, and partially succeeded by means of modularly coordinated sizing and compatible jointing within defined overall systems boundaries.[46] The world-wide availability of many IFC based components and subsystems will increase the flexibility of choice and fit in overall design integration, especially made possible by computerized selection, production and construction methods. To a large extent it is the case that

> We can reestablish craft in architecture by integrating the intelligence of the architect, contractor, materials scientist, and product engineer into a collective web of information.[47]

A central issue for interoperability of applications is broadening the content of building modeling repositories which function as nonproprietary, object-based model servers. Eastman at al write:

> An IFC repository can support integration of the data generated by multiple applications for use in other applications, support iterations on parts of the design, and track changes at the object level. They provide access control, version management, and various geometric, material and performance data that represent a building.[48]

The BIM representations are sets of computer aided architectural design visualizations produced by means of commercially available CAAD programs.

For all involved, but especially for designers, it is crucial to find quickly products which can be used in current circumstances. As computers can read today many kinds of descriptive and graphic data, semantic searching is possible and accordingly identifiers, which always have been part of product information, become more powerful and efficient.

Today, we are already able to search the Web and find building products based on user defined criteria, if one knows the product names and/or standard material names. Semantic searching will enable searches that accept a broad range of synonyms, with methods that understand class and inheritance relations and can deal with combinations of attributes.[49] A search command may be formulated, such as 'exterior shading, south exposure, horizontal, for 40 deg latitude, strongly supportive daylighting geometry, 6 foot mullion spacing, aluminum'.

With the increase of many IFC based building products and assemblies, usually referred to as "building elements", and an International Framework for Dictionaries (IFD) being developed in connection with IFC, most manufacturers and vendors will eventually join in this open format movement to stay competitive in an increasingly global market.[50] There obviously exist countless proprietary building element libraries containing data which design or construction firms use for current projects. They are made compatible with the CAAD application which these companies use.[51] It is a matter of time only until these private collections will adopt IFC or at least seek translation compatibility with them.

Different from conventional ways of using many drawings and separate files of data descriptions, the BIM/IFC model contains all data compatibly in one project data bank.

> Programs [computer applications] which support the IFC standard can export building models, developed by the architect or domain specialists in this neutral object format, and can import such models similarly interpreted.[52]

8.5 shows domain specific areas connected with the central BMU. Product data based on IFC formats enable the translation units to process compatibly.

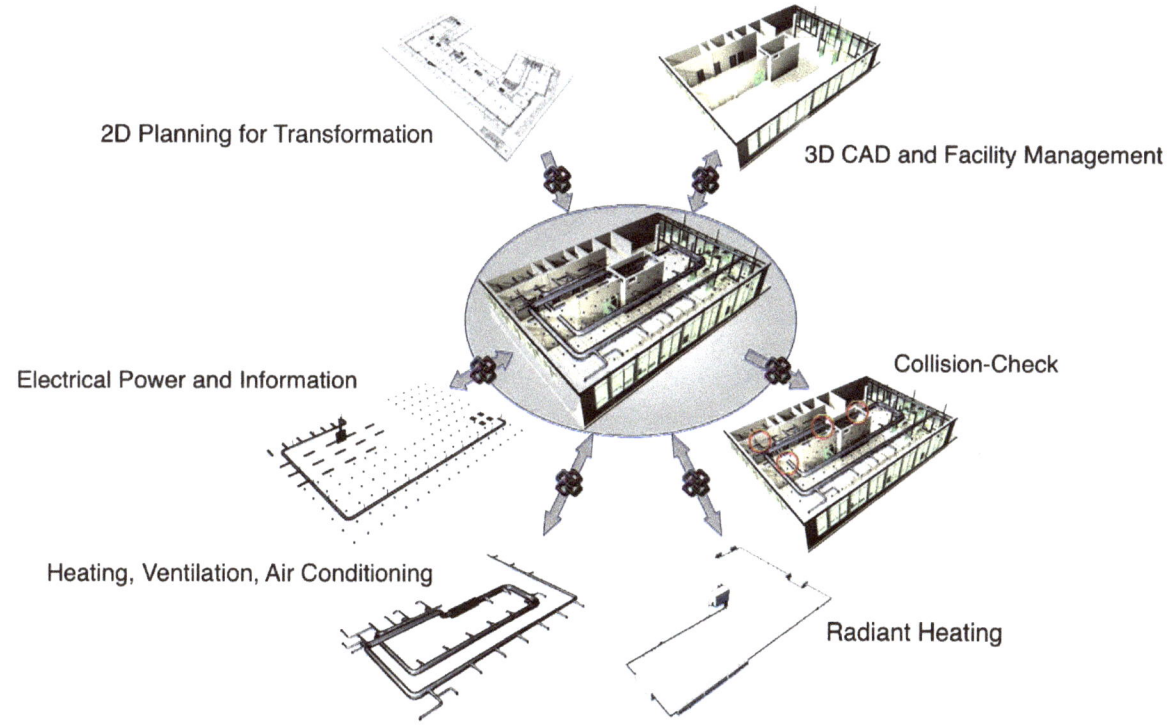

8.5 Data exchange between Central Building Modeling Unit and Domain Modeling Units (© permission)

Like the introduction of the building systems approach a generation ago gave the design and construction process an efficiency boost, which is reflected in the worldwide, to a large extent off-the-shelf building component market, so will the development of the BIM/IFC methodology be a watershed for providing intense coordination possibilities across the whole life-cycle span of architectural objects.

There always will be occasions in which the IFC approach is not applicable or only partially because of very unique circumstances and results to be achieved.

> A uniform direct exchange format to support all analysis types is not likely to be developed, because different analyses require different abstractions from the physical model, with properties that are specific to each analysis type.[53]

Examples of this type are the specialized computations necessary for the modeling and manufacturing processes to accommodate highly complex curvatures, such as In Frank Gehry's designs, or the use of one of a kind building assemblies, such as very idiosyncratic curtainwall systems.[54] Higher costs are most likely incurred by such individualizations.

Several, over the past two decades developed, programs for 2D/3D architectural modeling have adopted the IFC framework for interoperability. Plume and Mitchell write about this encompassing environment that

> ... the building model is [part of] the [global] repository of design information, model editors support the management of that information; design analysis is undertaken by specialist applications that are able to read the model data; and design decisions are made by the team members (generally humans, but just as realistically, could be computational design agents).

And,

> It is clear that once you have an interoperable, semantically rich model, then the opportunities for effective design resolution and strategic decision-making are significantly increased.[55]

Considering the rapidly increasing power of computing and automation with it, the translation among these building modeling applications for interoperability and decision making is a crucial issue in the collaborative IFC approach. IFC cannot propose design solutions on its own but developing programs will eventually be able to query IFC repositories about feasibility of alternatives in real-time.

As the strongest impact of decisions on design solutions occurs during the early stages of the process, these are also the most crucial times for preliminary domain specific inputs. Advanced virtual tools for the conceptual design level must, on one side, support the design thinking process and, on the other, provide quickly feedback for further design decision making. Such 'rule-of-thumb' type tools are not yet available for interaction and updating across all domains. They must be mainly based on the systems levels, rather than on details. Great care must be taken, that the choices in categorical input do not shortcut the generation of architectural design ideas or, in building model updates, negatively influence categorical functions of other project domains. They must flag such impacts for further evaluation.

The comprehensiveness of the BIM approach, with many directions waiting to be explored in detail, offers naturally a much broader outlook for what the influence of computerized virtuality can have than that of virtual shape making, although the latter occasionally may help through its randomness to stir design inspiration. The deeper understanding of design consequences from CSCW modeling, based on comprehensive virtual experiences, increases the confidence of designers in positing from the start prototypes which already point to the features needed in eventual design solutions. Some of the most pressing are those which can contribute toward environmental sustainability.

An operational aspect that is even more important with the CSCW approach than in the traditional unfolding of the design process is the appropriate matching of design progression and intensity levels of quantitative design analysis.[56] The designer traditionally calls for input from consultants according to project progress based on his own experience and knowledge in the specialty areas. Many performance simulation tools have become so advanced that they produce highly detailed and quantified output. Such intensity is in many cases not needed or even desired, especially not in the early, still very fluid stages of design when qualitative implications have priority for addressing. In very complex projects a more extensive learning process must occur for understanding all the implications of project development, especially by the designer, not only with regard to technical but also aesthetic consequences. This takes time. Therefore, the appropriate kind of analysis output is often more a question of making qualitative implications explicit rather than producing strong quantification through computational intensity. It makes sense to define this issue with the view that we analyze in order to synthesize and make judgments about proceeding in a particular direction under this premise. On the other hand and depending on the project, we frequently can understand through quantitative analysis much about its qualitative performance and utility; for example, from modeling of space utilization efficiencies or simulation of energy conservation efforts. In other words, we must as designers not be able to quantify everything we use, an obvious impossibility. But we need a basic understanding of how things work quantitatively. This is so for understanding how structural components work, plumbing systems function and sun shading performs, etc. One of the great benefits, which the rapid feed-back in the CSCW approach yields, is the multiple ideation and innovation effect from both the qualitative and quantitative output generated by the team members at every design iteration level.

The driving force of CSCW team work is the assessment for best possible performance in specialty areas and overall. But architectural projects which are determined by historical, cultural, environmental, technical, economic and aesthetic factors can never be optimized overall, as tradeoffs are required among these various influences of which many cannot be expressed numerically. This does not mean, however, that optimization should not be a guiding principle in specialty areas where quantification can be applied. Balances to satisfy complex performance are struck and decisions are eventually made through informed judgment on all input items. The designer's role as eventual decision maker is as important in this approach as in the conventional more linear one. This is also why, even with all the means digital virtuality makes available, talk about its generative capacity in the sense of design creativity, is misplaced – a view which shall not be taken as underestimation of its inspirational and practical values.

This line of thinking leads to the fundamental question: what limits virtuality in application? The answer is: the difference between representation and reality. While we understand through representation, we exist as reality and, in the wider context, exist in it. Architecture is part of the latter. Unless we abandon the axiom that architecture belongs to reality, architecture is not virtuality. Its representations are. During the process of design we think in the realm of virtuality. That our mental representations are documented by means of material representation, now often called 'virtual architecture', does not change this fact; nor does the increasing use of computer guided manufacturing and construction. What is on the computer screen is not architecture but physical representation of part of its mental content in visualized results of simulation. This explicitness is the great strength of computerized virtual modeling because it makes complexity with its many conflicts and necessary tradeoffs among components easier to understand.

The fundamental impetus in architectural design, as in any other human enterprise, cannot be the search for new forms per se, not for things just to have them, but the search for content-form unities which satisfy our needs and desires by means of observable and relational properties. As described, every component in architecture has both kinds, be it a door to accommodate passage or a wall defining space to accommodate gatherings. Out of this dual existence, components form complexity. Complexity can be defined as a whole of different but largely interdependent parts. Also mentioned, architecture is not self-organizing into such complexity. It does not develop on its own but is organized and designed. Usually and crucially, not everything which we like can be included. Choices have to be made. Therefore, its emergence comes in large part based on subjectivity. The predictive efficiency and certainty of the process is influenced accordingly. This is an existential fact of architecture and any other complex system which we cannot change even with the best information technology available. Paul Cilliers writes that

> ... meaning is constituted in a specific context where some components are included and others not. It would not be possible to have any real meaning if the number of relationships were not limited.[57]

There is not only the need for limiting the number of influencing design factors but the problem of assessing their mutual impact within complexity. When the number is reduced too much, imbalance will arise through neglect of important observable and relational aspects. The only way to set limits is by understanding importance and risk. Value judgment on the influence of one design factor versus another or others makes inclusion, beyond fundamentally necessary requirements, a matter of aesthetic decision. All what we said earlier about configuration and fit applies. Computations are helpful but cannot be decisive alone. Cilliers summarizes:

> ... There will always be limits, thus there will always be something that eludes our understanding of a complex system, but from different perspectives, following different strategies, these limits will be different. To keep on confronting these limits is what science – and life – is all about. Nevertheless, they will remain limits in the sense that we cannot say what it is that eludes us. We cannot calculate what it is that escapes our grasp. What we need, therefore, are ways of dealing with that which we cannot calculate, of coping with our ignorance. There is a name for this. It is called "ethics," and no amount of complexity theory will allow us to escape.[58]

What we include and what not of design factors in our work is essentially an ethical decision. In my view *aesthetics implies ethics*. From this position I will address a little further ahead, what I believe, is one of architecture's most important, if not the most important issue and obligation at the present time: to contribute toward sustainability.

Before we get to that, a few remarks on analysis and synthesis which play such a central role in the development of meaning in the design process and need elucidation of how and when we let them influence our decisions in this increasingly more powerful environment of virtuality. This is not the place and there is no need to go into a discussion about how the various design process models have positioned analysis and synthesis. There is an abundance of related literature.[59] For our present discussion it makes sense to use the most recent and sustained effort in this respect by John Gero and his collaborators. Gero proposed in 1990 the Function-Behavior-Structure (FBS) concept as model of the design process. He explains:

1. The *function [F]* of an object is defined as its teleology, that is, "what the object is for."
2. The *behavior [B]* of an object is defined as the attributes that are derived or expected to be derived from its structure, that is, "what the object does."
3. The *structure [S]* of an object is defined as its components and their relationships, that is, "what the object consists of." [60]

The FBS framework is made operational by the processes shown in 8.6:

1. *Formulation* (process 1) transforms the design requirements, expressed in function (F), into behavior (Be) that is expected to enable this function.
2. *Synthesis* (process 2) transforms the expected behavior (Be) into a solution structure (S) that is intended to exhibit this desired behavior.
3. *Analysis* (process 3) derives the "actual" behavior (Bs) from the synthesized structure (S).
4. *Evaluation* (process 4) compares the behavior derived from structure (Bs) with the expected behavior to prepare the decision if the design solution is to be accepted.
5. *Documentation* (process 5) produces the design description (D) for constructing or manufacturing the product.
6. *Reformulation type 1* (process 6) addresses changes in the design state space in terms of structure variables or ranges of values for them if the actual behaviour is evaluated to be unsatisfactory.
7. *Reformulation type 2* (process 7) addresses changes in the design state space in terms of behaviour variables or ranges of values for them if the actual behaviour is evaluated to be unsatisfactory.
8. *Reformulation type 3* (process 8) addresses changes in the design state space in terms of function variables or ranges of values for them if the actual behaviour is evaluated to be unsatisfactory.[61]

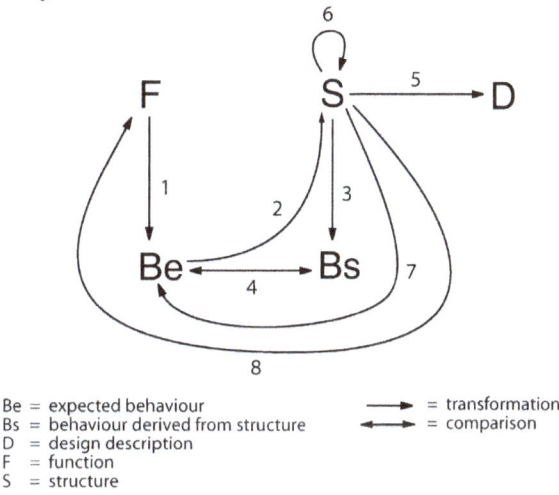

Be = expected behaviour
Bs = behaviour derived from structure
D = design description
F = function
S = structure

⟶ = transformation
⟷ = comparison

8.6 Function-Behavior-Structure framework (© permission)

The concept of purpose-context-realization as framework for design is similar to that of function-behavior-structure. Purpose and function are often considered synonyms. But it makes sense to avoid here the term function:

> Although it is well recognized that there is no function in structure and that there is no structure in function, human and design experience produces a connection between function and structure. Once that connection is learned it is very difficult to unlearn.[62]

The purpose and function of an artifact is our mental construct of what the performance and behavior of this artifact is to be. It is what we suppose it to be, not what it actually is. The later is its counterpart, the performance or behavior which is an integral part of structure. The term realization refers to this unity. What an artifact does, passively or actively, is part of what it is. Function, I repeat, is best explained as relationship between purpose and realization. In contrast to FBS, purpose-context-realization emphasizes the fundamental and categorical importance of context which influences every project in specific ways. Purpose finds realization in context.

As mentioned earlier, the first task in the design process is the development of the design prototype by using as much as possible of the information available at the time of design inception. This activity is a synthesis made possible by analysis of the purposive and contextual aspects of the project. In a sense, after it has been determined, purpose becomes one part of the present context, the other part being the overall environment (historical, cultural, financial and physical) in which the project is to be situated. Although there are precedents from earlier design solutions and client-generated requirements, a fair amount of additional information is usually collected and analyzed as the basis for synthesis of the prototype. In complex design, there is no synthesis without analysis. We cannot intelligently compose something new without understanding what the components are to be and do. William Peña named this first analytical phase of the design process "problem seeking".[63] The prototype is the first result of synthesis arising out of this information base.

That analysis also addresses synthesis is a natural part of the iterative sequence of design. We analyze what we have combined to judge its performance. This happens in the sequence of processes 2 through 4 in 8.6. Whether analysis or synthesis takes place first depends on what we consider our initial event in the chain of causation of a particular activity needs to be. In design we are, to speak with Heidegger, thrown into a given world of being and time. Some of it we understand because we have lived in it for a while. Some of it we even understand with regard to its importance to the anticipated project derived from constructive memory. Much, however, is not understood in this respect and needs analysis. This world, which is an existing synthesis for any encounter, becomes design context when we attempt to situate the project in it and start to analyze it for project development.

From this line of thought we may conclude that the design process, being so highly iterative, is from start to end driven by analysis and synthesis, back and forth, starting with analysis of the given situation and ending with analysis of a successful synthesis; with every iteration implying incremental judgment. This is naturally not so different from all our thinking processes in which part of impression is analytical and part of expression is synthetic. We 'express' our impressions, that is, combined thoughts from perception and conception, for validation and additional imagination. Therefore, it does not help to portray thinking and design processes in any linear fashion and single out an analysis-synthesis or a synthesis-analysis sequence without calling attention to the fact that it is only one of the phases in the process of iteration.

Again, we need to emphasize the importance of context here for the choice of prototype. It contains vast general knowledge and provides the resources for very specific understanding and inspiration when we analyze it with our project in mind. This speaks for the much more comprehensive approach of computer supported collaborative work in design with initial analysis-oriented prototype development rather than for the narrower approach with shape-oriented prototype which, to be successful for all kinds of complex architectural programs, will have to accommodate the many design factors through much additional iteration.

Analyses for syntheses are driven by aspects of purpose activated as design factors. This happens in uncountable instances throughout the whole design process nourished by the designers constructive memory which, in turn, is prompted by the present context. Pak-San Liew and John Gero write about this "situatedness" that

> Within a constructive memory system, the very act of constructing a memory of an associated design experience affects that memory through its grounding in the interaction with the environment. Any information about the current design environment, the internal state of the agent and the interactions between the agent and the environment is used as cues in the construction process.[64]

Any experience the designer ever had, architectural or not, can potentially turn into a design factor prompted and perhaps modified by the present circumstances. Subjectivity, heavily involved and never based on the same conditions, opens up possibilities for inspiration, creativity and variety. This is especially so in the formulation and choice of the prototype at the beginning of the process where the designer to a large extent depends on intuition. Prototypes are design concepts emerging at this early stage through constructive memory in relation to the main programmatic requirements. It is preliminarily determined by client, designer and consultants. Agreed upon priorities limit the constructive memory activity. Therefore projects, following problem seeking input to start with, impose many different constraints on prototype selection and initial design development. Shape making dominated projects, on the other hand, conventionally arrived at or by computerized virtuality, amount to an a priori aesthetic limitation on decisions and must be held flexible for potentially extensive change of appearance from beginning to end of design iteration.

Therefore, the way how the basis on which the prototype is selected differentiates the Purpose-Context-Realization model from the Function-Behavior-Structure model by initial emphasis on influences of context and a stronger view toward realization, and deemphasis on behavior-structure aspects. The former model is in search of content for impressions and expressions. It provides the background and understanding for the design iteration (6.6). The latter describes a version of design and testing itself (8.6). Its description does not address how we get to the prototype of the design process.

Our interest is teleological. Understanding and incorporation determines the performance of future design results. Earlier had experiences with content prompt and support understanding. We remember that among other criteria, a window performs with regard to day-lighting of an interior space and with regard to satisfying a certain preference of proportion. Daylighting can be measured and objectively judged. Proportion can be measured but only subjectively judged. And we remember that if well designed, a space performs as functionally anticipated. But it also performs in unanticipated ways, beyond original purposiveness. Spaces are generally used for various types of events, of which not all can be anticipated. Some aspects can be measured, others must be left to be directly judged and evaluated. The latter kind of decision happens more often than we assume. Context in the broadest sense always provides and often demands more than what we recognize and may decide, or even are able to consider. David Leatherbarrow goes so far as to claim that

> When the building is freed from technological and aesthetic intentionalities, we discover its lateral connections to an environmental and social milieu that is not anyone's making, still less of design and planning.[65]

A project or building cannot be "freed from technological and aesthetic intentionalities". They result in what its architecture is and does. What architecture does is inseparable from what it is. In other words, the quality of realization is reflected by performance in whatever way we may understand it. We discover because of its intentionalities, in which it reflects the demands of client, designer and many others, and the connections to its environment and social milieu. An as far as possible understanding of context in the broad definition of time, place and happenings is the way to attain much of architecture's intentionalities. According to Leatherbarrow:

> Performance in architecture unfolds within a milieu that is not of the building's making. A name for this milieu is *topography*, indicating neither the built nor the un-built world, but both.[66]

The performance of an architecture, a "building's making", unfolds and is influenced by whatever milieu (context) in which it finds itself. Etymologically, topography means "a description of place". Context means "a weave together". Architecture is part of the environment and milieu in which it is set, determines it to some extent and facilitates performances not fully thought of in advance. The 'with' (con) of context works both ways, from environment to architecture and then from architecture to its environment. Leatherbarrow concludes that

> For a theory of performativity we should seek nothing more and nothing less: instrumental reason and the rationality on which it depends, *plus* situated understanding that discovers in the particulars of a place, people and purpose the unfounded conditions that actually prompt, animate and conclude a building's performance.[67]

Places, people and purposes provide and encounter founded and unfounded conditions in a given context. Both kinds of conditions are subject to analysis and instrumentality. All are potential design factors, may enrich results and may lead to innovation. Their powers and effects are taken care of by our freedom and redundancy in design configuration and realization, not least aesthetically.

8.3 Sustainability and outlook

The general cultural and economic exuberance after World War II resulted in unprecedented urban growth and a major thrust in architectural output. It was the time of developing suburbs and expressways, the Seagram Building, the TWA terminal and the Monsanto "House of the Future". Industrialization and prefabrication of building entered construction with full force. But soon signs began to appear that not everything was well with the state of the world's environment and energy consumption. Rachel Carson's *Silent Spring* was on the New York Times bestseller list in 1962. The first oil crisis hit in 1973 and Fritz Schumacher's *Small is Beautiful* was published the same year. President Carter urged the public in 1979 to drive less and to adjust thermostats for energy conservation.

Designers and building owners were slow in adapting to these challenges for various reasons. Energy conservation did not decisively enter consideration as it did not play a perceptible role in construction costs. Energy used in building operation – natural gas and electricity, mostly produced from coal – was plentiful and nationally available, and prices only increased slowly. Few design students were told that good comfort in buildings could be achieved by architectural design decisions. The result was oversizing of comfort control systems and energy waste.[68] The general public did not urge architects to consider energy in what they designed because they did largely not understand its use, except perhaps for the homes in which they lived.

It took two decades of an increasing environmental movement and many, mostly government supported demonstration projects about conservation and alternative energy systems to raise awareness so that by the turn of the century sustainability became for many in the profession a guiding issue. The first energy conservation standards were published in 1975, *ASHRAE 90-1975*, rather tellingly, by the American Society of Heating, Refrigeration and Air Conditioning.[69] Other milestones were the *Building Energy Performance Standards* (BEPS) of 1980 which suggested building type baselines for the yearly energy consumption in new construction; the *Handbook of Energy Use for Building Construction* of 1981 which documented embodied energy in materials and assemblies from production, transportation and construction; and the *Architect's Handbook of Energy Practice* of 1982.[70,71,72] The 1990s saw eventually the emergence of results more broadly and in 1998 LEED (Leadership in Energy and Environmental Design) was organized. Its agenda also addresses health concerns, material recycling and waste streams.

> LEED is a point based system where projects earn LEED points for satisfying specific green building criteria. Within each of the six LEED credit categories, projects must satisfy particular prerequisites and earn points. The six categories include Sustainable Sites,

Water Efficiency, Energy & Atmosphere, Materials & Resources, Indoor Environmental Quality and Innovation in Design (projects can earn ID points for green building innovations). The number of points the project earns determines the level of LEED Certification the project receives. LEED certification is available in four progressive levels: Certified, Silver, Gold and Platinum.[73]

Strictly taken, sustainability is an absolute. A sustainably built environment is self-sufficient in the sense that it uses only renewable resources, which can be resupplied by nature without end and harm, and makes all resources it uses recyclable into a state in which they can be used again, that is, without side effects of pollution. It has an overall ecological efficiency ratio of 1. No such buildings, fully serving the complexity of our modern living conditions, exist. Daniel Williams is right when he postulates that

> dp ⟶ S, meaning *design and planning approaching sustainability*. A design is sustainable, or it is not. If it is not sustainable, changes can be made to make it sustainable. If it is sustainable, by necessity it will be changing and evolving. Sustainability is not static – it is iteratively changing, based on evolving knowledge that connects science and design. ...

To be sustainable

> The design must be capable of functioning "unplugged" from the external nonrenewable energy sources and resources in order to be sustainable.[74]

We are today in the early stages *toward* comprehensive sustainability. This does in most projects usually not yet include the major considerations of raw material depletion, embodied energy from production and assembly, and waste during construction and post-occupation disposal. Much progress has been made, considering where we were only a few decades ago. Arguably, we are about where automobiles are. Architecture can show improvements toward sustainability by means of hybrid solutions. But hybridization does only mean being partially sustainable. Even cars with "plug-in" or those running on hydrogen still are in a broad sense hybrids as long as the electricity used will not come fully from renewable, sustainably produced, nondepletable resources.

The meaning of sustainability has its foundation in the understanding that all of us, through whatever we are doing, have an impact on the resources of this planet and must participate in their maintenance. Some may be depleted in a rather short time and require conservation efforts, and others, which are renewable, require promotion. As designers and planners we must not only make sure that we ourselves understand how we can maximize the conservation of nonrenewable and the application of renewable resources in what we project but that we spread this understanding in every way possible among the general public.[75,76] This entails very specific aspects and actions which may vary according to regions, circumstances and communities. Many of the aspects are not obvious and their content must be acquired first as foundations for understanding what we design for. They belong to issues which one might call hidden meaning.[77]

Foremost is the understanding of efficiency in the systems context of a given purposiveness, whereby 'given' refers to the well analyzed and founded needs and desires of project performance requirements.[78] Efficiency is conventionally expressed as

$$e_p = \frac{\text{output}}{\text{input}}.$$

The subscript p shall indicate that the efficiency belongs to a process. The smaller the input is for obtaining an expected output, the larger is the efficiency. This efficiency ratio never reaches 1, as some part of the input will be 'lost' in the process and cannot be applied to produce output. In other words, waste occurs in the utilization of input to obtain output. We talk here about relative sustainability in comparison to the absolute sustainability which Williams describes.[79]

The efficiency may be expressed by identifying the input, the applied amount, as the usable part of the applied amount plus waste, the latter being the 'lost' portion of the input:

$$e_p = \frac{\text{output}}{\text{applied amount}} = \frac{\text{output}}{\text{usable amount} + \text{waste}}.$$

The useable amount is what enters the output. Therefore, output = useable amount. Assuming that in the construction of a particular wood framing 10 percent of the wood is wasted, the efficiency is 90 / 90+10 = 0.90.

Similarly a sustainability efficiency, related to the amounts of applied renewable and non-renewable resources, can be described as

$$e_s = \frac{\text{amount}_r}{\text{total amount}} = \frac{\text{amount}_r}{\text{amount}_r + \text{amount}_n}$$

where amount_r is the amount of applied renewable resource and
amount_n is the amount of applied nonrenewable resource.

e_s equals 1 when only renewable and 0 when only nonrenewable resources are used. For example, a room in a cold climate with windows uses 30 MBtu/sqft (floor area) per year for heating related to heat loss. Because of favorable orientation of its windows it has a useable solar heat gain during the cold weather season of 10 MBtu/sqft and e_s = 10/10+20 = 0.33. The same relationship applies to equipment which supplies renewable energy. When a wind mill requires for its manufacture and maintenance, rated over its useful life, 5 percent of the energy it is projected to supply then its sustainability (or renewability) efficiency is e_s = 0.95/0.95+0.05 = 0.95. If the electrical line losses from the same wind mill to the point of consumption are 25 percent, the overall sustainability efficiency is 0.70.

Another equation of this type can address main versus total floor area efficiencies of whole buildings or parts of them:

$$e_a = \frac{\text{main area}}{\text{total area}} = \frac{\text{main area}}{\text{main area} + \text{support area}}.$$

It is necessary to clearly define the main areas and support areas, for example, classrooms and hall ways in a school. A classroom wing which has a total area of 12,000 sq ft and a hall way support area of 3,000 sq ft has an e_a of 0.75, whereas one with 4,000 sq ft has an e_a of 0.67.

Such relationships confirm the claim by those of us who have been concerned over the years with various energy issues that 'passive' strategies in architecture are usually better than 'active' ones, pointing to design and engineering responses which yield highly positive results without or with relatively minor additional resource allocation, especially under whole building life cycle consideration. Building systems and materials of some kind are required to construct buildings. We may as well select and arrange them to also foster efficiency.

And, then there is that 'ultimate efficiency': avoidance of unnecessary building. It may well be in the future that one of the most valuable services a designer may render as part of a team which consults a client during pre-design activities is – here on grounds of sustainability – to help reduce the size of a project or avoid it all together when not needed. Among other expenditures, the avoidance of a square foot from being built saves in the range of 300 to 2,000 MBtu of embodied and 30 to 120 MBtu/sqft of operational energy yearly.

Obviously, only amounts in the same dimensional units can be used in the equations, such as Btu, sqft or dollars. But not all efficiency results must be expressed in the form of the above shown equations. One important category of this type is embodied (or embedded) energy in construction.[80] Typical multilayer wall components range from around 70 to 170 MBtu/sqft (vertical) of embodied energy; floor assemblies from around 150 to 280 MBtu/sqft (horizontal); overall residential construction from around 500 to 700 MBtu/sqft of floor area and overall office and school construction from around 1,100 to 1,700 MBtu/sqft of floor area. Related to yearly overall energy consumption per square foot and depending on climatic conditions, building type and energy conserving design features, the overall embodied energy may be between 10 and 40 times the yearly operational energy consumption per sf of floor area. 8.7 shows a scenario for embodied energy versus operational energy for housing and office buildings.

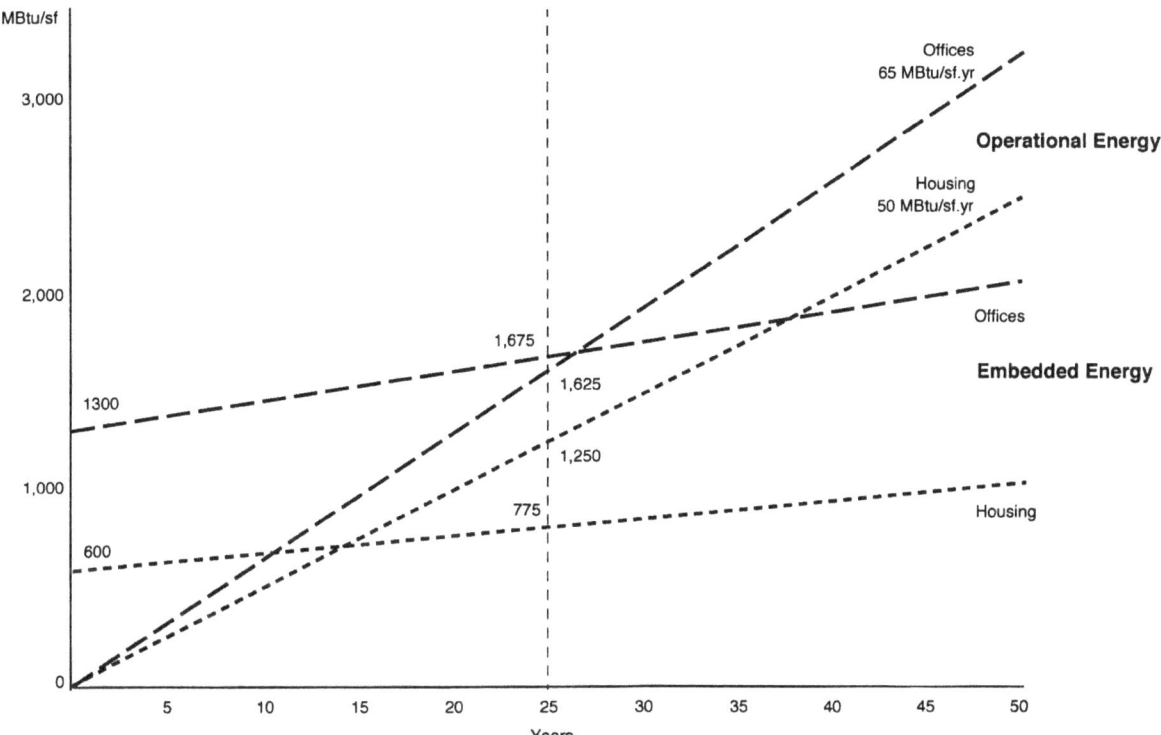

Assumptions: offices with 1300 MBtu/sqft initially embedded energy, 15 MBtu/sqft.yr for maintenance, repairs and replacement of the building components, and 65 MBtu/sqft.yr for operation; housing with 600 MBtu/sqft, 7 MBtu/sqft.yr and 50 MBtu/sqft.yr respectively. Looking at the half-way point of the assumed useful building life span of 50 years, the totally embedded energy is for the offices 1300+375 = 1,675 MBtu/sqft and for the housing 600+175 = 775 MBtu/sqft. The sum of the operational energy is for the offices 25x65 =1,625 MBtu/sqft and for the housing 25x50 = 1,250 MBtu/sqft. The embedded energy is for offices about 26 times the yearly operational energy (1675/65 = 25.8) and close to being passed by the sum of the yearly operational energy. The embedded energy is for the housing about 16 times the yearly operational energy (775/50 = 15.5) and has been passed by the sum of the yearly operational energy over ten years earlier. With improvements in energy conscious design (and perhaps small increases in embedded energy) the crossing points of operational and embedded energy can be considerably delayed (moved to the right).

8.7 Embedded energy versus operational energy in offices and housing

From such studies we can derive the possibilities for further shifts in the way the architectural profession views design at a time of increasingly scarcer and more expensive energy sources, and fears about global warming. The process of change, which had its impetus in the energy crises of the 1970s and 80s, was reinforced by an increase in understanding of building physics for providing interior environmental comfort conditions. One may regard these ongoing developments comparable to the over a century-long efforts in the advancement of structural analysis principles for how buildings were to be constructed. The most important guiding principles toward sustainability in architectural design are: maximizing solar orientation in siting and massing of buildings; using shading devices which are exterior or at least between glazing and are adjustable; placing insulation for enhanced thermal storage effect of walls and roofs; reducing exterior heat-islands by planting trees and other vegetation; providing operable windows for natural ventilation; placing windows for increased daylighting and controlling electric lighting accordingly by sensitive dimmers; favoring high wall and ceiling reflectances of exterior and interior materials; shifting thermal loads within buildings through the appropriate choice of heating and cooling systems; recovering heat in exhaust flues and from service water disposals; pre-cooling interior thermal mass by nighttime ventilation; coordinating mechanical systems operations with occupancy schedules; reducing electrical peak loads by shifting activity schedules accordingly; and, most generally, specifying materials and systems which are as far as possible renewable and require as little as possible work by machines and transportation.

Earlier, the TVA Building in Chattanooga (7.31 to 7.33) was given as an example for how sun-protection and daylighting utilization can be reflected in building expression. A few more examples will show how various other kinds of innovation toward sustainability can have considerable influence on appearance and with it meaning (8.8 to 8.21).

Plenk Residence, Salt Lake City

8.8 View from southwest

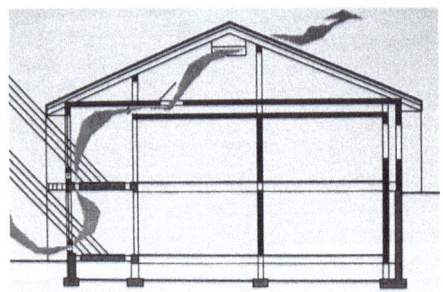

8.9 Lower level access and solarium   8.10 South-north section

A residence, by Kurt Brandle in 1980, features a double envelope in its south facade, north facade and second story ceiling (8.8 to 8.10). The windows in the south facade can provide large

306

solar heat gains. The concrete floors of the sun spaces and the gravel bed on the ground under the building have large heat storage capacity for such gains. During heat gain conditions warm air circulates in the double envelope clockwise, during heat loss conditions counter-clockwise, made possible by openings in the floors and ceilings of the sun spaces. Occasional overheating is eliminated by natural ventilation.

Gretsch-Unitas Building near Stuttgart

8.11 View from southeast

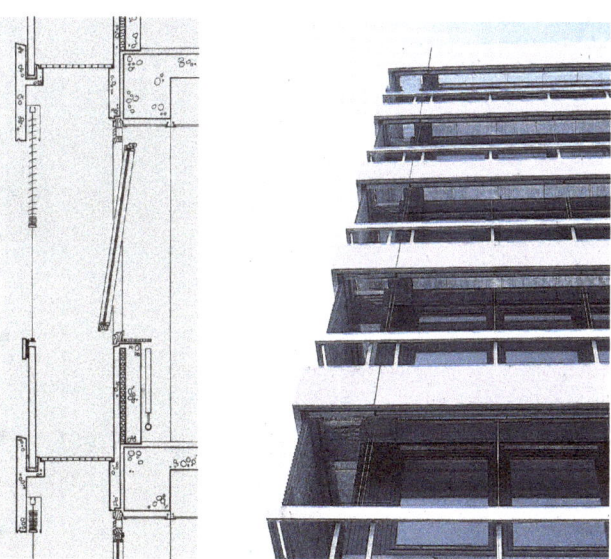

8.12 and 8.13 Facade section and details

The Gretsch-Unitas Office Building in Ditzingen near Stuttgart, by Kurt Möser in 1975, has naturally ventilated facades with venetian blinds as the outside 'skin' in 30 inch distance from the window plane (8.11 to 8.13). The space between blinds and windows causes a chimney effect through the metal grates. The blinds are automatically controlled, with manual override possibility, and serve also for reflecting the daylight deep into the interior. The reinforced concrete structure of the building provides solar thermal storage and is cooled by nighttime ventilation with external air.[81]

Since the time when these projects were built, enormous theoretical progress has been made in predicting the performance of such systems and the trade-off between their additional first costs and reduced life cycle costs from energy savings. 8.14 shows a comparative analysis in Klaus Daniels *Low-tech Light-tech High-tech: Building in the Information Age* of energy implications for exterior envelope systems including double skin facades.[82] It is crucial that designers become conversant with such data as background meaning not only for their own guidance in design evaluation but for helping the client to make informed decisions. All of these facades show low energy consumption but variations can be recognized.

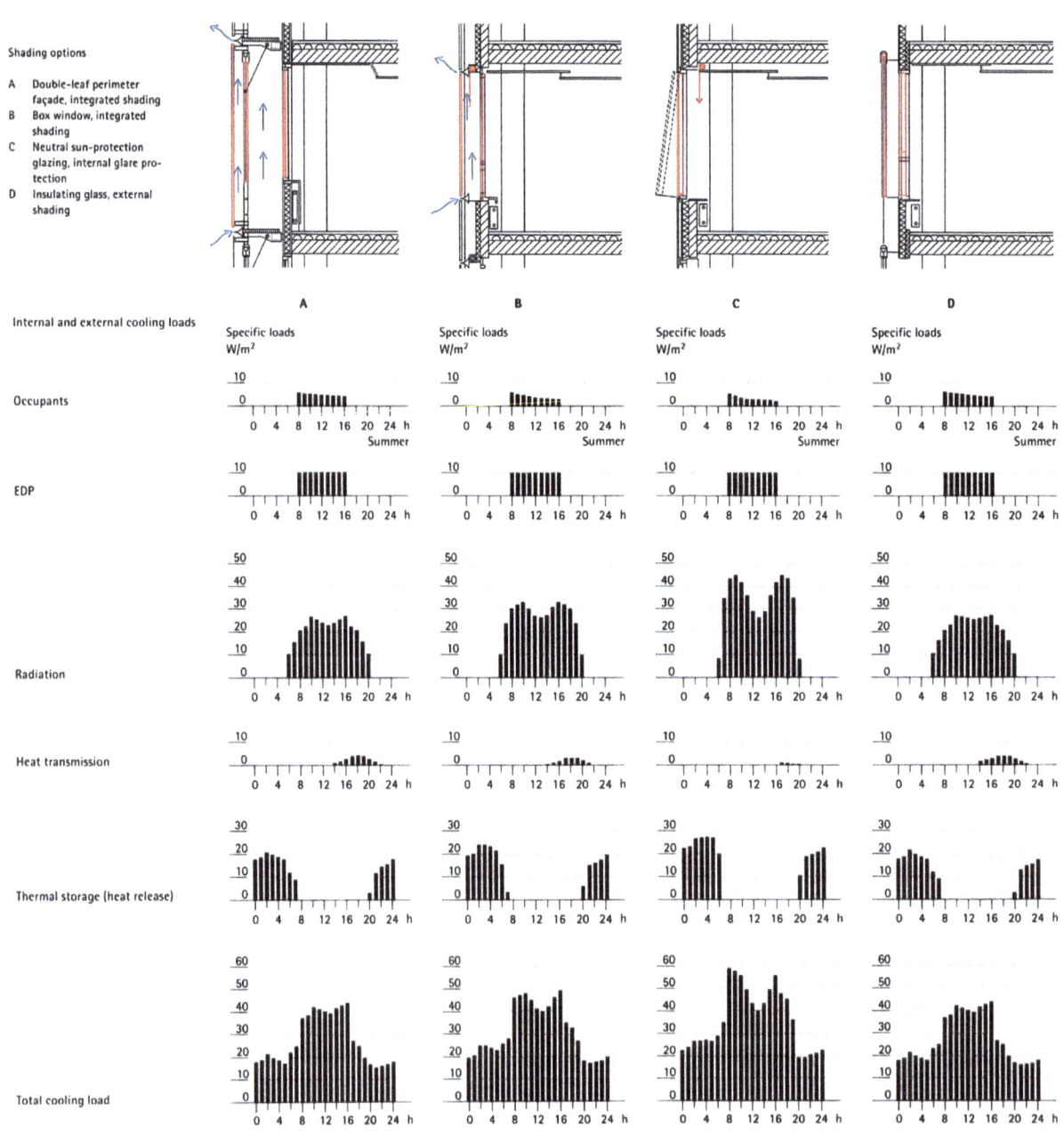

8.14 Analysis of high performance exterior envelope systems (© permission)

8.15 to 8.18 show one of the more recent examples of the many ventilated double envelope facades now existing worldwide; here an unavoidably west-oriented facade with high solar impact in the addition to an office complex in Berlin by Sauerbruch Hutton in 1999. The shallow tower allows for complete daylighting. The east facade has triple glazing with in-between venetian blinds. Operable openings allow for natural east-west ventilation exiting into the cavity of the double skin west facade which has inside insulating and outside single glazing. The chimney effect of this cavity supports its ventilation upwards. The colored louvers in the cavity can be adjusted for sun shading.[83]

8.15 View from west

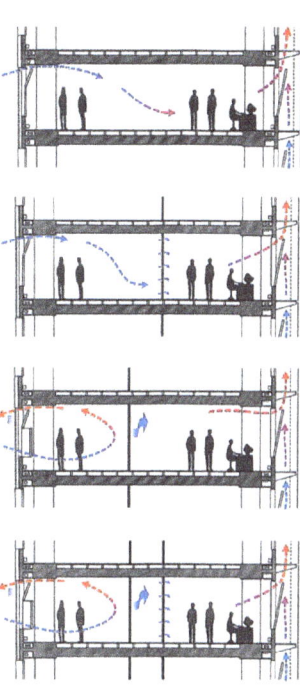

GSW Office Building, Berlin

8.16 Section with variations of natural ventilation (© permission)

8.17 West facade detail

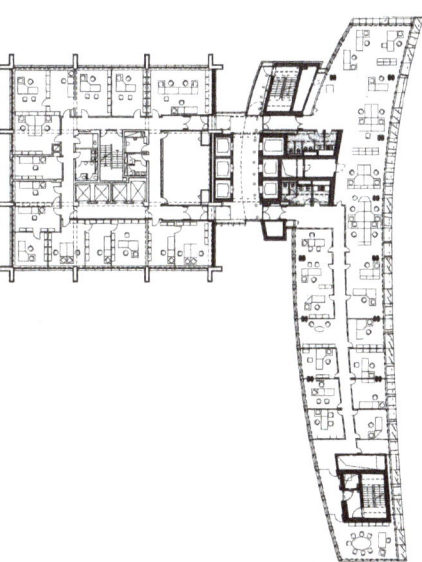

8.18 Floor plan, existing and new tower (© permission)

There is an abundance of studies showing particular subsystems of architecture optimized toward sustainability. Not as readily, we can find scenarios which bring together many of these systems for a large scale integrated approach. 8.19, by Kurt Brandle, shows in the south-north section of a mixed use downtown city block such systems relationships and interactions. The mix of activities in this scenario results in a large diversity of energy streams that lend themselves to energy trade-offs. Four groups of systems support the building functions and the needs of the occupants: environmental controls, building services, food production and transportation. All of these systems are interconnected by means of a district heating/cooling system and networks for electric power as well as communication. For example, the water loop heat pump system shifts solar heat gains from one side of buildings to the other where heat may be needed; the solar photovoltaic collectors, on the roof and as solar-adjusted shading devices on the facades, produce electricity for the buildings, the electro-cars, the battery storage bank or download to the electrical grid; the water type solar collectors provide heat for service water, absorption type cooling or green house heating; the greenhouses on the roof produce vegetables and flowers; rainwater is used for watering plants in greenhouses and on lawns; biological refuse throughout the project is composted and used as fertilizer; passive energy conservation strategies are used wherever possible, such as proper solar orientation and natural ventilation.[84]

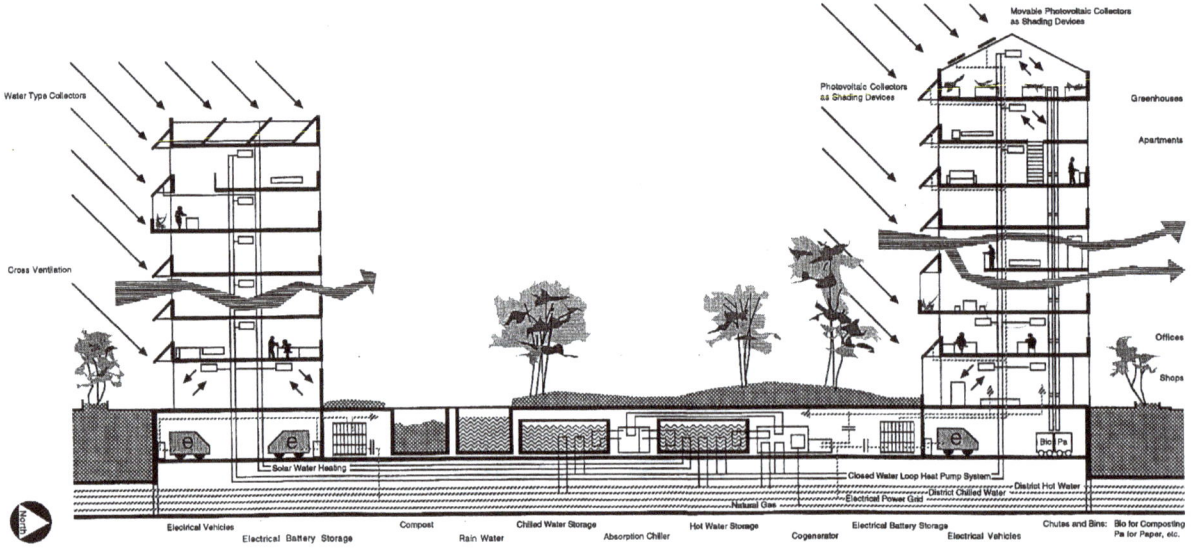

8.19 Passive and active systems integration for urban development

The prototype for an 'urban farm' was proposed in 2007, by Mithun Architects, for a site in downtown Seattle (8.20 and 8.21).

> The designers were attracted to the challenge of the sharp, angular plot and also benefited from its east-west orientation axis, which allowed them to put 34,000 square feet of photovoltaic (PV) panels on its south face to receive sunlight throughout the day. ... The lower floors of this triangular footprint are generally enclosed, while the upper floors are taken up by terraced plant nurseries and greenhouses with a long rectangular rooftop garden on top.
> The farm's 23 stories lift 1.35 acres of flora into a .72 acre site. Greenhouses, gardens, planters, and open-air tree nurseries will fill three terrace levels that grow fruits and vegetables and other types of native flora. A chicken run will also be on the lowest terrace.

This locally grown food will be sold to the community at large and also in the in-house restaurant and café below. ...

The most cutting-edge sustainability technology in the urban farm stores the power generated from the PV panels in a system housed below ground which converts energy into hydrogen gas and then converts it back into power when demand outpaces supply. Ninety percent of the building's power will come from these sets of PV panels, with the remaining 10 percent derived from panels along the Interstate 5 corridor. Black water, gray water, and rain water are to be treated and recycled on site through the use of greenhouse bio-membrane plants that can isolate and remove contaminants.

The consumers of this water and energy will live in 318 studio, one-, and two-bedroom apartments converted from shipping containers that are stacked on the south face of the building. Below them, labs and classrooms will offer residents and visitors the opportunity to learn about how the building "lives".[85]

Center for Urban Agriculture, Seattle

8.20 and 8.21 Views from southeast and northwest (© permission)

Such subsystems have their own efficiencies but are interdependent and, therefore, dynamically influence each other under impact from external conditions. Enormous complexity is involved which can be simulated and evaluated only to some extent by computation. This does not mean, however, that calculated efficiencies cannot serve for indication at least toward the 'right direction' and for the selection among subsystems. Sensitivity patterns of partial and overall energy consumption in actual operation will help to fine-tune the systems.

Here, it makes sense to pause and rethink what we are talking about overall. David Orr wrote in 2001 that

> ... the standard for ecological design is neither efficiency nor productivity, but health, beginning with that of soil and extending upward through plants, animals, and peoples. It is impossible to impair health at any level without affecting that at other levels. ... We now have armies of specialists studying bits and pieces of the whole as if these were, in fact, separable. In reality, it is impossible to disconnect the threads that bind us into the larger wholes up to that great community of the ecosphere. The environment outside us is also

inside us. ... The act of designing ecologically begins with the awareness that we can never entirely fathom those connections and with the intent to faithfully honor that we cannot fully comprehend and control.[86]

Efficiency is not the only standard for successful ecological design practice. But it is one of the tools toward achieving it. Efficiencies are references for comparison and without them we cannot aspire, being rational animals, to cautiously approach the standard of holistic health, out- and inside us.

To obtain overall efficiency of building complexes which use multiple resources is a somewhat utopian enterprise especially for reasons of the earlier mentioned non-uniformity of dimensional scaling. Use of monetary valuation has the problem of market fluctuations and distortion. Also the pollution impacts of various resource utilizations differ greatly, such as among energy sources. Eventually carbon footprint accounting may be the best candidate for dimensioning.

An overall efficiency equation taking into account all components of a building complex could look somewhat like

$$F = e_{c,1} * f_1 + e_{c,2} * f_2 + e_{c,3} * f_3 + \ldots + e_{c,n} * f_n \ .$$

The $e_{c,x}$ values represent the system component efficiencies. The f_x values represent the fraction of the component amount within the overall amount of the carbon footprint. If weighting because of component preferences is an issue, adjustments of the component fractions within the total would be applied. Weighted importance is value dependent. Design always has been and will be a value dependent activity which puts burdens of responsibility on those who practice it.

This overall efficiency refers to what is measurable. What we build is reality, is physical, and it is irresponsible not to measure as far as we possibly can. This still leaves much which is not measurable and belongs to that wider aspect of holistic health, about which Orr speaks and which must arise out of the overall judgment, resulting in this comprehensive aesthetic, perhaps deepest expressed by "love what surrounds you", whoever or whatever it is.

It is obvious that to address such kind of complexity responsibly is way beyond any individual's capacity and makes the strong case for computer supported collaborative work, as earlier discussed. We need computers for calculating results and collaborative efforts to comprehensively evaluate them. That overall efficiencies will be biased by aspects of design which arise from those domains contributing crucial but non-quantifiable inputs must not deter us. The risk from their influence is much smaller than the much larger one of exclusion.

In a 2007 survey 347 practicing architects gave the following answers about *Leading Factors Influencing Adoption of Green Building Practices*:[87]

> Each of the following factors could influence your likelihood to design green buildings. From your perspective, which three are most likely to increase the extent of your green building practices and procedures?

	%
Client demand	70
Regulatory requirements	59
Rising energy costs	57
Government/industry incentives	38
Personal sense of environmental responsibility	35
Long-Term Return on Investment	30

If sustainability is to be become the main issue of design integration as a matter of course and a compelling issue for architects to influence clients toward it, what is located in position 5, "our personal sense of environmental responsibility", must increase and move into position 1.

An extensive effort is presently gaining momentum in Switzerland undertaken by a group of public and private actors called the 2000 Watt Society, positing 2000 Watt as the eventual limit of total current energy use by every world citizen (8.22).

> This means that today's energy requirements of 6000 Watts per Swiss citizen have to be reduced by a factor of 3. Of the 2000 Watts – the average global need – only 500 Watts should be provided from nonrenewable resources. The remainder should come from renewable energy. These figures are in accordance with the needs of a sustainable society. This vision can only be achieved by contributions from diverse fields of activity: ecological, economical, and social.
>
> Projects which are being executed in the framework of the Basel pilot region project are based on long term considerations and should initiate in a visionary way procedures and technologies which are not yet competitive, but do however hold the potential to reach their ambitious goals.[88]

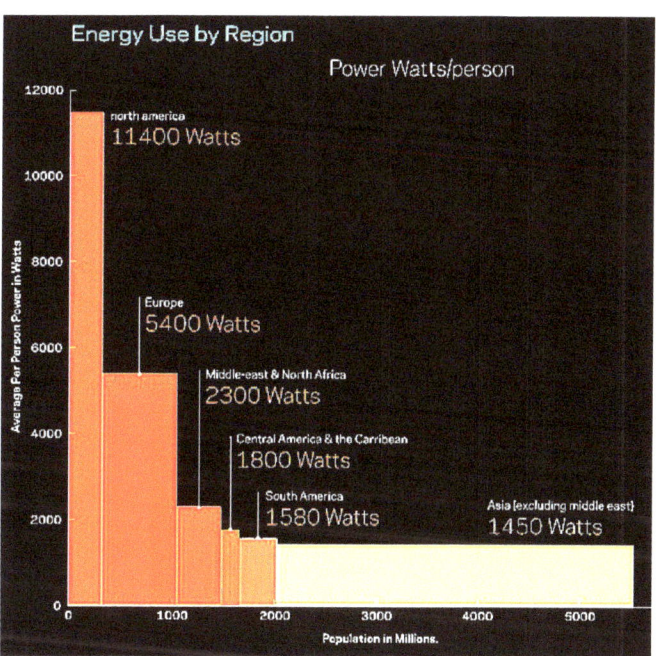

8.22 Present energy use by world regions
(© permission)

To achieve such a drastic reduction requires an enormous change of thinking and acting in all sectors using energy. It encompasses essentially everything we undertake. The region of Basel was chosen for a laboratory to show many efforts in this direction, especially also in planning and architecture. This city offers already many green features. From anywhere in its metropolitan area one can use a trolley car to the central plaza (Marktplatz) of downtown for shopping, such as for fresh farm produce grown in the area around the city (8.23 and 8.24, see also 3.28). The plaza is the main hub of the trolley network which was after World War II fortunately never abandoned in favor of automobiles.

8.22 shows that the energy use per capita in North America is around 11 400 W. With nearly half of this energy used for the production of and consumption in buildings, it is obvious that architectural design must play a central role in what is essentially a fight for human survival.[89]

8.23 Public transport network, Basel
(© permission)

8.24 Street car in Spalenvorstadt, Basel

    The least addressed issue of sustainability in architecture is the recycling of components and materials of buildings having outlasted useful life. It is necessary to see building recycling not only as a problem of design and construction but also as one of society and infrastructure overall. Material and process engineering will play an increasing role. Most materials can be reconstituted and used again, though perhaps for other functions than they had first. Energy efficiency and waste reduction point to approaches which as much as possible facilitate demountable rather than destructive removal of buildings. The earlier mentioned component methods of prefabrication, which typically allow decoupling in joints, may come again into focus, here for other reasons. The comparison with what happens in automobile recycling is helpful. While automobiles, with all their diversity, do not approach the individuality of buildings, they certainly use component materials which satisfy a large number of functional relationships. Therefore, it makes sense to look carefully how far their recycling lets us better understand what eventually has to happen in the recycling of buildings. For over a decade BMW has operated a large recycling program for discarded cars of their brand (8.25).

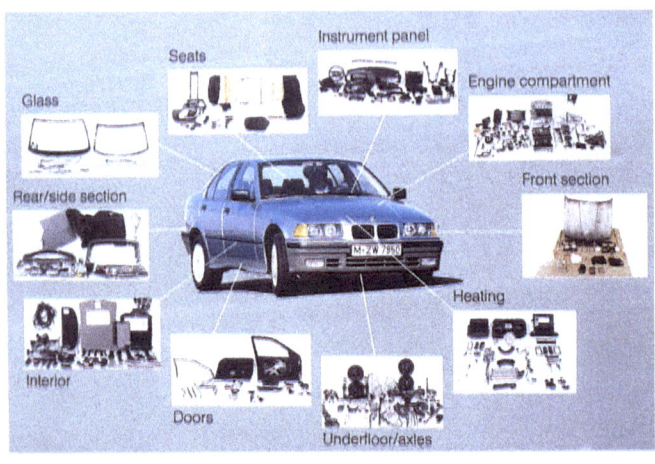

8.25 Automobile recycling at BMW (source)

The European Union demands that by 2015 over 90 percent of all passenger car materials are recycled.[90] I do not endorse the view that the automobile can serve as a model for machine-like buildings to inhabit. But the approaches to production with recycling as criterion are of interest. It should be understood that recycling here means not direct reuse but mainly reconstitution of materials and subsequent reproduction of building components.[91] As in general so in this regard, there is no question that architecture always stood and still stands in the tension between needs for utility and repetition on one hand, and desires for variety and embellishment on the other. The 20th century, more than any other time, broke open the conflicts of this tension and pointed in directions for easing it. Further advances in the mass production of building components and their use for repetitive needs can yield results in environmental and economic waste reduction. As mentioned earlier, all projects of today include many more mass-produced items than we usually recognize. But at the same time, computerized variation in production opens up ways of individuation. Crucial guide posts will be eventually set by our abilities to advance sustainability. We cannot sustain the development of unlimited, freewheeling kinds of Gehry, Libeskind, Hadid, Kohlhaas or Himmelblau designs. Nor can we return to the endless repetitions of many projects in the 1960s and 70s. What is needed is not a push in any extreme way of individuation or mass production but accept both for wherever fitting.

During the past two decades the spirit behind efforts to advance our affinity to nature has at times been called *Biophilia*. Eric Fromm referred to it in 1964 as part of our psychological being:
> I believe that the man choosing progress can find a new unity through the development of all his human forces, which are produced in three orientations. These can be presented separately or together: biophilia, love for humanity and nature, and independence and freedom.[92]

Edward Wilson connected biophilia's etymological meaning "love of living things" with our
> ... innate tendency to focus on life and lifelike processes.[93,94]

Biophilia is not a movement or method. It is our longing for nature which in modern times can be traced back to Jean-Jacques Rousseau who, being a creature of the Enlightenment, was at the same time a severe critic of the emerging over-reliance on the power of reason versus nature. Biophilia has its grounding and actionable direction in two centuries of research and understanding in the various fields of ecology.

Ecological concerns and concepts in the design of built environments are nothing new either. Some were realized, often spurring unexpected innovations. The garden city movement in Europe and the United States influenced positively the planning of many large and small communities throughout the past century. The importance of daylight and fresh air in buildings was intuitively understood since real estate speculation had produced deplorable housing densities with "courtyards" which prevented sunshine from ever reaching the windows of the lower levels of multistory apartment buildings. For decades now we have standards for minimum lighting and fresh air ventilation rates in buildings.[95] And, it has become recognized that greening within buildings has beneficial effects on mind and body. Indoor planting, for example, in atriums of commercial buildings and hotels, is now quite common. There is a wealth of information available on the relationship of ecologically sound environments and human welfare.[96]

When biophilia is taken to mean the affectionate and motivating attitude toward our natural environment and the life in all of creation, I agree. When it is taken, however, to mean a necessity of adhering to forms because they are derived in one way or another from nature, I do not. Nonhuman, organic nature is *instinctive,* and its shapes and influences arise from these instincts. But human nature is *rational* as well as instinctive. We are able to reason far beyond instincts. From this point of view, I believe that biophilia should not try to suggest anything to human activity, in design or otherwise, which does not acknowledge our freedom of choice derived from our being rational. Nature related forms do not guarantee a priori higher quality. When we agree that we have to build at all, because human activities require shelter, there are countless instances in which rational decisions to use artificial shapes and materials lead to environmentally more preferable solutions than nature related ones.[97] Therefore, many things we develop by design do not resemble natural forms.

In other words, what nature beyond us does is different from what we do, which shall not mean that we cannot learn from it. But we should refrain from emulating nature unless our being rational has the chance to judge the value of the results thoroughly. The design component of a building's floor plan is largely not a derivation from instinctive but rational thinking. Rectangularity is usually an ecologically preferred choice, as lending itself to more efficient fit of spaces. The I-beam of steel, which does not exist in nature, is for certain applications and with regard to ecological concerns a better shape than those we may find in nature. Heat pumps are based on processes in nature, but the choice of its refrigerant, because of its condensation and evaporation characteristics under pressure, is being applied in this particular way because of rational design and engineering not instinct. So it is with modern plumbing systems or many other modern inventions in architecture and other fields, such as medicine. With regard to the appearance of buildings and components Janine Benyus writes that

> This listening [looking at nature] in order to emulate is an inherently biophilic process, one that brings us into a close intimacy with our biological mentors. But the final design that comes from biomimicry process may or may not look organic or visually resemble the organism from which the lesson came. ...
>
> This focus on function points to a key difference between buildings that mimic nature to "look as nature" for decorative or symbolic purposes and those that mimic nature to "do as nature does" in order to enhance functional performance.[98]

I agree. But both, what "looks as nature" and what "does as nature", may have justification. Much of art 'looks' not 'does' and much in architecture is beautiful because it 'looks' not 'does'; though in a passive sense it 'does' because of influencing our aesthetic judgment.

Let's consider an example often cited to be organic: Fallingwater by Frank Lloyd Wright (8.26). Its placement and form are stunning and innovative. But what of it is organic? No biological form grows nor looks like it. It is not even integrated in any special way with nature. It sits on top of the water fall. Its form highly contrasts with its natural environment. Most buildings do so more or less. Now, one may say that the floor plan is organic in the sense an organ should perform, being supportive of the overall life within and around the building. But, this obviously is a much broader definition than what visual form implies. All well designed buildings must satisfy this fundamental condition, whether they display such so-called organic or biophilic shapes or not.

8.26 Fallingwater, Kaufmann Residence, Fayette County, PA

At a time when efforts toward sustainability are of central concern, buildings whether they 'look like nature' or anything else must become exceptions when sustainably inefficient. There may always be architectural projects of this kind. A prime example is the Sydney Opera House.[99] Let it be clearly understood that, as far as our present ecological outlook goes, the future possibility of such architecture must be bought on balance by high sustainability efficiency of the very much larger rest of architecture coming about. This latter line of thought raises an issue which Stephen Kieran brings into focus, writing that LEED

> ... even with all its enormous influence and benefits, sanctions architecture by addition, giving points for good behavior, but no points for beauty. LEED has added and abetted the design of a lot of really ugly buildings by a generation of point-counting A-students. LEED "bling" is here among us and threatens the very soul of what environmental design is attempting to accomplish, because it is not yet aesthetic.[100]

There never will be an environmental aesthetic, as there is no Roman or Baroque aesthetic or functional aesthetic, etc. – viewed as an inherent property of something, that is, being more than a reference to what we may or may not like in a particular epoch or area of contemplation. As discussed in Chapter 4, the aesthetic is the result of subjective judgment of individuals encountering the properties of things, at which they arrive with rationale and instinct, and judge them to be pleasant or not. Neither LEED nor any other system can prescribe the aesthetic a priori. All attempts to do so fail. As discussed, the aesthetic is not an extra. It arises from everything we do. On the other hand, we need ways to evaluate all kinds of aspects, such as what aesthetic opinions people may have and what LEED aims to do: assessing efforts toward sustainability. The latter contributes to a comprehensive aesthetic judgment of an architectural object. From this point of view, I believe that there is no evidence that buildings rated by LEED are less beautiful than others, considering what is built overall.[101]

To conclude. Recently 'evidence-based' is an adjective which seeks to attach itself to design work. Kirk Hamilton and David Watkins write that

> Evidence-based design is a process for the conscientious, explicit, and judicious use of current best evidence from research and practice in making critical decisions, together with an informed client, about the design of each individual and unique project.[102]

Evidence has been a potent resource since architects thought about the impact of decisions in practice. The problem is that architectural education programs do not sufficiently encourage an integrated approach where it counts most, that is, in the design studio. Even when this happens, what is learned as evidence, during these formative years and afterwards, is later often neglected. There is also the problem that consultants, who are major sources of evidence, are not engaged early enough to influence projects when still in the fluid stages.

When using not very common terminology, such as 'evidence-based', we must contemplate whether and how it advances our understanding. 'Evidence-based' points to our awareness of the present knowledge in the profession and the willingness to use it, very much like 'performance-oriented' implies. Both refer to underpinning functional concerns with experiential proof. How far such functional relationships can be traced and evaluated plays a crucial role. They require trade-offs because of functional interdependencies.

Regarding evidence, I return another time to my pet example, sun shading. For a long time it has been known that exterior shading devices can over the years save more than what they cost (because of reduced heat gains and improved daylighting). This is the case still now when we have highly improved shading properties of glazing compared to a few decades ago. Why, one must ask, are there only so few buildings in this country using such shading devices, which also make many facades look more interesting? One can ask such questions about many issues to which some of my earlier chapters allude or which the book, containing the above given quote, addresses.

The central question "From where do and should design ideas arise?" is too often not clearly addressed. It must arise in the first place from that for which buildings serve. To make this possible, designers must, to paraphrase Louis Kahn, listen to what every project wants to be and especially for what it wants to be – what the driving design factors of purpose, context and realization are. Many helpful inspirations are derived from precedents in building type documentation and post-occupancy research. Comprehensive information modeling will be able to support all decisions about our being part of overall existence through architecture. Eddy Krygiel and Bradley Nies write that

> Parametric modeling will go well beyond mapping relationships between objects and assemblies. Both model and designer will have knowledge of climate and region. The model will know its building type, insulation values, solar heat gain coefficients, and impact on the socioeconomic environment it resides within. It will inform the design team with regard to upstream impacts and downstream consequences of their choices.

And,

> The relatively recent emergence of various models of [such comprehensive] integration suggests a promising convergence of thought in distinct yet related disciplines. We might now have the information and tools required to achieve integration in the technological sense, but we must recover our understanding of resource consumption, global regard for the environment and social equity.[103]

I am not so sure that mankind ever had such a broad understanding to be recovered, and certainly not one with the urgency required now. What develops presently as the most important meaning of our time is the need to balance what we want and what is possible on this planet with billions more people wanting what those in industrialized nations already have. This means for architecture and planning to combine the advantages of collaborative building information modeling with our reasoning toward sustainability and to become exemplary for those who are only at the beginning of the steep learning curve which we hopefully have climbed already to some extent.

The fundamental relationship of architecture to its wider context, though in a quite different direction, has also been the focus of Christopher Alexander's recent efforts. Following his work on design patterns he concentrates on elucidating the cosmic order for which architecture is in one sense a welcome part and in another an imposition. He views positive aspects of wholeness as living structure in which centers are more or less the nodes of beneficial connectedness prompting our attention. Living structure comes about because of the "life" these centers have and generate among themselves. He lists five assertions about centers:

1. Centers arise in space.
2. Each center is created by a configuration of other centers.
3. Each center has a certain life or intensity. ...
4. The life or intensity of one center is increased or decreased according to the position and intensity of other nearby centers. ...
5. The centers are the fundamental elements of the wholeness, and the degree of life of any given part of space depends entirely on the presence and structure of the centers there.[104]

I derive from his writing that Alexander means with "center" a member of a set of components in a limited space and all of these components are connected with each other. With some components we have or develop a particularly intense positive relationship. We highly value them for whatever reasons. These are the centers which have more "life" for us than the others.

Doubt and even opposition is justified at the point where Alexander defines a principle which bridges the gap between the objective and the subjective. He writes:
> I have slowly become certain that the relatedness we experience in things with living structure is not a psychological trick or an illusion. What we experience as a link is, I am certain, real. The apparently self-like presence which I seem to see in the world – in the column bracket, in the tree stump, in the water of the pond, in the scudding clouds – is an actual thing *in* the thing. It is not a mental construct.[105]

And this "self-like presence",
> This "something" needs a name. ...
> Because it is so personal, and because it is also one thing, and because it is so related to all that is, so vital – I must coin a phrase for it. I call it "I". ...[106]
> The I-like substance is visible in things which have life, according to the degree of living structure which exists. I do not make it happen by being there. It is not subjective. It is there. Thus the I is not something imagined, but an actual thing, in matter itself.[107]

The link is real. But it is an active relationship of us with the object, not of the object with us, as Alexander often implies – unless it is similar to us at least to the extent that it can initiate such a relationship and respond accordingly.[108] What I perceive of something beyond myself is my mental construct, my representation of the object and this is not what we call or should call "I". Our nature is being people, objects with subjective minds; being apart from other objects. My empathy may arise relating to the other, be it a human, animal, plant or stone. This empathy is not in the "I" of the other but in me – not *of* the other but *about* it.

There is a capacity common to mind and matter, and in everything: energy. We can measure its incremental impact but do not know its initial origin nor its ultimate future, neither its smallest amount nor its largest. It flows from here to there and creates what we can observe and design. It is what we call nature in untold variations. It manifests itself in forms which we also call objects. Somehow along its uncountable paths it brought about mind, the interrelations of matter in brains which we call states of consciousness and awareness. One of its most amazing results is subjectivity, the possibility of objects who have it – here us – to relate and interact with other objects in responsible and forward looking ways. As discussed, some of these involvements are instinctive, some are deliberate; together they are aesthetic in the comprehensive sense. We have energy as our subjectivity, let it flow and seek the centers of life in architecture and elsewhere. The very human part of this process and its result is what we call understanding and, if it is about something specific, we call it meaning.

Like all our activities, design impacts the physical world with regard to utilization of material and energy, whereby energy is in essence material producing work and change. Some of the materials we use exist in abundance. Others do not, including many of those which we can transform for special purposes. We are not running out of clay to produce brick or silica to produce glass but we eventually will run out of coal, petroleum and gas to produce building components, assemble them and operate the resulting structures. Through production, assembly and operation and eventual disposal we often impact the environment negatively. We pollute because of waste. In order to sustain human survival in decent conditions we must reduce and in the long run stop the depletion of these limited resources by means of conservation, recycling and regeneration.

That such efforts cannot be achieved in an unregulated free market system is evident as preoccupation with profit maximization defies avoidance of resource depletion and favors externalization of unfavorable impacts. A well-based and comprehensive carbon footprint tax would go a long way toward sustainability as it would pertain to every process of production and operation. The tax proceeds could be used to advance development of renewable production, and to subsidize studies for conservation of nonrenewables and application of renewables. To emphasize, the earlier and the more intensive such studies are undertaken, the more effective they are in reducing design time, lowering building costs and avoiding resource depletion.

Our main contribution to the present Zeitgeist can be built on the enormous advantages which virtuality in design affords us toward sustainability. But at the very center of architectural design and any related theory must not be any a priori procedures for achievement, be they the application of fixed rules of programming or shape making by computer. Our problems in architecture today are not architectural in the sense of how to plan and build. We are not short of ways to find adequate design and construction methods or devise new ones. Our challenges are in understanding the human needs and desires of our time as foundation of design thinking. They are in the definitions of what is to be achieved for the comprehensive wellbeing of society and responsiveness to environmental concerns worldwide. We must bring the gained understanding in the public arena, especially through the many opportunities we as professionals have to inform via news channels or at city halls; letting it be known that architecture and all the built environment is, as David Orr writes, a form of education for all of us.[109] Then our decision making and that of the public will arise out of a well-based ecological premise. The ethics of the approach will be reflected in our overall understanding and its results. Our forms will follow sustainability. What sustainability means to us in this critical undertaking and which consequences we draw for architectural design will determine how history will look at what we contributed to our time.

There is an issue on which we touched at various times but never in any depth it deserves. I bring it to the fore here another time, more as reminder of importance than for resolution which I believe it ultimately defies. It is the phenomenon of the ideal which has its grounding in the understanding of idea in perfection – something being perfect only in conceptual thought not in existential reality.[110] As I frequently asserted, meaning is particular understanding derived from thinking. From impression and for expression we want to understand things as well as we possibly can in their ideal state as things in themselves. For meaning to be embedded in any physical form of design, such as in architecture, it must pass the threshold from being wanted to being possible, from being mental to being physical. We usually think the ideal but eventually have to settle for the practicable. Not that the ideal does not exist, but its appearance to us in reality and in our mind can only approach it, not show it in full. It can only be thought while being prompted by certain relational properties which we conceive as beyond its observable domain. These properties point to the wider meaning of the object, from its worldly being to its spiritual value. Here, the aesthetic – as the outcome of emotional and rational judgment – is at its highest level of impression. This is similarly so in design with expression and creativity most strongly relying on the inspiration of the designer and on his or her judgment, not only about the work as such but about its best possible effect on those who observe and live with it. Among the design properties we may find are responses to performance requirements, such as those relating to comfort conditions or resource conservation. Others may be features of simplicity or complexity enticing clarity or richness in perception. Again others may provide familiarity out of historical or other cultural notions. Most illustrations in this volume yield more or less understanding of such practicality. But often the ideal shines through in the ways these features play their role. What Joseph Rykwert wrote five decades ago very well sums up also my view:

> All the elements of our work: pavement, threshold, door, window, wall roof, house, factory, school – all these have their poetry; and it is poetry we must learn to draw from the programmes our clients hand us. Not to impose it by cheep melodramatisation, but to spell it from the common place elements which we fit together.[111]

Whether we gain impressions as observers or give expressions as designers, the things which we encounter evoke their meaning, their aesthetic and their poetry. I trust that the final two examples with their very different themes will serve as confirmations.

8.27 Law Library, University of Michigan, Ann Arbor, MI

The underground law library at the University of Michigan, by Gunnar Birkerts, is wrapped around a three-story lightwell. To study books by daylight with the possibility to look outside goes far beyond reading comfortably and provides an enjoyable experience not otherwise easily had.

8.28 Chapel at MIT, Cambridge, MA (© permission)

In the chapel of the Massachusetts Institute of Technology, by Eero Saarinen, one is drawn to the elevated marble block, the altar. A glittering metal filigree, by Harry Bertoia, extends to the circular skylight above, letting us grasp that there are powers to contemplate beyond our own world.

Notes and Bibliography of Chapter 2

1   Many of the bibliographic references on philosophy which I give in the course of our discussions have to do in one way or another with the issues the twelve terms represent. The following references point to works which I found particularly helpful as introductory background: Immanuel Kant (1783/1950) *Prolegomena to Any Future Metaphysics*, Bobbs-Merrill Education Publishing; Kant, Immanuel (1787/1998) *Critique of Pure Reason*, Paul Guyer and Allen W. Wood, trans. and ed., Cambridge University Press; Magee, Bryan (1988) *The Great Philosophers: an Introduction to Western Philosophy,* Oxford University Press; (1995) *The Cambridge Dictionary of Philosophy*, Robert Audi, ed., Cambridge University Press; Searle, John (1998) *Mind, Language and Society: philosophy in the real world*, Basic Books; Rescher, Nicholas (2000) *Realistic pragmatism: an introduction to pragmatic philosophy,* State University of New York Press; Chalmers, David J. (2002) *Philosophy of Mind: Classical and Contemporary Readings*, Oxford University Press.

2   Understanding has various connotations. They are usually grasped from the context in which the understanding arises. I suggest, for the present, to consider it an interpretation derived from something or communicated about something.

3   Descartes, René (1641/1901) *Meditations on First Philosophy,* John Veitch trans.1901, Meditation II, Section 8. http://www.classicallibrary.org/descartes/meditations/5.htm .

4   Ibid, Meditation VI, Section 9, p. 45:
"... because, on the one hand, I have a clear and distinct idea of myself, in as far as I am only a thinking and unextended thing, and as, on the other hand, I possess a distinct idea of body, in as far as it is only an extended and unthinking thing, it is certain that I, that is, my mind, by which I am what I am, is entirely and truly distinct from my body, and may exist without it."

5   Locke, John (1706) *An essay concerning human understanding.* London: Awnsham and Churchill at al., Book 1, Chapter 1, § 8, page 4.
Eighteenth Century Collections Online. From Gale. University of Michigan. 7 Sept. 2010:
http://find.galegroup.com.proxy.lib.umich.edu/ecco/infomark.do?&contentSet=ECCOArticles&type=multipage&tabID=T001&prodId=ECCO&docId=CW117467773&source=gale&userGroupName=umuser&version=1.0&docLevel=FASCIMILE .

6   Ibid, Book 2, Chapter 1, § 4 and 5, page 52.

7   Hobbes, Thomas (1651) *Leviathan, or, The Matter, Form, and Power of a Common-Wealth Ecclesiastical and Civil*, London, Chapter 3, 8-10, from EEBO, Early English Books on Line :
http://eebo.chadwyck.com.proxy.lib.umich.edu/search/full_rec?ACTION=ByID&SOURCE=pgimages.cfg&ID=V62954 .
For a modern version see Hobbes, Thomas, 1588-1679.: *Leviathan* [electronic resource] / Thomas Hobbes ; edited with an introduction and notes by J.C.A. Gaskin, Oxford : Oxford University Press, 1998, lv, 508 pages.

8   Locke (1706) *An essay concerning human understanding,* Book 2, Chapter 12, § 2, 96.

9   Ibid, Chapter 11, § 2, 90.

10   Ibid, Book 2, Chapter 8, § 8, 74.

11 Hume, David (1748) "*Of the* Idea of Power *or necessary* Connection" in *Philosophical Essays concerning Human Understanding. By the Author of the Essays Moral and Political*, London: A. Millar, Essay VII, 102.
See http://find.galegroup.com.proxy.lib.umich.edu/ecco/infomark.do?&contentSet=ECCOArticles&type=multipage&tabID=T001&prodId=ECCO&docId=CW3319914515&source=gale&userGroupName=umuser&version=1.0&docLevel=FASCIMILE .
For a modern language version see
http://library.nlx.com.proxy.lib.umich.edu/xtf/view?docId=hume/hume.05.xml;chunk.id=div.britphil.v37.2;toc.depth=1;toc.id=div.britphil.v37.1;brand=default;query= .

12 Ibid, Essay IV, 57 and 58.

13 Ibid, 58 and 59.

14 Kant, Immanuel (1783/1950) *Prolegomena to Any Future Metaphysics*, § 14, Indianapolis: Bobbs-Merrill Educational Publishing, 42, See also § 32, § 57 and § 59 (42-44, 62, 102 and 110).

15 See, for example, Kant, Immanuel (1787/1998) *Critique of Pure Reason*, Paul Guyer and Allen W. Wood trans. and eds., Cambridge: Cambridge University Press, 347. Kant's adoption of the term noumenon in this sense has been contested especially by Arthur Schopenhauer who emphasized that it meant by the Ancients simply "what is thought", not what exists in a thing but cannot be perceived by our senses.
 (http://en.wikipedia.org/wiki/Noumena#Schopenhauer.27s_critique).

16 Wittgenstein, Ludwig (1953) *Philosophical Investigations*, § 580, G. E. M. Anscombe trans., New York: The Macmillan Company.

17 Moore, George E. (1903/1951) "The Refutation of Idealism" in *Philosphical Studies*, London: The Humanities Press, 22.

18 Ibid, 26.

19 Merleau-Ponti, Maurice (1962) *Phenomenology of Perception*, Routledge & Kegan Paul, London, 138-139.

20 Searle, John (1983) *Intentionality*, Cambridge: Cambridge University Press, 1.

21 Rescher, Nicholas (2000) *Realistic Pragmatism,* State University of New York Press, Albany, 2000, 126-127.

22 Rescher, Nicholas (1973) *Conceptual Idealism*, Blackwell, Oxford, 169.

23 Searle, John (1997) "Does the Real World Exist?" in *Realism/Antirealism and Epistemology*, Christopher B. Kulp ed., Lanham MD: Rowman & Littlefield, Lanham, MD, p. 19-20 , 24 and 26.

24 Kant, *Prolegomena*, 38.

25 Putnam, Henry (1990) *Realism with a Human Face*, Cambridge, MA: Harvard University Press, 261.

26 Gardner, Sebastian (1999) *Kant and the Critique of Pure Reason*, London: Routledge, 42.

27 "... in the process of understanding, the intellectual impression received in the potential

intellect is that *whereby* we understand [quo], as the impression of colour in the eye is not that *which* is seen, but that *whereby* we see [quo]. On the other hand, that *which* is understood [quod] is the nature (ratio) of things existing outside the soul, as also it is things existing outside the soul that are seen with the bodily sight: for to this end were arts and sciences invented, that things might be known in their natures (naturis)." From "Confutation of the Arguments which seem to prove the Unity of the Potential Intellect" in Thomas Aquinas (1264/1905) *Of God and His Creatures,* An Annotated Translation (with some Abridgement) of the Summa Contra Gentiles by Joseph Rickaby et al, London: Burns and Oates, Book 2, Section 75 (Reply to Argument 2). (http://www2.nd.edu/Departments/Maritain/etext/gc2_75.htm) by Jacques Maritain Center. See also "objectum quo" in (1995) *The Cambridge Dictionary of Philosophy*, Robert Audi ed., Cambridge, UK: Cambridge University Press, 541.

28 Kant, *Critique of Pure Reason*, 136.

29 Ibid, 224.

30 Kant Immanuel (1790/2000) *Critique of the Power of Judgment,* Paul Guyer and Eric Matthews trans. and ed., Cambridge, UK: Cambridge University Press, 26.

31 Jackendoff, Ray (1990) *Semantic Structures.* Cambridge, MA: MIT Press, 7.

32 Gillett, Grant R. and John McMillan (2001) *Consciousness and Intentionality.* Amsterdam: John Benjamins Publishing Company, 46.

33 Price, Henry H. (1953) *Thinking and Experience*, London: Hutchinson House, 13.

34 The process of ostensive learning is perhaps best observed by looking at the way children intuit first experiences and accept them without reflection before asking "What is it?" and "What is the name?". We accept names of things as ostensively given – arbitrarily associated first, then passed down by tradition. See http://en.wikipedia.org/wiki/Ostension .

35 We will address later further aspects of generic and specific concepts.

36 Kant, *Critique of Pure Reason*, 172.

37 Kant, *Prolegomena*, § 13, p. 38.

38 Much work has been done on how original concepts come about, especially in the mental development of children. Classic texts in this field are by Jean Piaget, Jerome S. Bruner and Robert Kegan. For a collection of major essays on the subject see Margolis, Eric and Stephen Laurence, ed. (1999) *Concepts: core readings,* Cambridge, MA: MIT Press. http://cognet.mit.edu/library/books/view?isbn=0262631938 .

39 I hold that the color red is a concept. It is part of a mental representation of an object which comes about through recognition. According to Kant, *Critique of Pure Reason,* 232 and 193-194, "All cognition requires a concept, however imperfect or obscure it may be; …" and "… intuitions without concepts are blind." 'Red' is certainly an intuition and concept.

40 Kant, *Critique of Pure Reason*, 211.

41 Ibid, 232.

42 Ibid, 249.

43 For Kant's definition of transcendental idealism see *Critique of Pure Reason*, ibid, 426. And,

44 Kant, *Prolegomena*, § 13, 41.

45 For further understanding of the issues, we just discussed, I quote in the following some more of Kant's explanations with the page numbers in parentheses referring to Kant (1787/1998) *Critique of Pure Reason*.

> The effect of an object on the capacity for representation, so far as we are affected by it, is *sensation*. That intuition which is related to the object is called *empirical*. The undetermined object of an empirical intuition is called *appearance*. (155).

Kant uses in this quote 'object' first for something in physical nature and then for its mental counterpart in appearance. While one may say that something can be an object of consideration whether it is physical or mental, I use for our context 'object' for what I perceive in physical nature. A mental object I name as such.

> By *synthesis* in the most general sense, however, I understand the action of putting different representations together with each other and comprehending their manifoldness in one cognition [one representation]. (210).
> The synthesis of representations rests on the imagination, ... (281).
> The principle of the synthetic unity of apperception is the supreme principle of all use of the understanding. (248, title of § 17).

The resulting manifold, which Kant also calls the synthetic unity of consciousness,

> ... says nothing more than that all *my* representations in any given intuition must stand under the condition under which alone I can ascribe them to the identical self as *my* representations, and thus can grasp them together, as synthetically combined in an apperception, through the general expression *I think*. (249-250).

Imagination is the thinking process which recalls existing concepts and brings them together with new appearances. Understanding is the thinking process which uses generic concepts as rules for decisions on the nature of presently acquired, additional concepts.

> If the understanding in general is explained as the faculty of rules, then the power of judgment is the faculty of *subsuming* under rules, i.e., of determining whether something stands under a given rule or not. (268).
> Objects are ... given to us by means of sensibility, and it alone affords us intuitions; but they are *thought* through the understanding, and from it arise concepts. (155).

46 Magee, Bryan (1997) *The Philosophy of Schopenhauer,* Oxford: Clarendon Press, 84.

47 Searle, John (1998) "Meaning, Communication and Representation" in *Pragmatics: critical concepts*, vol 5, Asa Kasher ed., London: Routledge, 11.

48 Paradoxically, though we encounter observable objects directly, it is not at all easy for us to conceptualize what they are as such without using relational property descriptions. We do not perceive water as H_2O or the color red as a certain wave length of light. These identifiers are only names of our concepts which we attribute.

49 Kant, *Critique of Pure Reason*, 321.

50 Rapoport, Amos (2001) "Architectural Anthropology or Environment-Behavior Studies?" in *Architectural Anthropology*, Mari-Jose Amerlinck (ed.), Westport, CN: Bergin & Garvey, 28.

51 I believe the term 'environment-behavior studies', for the now well established field it designates, is an inadequate one, particularly also when one considers the interactions it

involves. 'Environment-people studies' would more clearly indicate what this overlapping enterprise has as its objective. Such studies go beyond environment-behavior interaction. People are more than behavior.

52 The American Heritage® Dictionary of the English Language, Fourth Edition, 2000, Houghton Mifflin Company, 485. Just above this quote, however, it gives an example for proving the point of confusion: "A flashing yellow light denotes caution". The name "a yellow flashing light" and its activity are denotations (facts). It connotes "caution" (meaning).
See http://www.yourdictionary.com/denote .

53 Garza-Cuarón, Beatriz (1991) *Connotation and Meaning*, Charlotte Broad (trans), Berlin: Mouton de Gruyter, 119.

54 Chandler, Daniel (2002) *Semiotics: The Basics*, London: Routledge, 141.

55 Goodman, Nelson (1985) "How Buildings Mean", Critical Inquiry, Vol. 11, No. 4 (June), pp. 642-653.

56 Ibid, 644-645.

57 Rossi, Aldo (1981) *A Scientific Autobiography*, Cambridge, MA: MIT Press, 19.

58 Sullivan, Louis H. (1896/1979) "The Tall Building Artistically Considered" in *Kindergarten Chats and Other Writings,* New York: Dover Publications, 208. Sullivan's text says: "It is the pervading law of all things organic, and inorganic, ... that form ever follows function."

59 Brand, Stewart (1994) *How Buildings Learn: What happens after they 're built.* New York: Viking, Penguin Books, 3. In 1943 Winston Churchill said "We shape our buildings, and afterwards they shape us". He spoke about rebuilding the war damaged Parliament Building the same as it was before (Winston Churchill-WSC, 28 October 1943 to the House of Commons; source www.winstonchurchill.org) .

60 Nasar, Jack L., Arthur E. Stamps III, Kazunori Hanyu (2005) "Form and function in public buildings" in *Journal of Environmental Psychology*, 25, 164–165,
http://facweb.knowlton.ohio-state.edu/JNasar/crpinfo/research/FormandFunctionJEP2005.pdf .

61 Ibid, 165

62 My design project for graduation, over half a century ago at the Technical University in Berlin, was a Lutheran Church on a site in Hamburg. I based its design symbolically on the constitutive sequence of Christian worship: hearing for belief, baptism for acceptance and communion for salvation. Non-rectangular fit in circular succession lent itself well for the spatial arrangement.

 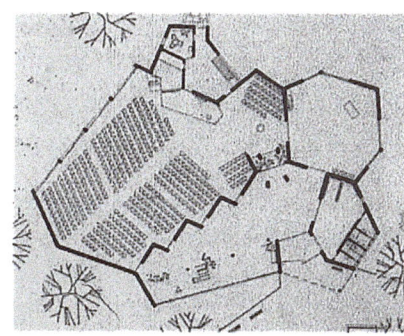

63 Nylund, Kjell and Peter Stürzebecher (1986) *Das Wohnregal im Schnittpunkt der Linien*, Berlin: Konopka Verlag, 65 pp. Although projects with considerable spatial variability in use have been built over several decades of housing, only a few and rather early studies about their success have been made, mainly in Germany and Scandinavia. For examples, see Werner, Jörg (1977*) Anpassbarer Wohnbau*, Munich: Callvey Verlag. Usually higher than typical front-end costs are an impediment. It is very likely that, when needs change, people rather move to places which have more suitable layouts rather than bear increased expenditures for built-in variability, felt throughout the amortization of front-end costs. See also http://www.afewthoughts.co.uk/flexiblehousing/browse.php?action=all&data=all&order=title&dir=ASC&message=all%20projects&messagead=alphabetically%20ordered%20by%20name .

64 Steward Brand gives in (1994) *How Buildings Learn: what happens after they 're built* many revealing examples of not how buildings 'learn' but how designers and non-designers find more or less innovative ways to adjust buildings according to their changing needs over time.

65 Venturi, Robert (1966) *Complexity and contradiction in architecture*. New York: Museum of Modern Art, 16.

66 Ibid.

67 Venturi, Robert and Denise Scott Brown (2004*) Architecture as signs and systems*, Cambridge, MA: Harvard University Press, 212.

68 Mannerism is variously defined as "habitual peculiarity", "adherence to a particular style", "idiosyncratic behavior", "artificial habit", etc.

69 Venturi, *Architecture as signs and systems*, ibid 214.

70 Ibid, 74.

71 With regard to the latter rhetorical question: It is simply a matter of taking care of a rather long ceiling span for 13th century construction, especially by the poor Dominican order and its congregation. For more on this issue see Richard A. Sundt, "The Jacobin Church of Toulouse and the Origin of its Double-Nave Plan", Art Bulletin, 71:2 (1989: June), 185-207.

72 Weber, Ralph (1994) "The Myth of Meaningful Forms" in Michael H. Mitias (ed.) *Philosophy and Architecture*, Amsterdam: Rodopi, 114.

Notes and Bibliography of Chapter 3

1 It is an English physician, Henry Stubbs, who is credited to have characterized a little earlier than Locke's essay the symptoms of illness as signs. See http://en.wikipedia.org/wiki/Semiotics .

2   Locke, John (1706) *An essay concerning humane understanding.* Fifth edition, London, Book IV, Chapter 21, § 4, p. 604. From Eighteenth Century Collections Online. Gale Group.

3 Chandler, Daniel (1994): S*emiotics for Beginners* [WWW document] http://www.aber.ac.uk/media/Documents/S4B/semiotic.html (at the beginning of the chapter on "Modality and Representation"). This work, with a too modest title, is a concentrated introduction to semiotics with extensive bibliography.

4 Peirce, Charles (1932) *Collected Papers of Charles Sanders Peirce*, Charles Hartshorne and Paul Weiss ed., Vol. V, 4th Printing, section 5.448 (note), 302.

5 *Ibid*, Vol. II, 4th Printing, section 2.274, 156.

6 Hausman, Carl R. (1993) *Charles S. Peirce's Evolutionary Philosophy,* Cambridge University Press, 68.

7 These triangular arrangements most likely originated with one given by Ogden C.K. at al (1923) *The Meaning of Meaning*, New York: Harcourt, Brace & Company, 11; also found confusing by Eco, Umberto (1976) *A Theory of Semiotics,* Bloomington: University of Indiana Press, 59-60, who then, however, introduces himself some complicating and confusing aspects. See also http://frank.mtsu.edu/~jcomas/burke/ogden.html .

8 Morris, Charles (1938/1971) *Writings on the General Theory of Signs*, The Hague: Mouton, 19, characterizes interpretants as "the takings–account-of". They take account of what happens to our semiotic understanding toward a final representation of an object in our mind.

9 Peirce, *Collected Papers of Charles Sanders Peirce*, Vol. V, 4th Printing, 5.407, 268.

10 Rescher, Nicholas (2000) *Realistic Pragmatism,* State University of New York Press, Albany, 53. This book is a very helpful introduction to pragmatism. One of the chapters contains a clear juxtaposition of what Rescher calls "metaphysical realism and the pragmatic basis of objectivity" from which I quoted earlier (Chapter 2, Note 21).

11 Rescher, Nicholas (2002) "Knowledge of the truth in pragmatic perspective" in *Hilary Putnam: Pragmatism and Realism,* James Conant and Urszula M. Zeglen ed., London: Routledge, London, 70.

12 Ibid, 74.

13 Ibid, 75.

14 Ibid 81-82.

15 Peirce, *Collected Papers of Charles Sanders Peirce*, Vol. II, idem, Chapter 3, § 1-6, 156-173. Although Peirce views signs generally as mental representations, he describes them as we believe they are in reality.

16 Ibid, section 2.230, 136.

17 *Critical Path Method*, Wikipedia. http://en.wikipedia.org/wiki/Critical_path_method .

18 Peirce, *Collected Papers of Charles Sanders Peirce*, Vol. V, § 2, 4.

19 Cassirer, Ernst (1944) *An Assay on Man*, Yale University Press, New Haven, 23-26.

20 Cassirer, Ernst (1923/1955) *The Philosophy of Symbolic Forms*, Yale University Press, RalphManheim trans., New Haven, Vol. 1, 106.

21 Ibid, 110.

22 Beneveniste, Emile (1985) "The Semiology of Language" in *Semiotics: an introductory anthology*, edited with introductions by Robert E. Innis, Bloomington: Indiana University Press, 1985, 239.

23 Lévi-Strauss, Claude (1972): *Structural Anthropology*, Claire Jacobson and Brooke Grundfest Schoepf trans., Harmondsworth: Penguin, p. 48.

24 Today mostly the term syntax is used. Charles Morris uses since 1938 the term syntactics as a field of inquiry which I find fitting better with the other two (Morris, Charles (1971) *Writings on the General Theory of Signs,* The Hague: Mouton). See also in Miriam-Webster online: http://www.m-w.com/dictionary/syntactics. It helps to understand the origin of the term Syntax. It was derived from the combination of the Greek expressions syn- (together) and taxis (arrangement). For more, see "Syntax" in Wikipedia http://en.wikipedia.org/wiki/Syntax#Syntactic_terms .

25 Morris, Charles (1946) *Signs, Language and Behavior,* New York: Prentice-Hall, 219, 352-355. He had defined pragmatics in 1938 (in *Foundations of the Theory of Signs*) as the study of "the relation of signs to their interpreters" (repeated in *Writings on the General Theory of Signs*, 43).

26 Rapoport, Amos (1982) *The Meaning of the Built Environment*, Beverly Hills, CA: Sage Publications, 38-9. Probably no one has to date written and referenced more work about pragmatics in the built environment than Rapoport. I highly recommend this book and his other publications for further studies.

27 *EDRA*, Proceedings of the annual Environmental Design Research Association Conference, Raleigh, N.C., 1969–present.

28 Blumer, Herbert (1969) *Symbolic Interactionism: Perspective and Method.* Englewood Cliffs, NJ: Prentice-Hall, 2 (my formalization).

29 Rapoport, *The Meaning of the Built Environment,* 57.

30 Moore, Keith Diaz (2000) "Introduction" in *Culture – Meaning – Architecture: Critical Reflections on the work of Amos Rapoport,* K. D. Moore (ed.), Aldershot, England: Ashgate, 17.

31 Groat, Linda N., "The Architect as Artist or Scientist?: A Modest Proposal for the Architect-as-Cultivator", ibid, 127-149.

32 Heidegger, Martin (1954/2000) "Bauen Wohnen Denken" in *Vorträge und Aufsätze*, Frankfurt: Vittorio Klostermann, 156. My translation. For text in English see Heidegger, Martin (1977) "Building Dwelling Thinking" in *Basic Writings*, David Farrell Krell ed, New York: HarperCollins, 357.

33 Ibid, 160-161 (in Krell ed., 359-360).

34 Mumford, Lewis (1967) *The South in Architecture*, New York: Da Capo Press, 114.

35 See in this regard Lefaivre, Liane and Alexander Tzonis (2003) *Critical Regionalism: Architecture and Identity,* Munich: Prestel Verlag; and Frampton, Kenneth "Towards a Critical Regionalism: Six Points for an Architecture of Resistance" in Foster, Hal ed., (1983) *The Anti-Aesthetic: Essays on Postmodern Culture*, Seattle: Bay Press, 16-30.

36 For ADA (Americans with Disability Act) Accessibility Guidelines see http://www.access-board.gov/adaag/about/index.htm and for the United Nations Manual on barrier free environments see http://www.un.org/esa/socdev/enable/designm/ . On design aspects see, for example, Peloquin, Albert (1994) *Barrier-Free Design,* New York: McGraw-Hill, and

Holmes-Seidle, James (1996) *Barrier-free design: a manual for building designers and managers,* Oxford: Butterworth Architecture.

37 See, for example, the series by various authors on *Building Type Basics for ...*, New York: John Wiley & Sons, 2000-, (so far 14 volumes for housing, offices, museums, etc.).

38 Hertzberger, Herman (1991/2005) *Lessons for Students in Architecture,* Rotterdam: 010 Publishers.

39 Ibid, 32.

40 Ibid, 42-43.

41 For several of the other projects see *Barrierefreies and integriertes Wohnen,* Forschungsbericht, Oberste Baubehörde im Bayerischen Staatsministerium des Innern Abteilung Wohnungswesen und Städtebauförderung, Franz-Joseph-Strauß-Ring 4 80539 München http://www.verwaltung.bayern.de/Anlage2309525/BarrierefreiesundintegriertesWohnen.pdf .

42 Faller, Peter (1997) *Der Wohngrundriss,* Stuttgart: Deutsche Verlags-Anstalt, Stuttgart, 30, my translation.

43 Innis, Robert E., *Pragmatism and the Forms of Sense,* University Park, PA: Pennsylvania State University Press, 2002, 230.

44 Kant, *Critique of Pure Reason*, 241.

45 Bolter, David and Richard Grusin (1999) *Remediation: Understanding New Media.* Cambridge, MA: MIT Press, 122 and 19.

46 Baudrillard, Jean (1996) "Symbolic Exchange and Death", Reprinted in Cahoone, Lawrence E. ed., *From Modernism to Postmodernism: An Anthology*, Cambridge, MA: Blackwell, 438.

47 Ibid, 439.

48 Ibid, 457.

49 Peter Eisenman, "The End of the Classical: The End of the Beginning, the End of the End" in *Perspecta,* Vol. 21. (1984), 159. See also
http://www.jstor.org.proxy.lib.umich.edu/stable/1567087 .

50 Bouman, Ole and Roemer van Toorn (1994) "The Invisible in Architecture" in *The Invisible in Architecture*, London: Academy Editions,12.

51 Hays, K. Michael (2001) "Prolegomenon for a Study Linking the Advanced Architecture of the Present to That of the 1970s through Ideologies of Media, the Experience of Cities in Transition, and the Ongoing Effects of Reification" in *Perspecta,* Vol. 32, Resurfacing Modernism. 104. See also
http://www.jstor.org.proxy.lib.umich.edu/browse/00790958/ap050019?frame=noframe&userID=8dd3af8b@umich.edu/01cce4405c1b3b91143d472e09&dpi=3&config=jstor .

52 Aristotle, *The Poetics*, Chapter 21, Ingram Bywater (trans.), The Gutenberg Project, Etext, October 2004, Champaign, IL.

53 Ibid, Chapter 22.

54 Richards, Ivor A. (1936, 1965) *The Philosophy of Rhetoric*, Oxford University Press, New York, 93.

55 Snodgras, Adrian and Richard Coyne (2006) *Interpretation in Architecture: Design as a way of thinking,* London: Routledge, 191.

56 Ibid 188.

57 Heidegger, Martin (1927/1957) *Sein und Zeit,* Tübingen: Max Niemeyer Verlag, 148-9 (§ 32), my translation. For English edition look Martin Heidegger, Martin (1996) *Being and Time,* Joan Stambaugh trans., Albany, NY: State University of New York Press, 139.

58 Ibid, 154-5 (German edition) and 144-5 (English edition).

59 Mac Cormac, Earl R. (1985) *A Cognitive Theory of Metaphor,* Cambridge, MA: MIT Press, 227.

60 Booth, Wayne C. "Afterthoughts on Metaphor: Ten Literal 'Theses' ", in (1979) *On Metaphor*, Sheldon Sacks ed., Chicago: University of Chicago Press, 173.

61 An elaborate treatment of contextual issues of metaphor is given in Stern, Joseph (2000) *Metaphor in Context,* Cambridge, MA: MIT Press. But as is the case with most fundamental discussions of metaphor, it looks at linguistic expressions only.

62 Davidson, Donald (1984/2001) *Inquiries into Truth and Interpretation,* Clarendon Press, Oxford, 24.

63 Ibid, 261.

64 Stern, Joseph (2000) *Metaphor in Context,* Cambridge, MA: MIT Press, 307.

65 "The initial letters of the Greek phrase 'Jesus Christ, Son of God, Savior' form the Greek word ICHTHUS, which means 'fish'. This symbol was used by believers in the early days of persecution as a secret sign of their shared faith. One person would draw an arc in the sand, and the other would complete the sign to show his brotherhood in Christ." From Walter E. Gast, Symbols in Christian Art and Architecture, http://www.planetgast.net/symbols/symbolsf/symbolsf.html (see "Fish").

66 For a vivid demonstration of "Ginger and Fred" connections see http://images.google.com/images?source=ig&hl=en&rlz=&q=ginger+and+fred&lr=lang_en%7Clang_fr%7Clang_de&oq=&um=1&ie=UTF-8&ei=80VrS9rPF8vYnAet6_T0AQ&sa=X&oi=image_result_group&ct=title&resnum=4&ved=0CCIQsAQwAw&biw=1374&bih=952 .
One commentator writes about this building: "Nicknamed 'Fred and Ginger', it sports a distorted circulation tower that suggests the swaying movement of an elegantly waltzing couple. The windows of the office stories undulate in the facade as if responding to music. Created as a straightforward structural design and then morphed into distortion, its effect is whimsical but manifests a redemptive seriousness of creative purpose." (Heran, Fil (2003) *Ideas that shaped buildings*, Cambridge MA: MIT Press, 330-332) What is here "structurally straightforward" and "redemptive seriousness"?

67 Jencks, Charles (2005) *The Iconic Building*, New York: Rizzoli, 27-28.

68 Ibid, 40.

69 Ibid, 41 and 43. Read in this regard also "The New Iconic Building?", excerpts from a discussion by Peter Eisenman and Charles Jencks: http://wirednewyork.com/forum/showthread.php?t=7877 .

.70 The AT&T Building's roof top is iconic in that it resembles the decoration on Chippendale-style highboy chests. The screens at the Institute du Monde Arab are useless for shading and daylight control, making drab interior spaces that require artificial lighting even when the sun shines on the facade. Confusion flourishes in Jencks' discussion of works and their architects in the rest of the book, perhaps most so about Rem Koolhas and his Peking CCTV tower, which in my view is an exercise of form seeking content as an 'icon' of the landmark kind.

71 Jencks, Charles (2005) *The Iconic Building*, 132.

72 de Saussure, Ferdinand (1916/1966) *Course in General Liguistics*, Charles Bally et al. (ed.), Wade Baskin (trans.), New York: McGraw-Hill, 66 and 114. This publication is based on lecture notes by students of De Saussure.

73 Ibid, 66 and 67.

74 De Saussure indicates on page 113 that "Linguistics … works in the borderland where the elements of sound and thought combine; *their combination produces a form, not a substance.*" The emphasized part of this quote is very unclear because he does not define "form" nor "substance". I define form as how something is realized as a result, which is in this case, sound or script realizing a concept physically for communication.

75 We will discuss later many other differences in a section on language and architecture.

76 Ibid, 66. De Saussure explains that "The two elements are intimately united, and each recalls the other".

77 For historical perspectives on concepts of form in architecture see "Form" in Forty, Adrian (2000) *Words and Buildings: A Vocabulary of Modern Architecture*, New York: Thames & Hudson, 172.

78 Kant (1787/1998) *Critique of Pure Reason*, 156.

79 On the other hand, the form of any mental existence, here the form of appearance (Kant), is solely thought. I believe that the forms in our mental representations are equivalent to the forms of the objects which they represent (but are obviously not the same).

80 Hegel, Georg W.F. (about 1828/1971) *Vorlesungen über die Ästhetik* (Lectures on Aesthetic), Part 1 and 2, Stuttgart: Philip Reclam, 53, my translation.
See also Hegel G.W.F. (1975) *Aesthetics: Lectures on Fine Art,* T.M. Knox (trans.), Oxford: Clarendon Press, 13.

81 Forty, Adrian (2000) *Words and Buildings: A Vocabulary of Modern Architecture,* idem, 172.

82 Kant (1787/1998) *Critique of Pure Reason*, 232. This is so because there is a rationale behind what occurs overall, beyond our rationale and broader than ours collectively. Unless there is a physical extension of a concept we cannot perceive by means of our senses.

83 McDowell, John H. (1994) *Mind and World,* Cambridge: Harvard University Press, 25-26.

84 Fales, Evan (1996) *A Defense of the Given,* Lanham, MD: Rowman & Littlefield, 103 and 149.

85 Ibid, 149.

Notes and Bibliography of pages 85-92

86 De Saussure, *Course in General Linguistics,* idem, 114.

87 Frege, Gottlob (1884/1980) *The Foundations of Arithmetic; a logico-mathematical enquiry into the concept of number,* J. L. Austin trans., Evanston: Northwestern University Press, x.

88 De Saussure, *Course in General Linguistics,* idem.

89 Ibid, 115.

90 McLuhan, Marshall (1964/1994) *Understanding Media,* Cambridge, MA: MIT Press, 7 ff.

Notes and Bibliography of Chapter 4

1 I avoid here the term cognition as far as possible because it is ambiguous through highly diffuse application in many fields which give it their own interpretation.

2 Damasio, Antonio R. (1994) *Descartes' Error: emotion, reason, and the human brain,* New York: Avon Books and (1999) *The feeling of what happens: body and emotion in the making of consciousness,* New York : Harcourt Brace; Damasio, Antonio R. (2003) *Looking for Spinoza : joy, sorrow, and the feeling,* Orlando, FL.: Harcourt; Edelman, Gerald H. (1992) *Bright Air, brillant fire: on the matter of the mind*, New York: BasicBooks, Harper Collins; LeDoux, Joseph E. (1996*) The emotional brain : the mysterious underpinnings of emotional life,* New York: Simon & Schuster; Le Doux, Joseph E. (2003) *Synaptic self : how our brains become who we are,* New York: Viking; Tucker, Don M. (2007) *Mind from body: experience from neural structure*, Oxford: Oxford University Press.

3 For examples, see Ciarrochi, Joseph, Joseph Forgas and John D. Mayer, ed., (2001) *Emotional Intelligence in Everyday Life,* Philadelphia: Psychological Press; Barrett, Lisa F. and Peter Salovey, Zeidner M, ed. (2002) *The Wisdom in Feeling: Psychological Processes in Emotional Intelligence.* New York: The Guilford Press; Matthews, Gerald, Moshe Zeidner and Richard D. Roberts (2002) *Emotional Intelligence: Science and Myth.* Cambridge, MA: MIT Press; Goleman, Daniel (2005) *Emotional Intelligence*, New York: Bantam Books.

4 Spinoza, Baruch (1677/1992) *Ethics,* Part II, Propositions 14 and 26, ed. Seymour Feldman, ed., Samuel Shirley, trans., Indianapolis: Hackett Publishing, 76 and 83.

5 See Online Etymology Dictionary http://www.etymonline.com/index.php?l=e&p=5 . See also http://en.wikipedia.org/wiki/Emotion.

6 A third aspect, not so much of interest for our concerns, is the fact that we are affected and react to internally caused bodily sensation, such as pain because of illness.

7 Internal sensation may arise from having reasoning as "second thoughts", daydreaming, dreaming in sleep, reaction to drugs, etc.

8 Damasio, Antonio (2003), 206. Damasio presents many examples about why he postulates that feelings presuppose emotions.

9 Ibid, 30.

10 James, William (1884/1920) "What is an Emotion?" in *Collected Essays and Reviews*, London:

Longmans, Green and Co., 247. From http://books.google.com/books?id=SmsbzTAgq7wC&printsec=frontcover&source=gbs_ViewAPI .
Reprinted in *The Nature of Emotion*, ed. M.B. Arnold, 1968, 17-36. See also Commentary on "What is an Emotion? in *Classics in the History of Psychology*, an internet resource developed by Christopher D. Green, http://psychclassics.yorku.ca/James/emotion.htm .
   And

11 See LeDoux (1996), 42 ff. for a very helpful exposition of James' view and theories which built on it.

12 Damasio (2003), 112.

13 Damasio, (1994), 150.

14 Here I disagree somewhat with Searle, John R. (2004) *Mind: a brief introduction*, New York : Oxford University Press, 237 ff. This concentrated text is an excellent introduction to aspects of the mind with a well selected bibliography for every chapter.
http://site.ebrary.com.proxy.lib.umich.edu/lib/umich/docDetail.action?docID=10085231 .

15 Arnold, Magda B. (1960) *Emotion and personality*, vol. 1. New York: Columbia University Press, 171-2.

16 Lazarus, Richard S. and Bernice N. (1994) *Passion and Reason: Making Sense of Our Emotions,* New York: Oxford University Press, 203.

17 Johnson, Mark (2007) *The Meaning of the Body: aesthetics of human understanding,* Chicago: University of Chicago Press, 74.

18 Ibid, XII. The term "embodied mind" has been used at least since 1965 when Godfrey Vesey used it in his book *The embodied mind*. See also Varela, Godfrey et al (1991) *The embodied mind: cognitive science and human experience,* Cambridge, MA: MIT Press.

19 Bennett W. Helm uses the terms "emotional reason" and "evaluative feelings" in his (2001) *Emotional Reason: Deliberation, motivation, and the nature of value,* Cambridge, UK: Cambridge University Press, 33-36. I believe this is confusing terminology as reason is not emotional and there are no feelings which evaluate. There is, as I discuss, what I call "emotion influenced reason". And, there are feelings as affects because of evaluations and judgments, and feelings which are grounds for judgments, but they themselves are not judgments. They often, however, motivate thought toward judgment.

20 Recent research shows that the brain accommodates at least in part learning and memory functions by means of synaptic plasticity: "In neuroscience, synaptic plasticity is the ability of the connection, or synapse, between two neurons to change in strength. … Since memories are postulated to be represented by vastly interconnected networks of synapses in the brain, synaptic plasticity is one of the important neurochemical foundations of learning and memory." From "Synaptic Plasticity" in Wikipedia, <http://en.wikipedia.org/wiki/Synaptic plasticity>, 17 January 2007.

21 Andreasen, Nancy C. (2005) *The Creating Brain*, New York: The Dana Press.

22 A side note: It is interesting that Kant speaks of "imagination, a function of the soul" but replaces "soul" in his own first edition copy of his (1781/1998) *Critique of Pure Reason* with

"understanding", 211, footnote b); "soul" perhaps implying emotion as part of understanding, an aspect which I think he should have expanded upon.

23 Searle, John R. (2004) *Mind: a brief introduction*, New York : Oxford University Press,(2004), 136-7. http://site.ebrary.com.proxy.lib.umich.edu/lib/umich/docDetail.action?docID=10085231 .

24 Kant, *Critique of Pure Reason*, idem, 248 and 232 (see also Chapter 2, Notes and Bibliopgraphy, 45).

25 LeDoux (1996), 175.

26 Damasio (1999), 43.

27 Gray, Jeffrey (2004), *Consciousness: creeping up on the hard problem,* Oxford: Oxford University Press, 89.

28 Waynbaum, Israel. "The Affective Qualities of Perception", in Niedenthal, Paula M. and Shinbu Kitayana, eds., Christine Madeleine Du Bois, trans. (1994) *The Heart's Eye*: *emotional influences in perception and attention,* San Diego: Academic Press, San Diego, 29.

29 Ibid, 31.

30 Ibid.

31 Schwarz Norbert, "Situated Cognition and the Wisdom in Feelings" in Barrett, Lisa F. and Peter Salovey, eds. (2000) *The Wisdom in Feeling: Psychological Processes in Emotional Intelligence,* New York: Guilford Press, 147.

32 Kalon in ancient Greek means beautiful and fair, <http://www.kypros.org/cgi-bin/lexicon> . See also Tartarkiewicz, Wladyslaw (1970) *History of Aesthetics,* Vol.1 Ancient Aesthetics, The Hague: Mouton, 25-26.

33 Dagobert D. Runes (1942) *Dictionary of Philosophy*. "Techne. The set of principles, or rational method, involved in the production of an object or the accomplishment of an end; the knowledge of such principles or method; art. Techne resembles episteme in implying knowledge of principles, but differs in that its aim is making or doing, not disinterested understanding." http://www.ditext.com/runes/k.html .

34 Tatarkiewicz, Wladyslaw (1970) *History of Aesthetics*, Vol. I, The Hague: Mouton, 112.

35 Plato, *Hippias Major*, Elpenor (electronic resource), 9. <http://www.ellopos.net/elpenor/greek-texts/ancient-greece/plato/plato-hippias-major.asp> .

36 Ibid, 37.

37 In *Phaedo* Socrates asks: "Is there or is there not an absolute justice? And an absolute beauty and absolute good?" Simmias agrees. "But did you ever behold any of them with your eyes?" Certainly not. "Or did you ever reach them with any other bodily sense? … Has the reality of them ever been perceived by you through the bodily organs? or rather, is not the nearest approach to the knowledge of their several natures made by him who so orders his intellectual vision as to have the most exact conception of the essence of that which he considers?" "Certainly." http://www.gutenberg.org/files/1658/1658-h/1658-h.htm .

38 Xenophon, *The Memorable Thoughts of Socrates*, Edward Bysshe trans., London: Cassell &

Company, 1888, 124-126 (Book 3, Ch. 8). <http://www.gutenberg.org/files/17490/17490-h/17490-h.htm> . The work is usually known as *Memorabilia*.

39 Plato, *Symposium,* Benjamin Jowett, trans., The Internet Classics Archive http://classics.mit.edu/Plato/symposium.1b.txt .

40 Beardsley, Monroe C. (1966) *Aesthetics from Classical Greece to the present*, New York: The Macmillan Company, 39ff.

41 Plato (about 360 BC) "*Timaeus"* in Jowett, B., trans. (1892) *The Dialogues of Plato*, Vol. III, 3rd edition, Oxford: Clarendon Press, 1892, 510. http://babel.hathitrust.org/cgi/pt?id=mdp.39015011712794;q1=heed;start=1;size=25;page=search;seq=756;view=image;num=510 . Note: 'beautiful' and 'fair' are often taken as synonyms.

42 Knight, William (1891) *The philosophy of Beauty*, London: John Murray, 26-27.

43 Aristotle (about 350 BC) *Metaphysics,* XIII, 3, W. D. Ross, trans, Internet Classics Archive http://classics.mit.edu/ .

44 See "Symmetry" in the Online Etymology Dictionary: http://www.etymonline.com/index.php?term=symmetry . and Beolingus Dictionary, under Definitions En: (http://dict.tu-chemnitz.de/).

45 Aristotle (c. 350 BC) *Nicomachean Ethics,* VI, 4, W.D.Ross, trans., http://www.constitution.org/ari/ethic_00.htm .

46 Plato (c. 360 BC) *Sophist*, Benjamin Jowett, trans., http://classics.mit.edu/Plato/sophist.1b.txt . Only the Stranger's views are quoted without intermittent responses.

47 Aristotle (c. 335 BC) *Poetics*, Section1, Part I, trans S.H. Butcher, The Internet Classics Archive by Daniel C. Stevenson, Copyright 1994-2000, Web Atomics. http://classics.mit.edu/Aristotle/poetics.mb.txt .

48 Halliwell, Stephen (2002) *The Aesthetics of Mimesis.* Princeton University Press, Princeton, 131.

49 Vitruvius (c. 30 BC) *The Ten Books on Architecture*, Morris H. Morgan, trans. (1914), Dover Publications, New York, 1960, 17 (Book 1, Ch. 3, Sec. 2).

50 *The Architecture of Marcus Vitruvius Pollio*, Joseph Gwilt, trans. (1826) London: Priestley and Weale, Book I, Chapter 3. http://penelope.uchicago.edu/Thayer/E/Roman/Texts/Vitruvius/home.html .

51 Vitruvius *The Ten Books on Architecture,* 72 (Book 3, ch. 1, sec. 2).

52 Ibid, 103 (Book 4, ch. 1, sec. 6).

53 Ibid, 174-175 (Book 6, ch. 2, sec. 1-5).

54 Plotinus, (c.265 AD) *The First Ennead,* Sixth Tractate, Section 1, Stephen MacKenna and B.S. Page trans, Philadelphia: The University of Pennsylvania, http://www.sacred-texts.com/cla/plotenn/index.htm .

55 Ibid, Section 2.

56 Ibid, Section 9.

57 Augustine, Saint, Bishop of Hippo (388-390) *De Diversis Questionibus*, 83, no. 78.

58 Augustine (c. 390) "True Religion (De vera religione)", in *The works of Saint Augustine: a translation for the 21st century,* Augustinian Heritage Institute, John E. Rotelle, ed., Edmund Hill, trans., New York: New City Press, 1990, Part 1, vol. 8, sections xxxii/59 to 61, p. 69 (The latin text uses 'artifice' that is better translated as 'craftsman' not "architect", see http://lysy2.archives.nd.edu/cgi-bin/words.exe?artifice .

59 Ibid, section 60, p. 70.

60 Ibid, section 61, p. 71.

61 Ibid, section 62.

62 Ibid, section 77, p. 82.

63 Ibid, section 55, p. 66.

64 Ibid, section 57, p. 68.

65 Ibid, section 56, p. 67.

66 Augustine (397-398) *Confessions and Enchiridion,* Albert C. Outler, ed. and trans., (1908) London: SCM Press, [1955], Book 6, Chapter 16, p. 133, http://name.umdl.umich.edu/AFZ6439 .

67 Aquinas, Thomas (1274) *Summa Theologica*, Part I, question 5, article 4. Grand Rapids, MI: Christian Classics Ethereal Library, Calvin College. http://www.ccel.org/ccel/aquinas/summa .

68 Ibid, Part I, question 39, article 8.

69 Ibid.

70 Ficino, Marsilio (1469) *Commentary on Plato's Symposium*, Sears R. Jayne, trans., Columbias, MO: University of Missouri Studies, XIX, No. 1, , 1944, p. 171 and I, iii, p. 128.

71 Alberti, Leon B. (about 1450/1988) *On the Art of Building in Ten Books*, Joseph Rykwert et al, trans, MIT Press, Cambridge MA, 156.

72 Ibid, 302.

73 Ibid, 156.

74 Ibid 420 (in glossary of translators).

75   Dürer, Albrecht (1528) *Das Lehrbuch der Malerei (The Painter's Manual)*.
(Source of this reference: Hart Nibbrig, Christiaan L. (1978) *Ästhetik*, Frankfurt am Main: Suhrkamp, 67). From Dürer's unfinished and unpublished manuscript.
See also "Van Schönheit" in http://helioda.macbay.de/Willkommen/74F66C35-F23C-4792-8843-A191CBB3B1E8.html .

76 Goethe, Johann W. (1788/89) *Der Sammler und die Seinigen,* fünfter Brief, in Gedenkausgabe der Werke, Briefe und Gespräche, Zürich 1948, Band 13, p. 286. See also http://www.zeno.org/Literatur/M/Goethe,+Johann+Wolfgang/Theoretische+Schriften/Der+Sammler+und+die+Seinigen .

77 Beardsley, Monroe C. (1966) *Aesthetics from the Classical Greece to the Present,* The Macmillan Company, New York, 156.

78 Descartes, René (1641) *Meditations on First Philosophy*, Parts 4 and 6,
http://www.earlymoderntexts.com/f_descarte.html .

79 Leibnitz, Gottfried Wilhelm (1686) *Discourse on Metaphysics Correspondence with Arnauld and Monadology,* George R. Montgomery, trans., Section xxiv, 41, Chicago: Open Court Publishing Company, 1916.
http://babel.hathitrust.org/cgi/pt?id=uc1.b3922798;q1=shocks;start=1;size=100;page=root;view=image;seq=71;num=41 .

80 Shaftesbury, Anthony A. C. (1711), *Characteristicks of men, manners, opinions, times,* London: John Darby, Vol. 2, p. 414-15.
http://galenet.galegroup.com.proxy.lib.umich.edu/servlet/ECCO?dd=0&locID=umuser&d1=0339601502&srchtp=ra&c=1&SU=0LRL+OR+0LRI&df=f&d2=411&docNum=CW3304279206&d7=414&h2=1&vrsn=1.0&af=BN&d6=411&d3=425&ste=10&d4=0.33&stp=Author&n=10&d5=d6&ae=T030440 .

81 Ibid, Vol. 3 (Miscellany III), p. 162.

82 Hutcheson, Francis (1725) *An Inquiry into the Original of our Ideas of Beauty and Virtue,* London: J. Darby, for Will and John Smith, Section 1, Paragraph 17, pp.13-14. Electronic access. See also
http://oll.libertyfund.org/?option=com_staticxt&staticfile=show.php%3Ftitle=858&chapter=65972&layout=html&Itemid=27 .

83 Ibid, 6-7.

84 Locke, John (1706) *An essay concerning humane understanding*, E. Holt, London, Fifth Edition, Book 2, Chapter 1, § 4, p. 52, Chapter 11, § 9, p. 92, etc.

85 Hutcheson, Francis (1725) *An Inquiry into the Original of our Ideas of Beauty ...,* idem, 14.

86 Hume, David (1752) "Of the Standard of Taste" in *Four Dissertations*, London, 1757, 208-9, reprinted in *Aesthetics*, Oxford Readers, Susan L. Feagin and Patrick Maynatd, Oxford GB: Oxford University Press, Oxford, 1997, 352.

87 There are things that have intrinsic value because we cannot live without them directly or indirectly, like water, minerals and vitamins, and solar radiation. If they would not exist, we would not be alive. Their necessity is not a question. Where there is no latitude of judgment there is absoluteness. This does not apply to a particular aesthetic. Beauty in something may approach intrinsic value for me but not necessarily for anybody else.

88 Hume, David (1739/1888) *A Treatise of Human Nature,* Book II, London: Printed for John Noon, 299. Hume is at times careless with terminology, here in saying "taste or sensation".
http://babel.hathitrust.org/cgi/pt?id=uc1.32106009586717;page=root;view=image;size=100;seq=15;num=xi .

89 Ibid, 617.

90 Hume, David. "Of the Standard of Taste", 233-4.

91   For more on the etymological definition of the term see, for example, Kovach, Francis (1973) *Philosophy of Beauty,* Norman, OK: University of Oklahoma Press, 1973, 5-10.

92   Relatively short overall accounts of aesthetics in historical perspective are Beardsley, Monroe (1966) *Aesthetics from Classical Greece to the Present,* New York: Mcmillan and Dieckmann, Herbert (2003) "Theories of Beauty to the mid-nineteenth Century" in *The Dictionary of the History of Ideas*, Vol. 1, Gale Group, University of Virginia Library, 195-206. A more extensive treatment in three volumes is in Tatarkiewicz, Wladyslaw (1970) *History of Aesthetics*, The Hague: Mouton. An elaborate treatment from a definitional point of view, pointing out confusions but itself sometimes confusing, is given in Sparshott, F. E. (1963) *The Structure of Aesthetics*, Toronto: University of Toronto Press. A thought provoking, historical appraisal, especially in reference to what Nietzsche thought to be the struggle with our longstanding "ascetic" misconception of beauty is in Faas, Ekbert (2002)*The Geneology of Aesthetics,* Cambridge: Cambridge University Press. The most recent and comprehensive treatment of aesthetics is in Kelly, Michael, ed. (1998) *Encyclopedia of aesthetics,* New York: Oxford University Press.

93   Baumgarten, Alexander G. (1750 and 1758) *Aesthetica,* § 1, ed. and trans. from Latin into German by Hans Rudolf Schweizer, *Ästhetik als Philosophie der sinnlichen Erkenntnis,* Schwabe & Co, Basel, 1973, 107. My translation from German.

94   Ibid, 115 (§ 14).

95   What I translate in these quotes as aesthetics is in the Latin text 'aesthetica' and in German 'Aesthetik'. We need to be careful with this 'Aesthetik' in not thinking of it as pointing to one thing only. The German 'Aesthetik' can mean 'aesthetics' (noun) as a field of study about aesthetic aspects or 'the aesthetic' (noun) as one aspect or several combined aspects of something. There will be much to say about the nature of 'the aesthetic'.

96   I try to avoid the term cognition because of its different meanings in the many fields of art, science and technology.

97   Ibid, 117 (§ 18, 19 and 20).

98   Ibid, 119 (§ 22).

99   Ibid (§ 24).

100   Ibid, 107 (§ 3).

101   Robert Dixon, *The Baumgarten Corruption, From Sense to Nonsense in Art and Philosophy,* Pluto Press, London, 1995, p. 48.

102   Ibid,152.

103   Ibid, 80.

104   Ibid, 82.

105   Baumgarten, Alexander G. (1750 and 1758) *Aesthetica,* 115 (§ 15).

106   Ibid, 115 (§ 17).

107   Kant, *Critique of Pure Reason*, 156. άισθητα και νοητα (aisthita kai noita) means "visibly and

understandably" [perceptual and conceptual], translation via http://www.kypros.org/cgi-bin/lexicon/ .

108 Kant, Immanuel (1790/2000) *Critique of the Power of Judgment, (First Introduction),* Paul Guyer and Eric Matthews, trans., Cambridge UK: Cambridge University Press, p. 24, with my alteration according to the German original.

109 Ibid, p. 89. Guyer and Matthews write that "The doctrine that the feeling of pleasure or displeasure reflects the relation of an object to the subject rather than the properties of the object by itself is one of Kant's most entrenched views" (note 5, ibid, 359).

110 For extensive discussions of objectivist versus subjectivist positions in aesthetic issues see, for example, Kovach, Francis (1973) *Philosophy of Beauty,* 55-93 and Sibley, Frank (2001) *Approach to Aesthetics: collected papers on philosophical aesthetics,* 71-87.

111 Sibley, Frank. "Aesthetic and Non-aesthetic" in *The Philosophical Review*, Vol. 74, No. 2. (Apr., 1965), pp. 137-138, reprinted in Sibley, Frank (2001) *Approach to Aesthetics*, John Benson et al, ed, Clarendon Press, Oxford, 35.

112 The Golden Section was for a long time considered an unassailable proportion to 'yield' beauty; but not anymore. For a short discussion on "The golden ratio and aesthetics" by Mario Livio, an astrophysicist, see http://plus.maths.org/issue22/features/golden/ . Proportion is only one property of an object. Usually many other properties play a role in our judgment whether we like an object or not.

113 If one wanted to make a differentiation between properties and their qualities, that is, between the observable and relational substances of which things are made and their aesthetic dimensions after aesthetic judgments, one could say that the "aesthetic" qualities of objects depend on their observable and relational properties.

114 Makkreel, Rudolf A. (1990) *Imagination and Interpretation in Kant*, Chicago: University of Chicago Press, 48-9.

115 Kant, *Critique of the Power of Judgment*, 103. He writes that "When we call something beautiful, the pleasure that we feel is … just as it were to be regarded as a property of the object that is determined in it in accordance with concepts; but beauty is nothing by itself, without relation to the feeling of the subject." Note the "as it were".

116 Dewey, John (1934/1958) *Art as Experience*, New York: Capricorn Books, 46.

117 A helpful book by Richard Shusterman and Adele Tomlin, eds. (2008) *Aesthetic Experience,* New York: Routledge, uses this term as the main theme of papers but does not address the differentiation of experience and result. Interesting in this regard is also an earlier paper by Shusterman "The End of Aesthetic Experience", *The Journal of Aesthetics and Art Criticism*, Vol. 55, No. 1 (Winter, 1997), pp. 29-41.

118 John Dewey writes in *Art and Experience* (page 40) that "... no experience of whatever sort is a unity unless it has esthetic quality." I believe that every experience has a unity of content and form, and has, because of our judgment on being pleased or displeased with it, aesthetic quality.

119 Langer, Susanne (1957) *Problems of Art: ten philosophical lectures,* New York : C. Scribner, 133-134.

120 Scruton, Roger (1983/1998) *The Aesthetic Understanding: Essays in the Philosophy of*

Art and Culture. South Bend, IN: St. Augustine's Press, 3. This passage echoes an earlier, also introductory one in his *The Aesthetics of Architecture* (page 1) where he writes "… that the division between practical reason and aesthetic understanding is in fact untenable, and that until the relation between the two is reestablished they must both remain impoverished." I believe that they are not only related but in effect one, completely interdependent, though we make the distinction for analytical purposes.

121 Hegel, Georg W.F. (1835-1838/1971) *Vorlesungen über die Ästhetik*, Stuttgart: Philip Reclam Jun., 37. My translations. See also http://www.textlog.de/3421.html . The references in parenthesis in notes 123 to 127 are to pages in Hegel, G.W.F. (1975) *Aesthetics: Lectures On Fine Art*, T.M. Knox, trans., Oxford: Oxford University Press.

122 Ibid, 38.

123 Ibid, 52 (Ref in Knox 12) The German word *Geist*, which is zentral to Hegel's philosophy, can be translated as spirit or mind, sometimes also as mentality and mental attitude.

124 Ibid, 64 (Ref in Knox 21-22).

125 Ibid, 129 (Ref in Knox 72).

126 Ibid, 178 (Ref in Knox 110).

127 Ibid, 179 (Ref in Knox 111).

128 Ibid. Reason is always involved in thinking as it provides conceptualization without which judgment and, consequently the aesthetic, would have no object. Strangely, Hegel draws here a conclusion against his own view of ideality and reality in objects. Beauty is not "*infinite* and free". It is dependent on the object properties in conjunction with our judgment.

129 Schiller, Friedrich von (1795) *Über die ästhetische Erziehung des Menschen, in einer Reihe von Briefen*. 10. Brief (*On the aesthetic education of man, in a series of letter*s. 10th Letter), my translation, http://www.kuehnle-online.de/literatur/schiller/werke/phil/aestherzieh/10.htm . For English version see http://www.gutenberg.org/files/6798/6798-h/6798-h.htm#2H_4_0014 .

130 Ibid, 24. Brief (24th Letter).

131 Ibid, 14. Brief (14th Letter).

132 Ibid, 15. Brief (15th Letter).

133 Schopenhauer, Arthur (1910) *The World as Will and Idea*, R.B. Haldane and J. Kemp trans, 7th ed, Vol. 1, 219.
http://www.archive.org/stream/worldaswillandi01schogoog/worldaswillandi01schogoog_djvu.txt .

134 Ibid, 221.

135 Ibid, 238-239.

136   For detailed reading on Schopenhauer's position in aesthetics see, for example, Neill, Alex (2008) "Schopenhauer and the foundations of aesthetic experience" in Richard Shusterman and Adele Tomlin, eds., *Aesthetic Experience*, Routledge, 178-193.

137 For developments in aesthetics in the 19th and 20th century see, for example, Beardsley, Monroe C. (1966) *Aesthetics from Classical Greece to the Present*, ch. 10-12, New York:

MacMillan Company; Tatarkiewicz, Wladyslaw (1974) *History of Aesthetics,* Vol. 3, The Hague: Mouton; Kelly, Michael (1998), *Encyclopedia of Aesthetics,* New York: Oxford University Press.

138 Francis Hutcheson writes in *An inquiry into the original of our ideas of beauty and virtue; in two treatises.* The fourth edition. London: Printed for D. Midwinter et al., 1738, 11, that "… the Ideas of Beauty and Harmony, like other sensible Ideas are *necessarily* pleasant to us …" or, we may suggest, they would not be called so. Then he goes on "… neither can any Resolution of our own, nor any *Prospect* of Advantage or Disadvantage, vary the Beauty or Deformity of an Object: For as in the external Sensations, no View of *Interest* will make an object grateful, …" In the first instance he refers to "Ideas of Beauty" which is internal sense (feeling) and in the second to external sensation. The first is effect and the second its cause. We cannot change through sensation the properties of given objects but our feeling about them is influenced by our interests, consciously or not.

139 Kant, *Critique of the Power of Judgment*, 96.

140 Ibid, 75. At another point he writes that "Here the representation is related entirely to the subject, indeed to its feeling of life, under the name of the feeling of pleasure or displeasure, which grounds an entirely new faculty for discriminating and judging that contributes nothing to cognition … ." (Ibid, 90).

141 Ibid, 104.

142 Kant, Immanuel (1790/2000) *Critique of the Power of Judgment, 89.*

143 Ibid, 114.

144 Another reason that I cannot agree with some of Kant's aesthetics is his separation of emotion from judgment on beauty. He writes: "Emotion, a sensation in which agreeableness is produced only by means of a momentary inhibition followed by a stronger outpouring of the vital force, does not belong to beauty at all. Sublimity (with which the feeling of emotion is combined), however, requires another standard for judging than that on which taste is grounded; and thus a pure judgment of taste has neither charm nor emotion, in a word no sensation, as matter of the aesthetic judgment, for its determining ground." (Ibid, 111).

145 Nietzsche, Friedrich Wilhelm, (c.1883) *Sämtliche Werke : Kritische Studienausgabe* herausgegeben von Giorgio Colli und Mazzino Montinari, München: Deutscher Taschenbuch Verlag, (1999), Vol. 10, 293.
See also *Nietzsches Werke: Historisch-kritische Ausgabe.* Electronic edition.
Werke: Kritische Gesamtausgabe VII-1 Nachgelassene Fragmente Juli 1882 bis Winter 1883-1884 (KG VII-1) [7 = M III 4b. Frühjahr — Sommer 1883].

146 Guyer, Paul (2005) *Values of Beauty: Historical Essays in Aesthetics,* Cambridge GB: Cambridge University Press, chapter 5 and Wicks, Robert "Dependent Beauty as the Appreciation of Teleological Style" in (1997) *The Journal of Aesthetics and Art Criticism*, 55, 387-400.

147 Berleant, Arnold and Ronald Hepburn "An Exchange on Disinterestedness", *Contemporary Aesthetics,* Vol. 1, 2003. http://www.contempaesthetics.org/newvolume/pages/article.php?articleID=209#FN4link .

148 Ibid.

149 For more on the controversial discussion of interest and disinterest in aesthetic experience as well as free and adherent beauty see Guyer, Paul (2005) *Values of Beauty: Historical Essays in Aesthetics*, chapters 4 and 5; Kreitman, Norman "The Varieties of Aesthetic Disinterestedness", *Contemporary Aesthetics,* Volume 4, 2006,
http://www.contempaesthetics.org/newvolume/pages/article.php?articleID=390, and Stolnitz, Jerome "On the Origins of 'Aesthetic Disinterestedness' ",
The Journal of Aesthetics and Art Criticism, Vol. 20, No. 2 (Winter, 1961), pp. 131-143.

150 Mothersill, Mary "Beauty" in *A Companion to Aesthetics*, Blackwell, David Cooper ed., 1995, 46. This aspect is treated by her more broadly in *Beauty Restored*, Oxford: Clarendon Press, 1984, 220 and 278.

151 Mothersill, Mary (1984) *Beauty Restored*, Oxford: Clarendon Press, 115.

152 Goldberger, Paul "House Proud", *The New Yorker*, July 2, 2001.

153 My comment on the discomfort in the Lake Shore Drive apartments is based on comments by people who lived there and I visited in the 1960s. I don't know whether this problem has been corrected since. The Barcelona chair's back gives insufficient lumbar support for seating comfort.

154 Frampton, Kenneth (1983) "Towards Critical Regionalism: Six Points for an Architecture of Resistance" reprinted in Frampton, Kenneth (2002) *Labour, Work and Architecture*, 88. See also http://www.colorado.edu/envd/courses/envd4114-001/Spring%2006/Theory/Frampton.pdf , 28

155 Fitch, Marston (1972) *American Building*, vol. 2, Schocken Books, New York, 1.

156 Shusterman, Richard (2000), *Pragmatist Aesthetics*, Oxford: Rowman & Littlefield, 278.

157 Harries, Karsten (1997) *The Ethical Function of Architecture,* Cambridge, MA: MIT Press, 25-26.

158 As quoted by Michael Kimmelman in 'Normally architects render a service. They implement what other poeple want. This is not what I do.' In "The Ascension of Peter Zumthor." *The New York Times Magazine*, March 13, 2011, 37.

159 Kant writes that "We can, however, trace all actions of the understanding back to judgments, so that the *understanding* in general can be represented as a *faculty for judging*. ... Thinking is cognition through concepts. Concepts, however, as predicates of possible judgments, are related to some representations of a still undetermined object." (Guyer et al (1781/1998) *Critique of Pure Reason*, 205). As mentioned earlier, judgment occurs to sort out concepts and provide aesthetic valuation.

160 James, William (1907) "What Pragmatism Means" in *Pragmatism*, New York: Longmans, Green and Co., 1922, 54-55.
http://babel.hathitrust.org/cgi/pt?seq=7&view=image&size=100&id=uc2.ark%3A%2F13960%2Ft39028v34&q1=looking&u=1&num=54 .

161 Merleau-Ponty, Maurice (1962) *Phenomenology of Perception*, London: Routledge & Kegan Paul, xix.

Notes and Bibliography of Chapter 5

1 For further study see, for example, Moreland, J. P. (2001) *Universals*, Montreal: McGill-Queen's University Press; Mellor, D. H. and Alex Oliver, eds. (1997) *Properties*, Oxford University Press;

Schoedinger, Andrew B. ed. (1992) *The Problem of Universals*, Atlantic Highlands, NJ: Humanities Press; Armstrong D. M. (1989) *Universals: an opinionated introduction*, Boulder: West View Press.

2   Wittgenstein, Ludwig (1953) *Philosophical Investigations,* G. E. M. Anscombe trans., New York: The Macmillan Company, 32, § 67.

3   Baylis, Charles A. (1951) "Universals, Communicable Knowledge, and Metaphysics" in Andrew B. Schoedinger ed. (1992)*The Problem of Universals*, 182.

4   Lewis, David (1997) "Modal Realism at Work: Properties" in *Properties*, Mellor D. H. and Alex Oliver, eds., Oxford University Press, 175 (footnote).

5   Hume, David (1740) *An abstract of a book lately published; entituled, A treatise of human nature, &c. Wherein the chief argument of that book is farther illustrated and explained.* London: printed for C. Borbet [sic], at Addison's Head, over-against St. Dunstan's church, in Fleet-street, 32, http://mirlyn.lib.umich.edu/Record/004773773 .

6   Goodman, Nelson (1972) "Seven Strictures of Similarity" in *Problems and Projects*, Indianapolis: The Bobbs-Merrill Company, 446.

7   My concept of concepts is a rather instrumental and limited one, geared toward our needs. There is a considerable body of literature on the subject, such as Margolis, Eric and Stephen Laurence, eds. (1999) *Concepts: core readings*, Cambridge MA: MIT Press, especially the first and last chapters; Villanueva, Enrique, ed. (1998) *Concepts*, Atascadero, CA: Ridgeview Publishing; Morris Weitz (1988) *Theories of Concepts: A History of the Major Philosophical Tradition,* London: Routledge.

8   Quatremère de Quincy, A.-C. (1788-1825) "Type" in *Encyclopédie Méthodique, Architecture*, vol. 3, part II. Paris. Introduction and English translation by Anthony Vidler In Oppositions 8 (Spring): 147-150. Reprinted in *Oppositions Reader* (1998), K. Michael Hayes ed., New York: Princeton Architectural Press, 618.

9   Alberti, Leon Battista (1486, 1988) *On the Art of building in Ten Books,* Joseph Rykwert et al trans, MIT Press, Cambridge, 92.

10   Ibid 149. Alberti's descriptions of residential space arrangements, for example, are a wide ranging cultural commentary on part of the domestic life of his time: "The husband and wife must have separate bedrooms, not only to ensure that the husband be not disturbed by his wife, when she is about to give birth or is ill, but also to allow them, even in summer, an uninterrupted night's sleep, whenever they wish. Each room should have its own door, and in addition a common side door, to enable them to seek each other's company unnoticed. Off the wife's bedroom should be a dressing room, and off the husband's, a library. The grandmother, being weary with old age and in need of rest and quiet, should have a bedroom that is warm, sheltered, and well away from the din coming from the family or outside; …" These descriptions amount to a programmatic typology for housing.

11   The first volume of Sebastiano Serlio's main work *General Rules of Architecture (Regole generali d'architettura)* appeared in 1537: http://babel.hathitrust.org/cgi/pt?id=ucm.5326946993;page=root;view=image;size=100;seq=5 .
See also Kruft, Hanno-Walter (1994) *A History of Architectural Theory*, Ronald Taylor et al., trans., New York: Princeton Architectural Press, 74-75.

12 See, for example, Furttenbach, Joseph (1635), *Architectura Universalis*, Ulm, http://digi.ub.uni-heidelberg.de/diglit/furttenbach1635 .

13 Diderot, Denis (1751/1967) *Encyclopédie ou Dictionnaire raisonné des Sciences, des art et des métiers.* Facsimile of the first edition of 1751-1780. Stuttgart-Bad Cannstatt: Friedrich Fromann Verlag, see "type". Translated and quoted in Lavin, Sylvia (1992) *Quatremère de Quincy and the Invention of a Modern Language of Architecture*, Cambridge: MIT Press, 90-91.

14 Vidler, Anthony (1977) "The Idea of Type: The Transformation of the Academic Ideal, 1750-1830". *Oppositions* 8, 95.

15 Vidler, "The Production of Types", ibid 93.

16 Blondel, Jacques Francois (1777) *Cours d'Architecture*, Paris, vol. 2, 229, my translation. For French original see
http://books.google.com/books?id=O_YTAAAAQAAJ&printsec=frontcover&dq=blondel+cours+d'architecture&source=bl&ots=c4hPgqsAAW&sig=uPcDY0hj6ccw-dd7P5ToFMqYc8U&hl=en&ei=RDsmTZbwJcm-nAejnfSKAg&sa=X&oi=book_result&ct=result&resnum=8&sqi=2&ved=0CFoQ6AEwBw#v=onepage&q=teatre&f=false .

17 Durand, J.N.L. (1809) *Précis des Leçons d'architecture données à l'Ecole Polytechnique*, Paris, Vol. I, 17, my translation.
For French original see http://www.google.com/books?id=S9vnzwtsKq8C&printsec=frontcover&source=gbs_ge_summary_r&cad=0#v=onepage&q&f=false.

18 Vidler, "The Idea of Type", ibid, 107.

19 The word "character" appears in the English translation of Durand's *Précis des leçons d'architecture* at least 29 times, "grandeur" at least 12 times, "convenance" at least 10 times, "fitness" or "appropriateness" at least 74 times, "dispostion" at least 67 times, "arrangement" at least 17 times.

20 Laugier, Marc-Antoine (1753/1977) *An Essay on Architecture*, W. and A. Hermann, trans., Los Angeles: Hennesey & Ingalls, 12-13.

21 For a positioning of Laugier in the search for universal origins of architecture see, for example, Hvattum, Mari (2004) *Gottfried Semper and the Problem of Historicism*, Cambridge GB: Cambridge University Press, 29-42. See also http://en.wikipedia.org/wiki/Marc-Antoine_Laugier .

22 Quatremère de Quincy, A.-C. (1825), "Type" in *Oppositions reader : selected readings from a journal for ideas and criticism in architecture, 1973-1984,* K. Michael Hays, ed., New York: Princeton Architectural Press, 1998, 618 (original in *Encyclopédie Méthodique,* Architecture, vol. 3, pl. II, Paris, 1825).

23 Lavin, Sylvia (1992) *Quatremère de Quincy*, 98.

24 Quatremère de Quincy, A.-C. (1825) "Type", 618.

25 Ibid.

26 Rossi, Aldo (1984) *The Architecture of the City*, Cambridge, MA: MIT Press, 41.

27 Semper, Gottfried (1834) "The History of Building", Inaugural Lecture as Professor of Architecture, Dresden Art Academy, my translation from Laudel, Heidrun (1991) *Gottfried Semper, Architektur und Stil*, Dresden: Verlag der Kunst, 223-224.

28 Quatremère de Quincy, A.-C. (1800) "Sur la manière d'imiter la bonne Architecture grecque" and "Fin del la manière d'imiter la bonne Architecture grecque" in *Journal de bâtiment civils*, no. 29 and 30 (December 27 and 30). My translation. French version reprinted in Lavin, Sylvia (1992), *Quatremère de Quincy and the Invention of a Modern Language of Architecture*, Cambridge, MA: MIT Press, 194 and 196.

29 From a letter to publisher Eduard Vieweg, 1843. My translation from Laudel, Heidrun (1991) *Gottfried Semper: Architektur und Stil*, 235.

30 Semper, Gottfried (1850) "The Basic Elements of Architecture", Semper Archive, Ms 58, fols. 15-30. Reprinted in Herrmann, Wolfgang (1984) *Gottfried Semper: In Search of Architecture*, Cambridge, MA: MIT Press, 198. This quote contemplates about text in Vitruvius, *The Ten Books on Architecture*, Book II, chapter 1, section 1 and 2. For similar text see Gottfried Semper (1851/1989) *The Four Elements of Architecture and other Writings*, Harry F. Mallgrave and Wolfgang Herrmann, trans., Cambridge GB: Cambridge University Press, 102.

31 "Science, Industry and Art" in *Gotffried Semper: The Four Elements of Architecture and other Writings*, Harry F. Mallgrave and Wolfgang Herrmann, trans, Cambridge: Cambridge University Press, 130-167. The neglect to discuss the Crystal Palace itself in depth has its grounds in Semper's somewhat strange, conservative attitude toward advancements in building construction and building materials. Iron which becomes so prominent during the nineteenth century plays essentially no role in Semper's theories or practice, and he cannot foresee a role in "monuments", though perhaps in buildings for industry or transport (in greenhouses it is already been used extensively). The Eiffel tower is built less than forty years later. More important and decisive for his following work is his investigation of what many of the exhibits from all over the world, especially those from less developed societies, represent with regard to the origins of architecture; not as cave, tent or primitive hut but as material manifestations of laws of nature in artifacts throughout history.
See also http://en.wikipedia.org/wiki/The_Crystal_Palace .

32 As quoted in Herrmann (1984) *Gottfried Semper: In Search of Architecture*, 179.

33 "Science, Industry, and Art" in Semper (1852) *The Four Elements of Architecture*, 136.

34 Hvattum, Mari (2004) *Gottfried Semper and the Problem of Historicism*, Cambridge GB: Cambridge University Press, 136.

35 Panelized cottages were already produced and shipped in the late seventeenth century from the American east coast and from England. By the 1820s houses built in sections and packaged in London are sent to South Africa and Australia.* The *Manufacturer and Builder* magazine published in 1876 two- and three-story prefabricated houses.** Cast iron building components are used since the late 1700s. Large scale off-site production starts for multistory, load bearing facades in New York and other cities in the Eastern United States by the Bogardus Company around 1850.*** A boathouse in Sheerness, England, finished in 1860, is probably the first completely iron framed, multistory building.**** The first, steel framed skyscrapers in Chicago and New York follow three decades later. The first precast concrete buildings are assembled around 1900.*****

For more on construction types, using prefabrication, and extensive bibliographies see: Brandle, Kurt (1974-1976) *The Systems Approach to Building*, Associated Schools of Architecture Learning Packages, distributed to all schools of architecture and often located in school of architecture libraries, and Dominguez, Karen J. (1989) "Industrialized Construction" in *Encyclopedia of Architecture*, New York: John Wiley & Sons, vol. 3, 1-20.

* Herbert, Gilbert "The Portable Colonial Cottage" in *Journal of the Society of Architectural Historians*, vol. 31, no, 4 (Dec. 1972), 261 (electronic resource).

** Margaretta J. Darnell "Innovations in American Prefabricated Housing: 1860-1890" in *Journal of the Society of Architectural Historians*,vol. 31, no.1 (March 1972) 51-55.

*** (1970) *The Origins of Cast Iron Architecture,* New York: Da Capo Press, and , Margot and Carol (1998) *Cast-Iron Architecture in America: the significance of James Bogardus*, New York:W.W, Norton.

**** Fletcher, Bannister (1963) *A History of Architecture,* Charles Scribner's Sons, 17th ed., 1045.

***** Moore, Richard, "An early system of large-panel building" in *Journal of the Royal Institute of Architects*, vol. 76 (Sept. 1969), 383-386.

36 Muthesius, Hermann (1911) "Wo stehen wir?" in *Jahrbuch des Deutschen Werkbundes,* 1912, vol. 1, 11/26. German text:
http://www.tu-cottbus.de/theoriederarchitektur/Archiv/Autoren/Muthesius/Muthesius1912a.htm .
The claim "Wenn irgendeine Kunst, so strebt die Architektur nach dem Typischen. Nur hierin kann sie ihre Vollendung finden" is also the first of ten principles which Hermann Muthesius brings into a very contentious debate about style and type in 1914 on occasion of the Werkbundausstellung in Köln. See also Muthesius, Hermann (1902) *Style-Architecture and Building-Art: transformations of architecture in the nineteenth century and its present condition,* with introduction by Stanford Anderson, Santa Monica, CA: Getty Center for Art and Humanities, 1994. On the Werkbund and matters of style and type see Banham, Reyner (1960) *Theory and design in the first machine age,* New York: Praeger, 68-78.

37 Brolin, Brent C. (2000) *Architectural Ornament: Banishment and Return.* New York: Norton & Company, 224.

38 Franck, Karen A. (1994) "Types Are Us" in *Ordering Space: types in architecture and design*, Franck and Schneekloth, eds., New York: Van Nostrand Reinhold, 346.

39 Moneo, Rafael (1978) "On Typology" in *Oppositions* 13, Summer 1978, 23.

40 Quatremère de Quincy, A.-C. (1825), "Type", in *Oppositions Reader*, New York: Princeton Architectural Press, 618.

41 Rossi, Aldo (1981) *A Scientific Autobiography*, Cambridge, MA: MIT Press, 35.

42 Taut, Bruno (1929) *Modern architecture,* London: The Studio, 9.

43 A discussion on 'style' with focus on the arts is given in Berel Lang's entry of "Style" in Kelly, Michael, ed. (1998) *Encyclopedia of Aesthetics.*
    And,

44 A description of the terminological origin of 'style', especially with regard to architecture, is in Chapter 1 of Mallgrave, Harry F. (1983) *The Idea of Style: Gottfried Semper in London*, 2-20. UMI Dissertation Services, Ann Arbor, MI, 1993.

45 Quatremère de Quincy, *Encyclopédia Méthodique,* idem, vol. 3, 411, my translation. http://visualiseur.bnf.fr/CadresFenetre?O=NUMM-85720&M=pagination .

46 Brolin, Brent C. *Architectural Ornament: Banishment and Return.* Norton & Company. 2000, 18-54.

47 Kant, *Critique of the Power of Judgment*, 186.

48 *Aus Schinkel's Nachlass*, A.F. von Wolzogen, Berlin, 1862, vol. 2, 209. As quoted in Mallgrave, Harry F. *The Idea of Style: Gottfried Semper in London*, 48-49: "Da Zweckmässigkeit das Grundprincip alles Bauens ist, so bestimmt die möglichste Darstellung des Ideals der Zweckmässigkeit, das ist der Charakter oder die Physionomie eines Bauwerks, seinen Kunstwerth." My translation.

49 Pugin, Augustus W.N. (1836/1898) *Contrasts; or, A Parallel Between the Noble Edifices of the Middle Ages and Corresponding Buildings of the Present Day, Showing the Present Day Decay of Taste.* Second edition. Edinburgh: John Grant, 1. http://books.google.com/books?id=5DjYAAAAMAAJ&printsec=frontcover&cd=1&source=gbs_ViewAPI#v=onepage&q&f=false .

50 Gottfried Semper in a letter to Eduard Vieweg, Publisher (26 September 1843) as documented in Herrmann, Wolfgang "Semper and Eduard Vieweg" in *Gottfried Semper und die Mitte des 19. Jahrhunderts*, Symposion 1974, ETH Zürich, Basel: Birkhäuser Verlag, 1976, 216, my translation.

51 "Science, Industry, and Art" in Semper, Gottfried (1852) *The Four Elements of Architecture*, 136.

52 Muthesius, Hermann (1902) *Stilarchitektur und Baukunst: Wandlungen der Architektur im XIX. Jahrhundert und ihr heutiger Standpunkt,* Mülheim-Ruhr: Schimmelpfeng. My Translaltion. http://www.tu-cottbus.de/theoriederarchitektur/D_A_T_A/Architektur/20.Jhdt/MuthesiusHermann/StilarchitekturundBaukunst.htm .

53 Paul Gapp, then architectural editor for the Chicago Tribune, wrote the following about the 860-880 Lake Shore Drive Apartments in an article published March 31, 1991 that "Chicagoans called Ludwig Mies van der Rohe's twin 26-story apartment towers the 'glass houses' when they were built between 1948 and 1951. ... His lakefront tour de force influenced architects everywhere and in this respect eventually helped change the look of virtually every American city." Quoted from http://www.tnemec.com/project/view/?j=258 . True. Mies' "glass houses" had a great influence, not only on high-rise apartment buildings but also on other building types.

54 "Cosmos" as described in Wikipedia: 'In its most general sense, a *cosmos* is an orderly or harmonious system. It originates from a Greek term κόσμος meaning *order, arrangement, ornaments.* The word cosmetics originates from the same root. The study of the cosmos (from whatever perspective) is termed "cosmology" '. http://en.wikipedia.org/wiki/Cosmos . "Cosmos" as described in Online Etymology Dictionary: 'c.1200 (but not popular until 1848, as a translation of Humboldt's *Kosmos*), from Gk. *kosmos* "orderly arrangement" (cf. Homeric *kosmeo,* used of the act of marshaling troops), with an important secondary sense of "ornament, decoration, dress." Pythagoras is said to have been the first to apply this word to "the universe," perhaps originally meaning "the starry firmament," but later it was extended to the whole physical world, including the earth. ...' http://www.etymonline.com/index.php?l=c&p=55 .

55 Bloomer, Kent C. (2000) *The Nature of Ornament.* New York: W.W. Norton & Company, 16-17. With regard to my suggestion to view ornamentation, it is very helpful to read Bloomer's whole chapter on "The Term Ornament".

56 My view and that of Bloomer about ornament is obviously different from that of John Ruskin, Gottfried Semper, Owen Jones and many others before and after them. For example, the

architectural historian John Summerson (1963) spoke very narrowly of "surface modulation" (in *Heavenly Mansions and other essays on architecture,* New York, W. W. Norton, p. 217).

57 Vitruvius. *The Ten Books on Architecture*, Morgan, trans., 107-109.

58 Alberti, Leon, Battista. *On the Art of Building In Ten Books.* 156. When Alberti writes on page 156 that "… ornament, rather than being inherent, has the character of something attached or additional", it should not be taken as ornament being always from a source outside and attached but also being additional in the sense of expansion of what exists, that is, configurational as I view it.

59 Venturi, Robert; Denise Scott Brown and Izenour, Steven (1972) *Learning from Las Vegas*, Cambridge, MA: MIT Press, 88.

60 Bloomer, Kent C. (2000) *The Nature of Ornament,* 44.

61 My definitions of ornament and decoration are very different from those of James Trilling in his *Ornament: a modern perspective*, Seattle: University of Washington Press, 2003, 21 and 23. He writes that "All ornament is decoration, but not all decoration is ornament." In my view all decoration is ornament, but not all ornament is decoration. Ornament is terminologically more comprehensive than decoration.

62 Ramage, Michael "What is, and what is not, ornament? What is its use?" in
http://ocw.mit.edu/courses/architecture/4-645-selected-topics-in-architecture-architecture-from-1750-to-the-present-fall-2004/assignments/responses_5_3.pdf .
For other images of the Palazzetto dello Sport see
http://www.google.com/search?q=palazzetto+dello+sport&hl=en&prmd=imvns&tbm=isch&tbo=u&source=univ&sa=X&ei=QPi2Ts6iKIqvsALCsrjYDA&ved=0CE4QsAQ&biw=1258&bih=906&sei=%20TPi2TvGqPKr3sQLL_YX1Aw .

63 For a discussion of modular coordination principles in these and other projects see Brandle, Kurt "Co-ordinating Dimensions for Building Components" in *Build International*, Jan./Feb. 1971, 46-57. For an extensive report on "SCSD: the project and the schools" see
http://crs.arch.tamu.edu/media/cms_page_media/713/eflhistory.pdf .

64 See examples of hotel atriums by John Portman and Associates at
http://www.portmanusa.com/projectfilter.php?sector=hospitality&csector= .

65 For an extended discussion see Mallgrave, Harry F. (1983)*The Idea of Style: Gottfried Semper in London*, 194-198, UMI Dissertation Services, Ann Arbor, MI, 1993.

66 Bötticher, Karl (1852) *Die Tektonik der Hellenen,* Potsdam: F. Riegel, vol. 1, XV. My translation. For the original German text see http://www.google.com/books?id=y8cOAAAAQAAJ&pg=PA206&dq=Die+Tektonik+der+hellenen .

67 In a later, strongly revised, much easier to read edition "Kernform" (core-form) is replaced by the more explicit "Werkform" (work-form), pointing to the physical nature of realization. See Bötticher, Karl (1874) *Die Tektonik der Hellenen*, Berlin: Ernst & Korn, vol.1, §. 4. Werkform der Bauglieder, section 7, page 20, http://books.google.com/books?id=prEaAAAAYAAJ&pg=PR6&lpg=PR6&dq=Tektonik+der+Hellenen&source=bl&ots=2WSXewX_HX&sig=N7PgGXKmRZRhw457NI8rPE64A4&hl=en&ei=DrYNSqPmE4TwMq0kK0G&sa=X&oi=book_result&ct=result&resnum=1#PPR8,M1> .

68 From quote 143 in German, p. 297, in Mallgrave, *The Idea of Style: Gottfried Semper in London*. My translation.

69 For a description of this evolution see Vitruvius, *The Ten Books on Architecture,* 102-104.

70 From http://www.johnoutram.com/projectsmenu.html (click projects name, then Houston, Rice University, then second photograph, then go to last paragraph of Martell Hall caption).

71 Jones, Owen (1856/1986) *The Grammar of Ornament*. London: Studio Editions, London, 5. Much of Jones' writing shows clearly the confusion that arises when 'ornamentation' and 'decoration' mixed in with 'beauty' are used without giving definition to any of them.

72 Harries, Karsten (1997) *The Ethical Function of Architecture*. Cambridge, MA: MIT Press, 48.

73 Loos, Adolf (1930/1982) *Trotzdem, 1900-1930,* Wien: G. Prachner, Vorwort, 3.

74 Broch, Hermann (1931/1978) "Zerfall der Werte (3)" in "1918 – Huguenau oder die Sachlickeit" in *Die Schlafwandler*, Frankfurt am Main: Suhrkamp Verlag, 444.

75 From Artifice, Inc., http://www.artificeimages.com/architects/Coop_Himmelblau.html .

76 Venturi, Robert, Denise Scott Brown, Steven Izenour (1977,1972) *Learning from Las Vegas*, Cambridge, Mass.: MIT Press, 103.

77 Ibid, 87.

78 Lynch, Kevin (1960) *The Image of the City*, The Technology Press & Harvard University Press, Cambridge, Chapter III.

79 In this regard see also Goodman, Nelson (1975) "The Status of Style" in *Critical Inquiry,* vol. 1, No. 4, 799-811.

Notes and Bibliography of Chapter 6

1 Kant, Guyer et al, *Critique of Pure Reason*, 158.

2 Ibid 163-164.

3 Ibid 316.

4 White, F.C. (1997) *Schopenhauer's Early Fourfold Root: Translation and Commentary*, Ashgate Publishing Ltd, Aldershot, England, p. 27.

5 The following references, in addition to those related to upcoming quotes, are on literature which I found particularly helpful as background reading: Ellis, Brian (2002) *The Philosophy of Nature,* Montreal: McGill-Queen's University Press; Keil, Geert (2000) *Handeln und Verursachen,* Frankfurt/M: Vittorio Klostermann; Kim, Jaegwon (1995) "Causation" in *The Cambridge Dictionary of Philosophy,* Cambridge: Cambridge University Press, 110-112; Child, William (1994) *Causality, Interpretation and the Mind,* Oxford: Clarendon Press; Sosa, Ernest and Michael Tooley, ed. (1993) *Causation,* Oxford: Oxford University Press; Davidson, Donald (1980) *Essays on Actions and Events,* Oxford: Oxford University Press; Mackie, J. L. (1974) *The Cement of The*

Universe: A Study of Causation. Oxford: Clarendon Press, Oxford.

6 Hume, David (1740/1993) "An Abstract of a Treatise on Human Nature" in *David Hume*, Eric Steinberg, ed, Indianapolis: Hackett Publishing Company, 129.

7 Hume, David (1748/1993) "An Enquiry Concerning Human Understanding", Idem, 49 and 51.

8 Kant, Immanuel (1787/1998) *Critique of Pure Reason,* Paul Guyer and Allen W. Wood, trans. and eds., Book II, Sec. iii, 3.B Second Analogy, (versions in first and second editions), Cambridge: Cambridge University Press, 304.

9 Ibid, 21 (in Introduction by Guyer and Wood).

10 Rescher, Nicholas (2000) *Realistic pragmatism: an introduction to pragmatic philosophy,* Albany, State University of New York Press,133-4.

11 Anscombe, G.E.M. (1993) "Causality and Determination" in Sosa, Ernest and Michael Tooley *Causation,* Oxford: Oxford University Press, 101.

12 Searle, John R. (1983) *Intentionality*, Cambridge University Press, Cambridge, 131.

13 Hartshorne, Charles and Paul Weiss, eds. (1931-1958) *The Collected Papers of Charles Sanders Peirce,* Vol. V, 4th Printing, section 5.9, p. 6, Cambridge, MA: Harvard University Press.

14 Broad, Charles, D. (1923) *Scientific thought.* London: Kegan Paul, trench, Trubner & Co and Routledge (2000), 393.

15 Russell, Bertrant (1948) *Human Knowledge,* New York: Simon and Schuster, 429-430, etc.

16 Hume, David (1740/1888) *A treatise of human nature,* L.A. Selby-Bigge, ed., Part III, Section XV, 173, Oxford: Clarendon Press.
http://babel.hathitrust.org/cgi/pt?view=image;size=100;id=mdp.39015000678832;page=root;seq=201;num=173 .

17 Hume, David (1740) "An Abstract of A Treatise of Human Nature, &c." in *David Hume*, Eric Steinberg, ed, Indianapolis: Hackett Publishing Company, 1993, 130.

18 For more than a century several philosophers, among them Ernst Mach and Bertrand Russell, held that strict causal regularities are not possible. Most recently Nancy Cartwright argued convincingly that there are, therefore, only singular causal relationships and that strict causal laws do not apply (Cartwright, *Nancy* (1983) *How the Laws of Physics Lie,* Oxford: Clarendon Press).

19 Venturi, Robert (1966) *Complexity and contradiction in architecture,* New York: Museum of Modern Art, distributed by Doubleday, Garden City, NY.

20 Kistler, Max. "Causation as Transference and Responsibility" in *Current Issues in Causation,* Wolfgang Spohn et al, eds, Mentis Paderborn, 2001, 131. See page 14 of
http://max.kistler.free.fr/articles/MK11.pdf .

21 The small Critical Path sample diagram shown in 3.5 is explained by "PERT (Program Evaluation and Review Technique) chart for a project with five milestones (10 through 50) and six activities (A through F). The project has two critical paths: activities B and C, or A, D, and F – giving a minimum project time of 7 months with fast tracking. Activity E is sub-critical, and has a

float of 2 months. t=time in months. The essential technique for using CPM is to construct a model of the project that includes the following:
> 1. A list of all activities required to complete the project (also known as Work Breakdown Structure),
> 2. The time (duration) that each activity will take to completion, and
> 3. The dependencies between the activities."

(from http://en.wikipedia.org/wiki/Critical_path_method) .

22 Schutz, Alfred (1932/1967) *The Phenomenology of the Social World*, trans. George Walsh and Frederick Lehnert, Evanston IL: Northwestern University Press, 100.

23 Ibid, 132 to 135.

24 See, for example, such strained justifications for this concept in architecture as given in Wigley, Mark (1997) *The Architecture of Deconstruction: Derrida's Haunt*, Cambride, MA: MIT Press.

25 Ibid, 50.

26 Mackie, John L. (1974) *The Cement of The Universe: A Study of Causation.* Clarendon Press, Oxford, 293.

27 Stout, Rowland (1996) *Things That Happen Because They Should.* Oxford University Press, 84.

28 Ibid, 85.

29 Peirce, Charles S. (1931-1935) *The Collected Papers of Charles Sanders Peirce,* ed. Charles Hartshorne and Paul Weiss, Cambridge, MA: Harvard University Press, vol. 7, ch. 3 (The Logic of Drawing History from Ancient Documents), 202.

30 Ibid, vol. 5, lec. 7 (Pragmatism and Abduction), 181.3.

31 Child, William T. (1994) *Causality, Interpretation and the Mind.* Oxford: Oxford University, 112.

32 For more on counterfactuals see "Counterfactual Theories of Causation" at http://plato.stanford.edu/entries/causation-counterfactual/ .

33 Frankl, Paul (1914/1968) *Principles of Architectural History: The Four Phases of Style, 1420-1900,* James O. Gorman, trans., Cambridge, MA: MIT Press, 161.

34 See Conrads, Ulrich (1971) *Programs and manifestoes on 20th-century architecture*, Cambridge, MA: MIT Press.

35 See, for example, *Architektur Wettbewerbe*, Stuttgart: Krämer Verlag.

36 Hatch Richard C, (1984) "Toward a Theory of Social Architecture" in *The Scope of Social Architecture*, C. Richard Hatch, ed, New York: Van Nostrand Reinhold, 7.

37 Schneekloth, Lynda H. and Robert G. Sibley (1995) *Placemaking: the art and practice of building communities.* New York: John Wiley & Sons, 6.

38 Anderson, John (2001) in *Communities by Design*, The American Institute of Architects.

39 From an earlier website of Pratt Institute Center for Community and Environmental Development (PICCED), Brooklyn, New York, about 2005. For present website see http://prattcenter.net/how-we-work .

40 from http://www.designadvisor.org/frameset.html?http://www.designadvisor.org/gallery/parkview.html .
See also "California Hilltown", Architectural Record, July, 1990, 84-87.

41 Markus, Thomas (1993) *Buildings and Power: Freedom and Control in the Origin of Modern Building Types, London:* Routledge, 23.

42 King, Anthony D., ed. (1979) *Buildings and Society: Essays on the social development of the built environment*, London: Routledge & Kegan Paul, 1.

43 "Rudolph" in Perspecta 7, Yale School of Architecture, 1961, 51.

44 For example, Mies' Crown Hall on the IIT Campus is not a comfortable space to work in. It is noisy and provides for very little privacy. And, it does not provide good daylighting, having for all facade orientations the same very large windows without adequate shading control.

45 From "Ein deutscher Prinzipienritter" (A German Doctrinaire) by Hanno Rautenberg, *DIE ZEIT*, 28, 6. Juli 2006, 39.

46 Moneo, Rafael (1978) "On Typology" in *Oppositions* 13 (Summer), 37.

47 Eisenman, Peter (1984) "The End of the Classical: The End of the Beginning, the End of the End" in *Perspecta* 21, 168. Reprinted in Hays, Michael, ed (1998) *Architecture Theory since 1968*, Cambridge, MA: MIT Press, 524-538.

48 In an increasingly interdependent world, attempts toward extreme arbitrariness and autonomy lead to authoritarianism. The consequence is neglect of general welfare. In our field it leads to brushing aside of crucial design factors for the sake of 'signature' architecture, not to belittle the qualities of awe and beauty it may evoke. Inclusion, not exclusion, is the paradigm for broadly meaningful architecture at least to the point where local societal and environmental needs find reflection.

49 Vande Moere, A. (2005). "Form Follows Data: the Symbiosis between Design and Information Visualization", *International Conference on Computer-Aided Architectural Design (CAADfutures'05)*, OKK Verlag, Vienna, Austria, pp.31-40. See also
http://www.neme.org/main/815/form-follows-data .

50 Alexander, Christopher (1968) *Notes on the Synthesis of Form*, Cambridge, MA: Harvard University Press, 15-16.

51 Peña, William, Steven A. Parshall (2001) *Problem Seeking: an architectural programming primer.* New York: John Wiley, 20 and 24. The first edition was published in 1969.

52 Hershberger, Robert G. (1999) *Architectural Programming and Predesign Manager*. New York: McGraw-Hill, 5.

53 White, Eduard T. (1972) *Introduction to Architectural Programming*. Tucson AZ: Architectural Media, 28.

54 Peña and Parshall (2001), 183.

55 See especially *EDRA, Proceedings of the annual Environmental Design Research Association Conference*, Raleigh NC, since 1969.

56 Lang, Jon T. (1987) *Creating architectural theory: the role of the behavioral sciences in environmental design.* New York: Van Nostrand Reinhold.

57   Some of the more recent publications on POE and BPE (Building Performance Evaluation) are: Anderzhon, Jeffrey W. et al (2007) *Design for Aging Post-Occupancy Evaluations.* The American Institute of Architects. Hoboken, NJ; John Wiley & Sons; *Guide to Post Occupancy Evaluation*, Higher Education Funding Council for England, 2006, http://www.smg.ac.uk/documents/POEBrochureFinal06.pdf; Preiser F.E., Jacqueline C. Vischer, ed (2005) *Assessing building performance.* Oxford: Elsevier. This book describes especially the wider framework of BPE versus POE; Baird, George et al (1995) *Building Evaluation Techniques.* New York: McGraw-Hill.

58   Anderzhon, Jeffrey W. et al (2007) *Design for Aging Post-Occupancy Evaluations.* The American Institute of Architects. Wiley & Sons, Hoboken, NJ, xiii (foreword by Margaret Calkins).

59   Preiser, Wolfgang E.F., Harvey Rabinowitz and Edward T. White (1988) *Post-Occupancy Evaluation.* New York: Van Nostrand Reinhold Company, 53-57. A third level mentioned, "investigative POEs", is between the other two. All POEs are investigative, more or less.

60   Hartkopf Volker, et al "Integration of Performance" in Rush, Richard ed. (1986)*The Building Systems Integration Handbook,* John Wiley & Sons, New York, 231- 316.

61   *SCSD: the project and the schools*, New York: Educational Facilities Laboratories, 1967. Also see "The Performance Concept" and "The SCSD Project" in Ehrenkrantz Ezra (1995) *Architectural Systems.* New York: McGraw-Hill, 43-48 and 133-136.

62   For a comparison chart about performance specifications versus prescriptive (design) specifications see https://acc.dau.mil/CommunityBrowser.aspx?id=294564 .

63   Ehrenkrantz, Ezra D. (1989) *Architectural Systems*, New York: McGraw-Hill, 43.

64   With everything we do, so in design, we find ourselves in a context. Therefore, it applies also more broadly for architectural design, what Maurice Merleau-Ponti writes about the human body's spatiality, that it is not "... a spatiality of position but a spatiality of situation." (Phenomenology of *Perception*, 1962, 100). Wherever we are and do something, we are in and part of circumstances.

65   For interesting observations in this regard see, for example, Forty, Adrian "The modern Hospital in England and France: the social and medical uses of architecture" and Hancock, John "The apartment house in urban America" in King, Anthony D., ed.(1980*) Buildings and society*. London: Routledge & Kegan Paul.

66   Buder, Stanley (1967) *Pullman: An Experiment in Industrial Order and Community Planning 1880-1930,* New York: Oxford University Press, 43. For a bibliography on further resources about Pullman see http://www.pullmanil.org/links.htm .

67   For literature on the industrialization of building see, for example, Kelly, Burnham (1951) *The Prefabrication of Houses.* New York: Wiley and Sons; Testa, Carlo (1972) *The Industrialization of Building.* New York: Van Nostrand Reinhold; Bender, Richard (1973) *A Crack in the Rear View Mirror: a view of industrialized building.* New York: Van Nostrand Reinhold.; Brandle, Kurt (1976) *The Systems Approach to Building.* ACSA Learning Package, Salt Lake City: Graduate School of Architecture, University of Utah; Ehrenkrantz, Ezra (1995) *Architectural Systems,* New York:

McGraw-Hill. Although there is today still much realization by traditional means of construction, all present construction greatly benefits from the inclusion of many components which mass production and its huge 'of the shelf' market make available. The structural concrete double-T ceiling system is one example. Integrated lighting/HVAC subsystems for suspended ceilings are another.

68   Jacobs, Jane (1961) *The Death and Life of the American City. New York: Random House.* Blake, Peter (1964) *God's own junkyard; the planned deterioration of America's landscape.* New York: Holt, Rinehart and Winston; Gans, Herbert (1968) *People and Plans; essays on urban problems and solutions.* New York: Basic Books; Lynch, Kevin (1960) *The Image of the City.* Cambridge MA: MIT Press; Norberg-Schulz, Christian (1963) *Intentions in Architecture.* Cambridge MA: MIT Press; Perin, Constance (1970) *With Man in Mind.* Cambridge MA: MIT Press; Newman, Oscar (1973) *Defensible Space: crime prevention through urban design.* New York: Mcmillan.

69   Jones, J. Christopher et al, ed. (1963) *Conference on Design Methods*; Gregory, Sydney, ed. (1966) *The Design Method*; Moore, Gary T., ed. (1970) *Emerging Methods in Eenvironmental Design and Planning*; Rapoport, Amos (1970) *House Form and Culture.*

70   Lye, John (1997) Some Post-Structural Assumptions. http://www.brocku.ca/english/courses/4F70/poststruct.php .

71   See Miriam-Webster online: http://www.merriam-webster.com/dictionary/postmodernism .

72 The term *Deconstruction*, as often used today in architectural theory, is a linguistic monster. One cannot at the same time de- and construct. When Derrida adopted Heidegger's "Destruktion" from *Sein and Zeit* (*Being and Time*, Joan Stambaugh, trans., Albany, NY: State University of New York Press, 1996, 20-27, § 6) and coined the term "deconstruction", he twisted the meaning of the German term ostensively into a direction it does not have. Destruktion, as clearly explained by Heidegger, is taking apart components of what is given to gain better understanding of it. For our interest, it means to look at properties of objects and their causal relationships within the whole. Destruktion, in Heidegger's sense, is best translated as destructuring. Its other meaning of destroying is not applicable here. If one wants to play with words, one could say with regard to the overall process: we 'de- plus construct' for advancing understanding of what we encounter. This is not what Derrida had in mind. Heidegger writes in 1955, referring to *Being and Time,* that "Destruktion does not mean destroying but pulling apart, taking down and putting aside ... Destruktion means to open our ears, to make ourselves free for that which speaks to us out of tradition as the Being of being." (What is Philosophy?, New York: Twayne Publishers, 1958, 70 and 72, my trans). Barbara Johnson writes that "*Deconstruction* is not synonymous with *destruction*, ... It is in fact much closer to the original meaning of the word *analysis*, itself, which etymologically means 'to undo' – a virtual synonym for 'to de-construct'. ... If anything is destroyed in a deconstructive reading, it is not the text, but the claim to unequivocal domination of one mode of signifying over another. A deconstructive reading is a reading that analyzes the specificity of a text's critical difference from itself." (Johnson, Barbara (1980) *The critical difference: essays in the contemporary rhetoric of reading,* Baltimore: Johns Hopkins University Press, 5). A "text's [or anything else's] critical difference from itself" Is typical post-modern jargon: nothing can be a difference from itself, unless the itself is changed and then it is something else not itself

anymore. Everything different from itself is different. More broadly and straight forwardly, one might simply say: What else might this (thing, text) mean?

73 Ghirardo, Diane (1996) *Architecture after Modernism.* London: Thames and Hudson, 36-37.

74 Vidler, Anthony "Deconstruction Boom", *Artforum International*, New York: Dec 2003. Vol. 42, Iss. 4; p. 33. Vidler refers to the 7 architects featured in the "Deconstructivist Architecture" show of 1988 at the Museum of Modern Art, New York.

75 Examples of literature which show how designers organize the multitudes of cause-effect relationships: Schirmbeck, Egon (1983) *Idee+Form+Architektur*, Stuttgart: Karl Krämer Verlag; Ching, Frank (1996) *Architecture: Form, Space and Order*, New York: Van Nostrand Reinhold; Lawson, Bryan (1997) *How Designers Think*, Oxford: Architectural Press; Righini, Paul (2000) *Thinking Architecturally*, Cape Town: University of Cape Town Press; Hearn, Millard (2003) *Ideas that shaped buildings*, Cambridge: MIT Press; Clark, Roger and Michael Pause (2004) *Precedents in Architecture: analytic diagrams, formative ideas and partis,* New York: Wiley & Sons.

Notes and Bibliography of Chapter 7

1 Helpful introductions which address the main issues on language in general are, for example, the entries of "meaning", "philosophy of language", "philosophy of mind" and "proposition" in *The Cambridge Dictionary of Philosophy*, Cambridge GB: Cambridge University Press, 1995, and the entries on "analytic philosophy", "language" and "semantics" of the *Encyclopedia Britannica Online*, http://www.britannica.com. Books by single philosophers on language, I found very helpful, are John R. Searle (1998) *Mind, Language and Society: philosophy in the real world,* New York: Basic Books; Michael Losonsky (2006) *Linguistic Turns in Modern Philosophy,* New York: Cambridge University Press; Peter M.S.Hacker, "Analytic Philosophy: Beyond the Linguistic Turn and Back Again" in Michael Beaney, ed. (2009) *The Analytical Turn: Analysis in Early Analytical Philosophy and Phenomenology*, New York: Routledge.

2 Locke, John (1690) *An Essay Concerning Humane Understanding,* Vol. 1, Book 2, 29.1 and 33.19. Project Gutenberg: 2004, based on 2nd edition, http://www.gutenberg.org/files/10615/10615.txt .

3 Humboldt, Wilhelm von (1820/1903ff.) *Gesammelte Schriften*. Issued by Königlich Preussische Akademie der Wissenschaften, 17 vols., Berlin: B. Behr (1905) vol. IV, 14, my translation. http://books.google.com/books?id=ZQlcAAAAMAAJ&pg=PP8#v=onepage&q&f=false .

4 Ibid, (1907) vol, VII, first half, 53, http://books.google.com/books?id=AwhcAAAAMAAJ&pg=PP7#v=onepage&q&f=false .

5 Ibid, "Über Denken und Sprechen", item 6, Berlin: Behr (1908) vol. VII, second half, 581, my translation. http://books.google.com/books?id=QRgeAQAAIAAJ&pg=PA581&source=gbs_toc_r&cad=4#v=onepage&q&f=false .
See also: Source: Mauthner-Gesellschaft/Verein der Sprachkritiker http://www.blutner.de/philos/Texte/humboldt.html .

6 Heidegger, Martin (1944) "Hölderlin und das Wesen der Dichtung" in *Erläuterungen zu Hölderlins Dichtung.* Frankfurt: Klostermann, 37-38, my translation.

7 Heidegger, Martin (1959/1971) *Unterwegs zur Sprache.* Pfullingen: Günther Neske, 164-166, my translation.
    And,
8 On these issues see also Lafont, Cristina (1999) *The Linguistic Turn in Hermeneutic Philosophy*, Cambridge, MA: MIT Press.

9 Ludwig Wittgenstein writes in *Tractatus*, 7 that "Whereof one cannot speak, thereof one must be silent".

10 Jürgen Habermas "Comments on John Searle's 'Meaning, Communication, and Representation' " (1988) in Habermas, Jürgen (2000) *On the pragmatics of communication*, Maeve Cooke ed, Cambridge MA: MIT Press, 258.

11 On this see also Lafont, Cristina (2005) "Heidegger on meaning and reference", *Philosophy & Social Criticism,* vol 31 no 1, p. 11.

12 For a discussion of "Sinn und Bedeutung" and related terminology in English see Section 3.b of http://www.iep.utm.edu/freg-lan/#SH3b . For an translation of Frege's text see http://en.wikisource.org/wiki/On_Sense_and_Reference .

13 Wittgenstein, Ludwig (1922) *Tractatus Logico-Philosophicus,* London: Kegan Paul, Trench, Trubner & Co., 31 (§ 1.11), 39 (§ 2.1, 2.12, 2.13), 43 (§ 2.221).
http://books.google.com/books?id=w-PWAAAAMAAJ&printsec=frontcover&dq=Tractatus&hl=en&ei=Hp9ZTb7IDsHYgAf7xaD0DA&sa=X&oi=book_result&ct=result&resnum=1&ved=0CCoQ6AEwAA#v=onepage&q&f=false .

14 Jacquette, Dale (1998) *Wittgenstein's Thought in Transition*, West Lafayette, IN: Purdue University Press, p. 35. This book is a detailed introduction to the issues in Wittgenstein's main works, the *Tractatus* and *the Philosophical Investigations.*

15 Wittgenstein (1922) *Tractatus*, 47 (§ 3.1431).

16 Wittgenstein, Ludwig (1953) *Philosophical Investigations,* G.E.M. Anscombe, The Macmillan Company, New York, 11-12, (§ 23). See also
http://books.google.com/books?id=JoPYriJM1cwC&printsec=frontcover&dq=wittgenstein+philosophical+investigations&hl=en&ei=OzvFTdTuC4fVgAeG0LXLBA&sa=X&oi=book_result&ct=book-thumbnail&resnum=1&ved=0CDAQ6wEwAA#v=onepage&q&f=false .

17 Ibid, 20-21 (§ 43). Sometimes the expression "Meaning is use" is given in the literature, which is ambiguous, if not misleading. Wittgenstein, I believe, says that "Use has Meaning", that is, when thought about use helps us to understand.

18 Ibid, 149 (§ 560). This may seem to be simplistic advice. But it is very practical, considering the ambiguity of the term meaning. But Wittgenstein also makes some strange remarks on what and what not to assume what 'understanding' and 'meaning' are, and one must be careful not to see them contradictory to what else he says. We encounter, for example, "Try not to think of understanding as a 'mental process' at all.– For *that* is the expression which confuses you. ..." (§ 154) And, "... nothing is more wrong-headed than calling meaning a mental activity! Unless, that

is, one is setting out to produce confusion. ..." (§ 693) I believe he is driving at understanding and meaning being result rather than process. The mental process which leads to understanding and meaning is thinking. As result, however, understanding and meaning have mental status. What else could understanding and meaning be but mental? As there are intermediate results of the emotion-and-reason process (Figure 4.1) and as understanding and meaning are part of our ongoing processes in memory, it is easy to mix up process and result. For further reading on this aspect I refer particularly to Colin McGinn (1984) *Wittgenstein on Meaning*, Oxford: Basil Blackwell, 102-105.

19 Ibid, 32 (§ 66 and 67).

20 Ibid, 81 (§ 199).

21 Ibid, 153 (§ 580).

22 Gillett, Grant R. and John McMillan. (2001) *Consciousness and Intentionality.* Amsterdam: John Benjamins Publishing Company, 5.

23 Fodor, Jerry A. (1975) *The Language of Thought*, Cambridge, Massachusetts: Harvard University Press.

24 Aydede, Murat, (2004) "The Language of Thought Hypothesis" in *The Stanford Encyclopedia of Philosophy* (Fall 2004 Edition), Edward N. Zalta, ed., http://plato.stanford.edu/archives/fall2004/entries/language-thought/ .

25 Searle, John R. (1998) *Mind, Language and Society.* New York: Basic Books, 10.

26 Rowe, Peter (1987) *Design Thinking.* Cambridge, MA: MIT Press.

27 Alexander, Christopher (1979) *The Timeless Way of Building*, Oxford: Oxford University Press, 186.

28 Ibid, 253.

29 Ibid, 187.

30 The Blackforest farmhouse has an organization which evolved over generations of farmers. Often it is built with its north side unto a hill so that hay can be brought from the hill for storage under part of the roof above the stables. The animals are below and can be served directly by throwing the feed down. A heavy stone wall between this barn section of the house and the farmer's two story living section serves as structural, sound, thermal and fire barrier. In winter it is a 'warm wall' because of the warmth from animals. The south side has many windows, a large roof overhang for shading and frequently a long balcony, which also serves for shading the windows below. All of these features represent meaningful functional relationships in architecture here arrived at without a professional designer.

31 Fischer, Günther (1991) *Architektur und Sprache.* archpaper-edition, Stuttgart: Karl Krämer Verlag, 52-77.

32 Ibid, 85. My translation.

33 See, for example, Ehrenkranz, Ezra (1956) *The Modular Number Pattern; flexibility through standardisation*, London: A. Tiranti. and Brandle, Kurt "Co-ordinating Dimensions for Building Components" in *Build International,* Jan./Feb. 1971, 46-57.

34 See footnote 35 in the bibliographies of Chapter 5.

35 For in a nutshell introductions to aspects of Space Syntax see Peponis, John and Jean Wineman (2002) "Spatial Structure of Environment and Behavior" in *Handbook of environmental psychology*, Robert Bechtel and Arza Churchman ed., New York: J. Wiley, 271-291, and Bafna, Sonit (2003) "SPACE SYNTAX: A Brief Introduction to Its Logic and Analytical Techniques", *ENVIRONMENT AND BEHAVIOR*, Vol. 35 No. 1, 17-29.

36 Peponis, John (2001) "Interacting Questions and Descriptions" in *Space Syntax*, Proceedings, 3rd International Symposium, Atlanta, published by A. Alfred Taubman College of Architecture and Urban Planning, University of Michigan, Ann Arbor, MI, page XVI.

37 For a discussion and bibliography of modern views on space in architecture see, for example, Zevi, Bruno (1957/1993) *Architecture as Space*, New York: Da Capo Press; Van de Ven, Cornelis (1987) *Space in Architecture*, Assen/Maastricht: Van Gorcum & Company; and "Die Wahrnehmung des Raumes" in Moravanszky, Akos ed. (2003) *Architekturtheorie im 20. Jahrhundert*, Wien: Springer-Verlag, 121-251.

38 Hillier, Bill (1996/2007) *Space is the machine,* Cambridge, GB: Cambridge University Press, Cambridge, 20. http://www.ninsight.at/ak_stdb/SpaceIsTheMachine.pdf .

39 Ibid, 27.

40 Ibid, 327.

41 Ibid, 326.

42 Scruton, Roger (1979) *The Aesthetics of Architecture,* Princeton, NJ.: Princeton University Press, 158. The given quote is at the beginning of chapter 7, unfortunately called "the Language of Architecture". In fact the chapter clearly refutes the "of" and does not have much sympathy even for an analogy of language and architecture. While I do not agree with Scruton in every point, I find this chapter an excellent exposition of why "language of architecture" is highly problematic and misleading terminology.

43 Whyte, William (2006) "How do buildings mean? Some issues of interpretation in the history of architecture", *History and Theory,* vol. 45 (May), 169.

44 Ibid 153 (abstract).

45 Ibid 175-176. This quote refers to *Eero Saarinen on His Work*, Aline B. Saarinen ed., New Haven: Yale University Press, 1968, 68.

46 Examples are Niels Luning Prak *The language of architecture;* Bruno Zevi *The modern language of architecture* and Charles Jencks *The language of post-modern architecture*. There are, across various fields, many books in print with titles of 'The Language of …'. Few of them have anything to do with the structural aspects of language and would be better more generally called something like 'The Nature of …'. For reading on rather pointed architecture/language comparisons, again with caution because of missing differentiations with regard to "language of architecture" versus "language about architecture", see Forty, Adrian (2000) "Language and Drawing" and "Language Metaphor" in *Words and Buildings*, New York: Thames & Hudson, 29-41 and 63-85, respectively.

47 Markus, Thomas A. and Deborah Cameron, *The Words Between the Spaces*, London: Routledge, London, in prologue. This book touches on many themes which are relevant to our present concerns.

48 Ibid, 8.

49 Gardiner, Alan. *The Theory of Speech and Language.* Oxford: Oxford University Press, 1951, 35.

50 De Saussure, *Course in General Linguistics*, p. 67.

51 Krampen, Martin (1979) *Meaning in the Urban Environment*, London: Pion, 181. This book also contains probably the most comprehensive bibliography on meaning and semiology for its time of publication.

52 Such as Sommer, R. (1965) "The significance of space", *Journal of American Institute of Architects,* May 63-5; Hershberger, R.G. (1972) "Toward a set of semantic scales to measure the meaning of architectural environments", *EDRA Three*, Proceedings, University of California, Los Angeles, 6-4-1 to 6-4-10.

53 Canter, David (1975) "Buildings in Use" in *Environmental Interaction: Psychological Approaches to our Physical Surroundings*, 196. Though thirty years old, this account provides many helpful insights on the 'measurement' of meaning.

54 See note 51 above and Groat, Linda (1995) "Meaning in Post-Modern Architecture: An Examination using the Multiple Sorting Task" in *Giving Places Meaning*, Linda Groat ed., London: Academic Press, 140-160.

55 Hershberger, Robert G. (1972) "Toward a set of semantic scales to measure the meaning of architectural environments" in *EDRA Three Proceeding*s, University of California, Los Angeles, 6-4-1 to 6-4-10.

56 Hershberger Robert G. (1969) *A Study of meaning in Architecture*, Doctoral Dissertation at the University of Michigan, 204-7.

57 Habermas, Jürgen (1984) *The Theory of Communicative Action*, Thomas McCarthy trans., Boston: Beacon Press.

58 Hershberger (1969), idem, 7.

59 Hershberger's work, though obviously somewhat dated, provides a good background for our interests, although there are considerable differences between his and my views, especially with regard to scaling categories.

60 This is in line with Kant's fundamental dictum, that "There is no doubt whatever that all our cognition begins with experience"; that is, experience of an expression (Guyer ed, Kant (1781/1998) *Critique of Pure Reason,* p. 136).

61 This agrees with Kant's emphasis that perception requires imagination (Guyer, ed, Kant (1781/1998) 238-239 and 256-257). I believe that 'creative thought' is a more neutral term for what Kant calls "productive imagination" and 'reproductive thought' for "his reproductive imagination", although the literal translation from his work is "imagination" (Einbildung).

62 Kant: "… insofar as they are to relate to an object our cognitions must also necessarily agree with each other in relation to it [the object], i.e., they must have that unity that constitutes the concept of an object." (Guyer, ed, Kant (1781/1998) *Critique of Pure Reason,* 231).

63 From this point of view it can be easily understood why I believe that De Saussure's use of 'concept' for the semantic component in his linguistic sign theory (Figure 3.53) is not a good one,

at least not for our interests, and why I replaced it with 'content'.

64 Tschumi, Bernard (1994) "Disjunctions" in *Architecture and Disjunction*, Cambridge: MIT Press, 207.

65 Psarra, Sophia (2009) *Architecture and Narrative*. London: Routledge.

66 Lowri, Glenn D. (2004) "Introduction" in *MoMa Highlights*, New York: Museum of Modern Art, 21.

67 From http://www.etymonline.com/index.php?l=n&p=1 : *narration* , early 15c., from O.Fr. *narration* "a relating, recounting, narrating," from L. *narrationem* (nom. *narratio*), from *narrare* "to tell, relate, recount, explain," lit. "to make acquainted with," from *gnarus* "knowing," from PIE suffixed zero-grade *gne-ro-*, from base *gno-* "to know" (see *know*).

68 Psarra (2009), idem, 2.

69 Rittel, Horst W J and Melvin M. Webber (1973) "Dilemmas in a General Theory of Planning", *Policy Sciences* 4, 155-169.

70 I am perhaps more familiar with this building through its history of evolution than with any other building with which I was not involved directly. I was lucky to have had Scharoun as a teacher in urban design the year after he won the competition for The Philharmonie. The class project of my three member student team was chosen for the urban planning exhibit of 'Die Stadt von morgen', which Scharoun organized, as part of the 1958 International Building Show in Berlin.

71 For additional descriptions of this building see http://ennead.com/#/projects/michigan-biomedical-science-building and http://www.umaec.umich.edu/projects/BSRB/index.html .

Notes and Bibliography of Chapter 8

1 See, for example, anthologies by Mallgrave, Harry Francis, ed. (2008) *Architectural Theory*, vol. 2, Oxford: Blackwell; Moravanszky, Akos, hrsg. (2003) *Architekturtheorie im 20. Jahrhundert*. Wien: Springer; Di Cristina, Giuseppa, ed. (2001) *AD: Architecture and Science,* Chichester: John Wiley & Sons; Hays, K. Michael, ed. (1998) *Architecture Theory since 1968*. Cambridge MA: MIT Press; Hays, K. Michael ed. (1998) *Oppositions Reader*, New York: Princeton Architectural Press. For authors of monographs and articles see, for example, Gilles Deleuze, Jacques Derrida, Umberto Eco, Peter Eisenman, Charles Jencks, Jeff Kipnis, Rem Koolhas, Rob Krier, Sanford Kwinter, Daniel Libeskind, Gregg Lynn, José Moneo, Stephen Perrella, Aldo Rossi, Nikos Salingaros, Manfredo Tafuri, Bernard Tschumi, Robert Venturi and Mark Wigley.

2 Ghirardo, Diane (1996) *Architecture after Modernism,* London: Thames and Hudson.

3 Douglas Harper *Online Etymology Dictionary*: http://www.etymonline.com/index.php?l=v&p=7 .

4 Ibid.

5 Perrella, Stephen and Rebecca Carpenter (2001) "The Möbius House Study" in *AD: Architecture and Science*, Giuseppa Di Cristina ed.,159 (Note 2). The reference to Deleuze and Guattari is based on these philosophers positions on identities and differences which offer exceptional freedoms of thought and living. "For Deleuze, there is no one substance, only an

always-differentiating process, an origami cosmos, always folding, unfolding, refolding." See toward end of section on "Metaphysics" in (http://en.wikipedia.org/wiki/Deleuze) and http://plato.stanford.edu/entries/process-philosophy/ .
For images from The Möbius House Study and other studies of hypersurfaces see also http://x2.i-dat.org/~cs/places/speed.pdf .

6   Representative for this thinking is the collection of articles in Di Cristina, Giuseppa, ed. (2001) *AD: Architecture and Science*, Chichester: John Wiley-Academy. Other and more recent views are given in many of the 26 titles in the series on "The IT Revolution in Architecture", Antonio Saggio ed., Basel: Birkhäuser, 1999-2006. In one of these booklets, *Induction design: a method for evolutionary design,* 5-6, Makato Sei Watanabe writes that "Essentially, design begins by selecting a single line. It is not a matter of choosing any line, say this one or any other one. Design is a matter of choosing a specific line, the only possible one. ... This line needs to be a good one. In this case, good means, first of all useful. Useful means that it solves the conditions posed by the project. ..." Does the author understand the contradiction in the priorities he is describing? If choosing a line or any other useful action toward architectural realization is to be taken, it requires first thinking about purpose and context, although because of the complexity of factors involved, purpose is at this point propositional rather than ultimate. "Useful" design, that is purposive design, does not "begin by selecting a single line" but with design thinking which aims at understanding content as the basis of form which then will have as consequence many lines and other physical as well as relational properties.

7   De Kerckhove, Derick (2003) "Searching for the Principles of Web Architecture" in *The Charter of Zurich: Eisenman, De Kerckhove, Saggio,* Furio Barzon ed., Basel: Birkhäuser, 39.

8   Whyte. Jennifer (2002) *Virtual Reality and the Build Environment*, Oxford: Architectural Press, 45.

9   Borradori, Giovanna (2001)"Against the technological interpretation of virtuality" in *AD: Architecture and Science*, Giuseppa Di Cristina ed, Chichester: Wiley-Academy, 208.

10   Eisenman, Peter (2003) "A Matrix in the Jungle" in *The Charter of Zurich*, 35.

11   Ibid, 36.

12   For an example of evoking chaos see Barzon, Furio (2003) "Nine Keys for a Matrix", in *The Charter of Zurich*, 11. In "History", a forward to Michael Leyton's *Shape as Memory*, Birkhäuser, Basel, 2006, 5, Antonio Saggio writes that Leyton "… explains in an incontrovertible manner that symmetry simultaneously kills both history and form!". This is an example of a favored device in some of postmodern writing, namely incessant change of traditional word meaning (here symmetry, history and form), with the consequence of misunderstanding in communication. Leyton's text itself is a masterpiece of such obfuscation of meaning.

13   Venturi, Robert (1966), idem, 20.

14   In Deleuze's work, arguably closest related to anything architectural and most often referred to, is "The Pleats of Matter" in (1988/1993)*The Fold: Leibnitz and the Baroque*, Chapter 1, Minneapolis: University of Minnesota Press; reprinted in (2001) *AD: Architecture and Science* 39-43. Folding is associated with Baroque without explanation what is meant by "folds". Here, folds do all kinds of things which have nothing to do with folding and thus attain mysteriousness. He starts with "The Baroque refers not to an essence but rather to an operative function, to a trait. It endlessly produces folds. It does not invent things: there are all kinds of folds coming from

the East, Greek, Roman, Romanesque, Gothic, Classical folds …" It seems that his "folds" are influences, notions, layers or aspects. Why not to use such words which add explanatory power to the context in which they are used? It seems that linguistic explicitness is not a sought-after quality in some of the recent philosophical writing. Half way through the chapter: "Plastic forces are thus more machinelike than they are mechanical, and they allow for the definition of Baroque machines. It might be claimed that mechanisms of inorganic nature already stretch to infinity because the motivating force is of an already infinite composition, or that the fold always refers to other folds. …" Such sentences, and they occur throughout Deleuze's writing, are not only "difficult and opaque", as Tom Conley in the translator's foreword mentions, but simply incomprehensible because words with familiar meanings, are given other never explained content, if any. What are "plastic forces"? How are forces "more machinelike than …mechanical"?

15 Lynn, Greg (2001) "Architectural Curvilinearity: The Folded, the Plint and the Supple" in *AD: Architecture and Science*, 32.

16 Eisenman, Peter "Folding in Time: The Singularity of Rebstock", ibid, 52.

17 In his article Eisenman refers to *Siedlung* as a particular urban form during the first part of the 20th century. All what *Siedlung* means is settlement, usually assembly of housing, with obviously many forms from the ancient times to this day. Because of various reasons, especially concerns for health but also because of shopping, street layouts, parking, etc., settlements during the 20th century developed patterns. But there is not only one kind of *Siedlungsform* and often there is considerable variety among the parts of the *Siedlungen*.

18 Perrella, Stephen "Hypersurface Theory: Architecture>< Culture" in *AD: Architecture and Science*, 139 and 142.

19 For a discussion of some of the problems involved see Colajanni B. et al (2006) "Which new semantic for new shapes?" in *Digital Architecture and Construction,* Ali a. and Brebbia C.A. ed, Southampton: WIT Press, 1-10.

20 Oxman, Rivka (2008) "Digital architecture as a challenge for design pedagogy: theory, knowledge, models and medium", *Design Studies*, Volume 29, Issue 2, March, 99-120, Section 4.4.1.

21 From "Emergent Architecture", Jan. 15, 2010 (an earlier website, see http://m-rad.com/index.php?/product-design/bat-wing/).

22 As, for example, in Oxman (2008) "Digital architecture as a challenge for design pedagogy: theory, knowledge, models and medium".

23 Friedman, Mildred (1999) "the reluctant master" in *Gehry talks : architecture + process*, Mildred Friedman ed., New York: Rizzoli, 34.

24 Benjamin, Andrew (2000) *Architectural Philosophy,* London: The Athlone Press, 10-11.

25 Ibid, 202-203.

26 Derrida, Jacques (1991) "58 min 41 sec, Summary of Impromptu Remarks" in *ANYONE*, Cynthia Davidson ed., New York: Rizzoli International Publications, p. 39-45.

27 My last sentence was prompted by a book by John Silber (2007) *The Architecture of the Absurd: How "Genius" Disfigured a Practical Art*, New York: The Quantuck Lane Press. This book largely parallels my views on deconstructivist tendencies in architecture.

28 Ford, Alan (2007) *Designing the sustainable school*, Bastow : The Images Publishing Group Pty Ltd., 142. For photographs of the school, to which reference is made in the quote, see Central Los Angeles Area High School # 9: http://www.coop-himmelblau.at/ .

29 Derrida, Jacques (1976) *Of Grammatology*, Gayatri C. Spivak trans. Baltimore: Johns Hopkins University Press, 50.

30 Jencks, Charles (2002) *The New Paradigm in Architecture*, New Haven: Yale University Press, 1-7.

31 Ibid, 3. Jencks writes that the architecture of the new paradigm, he advocates, "...may be explicitly based on complexity theory, and emerge as a surprise to the designer from the belly of a computer." But theoretical computations cannot work with complexity without inputs representing conditions for the cause/effect process in the computer, nor may the results be accepted without evaluation. Complexity theory does not guarantee positive surprises to the designer.

32 Ibid, 2.

33 Harries, Karsten (2009) "Theory as Ornament", *Relearning from Las Vegas*, Aron Vinegar and Michael J. Golec, ed, Minneapolis: University of Minnesota Press, 86.

34 Ibid, 87.

35 Hegel, Georg W.F. (1835-1838/1971) *Vorlesungen über die Ästhetik*, Stuttgart: Philip Reclam Jun., 50. My translations.

36 Harries, Karsten (2009), 87.

37 Hegel, *Vorlesungen über die Ästhetik*, 50.

38 Ibid, 49.

39 Wolfe, Tom (1975) *The Painted Word*, New York : Farrar, Straus and Giroux, 6. He refers to tendencies of "literary" nature in the 1960s and 1970s (not only in painting itself but also in words of criticism).

40 http://en.wikipedia.org/wiki/Iris_Clert .

41 A prototype is an object of typical properties which serves as a model for the same or similar future objects. Objects derived from prototypes thus have by definition to a large extent generic properties and, therefore, belong to a class of objects. In general, design prototypes are the result of inferences from past and present experiences. John Gero defines a design prototype as "... a conceptual schema for representing a class of a generalized grouping of elements, derived from like design cases, which provides the basis for the commencement and continuation of a design. Design prototypes do this by bringing together in one schema all the requisite knowledge appropriate to that design situation." (Gero, John (1990) "Design prototypes: A knowledge representation schema for design", *AI Magazine* 11(4), 1).

42 Leach, Neal et al. ed. (2004) "Swarm Tectonics" in *Digital Tectonics*, Chichester UK: John Wiley & Sons, 75.

43 Kristin Shea (2004) "Directed Randomness", ibid, 89.

44 My explanations of the worldwide effort to coordinate and unify building systems and

components, and some of the terminology which I use are derived from the buildingSMART Alliance and the IAI Industrieallianz für Interoperabilität.
http://www.buildingsmartalliance.org/index.php/about/ and http://www.buildingsmart.de/ .

45 Eastman, Chuck, Paul Teicholz, Rafael Sacks and Katheleen Liston (2008) *BIM handbook: a guide to building information modeling for owners, managers, designers, engineers, and contractors*, Hoboken NJ: Wiley. See also websites with additional BIM literature.

46 For example, see Brandle, Kurt (1974-1976) *The Systems Approach to Building*, Associated Schools of Architecture Learning Packages, 51 ff.

47 Kieran, Stephen and James Timberlake (2004) *Refabricating Architecture: How Manufacturing Methodologies Are Poised to Transform Building Construction,* New York: McGraw-Hill, 115.

48 Eastman (2008), *BIM handbook*, 88.

49 Ibid, 303.

50 In January 2008 the General Services Administration of the U.S. Government published a "Statement of Intentions to support Building Information Modeling with Open Standards" including support for IFC.

51 One company which offers such work is SmartBIM Object Creation Services http://www.reedconstructiondata.com/bim/ . For BIM demonstrations of this company see their SmartBIM Flash Demos.

52 *Anwenderhandbuch Datenaustausch BIM/IFC* (2006), München: IAI Industrieallianz für Interoperabilität, 14, my translation.

53 Eastman (2008), 171.

54 An example is the strongly differentiated curtain wall in the 100 11th Avenue Condominium Building, New York City, as described by Eastman (2008), 405-418.

55 Plume, Jim and John Mitchell (2007) "Collaborative design using a shared IFC building model – Learning from experience" in *Automation in Construction* 16, 34.

56 For the discussion of this issue see, for example, "Operative Performativity" in Kolarevic, Branko and Ali M. Malkawi eds.(2005) *Performative architecture: beyond instrumentality.* New York: Spon Press, 238-246.

57 Cilliers, Paul (2002) "Why we cannot know complex things completely" in *Emergence*, 4(1,2), 81. Electronic Access.

58 Ibid, 83.

59 See, for example, Jormakka, Kari et al (2008) *Basics Design Methods*. Basel: Birkhäuser; Lawson, Bryan (1997) *How Designers Think: the design process demystified.* Oxford: Architectural Press; Jones, J. Christopher (1992) *Design Methods.* New York: Van Nostrand Reinhold; Rowe, Peter (1987) *Design Thinking.* Cambridge, MA: MIT Press; *Design methods: theories, research, education and practice.* San Luis Obispo CA: Design Methods Institute, (informal reports since ca. 1970).

60 Gero, John S. and Kannengiesser, Udo "An ontology of situated design teams", *AI EDAM*

(2007), 21 (3): 295. Cambridge University Press. See also http://cs.gmu.edu/~jgero//publications/2007.html .

61 Ibid, 296.

62 Gero, John S. (1990) "Design prototypes: A knowledge representation schema for design", *AI Magazine* 11(4),31. See also http://cs.gmu.edu/~jgero//publications/1990.html .

63 Peña, William, Steven A. Parshall (2001*) Problem Seeking: an architectural programming primer.* New York: John Wiley (first edition in 1969).

64 Liew, Pak-San and John S. Gero (2003) "Operational characteristics of a constructive memory system for design agents", in M-L Chiu et al. eds., *Digital Design: Research and Practice*, Kluwer, 137-147. See also http://cs.gmu.edu/~jgero//publications/2003.html .

65 Leatherbarrow, David (2005) "Architecture's unscripted performance" in Kolarevic, Branko and Ali M. Malkawi eds, *Performative Architecture: Beyond Instrumentality*, New York: Spon Press, 16.

66 Ibid.

67 Ibid, 18.

68 I remember how few published resources on energy conservation were available when I started teaching building systems and environmental controls at the University of Utah in 1969.

69 *ASHRAE 90-1975* was the first standard for Energy Conservation in New Buildings. Reference: ASHRAE Fundamentals 1981, p. 38.4.

70 *Building Energy Performance Standard*, Notice of Proposed Rulemaking, *Federal Register.* April 1980, Washington, D.C.
   And
71 Stein R.G. at al, *Handbook for Energy Use in Building Construction*, U.S. Department of Energy, DOE/CE/20220-1, March 1981, *National Technical Information Service*, Springfield, VA.
   And,
72 *Architect's Handbook of Energy Practice* (1982), Washington, D.C.: American Institute of Architects.

73 From FAQ about the LEED Green Building Certification System, http://www.usgbc.org .

74 Williams, Daniel E. (2007) *Sustainable Design: Ecology, Architecture and Planning*, Hoboken NJ: John Wiley & Sons, 17.

75 That there is a common interest in specific information on how the built environment impacts resources I could observe again and again since teaching classes on energy conservation in building within the Continuing Education program at the University of Utah in 1974.
   And,
76 For a bibliographic resource guide see *Green Design / Sustainable Architecture: Resources,* Environmental Design Library, University of California, Berkeley, 2009, http://www.lib.berkeley.edu/ENVI/GreenAll.html . For individual volumes see, for example, Vallero, Daniel and Chris Brasier (2008) *Sustainable Design: the science of sustainability and green engineering,* Hoboken NJ: John Wiley & Sons; Hegger, Manfred et al (2008) *Energy Manual: Sustainable Architecture*, Basel: Birkhäuser; Williams, Daniel E. (2007) *Sustainable*

Design: Ecology, Architecture and Planning, Hoboken NJ: John Wiley & Sons; Kim Tanzer and Rafael Longoria, eds. (2007) *The Green Braid: towards an architecture of ecology, economy, and equity*; Mendler, Sandra et al (2006) *The HOK guidebook to sustainable design.* Hoboken : John Wiley & Sons, 2006; Brown, G.Z., Mark DeKay (1985/2001) *Sun, wind & light: architectural design strategies*, New York : J. Wiley & Sons; Daniels, Klaus (1998) *Low-Tech Light-Tech High-Tech*, Basel: Birkhäuser; Daniels, Klaus (1997) *The technology of ecological building: basic principles and measures, examples and ideas*, Basel: Birkhäuser; Yeang, Ken (1995) *Designing with Nature,: The Ecological Basis for Architectural Design*; Todd, Nancy and John Todd (1994) From eco-cities to living machines: principles of ecological design. Berkeley CA: North Atlantic Books; Lyle, John T. (1994) *Regenerative Design for Sustainable Development*; For older, but still relevant volumes see, for example, (1982) *Architect's Handbook of Energy Practice,* Washington DC: The American Institute of Architects. With volumes on energy analysis, building envelope, daylighting, HVAC systems, passive heating and cooling, etc.; Mazria, Edward (1979) *The passive solar energy book,* Emmaus, Pa.: Rodale Press; Brändle, Kurt et al (1979) *Energie-bewusstes Bauen* (Energy Conscious Building Stuttgart: Verlagsanstalt Alexander Koch; Watson, Donald ed. (1979) *Energy Conservation through Building Design*. New York: McGraw Hill; Stein, Richard G. (1977) *Architecture and energy,* Richard G. Stein..Garden City NY: Anchor Press.

77 An extensive compilation of issues to be looked into is given in "Ten Key Steps" of *The HOK Guidebook to Sustainable Design*, ibid, 41-170.

78 Some of the following remarks are based on Brandle, Kurt (1996) "Efficiency in Creation" in *Recreation: currents & tides in architectural education, Proceedings*, ACSA Western Regional Meeting, University of Hawaii at Manoa, Honolulu, Hawaii.

79 Some systems apparently reach efficiencies larger than 1. An example is the coefficient of performance of heat pumps. What happens here, however, is an increase of output because of heat addition from an ambient source, such as air or water, a source external to the system. In a sense we may call the gain 'free energy', although a heat pump must be operating to occasion the gain. Cooling a room by ventilating it with fresh air has an efficiency of 1. But somebody must open the windows to allow for the heat exchange to happen and the outside energy source is 'free'.

80 For embodied energy definitions and data see *Buildings Energy Data Book*, U.S. Department of Energy, http://buildingsdatabook.eren.doe.gov/SearchResults.aspx?search=embodied and Stein, R.G. at al. (1981) *Handbook for Energy Use for Building Construction*, Springfield, VA: National Technical Information Service (Product Code: DOECS202201), 81-93.

81 For further details see Brändle et al (1979) *Energiebewusstes Bauen*, 10, 22 and 35.

82 Daniels, Klaus (1998) *Low-tech Light-tech High-tech: Building in the Information Age,* Basel: Birkhäuser Verlag.

83 For details on this building see (2006) *gsw headquarters berlin sauerbruch hutton: archive,* Baden, Switzerland: Lars Müller Publishers.

84 8.19 is a summary in form of a drawing of the systems discussed in a seminar on energy systems and conservation at the College of Architecture, University of Michigan, 1996; discussed also in Kurt Brandle (1996) "Efficiency in Creation" in *Recreation: currents & tides in architectural education, Proceedings*, ACSA Western Regional Meeting, University of Hawaii at Manoa, Honolulu, Hawaii.

85 Mortice, Zach "From Farm to Market, Down the Stairs, Around the Block", *AIArchitect*, vol. 14, Oct. 26, 2007, http://info.aia.org/aiarchitect/thisweek07/1026/1026d_mithun.cfm .

86 Orr, David "Architecture, Ecological Design, and Human Ecology" in *The Green Braid* (2007), Tanzer, Kim and Rafael Longoria eds, New York: Routledge, 28.

87 *The 2007 Autodesk/AIA Green Index*, page 6
http://images.autodesk.com/adsk/files/2007_autodesk_aia_greenindex.pdf .

88 From a former website "The Basel pilot region of the 2000 Watt Society".
See also http://en.wikipedia.org/wiki/2000-watt_society
and http://ourworld.unu.edu/en/2000-watt-society/ .

89 According to the *Buildings Energy Data Book*, U.S. Department of Energy, idem, Table 1.1.3 the operational energy consumption of buildings in 2009 is 39.9 percent of the total. http://buildingsdatabook.eren.doe.gov/TableView.aspx?table=1.1.3 . For embodied energy in building (production and construction) 6 to 8 percent of total energy needs to be added.

90 Since 2007 all automobiles in Europe must be taken back under EU law by their manufacturers for recycling. (From: Recycling von Altfahrzeugen, Informationen der BMW Group, 2004). "About 75 percent of end-of-life vehicles, mainly metals, are recyclable in the European Union. The rest (~25%) of the vehicle is considered waste and generally goes to landfills. Environmental legislation of the European Union requires the reduction of this waste to a maximum of 5 percent by 2015." From http://www.tms.org/pubs/journals/JOM/0308/Kanari-0308.html . For details see http://eur-lex.europa.eu/LexUriServ/LexUriServ.do?uri=CONSLEG:2000L0053:20050701:EN:PDF .

91 For efforts in recycling and reuse of building components see the library of the Building Materials Reuse Association http://www.bmra.org/ and the *Construction & Demolition Recycling* magazine. See also Kibert, Charles J. (2005) *Sustainable construction: green building design and delivery*, Hoboken, N.J.: John Wiley.

92 Fromm, Eric (1965/1994), *On being human. New York: Continuum,* 101.
http://books.google.com/books?id=5UxTf77f_w4C&printsec=frontcover&cd=1&source=gbs_ViewAPI#v=onepage&q=biophilia&f=false .

93 Wilson, Edward O. (1984) *Biophilia*, Cambridge, Mass.: Harvard University Press, 1.
And,
94 *bios*, Greek,"life, course or way of living" and *philia* and *philos*, Greek, "affection" and "loving" respectively. From http://www.etymonline.com .

95 By the 1930's several studies looked at the interdependence of fenestration and natural lighting. In the 1950s and 1960s British and German standards prescribed daylight factors, which are minimum ratios of natural lighting intensities (see Burberry, Peter (1977) *Environment and Services*, London: B T Batsford, 39). Efforts to establish a building ventilation code by the American Society for Heating and Ventilating Engineers were under way at least by 1915 ("Building Ventilation", August 20, 1922, © The New York Times, http://query.nytimes.com/gst/abstract.html?res=9C04E6DA1E3FE432A25753C2A96E9C946395D6CF&scp=1&sq=building+ventilation&st=p .

96 See, for example, *Understanding the Relationship between Public Health and the Built Environment*, a report prepared for the LEED-ND Core Committee, May 2006 https://www.usgbc.org/ShowFile.aspx?DocumentID=3901 .

97 This is why I prefer the term 'ecological design' to the term 'biophilic design'. The term ecology implies the rational as well as the instinctive of human being and the study of nature (-logia means "study of" http://www.etymonline.com/index.php?l=e&p=1 .

98 Janine Benyus "A good place to settle: biomimicry, biophilia, and the return of nature's inspiration to architecture" in *Biophilic Design,* Kellert, Stephen et al eds. (2008) Hoboken NJ: John Wiley & Sons, 29.

99 The Sidney Opera House reminds us of sails or sea shells. It is problematic as a "biophilic" design and has nothing to do with efforts toward sustainability. It is a tour-de-force with enormous amounts of embedded energy in its construction to even exist the way it does.

100 Kieran, Stephen (2008) "Evolving an Environmental Aesthetic" in Kellert, *Biophilic Design*, ibid, 244.

101 Whether LEED led so far to more or less beautiful buildings, compared with architecture not considering it, is a matter of judgment. In addition to providing tangible results toward sustainability, it certainly has helped to bring the issue into mainstream. That it uses addition of 'quality points' is its nature as a measuring device. Architecture itself is additive which has nothing to do with whether its results are beautiful or not. Beauty depends on what we add together and how we integrate it.

102 Hamilton, D. Kirk and David H. Watkins (2009) *Evidence-Based Design*, Hoboken, NJ: John Wiley & Sons, 9.

103 Krygiel, Eddy and Bradly Nies (2008) *Green BIM: successful sustainable design with building information modeling*, Hoboken NJ: John Wiley & Sons, 226-7.

104 Alexander, Christopher (2002) *The Nature of Order, Book One: the Phenomenon of Life,* Berkely, CA: Center for Environmental Structure, Book 1, 122.

105 Ibid, Book 4, 61.

106 Ibid, 63.

107 Ibid, 65.

108 See, for example, ibid, Book 4, 60. He writes "When there is a living structure, it is related to me, to you, to every person. ... It is the most fundamental experience. No other experience is as comforting. ... All of it, when it has the right structure, is undeniably related to you. It is related to YOU: A matter of degree, but the degree is not the main issue."

109 Orr, David W. (2006) *Design on the Edge*, Cambridge: MIT Press, 7.

110 The etymological connection of idea and ideal from Douglas Harper Online Etymology Dictionary: ideal (adj.) early 15c., "pertaining to an archetype or model," from L.L. idealis "existing in idea," from L. idea in the Platonic sense ... Sense of "perfect" first recorded 1610s. The noun meaning "perfect person or thing" is first recorded 1796 in a translation of Kant, http://www.etymonline.com/index.php?l=i&p=1 .

111 Rykwert, Joseph (1957) "Meaning and Building" in *The Necessity of Artifice*, New York: Rizzoli, 1982, 16.

Illustration Credits and Information

This list gives information about images with copyright for which permissions to publish was received. They are identified at the end of the image captions by (© permission). All other images are mine or are in the public domain. Occasionally, other information is provided. These images are identified at the end of the caption by (source). Every conceivable effort has been made to obtain permissions and to comply with related requirements. If you know of any insufficiency, please let me know at kbrandle@umich.edu .

2.4 Courtesy Richard Meier & Partners Architects.

2.6 Licensed under Creative Commons Attribution-No Derivatives Works 3.0 License, David Baker + Partners Architects, San Francisco,
see at http://www.dbarchitect.com/projects/slideshow/50.html#449 .

2.10 Matthäus Merian (1642) Topographia Helvetiae, Rhaetiae et Valesiae.
http://commons.wikimedia.org/wiki/Category:1642_in_Switzerland .

2.12 Library of Congress, Map Collections, Washington DC .
http://hdl.loc.gov/loc.gmd/g4104c.pm001530 .

2.18 From the Historic American Buildings Survey (Library of Congress), HABS IL-1029.
http://hdl.loc.gov/loc.pnp/hhh.il0041 .

2.19 Courtesy Sert, Jackson and Associate.

3.4 Courtesy RB+B Architects, Inc. (Architect of Record) and ATS&R (Programming Consultant).

3.5 Jeremy Kemp, http://en.wikipedia.org/wiki/Program_Evaluation_and_Review_Technique .

3.9 Courtesy Peter Zumthor.

3.10 to 3.14 Courtesy Ronald Keenberg, IKOY architects.

3.15 Courtesy Architectuurstudio HH, Herman Hertzberger.

3.18 Courtesy Steidle Architekten.

3.22 Courtesy Kohler Company.

3.23 Courtesy Rainer Fundel of Fundel, Holste, Kermann, Priesemeister, von Mann, Architekten; drawing in *Bauen für Kinder – Wohnen mit Kindern*, Wettbewerbsbroschüre, Innenministerium Baden-Württemberg, 1979.

3.32 Courtesy Stijn Rolies, Danda Gallery.

3.35 Courtesy HiMY SYeD, Photopia.

3.37 Courtesy Antonis C. Antoniades. See also Anthony C. Antoniades (1992) *Poetics of Architecture*, New York: Van Nostrand Reinhold, Chapter 2 "Metaphors", 29-48. This book has an extensive section on metaphors in architectural design.

3.38 Ibid.

3.41 Courtesy Photo Archives, Ohio State University
and

3.42 Courtesy Barbara T. Young, photo by Paul E. Young.

3.43 Courtesy Venturi, Scott Brown and Associates, Inc., photo by Matt Wargo.

3.47 Courtesy Ricardo Bofill Taller de Arquitectura.

4.10 Photo by Taxiarchos228. This file is licensed under the Crative Commons Attribution 3.0. For license description see http://creativecommons.org/licenses/by/3.0/deed.en . http://de.wikipedia.org/wiki/OCAD_University . See also http://en.wikipedia.org/wiki/OCAD .

4.11 Courtesy Molenaar & Van Winden architecten / WAM architecten, photo by Roel Backkaert. See also http://www.wam-architecten.nl/projecten/Intell_Hotel_Zaandam.php .

4.13 Courtesy Axel Menges Verlag.

5.7 From Durand J.N.L. (1809) Précis des Leçons d'Architecture données à l'École Polytechnique, Premier Volume, contenant trente-deux planches, 2e Partie, Planche 2, 114-115. Image is in public domain. From http://books.google.com/books?id=S9vnzwtsKq8C&printsec=frontcover&dq=inauthor:%22Jean-Nicolas-Louis+Durand%22&hl=en&ei=4re5TsLVJKi2sQKqtrStCA&sa=X&oi=book_result&ct=result&resnum=6&ved=0CFAQ6AEwBQ#v=onepage&q&f=false .

5.8 Semper, Gottfried (1879) *Der Stil in den Technischen und Tektonischen Künsten oder Praktische Aesthetik*. München: Friedrich Bruckmann, vol. 2, 263.

5.9 Photo by Philip H. Delamotte, http://en.wikipedia.org/wiki/Philip_Henry_Delamotte .

5.10 and 5.11 Courtesy Kimball Art Museum, Fort Worth, Texas; photos by Robert LaPrelle, Kimbell Art Museum.

5.12 to 5.14 Courtesy Foster + Partners.

5.17 Paul Righini (1999) *Thinking Architecturally – an Introduction to the Creation of Form and Place*, University of Cape Town Press, 150. Courtesy of Paul Reghini and University of Cape Town Press.

5.28 Courtesy Zaha Hadid Architects, photo by Virgile Simon Bertrand.

5.29 Wilhelm Lübke (1890) http://de.wikipedia.org/wiki/Georgskirche_(Reichenau) .

5.31 Karl Künstle (1906) http://de.wikipedia.org/wiki/Basilika_Vierzehnheiligen, by Balthasar Neumann.

5.33 Courtesy Gerhard and Karin Kirsch. See also Kirsch, Karin (1989) *Die Weissenhofsiedlung: experimental housing built for the Deutsche Werkbund, Stuttgart, 1927*, New York: Rizzoli.

5.34 Courtesy Hugo Kliczkowski, Asppan S.L., Onlybook S.L. See also Cuito, Aurora and Cristina Montes (2002) *Gaudi: Complete works*, Barcelona: LOFT Publications.

5.35 Courtesy Robert Mark, Princeton University.

5.36 Courtesy Robert Darvas, University of Michigan.

5.37 Photo by Wladyslaw, Attribution: Taxiarchos228 (at the German Language Wikipedia), GNU Free Documentation License, see also http://en.wikipedia.org/wiki/Santiago_Calatrava#Awards .

5.42 Photo by Raphael Azevedo Franca. Image is in public domain: http://en.wikipedia.org/wiki/Katsura_Imperial_Villa/ .

5.43 Courtesy Archives of Tuxford School District, Nottinghamshire.

5.44 *The Story of CLASP*, Building Bulletin 19, Ministry of Education, HMSO, June, 1961, 33.

5.45 and 5.46 Courtesy of Ehrenkrantz Echstut & Kuhn, Architects.

5.48 Courtesy Edition Axel Menges GmbH.

5.52 Courtesy Universitätsbibliothek Eichstätt-Ingolstadt, photo by Maria Eckerle.

5.53 Courtesy Günter Behnisch.

5.60 Courtesy Ricardo Frantz.

5.61 Photo by Ingersoll. Image is in public domain. See also http://en.wikipedia.org/wiki/Semper_Oper .

5.62 *Encyclopédie, ou dictionnaire raisonné des sciences, des arts et des métiers (Encyclopedia, or a Systematic Dictionary of the Sciences, Arts, and Crafts),* vol. 18, Paris, 1751-1772. http://www.alembert.fr/PLANCHES/slides/ARCHITECTURE25.html . See also http://en.wikipedia.org/wiki/Classical_orders .

5.65 Photo by DAVID ILIFF. License: CC-BY-SA 3.0
For license description see http://creativecommons.org/licenses/by-sa/3.0/deed.en).
See also http://en.wikipedia.org/wiki/Casa_Mila .

5.76 and 5.77 Courtesy John Outram.

5.83 Courtesy Hans Hollein.

5.87 Courtesy Gehry Partners.

5.96 Courtesy Office for Metropolitan Architecture (OMA).

5.97 Courtesy Venturi, Scott Brown and Associates, Inc.

6.7 From Google Earth. © Google-Imagery © Digital Globe, Geo Content, Aero West, Landeshauptstadt Stuttgart, GeoEye. Used according to its Permission Guidelines for Google Maps and Google Earth (distinctive aspects):
http://www.google.com/permissions/geoguidelines.html .

6.10 Library of Congress Record:
http://hdl.loc.gov/loc.gmd/g3850.ct000509
See also http://en.wikipedia.org/wiki/Pierre_L%27enfant .

6.11 United States National Park Service.

6.13 Matthäus Merian (1642) Topographia Helvetiae, Rhaetiae et Valesiae.
http://commons.wikimedia.org/wiki/Category:1642_in_Switzerland .

6.21 and 6.22 From *Harper's Magazine* 70 (February 1885), 453 and 454.

6.23 Sandleiten, *Prolegomena* 37, Institut für Wohnbau, Technische Universität Wien, Vienna, 1981, 8.

6.26 See http://en.wikipedia.org/wiki/File:LevittownPA.jpg . Image is in public domain.

6.27 Courtesy S. David Marable, Levittown Internationally Known Communities, Inc. and LevittownExhibitCenterNorth.com.

6.28 Courtesy Svenska Bostäder.

6.30 RESTON, Simon Enterprises Developer and Whittlesley & Conklin City Planners, Masterplan Proposal, May 1962. See also http://www.restonmuseum.org/main_/rht_masterPlan.htm .

6.31 Courtesy Estate of James Rossant, architect and planner.

6.32 United States Geological Survey. See http://en.wikipedia.org/wiki/Pruitt-Igoe .

6.33 Photographer Evp. This file is licensed under the Crative Commons Attribution 3.0, http://creativecommons.org/licenses/by/3.0/deed.en .
See also http://en.wikipedia.org/wiki/Embarcadero_Freeway .

7.3 Courtesy Gustav Burlet.

7.5 Courtesy John Peponis and Jean Wineman.

7.8 Courtesy Sophia Psarra.

7.16 and 7.17 Courtesy Akademie der Künste, Berlin.

7.21, 7.22, 7.24 and 7.25 Courtesy Ennead Architects.

8.1 Courtesy Eisenman Architects.

8.3 Courtesy Thomas Wiscombe.

8.5 Courtesy Thomas Liebich. From *BIM/IFC Anwenderhandbuch*, page 14, buildingSMART e.V. with my adjustments into English.

8.6 Courtesy John Gero.

8.14 Courtesy Birkhäuser Verlag, Basel. From Klaus Daniels' (1998) *Low-tech Light-tech High-tech: Building in the Information Age, 161-162*.

8.16 and 8.18 Courtesy Sauerbruch Hutton. See also *GSW Headquarters, Berlin, Sauerbruch Hutton Architects*, Baden: Lars Müller Publishers, 2000.

8.20 and 8.21 Courtesy Mithun, Inc (© Mithun I mithun.com).

8.22 Courtesy Novatlantis – Sustainability at the ETH Domain.

8.23 Courtesy BVB Basler Verkehrs-Betriebe.
See also http://de.wikipedia.org/wiki/Basler_Verkehrs-Betriebe .

8.25 BMW AG. From *A Consistent Initiative to Protect the Environment: BMW Recycling*, BMW AG, Public Affairs/T-RC, 1992, 24.

8.28 Courtesy Michael Frechette.

Index

There are no entries for 'architecture' as the whole book is about architecture.

aesthetic(s): 6-8, 95, 104, 108, 111, 119-128, 130, 136-138; as pleasure or displeasure 6, 19, 102-103, 118, 119, 123-125,128, 130, 134, 137, 164, 291, 343; as mental state (the aesthetic) 6, 120, 125-126, 133-135, 137, 138; and function 232; as derived from judgment 122-126, 128, 130-134, 137, 154; and interest 132; a particular aesthetic not inherent nor intrinsic 118, 339; as part of meaning 119, 120, 124, 125; ethical dimension 298; modern 132
aesthetics as field of inquiry 120, 122, 127, 128, 134, 138, 290, 336, 337, 340
aesthetic experience 95, 119, 124, 125, 130, 341
aesthetic judgment, see judgment
aesthetic understanding 119, 341, 342
affection 49, 96, 117, 118, 369
Akron Art Museum, Akron OH 187
Alberti, Leon Battista 116, 147, 164, 338, 345, 350
Alexander, Christopher 157, 221, 234, 250, 251, 254, 318
Alhambra Castle, Granada 178
Alsop, Will 106
Altes Museum, Berlin 159
ambiguity 37, 43, 44, 89, 94, 123, 197, 284
amplification as ornamentation 7, 164, 165, 167-169, 172, 174-176, 180-189, 288
analysis, analytical 8, 9, 18, 59, 131
Anderson, John 212
Andreasen, Nancy C, 335
Anscombe, G.E.M. 193
Antoniades, Anthony 80
appearance: of physical objects 11, 16-22, 89, 111, 112, 118-123, 191, 267; as representation in our mind 19-25, 30, 34, 47, 48, 88, 89, 122, 193, 200, 326, 333, 342

appraisal, instinctive (indeliberate) or reflective 97-102
Aquinas, Thomas 115
Aristotle 72, 85, 110, 111, 115
Armory, Ohio State University 81, 82
Arnold, Magda 98
attribute and attributed 4, 18, 19, 31, 87, 89, 260, 261, 295; as property 4, 18, 19
Atwood, Charles 38
Auditorio de Tenerife, Santa Cruz, Tenerife 168
Augustine of Hippo 113-115
Aydede, Murat 246
Baird, George 2
Baker (David) and Partners 28
Batwing Project 286, 287
Bauakademie, Berlin 159
Baudrillard, Jean 70, 71
Bauhaus Dormitory, Dessau 177
Baumgarten, Alexander G. 120-127, 158
Baylis, Charles A. 143
Bellahøj Housing, Kopenhagen 161
Beardsley, Monroe 110, 117, 130
beauty 2, 6, 108-118, 336
beautiful versus ugly 108, 114-115, 121, 123, 124, 134, 159
beauty as affect(ion) not cause 117-123, 133, 134
beauty: in Ancient Greece 108; as ideal form of its content (Plato and Socrates) 108-110, 336 ; as desired outcome of practical reasoning and mimesis (Aristotle) 110-111; as correspondence of whole and part (Vitruvius) 112; as God inspired order and truthfulness (Augustine) 113-115; as pleasant when perceived (Aquinas) 115; as harmony of parts and whole (Alberti) 116; as a matter of education and taste (Shaftesbury) 117; as form evoking pleasure (Hume) 118; not inherent nor

intrinsic 116, 118, 339; disinterested (or free) 131-133, 137, 336; as value 134, 231, 343
Beauvais Cathedral, France 167
Behnisch & Partners 172
Beneviste, Emile 58
Benjamin, Andrew 288
Benyus, Janine 316
Berleant, Arnold 132, 133
Bessunger Strasse Apartments, Darmstadt 172
BIM (building information modeling) 293-296
biophilic 316, 370;
Birkerts, Gunnar 321
Bloomer, Kent 164
Blumer, Herbert 59
body: and mind 5, 7, 12, 95-100, 192, 196-202, 282; and consciousness 15
Bofill, Ricardo 85
Bolter, Jay David 69
Booth, Wayne 75
Borradori, Giovannia 282
Bouman, Ole 331
Brand, Stewart 37
Brandle, Kurt 142, 306, 310
Breuer, Marcel 180
Broad, Charles D. 194
Brolin, Brent 154
Buder, Stanley 230
building type 31, 39, 41, 42, 160, 188, 226, 230, 233;
Bulguksa Temple, South Korea 178
Burnham, Daniel 38
Calatrava, Santiago 80, 168
Calkins, Margaret 226
Cameron, Deborah 256
Canter, David 260
Carpenter, Rebecca 281
Casa Milá, Barcelona 165, 167, 177
Cassirer Ernst 56, 57, 68
Caudill Rowlet Scott 277
causation 7, 138, 144, 191-195; world-to-world, world-to-mind, mind-to-world, mind-to-mind 195-205; design factors as causes 7, 201
cause and effect 191-195
cause-events and effect-events 195; design as chain of cause and effect sequence 194; cause-effect chain in impression (observation) 203; cause-effect chain in expression (design) 203; design result as effect-event 195-206
cause-object, effect-object 195-203
CCTV Headquarters, Beijing 187, 333
Central Library, Catholic University, Eichstätt 172, 173
Centre Pompidou, Paris 61, 168, 169
Chandler, Daniel 34, 47
change: as cause, effect or event 194, 195
Child, William 208
Cilliers, Paul 298
CLASP (Consortium of Local Authorities Special Programme) System 169, 170
Classical Column Orders 176
concept, conception, conceptualization 3-5; as reason 31; as mental representation 16-25; from impression and for expression 45; as derived from object, appearance and judgment 18-21; and aesthetic judgment 126; specific or generic 18, 21, 23, 139; in metaphors 73-83
concept as mental sign (content of form) 88
concept as signified (De Saussure) 87
concept of body (of physical object) 90
concept-with-feeling as understanding 99, 126
configuration, configurational 7, 131, 164-172, 188-190, 216, 222, 229, 250, 250-253
connotation 33-35, 77, 241, 242
consciousness 4, 15, 16, 23, 48, 57, 101, 127, 137, 144, 319, 326
content 5-8, 10, 15, 37, 57, 64, 86-94, 189, 267; from impressions and for expression 52, 93; as design factor 221; its sources in form of design 222; content is semantic 263, 264; see also meaning; see also semantics
content-form relationship 5, 8, 37, 45, 86-92, 127-129, 133, 218; in design narratives 262-264, 266-275
content-form unity see content-form relationship
content thinking 91, 245-248; and form thinking as emotion-and-reason process 247; creates meaning 247
context, contextual 7, 8; as basis for

understanding 103; and realization 154, 157, 228; as design factors 218, 220-222; as frame of reference 228; historical 230; with global and local dimensions 229; its neglect 284-286; as "situatedness" 300
Coop Himmelblau 162, 187
Coyne, Richard 73, 74
critical path method 52, 53, 54, 204, 352
CSCW (computer-supported co-operative work) 292-297
cue 35, 36, 59, 225, 227, 300; from denotation and connotation 35
Culture and Convention Center, Luzern 106
Dagobert D. Runes 336
Damasio, Antonio 4, 95-98, 100, 102
Daniels, Klaus 308
Davidson, Donald 75
Deconstruction and deconstruction 9, 235-237, 356, 364
denotation 33-35, 52, 58, 241, 242, 267, 327
decoration, decorated, decorative 7, 137, 164, 165, 176, 177, 182-190, 333, 349; not synonymous with ornament 164, 165
"decorated shed" 164, 188
Deleuze, Gilles 281, 284, 362-364
Denver Art Museum, Denver 106, 107
De Kerckhove, Derrick 281, 282
De Overloop, Home for Elderly, Almere 105
Derrida, Jacques 205, 288, 289, 356
Descartes, René 4, 12, 13, 117, 282, 288
design 89, 139, 254-259, 258; synthesis based on 223, 236, 300; in pattern language 250, 251; for finding content, understanding, meaning, function 254; from form to content 8, 264; impressions and expressions for 262, 263; as basis for design narratives 262-265; in Function-Behavior-Structure or purpose-context-realization model 297-299, see also synthesis
design analysis 267, 296, 297
design factors: 4, 7-9, 34, 36, 41-43, 46, 94, 154, 164, 218-223 ; as causes 7; and judgment 190; in design narrative analysis 262-269; their impact and conflicts 43, 46, 298

design narratives: 8, 9, 258, 264, 265, 267, 269; as record of design process 269
design progression as iteration process 207, 263
design thinking: 8, 85 (in metaphors), 202, 221, 245 (as object thinking), 246, 247, 278; and language thinking 248, 259; in impression (observation) and expression (design) 202- 204; as process 263; see and also design narratives as structured and explicit design thinking; in programming 223
Dewey, John 95, 125
Di Cristina, Giuseppa 362, 363
Dixon, Robert 121, 122
Domenig, Günther 286
"duck versus decorated shed" 188, 189
Duncan Hall, Rice University, Houston 179, 180
Durand, J.N.L. 148-150, 153
Dürer, Albrecht 116, 158
Eastman, Chuck 294
Eco, Umberto 329
Edelman Gerald H. 4
effect 7; see causation, cause and effect
effect-object see cause-object
Ehrenkrantz, Ezra D. 227, 355
Eisenman, Peter 71, 81, 217, 218, 283-285
emotion, emotional 5, 6, 32; as feeling of pleasure or displeasure 19, 102; in aesthetics and feelings 95-100 ; as cause of feeling 96; in Kant 343; and reason in interdependence 95, 98, 99, 101-103, 131-133, 137; emotion-reason process as thinking 98-100, 243; 247; as perception and conception 126; in understanding 99;
emotional and rational judgment of design factors 254
emotional Intelligence 95
energy efficiency 304-313; passive and active systems 306-311
energy efficient facades 308
energy systems integration in buildings 310, 311
Ennead Architects 273-275

Environmental Design Research Association 59

event in causation 192

expression: 1, 4, 5, 7, 11, 25, 32, 93; for design from understanding, judgment and meaning 23, 25, 32; and function 41; from content to form 264; as mind-to-world causation 202; difference to impression 202-204; based on impression 262, 263; and language 248, 249, 258, 259; in architecture versus language 72; in metaphors 72-85; in design process 101, 207, 208, 222, 262, 263; in signs 93; determines signifier 240

Fales, Evan 91, 92

Faller, Peter 1, 66

feeling 5, 6; of pleasure or displeasure 19, 102, 118; from emotion 95-103 (see also aesthetics); in understanding 96, 99; about beauty 117-119 (see also aesthetics and beauty); versus sensation 19, 96-102

Ficino, Marsilio 115

Fischer, Günther 252

Flin Flon Town Hall, Flin Flon 60, 61

Fodor, Jerry 246

form 5-7, 189, 266-276; in impression and expression 5; content-form relationship 5, 8, 37, 45, 86-92, 127-129, 133, 218; in design narratives 262-264, 266-275; determining content 215, 216; and function 288; versus shape 42, 90, 216, 236, 254; and performance 292; and nature 315, 316; organic 30, 153, 159, 160, 315, 316; form is syntactic 263, 264

form follows function concept: 'form follows content' 37; "Form Follows Data" 218; 'form follows ego' 9; "Form follows function" 41; "form ever follows function" (Sullivan) 37, 91, 327; 'form ever follows function[s]' 37; form follows content 37, 91; see also realization

form thinking 91, 245, 247

Forty, Adrian 89, 333, 355

Fossil Ridge High School, Fort Collins 54

Foster+Partners 84, 155

Frampton, Kenneth 135

Frankl, Paul 211

Frege, Gottlob 92, 241

Friedman, Mildred 287

function, functional 4, 6, 27, 37, 38, 41, 43, 45, 154; and complexity 37, 43; and amplification (configuration) 172,185; potential neglect 217; in design factors 216; and type 147, 151, 153, 154, 157; and style 159, 232; as correspondence of purpose and realization 230; see also form follows function concept

Fundel, Rainer 67

Gardiner, Alan H. 256

Gardner, Sebastian 17

Garza-Cuarón, Beatriz 33

Gaudi, Antoni 165, 177

Gehry, Frank 3, 40, 81, 162, 181, 182, 287, 296, 315

generic versus specific concepts, or properties 18, 21, 23, 72, 92,145, 146; and resemblance 72, 139-142, 150, 155; in metaphors 78

Gero, John 298. 300, 365

Ghirardo, Diane 234, 280

Gillett, Grant R. 20, 244

Glen Avenue Parking Garage, University of Michigan, Ann Arbor, MI 174

Goethe, Wolfgang J. 116, 159

Goodman, Nelson 34, 145

Graves, Michael 160, 186

Gray, Jeffrey 102

Gretsch Unitas Building, Ditzingen near Stuttgart 307

Groat, Linda 2, 62, 260, 361

Gropius, Walter 160, 177, 231

Grusin, Richard 69

GSW Office Building, Berlin 309

Guangzhou Opera House, Guangzhou 163

Guggenheim Museum, New York 85, 86

Guyer, Paul 131, 193, 324, 344

Haas Haus, Vienna 181, 182

Habermas, Jürgen 240, 259, 261

Hadid, Zaha 162, 315

Halliwell, Stephen 111

Hamilton, Kirk 317

Hanyu, Kazunori 327

Harries, Karsten 137, 184, 290, 291
Harvard Science Centre, Cambridge MA 39, 42, 43, 56, 168, 179
Hatch, Richard 212
Hausman, Carl R. 48
Hays, Michael 71
Hegel, Georg F. 89, 126-128, 159, 288, 290, 291
Heidegger, Martin 4, 9, 63, 74, 76, 235, 239, 240, 245, 288, 289, 300, 356
Heinrich Hübsch Trade School, Karlsruhe 40
Hentrich-Petschnigg and Partners 68
Helm, Bennet W. 335
Hepburn, Roland W. 132
Hershberger, Robert 223, 260, 261, 361
Hertzberger, Herman 64, 104
Hillier, Bill 253, 254
Hobbes, Thomas 13, 117
Hofmann, Hans 55
Hollein, Hans 181
Hongkong-Shanghai Bank, Hongkong 61, 155, 156
Hoppe Schönthal and Matuschek 231
Hubacher and Issler 162
Humboldt, Wilhelm von 238-240, 245
Hume, David 4. 14, 18, 31, 118, 119, 144, 192, 196, 197, 209
Hundertwasser Haus, Vienna 177
Hutcheson, Francis 117, 118, 130, 343
hypersurface 280, 281, 285, 363
icon, iconic 5, 51-58, 83-88, 93, 164,188, 241, 247, 248, 333;
metaphors 5, 72-85; 104; architecture is often iconic, symbolic and 289; in relation to 'Duck' and 'Decorated shed' 188; see also semiotics
IFC (Industry Foundation Classes) 293-296
IKOY Partnership 60
impression 1, 3-5, 7, 8, 22, 23, 25, 32, 58, 93; from observation for judgment, understanding and meaning 23, 25, 32; concepts are results of 45; as world-to-mind causation 199; difference to expression 202-204; from form to content 264; as basis for expression 262, 263; and language 248, 249, 258; in metaphors 9, 72, 85; in design process 101, 198, 207, 208, 222, 262, 263; in signs 52; for analysis 259
Index, indexical 5, 51-53, 57, 58, 93; and simultaneously symbolic, iconic or both 57, 87, 257; see also semiotics
Innis, Robert 69
Inntel Hotel, Zaandam, Amsterdam 106, 107
Integrated Housing, Munich-Nymphenburg 65, 66
intentionality 15, 16, 97, 130-132, 200, 202, 206
interpretant 48, 49, 329
interpretation 5, 45, 68; through metaphor 72-76
Jackendoff, Ray 20
Jacobson, Arne 78, 179
Jacquette, Dale 242
Jahn, Helmut 104
James, William 4, 95, 97, 138, 243
Jencks, Charles 2, 85, 279, 289
Jewish Museum, Berlin 84
Johnson, Barbara 356
Johnson, Mark 99
Johnson, Philip 76, 85
judgment 4, 6, 7, 11, 13, 14, 19, 21-25, 45; and understanding and meaning 21, 25; as aesthetic judgment 120. 122, 126, 132-136, 154, 317; aesthetic judgment as design factor 42, 154; influence of interest on 132; about value and appraisal, 98, 100, 103, 108, 114, 133, 216; emotion and reason 98, 103, 114, 115, 126, 128; on beauty 116-119; fallible and relative 114; and diverse 119; on "aesthetic kind of representation" (Kant) about pleasure or displeasure 122; of representation 133; about impact of properties 123, 124; in the design process 207
Kahn, Louis 3, 42, 154, 155, 231, 318
Kaiser Wilhelm Memorial Church 84
Kaleva Church, Tampere 80, 85
Kant, Immanuel 4, 14, 15, 17-19, 21-25, 31, 49, 68, 89, 101, 121-123, 126-131, 139, 158, 159, 191, 193, 279, 288, 290, 323
Karl Marx Allee, Berlin 162

Katsura Imperial Villa, Kyoto 169, 170
Kemp, Jeremy 53
Kerckhove, Derrick de 281, 283
Kieran, Stephen 317
King, Anthony D. 215
Kistler, Max 200
Kirsch, Gerhard and Karin 372
Kloeckner Building, Bremen 68
Knight, William A. 110
Kohler Company 67
Kohn Pedersen Fox Associates 142, 184
Kramm und Meyer, Architekten 171
Krampen, Martin 259, 260
Krygiel, Eddy 318
Kunsthalle Karlsruhe 124
Lake Shore Drive Apartments (860-880) 135, 161, 344, 349
Lang, Jon T. 225
Langer, Susan 126
language, semiotic/symbolic nature of 53, 56-58, 87; in difference to architecture 72, 78; *about* versus *of* architecture 85, 244, 248, 249, 250, 254, 256, 291, 360; as externalizing thinking and understanding 239; in metaphors 72
language thinking 8, 91, 245-248, 257, 258, 259, 278; and design thinking 259
language-games 243-245
Laugier, Marc-Antoine 149
Lavin, Sylvia 150, 346-347
Lazarus, Richard and Bernice 98
Leach, Neil 292
Leatherborrow, David 301, 302
LeDoux, Joseph 95, 101
LEED (Leadership in Energy and Environmental Design) 302, 303, 317, 370
Leibnitz, Gottfried W. 117, 284
Les Espaces d'Apraxas, Marne-La-Vallée 85, 86
Levittown, PA 233
Lévi-Strauss, Claude 58
Libeskind, Daniel 84, 106, 315
LIMA Housing, Berlin 64, 65
Liew, Pak-San 300
Locke, John 4, 13, 14, 47, 48, 117, 118, 238, 328
Loeble, Schlossman and Bennett 161

Loos, Adolf 168, 184
Loos Haus, Vienna 185
Lowry, Glenn D. 264
Lye, John 234
Lynn, Greg 284
L'Enfant, Pierre 209
Luckenbach Ziegelman 173
Mac Cormac, Earl R. 75
Mackie, John 206
Magee, Bryan 25
Makkreel, Rudolf 124
Mannerism 44, 328
Markus, Thomas 213, 256
Maulbronn Abbey 142, 143, 147
McDowell, John H. 91
McLuhan, Marshall 70
McMillan, John 20, 244
meaning 1-3, 6, 10, 11, 26 ; as presently considered understanding 4, preliminary definition of 11, as selective and selected understanding 11, 23, 34; impressive and expressive 1, 202, 262, 263; and functions 41, 42, 180; not intrinsic 45; in reality 50; from content and context 283; and communication 41, 59, 143, 237; in denotation and connotation 33, 34, 45; emergence of 35, 269. 289.290; as signs (in semiotics) 52-59, 242; being inevitable 71, 138; in metaphors 72-79; and language 92, 237, 240ff.; as result of the emotion-reason process 99; aesthetic as part of 119-125; in art 126; and somaesthetics 135; and style 163; in purposive causation 200, 216, 223-225; in conceptualization 194; perceptive/conceptive differences of 255; input and output during design progression 202, 203, 207; meaning as power 211-213; in reference 241, 242; from explanation and from its use 243; assessment of 11, 259-261; through narration between content and form 262-275; ambiguity of 358; in hypersurfaces 285-287; "We think only in signs" (Derrida) 289; "from a concern with meaning to a concern with form" (Benjamin) 288; in sustainability and efficiency 303ff.; see

also semantics; see also content
"medium is the message" 93
Meier, Richard and Partners 26, 52
Merleau-Ponti, Maurice 15, 138, 355
metaphor 5, 72ff.; and interpretation 74, 75; and context-dependence 75; linguistic metaphor in its conventional form 73; linguistic metaphor in its complete form 76; in design and observation of physical objects 76-79; importance of 82; 'dead' metaphors 83; and iconic aspects 83; as architectural paradigms 84
Mies van der Rohe 76, 104, 135, 161, 165, 216, 217, 349, 354
Milwaukee Art Museum 80, 81
Mitchell, John 296
Mithun Architects 310
modern, Modernism 6, 10, 71, 132, 151-154, 157, 158, 160, 168, 177, 184, 188, 189, 211, 229, 230, 232, 235, 236, 263, 269, 270, 279, 280, 282, 283, 291, 302, 315; and ornament 168, 184, 188, 189; as terminology 229
Mohl, Heinz 40, 124
Moneo, Rafael 154, 217
Moore, Gary 234
Moore, George E. 15
Moore, Keith Diaz 62
Morris, Charles 58, 330
Mothersill, Mary 130, 133, 134
Multnomah County Justice Center, Portland OR 186
Mumford, Lewis 63, 234, 279
Museum for Arts and Crafts, Frankfurt a. M. 27
Möser, Kurt 307
narratives, see design narratives
Nasar, Jack L. 41
National Mall, Washington 209
Nervi, Pier L. 168
Neue Staatsgalerie, Stuttgart 178, 179, 185, 208, 209
Nies, Bradley 318
Nietzsche, Friedrich 130, 131, 282, 289, 340
Norberg-Schulz, Christian 2, 279
Nouvel, Jean 85, 106
object 4-7; as things under consideration 12, 13; and subject 14, 130; and representation 15, 112; may be physical or mental 326 (note 45); and concepts (understanding) 18-22; and properties 18, 19; and content-form unity 89-91; and aesthetics 130, 131; and signs 48, 49, 51, 52, 88; as realizations and forms of content 89-91; and aesthetic judgment 123; as types 146, 154
object thinking 18, 19, 74; in metaphors 90; as content thinking and form thinking in unity 91
Office of Metropolitan Architecture 187
ornamentation, ornament 6. 7, 164, 184, 188, 189, 216; and beauty 116; not synonymous with decoration 164, 165; as amplification and/or decoration 171, 174-177, 180, 181, 183-187, 189; determines style 186; as strong design factor 216
Orr, David 311, 312, 320
Outram, John 179
Oxman, Rivka 286
Palazzetto dello Sport, Rome 168
Parkview Commons, San Francisco 27, 28, 213
Parshall, Steven A. 223
pattern language 157, 250, 251
Paxton, Joseph 152
Peirce, Charles 4, 48-52, 55, 57, 58, 87, 93, 194, 206
Peña, William 223, 224, 300
Perrella, Stephen 281, 285
Peponis, John 252, 360
Philharmonic Hall, Berlin 80, 81, 136, 270-272, 362
Piano. Renzo 85, 86
Piano and Rogers 168
Piazza del Campo, Siena 53
Plato 12, 13, 88, 108-113, 115, 129, 130
Plenk Residence, Salt lake City 306
Pietilä, Reima 80
Plotinus 112, 114, 116
Plume, Jim 296
Portland Building, Portland OR 186
Postmodernism, postmodern 31, 71, 154, 232, 235, 236, 259, 363

Index 381

post-occupancy analysis 64, 226, 227, 249, 303
Powerplant, Birsfelden 55
pragmatics 5, 58, 59, 62, 64, 66-68, 70, 72, 93, 225, 330; and 'dream worlds' 70
Pragmatism 50, 329
Prairie Shores Apartments, Chicago 161
Pratt Institute Center for Community and Environmental Development (PICCED) 213
prefabrication, prefabricated 39, 60, 224, 227, 252, 294, 302, 314, 347, 348
Price, Henry H. 20
programming 222-224, 228, 301, 320; and building evaluation 227, see also purpose
properties 4-8, 14, 18, 19; of concepts 18, 21, 45; versus attribute 18, 87; in representations 93; observable (physical) or relational (referred to) 25-28, 30-35, 37, 55, 57, 89, 93, 143, 256, 267; in design 34, 144; observable properties are form as exemplification 34, 35; and cues 36; and function 37, 38, 41; selection of 45; as physical signs 52; in metaphors 74, 75, 77-79, 83; in aesthetics 122-125; and resemblance 140-142; in architecture versus language 248, 254-256; as used in design narratives 267-269
prototype 6, 21, 65, 153, 286, 292, 293, 296, 300, 301,310, 365
Psarra, Sophia 264, 265
Pullman, George 231
Pullman Town near Chicago 230
purpose, purposive 6-8, 23, 56, 103, 116, 137, 147, 154, 157-159, 211, 218,-224, 228, 230; based on need and desire 248, 303; and context 9, 23, 36, 154, 171, 176, 215, 220, 238, 262; and realization 215, 220, 221, 299, 301, 318; and function 37, 38, 42, 154, 254, 299; and form 42, 61, 217, 262; and ornament 116, 291; and configuration 171, 190; architecture not free of 217; and design factors 35, 41, 154, 165, 219-222, 254; see also programming; see also realization
Putnam, Henry 17, 50
Quatremère de Quincy, A.-C. 149-151, 153, 154, 158

Rapoport, Amos 2, 32, 58, 234, 330
RB+B Architects 53
realization 5. 7, 8, 11, 23, 32, 37,89,157, 218; and syntactics 58, 60; form is 87, 90, 93, 110, 118, 145, 216, 221, 280, 350; more than physical matter 93; and aesthetic preference 184; design factors of 218-222, 236; as amplification (ornamentation) 184; self-realization as part of 229; and   mass production 233, 356; world of realization versus world of language 289;   see also context; see also purpose
reason, reasoning 5, 6, 14,; and emotion (including sense) in interdependence 23, 95-103, 131-133, 137; emotion-reason process as thinking 98-100, 247; in aesthetics (including beauty) 110, 114, 116, 121-123; and judgment 98, 108, 114, 133; and imagination 123; derived from cause and effect 192; see also understanding; see also concept
Rebstockpark, Frankfurt 284, 285
recycling 43, 302, 314, 315, 319
reference, referential 4,5, 8, 21, 90, 93, 25, 26; 33; concepts are 25; in denotation and connotation 33-35; process of 49; signs as 5, see more in semiotics; and cues 35; in metaphors 73, 75, 79; differences between language and architecture 87; 240, 241, 253, 257; referential versus self-referential 62,81, 87, 90, 93; language is purely referential 87, 253; and semantic efficiency 258
Reichstag Building, Berlin 84
Reliance Building, Chicago 38
representation, represent: mental 4, 5, 7, 19-21, 24, 31, 88, 89, 90. 91, 131, 200, 137, 246, 326, 333; physical 20, 37, 42, 49, 213, 241, 249, 257, 277, 297; computerized, virtual 9, 236, 280-283, 287, 292, 297;, of architecture by language 8, 248-251; in signs see semiotics;appearance as early 57, 122; is subjective 112, 122, 123, 261; as emotion-reason process and understanding 133 aesthetic as 112, 122, 123, 126; in

narratives (content-form) 265-275
Rescher, Nicholas 4, 16, 50, 193
Reston, VA 232, 233
Revell, Viljo 78
Richards, Ivor 72
Rietholz Apartments, Zollikerberg 162
Righini, Paul 160
Rittel, Horst 267
Rødovre Town Hall, Rødovre 78, 179
Rogers, Richard 168
Rossant, Conklin 232
Rossi, Also 35, 150, 157, 180, 217
Roth Residence, Weil am Rhein 266
Rowe, Peter 248
Rudolph, Paul 217
Russell, Bertrant 194, 241, 242
Rykwert, Joseph 116, 320
Saarinen, Eero 80, 231, 255, 321
Sainsbury Wing, National Gallery, London 41, 83
Saint John's Abbey, Collegeville MN 180, 181
Salk Institute for Biological Studies, La Jolla 3
Sandleiten Housing, Vienna 231, 232
San Vitale Church, Ravenna 178
Sauerbruch Hutton 309
Saussure, Ferdinand de 70, 87, 88, 92, 93, 245, 257, 333, 361,
Scharoun, Hans 80, 81,136, 231, 270, 271, 362
Schiller, Friedrich 128, 159
Schinkel, Karl F. 158, 159
Schliemann, Todd Preface, 275
Schneekloth, Linda H. 212
Schopenhauer, Arthur 128-130, 191, 342
Schutz, Alfred 205
Schullin Jewelry Store, Vienna 181
Science Center, Harvard University 39, 43, 43, 56, 168, 179, 355
Scott Brown, Denise 41, 44, 83
Scruton, Roger 126, 130, 254, 279, 360
SCSD System (School Construction Systems Development) 169, 171, 252, 350
Seagram Building, New York 76, 77, 104, 105, 302
Searle, John 4, 15, 16, 25, 101, 193, 247, 335, 357
Secondary Modern School Tuxford, Nottinghamshire 170
self-referential 62, 87, 90, 93
semantics 4, 5, 8, 34, 58, 70; connection to pragmatics 68; and 'dream worlds' 70; and physical, architectural nature 252; content is 263; interdependence with syntax 263; efficiency 258; 268; see also meaning; see also content
semiotics, sign 4, 5, 8, 48-58, 90, 93, 94 ; physical sign and mental significance 47-51, 57, 68, 87; in denotation and connotation 33; in representation and communication 47-51; iconic, symbolic and indexical 51-54; and representation 93, 257; as media 94; signifier and signified 87-89;and interpretation 48, 49, 242; verbal versus physical sign nature 92; expressions as physical, impressions as mental signs 93; content is semantic; see also reference; see also representation
Semper, Gottfried 151-153, 159, 174-176 , 347-351
Semper Oper, Dresden 176
sensation 4-6, 13-15, 17, 126, 132; and intentionality 15; for perception and conceptualization 17; is experience 31, 96; is denotative 32; provides appearance of object 18-22; not synonymous with feeling 19, 96-102; is basis for the emotion-reason process 98, 99, 102; also from inner sense 98,118-191; and the body 102; and beauty 118; see also somaesthetics
Sert, Jackson and Associates 39
shape making versus form realization 42, 63, 236, 280, 284, 285, 288, 301; is crucial 281
Shaftesbury, 3rd Earl of 117, 118, 130
Sharp Center for Design, Toronto 106, 107
Shea, Kristina 292
Shusterman, Richard 135, 341, 342
Sibley, Frank N. 123, 124
Sibley, Robert G. 212
Siena Cathedral, Siena 175
signs see semiotics

simile 73, 74
simulacrum 9, 31, 71, 281
Sitten, Switzerland 214
Snodgrass, Adrian 73, 74
Socrates 106, 108-111, 336
somaesthetics 135, 137
Space syntax 252-254, 360
specific concepts or properties, see generic versus specific concepts
Spinoza, Baruch 95, 117
St. Georg Church, Reichenau 165
Stamps, Arthur E. 327
Steidle and Partners 64, 65
Sterling, James 179, 184, 208,
Stern, Joseph 76
Stout, Rowland 206
Strauss, Susan Preface, 275
structuralism 70, 235, 237
style 6, 7, 44, 84, 139, 157-160, 163, 186, 280; change of 118; and subjectivity 157, 189; is normative 161, 162; of society or individuals 158; as expression of basic idea 159; and type 160-163; as medium 184; and ornament 186; style as synthesis and form 189, 236
international style 229, 232
Sullivan, Louis 6, 37, 41, 91, 149, 159, 231
sustainability 7, 9, 10, 43, 62, 213, 220, 225, 228, 236, 261, 279, 296, 298, 300, 302-304, 310-315, 317-320, 367- 370 see also LEED
symbol, symbolic 5, 21, 25, 51-59, 93, 151 180, 316, 327, 332; in metaphors 76, 77, 80, 85, 93; in linguistic versus physical aspects like architecture) 57, 87, 88, 241, 246, 247, 258; simultaneously iconic, indexical or both 5, 93, 248, 257, 289 ; in relation to 'Duck' and 'Decorated shed' 188, 189; see also semiotics
syntax, syntactic 5, 8, 58, 59, 72, 144, 208; in language 58, 87, 246; in architecture 60-62, 66, 72, 93, 144, 247, 72, 208; in architecture versus language 59, 61, 62, 66, 68, 70, 72, 93, 246, 249-252; and complexity 144; form is 263; interdependence with semantics 263; form is syntactic 263, 264; and 'dream worlds' 70
synthesis, synthetic 8, 9, 11, 17, 22-24, 102, 218, 326; in design 11, 139, 260; analysis for 223, 236, 250, 297, 300; in pattern language 250, 251; to create configuration and realization 254; for form from content 8, 264; in the Function-Behavior-Structure model or the purpose-context-realization.model 297-299; see also analysis
Taos, NM 35, 135, 136
Tatarkiewicz, Wladislaw 336, 340
Tennessee Valley Authority Building, Chattanooga TN 277
Thamesmead near London 162
The Architects Collaborative 277
Therme, Vals 55, 56
things in themselves 14, 15, 17, 50, 51, 90; and uncertainty 51; and the aesthetic 128, 129; not space and time 191; and the desire to understand 320
thinking, thought 7, 11-15, 18-22, 24, 26,31,44 (comprehensiveness of process). 100, 323 (thinking body); about objects and their properties 18, 19, 25, and conceptualization 19-22, 45; as judgment 19, 21-24, 44, 98, 103, 145, 344; as emotion-reason process 98ff.; as "unity of apperception" 24; as denotation and connotation 34; about signs 47; and interpretation 58, 323, in metaphors 5, 72-76; as object thinking see object thinking; as language thinking see language; content-form unity as object of see content form unity
Toorn van, Roemer 331
Toronto City Hall, Toronto 78, 79
Tschumi, Bernhard 263, 285
TWA Building, New York 80, 81, 255, 302
type, typology 6, 146-149; 187-188; as building type 31, 39, 41, 42, 160, 188, 226, 230, 233; as prototype 6, 21, 286, 292, 293, 296, 301; and resemblance 139-142, and function 41, 148, 149, 151, 153, 219; is normative 156, 161; and mass

production 153, 157, 161, 162, 233, 356; and style 160-163

understanding 1-11; meaning as selected 11, 23; as idea 13, 14; and experience 5, 14 (Hume), 17 18 (Kant), 279; and judgment 19, 21-23; as process and result 21-22; as emotion-reason process 99-103; and properties of objects 25-29; denotative and connotative 33, 34; with feelings 99-103; for more see meaning (especially entries beyond page 50)

Ungers, Oswald M. 185, 217
United Air Lines Terminal, Chicago 104
Vande Moere, Andrew 218
Venezuela Pavillon, Montreal 103, 104
Venturi, Robert 41, 43, 44, 83, 164, 188, 197, 279, 283, 284
Vidler, Anthony 148, 235
Vierzehnheiligen Church near Bamberg 166
Villanueva, Carlos 103
virtuality, virtual 9, 68, 69, 280, 281, 292, 296, 301, 320; space, reality 281 282; limtis of 297
Vitra Company, Weil am Rhein, Chair Museum and Fire Station 162, 163
Vitruvius 43, 112, 116, 147, 164, 291, 347
Vällingby near Stockholm 232, 233
Wacker Drive (333), Chicago 142, 184, 185
Wagner, Otto 181
WAM Architects 106
Washington DC Plan 209
Watkins, David 317
Waynbaum, Israel 105, 107
Weatherhead School of Management, Case Western University, Cleveland 3, 40, 163, 181, 183
Weber, Ralph 45
Weissenhof Apartments, Stuttgart 165, 166
Wexner Center of the Arts 81, 82
White, Eduard T. 224
Whyte, Jennifer 282
Whyte, William 255
Wienzeile, Vienna 181
Wies Church, Southern Bavaria 276
Wigley, Mark 205, 353
Wiscombe, Tom 286

Wittgenstein, Ludwig 4, 15, 139, 242-245, 358
Wright, Frank Lloyd 85, 160, 231, 316
Wöhrle Residence, Weil am Rhein 142
Wolfe, Tom 291
Xenophon 109
Zeitgeist 9, 158, 159, 279; and virtuality; 320
Zentralsparkasse, Vienna 286
Zimmer Gunsel Frasca 186
Zimmermann, Dominikus 276
Zumthor, Peter 56, 137, 344

Index

www.ingramcontent.com/pod-product-compliance
Lightning Source LLC
Chambersburg PA
CBHW061117010526
44112CB00024B/2900